Quantitative Methods in the Humanities and Social Sciences

Quantitative Methods in the Humanities and Social Sciences is a book series designed to foster research-based conversation with all parts of the university campus – from buildings of ivy-covered stone to technologically savvy walls of glass. Scholarship from international researchers and the esteemed editorial board represents the far-reaching applications of computational analysis, statistical models, computer-based programs, and other quantitative methods. Methods are integrated in a dialogue that is sensitive to the broader context of humanistic study and social science research. Scholars, including among others historians, archaeologists, new media specialists, classicists and linguists, promote this interdisciplinary approach. These texts teach new methodological approaches for contemporary research. Each volume exposes readers to a particular research method. Researchers and students then benefit from exposure to subtleties of the larger project or corpus of work in which the quantitative methods come to fruition.

Sandra R. Schloen • Miller C. Prosser

Database Computing for Scholarly Research

Case Studies Using the Online Cultural and Historical Research Environment

Springer

Sandra R. Schloen
Forum for Digital Culture
The University of Chicago
Chicago, IL, USA

Miller C. Prosser
Forum for Digital Culture
The University of Chicago
Chicago, IL, USA

ISSN 2199-0956 ISSN 2199-0964 (electronic)
Quantitative Methods in the Humanities and Social Sciences
ISBN 978-3-031-46694-6 ISBN 978-3-031-46696-0 (eBook)
https://doi.org/10.1007/978-3-031-46696-0

This Springer imprint is published by the registered company Springer Nature Switzerland AG
The registered company address is: Gewerbestrasse 11, 6330 Cham, Switzerland

Acknowledgments

This book was inspired by over 20 years of consulting with academic research projects and helping scholars manage and use their research data using the Online Cultural and Historical Research Environment (OCHRE) platform. Our work has brought us into contact with scholars involved in a wide range of research projects. Their testing, recommendations, encouragement, and other feedback have been invaluable. Our special thanks go to early OCHRE adopters and supporters: Aaron Burke, Dennis Campbell, (the late) Philip Engblom, Gene Gragg, James K. Hoffmeier, (the late) Harry Hoffner, Janet Johnson, Scott Lidgard, Daniel Master, (the late) Lawrence E. Stager, Matthew W. Stolper, Edward Stratford, and Ron Tappy. Many new friends have since joined our ranks, each new project bringing new questions, new challenges, and fresh energy to the OCHRE endeavor.

Our early home at the Institute for the Study of Ancient Cultures (formerly the Oriental Institute) of the University of Chicago was fruitful ground in which to grow and enrich the OCHRE platform. Our current home at the Forum for Digital Culture of the University of Chicago is a similarly fertile and stimulating environment with a supportive team of computational and academic colleagues for which we are grateful.

We acknowledge with sincere thanks our technical support team, primarily Charles Blair (Director of the Digital Library Development Center at the University of Chicago Library) and H. Birali Runesha (Associate Vice President for Research Computing and the Director of the Research Computing Center at the University of Chicago). By extension we also thank other staff of the DLDC and RCC who have been important sources of support and help over the years, notably Elisabeth Long, Peggy Wilkins, Fred Seaton, and Matthew Vincent. Special thanks to Charles Blair for his helpful feedback following a thorough reading of a draft of this book.

Sandra Schloen recognizes long-time partner David Schloen as a co-designer of the OCHRE platform, but more than that, as an indispensable and inspirational user, fundraiser, and general booster, invaluable to the long-term success of OCHRE. Sandra is also greatly appreciative of Robert Schloen, Anna Schloen, and Sophia Lau, along with Stuart and Doris Cooke, for accepting OCHRE as a family affair, and for their enthusiastic support on countless adventures.

Miller Prosser acknowledges the inspiring support and encouragement provided by Lee A. Cook, whose own digital expertise challenges, informs, and provides critical perspective. Miller also acknowledges the community of brilliant researchers who have contributed to and corrected our work over the years.

We have had the great fortune of working with many intelligent, ambitious, and productive college and graduate students, cheerfully toiling over complex data sets, often in basement labs or in hot archaeology dig houses. We are inspired and motivated by their enthusiasm. We are similarly inspired and motivated by the dedication and passion of our academic colleagues to their research projects and to their commitment to working with us to maximize technology to achieve their goals. As we share our computational perspective in the pages that follow, we hope to inspire and motivate our readers in return.

Contents

List of Figures

List of Table

Chapter 1
Introduction

It is about more than just staying organized. It is about more than just being digitized. It is about more than having the right tool for the task. It is about a total solution for working with research data of any type at all phases of the process, from planning, through data capture, analysis, visualization, publication, preservation, and collaboration. This is the ambitious solution we propose in this book.

The ideas and practical techniques we discuss are the ever-evolving result of many years of work with academic researchers. The promise of the computer age was slow to be fulfilled in the halls of academia. Computers were supposed to make life easier. Yet, as we survey the world of academic computing, particularly in the humanities and social sciences, we are hard-pressed to find a computational solution that adequately addresses the needs of academic projects from beginning to end. As the data revolution has impacted all areas of research, and as technology-based solutions have become imperative, the authors of this book have witnessed first-hand the struggle by scholars to apply technology effectively in their research.

What follows is an argument in favor of an innovative approach to modeling and managing complex research data. This approach is implemented in the Online Cultural and Historical Research Environment (OCHRE). The slogan of OCHRE is "a place for every *thing* and everything in its place." OCHRE is designed to accommodate the most basic need of academic research: the ability to observe anything and everything needed to understand a given subject and to keep track of what has been said about it. This is made possible by using a framework for data that is on the one hand flexible and on the other hand comprehensive.

This approach has been applied successfully over the past twenty years in a wide range of fields: archaeology, history (economic history, legal history, history of science), language studies, literary studies, paleontology, philology, and sociology. And, in principle, it is applicable to any field of research. Not all these research areas will be discussed below. However, the examples, illustrations, and case studies from active research projects presented in this book can be extrapolated to many other kinds of research.

S. R. Schloen, M. C. Prosser, *Database Computing for Scholarly Research*, Quantitative Methods in the Humanities and Social Sciences,
https://doi.org/10.1007/978-3-031-46696-0_1

Scholarly research generates a wide range of data in a wide variety of formats. In recent times, most of this data is produced in some sort of digital format—a word processing document, a spreadsheet, or an image file, to name some common examples. Most digital tools employed by researchers were first developed for use in the business world. But research data in the humanities and social sciences often differs significantly from business data, being less predictably structured and more nuanced.

As computing has come to impact the world of research, scholars are faced with a challenge: how does one organize and manage data to allow meaningful, powerful, and accurate research? Many scholars find themselves losing control of their research data or coming to the realization that although the data is in a digital format, it is not very useful for research. Technology has become so easy to use that scholars can create data simply by using word processing or spreadsheet software, or by drawing maps with a Geographic Information System (GIS), or by building a database using a popular, commercially available tool like FileMaker. The accessibility and usability of software make it easy to get started right away. But these tools do not tell users how to model and manage their data to achieve their research goals. Without careful consideration, a spreadsheet or database may be little better than a cabinet of 3″ × 5″ index cards.

The academic world has reached a technological maturity that goes beyond basic digitization. Researchers must now consider broader impacts of their data, such as integration of research data with other widely available digital resources, collaboration among scholars with common interests, and long-term preservation of digital assets that ensure their continued accessibility to future generations of scholars.[1] How should we collect and manage data to serve these goals of integration, collaboration, and preservation? With intentional and purposeful data representation, organization, and integration, based on a set of sound technological principles, research data transforms into something more than a series of well-organized notes.

If you struggle with applying computational tools to your research, you are not alone. If your collections of data are spiraling out of control, you may be looking for a better solution. If your investment in digital data is not paying tangible dividends, it may be time for a new strategy. In this book, we recommend a strategy that makes as much data as possible available to as many people as possible for as many purposes as possible.

---

[1] See Huggett (2015a, p. 90) who reflects on the questions, "What effect does the process of structuring data for a database have on the way that we think about that data, on the way we go about recording that data, the way in which we retrieve that data, and the way in which we subsequently analyse that data [11]?".

About This Book

The goal of this book is to offer scholars insight into how to capture and manage research data so that it is useful for research, both now and in the future. It is aimed at scholars who are ambitious for their data, not content to merely collect or digitize data but to integrate, analyze, and process data to serve research goals; scholars in the humanities and social sciences who are faced not only with well-organized, highly structured data, like that often generated in the hard sciences and which is intuitively more easily represented and organized, but who are also dealing with unstructured or semi-structured data which is much more challenging to manage; scholars who have reached the limitations of business-oriented tools like FileMaker, Microsoft Access, or MySQL and need better models or more effective strategies. We hope that scholars and technical support staff will find guidelines and examples here to inform their work with research data. Recognizing that this book may be picked up by a wide range of readers, each coming to it with a different blend of academic and technical interests, it is intended to be accessible for those who do not have a technical background.

This book is divided into three major sections. In this chapter and Chap. 2 we make a case for why a fresh computational perspective on research data is needed, particularly in the humanities. Readers who already understand the problems of data management and want to get straight to practical solutions may move quickly on to the next section.

The second section (Chaps. 3, 4, 5, 6, 7, 8, and 9) expounds key principles and practices that we argue are vital to successful data management. The OCHRE database platform is based on these principles and enables these practices. Throughout this section, the real-world application of the concepts being discussed is illustrated by examples drawn from a wide variety of academic projects that use OCHRE. In addition, occasional technical details are supplied where relevant to satisfy the curiosity of technology specialists. However, this book is not a comprehensive manual for OCHRE, which is documented elsewhere (see Schloen and Schloen 2012 and the OCHRE website at https://ochre.uchicago.edu).

The third section (Chaps. 10, 11, and 12) offers three specific and detailed case studies, each of which follows a single project from the original conception of its data through the stages of data representation, management, analysis, and publication, taking into account the concepts introduced in the first two sections and implementing the principles under consideration. Although not all projects use all aspects of the OCHRE platform, the case studies were chosen to provide a more fulsome picture of active research projects engaging with the range of features available in OCHRE. Since the OCHRE system was originally developed for archaeologists, the first case study focuses on the Tell Keisan Archaeology Project in northern Israel. But since the OCHRE data model applies just as well to textual studies and philological research data, the second case study presents data management strategies applied to the corpus of ancient texts discovered at Ugarit (Ras Shamra), Syria. The third case study deals with early Greek coin hoards from the eastern Mediterranean. Although these three case studies each pertain to a specific region and period, the strategy implemented in OCHRE can be applied to any cultural or historical setting.

About OCHRE

The Online Cultural and Historical Research Environment (OCHRE) is a database platform quite unlike most others. This is warranted, welcomed, and intentional. OCHRE was designed by scholars for scholars in response to the shortcomings of popular database software intended for business applications. In the early 1990s, David and Sandra Schloen, both formally trained in computer science, concluded that a radically different approach was needed for scholarly data. Taking a fresh look based on first principles of data management and database design, they devised an innovative, item-based approach that makes extensive use of hierarchical data structures to model the highly variable, often unstructured, data generated across space and time by research in the humanities and social sciences.

Thirty years later, OCHRE is being used by hundreds of scholars and their students at dozens of institutions around the world in support of a wide variety of research projects. As a "multi-project, multiuser database system that provides a comprehensive framework for diverse kinds of information at all stages of research [OCHRE] can be used for initial data acquisition and storage; for data querying and analysis; for data presentation and publication; and for long-term archiving and curation of data" (Schloen and Schloen 2012, p. 1). As a data repository, OCHRE manages almost ten million database items that have been carefully collected and curated by OCHRE project teams. As academic software, it is hosted and supported within academic institutions, primarily the University of Chicago, where its use is supported by the staff of the OCHRE Data Service (ODS). As a unique database platform, OCHRE is instructive because it is different and because it offers a new perspective on data management and computational strategies. This is a feature, not a bug.

About the OCHRE Data Service

Throughout this book, and especially in the case studies, we describe how "we organized the taxonomy" or "we added data." Often it really is *we*, the staff of the OCHRE Data Service, working closely with project personnel to support project goals. This is a research model in which the research team works closely with the data service over the entire course of the project. Far from being a fifth wheel, the data service facilitates the use of digital tools and consults on digital approaches to research, sparing the humanities or social sciences researcher from having to manage technological details that are not likely in their wheelhouse.[2]

The OCHRE Data Service (ODS) is a component of the Forum for Digital Culture (https://digitalculture.uchicago.edu) of the University of Chicago. Without institutional context, a data service would not thrive. The ODS benefits from its close association with the Digital Library Development Center (DLDC) of the University of Chicago which provides data hosting and system administration for OCHRE. The ODS also partners with the University of Chicago's M.A. program in Digital Studies of Language, Culture, and History (DIGS), in which Miller Prosser teaches, and which embodies the interplay between teaching and research in an academic environment. Students in the DIGS program work with OCHRE data, learn from ODS staff, and contribute to research projects using OCHRE. We wish to acknowledge the role that all three tiers play in the success of digital research projects: (1) the investigators and the core research teams, including student assistants, (2) the data service which serves as a liaison, and (3) the institutional support infrastructure.

The ODS is managed by Sandra Schloen, who is Director of Technology of the Forum for Digital Culture. The ODS staff is highly integrated within some project teams but supports other projects more casually. For example, Prosser is the data manager for the Persepolis Fortification Archive project and oversees its photographers and its many terabytes of digital images. S. Schloen is often embedded within archaeology teams to serve as the onsite data manager for projects using OCHRE. The ODS has trained project personnel as field data managers for archaeology projects, digital photographers, metadata specialists, GIS experts, text editors, and various other roles. These specialists ensure that projects are not spinning their wheels as they implement strategies for data capture, description, analysis, and publication stages of the project. Our expertise and experience, combined with the provision of a robust computational platform, ensure that a research project does not need to reinvent the wheel when there have been many who have gone down the path before. Each project brings its own flavor, and new challenges, but need not start from scratch computationally.

To sum up, a digitally oriented research project in the humanities or social sciences has a much higher chance of success if it is supported by a data service staffed by personnel trained both in computational and humanities domains and that is situated in a stable, institutional context. In this model, the data service helps a research project keep the wheels of progress rolling in the right direction.

[2]We describe the OCHRE Data Service here, but see Cox and Verbaan (2018), especially their chapters 7–10, for a broader discussion of research data services.

Appendix A: Introducing Our Pioneering OCHRE Projects

Our work at the OCHRE Data Service, interacting with scholars on real research projects, has spurred on the development of the OCHRE platform to solve real problems and has inspired fresh solutions to troublesome issues that commonly plague attempts to digitize research data or apply computational methods, regardless of the discipline or subject matter, and allows us to introduce a selection of our colleagues and their projects, listed here from A (Ashkelon) to Z (Zincirli), who illustrate a variety of motivations for adopting a system like OCHRE, and who in turn have inspired our efforts to continually enhance OCHRE to serve their projects, and others like them, effectively. These projects pioneered early versions of OCHRE as collaborators, requesting and testing key new features. In the chapters to come, examples will be taken primarily from these projects.

Ashkelon, the Leon Levy Expedition

Long-time OCHRE user, Daniel Master, Professor of Archaeology at Wheaton College, had long been waiting for technology to live up to his visions for it. As co-director (2007–2016) of the large-scale archaeology project sponsored by Harvard University which begun in 1985 at the picturesque site of Ashkelon on Israel's southern coast, Master faced the challenge of managing four decades' worth of data while transitioning the project to use online digital data collection methods. Daisy-chaining extension cords from the outlets of the public restrooms managed by the National Park Service on the site, Master powered laptops deep in the excavation areas. But eking out bandwidth from early modems to power OCHRE was like wringing water from stone. Master's determination to use OCHRE to practice digital archaeology inspired the creation of a mode in which OCHRE can be used offline. Caching a preselected subset of the database onto the field supervisor's laptop allowed OCHRE data entry to be performed without the need for internet access on the site. Upon returning to the hotel after the dig day, the offline transactions were uploaded to the database—a process that was successfully repeated day after day, week after week, year after year, throughout the excavation seasons.

Having dealt with many of the frustrations of the early days of personal computing and having learned lessons regarding best practice for OCHRE usage, Master was able to start fresh, with co-director Mario Martin of Tel Aviv University, with a new project at Tel Shimron, historically an agricultural center in northern Israel. Whether digging new, born-digital data at Tel Shimron or working on Web-based digital companions for Ashkelon publications, Master and his team continue to inspire new features and get the most out of OCHRE at all stages of the data lifecycle.

Computational Research on the Ancient Near East (CRANE)

Principal investigator Timothy Harrison, Director of the Institute for the Study of Ancient Cultures, was dreaming big when he assembled the multi-institutional, international, and interdisciplinary research team known as CRANE.[3] The project brings together a wide variety of data to study the rise and development of complex societies in the watershed region of the Orontes River in southeast Turkey and northwest Syria: from legacy data collected by historical excavations to fresh data from ongoing field seasons, from detailed site-based archaeology to wide-ranging regional surveys, from quantitative data for petrographic analysis or radiocarbon dating to qualitative descriptions of walls and pits, and from mundane counts and weights of ceramics or bones to high-tech simulations and augmented reality that visualizes and imagines past behavior. This cross-project collaboration is supported by the OCHRE platform which allows for varying, and even competing, data recording systems. Projects participating in CRANE collected data to their own specifications and methodologies, yet these are respected and accepted by a generic and flexible, hierarchically organized, item-based approach offered by OCHRE.

CRANE projects performing survey archaeology developed hierarchically organized data structures that were broad and shallow, representing many sites spanning hundreds of kilometers, but each described only cursorily. Site-based excavation projects generated narrow, deep hierarchies representing archaeological items in context with findspots often recorded to centimeter-level accuracy, for example, seeds, found within a pot, found within a locus, found within a square, situated within a grid, situated within an area of the site. As the CRANE team pushed the need for integration among projects and as shared descriptive taxonomies were developed, somewhat to our surprise we discovered along the way that perhaps we are not so different after all in how we do our analysis (Fig. 1.1).

Corinth Excavations, Roman Pottery from East of the Theater

Kathleen Warner Slane, Professor Emerita of Roman Art and Archaeology, Department of Classics, Archaeology, and Religion, University of Missouri, Columbia, had accepted the daunting task of publishing over twelve tons of Roman pottery excavated at ancient Corinth from 1981 to 1990. At an early consultation with Slane, we were presented with a two-page, single-spaced description of the data relevant to the pottery analysis at this site. With an inspiring determination not to be overwhelmed by an ever-growing set of digital material, Slane had carefully tracked versions of a master database, numerous spreadsheets, and dozens of folders of documents of various types. Typical of many projects, there were thousands of images stored in various directories: traditional images of sherd fragments

[3] https://www.crane.utoronto.ca/. Since 2012, the project, originally based at the University of Toronto, has been awarded over 4.5 million dollars from the Social Sciences and Humanities Research Council of Canada.

Fig. 1.1 A tree-ring sample is analyzed and photographed by CRANE project co-investigator and dendrochronologist S. Manning and specialist B. Lorentzen at the Cornell University laboratory. (Photograph courtesy of the Tayinat Archaeological Project)

here, digitized sherd profile drawings there, and scans of slides somewhere else. As an early adopter of technology, she had pushed the Panorama database she maintained on her Mac to the limit, coding, sorting, and describing thousands of potsherds of interest. For Slane, OCHRE became an integrative repository in which this data was itemized and organized, preparing it for further analysis.

Along with contextualizing the pottery within "Lots" (the units of excavation), classifying it by ware, and creating catalogs of exemplary types, Slane was also counting and weighing. The qualitative data was thus bolstered by quantitative data which inspired its use with OCHRE's statistical features, and also its use with OCHRE's visualization wizards, for creating both Harris Matrices[4] and charts (e.g., pie charts showing proportions of selected wares). We look forward to continued efforts to help make this data accessible through an online, digital publication.

[4] A Harris matrix is a highly structured sequence diagram used by archaeologists to depict stratigraphic relationships over time. See Edward C. Harris (1979).

Critical Editions for Digital Analysis and Research (CEDAR)

CEDAR is a cross-departmental, multi-project initiative at the University of Chicago that "demonstrates that the same underlying data model and software can be used for research on very different literary corpora written in different historical periods using different languages and writing systems, and studied today by different communities of scholars"[5] (Fig. 1.2).

CEDAR illustrates how a shared platform can be utilized, along with a common set of tools, for performing textual criticism on any literary corpus that has a history of transmission, editing, or translation, thereby maximizing the investment in the technology and ensuring its support via a wide base of stakeholders. Multiple overlapping hierarchies are put to creative use as individual texts are extracted from a master pool of content. The core content is reused for similar texts, making it easy to see where texts are the same and where they differ. The original CEDAR team consisted of a biblical branch, focusing on *Genesis*, under the supervision of Jeffrey Stackert of the University of Chicago Divinity School; a Shakespeare branch, specifically the *Taming of the Shrew*, with English professor Ellen MacKay, also of the University of Chicago; and a Sumerian branch working on the ancient *Epic of Gilgamesh* with then-director of the Institute for the Study of Ancient Cultures, Christopher Woods. This project has been so successful at finding common ground that new subjects, including Herman Melville's works (modern), the poetic *Piers Plowman* (medieval), and the magical, but highly variant, *Book of the Dead* (ancient), have been added to the CEDAR repertoire.

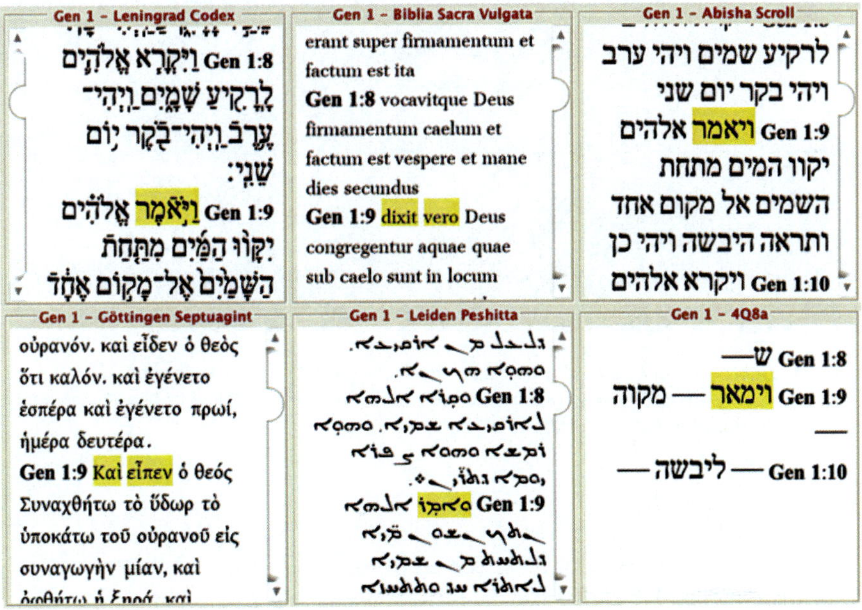

Fig. 1.2 Multiple manuscripts of Genesis are shown in CEDAR's Comparative View

[5] https://cedar.uchicago.edu.

The Electronic Chicago Hittite Dictionary (eCHD)

The Chicago Hittite Dictionary Project[6] began at the Institute for the Study of Ancient Cultures in 1975 as an endeavor to create a traditional, printed concordance for lexicographical research for all parts of the corpus of Hittite texts. As the use of technology became more prevalent in the early 2000s, the CHD team was challenged by a key funding agency to provide an electronic, online version of this comprehensive dictionary—something that went beyond merely delivering searchable PDFs. Entrenched in manual methods that depended on maintaining file drawers full of cross-referenced index cards as their primary data store, they turned to OCHRE (Fig. 1.3).

Fig. 1.3 Cabinets in the CHD office contain cards filed alphabetically for each word. (Photograph courtesy of A. Baumann, Managing Editor of the Publications Office at the Institute for the Study of Ancient Cultures of the University of Chicago)

[6] https://hittitedictionary.uchicago.edu.

Inspired by the enthusiasm of one of the original Senior Editors of the dictionary, the late Harry Hoffner, OCHRE was enhanced to process the highly structured documents of the CHD using the character formatting and paragraph styles to break down the document into individual glossary entries. Each lemma became an organized collection of attested grammatical forms and an often extensive, deeply nested hierarchy of semantic meanings. With assistance from dedicated graduate student in the University of Chicago Near Eastern Languages and Civilizations (NELC) program, Dennis Campbell (PhD '07), the lexical content was richly described, including grammatical details and orthographic variations, and internally cross-referenced. In addition, examples of word usages, listed Oxford English dictionary style, were supplemented by selected extracts of transcriptions of digitized Hittite texts also managed by OCHRE. The flexibility of the OCHRE approach is well suited to even a complex writing system like the Sumero-Akkadian cuneiform used for Hittite and for extensive documentation of both the lexical details and the relationship of the lexicon to the text corpus. While work on the printed edition of the CHD continues, the digital version delivers powerful browsing and searching tools to the end user.

The Florentine Catasto of 1427

The Catasto of 1427 is renowned as the first, major governmental census and tax assessment conducted in modern times. This extraordinary historical document enumerates the demographic, economic, and geographic relationships among the people and places of Florence. Citizens declare their names and family members, their ownership or rental of property, their occupation, their parish affiliation, their neighbors, and the streets on which they live. But this is not a systematic accounting. Giovanni declares Antonio as his father but neglects to provide a family name. The shoemaker declares vaguely that he rents a workshop across the street from the monastery. Streets change names as they meander across districts. The Catasto registers are replete with gaps, idiosyncratic details, and inconsistent spellings, but nonetheless are a wealth of information pertaining to the wealth of the people of Florence.

University of Chicago art historian, Niall Atkinson (Associate Professor of Art History, Romance Languages and Literature, and the College), had conceived of a research project to transform the mundane details "embedded in these Florentine tax returns" into a "data-rich digital topography of the remarkable urban society of Renaissance Florence precisely at the historical moment in which it was producing some of the most important artistic and architectural monuments of the western canon."[7] But he, along with research assistant Carmen Caswell, was finding the

[7] From Atkinson's project description in the OCHRE Project Gallery, https://voices.uchicago.edu/ochre/project/florentine-catasto-of-1427/.

digitized transcription of these records to be intractable. The Excel spreadsheet, comprised of 16,136 entries with a span of columns that ranged from A, B, …, AA, AB, …, FD, defied manageable manipulation and analysis. Progress identifying and untangling a myriad of relationships was painfully slow. With any declaration listing up to four owners, seven renters, and ten neighbors, each described at the whim of the declarer, the data was partial and haphazard. The variety and number of "relationships" begged for a "relational" solution, but this would be a formidable task culminating in a complex computational system.

Reimagining this data as a "network"—social, topographic, and technological—the OCHRE Data Service transformed the gnarly spreadsheet into an item-based "graph" of information. Each person, each family, each institution, each property, each parish, and each street was defined as its own item, described with whatever details were known about it, and linked to each declaration that referenced it. The process of freeing these items from the confines of their sparsely populated table rows imposed data integrity. The research team was energized to explore this network and resolve ambiguities with renewed enthusiasm, excited by the possibilities for visualization, network analysis, quantitative analysis, and mapping, afforded by an item-based approach.

The Jaffa Cultural Heritage Project (JCHP)

Directors Aaron A. Burke (Professor of the Archaeology of Ancient Israel and the Levant, UCLA) and Martin Peilstöcker (Johannes-Gutenberg Universität, Mainz, Germany) were the latest in a long line of investigators at the famous coastal site of Jaffa on the south side of modern-day Tel Aviv, Israel. Indeed, this project records a veritable, virtual *Who's Who* of the history of excavations at this impressive site from the 1940s to the present day.[8]

This project needed a collaborative data management system that was sufficiently flexible structurally to allow for the representation of multiple, attributed observations from different points of view—observations of the same space but over different periods of time. OCHRE's item-based, hierarchical structures, and its flexible system for defining descriptive properties, allowed the legacy data, collected to different standards and with vastly different recording schemes, to mingle with the born-digital data of the modern excavation, distinct yet integrated (Fig. 1.4).

[8] http://www.nelc.ucla.edu/jaffa/.

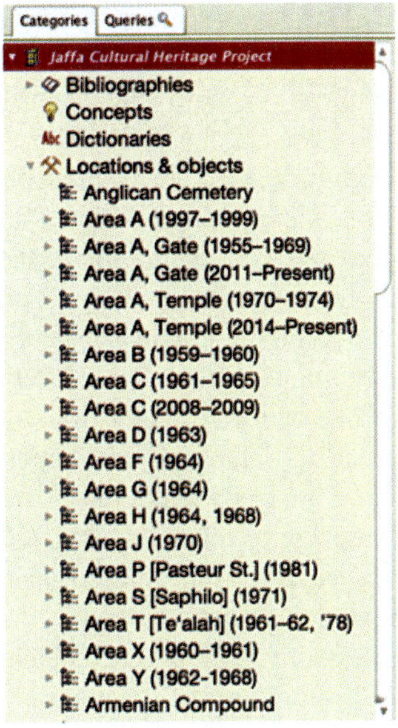

Fig. 1.4 A long list of hierarchies supports the integration of a long history of excavation at Jaffa

Lives, Individuality, and Analysis (LIA)

Curator Emeritus (Earth Sciences) at the Field Museum in Chicago, Scott Lidgard, was a kindred spirit from the start. The title of his 2017 book, coedited with collaborator Lynn Nyhart (Emeritus Professor, Department of History, University of Wisconsin-Madison), *Biological Individuality: Integrating Scientific, Philosophical, and Historical Perspectives,* gives a clue as to the scope and diversity of Lidgard's own interests (Lidgard and Nyhart 2017). "Describing and explaining the history of life"[9] while concurrently studying the history-of-science-of-the-study-of-the-history-of-life, made for complex data. Studying parts and wholes (in the context of bryozoans) and conflicting (scientific) taxonomic hierarchies, along with documenting detailed information describing the influences among nineteenth-century scientists regarding these issues, made it imperative to have an especially flexible data model.

Extensive conversations with Lidgard on matters of science, philosophy, history, and data contributed uniquely to the enhancement of OCHRE in early stages of its development. Careful curation of historical data by this project's research assistants, as they cataloged the books authored by the scientists of the day and the letters exchanged among them, inspired new features that have since benefitted other historically oriented projects.

---

[9] From Lidgard's personal website at https://www.fieldmuseum.org/about/staff/profile/101.

Old Assyrian Research Environment (OARE)

While a graduate student in the University of Chicago's Near Eastern Languages and Civilizations (NELC) program, Edward Stratford (PhD '10; Associate Professor, Department of History, Brigham Young University) was busy wrangling ancient texts, sourced from tablets found at the site of Kültepe-Kaneš in central Turkey. His goal was to study the social and economic networks of this early second-millennium Assyrian trading colony. Working in close consultation with OCHRE developer S. Schloen, a sophisticated import tool was created to provide an efficient means of entering textual content. After accepting a document pasted from an external source or one opened directly from a Microsoft Word file, OCHRE would process the text, creating database items representing a sign-by-sign transliteration and word-by-word analysis, while matching against a master cuneiform sign list, and tagging by language or other features. OCHRE would interpret text formats like italics, bold, and superscripting based on project specifications; for example, lower-case plain text would represent textual content in the Old Assyrian language. Since those early days, almost 25,000 texts have been imported by OCHRE projects, in sign-by-sign transliteration, in languages that include not only Old Assyrian from Stratford's corpus but also languages as varied as Akkadian, Aramaic, Coptic, Demotic, Elamite, English, Greek, Hebrew, Hittite, Neo-Babylonian, Syriac, and Ugaritic.

Stratford's data that focused on social and economic trade networks was somewhat unusual[10] due to the short timeframe covered by the Old Assyrian texts. Many of the events dated to within a year, with similar people and places referenced over and over. Could the teams of black (ṣallāmum) donkeys (ANŠE) on the trade route to Kaneš be the same ones mentioned in multiple texts, repeating their journeys, carrying different goods? This study inspired a specialized OCHRE query mechanism that could find texts based on the co-occurrence or sequence of a specified list of words regardless of their original spellings. A search for the mention of "any number of black donkeys" in this corpus returns a variety of results such as: 4 ANŠE ṣa-lá-mu (ICK 1.150); 7-x ANŠE.*ḪI.*A ṣa-lá-mu (ICK 1.188); 2 ANŠE [ṣa-lá-me] (ICK 1.189); 2 ANŠE ṣa-lá-me (KTS 1 30); 6 ANŠE.ḪI.A ṣa-lá-me (KTS 2 22); and 4 ANŠE.ḪI.A ṣa-lá-mu (KTS 2 38). When working with complex textual material, basic string matching is simply inadequate.

The Persepolis Fortification Archive Project (PFA)

The titan of OCHRE projects is the Persepolis Fortification Archive (PFA), directed by Matthew W. Stolper, Professor of Assyriology Emeritus at the Institute for the Study of Ancient Cultures of the University of Chicago.[11] Faced with an uncertain

---

[10] From the abstract to Stratford's book on the subject: "This volume focuses on a set of documents pertaining to a series of events that took place in one year. They reveal a tapestry of trade disruptions, illnesses, and commerce, as well as illuminate the relationships between texts and their material context, between narrative and time, and between economic forces and individual agency" (Stratford 2017).

[11] https://isac.uchicago.edu/research/projects/persepolis-fortification-archive.

future for tens of thousands of cuneiform tablets and fragments[12] discovered by the (then) Oriental Institute in 1933 at Persepolis (a site in modern-day southwestern Iran), Stolper spearheaded an ambitious effort (from 2002 to 2023) to document, transcribe, and photograph this collection. The tablets were inscribed with Elamite cuneiform texts, inked Aramaic texts, or both, often with seal impressions stamped or rolled on the clay. Stolper assembled an international team of experts in the Elamite language, the Aramaic language, and seal impressions, along with an army of students to photograph the tablets using various sophisticated methods.[13]

Confronted with the task of managing the variety of artifactual, textual, and photographic data generated by this project, Stolper turned to OCHRE. The online accessibility of OCHRE allowed his team around the USA and Europe to contribute content attributed to them. OCHRE Events track workflow as texts are collated and transcribed, as tablets are moved in and out of the photography lab, and as students are assigned tasks by their professor. The intensive photography effort inspired a streamlined interface in which the photographer snaps a picture, and then OCHRE adds it to the database, auto-names it, links the image to the appropriate database item, creates a thumbnail, and uploads both the high-resolution and thumbnail images to a secure server location where all are backed up that same night.

Having a single repository in which to record and integrate this detailed set of data proved to be empowering. Over the past fifteen years, this project alone has amassed over 1.7 million database items and over 100 terabytes of digital images, all managed by the powerful, flexible, and comprehensive data management system provided by OCHRE.

The Sereno Research Lab

A tour of the research lab of Paul Sereno, paleontologist (Professor of Organismal Biology and Anatomy) at the University of Chicago, is a journey in time and space.[14] Sereno shares vivid stories of his adventures around the world, introducing his dinosaurs by name and remembering every detail of where, when, and how they were found. Research assistants, determined to capture this data systematically, began by scanning his handwritten field notebooks, logging them within OCHRE—Niger 1993, Morocco 1995, Patagonia 1996, Gadoufaoua 1997, India 2001, Inner Mongolia 2004, Tibet 2006, Xinjiang 2007, and more. Collections of photographs were organized, spreadsheets listing artifacts were integrated, PDF copies of publications were cataloged, and specimens throughout the lab were inventoried and barcoded, creating a digital treasure trove.

---

[12] For background on the project, see Stolper (2007).

[13] See the PFA project website (https://isac.uchicago.edu/research/projects/persepolis-fortification-archive) for a description of the various photographic methods employed by the project, from conventional photography to high-resolution scanning, and Reflectance Transformation Imaging.

[14] https://paulsereno.uchicago.edu/fossil_lab/fossil_lab_gallery/.

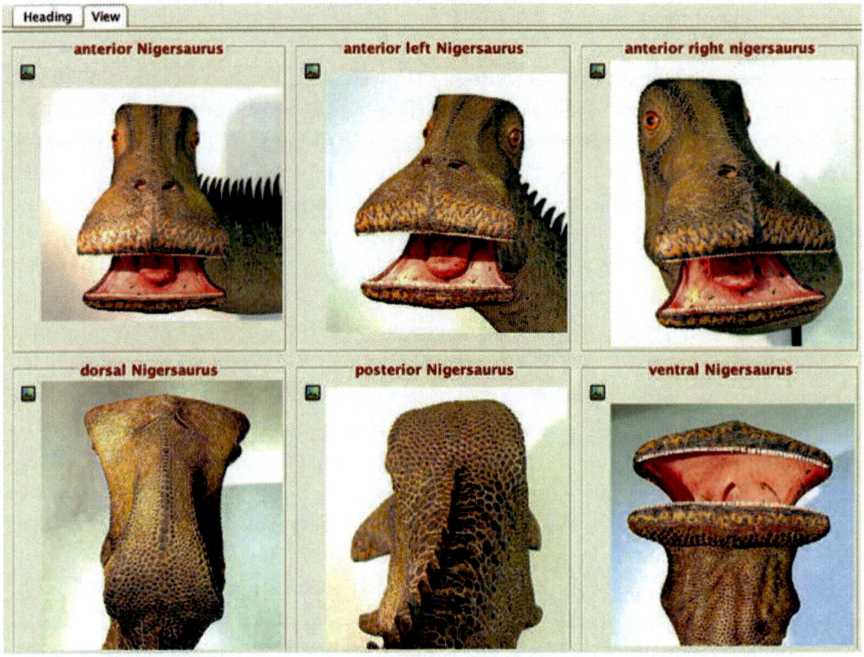

Fig. 1.5 The Nigersaurus, shown in OCHRE's Image Gallery, was made life-like by Tyler Keillor, fossil preparator and paleoartist in Sereno's laboratory since 2001

But while dinosaur hunting in the shifting sands of the Sahara Desert in central Niger, Sereno and his team discovered the site of Gobero where bones of crocodiles, hippos, fish, and humans mingled, along with stone harpoon blades and broken pottery. A new story emerged, that of life in a Green Sahara, and Sereno turned to OCHRE to document the discoveries there, richly illustrating that the recording possibilities of OCHRE know no bounds in time or space (Fig. 1.5).

The Zeitah Excavations

Ron Tappy, Professor Emeritus of Bible and Archaeology at Pittsburgh Theological Seminary, used carefully thought-out, paper-based documentation for the Zeitah Excavations (southern Israel) which he directed for over 10 years, beginning in the summer of 1999. This was around the time that the FileMaker database system became popular, owned and promoted by Apple, and *Microsoft Office 2000* released powerful new versions of its personal computing productivity software. Tappy's pages of detailed recording sheets, meticulously filled in by the excavation team, seemed ripe for automation, and he was fortunate to find a programmer, with a recreational enthusiasm for archaeology, to create a customized relational database which was a standard solution at the time.

But Tappy had concerns that his database was a "black box" over which he had little control. He also worried about his dependency on a technical specialist who may or may not be available to support the project in subsequent seasons. He was enticed by OCHRE's transparency. Even with no specialized technical skills, Tappy was empowered by OCHRE to create his own structures and descriptors to mimic his comprehensive paper-based system. Indeed, Tappy inspired new ways to add detail and nuance to OCHRE's descriptive possibilities. Tappy was also able, on his own, to create an extensive set of queries to rediscover his data later for further analysis. Although we like to think that OCHRE makes it easy for projects to share data, it is also true that OCHRE makes it easy to design a completely custom environment for one's own project data.

The Zincirli Excavations

When archaeologist David Schloen, director of the Zincirli Excavations,[15] traveled to southern Turkey in the early days of the project, he would check as baggage an empty suitcase nested within another empty suitcase for the sole purpose of having the capacity to carry home the reams of paperwork generated by the team throughout the summer's excavation. During the subsequent winter, archaeology students at the Institute for the Study of Ancient Cultures would be conscripted to transcribe that paperwork into a digital format, in the hope of capturing the "data" therein.

In addition, over sixteen years of excavation, many field staff, students, and specialists of all kinds would come and go, generating an intimidating digital collection. The faunal expert would study the bones, leaving behind a spreadsheet full of coded entries, arcane measurements ("Breadth of the biting surface of a tooth"), and obscure notation. The lithic expert would study the chipped stone, contributing a document describing the "retouched lateral proximal surface of the chert bladelet." Charcoal samples sent to specialists on the CRANE project would generate Bayesian statistics for dating calibrations. The ceramic specialist was onsite each season to analyze the "Iron Age bowls with thickened folded rims" and other pottery forms of interest. The detail, variety, and diversity of data would have posed a significant problem were it not for the flexible data representation schemes allowed by the OCHRE database system. The 162,000+ fully described extensively linked database items managed by OCHRE for this project reflect a successful data integration strategy (Fig. 1.6).

Appendix B: The OCHRE Origin Story

Over the long period of its development, OCHRE has ridden the tumultuous waves of the technology revolution, navigating rapid changes and instability in the software industry, in order to chart a course, whereby it could be pressed into service for

[15] https://zincirli.uchicago.edu.

Fig. 1.6 Aerial drone footage (pilot R. Schloen) added to the detailed and disparate data amassed at the site of Zincirli, Turkey, during sixteen years of excavations. (Photograph by M. Prosser, courtesy of the University of Chicago Zincirli Excavations)

many diverse projects. A brief look at the history of its development will explain why and how it came to be and will describe decisions that were made along the way. After over thirty years of fine-tuning the process of managing academic research data, and with feedback and suggestions from hundreds of active users, the OCHRE platform has evolved to become a workhorse on behalf of humanities research and a warehouse for millions of database items.

The story of OCHRE begins with the academic research of David Schloen, Professor of Archaeology at the Institute for the Study of Ancient Cultures and the Department of Near Eastern Languages and Civilizations of the University of Chicago. In the late 1980s, he was working on a Ph.D. at Harvard University. As part of his dissertation research, he studied textual and archaeological evidence from ancient Ugarit (Ras Shamra) in Syria to explore the "patrimonial household model" of ancient societies (Schloen 2001b). Having earned a degree in computer science and conveniently married to software engineer Sandra Schloen, it was logical to devise a database system to represent this evidence.

By this time, the creation of databases to support research had been popularized by user-friendly programs like dBase III and Paradox. These were "relational" databases where data was stored in tables having columns that identified descriptive qualities of rows of data. When multiple tables were needed for different types of data, they were naturally linked by common "key" fields. But even then, it quickly became apparent that the relational model was inadequate for representing the complexity of the data being derived from the Ras Shamra text corpus. Trying to capture too many relationships among too many things proved to be unwieldy. Rather, Schloen and Schloen devised a new item-based model that turned out to be widely applicable to all sorts of data born from the context of humanities research.

INFRA: An Integrated Facility for Research in Archaeology

By 1993, the Schloens had implemented a working database management system using Paradox that represented the salient features and content of thousands of Ugaritic tablets. Over thirty descriptive properties were used to record details such as Findspot, Findspot Depth, Tablet Length, Width and Thickness, Text Type, and Subtype (e.g., Legal: Sale-of-Property, Administrative: Account-of-Silver), Language, Text Condition, and Date of Text (e.g., Reign of …). Using an item-based model, variables and their corresponding values could be assigned as properties to tablet items either once, or multiple times, or not at all, depending on what information was available in the fragmentary record. As software tools improved to allow more sophisticated scripting, database-aware forms, and other user interface elements like menus and picklists, and as the Schloens' ambition for what had become a robust archaeological database system kept pace, the system developed into the Integrated Facility for Research in Archaeology (INFRA).

Barely off the ground, but in response to new paradigms in the field of technology, INFRA was rewritten in the mid-1990s to take advantage of object-oriented programming strategies which, conceptually, were ideally suited to the implementation of an item-based approach. Borland's Delphi rapid application development environment for Windows[16] was used for the frontend visual components which interacted with a Microsoft Access database engine[17] for the storage and organization of the underlying data. Thus equipped, INFRA became the tool used by D. Schloen and his students for recording field excavation data. Beginning in the summer of 1997, INFRA was used for a variety of other field projects in the Near East, including the Institute for the Study of Ancient Cultures project at Yaqush and the Leon Levy Expedition to Ashkelon. Other early adopters in the early 2000s included James K. Hoffmeier excavating at Tell el-Borg (Egypt), assisted by University of Chicago student Aaron Burke who served as the data entry specialist; Ron Tappy of the Zeitah Excavations; and Michel Fortin of l'Université Laval who adopted the item-based INFRA model and adapted it for other use (Fig. 1.7).

[16] INFRA was re-written first in 1995 using Borland's Delphi, based on Turbo Pascal, then in 1996 using Delphi 2, with Object Pascal for 32-bit Windows.

[17] An ODBC (Open Database Connectivity) driver provided the interface between the application frontend and the database backend.

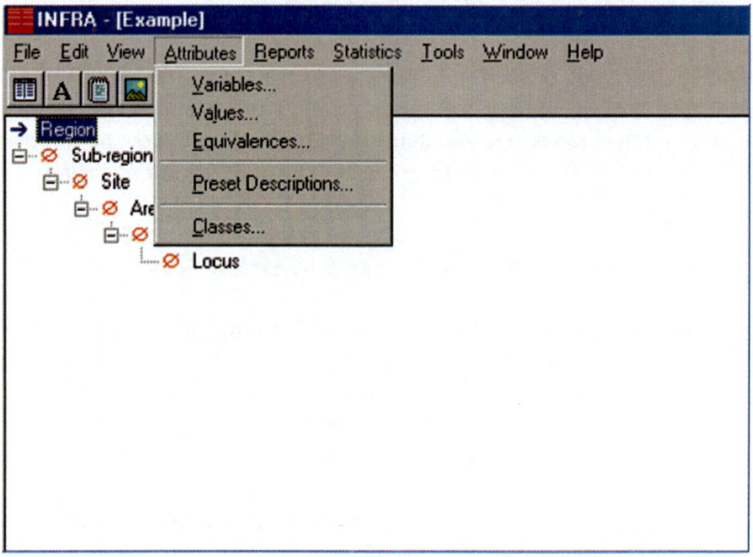

Fig. 1.7 A screenshot from Aaron Burke's user manual (Feb 2002) illustrates INFRA

As the computer industry grew and as software tools matured, technical familiarity and ability also grew within the academic community. Archaeologists turned-database-experts busied themselves designing database applications to capture archaeological data, each application in effect a digital recording system based on a specific field project's paper recording system with forms on the screen mimicking the paper record. But whether explicitly and consciously or not, the limitations of the table-based, relational model hamstrung such efforts to digitize archaeological data because conceptual barriers limit, in principle, what can be achieved with the relational approach. D. Schloen (2001a) expressed it thus:

> Most archaeologists use off-the-shelf commercial database software which is geared towards business applications and is not well-suited to representing archaeological data. Archaeological information is different than most business data because it is *spatially organized*, *temporally sequenced*, and *highly variable* to a much greater degree. As a result, conventional approaches to data management fail to realize the full potential of modern information technology for the advance of archaeology as an information-rich discipline.

XSTAR: The XML System for Textual and Archaeological Research

The 1990s was a time of rapid change in the computer industry. As INFRA was being field-tested and under constant enhancement, somewhat serendipitously two new developments in information technology caught up with the vision for INFRA and enabled its improvement in significant ways.

The first development was a new programming language, created at Sun Microsystems, called Java. Officially released in May 1995, Java has become one of the most popular and versatile programming languages in use today, allowing software developers to create "write once, run anywhere" code—code that is not system dependent and which is therefore compatible with Windows, Macintosh and Linux-based computers.[18] On the occasion of Java's 25th anniversary, a Java Magazine blogger remarked: "Little did anyone know that the programming language Sun was about to create would democratize computing, inspire a worldwide community, and become the platform for an enduring software development ecosystem of languages, runtime platforms, SDKs, open source projects, and lots and lots of tools" (Morales 2020).[19] While it is hard to remember or imagine a time before the Internet was in widespread use, Java was also significant at the time for supporting client–server capabilities that made it easier to write full-featured applications that facilitated Internet-based interaction with local personal computers which had become part of every academic's toolkit.

The second technological development that had a major impact on the future of INFRA was the arrival of the Extensible Markup Language (XML).[20] XML was invented as a reaction against HTML, the language upon which the World Wide Web was built and which provides the means for an application to "format text and multimedia" but which "is not very useful when it comes to describing information."[21] In introducing XML to its readers in May 1998 PC Magazine enthused, "Unlike HTML, XML allows you to define your own tags. This single feature frees you from the constraints of predefined tags and lets you structure the data in an XML document any way you like."[22] Even better for the Schloens, XML freed their item-based research data from the constraints of relational tables. The document-centered structure of XML suited perfectly the item-based approach, where each item could be fully and flexibly described, even uniquely so if necessary, by a discrete XML document, and where the descriptive properties (variables and their values) of database items converted easily to tags in the XML syntax.

Initially invented as a portable, human-readable, self-describing format for sharing both structured and semi-structured documents among differing applications, it took a few years for database technology to catch on to XML. While relational databases were dominant, they were not well suited to managing hundreds or thousands of individual XML documents. The tagline of an August 2001 article in a technology magazine entitled "Databases Embrace XML" read: "Whether as a data transport or native storage scheme, databases, often called the 900-pound gorilla of

[18] https://en.wikipedia.org/wiki/Write_once,_run_anywhere.

[19] First on the list of greatest Java apps ever written is the software that controlled the Spirit Mars Exploration Rover as it explored the red planet in 2004.

[20] The World Wide Web Consortium's (W3C) first created the official XML 1.0 Specification in 1998.

[21] PC Magazine, May 26, 1998, p. 230.

[22] See also Randall (1997).

IT, are making room for XML" (Barrett 2001). One such database was Tamino,[23] developed by European company Software AG, one of a new class of hierarchical and object-oriented databases designed specifically to store XML documents natively, not in relational structures or as binary objects.[24]

With Java as a new cross-platform, object-oriented programming language having features appropriate for developing Internet-based applications, and with XML-based database technology available to represent and manage countless numbers of item-based documents, S. Schloen began rewriting INFRA from scratch. This choice of tools was justified for reasons summarized by a Sun Microsystems Technical White Paper from 2001: "XML makes data portable. The Java platform makes code portable. The Java APIs for XML make it easy to use XML. Put these together, and you have the perfect combination: portability of data, portability of code, and ease of use" (Sun Microsystems 2001). While perhaps a bit of a gamble to embrace such fledgling technology, given the here-today-gone-tomorrow nature of the industry, the merits of using this combination of technology have been proven by the passing of time. Decades later—an eternity on the technology time scale—Java and XML are both still going strong!

The INFRA rewrite was also an opportunity to include an expanded feature set based on feedback from existing INFRA users and with a view to accommodating textual and lexical data for which, as we will demonstrate in the pages that follow, the item-based approach turns out to be especially appropriate. In 2001, with the support of Charles Blair of the Digital Library Development Center (DLDC) at Regenstein Library at the University of Chicago, the XML database Tamino, with its Java application programming interface (API), was installed to serve as the basis of the newly renamed, greatly enhanced, cross-platform, client–server[25] application: the XML System for Textual and Archaeological Research (XSTAR).

The use of "Textual"—the T in XSTAR—in the new name for this system reflected an intentional shift in emphasis from strictly archaeological data toward inclusion of lexical and textual content. In July 2001, S. Schloen prepared a document for then-director of the Institute for the Study of Ancient Cultures, Gene Gragg, and CHD editors Harry Hoffner and Theo van den Hout, mocking up sample entries of the CHD using XML. Lexical entries as database items linked to word items occurring on textual items (e.g., inscriptions) found in context with archaeological items (e.g., clay tablets) proved to be a powerful model for integrating the richly linked information that comprised the technically dense, highly annotated, semi-structured content of the CHD. With the support of Gragg and the CHD staff, XSTAR served as the basis for the first electronic edition of the CHD (eCHD). The

[23] "Tamino" is an acronym: Transactional Architecture for Managing Internet Objects.

[24] "Tamino's key differentiator is native storage and retrieval of well-formed or valid XML documents, along with the integrated management of Internet objects and SQL data, transaction support, high performance, and high scalability" (Schöning and Wäsch 2000).

[25] In this scenario, the Java application that runs locally on a user's personal computer (Windows, Mac, or Linux) acts as the "client" which interacts over the Internet with the Tamino "server" which is running remotely in a data center.

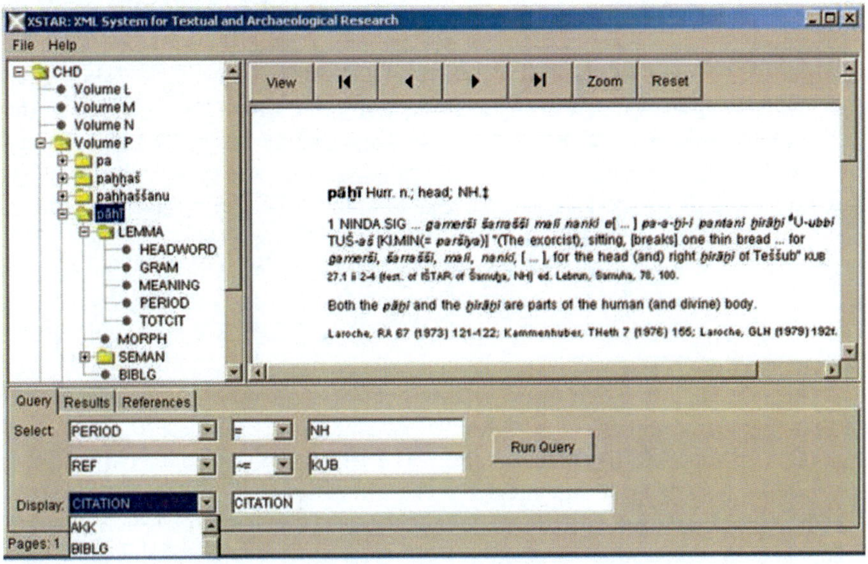

Fig. 1.8 The electronic Chicago Hittite Dictionary was first digitized in XSTAR

Persepolis Fortification Archive (PFA) project, led by Matthew W. Stolper of the Institute for the Study of Ancient Cultures, turned to XSTAR shortly after, as a database environment within which to represent its multifaceted archive—tablets impressed with Elamite texts, inked with Aramaic inscriptions, rolled with seal impressions, painstakingly studied, transcribed, translated, and imaged. These projects and their students offered valuable feedback that motivated ongoing development work. As the system grew, and as the item-based approach proved powerful enough to encompass cultural and historical data of all kinds, the system was once again renamed, this time as the Online Cultural and Historical Research Environment (OCHRE) (Fig. 1.8).

OCHRE: The Online Cultural and Historical Research Environment

By well into the new millennium, with extensive usage that inspired new features like expanded query options, integration of Geographic Information Systems (GIS) tools, and import/export mechanisms, OCHRE had become a mature, robust, well-tested application. The ongoing investment of time, data, and scholarly energy by several key projects at the Institute for the Study of Ancient Cultures, specifically the eCHD and PFA as well as several archaeology projects, created the need for a more formalized structure for OCHRE support and consulting. With encouragement by D. Schloen, support from then-director Gil Stein, and more formalized ties to Blair and the DLDC, the OCHRE Data Service was inaugurated in September 2011 under the management of OCHRE developer S. Schloen, with the mandate to provide support and services for projects anywhere using the OCHRE research platform.

Hired as the first full-time research database specialist of the OCHRE Data Service, Prosser arrived on the OCHRE scene in 2011 with a keen sense as to the nature of the problems that OCHRE addresses and a sense of relief for the solutions that it offers. Having ventured into the use of quantitative methods for his own dissertation research on the Ras Shamra textual archive, he had pushed a relational database approach (Microsoft Access) as far as possible for a technically savvy and determined user. Now, an OCHRE expert and consultant, Prosser (2018) has created a full-featured project for the study of the same set of texts from Ras Shamra that had started D. Schloen down this path, bringing OCHRE and its precedents full circle.

Today, OCHRE is a rich database environment supporting dozens of research projects in the humanities and social sciences. Still a Java client–server application running atop the XML database Tamino, OCHRE hosts a vast collection of disparate project data, itemized but integrated. This includes tens of thousands of texts, mostly ancient, and the millions of itemized signs and words of which they are comprised. From the words attested in these texts, tens of thousands of dictionary entries with detailed grammatical description have been documented in OCHRE. Hundreds of thousands of locations or objects in archaeological contexts across all scales and measures have been logged and described—everything ranging from entire geographic regions to microscopic botanical remains, from petrified dinosaur bones in ancient riverbeds to fish scales found in refuse pits and from painted, glazed Roman goblets in ancient Corinth to porcelain teacups found at the Amache National Historic Site in central Colorado. As supporting evidence for the artifacts and texts, millions of images, documents, and other external resources have been cataloged. The OCHRE Data Service, part of the Forum for Digital Culture of the University of Chicago since 2023, continues to provide technical support and data services (conversion, importation, archiving, etc.) for projects everywhere that depend on the OCHRE platform for the management of their research data.

Chapter 2
The Case for a Database Approach

Introduction

According to the Greek legend, Procrustes, son of Poseidon, controlled a stronghold on Mount Korydallos on the sacred way between Athens and Eleusis. There he had a bed in which he would invite passing travelers to spend the night under his roof. But turning his trade against his victims, Procrustes would set to work with his smith's hammer. If the guest proved too short, he would stretch them to fit; if the guest proved too tall, he would cut off the excess length. Nobody ever fitted the bed exactly (Fig. 2.1).[1]

As we make our case for a database approach, we argue against overly rigid restrictions that hinder, coerce, or otherwise force-fit data into a mis-sized bed. Data-rich research projects too often find themselves forcing data into structures that are ill-fitting—a complex text reduced to a single document with a predefined format or data limited by an inflexible controlled vocabulary. Such projects deserve instead a computational approach that allows for the integration of all data in a way that fits naturally, intuitively, and productively into the research program. A guiding principle of OCHRE is to provide "a place for every *thing* and everything in its place"—a structure within which data can fit, without distortion or compromise.

As we begin our case for a database approach, it seems necessary to clarify what we mean by *database*, a term that is often used loosely to refer to any collection of data in some digitized format. A spreadsheet, for example, with rows and columns of data, or a folder of word processing or other document files, or a collection of images in an online site, might all be called databases, colloquially and imprecisely. This also raises the rudimentary question of what *data* is, a question with which we begin our discussion in this chapter. We then review various approaches to

[1] https://en.wikipedia.org/wiki/Procrustes.

S. R. Schloen, M. C. Prosser, *Database Computing for Scholarly Research*, Quantitative Methods in the Humanities and Social Sciences,
https://doi.org/10.1007/978-3-031-46696-0_2

Fig. 2.1 This scene on this Attic red-figured kylix depicts Theseus giving Procrustes a taste of his own medicine (https://www.researchgate.net/figure/Theseus-adjusting-Procrustes-to-the-size-of-his-bed-Photograph-provided-by-Marie-Lan_fig5_277558596 Wikimedia Commons)

collecting, organizing, and publishing digital data that, in one way or another, might be thought of as constituting a database, at least in the informal sense of this word. Against this backdrop, we consider more formally the role of a database in support of the management and analysis of research data. Comparing OCHRE with existing database paradigms helps explain the rationale for a new approach and justify design considerations. Because our work and database experience are contextualized within the domains of humanities and social sciences research, our focus is on *research data*—which is gathered and modeled for the purpose of addressing research questions. Throughout, we advocate for the use of a comprehensive database environment that can faithfully and flexibly represent all types of data in a unified, compatible, and integrated manner in support of research goals.

What Is Data?

Digitized data is information that has been transformed into some format suitable for use by a computer process or by a human process that makes use of a computer. As Cox and Verbaan (2018, p. 19) point out, "The term 'data creation' may often be a more accurate term than 'data collection' or 'data capture', which imply that data are something existing before the researcher intervenes to actively construct them." These authors observe that there are significantly different views among disciplines or researchers as to what constitutes data, its importance, and the terminology used to describe it. They remind us that scholars in the humanities and social sciences do not necessarily think of their research material as "data" but, rather, as documents, manuscripts, codices, surveys, transcripts, artwork, maps, and the like. Data is often perceived to be numeric, the stuff of science and statistics. Therein lies the challenge of transforming observable units of inquiry of all kinds into forms conducive to computation and analysis. The following comprehensive definition of "research data" from the Concordat on Open Research Data developed in the UK resonates with us as it places data squarely within the context of serving research questions and encompasses both quantitative and qualitative information.

> Research data are the evidence that underpins the answer to the research question, and can be used to validate findings regardless of its form (e.g. print, digital, or physical). These might be quantitative information or qualitative statements collected by researchers in the course of their work by experimentation, observation, modelling, interview or other methods, or information derived from existing evidence. Data may be raw or primary (e.g. direct from measurement or collection) or derived from primary data for subsequent analysis or interpretation (e.g. cleaned up or as an extract from a larger dataset), or derived from existing sources where the rights may be held by others. … They may include, for example, statistics, collections of digital images, sound recordings, transcripts of interviews, survey data and fieldwork observations with appropriate annotations, an interpretation, an artwork, archives, found objects, published texts or a manuscript.[2]

The Challenge of Research Data

The above definition of research data hints at the wide range of types of data, along with their potential sources, which can quickly (or slowly) overwhelm a research project. Cox and Verbaan (2018) recognize that the "proliferation of data types is central to the challenge" of research data management (RDM). While we begin this next section by agreeing with that observation, there are additional factors that make the management of research data in the humanities and social sciences a genuine, nontrivial challenge from a computational perspective.

Research Data: Highly Diverse

Research data generated by scholarly pursuits tends to be wildly diverse. A typical research project will record data in many different formats and manage it using multiple applications. This may include both *quantitative* data that is well structured

---

[2] U.K. Research and Innovation Concordat on Open Research Data (https://www.ukri.org/wp-content/uploads/2020/10/UKRI-020920-ConcordatonOpenResearchData.pdf).

and which might be more naturally and intuitively organized, along with *qualitative* data that tends to be more freely formatted. Our work with archaeology projects finds us wrangling an accumulation of databases, spreadsheets, documents, images, and maps, created by different project personnel often over extended timeframes. The range of data generated by an excavation includes prose journal entries logging daily progress in tandem with stratigraphic analysis; identification and quantification of ceramic remains as well as faunal and botanical specimens; cataloging and processing of cultural artifacts of all kinds; scientific analysis of environmental evidence like radiocarbon, pollen, or petrographic samples; and evaluation and interpretation of historical and cultural events. Add to this an extensive photographic record of object photographs, field photographs, and aerial photographs, supplemented by videos or 3D models. The list goes on.

Diversity plagues textual studies, too as the scholar attempts first to decipher or capture what is written, and then, hopefully, to present an interpretation of the text. The problem for textual studies is compounded when the texts are written on sources which are archaeological in nature—inscribed on monumental ancient architecture, inked on fragile papyri, or impressed by stylus as cuneiform script upon clay tablets. These various textual media are archaeological objects to be treated separately from the texts which they preserve, often spatially situated in association with a coordinate, findspot, or other excavation context. They are physical objects that can be measured or analyzed for material composition. To further complicate matters, objects may have multiple texts written on them, perhaps using complex or dead languages or scripts, the study of which is itself a work of scholarship.[3] A text can be analyzed for epigraphy, paleography, grammar, syntax, and semantics. The process of representing a text as digital data should be informed by the realization that a text is not a stable thing. It is not a museum object that will have the same characteristics on each subsequent museum visit. A text is fluid, either as a function of revision or interpretation (Bryant 2002). A text is an expression of the inherent fuzzy thinking that defines human understanding. The challenge is to represent the text as data in a way that acknowledges and preserves these fluid and crisscrossing elements.

During the planning phase of a research project, it is essential to consider the diversity of the project's data and to choose appropriate data management strategies. Devising a consistent naming convention for images files or deciding on metadata fields for a catalog will help, but a comprehensive research platform like OCHRE can support higher ambitions for one's project data. If data is captured cleanly, recorded in meaningful parts, tagged with appropriate descriptors, and integrated with other project data, then the consequent stages of the project will proceed with much greater potential. Pause to consider your own research data and revel in its diversity. Then, imagine it all at your fingertips where it can be queried, reused, reconfigured, exported, published, shared, and archived with relative ease.

[3] For our purposes, a text is both the observable signs used to communicate an idea and the interpretation of those signs by the reader.

Research Data: Dispersed in Space and Time

Our roots in archaeological data management highlight another key feature of research data—that they often represent information dispersed across both space and time. These spatial or temporal contexts are not just incidental facts. They are key qualities, crucial to the research questions, which must be recognized as elements of study to be represented explicitly and accurately as data. Spatial contexts will vary greatly depending on the type of research being conducted, ranging from cross-continental expanses as migration patterns are studied by human geneticists to centimeter-level recording of a coin's findspot by an archaeologist. Likewise, some projects have sufficient evidence to record temporal periods down to the exact day of a certain year, while others can specify only a decade, a king's reign, a settlement phase, a cultural horizon, or a geological eon. Building a bespoke GIS database to manage spatial data or organizing content in a separate timeline widget only adds to the decentralization of project data. Much better is a computational research platform that provides infinite support for both space and time across all scales of measure.

Research Data: Vary as to Level of Detail

Research data varies greatly as to the level of detail available, or needed, for proper study. Again, because our work originates in the context of archaeology, data was often as fragmentary as the objects that were being unearthed. For example, a collection of faunal data might contain many long-bone shafts from indeterminate mammals. Maybe in a few cases, the faunal expert would be able to state with confidence that the bone was a femur of a red-tailed deer. Adding such a detail merely as a descriptive note seems inadequate, since we are more likely to want to be able to find these more interesting specimens again in our database. A highly detailed descriptive scheme is in order so that we can capture explicitly, and clearly as structured data, the full extent of what we do know, while having the flexibility to capture explicitly, and clearly as structured data, the cases where we do not have the same level of detail available.

Similarly, in the case of textual studies, one scholar may analyze a text as to its grammatical or other structural properties, satisfied to break down a text into high-level elements like clauses, phrases, and sentences. In other cases, for example, when studying ancient texts inscribed in clay using cuneiform script, like many of those we have seen in our work at the Institute for the Study of Ancient Cultures, each word or even character might be a distinct unit of observation whose nature first needs to be understood before the scholar can begin to consider the meaning of the text. Such a text would need to be analyzed at a much finer level of detail. The research platform needs to be sufficiently flexible to represent whatever level of detail is available or is deemed appropriate by the scholar.

Research Data: Disorganized (Or Semi-structured)

They say you can learn a lot about a person by the tidiness of their desk. The organizational strategies used in designing a spreadsheet can similarly yield a psychological profile of the scholar who produced it. From our experience, research data is often quite literally disorganized. The law of entropy also seems to apply: data organization tends toward chaos, especially when a project's data grows to a cumbersome size or languish over time. Recording procedures change, student assistants come and go, inconsistencies in data entry are introduced, new ideas are adopted, and technology inexorably requires upgrades along the way.

In fairness to scholars in the humanities and social sciences, this is a legitimate problem because the data, often by its very nature, lacks structure or an obvious organizing principle; that is, it is *semi-structured.* This presents challenges different from those faced by scientists who, by contrast, often have highly structured data that practically organizes themselves. This is not to say that science does not have its share of troubles too, and we believe that many of the strategies we advocate here are widely applicable to the sciences. But scientific data often is more well defined, more standardized, and has more built-in structure that translates easily into spreadsheet columns or database fields. Humanities and social sciences scholars benefit greatly from the use of a framework within which to organize even unstructured or semi-structured data and to capture effectively, and explicitly as possible, whatever structure can be found in their research data.

Research Data: Dirty

A 2014 *New York Times* article drew attention to another problem inherent in large collections of data—it is dirty. This has spawned an industry of data scientists or data janitors as they are sometimes called, charged with the task—a very necessary and important one—of cleaning dirty data. "Data scientists … spend from 50 percent to 80 percent of their time mired in this more mundane labor of collecting and preparing unruly digital data, before it can be explored for useful nuggets" (Lohr 2014). The value of any data will be in proportion to the trouble taken to prepare it for analysis and research. "It's an absolute myth that you can send an algorithm over raw data and have insights pop up" (ibid.).[4] The diversity of the data, the variation among data formats, and the ambiguity of descriptive language all limit the value that can be gained by automated means. While improvements in artificial intelligence, natural language processing, and other software algorithms will continue to advance the outcomes of such techniques as demonstrated, for example, by IBM's Watson computer which showed promise in aiding in decision-making processes

[4] This sentiment was expressed by Jeffrey Heer, a professor of computer science at the University of Washington and a cofounder of Trifacta, a start-up based in San Francisco.

for information-intensive fields (e.g., healthcare),[5] we have no basis for assuming that anytime soon computers will be able to spare us the hard work of maintaining clean, well-organized data. Our experience integrating legacy data sets (those compiled by pre-digital means) with born-digital data has taught us that it is sometimes necessary to simply roll up our sleeves and do janitorial work.[6] Data collected without the constraint of a picklist[7] or a controlled vocabulary will exhibit every imaginable inconsistency. Investing effort in cleaning up data so that it can be rationally and thoroughly integrated with other data within the research platform maximizes its value and helps ensure that meaningful information does not slip through cracks in the data structures. As mundane as the task of fixing typographical errors, standardizing terminology, eliminating cruft, and resolving idiosyncratic abbreviations may seem, the result is not only very satisfying but can amplify the amount of data available to the research enterprise.

Research Data: Support Disagreements

Even clean, well-organized data will not unequivocally answer research questions and may be used instead to support disagreements as scholars use data to offer differences of opinion or to draw different conclusions. "The computer says" is not reason enough to support a scholarly argument, even one that is data-driven. Rather than serving as some authoritative voice, the computer should be able to capture the essence of the discussion, describe its basis in data, and attribute content as to its source, as scholars make arguments, express disagreements, and reflect a degree of uncertainty. Whether one agrees with him or not, Nietzsche's famous statement that "there are no facts, only interpretations"[8] highlights the need for the representation of research data to accommodate multiple and attributable points of view. The use of attribution, multiple observations or text editions, integrated bibliography, and other features in OCHRE provides support for this extra dimension of scholarly disagreement and can help document the history of scholarship on a given topic.

[5] It now seems inevitable that large language models will play a role in health care and beyond (Dave et al. 2023).

[6] Good tools are available to help with such tasks, like OpenRefine, "a free, open-source, powerful tool for working with messy data" (https://openrefine.org).

[7] By "picklist" we mean a user interface mechanism to provide a list (usually drop-down) of only valid values from which the user can choose.

[8] See Friedrich Nietzsche, *The Will to Power*, translated by Walter Kaufmann and R. J. Hollingdale (1968), section 481.

In Contrast to Research Data

There are any number of ways to create and organize research data. Scholars use different methods based on what seems natural and often to very good effect. But just as often we fall prey to common misconceptions that give a false sense of accomplishment as it pertains to the data creation process, the data organization choices, and the success of the outcomes.

Research Data: Not to Be Confused with Mere Digitization

The mere process of digitization does not necessarily create useful research data. The information page of your passport can be scanned and saved as a document (e.g., a PDF) or as an image to produce a digital copy of your passport information but that does not make the information in the passport accessible as research data. If we had thousands of passport images, we could not compile and study the distribution or frequencies of names and dates of birth without first passing the images through some sort of text recognition or computer vision process. Archaeologists scan field notebooks created by the field staff while excavating the site. The scanned documents will be important as a reference source and will become part of the digital assets of the project. But data in this format cannot be analyzed, summarized, or otherwise usefully processed for research. So, while digitization for record-keeping is often a good first step, it should not represent one's only ambition for such information.

To give another example, GIS data composed of numerous polygons, line segments, and points is often painstakingly traced from an archaeological top-plan or derived from extensive collections of electronically captured geophysical survey data. But unless there is an associated level of corresponding detail about these shapes—identification, context, relationships to other shapes, and so on—we are left only with graphics that are not useful as research data. To use such data effectively, it needs to be carefully articulated, fully described, and integrated with other relevant information about the objects being represented by the digitization. While it may require a significant investment of time and effort, it is essential to enrich digitized content with supporting data to make it meaningful.

Research Data: Not to Be Confused with Mere Description

Digitization efforts of the abovementioned field notebooks might be taken one step further to create a transcription of the information, either as an electronic document or as a spreadsheet of columns of data with values like the diameter of a coin or the length of a wall, mixed with columns of descriptive prose. Although it is natural to record entries such as "3 bronze arrowheads and a flint blade frag" or "tablet; obverse has a wormhole, reverse is partially damaged," it is difficult to use these descriptions for research. It would be impossible to perform statistical analysis of the distribution of bronze arrowheads. Similarly, it would be difficult to query for tablets with undamaged surfaces. To address research questions, purely descriptive data should be enhanced with properly structured discrete fields or attributes that target key information. While long narrative entries are informative and easily readable, such descriptions tend to be unscientific, anecdotal, rife with typographical errors and idiosyncratic abbreviations, and marked by inconsistently applied formatting, making even character string searching haphazard at best.

The purely descriptive method of recording observations follows the paradigm of an old-fashioned notecard system where some noteworthy element is used for organization (e.g., a call number or a keyword) and all other information is recorded in a narrative form that must be interpreted by the scholar each time it is accessed. In a world where sharing of primary data and collaboration among colleagues is desirable, and where statistical analysis and other computational methods are easily accessible, we can do better than digital notecards. The use of free-format text or unstructured string fields should be discouraged, used sparingly, or supplemented with structured data to create effective research data.

The 2015 workshop *Mobilizing the Past for a Digital Future: The Future of Digital Archaeology* gathered "leading practitioners of digital archaeology in order to discuss the use, creation, and implementation of mobile and digital, or so-called 'paperless,' archaeological data recording systems" (Walcek Averett et al. 2016, p. vii). While the outcomes of two days of sessions were not, exactly, the how-to manual of best practice they had hoped for, the published proceedings offer up a rich, varied, stimulating, and self-reflective discussion based on real-world experience that "ultimately proved that there are many ways to 'do' digital archaeology, and that archaeology as a discipline is engaged in a process of discovering what digital archaeology should (and, perhaps, should not) be ..." Contributor Stephen Ellis (2016, p. 64), whose team members at Pompeii were early adopters of iPads for data collection, emphasized that "both structured and unstructured recording should, and can, be performed regardless of the medium," whether using a paper-based system or digital tools. But we are not surprised by his assessment that "...in reality, our post-excavation processing of the data has drawn immeasurably more valuable information from the structured data."

Research Data: Not to Be Confused with Mere Content Management

Content Management Systems (CMS) represent a broad category of software used to organize and present digital assets like images and documents. They have been widely adopted in corporate and academic contexts and vary in available features, tools, licensing, and cost. CMS platforms focus on cataloging data which is typically entered into configurable pages, forms, tables, or other simple structures for the purpose of sharing or publication. Catalog entries are enriched with often substantial amounts of metadata which might document authorship and copyright, for example, and which can form the basis for extensive filtering or querying of the available content. In the academic sphere, the Omeka platform is a popular CMS that provides "web publishing platforms for sharing digital collections and creating media-rich online exhibits."[9]

While CMS platforms make static data widely accessible via pleasing displays and efficient navigation tools, they are no substitute for a research database platform. If one's ambition is fulfilled by pleasing, well-organized, easily navigable webpages bursting with content and metadata, then a CMS may be an excellent choice. But be aware of their restrictions. On most CMS platforms, there are very few options for querying, reusing, or integrating data in ways beyond a simple page display.[10] With content delivered pages at a time at the request of a human viewer, a CMS serves a valuable role as reference but has limited scope for research.

Research Data: Not to Be Confused with Mere Razzle-Dazzle

As technological advances continue to amaze and impress, there is a temptation to be captivated by technology for its own sake and to pass off as research that which is merely an impressive display or application of the latest gadget. Pinching and swiping at midair while wearing fancy goggles in a virtual reality environment, navigating an avatar through video game quality graphics, endlessly rotating, skewing and morphing a 3D model, building color-coded node-graph cluster diagrams, or piloting a quadcopter for aerial photography can be great fun, and can serve in many helpful ways to educate, elucidate, illustrate, and amuse.[11] Cutting edge digital interface tools, such as virtual reality, succeed as tools for engaging students and the public in museums and the classroom and can be an effective way to visualize data.[12] But not everyone is enamored by the "recent intensification of digital methods in archaeological research" noted here as the *Mobilizing the Past* participants grappled with the impact of "cyber archaeology" (Gordon et al. 2016, p. 5).

> …to be able to offer "unprejudiced" representations of the past by enrolling digital media into a campaign of achieving more and more precision, speed, resolution, supposed immersion, and purported objectivity and "virtual reversibility" of excavation via totalised forms of recording…deploying the wow-factor to draw people into…an unproductive, and in many cases fallacious, conversation about the revolutionary nature of the methodologies. (Perry 2015)

We are well cautioned not to use technology uncritically and to be careful of the claims we make for digital methods. Maximizing the value of digital tools and their end products requires that they be tightly integrated with research data and with established processes of analysis and scholarship. Care must be taken not to neglect the work of building rich data foundations in support of these valuable, and often more compelling, technologies.

---

[9] See https://omeka.org/. WordPress and Drupal are similar platforms widely used in academic circles.

[10] We have had some success with CMS tools that can accommodate calls to an API as a means of fetching data, as does the more recent Omeka S version.

[11] On the use of virtual reality tools foreign language teaching, see Dobrova, et al. (2017).

[12] On the use of virtual reality tools to stimulate student engagement, see Lau and Lee (2015).

Research Data: Not to Be Confused with Mere Markup

Markup is an encoding strategy that uses an inventory of elements (tags) to define the structure, formatting, semantics, and other aspects of data. In-line markup places these elements directly in the data file. Standoff markup places these elements outside the data being described. Perhaps the most ubiquitous form of markup, HTML (Hypertext Markup Language) creates the structure of a web page and its content. An HTML document is not a database. One may derive an HTML document from an underlying database in which the research data is stored in a more granular format. But the output as HTML, while being an acceptable and usable format for publishing and sharing information, does not necessarily resemble the format in which the data is stored in the underlying database. In fact, it rarely does.

There are many other markup standards[13] which were mainly intended to be used to define a common *schema*—which describes the structure and constraints of a data format (Garcia-Molina et al. 2008, p. 5) for documenting and sharing published files across computer systems. For example, the Lexical Markup Framework defines the structure and semantics of a markup schema used for sharing and publishing dictionary lexical data in predictable formats (Francopoulo 2012). Similarly, the Text Encoding Initiative (TEI) guideline for text edition encoding provides an extensive vocabulary of elements and attributes to encode digital text editorial practice using the Extensible Markup Language (XML)—a plain text notation that uses embedded markup tags to describe the semantics of textual data. Applying the TEI guidelines to textual content typically results in a single, static TEI-XML document per text edition, formatted in accordance with the chosen standard, and as such is useful within a community of scholars that have adopted the same standard. Editing tools are available to help users create "well-formed" documents that conform to a schema. But better still would be a more dynamic, more flexible database approach to research data which represent data in a computationally accessible form, from which one can produce any number of published forms of the data according to any number of markup standards.

Research Data: Not to Be Confused with Metadata

The term *metadata*, commonly described as "data about data," is also reminiscent of an earlier day when brick-and-mortar libraries contained card catalogs full of index cards that described other resources—the actual books—that were on the library's

[13] For the Geography Markup Language, see Sharma and Herring (2018). The CIDOC Conceptual Reference Model (CIDOC-CRM) has been adopted by many in the archeology or cultural heritage communities. See also the textual markup guideline maintained by the Text Encoding Initiative (TEI) https://tei-c.org/. Many other markup standards exist for domain-specific purposes.

shelves. The title, author, date of publication, and call number would all be considered metadata about the book. Metadata standards, like the well-known Dublin Core, prescribe what kind of metadata should be collected about which kinds of objects.[14] Dublin Core, specifically, provides a generic, structured vocabulary for describing anything "that can be named"—books, artwork, songs, people, services, …; in short, anything. Limited to fifteen descriptors like "title," "description," and "date," it is not intended to describe domain-specific research data. Many other metadata schemas have been developed for specific domain areas. For example, a study of shipwrecks, parks, gardens, and archaeological sites of interest in the UK might reference the MIDAS Heritage metadata schema.[15] A study of Renaissance art might use the Categories for the Description of Works of Art (CDWA) Getty vocabulary.[16]

With burgeoning collections of data that vary greatly in the kinds of data being collected, one may wonder whether there is still a useful distinction to be made between data and metadata. The massive Twitter archive at the Library of Congress initially included approximately 21 billion tweets dating from 2006 to 2010. Each of these tweets had more than 50 associated metadata fields such as "place" and "description."[17] With each tweet limited to the maximum of 140 characters, the metadata greatly outweighed the primary data. On some level, metadata is still just data.

Metadata schemas are useful starting places to help make one's data findable and to situate it in the context of other relevant data. Applying a relevant metadata standard to a data set and its resources, for example, usefully describes it using terms that are semantically meaningful to other researchers, in the hope of making the data set more discoverable and intelligible. However, research data should not be reduced to the restrictions of metadata schemas or forced to fit a predefined set of limited descriptors. While it is good to plug into standard conventions, a scholar should not be limited by them.

Research Data: Not to Be Confused with Big Data

Speaking of the Twitter archive, we should clarify that our definition of research data is not synonymous with "big data." The handling of big data is a rather different problem that emerged in response to huge volumes of transactional data being generated either *en masse* by Web usage or social media activity, like the Twitter

[14] The term "Dublin Core" is a trademark. For more information, see https://dublincore.org/.

[15] https://historicengland.org.uk/images-books/publications/midas-heritage/.

[16] https://www.getty.edu/research/publications/electronic_publications/cdwa/.

[17] http://www.loc.gov/today/pr/2013/files/twitter_report_2013jan.pdf.

archive, or in an automated way, for example, by medical sensors, traffic cameras, or electronic devices. ("Volume" is the first of the original 5 V's used to describe big data, the others being velocity, variety, veracity, and value.) The ever-growing Internet of Things (IoT)—things like your fitness tracker or Alexa-enabled crock-pot, along with a huge range of consumer, commercial, and industrial devices—is generating massive amounts of data. Big data calls for data mining strategies or statistical methods that look for patterns and trends in large quantities of data, and it raises different issues of data collection, representation, and access. Big data also redefines the notion of sharing data. Whereas it is generally desirable to share data among collaborators and the research community of users, the sheer scale and scope of data have made it more important to facilitate sharing among computational processes rather than human consumers.

Big data researchers deal with such large quantities of data that they have the luxury of being selective, typically throwing out data that seems under-represented, inconsequential, or statistically irrelevant—in effect "noise." In studying a corpus of 30,000 historical novels, for example, researchers might eliminate words that were not properly transcribed by OCR,[18] common words that occur too many times ("it," "and"), or words that are not attested in a control dictionary. Studies using big data often involve "machine learning" (ML) techniques, assigning the task of crunching the data to computer algorithms based on artificial intelligence, rather than to human scholars, in the hope of gleaning new insights or becoming more productive. To tag such a corpus of literature manually would otherwise take an enormous effort. However, sometimes an enormous effort is required and justified. Research in the humanities and social sciences sometimes cannot accept noise in the data demanding careful curation instead, whether digital or not. Our colleagues at the Institute for the Study of Ancient Cultures celebrated the completion of the *Chicago Assyrian Dictionary* in 2011—twenty-six volumes and ninety years after the project was initiated in 1921 by the founder of the (then) Oriental Institute, James Henry Breasted.[19] While not a digital project, this was an enormous effort!

Big data can, indeed, be used for research purposes, but it is not the focus of our discussion. We are not concerned about how to collect over half-a-billion tweets each day generated by the public-at-large or with mining subjects and predicates from millions of Wikipedia pages in order to study how humans navigate complex information systems (Aguinaga et al. 2015) or with scraping public data sets for grist for statistical analyses or computational exercises. Our interest, instead, resonates with what has been called in the scientific community "the long tail" of research where:

[18] Optical character recognition (OCR) refers to the conversion of typed, printed, or handwritten text into machine-readable encoded text.

[19] The completion of the Chicago Assyrian Dictionary as reported by the *New York Times*: https://www.nytimes.com/2011/06/07/science/07dictionary.html.

> …individuals and small teams collect data for specific projects. These data tend to be small in volume, local in character, intended for use only by these teams, and are less likely to be structured in ways that allow data to be transferred easily between teams or individuals. While "big data" is getting the attention, small science and the long tail appear to constitute the major portion of scientific funding. Making data from the long tail discoverable and reusable is emerging as a major challenge. (Wallis et al. 2013, p. 3)

Data collection and management strategies used in our project work emphasize quality even when dealing with quantity and aim to serve individual scholars or research projects which are collecting and curating primary data, carefully and with intent, whether big[20] or small. The goal is to model data in ways that support research questions and to publish data in ways that serve the research community. This might include serving the goals of research based on big data too, by managing inputs, outputs, and analysis generated by such research, with the aims of promoting discoverability and reusability of relevant data, encouraging reproducibility of workflows, and facilitating publication of results.

Big data touches on the debate in Digital Humanities (DH) over the merits of "close" versus "distant" reading of literary texts. While a detailed analysis of this issue is beyond the scope of this book, it leads us to the work of Katherine Bode, an Associate Professor of Literary and Textual Studies at the Australian National University. Bode "struck a nerve" in the DH community by articulating a "long-standing critique of large-scale text analysis methods: a neglect of book history" (McGrath 2019). In reviewing Bode's (2018) book, *A World of Fiction*, McGrath explains:

> Many distant readers, [Bode] argues, treat data as a transparent window that allows us to see all of literary history without restriction. Bode insists that we look at the window itself: that we learn about the history of the design of the frame, the architect who designed it and the builder who assembled it, the materials used by the glazier to construct the panes, how the window in the structure compares to others in the vicinity, who owns the structure and how much they paid for it, what the breeze is like when window is opened (if it opens at all), and how recently it's been dusted. Only then can we accurately assess the quality of the view. (McGrath 2019)

In making a distinction between (big) data and *curated* data, Bode calls for a more intentional approach to creating a *scholarly edition*—"a new scholarly object for (data-rich) literary history" (Bode 2018, p. 46)—backed by literary data which should "be carefully documented and understood as itself a scholarly product with argumentative aims" (McGrath 2019). She exemplifies this approach in her own work, *A World of Fiction*, publishing it in tandem with a carefully curated, publicly available data set[21] on which she based her own computational analyses. Taking liberties with established systems of textual and bibliographic metadata, she invented descriptive categories relevant to her research goals, such as the notion of

[20] As of July 2023, the OCHRE database is managing almost 10,000,000 intentionally and carefully curated database items generated by almost one hundred projects.

[21] Commended as being accessible even to the technically uninclined, the data set is hosted online at "To be continued: *The Australian Newspaper Fiction Database*" (https://readallaboutit.com.au/).

"Inscribed gender" to account for a female author like George Eliott who wrote under a male name. While wholly appreciating the role of large-scale data analytics for literary analysis, we applaud Bode's emphasis on the scholarly edition and her freedom in tagging data beyond conventional boundaries. We pause to add that one scholar's "close" might be another scholar's "distant" and we take up the question of *How far is far enough*? elsewhere in this book (Fig. 2.2).

While digitization, description, eye-catching visualizations, metadata tagging, and content management are legitimate data representation strategies, we are seeking "immeasurably more" value from research data on the strength of more-than-mere digital methods. And while not denying the importance of big data, sometimes less is more—less data more coherently and explicitly organized can provide more value than reams of loosely structured information. Of course, such generalizations depend entirely on the sort of research questions being asked of the data but let us be sure to be suitably ambitious about getting the most from our research data. To this end, our overarching goal is to design a database system that makes available as much data as possible to as many users as possible for as many purposes as possible.

Fig. 2.2 Professor Matthew W. Stolper performing a "close reading" of a Persepolis Fortification tablet in his office at the Institute for the Study of Ancient Cultures of the University of Chicago (by Pfa16, own work, licensed under Creative Commons Attribution-Share Alike 4.0 International, https://commons.wikimedia.org/w/index.php?curid=57530401)

What Is a Database?

C. J. Date, a pioneer and long-standing authority in the field of database systems, describes a database as "a computerized record-keeping system…whose overall purpose is to store information and to allow users to retrieve and update that information on demand" (Date 2004, p. 6). Another answer given in a well-known college textbook, *Database Systems: The Complete Book*, is that "in essence a database is nothing more than a collection of information that exists over a long period of time" (Garcia-Molina et al. 2008, p. 1). This rather mundane definition is then followed by 1045 pages of more than what one probably ever needs to know about databases. But on page 1, the authors summarize the five key features of a database management system, paraphrased here: (1) It allows users to add new data and define its structure; (2) it gives users the ability to query and modify the data; (3) it supports the storage of very large amounts of data over a long period of time; (4) it enables durability, i.e., safeguards against errors and other points of failure; and (5) it controls access to data by many simultaneous users.

There is much to be said about databases in general, but we will focus here on a few key points to inform our discussion. Data consists of basic entities that represent "anything that is of significance to the individual or organization concerned" (Date 2004, p. 6) with "relationships linking those basic entities together" (p. 12). Any entity is uniquely identifiable and distinguishable from any other entity (pp. 269–271). Furthermore, any entity ("any object about which we wish to record information") and the connecting relationships between entities "can be regarded as having properties, corresponding to the information we wish to record about them" (p. 14).

Every database system has as its conceptual underpinnings a *data model*: "an abstract, self-contained, logical definition of the objects, operators, and so forth, that together constitute the abstract machine with which users interact. The objects allow us to model the *structure* of the data. The operators allow us to model its *behavior*" (Date 2004: 15).

Although we doubt it is necessary to justify the need to model data intentionally and to use a database of *some* kind, Date reminds us of the benefits of a database approach: the data can be shared among many users for many purposes; redundancy can be reduced; inconsistency can be avoided (e.g., by not having separate copies of the same data managed differently); security can be enforced to control who has access to what data; and standards can be observed, making the data more useful for sharing and interchange (ibid., p. 18).

In the sections that follow, we will keep these basic concepts in mind concerning database systems and their underlying data models as we evaluate the suitability of different data models for representing research data. As we review common strategies of data management, we will put them to the test, regarding both structure and behavior:

- Does the data structure allow the representation of *uniquely identifiable entities* for "anything that is of significance"?

- Does the data structure allow for representing *relationships* among those entities?
- Does the data structure allow for describing *properties* "corresponding to the information we wish to record" about the entities?
- Does the database behavior allow for *querying* data?
- Does the database behavior provide for data *integrity* (its overall accuracy, completeness, consistency, and therefore, reliability)?
- Does the database behavior provide support for *long-term sustainability* of the data we need to keep? (While this is not so much a technical consideration as an organizational or institutional concern, when the data structure plays a role, it will be noted here.)
- Does the database behavior allow data *sharing*?

Keep in mind your own data throughout the ensuing discussion. What are the things of significance to your research, and what are the relationships between them? What do you wish to record about those things? How will you want to find them for further analysis? How will their organization spiral out of control if you are not careful and intentional? How upset would you be when your student assistant graduates? With whom do you wish to share your raw data? Your analytic techniques? Your results?.

There are no right answers to these questions; the right answer is the one that is right for you and your project team and your research goals (Fig. 2.3). Solutions entail balancing trade-offs among many factors, weighing pros and cons. As we survey typical approaches to the management of research data, we explain and justify the decisions we made when designing and building the robust and comprehensive OCHRE database system. We assign a "suitability score" for each approach in light of what we believe to be the best method for representing and managing the data of complex research projects in the humanities and social sciences.

Research Data as Single Tables: The Flat File Data Model

A very simple and widely used method of modeling data involves the use of *flat files* in which data is structured as tabular rows (records) and columns. A number of well-known data formats are based on the flat file model, for example, the CSV (comma-separated value) format using plain text, the "data frames" used by data analysis programs written in Python or R, and spreadsheet formats like Microsoft Excel and Google Sheets. The first row of the file normally lists column headings that describe the data values in each subsequent row. The rows contain one data value per column, even if it is just a blank or null value, corresponding to the sequence of the headings. In the case of a CSV file, easily created using any simple text editor, the headings and corresponding values are separated by commas (Fig. 2.4); for TSV files, they are separated by tabs. Optionally, rather than using a delimiter like a comma or tab, data fields can have a fixed width instead, creating the needed alignment with the column headings.

Fig. 2.3 What is right for you? …"'visual thinkers' might remember the bright blue cover of the novel they read last summer, rather than who wrote it, or its title" (https://slate.com/human-interest/2014/02/arranging-your-books-by-color-is-not-a-moral-failure.html. Image by See-ming Lee 李思明 SML, Creative Commons Attribution-Share Alike 2.0)

```
"URI","Title","RecordId","Tpq","Taq","Coin Type URI","Description",
"Findspot","Findspot URI","Reference","Date Record Modified"
```

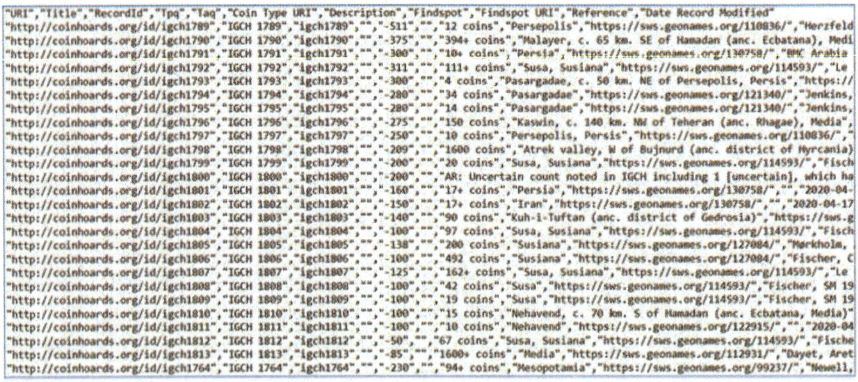

```
"URI","Title","RecordId","Tpq","Taq","Coin Type URI","Description","Findspot","Findspot URI","Reference","Date Record Modified"
"http://coinhoards.org/id/igch1789","IGCH 1789","igch1789","","-511","","12 coins","Persepolis","https://sws.geonames.org/110836/","Herzfeld
"http://coinhoards.org/id/igch1790","IGCH 1790","igch1790","","-375","","394+ coins","Malayer, c. 65 km. SE of Hamadan (anc. Ecbatana), Medi
"http://coinhoards.org/id/igch1791","IGCH 1791","igch1791","","-300","","10+ coins","Persia","https://sws.geonames.org/130758/","BMC Arabia
"http://coinhoards.org/id/igch1792","IGCH 1792","igch1792","","-311","","111+ coins","Susa, Susiana","https://sws.geonames.org/114593/","Le
"http://coinhoards.org/id/igch1793","IGCH 1793","igch1793","","-300","","4 coins","Pasargadae, c. 50 km. NE of Persepolis, Persis","https://
"http://coinhoards.org/id/igch1794","IGCH 1794","igch1794","","-280","","34 coins","Pasargadae","https://sws.geonames.org/121340/","Jenkins,
"http://coinhoards.org/id/igch1795","IGCH 1795","igch1795","","-280","","14 coins","Pasargadae","https://sws.geonames.org/121340/","Jenkins,
"http://coinhoards.org/id/igch1796","IGCH 1796","igch1796","","-275","","150 coins","Kaswin, c. 140 km. NW of Teheran (anc. Rhagae), Media",
"http://coinhoards.org/id/igch1797","IGCH 1797","igch1797","","-250","","10 coins","Persepolis, Persis","https://sws.geonames.org/110836/","
"http://coinhoards.org/id/igch1798","IGCH 1798","igch1798","","-209","","1600 coins","Atrek valley, W of Bujnurd (anc. district of Hyrcania)
"http://coinhoards.org/id/igch1799","IGCH 1799","igch1799","","-200","","20 coins","Susa, Susiana","https://sws.geonames.org/114593/","Fisch
"http://coinhoards.org/id/igch1800","IGCH 1800","igch1800","","-200","","AR: Uncertain count noted in IGCH including 1 [uncertain], which ha
"http://coinhoards.org/id/igch1801","IGCH 1801","igch1801","","-160","","17+ coins","Persia","https://sws.geonames.org/130758/","","2020-04-
"http://coinhoards.org/id/igch1802","IGCH 1802","igch1802","","-150","","17+ coins","Iran","https://sws.geonames.org/130758/","","2020-04-17
"http://coinhoards.org/id/igch1803","IGCH 1803","igch1803","","-140","","90 coins","Kuh-i-Tuftan (anc. district of Gedrosia)","https://sws.g
"http://coinhoards.org/id/igch1804","IGCH 1804","igch1804","","-100","","97 coins","Susa, Susiana","https://sws.geonames.org/114593/","Fisch
"http://coinhoards.org/id/igch1805","IGCH 1805","igch1805","","-138","","200 coins","Susiana","https://sws.geonames.org/127084/","Mørkholm,
"http://coinhoards.org/id/igch1806","IGCH 1806","igch1806","","-100","","492 coins","Susiana","https://sws.geonames.org/127084/","Fischer, C
"http://coinhoards.org/id/igch1807","IGCH 1807","igch1807","","-125","","162+ coins","Susa, Susiana","https://sws.geonames.org/114593/","Le
"http://coinhoards.org/id/igch1808","IGCH 1808","igch1808","","-100","","42 coins","Susa","https://sws.geonames.org/114593/","Fischer, SM 19
"http://coinhoards.org/id/igch1809","IGCH 1809","igch1809","","-100","","19 coins","Susa","https://sws.geonames.org/114593/","Fischer, SM 19
"http://coinhoards.org/id/igch1810","IGCH 1810","igch1810","","-100","","15 coins","Nehavend, c. 70 km. S of Hamadan (anc. Ecbatana, Media)"
"http://coinhoards.org/id/igch1811","IGCH 1811","igch1811","","-100","","10 coins","Nehavend","https://sws.geonames.org/122915/","","2020-04
"http://coinhoards.org/id/igch1812","IGCH 1812","igch1812","","-50","","67 coins","Susa, Susiana","https://sws.geonames.org/114593/","Fische
"http://coinhoards.org/id/igch1813","IGCH 1813","igch1813","","-85","","1600+ coins","Media","https://sws.geonames.org/112931/","Dayet, Aret
"http://coinhoards.org/id/igch1764","IGCH 1764","igch1764","","-230","","94+ coins","Mesopotamia","https://sws.geonames.org/99237/","Newell,
```

Fig. 2.4 A CSV export option lists coin hoard details aligned with descriptive headings (from http://coinhoards.org/results)

Evaluating the Flat File Data Model

Due to their simplicity, flat files have been ubiquitous for decades and are still widely used as a means of sharing data. Most software applications can read and write flat files. CSV and TSV text files have the advantage of being human-readable, and their structure is explicit and self-documenting, which makes them suitable for archiving data. But their simplicity is also their downfall.

Flat file formats often do not support the use of data types; e.g., in a CSV file, it is not possible to distinguish numbers from character strings, so care must be taken when using data from such files. More problematic, however, is that they are rigidly structured as two-dimensional tables and do not provide a way to indicate relationships or links between rows of data within a single file or across multiple files. That is why they are called "flat." Querying is restricted to string matching within a single file (table) and the rigid structure introduces redundancy and risks inconsistency since recurring data values must be repeated row by row. For example, a flat file that listed authors and their published books with one row per book would need to repeat the author information in successive rows. This increases the chance of compromising data integrity and introducing errors when adding, deleting, or updating author information. Their suitability for use in a database approach is limited, and so we assign a suitability score of **D**.

Research Data as Linked Tables: The Relational Data Model

The relational data model can be pictured as a set of *linked* tables, each consisting of rows (called "tuples") and columns. The tables in a relational database are linked by values known as keys. A *primary key* is an identifying value in a row of a table that uniquely identifies that row. The familiar and long-established relational database approach was devised at IBM in the late 1960s by E. F. Codd, who claimed that "the relational view (or model) of data … appears to be superior in several respects…" to the prevailing strategies of his time (Codd 1970). Since then, there is no doubt as to the enduring popularity of the table-based, relational approach as exemplified by database systems ranging from high-end corporate systems like Oracle Database and IBM's DB2 to desktop productivity tools like Microsoft Access and FileMaker which are accessible to scholars and students. The relational data model has been widely adopted because it is well suited for highly structured business data where there are many instances of the same kinds of things—employees with names and addresses, widgets with part numbers and product descriptions, sales by month and by district. Indeed, relational databases are so ubiquitous that they are usually what nonspecialists think of when they hear the word "database."

Scholars who are digitizing a collection of structured data often begin by entering it into a table, i.e., a flat file, using software that supports this format, whether it be a table in a word processing document, an HTML <table> on a web page, a spreadsheet, or a table in a relational database. Highly structured data will be easily broken out into its descriptive characteristics: Name, Description, Location, Shape, Length, Weight, Color, Frequency, etc. We can all think of many examples of this approach: a table of Roman pottery from the city of Corinth, a chart of grammatical paradigms of the verbs used in the Iliad, a list of authors and book details in the bibliography of a research study, the collated responses to a multiple-choice questionnaire, and so on. We have no complaint with well-organized, highly structured, rigorously formatted table-based data.

However, the relational data model emphasizes the importance of *normalization*, a process that breaks apart a single table into multiple linked tables to reduce data redundancy. For example, a database that tracks published books may have one table for Authors detailing the AuthorID, name, and date of birth, and another for the Publishers, with each table having a *key field*. A third table, Publications, would *join* the master tables, adding transactional data such as the details of a specific publication, thereby linking both the Authors and the Publishers. Rigorous rules maintain data integrity by ensuring that master data is not deleted if transactional data is dependent upon it (Fig. 2.5).

The relational data model is effective because it "(1) provides a simple, limited approach to structuring data, yet is reasonably versatile, so anything can be modeled; and (2) provides a limited, yet useful, collection of operations on data" (Garcia-Molina et al. 2008, p. 21). The versatility of the relational database model

PubID	Publisher	StreetAddress
56724	NewHouse	123 Main
26547	Academe	234 Elm
97722	PhotonHouse	345 Oak

AuthorID	firstName	lastName	dob
1348906	Jenkins	Richard	4/2/67
9802367	O'Gary	Sharon	6/3/99
784593	Mueller	Otto	3/13/56
613478	Mbaate	Joseph	5/1/88
9782456	Werling	Angela	10/20/77

ISBN	AuthorID	PubID	Title
1-23456-789-0	1348906	56724	Elements of Grammar
1-34567-890-X	613478	56724	Introduction to Philosophy
1-45678-901-2	9782456	56724	A History of Gaming

Fig. 2.5 Normalized tables are joined by key fields to eliminate data redundancy

makes it useful for research projects in the humanities and social sciences that have homogeneous data sets, highly predictable objects of study, and basic goals for analysis and publication. A typical archaeological project may use a series of tables that allow for entry of new objects, identified by key fields, described by properties, normalized into separate tables, and joined appropriately. Tables of pottery, artifacts, faunal data, and botanical finds will be joined to a table that describes the excavation contexts and linked to another table that catalogs the images. As long as the researchers are content to restrict the digital record to the fields and values allowed by the predefined system, with proper supervision, careful attention to detail, and rigorous controls for data entry, tables in a well-designed, relational-style database can go a long way to serving the data management needs of a project.

Also, working in favor of the relational approach is the success of Structured Query Language (SQL), long a hallmark of relational databases.[22] While "neither the faster nor the most elegant way to talk to databases … it is the best way we have" said InfoWorld as recently as November 2019,[23] despite the rise of competing options. The easy, accessible, portable, and ubiquitous "`SELECT ... FROM ... WHERE`" expression still rules, with many variations and spin-offs.

```
SELECT Authors.AuthorName, Title
FROM Publications
INNER JOIN Authors ON Publications.AuthorID=Authors.AuthorID
WHERE Date<1980;
```

A major benefit of the relational approach is its focus on enforcing data integrity and minimizing data redundancy. Over the years, we have heard researchers suggest that data redundancy is a good thing, a backup of sorts.[24] To this we say "No!" It is never a good idea for copies of the same data to exist in different places or to be managed by different users. This is asking for trouble. Good database systems are designed to avoid redundancy. What if data is corrected in one "database"? How are the corrections going to be propagated to other versions of the data? Who is going to bother to do this? How are "they" going to know that updates are needed? How

[22] SQL has been an ANSI (American National Standards Institute) standard since 1986 and an ISO (International Organization for Standardization) standard since 1987. SQL was taken up by IBM, Microsoft, Oracle and others and includes implementations in systems like MySQL and PostgreSQL, to name two of the most popular.

[23] https://www.infoworld.com/article/3219795/what-is-sql-the-lingua-franca-of-data-analysis.html.

[24] Do not confuse data redundancy with a backup. A backup is an archived version of the primary data, hopefully never needed to be seen or used again. It is not another copy of the viable data, or some portion thereof, intended to be used in a different context for a different purpose or by different users. LOCKSS, "Lots of Copies Keep Stuff Safe," seems to be a poor man's sustainability option. It is not clear, exactly, where LOCKSS (or CLOCKSS, Controlled LOCKSS) is headed, so be careful.

are inevitable differences reconciled? One of our core mantras is the old database adage to “get it once, get it early, and get it right.” In other words, store the data in one place in the database, without redundancy; enter it into the database as early as possible in the process of working with it; and clean the data before storing it to ensure it is internally coherent and consistent.

Working against the relational approach are some practical and conceptual problems of data management. What happens when something unusual is found, something that does not fit the Procrustean bed? The Katumuwa stele (KTMW), discovered at the ancient site of Zincirli in Turkey, is one-of-a-kind for that project (Herrmann Rimmer and Schloen 2014). In which table should such a unique object be recorded? Although a special find, the registrar’s table of beads, coins, and other artifacts was not suitable. Although made of basalt, it did not fit well in the table of stone objects being studied by the geologist along with grindstones, slingshots, and basalt bowl fragments. Although an inscription, it did not fit well in the philologist’s document detailing brief scribbles on broken potsherds and fragmentary words carved on broken marble slabs. Although crafted with an artistic scene, it did not fit the styles and themes cataloged from painted vessels. Force-fitting the stele into any of these structures would not do justice to its description. Do we take the time and trouble to add a new table for this single example of a stele (in the hope of finding others), in order to provide “a place for every *thing*”? (Fig. 2.6).

Likewise, what happens when one of the many similar objects in a table displays unique or noteworthy features that we might especially want to be able to find again in the data? Do we take the time and trouble to add new columns to an existing table structure to capture descriptive details leaving the table *sparse*, with empty table cells that do not apply to many of the items? Do we lump the noteworthy

Fig. 2.6 The Katumuwa stele from the site of Zincirli, Turkey. (Photograph by E. Struble, courtesy of the University of Chicago Zincirli Excavations)

observations into an existing column, say a free-form, all-purpose note, resulting in a hodge-podge of idiosyncratic descriptions in an unformatted text field which will leave us dependent on string matching to find the information again? None of these are great options. Highly variable data wreaks havoc with nicely organized tables and the table model becomes less accommodating.

Likewise, what happens when there are multiple qualities to be recorded of a single property that has been assigned to one table column? What if the blade artifact is comprised of both metal and stone materials? What if a given word in a text is serving as both a noun and an adjective? In a properly modeled relational database, the tables to record this type of variability would ideally be configured before data entry begins, which requires a sort of advanced knowledge that is rarely possible. Otherwise, changing the database structure later requires difficult and risky schema evolution. Therefore, hobbyists and casual users of relational databases often devise creative ways of accommodating multiple values in a single table column. More values in assorted combinations could be added to the picklist of options ("Metal and stone"). Free-form additions could be allowed. Commas or other punctuation could be used to separate multiple values ("Metal, stone" or "Metal/stone"). New columns might be added to the table creating a proliferation of checkboxes (Metal?-Yes; Stone?-Yes). But each of these accommodations inevitably results in messy and inconsistent data, making it less certain that one would be able to find reliably all stone blades, or all artifacts made from a mix of metal and stone. In the best-case scenario, the relational database designer might need to add new fields, new keys, perhaps even new tables, to accommodate more types of relationships (e.g., many to many), adding to the overall complexity.

In addition to the structural challenges presented by the table, what happens when we want to share data with a colleague or to compare our stone blades with those found at neighboring sites? The downside of the relational model is that it leads to a proliferation of custom, one-off project databases having been designed with little to no effective standardization or collaboration. Each project becomes deeply entrenched in its way of doing things and deeply committed to the investment put into creating a custom database. Sharing information among bespoke database systems will be a problem familiar to anyone who has tried.

Evaluating the Relational Data Model

There are signs in the technology industry that the relational model is showing its age. With the emergence of big data research for which the relational model is not well-suited computationally, the predominance of the World Wide Web as a platform for distributing data, and the proliferation of alternate approaches, it is fair to conclude that "the dominance of relational databases…is cracking."[25] As Emil Eifrem (2021), the CEO and Cofounder of Neo4j (maker of a non-relational database product), observes:

[25] Pramod Sadalage; http://www.thoughtworks.com/insights/blog/nosql-databases-overview.

> The relational database was invented in the late '70s. And while Larry Ellison has bought many yachts and a few Hawaiian Islands with the fruits of the commercial success of the relational database, the technology has remained remarkably the same...That is, until the early part of the previous decade. All of a sudden, this huge market was attacked from all fronts by a number of massive, secular trends – the shift to the cloud, sensor proliferation, big data, new patterns in architecture like microservices, and of course AI and machine learning. These trends converged into a perfect storm that gave birth to NoSQL and the rise of non-relational databases.

Since 2009, the NoSQL ("not only SQL") movement has been challenging the long-standing assumption of the superiority of the relational model and has been leading a move away from dependence on that approach. Flexibility, simplicity, efficiency, and accessibility are all goals of NoSQL database systems, and there are many examples of such systems in this rapidly developing and changing arena.[26] As Robinson, Webber, and Eifrem (2015, p. 14) say, "We work against the grain whenever we try to model and query connectedness in a relational database."

The value, utility, and durability of the relational model for a database approach cannot be denied. Rows of tabular data representing entities of interest can be uniquely identified by key fields. Those rows, or records, within a table can be related to items within other tables by using "joins" on those key fields. Columns can be added to the tables to capture information of interest about the entities. SQL provides query functionality that has stood the test of time. Data integrity and consistency can be assured by data management systems that carefully implement the rules of the relational model. Sustainability is subject to the resolve of the data managers but is bolstered by the pervasiveness of the format, with experienced help easy to find. However, sharing is made difficult by both the flexibility (everyone will do it their own way) and the inflexibility (once it is built it is not trivial to change) of a relational table. Inflexibility also means that data must conform to the structure of the table, bringing to mind the disastrous outcomes of the Procrustean bed, and so we assign our suitability score: **B+**.

Research Data as Trees: The Hierarchical ("Document") Data Model

Before there were tables, there were trees. In the era of the Apollo space missions in the 1960s, the mainframe computers that replaced human "computers" (who are vividly portrayed in the popular 2016 film *Hidden Figures*) used IBM's Information Management System (IMS). This was a "high-performance, hierarchical database system that could retrieve, organize and store data quickly" and the "Apollo 11 Moon mission was one of the first major projects for which computerized information management tools were essential to its success."[27]

---

[26] For "your ultimate guide to the non-relational universe!" see http://nosql-database.org.

[27] https://www.ibm.com/ibm/history/ibm100/us/en/icons/ibmims/.

IMS was the world's first commercial database system when it was launched in 1968. It had two main parts: "the database system supporting a hierarchical, tree-like structure data model; and transaction-processing software for handling complex, high-volume transactions" (ibid.). For a long time, IMS was the "workhorse for very large workloads" serving applications in manufacturing, retail, and the financial industry, among others, all around the world.[28]

The hierarchical data model has an intuitive, predictable structure, well suited to highly structured data, with database records linked in parent-child relationships. Each record, a collection of predefined fields, could have many child items, but only one parent. This data model is easy to work with and efficient for processing one-to-many relationships. But with increased sophistication and complexity in data and their relationships, the hierarchical data model gave way to more flexible schemes, like the relational data model described above and the graph data model described in the next section.

The hierarchical data model has made a comeback in recent years as part of the trend toward digitizing and publishing textual documents, like those that are commonplace in the humanities and social sciences.[29] Unlike more transactional, highly structured data, document-based data is often described as being *semi-structured*, or schema-less. Semi-structured data tends to be a mixture of organized content and free-flowing prose. Since it need not conform to a specific schema, it can be *self-described* using XML notation. The advantage of XML is that the descriptive notation need not be prescribed in advance but can consist of custom-made, meaningful tags invented by a researcher as needed to adequately describe the research.

It may be surprising to discover how much hierarchical structure is inherent in a document which, at first glance, appears to be mostly narrative. The Text Encoding Initiative (TEI), for example, makes effective use of a flexible and generic XML schema for exposing structure within documents. As stated on the TEI website:[30]

> The TEI Guidelines for Electronic Text Encoding and Interchange define and document a markup language for representing the structural, renditional, and conceptual features of texts. They focus (though not exclusively) on the encoding of documents in the humanities and social sciences, and in particular on the representation of primary source materials for research and analysis.

When formatted as TEI-XML, a text is represented as a hierarchy of elements, specifically, an ordered hierarchy of content objects (OHCO),[31] which includes both metadata and textual data. A TEI document may represent a whole, unitary text or

---

[28] As a computer science graduate in the early 1980s, S. Schloen began her professional career by maintaining an IMS application on an IBM System/360 mainframe for one of the world's largest oil companies.

[29] Website developers will recognize the hierarchical document model in the Document Object Model (DOM) interface that lets them manipulate the content, structure, and style of a web page programmatically (e.g., using JavaScript).

[30] https://tei-c.org/guidelines/.

[31] This simplified view of a text does not do justice to the complexity allowed by TEI, but is a general starting point for a well-documented discussion of texts represented by hierarchical XML.

one component of a text where various independent documentary components refer to each other.[32]

Throughout this book, we explore the question of whether research data should be stored as whole documents, partial documents, or more granular elements. We encapsulate this discussion in the phrase *How far is far enough?* when deciding the degree to which research data is broken down into smaller parts. While this is an open question that must be answered by each research project, the data schema and database must not be a limitation. An entire document may be considered a single object of study in one case, but it may also be the case that every word, every character, and every punctuation mark needs to be considered as a discrete, observable item.

Case Study: The Electronic Chicago Hittite Dictionary (eCHD)

OCHRE is designed to accommodate granular data elements of a document and capture their structure, so that document-based data becomes more valuable for analysis and study. This is evident in the electronic version of the Chicago Hittite Dictionary. The CHD team has produced many complex volumes of dense, highly detailed, extensively annotated, and richly formatted content describing the vocabulary of an ancient society. On the face of it, one would not look at a dictionary volume—either a printed copy or a digitized version—and think, "Aha, a database!" A word processing document, of course, and also a useful, searchable PDF, but a database?

With the ambition of making the document content more accessible and more searchable, and wanting to expose more explicitly various relationships inherent in the data, we set about reorganizing CHD content into a database format. The CHD editors had followed carefully prescribed conventions in the formatting: lowercase, italicized words represented Hittite language, uppercase words without special formatting represented Sumerian loanwords, bolded abbreviations described grammatical properties, and a system of numbering the various meanings of a dictionary entry (e.g., 1, a, 1', a') outlined a natural hierarchy of meaning from the more general to the more specific.[33]

By capturing these distinctions using custom XML tags and parsing the documents' string-based content into component parts based on the word processing formats that had been applied,[34] we were able to identify the structure within these documents, allowing querying and analysis that goes far beyond mere string matching. And while this self-describing, flexible framework was initially proposed to suit

[32] https://www.tei-c.org/release/doc/tei-p5-doc/en/html/DS.html.

[33] See Chap. 4 for a discussion of OCHRE's implementation of the Lexical Markup Framework.

[34] The original, now discontinued OpenOffice, used the OpenDocument format which was XML-based. This was innovative at the time and very helpful. CHD documents were saved in this format, which exposed the formatting clearly as XML elements and attributes. These were then transformed (using XSLT) to a more semantically meaningful document for import to OCHRE.

the content of the CHD, we have since used the same framework for creating online editions of Akkadian, Aramaic, Demotic, Elamite, Greek, Old Assyrian, and Ugaritic dictionaries. Even though there are many differences between these ancient languages, XML does not require complete conformity. Different projects share what is helpful, add new tags as necessary, and consider the rest to be valid customizations.

Consider, for example, the headword from Volume P of the CHD:

pakkušš- v.; to pound, crack, crush, grind (grain); OH/NS.†[35]

The structure of this entry can be exposed, explicitly, using custom XML tags. Note that the nesting of tags creates a naturally hierarchical structure—tags within other tags—a feature that OCHRE exploits, as we shall see.

```
<dictionaryUnit>
 <entry>
  <lemma areAllKnownOccurrencesCited="true">
   <citationForm>pakkušš-</citationForm>
   <partOfSpeech>verb</partOfSpeech>
   <meaning>
    <gloss>to pound, crack, crush, grind (grain)</gloss>
   </meaning>
   <period>OH/NS</period>
  </lemma
 </entry>
</dictionaryUnit>
```

Problems with the document model arise when there is the desire to mark up the same document for different purposes. A literary document, for example, might be described for grammatical, metrical, or form-critical analysis. This typically, even inevitably, leads to the situation where tags that are bracketing character strings to be marked up need to overlap. This violates the rules of traditional markup. The problematic need for multiple, overlapping hierarchies to describe a document is a well-known restriction of the document markup model (see Schloen and Schloen 2014). Simply put, imagine wanting to mark up a book based *both* on its page layout `(book > page > line > word)` *and* its sentence structure `(book > chapter > paragraph > sentence > word)`. Unless there are unrealistic policies like each sentence must start a new line and each chapter must start a new page, we get into trouble right away trying to interweave conflicting hierarchical structures.

Various schemes have been devised to circumvent the restriction on multiple, overlapping hierarchies, the best known of which is based on standoff markup. The standoff markup approach departs from the usual markup technique of using in-line tags and instead uses a strategy of uniquely identifying granular components of a

[35] See CHD (Güterbock and Hoffner 1997), Volume P, p. 58.

document and then relating these components together using a system of links. Uniquely identified entities, with relationships linking those entities together—this is heading in the right direction to how Date described a database approach. In addition, the ability to define custom tags allows a document's designer to create whatever descriptive properties are needed to record the desired information about the entities.

So far, we are on track to base a "database" on the hierarchical document model, albeit somewhat awkwardly, but what about the requirement that data be easily queried? XML provides a query mechanism, XQuery, the syntax for which is based on a FLWOR ("flower") expression, where FLWOR is an acronym for "for … let … where … order by … return" (Doan et al. 2012, p. 357). XQuery expects a document to be represented as a top-level root node with a set of subtrees and it is tuned to work with hierarchically organized XML elements which are, optionally, qualified by attributes. A search for all verbs from the CHD, for example, might look like this simple FLWOR expression:

```
for $entry in input()/dictionaryUnit
where $entry/lemma/partOfSpeech = "verb"
return $entry/lemma/citationForm
```

Along with XQuery, the XML standard is complemented by XSLT (Extensible Stylesheet Language Transformations) which allows structured XML documents to be transformed easily into other well-formed documents. This accommodates reformatting of documents when needed, facilitating the sharing of documents among users and applications.

Evaluating the Hierarchical (Document) Data Model

Ted Nelson, who purportedly coined the terms *hypertext* and *hypermedia*, was an early detractor of the hierarchical model. "Hierarchy maps only some of the relationships in the world, and it badly maps the rest … Hierarchy is less and less appropriate as we try to represent more and more of the world" (Nelson 2015, p. 141). But database systems based on the hierarchical model have served well in providing reliable, accessible, and sustainable solutions for managing structured data. And document notation methods, with a strong emphasis on the value of hierarchy, have helped to highlight and expose the analytic potential inherent in semi-structured data. Just because new technologies and new methods have come along, it does not necessarily make old methods obsolete. But while we applaud many features of the hierarchical model, as with the relational model, we also welcome other approaches more appropriate to the explosion of new data, to the expression of semi-structured data, and to new expectations for data-driven research. Suitability score: **B-**.

Research Data as Networks: The Graph Data Model

A graph database organizes information in a network consisting of "a set of items … with connections between them" (Newman 2003, p. 168). (The term "graph" is borrowed from mathematical graph theory, which was developed to analyze network structures.[36]) A network is a useful and widely applicable model for representing data of all kinds. Items are represented as *nodes* in the network (also called vertices), and they are related to other items by *links* (edges). Social networks, transportation networks, biological networks, and so on are simple, yet powerful, schemes for organizing data in a way that makes the data useful for statistical analysis and other forms of research. The simplicity of the network model also scales well for application to "big data"—more nodes and more links between them.

The graph data model underlies the recent resurgence of non-relational "NoSQL" databases, but it has been around for a long time. It emerged in the early 1970s in the period when the sequential medium of magnetic tape was giving way to direct access storage devices like hard disk drives.[37] Charles Bachman, considered by some to be the inventor of the database management system (Haigh 2016), compared this paradigm shift to that of the Copernican revolution, describing in the *Programmer as Navigator* "a radically new point of view" where the programmer can act as "a full-fledged navigator in an n-dimensional data space."

> The availability of direct access storage devices laid the foundation for the Copernican-like change in viewpoint. The directions of "in" and "out" were reversed. Where the input notion of the sequential file world meant "into the computer from tape," the new input notion became "into the database." This revolution in thinking is changing the programmer from a stationary viewer of objects passing before him in core into a mobile navigator who is able to probe and traverse a database at will. (Bachman 1973, p. 654)

Traversing a database at will, with one item inviting movement toward another based on some criteria, was a novel idea and laid the framework for a network-graph database approach where items led inexorably to other items as an agent followed the links between items. The primitive technology of the 1960s and 1970s limited the development of these ideas, but the network approach has been revitalized as new database technologies were specifically designed for it and as massive amounts of both data and computational power became available, allowing software engineers to implement graph-traversal algorithms to find nearest neighbors and the shortest paths between items and to detect communities of items, among other operations, as they navigate vast n-dimensional spaces.

---

[36]The term "graph" is not intended to evoke images of data visualizations often informally referred to as graphs, like pie graphs and bar graphs. Instead, we will refer to those as charts or diagrams, reserving the use of "graph" for its mathematical meaning derived from graph theory and adopted by computer science as a data structure. Wikipedia provides a satisfactory introduction to graphs (https://en.wikipedia.org/wiki/Graph_(discrete_mathematics)).

[37]The Network Data Model (NDM) was proposed in 1971 by the Data Base Task Group (DBTG) of the Programming Language Committee (subsequently renamed the COBOL committee) of the Conference on Data Systems Language (CODASYL), the organization responsible for the definition of the COBOL programming language.

The purveyors of the industry-leading graph database product Neo4j note that: (1) graphs relate everything, (2) graphs create context lacking in big data analytics, (3) graphs are critical for the success of artificial intelligence (machine learning) strategies, (4) graphs make data science project management easier and more effective, and (5) graphs will facilitate advancements in AI (James (2021). Accordingly, they predict that the future of databases will include a larger market share for graph databases. In the context of commercial business applications, Robinson, Webber, and Eifrem (2015, p. 24) argue that "it is clear that the graph database is the best technology for dealing with complex, variably structured, densely connected data—that is, with datasets so sophisticated they are unwieldy when treated in any form other than a graph."

The rise in popularity of the graph data model has been felt in all areas of research, including studies in the humanities and social sciences. For example, in his book *An Archaeology of Interaction: Network Perspectives on Material Culture and Society*, Carl Knappett (2011) applies lessons learned from network theory and network analysis to the study of archaeology. He summarizes the features of networks that are most relevant in this context as follows (p. 10) (Fig. 2.7):

1) Networks force us to consider relations between entities.
2) Networks naturally represent spatial relations, with the flexibility to be both social and physical.
3) Networks provide a strong method for articulating scales.
4) Networks can incorporate both people and objects.
5) Networks incorporate a temporal dimension … unravel the complexities of how spatial patterns are generated by processes over time.

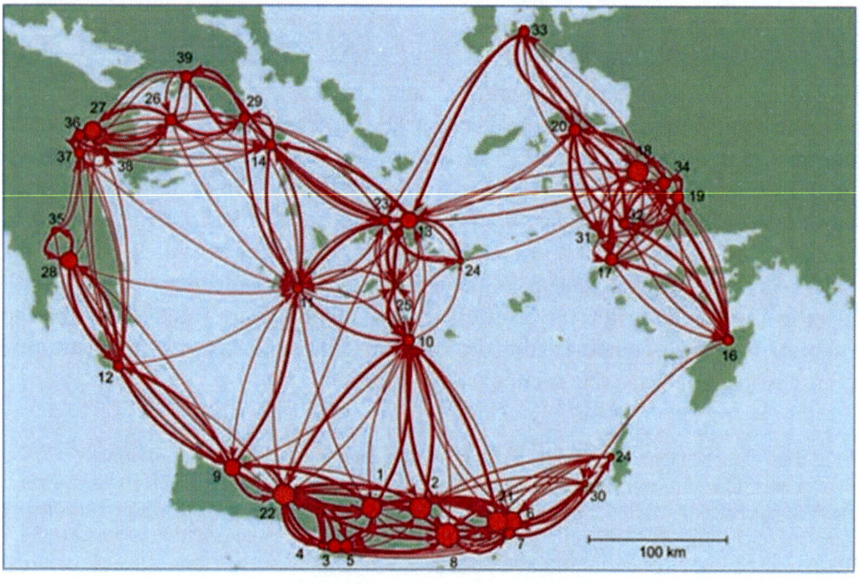

Fig. 2.7 A network model shows both local and regional connections among Middle Bronze Age Aegean sites (Knappett 2013)

The World Wide Web as a Graph of HTML Documents

It is worth digressing here to note that the World Wide Web is a vast network of data in which the nodes are web pages linked together by URLs ("hyperlinks"). In fact, by putting their data on the Web and linking one web page to another, researchers have long used the Web as a simple kind of graph database that is accessible to everyone through Web browsers that provide a standard user interface. The web pages that serve as nodes of the network are "documents," i.e., text files that are "marked up" with embedded "tags" set apart by angle brackets (e.g., <div>, which indicates a section of a document). These documents are delivered to users on the Internet in response to a request of some kind, usually by simply clicking on a link. A mouse-click on a navigation button or a keyboard interaction in a data entry field on a form may trigger the fetching and displaying of the "Next" or "Previous" document. Exactly how a document is to be presented in a Web browser is specified by means of markup tags that conform to the HyperText Markup Language (HTML). HTML (and its predecessor SGML, the Standard Generalized Markup Language) is a standardized system of tags used to describe how a formatted document is to be presented. Cascading Style Sheets (CSS) complement HTML by providing a concise notation for applying formats and for saving a collection of styles that can be applied in a variety of contexts to a variety of documents (Fig. 2.8).

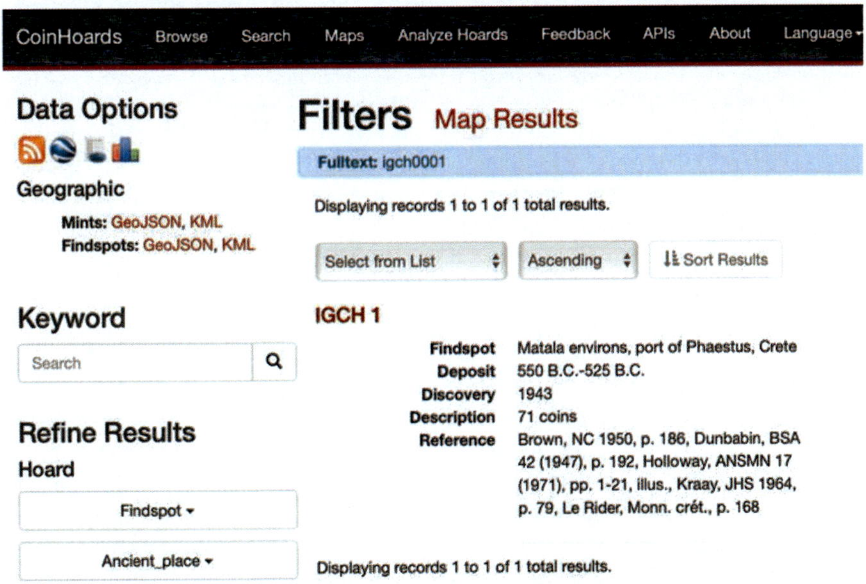

Fig. 2.8 Coinhoards.org is an example of a well-formatted, easy-to-use website that is useful for human browsing, with keyword search and other filters provided

As the basis for a database approach for managing research data, HTML has severe limitations. It defines a fixed set of tags to indicate how data should be *presented* to human readers but does not indicate the *semantics* of the data. It dictates the layout and styling of the data (e.g., this character string should be in italics) but not what it means (e.g., this character string represents the author of the book). The simple HTML notation and network linking structure of the Web spawned an entire industry and *hypertext publication* became ubiquitous as the strategy for delivering pages of formatted data to users on the Internet. This was great for human reading of information but not for automated search and retrieval. The lack of semantic indicators within HTML documents stimulated the development of sophisticated methods for indexing and searching the contents of web pages by Google and others, but the Web remains inadequate as a database. It can deliver pages of information at the request of human users who want to browse and read nicely formatted data, and who are happy to receive six million results from a simple search, letting Google prioritize those results on their behalf. But from a research perspective, websites are unpredictable and ephemeral. They are often a dog's breakfast of fragile, poorly formatted code and haphazardly tagged content. Data can be "scraped" from such pages, but not in consistent ways or with dependable outcomes. That many will recognize "404" as an error code for a "page not found" is a testament to the plethora of broken links across the Web. Sustainability is at the whim of website hosts and subject to the vagaries of obsolescence, neglect, and obscurity.

The Semantic Web as a Graph of Linked Data

The Semantic Web initiative launched by Tim Berners-Lee in 2001 was intended to rectify the lack of structured semantics on the Web by creating a "Web of data" not just a "Web of documents."[38] In other words, the goal was to make the Web a much more powerful graph database from which data can be searched and filtered in sophisticated ways and retrieved reliably. Among other things, the Semantic Web has encouraged the creation of "Linked Data" on the Web by means of structured metadata and standard protocols that make the semantics of the data machine-readable as well as human-readable.

In traditional Web hypertext publishing, document content is linked using HTML anchors and references. But in the case of Linked Data (LD), granular data objects are related using Web standards beyond HTML, including XML (the Extensible Markup Language) for semantic tagging of data; RDF (the Resource Description Framework) which encodes meaningful relations among data objects using subject-predicate-object triples; URIs (Universal Resource Identifiers) for uniquely identifying data objects on the Web, thus serving as database keys; OWL (Web Ontology Language) for specifying semantic classes and subclasses of entities; and SPARQL (SPARQL Protocol and RDF Query Language) for querying data stored as RDF triples (Fig. 2.9).

[38] https://en.wikipedia.org/wiki/Semantic_Web.

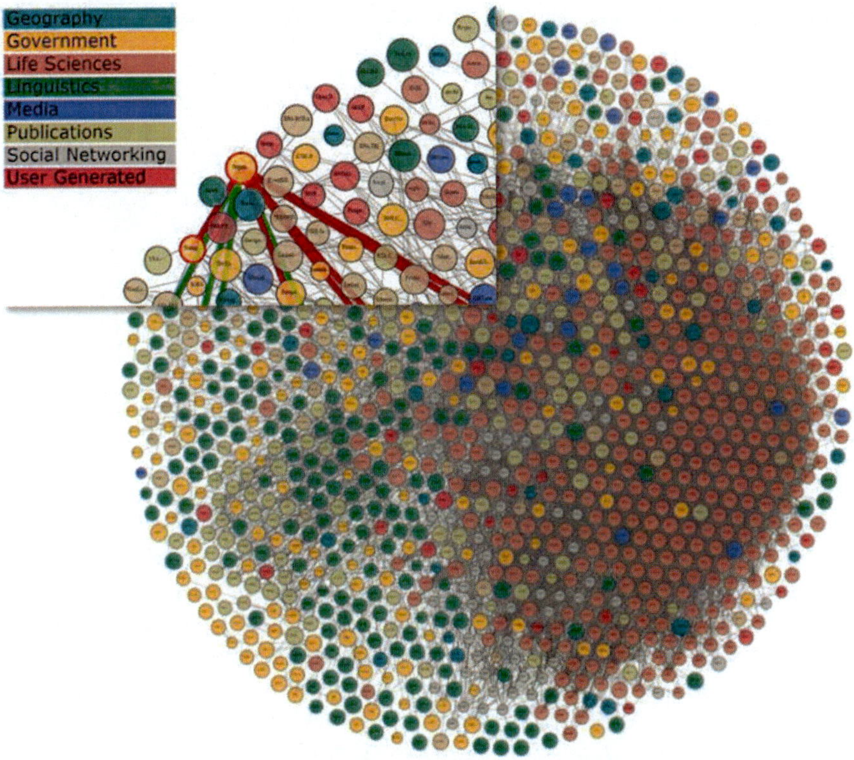

Fig. 2.9 The Semantic Web as illustrated by the Linked Open Data community (from http://cas.lod-cloud.net/)

Linked Open Data (LOD) is Linked Data with the additional caveat that the data is available and freely usable by the community without restriction. Tim Berners-Lee, the inventor of HTML and proponent of the Semantic Web, stated four core principles of Linked Data (Berners-Lee 2009):

1. Use URIs as names for things (any kind of object or concept).
2. Use HTTP URIs so that people can look up those names.
3. When someone looks up a URI, provide useful information, using the standards (RDF, SPARQL).
4. Include links to other URIs so that they can discover more things.

With uniquely identified data objects described with useful information, and with relationships among them, a case for a database approach based on the Semantic Web is off to a good start. To satisfy the need for querying, the querying language known as SPARQL (pronounced "sparkle") facilitates querying the subject-predicate-object tuples (or triples) defined by the RDF standard and provides the mechanism to query well-structured data on the Web (Fig. 2.10).

However, the Semantic Web still does not adequately meet the needs of researchers, although it has made progress toward a more comprehensible system of publishing and finding data using LD protocols. Emerging database management systems

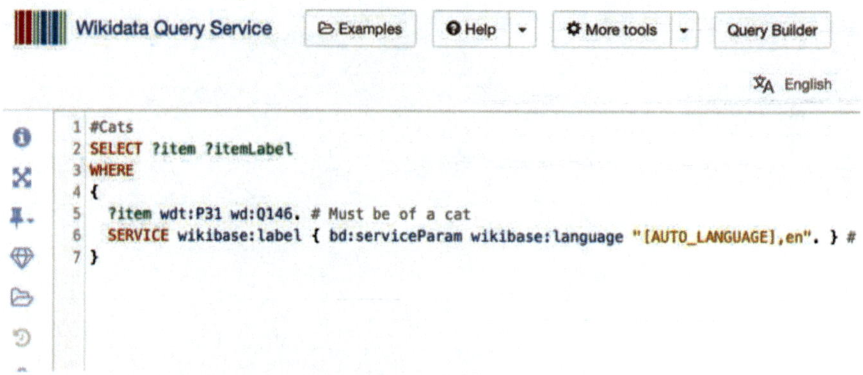

Fig. 2.10 SPARQL queries enable the lookup of data from endpoints of the Semantic Web. This Wikidata example uses SPARQL to find famous house cats

based on standards like RDF, and thereby supporting the use of subject-predicate-object triples, are providing more standardized options for managing research data. But much remains to be improved. Entities, albeit uniquely identifiable, are represented by a web page (or document) of information, from which details of interest need to be picked.[39] Relationships among entities become spaghetti-like and difficult to navigate with the proliferation of hyperlinks. In short, although item-based, and richly linked—"where anything can link to anything" (Berners-Lee et al. 2001, p. 37)—it seems *too* unstructured. Querying is provided by SPARQL but, despite being applauded for its sentence-like syntax, it is still rather obscure. One needs to know already that a house cat is represented by Q146 in order to find instances of them.[40] Data consistency and integrity receive failing grades when the Web of data devolves into a graveyard of broken links, although more is being done to improve stability through persistent identifiers managed by authorized services.[41]

While data sharing is front and center as a motivation for this approach and is supported by the openness of the Web, the quality and reliability of data, and the authority behind its "meaning," is not a given. Why does Wikidata get to declare what "Ras Shamra" is? In addition, the decentralization of the platform, still-evolving tools, the lack of coordinated efforts, and the "monumental technical and sociological challenges inherent in creating a global Semantic Web"[42] makes the WWW still feel like a Wild West Web. Some believe that the Semantic Web is

---

[39] Websites using structured formats like XML, or its simpler cousin JSON (Javascript Object Notation) do make this process more user-friendly and predictable.

[40] The most useful SPARQL query endpoints include preconfigured sample queries that give the user various models as help for getting started.

[41] On Digital Object Identifiers (DOI), for example, see https://www.doi.org/.

[42] https://www.explainablestartup.com/2016/08/the-history-of-semantic-web-is-the-future-of-intelligent-assistants.html.). As summarized by a more systematic critique, "The Semantic Web: Two Decades On": "a lack of usable tools, a lack of incentives, a lack of robustness for unreliable publishers, and overly verbose standards, in particular, are widely acknowledged as valid criticisms of the Semantic Web" (https://aidanhogan.com/docs/semantic-web-now.pdf, p. 13).

already dead, superseded by strategies based on artificial intelligence (AI) for finding data and making it accessible.[43] It remains to be seen whether the Semantic Web ultimately lives up to Berners-Lee's "dream for the Web [in which computers] become capable of analyzing all the data on the Web—the content, links, and transactions between people and computers … where the whim of a human being and the reasoning of a machine coexist in an ideal, powerful mixture" (Berners-Lee and Fischetti 1999, pp. 157–158). Berners-Lee himself, reflecting on the World Wide Web in 2022, admits that "there are lots of things we need to fix."[44]

Evaluating the Graph Data Model

At its best, a graph database carefully manages networks of item-centric data in which the nodes of the network represent discrete units of information. Links join related items and these links can be elaborated, weighted, and ascribed direction as needed.[45] GraphBase, a leading commercially available graph database management system, is described as "a database system optimized for managing highly-related data" and as a "faster, more flexible and future-proof way" to manage such data.[46] As recently as 2019, a new query language, Graph Query Language (GQL) was being ratified as an international standard through an initiative led by Neo4j, Inc., and supported by other industry backers, plugging a gap in the world of graph databases by supplying a required feature of a database solution, that of standardized query capabilities.[47] A database management system that supports the graph data model must provide a way to uniquely identify items (nodes). And, ideally, following an item-centric approach, the system will have constraints to ensure data integrity by eliminating redundancy, with only one instance of each item of information. The simplicity of the data structure—nodes joined by links—makes it easy to extract subsets of the data for sharing, to reformat data for reuse, and to design computational processes to visualize and manipulate the data. However, most graph databases create networks that are too unconstrained, placing a great burden on their users to keep the data semantically consistent. This is true not just of Semantic Web databases that rely on RDF triples and SPARQL but also databases built using Neo4j and other graph database systems that use non-RDF graphs. They rely on a

[43] See, for example, "RIP: The Semantic Web" (https://blog.diffbot.com/rip-the-semantic-web/) and "Whatever Happened to the Semantic Web?" (https://twobithistory.org/2018/05/27/semantic-web.html).

[44] https://www.techradar.com/news/the-inventor-of-the-world-wide-web-says-his-creation-has-been-abused-for-too-long.

[45] Neo4j, for example, is structured as a *labeled property graph* (LPG), in contrast to Semantic Web graphs based on RDF.

[46] https://graphbase.ai.

[47] Neo4j developed its own query language, Cypher, which is a strong influence on the standard being devised. See https://neo4j.com/press-releases/query-language-graph-databases-international-standard/.

network model that is powerful and flexible, but unconstrained and often inefficient. We therefore assign a suitability score of **A-**.

OCHRE as a Database Approach

The Online Cultural and Historical Research Environment (OCHRE) was conceived of as a database solution to the problems of representing research data for the humanities and social sciences, intentionally designed to deal with the challenges of diverse, often semi-structured, data and based on sound principles of data representation and database design. OCHRE aims to provide a one-size-fits-all platform without sacrificing flexibility, without making undue demands on the data, and without unnecessary complexity. Users coming new to OCHRE, especially those with a technological background, find it to be somewhat of a conundrum. It cannot be based on a relational model because there are no tables. But neither is it implemented in a graph database, so how can it be using the graph data model? It claims to use XML but there are no documents in evidence. Why did we not just use Excel? or MySQL? or Neo4J? or ArcGIS? or <insert-the-flavor-of-the-month>?

Research Data as a Hybrid: The Semi-structured Data Model

The semi-structured data model is a hybrid data model that combines features of the *relational* data model based on linked tables, the *hierarchical* data model based on tree structures, and the *graph* data model based on networks of nodes and links. A concise description of the semi-structured data model can be found in *Database Systems: The Complete Book* (Garcia-Molina et al. 2008, p. 484 ff.).

We have explored the defining features of a variety of approaches to modeling data, keeping in mind the challenges posed by semi-structured data which is typical of research in the humanities and social sciences. As a research platform, OCHRE aims to take advantage of the best features of each of these data models.

- From the *relational data model*, OCHRE learns the value of maintaining data integrity and avoiding data redundancy, adopting a modified form of normalization, even though it is not table-based.[48] Rather than repeating an item (e.g., a character string) redundantly, the item is represented once, assigned a unique identifier (a key) and then is referenced by that key thereafter. The OCHRE property "Material = Stone" that describes a basalt stele or an alabaster juglet or a limestone slingshot is a combination of a variable ("Material") and a value ("Stone"). Every item described as "Stone" (by an element in its XML docu-

[48] See Software AG, "Tamino: Advanced Concepts" (2015, p. 13) for a helpful, illustrated discussion on normalizing XML.

ment) references the same unique identifier that identifies the "Stone" value. "Stone" exists just once in the database, but it is reused in the description of thousands and thousands of stone objects.

- Learning from the *hierarchical data model*, OCHRE leverages the benefits of tree-like structures to provide context (via containment) and to impute qualities (via inheritance). That is, items within a tree-like structure are contained by their higher-level items and inherit their characteristics. Applying the hierarchical document model to semi-structured textual data lets OCHRE identify, and make more explicit for analysis, the implicit structure therein. Tools and strategies based on the hierarchical document model, most notably XML, support the management and manipulation of semi-structured data while not compromising its textuality.
- The *graph data model* underscores the value of an item-centric approach. Having only one instance of an item to track, and around which to manage the whole constellation of data related to that instance, greatly simplifies the data management task. OCHRE's item-based approach, where individually identified units of data (items) are related using links and described by properties can be correctly described as an implementation of a labeled property graph (LPG). But each database item is represented by its own XML document within the XML database, creating synergy between the graph model and the hierarchical document model.
- The *Semantic Web* reinforces the importance of accessibility and sharing, identifying entities of interest and exposing them for use and reuse within the community that is the World Wide Web. The notion of a "Web" highlights the importance of relationships between entities, and the need to make these findable, comprehensible, and navigable. When an entity (a database item) is first created in OCHRE, it is assigned a unique identifier and given an addressable URL based on that identifier. Making research data as accessible as possible from its moment of creation or capture has always been a top OCHRE priority.

In the same breath with which Ted Nelson objects to hierarchy, he states: "Hierarchy is not in the nature of the computer. It is in the nature of the people who set up computers" (Nelson 2015, p. 141). Because hierarchy is so natural to our human way of thinking about so many things, OCHRE embraces hierarchy and puts it to work on behalf of research data management. We are inspired by *the tree of Diderot and d'Alembert*, produced for the eighteenth-century *Encyclopédie*, which uses a deeply nested hierarchy to represent "the structure of knowledge itself" as known to the world of the Enlightenment (Fig. 2.11).[49]

That a hybrid model seems appropriate to us for managing research data reflects our perspective on the complexity of research data and our goal not to force it into pre-imagined, predefined constraints. Maximizing one's options to reformat, reuse, and repurpose data seems highly desirable, even critical.

[49] https://en.wikipedia.org/wiki/Encyclopédie.

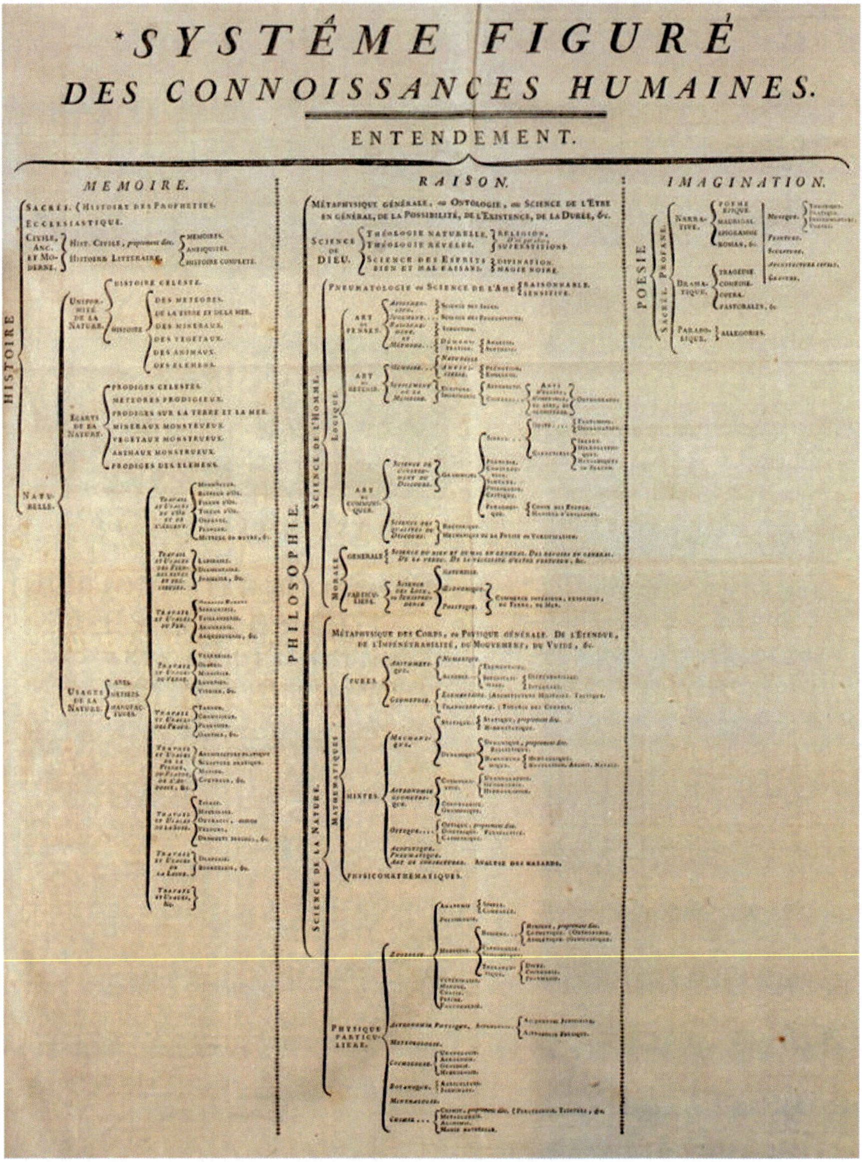

Fig. 2.11 French philosophers attempted to organize human knowledge as a tree (Public domain, https://commons.wikimedia.org/w/index.php?curid=66423)

Contrast the hierarchical view of knowledge with a network view of categories of information inferred from the cross-references between the articles of the *Encyclopédie*, produced by the ARTFL project at the University of Chicago using machine learning and data mining techniques to explore how knowledge was classified in the eighteenth century (Blanchard and Olsen 2002). Whether data is used

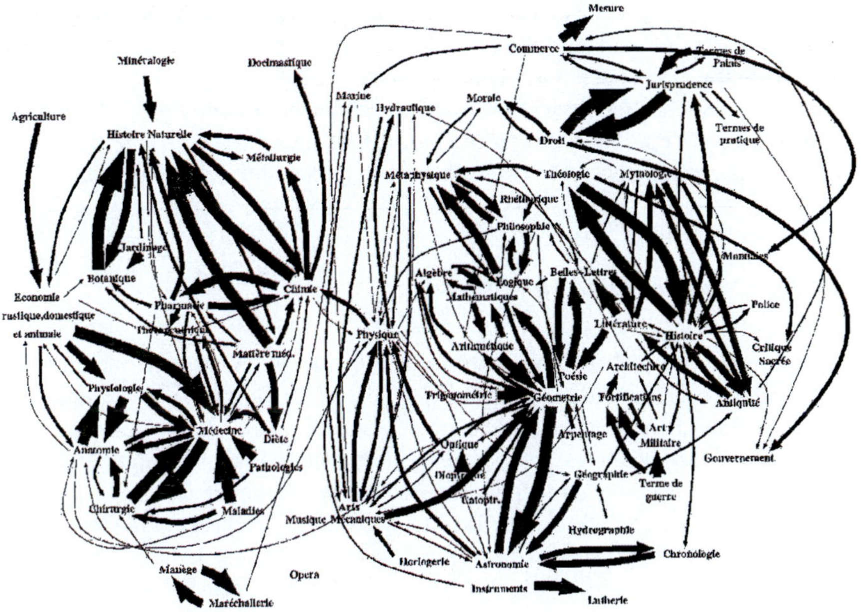

Fig. 2.12 This map of references between categories in the *Encyclopédie* visualizes knowledge as a graph (Blanchard and Olsen 2002)

as a tree, a graph, a document, or a table is neither right nor wrong. The task and the tools depend on the research questions. Undue constraints on the data should not be an obstacle (Fig. 2.12).

Evaluating the Hybrid (Semi-structured) Data Model

With a flexible syntax for defining the structure of data using XML Schema[50] and a powerful querying language (XQuery) for querying the data, a semi-structured XML database proves to be an excellent way to implement a database approach for managing research data, provided that the XML data objects it contains are sufficiently atomized. Both hierarchical relationships and cross-hierarchy links can be represented easily. The non-proprietary, text-based XML format is suitable for long-term archiving, working in favor of sustainability. The use of XML Schema, which provides a standard notation for documenting the structure of an XML document, along with the possibility of nimble reformatting (thanks to XSLT), facilitates successful sharing among both human and computational processes.

50 https://www.w3schools.com/xml/xml:schema.asp. Special-purpose tools like RELAX NG, and many XML editors will validate an XML document against a given schema.

In the next section of this book, we move on to explain how various features of the data models are worked out in practice and implemented within the OCHRE research platform. In so doing, we hope to inspire and equip you with computational strategies on which to base your own research data management. By illustrating the potential of a system that has learned from the best features of a long history of computational approaches, we also hope to justify a suitability score of **A+**.

The Challenge of Data Integration

The development of OCHRE as a tool for collecting and integrating data has followed broader trends in the business world, as technology has allowed the amassing of vast amounts of corporate data, from many sources and via assorted mechanisms. Those of us in the humanities and social sciences tend to think of corporate data as comparatively much more structured and predictable: customer and product identifiers, sales, expenses, and so on, and in truth, it generally is. But even in this context there is wide variability in how data is recorded. On my bank statement I am *Sandra Schloen*; on my credit card, *Sandra R. Schloen*; on my department store shopping account, *Sandy Schloen*; on my car insurance, *Schloen, S.*; and on my mortgage statement, *Schloen, David and Sandra*. Imagine trying to integrate my financial data computationally.

Imagine, next, two friendly archaeologists from neighboring sites comparing their collections of Greek coins. One of the projects measures the coin diameters in centimeters, the other in millimeters. One project calls the bronze coins "bronze" the other "copper alloy"; both use simply "metal" in some cases where corrosion makes it hard to tell. One uses a picklist that fills in table cells with "tetradrachm" and "stater"; the other types into a free-form column "tetr." and "st." Both use notes to describe the mint, the motifs, and the ruler whose profile is on the "obverse" (or "obv.") using all manner of shorthand and abbreviations. Aligning even these simple data sets so that a single analysis could combine data from both projects is a nontrivial problem, and it represents the problem of *semantic heterogeneity* specifically, and data integration more broadly. Asking, or expecting, these colleagues to agree on, and adopt, a common data structure and terminology has never seemed to us to be viable, and our experience has been that attempts to impose a standardized solution fall far short of the goal of achieving data compatibility.

Indeed, when D. Schloen started up the Zincirli project in Turkey, his team devised a recording system simplified from the method used at Ashkelon where he had worked for many years. The confusing naming of excavation contexts as Layers, Features, and Layer/Features was reduced to "Locus" prefaced by the year it was opened, e.g., L12-1001. But returning in successive seasons to continue excavating a Locus that had been labeled with a prior year also got to be confusing, and so when the team began a new project at Tell Keisan in Israel they adopted more generic terminology "Stratigraphic unit," dropped the year qualifier, and added an Area prefix, e.g., A-101. When a sister project was initiated with new Spanish colleagues at Cerro del Villar, in Malaga, Spain, it was agreed that "Unit of excavation" (UE), translated as "Unidad de excavación" (UE), was more bilingual-friendly, and so the terminology was adjusted once again. One excavator, with four different recording schemes—how does a database keep up?

While adopting digital methods at Pompeii, director Steven Ellis attributed the project's success not least to "…the fact that the vast majority of field data for all archaeological projects is really rather simple and easily handled by such apps" (Ellis 2016, p. 57). But he admitted that "some more difficult aspects were encountered along the way to recording digitally in the field…" that being the challenge of data integration:

> It is one thing to convert a paper-based project to a paperless system, but it is another to convert *all* of the project's team members to that system…It is a common practice for 'specialists' on archaeological projects, for example, to bring with them their own rather idiosyncratic systems, honed over decades and on multiple types of projects, to record their data. A good many of the specialists on the Pompeii excavations maintained these time-honored, paper-based recording systems. Naturally that data made its way into our system using more traditional, and achingly time-consuming methods of data entry, and the time spent doing that was a reminder of how such resources of a project can be better spent. The integration of paper-based records into a digital system also exposed just how limited the range and potential utility of 'traditional' data can be (ibid.).

Having put his finger on the problem, Ellis' team came up with its own solution: "a centralized and integrated system for data structure that is beneficial for everything from data security to site-wide and multivariate analyses to the management of productivity and publication goals" (ibid.). While we choose to entrust this responsibility to something other than a relational database system in practice,[51] we otherwise agree in theory on the value of an integrated system "for everything."

Over lunch at the Quadrangle Club at the University of Chicago with Zachary Ives,[52] computer science professor and co-author of *Principles of Data Integration*, he reminded us of a point from his textbook: "Human nature is such that if two people are given exactly the same requirements for a database application, they will design very different schemata. Hence, when data come from multiple sources, they typically look very different" (Doan et al. 2012, p. 21). According to Ives, this fact helps professors spot cheating among their students when results of a class assignment are suspiciously similar. While there are often technical reasons (one data set is queried using SQL, another using XQuery) or social reasons (the expectation that scholars cooperate) or practical reasons (making terminology more Spanish-friendly) why data integration is problematic, "semantic heterogeneity turns out to be a major bottleneck for data integration" (ibid.).

---

[51] The team at Pompeii uses a custom FileMaker 12 application which seems to be well-designed but highly specific to their needs at Pompeii (http://classics.uc.edu/pompeii/ Pompeii Archaeological Research Project: Porta Stabia [PARP:PS]).

[52] Ives was the speaker for a workshop sponsored by the Neubauer Collegium at the University of Chicago, "Data Integration to Facilitate Data Science," October 4, 2019, https://neubauercollegium.uchicago.edu/events/data-integration-to-facilitate-data-science.

The Case for a Data Warehouse

There are two main strategies for tackling the problem of data integration. One is to build a *data warehouse* that ingests data from disparate sources into a single repository, resolving differences in the data structures by mapping the original structures onto a compatible framework defined by the *warehouse schema*. At the other end of the spectrum is the strategy of performing *virtual integration*, on-the-fly, leaving data in its original format but fetching and transforming it on demand, aligning sources via a *mediated schema*, in response to specific queries. There are pros and cons to both approaches that consider complexity, performance, data governance, data quality, user effort, tolerance for incompleteness, and other factors, and there are hybrid approaches that attempt to maximize the pros while minimizing the cons.[53]

OCHRE is decidedly in the data warehouse camp,[54] opting to invest the effort up front to populate the repository (often requiring substantial data cleaning), and to commit to the ongoing governance of the data for the long term. For scholars carefully curating research data, this approach not only keeps the data under their control but generally results in "better performance, better data quality, and the ability to express more complex queries or perform more sophisticated data transformations" (Doan et al. 2012, p. 271). In the warehouse approach, since the schema mapping onto a common framework is done just once when loading the data, it can be done more richly, resolving errors and inconsistencies in the data, while carefully mapping the full data set to the warehouse schema. This is in contrast to virtual integration which fetches relevant, selective bits from the original (un-cleaned!) source on demand. Semantic heterogeneity is resolved by mapping onto the warehouse schema and building thesaurus relations as needed. Warehouse data can be indexed and primed for efficient retrieval. Queries can be formulated based on a predictable structure (that is, the warehouse schema).[55]

Over years of usage, OCHRE has evolved a sophisticated import tool that sets a demanding standard for data quality and leaves nothing behind.[56] The OCHRE Data Service consults with projects on this nontrivial process. Scholars are not expected to reinvent the wheel or muddle through the conceptual and technical challenges on their own. In addition, because data goes through this rigorous import process,

---

[53] For an in-depth discussion, we recommend Doan et al. (2012), especially section 1.3. The advent of cloud computing has also spawned a massive industry with options for cloud-based data warehouses, data lakes, lake houses, data meshes, etc. Each strategy has a range of features with corresponding pros and cons. Amazon Web Services and Microsoft's Azure products are big players in this game, for example.

[54] For an example of a system in a similar academic space that is based on virtual integration, see the Digital Archaeology Record (tDAR), "your online archive for archaeological information" (https://core.tdar.org/).

[55] For additional benefits of a warehouse strategy, see Doan et al. (2012, p. 319).

[56] This is OCHRE's version of the "pipeline of procedural ETL (extract/transform/load) tools" typical of a data warehouse (ibid.).

projects get back better, cleaner, more consistent data than what was originally given to OCHRE.

OCHRE as Master Data Management (MDM)

OCHRE's reliance on a data warehouse strategy is solidly in the mainstream. In a corporate, rather than an academic setting, this strategy is known as *master data management* (MDM), defined by a leading business consultancy, Gartner, as:

> a technology-enabled discipline in which business and IT work together to ensure the uniformity, accuracy, stewardship, semantic consistency and accountability of the enterprise's official shared master data assets. Master data is the consistent and uniform set of identifiers and extended attributes that describes the core entities of the enterprise…[57]

Pitching itself as *the* Master Data Management company, Stibo Systems consults on the core processes "used to manage, centralize, organize, categorize, localize, synchronize and enrich master data according to the strategies of your company."[58] MDM solutions emphasize the need to be "end-to-end," managing a wide range of data beyond the core data of the enterprise. MDM includes data that is unstructured (e.g., from articles, reports, and other documents), transactional, metadata, hierarchical (managing relationships between data), and reference data (e.g., real-world data apart from the enterprise—measurements, currencies, time zones, countries, etc.).[59] Substituting "your research project" for "the enterprise" and "your company" in the quotations above gives a succinct statement of our goals for OCHRE for research data management and analysis within the academic community.[60]

An early proponent of MDM recognized not only the importance of the "core business entities used in traditional or analytical applications across the organization, and subjected to enterprise governance policies, along with their associated metadata, attributes, definitions, roles, connections and taxonomies," but also the need to "extend the realm of possibility to incorporate datasets that might not fit the standard mold" (Loshin 2006). If ever there were data that did not fit the standard mold, it is research data from the humanities and social sciences!

Key to successful MDM is data cleansing, transformation, and integration.[61] As we argue throughout this book, the item-based approach, as exemplified by OCHRE, is ideally suited for data transformation,[62] and most importantly, for data integration. In response to the challenge of data integration, and as computational processes attempt

---

[57] https://www.gartner.com/en/information-technology/glossary/master-data-management-mdm.

[58] https://www.stibosystems.com/what-is-master-data-management.

[59] https://profisee.com/master-data-management-what-why-how-who.

[60] Consultants at the OCHRE Data Service guide academic researchers in the adoption and implementation of data management strategies. Our experience has been that without such a consultation service, this stage of the process can often derail a research project.

[61] https://www.informatica.com/services-and-training/glossary-of-terms/master-data-management-definition.html. See Berson and Dubov (2011, pp. 21–23).

[62] XML is well-known for its nimbleness and its ease of transformation using eXtensible Stylesheet Language Transformations (XSLT), for example.

to deal with the "volume, velocity and variety of today's ['big'] data" in more productive ways (Hunger et al. 2021, p. 5), the return of the *graph database*, has emerged as "the clear alternative" to more traditional, and rigid, relational database options. In stark contrast to the relational data model, "graph databases support a very flexible and fine-grained data model that allows you to model and manage rich domains in an easy and intuitive way" (ibid., 9).[63] Furthermore, a graph data model can be thought of as "structured yet schema-free" (Robinson et al. 2015, p. 109) as opposed to relational tables which predefine column structures that constrain row data. "Easy" and "intuitive," "flexible and fine-grained," "structured yet schema-free"—this is how we like to think of OCHRE and its item-based approach.

The Case for XML

As *Principles for Data Integration* emphasizes, "XML has played an important role in data integration because it provides a syntax for sharing data. Once the syntax problem was addressed, people's appetites for sharing data in semantically meaningful ways were whetted."[64] As a general-purpose markup language, XML has been used to generalize and replace HTML as a format for sharing or exporting data. XML's support for semi-structured data gives unparalleled flexibility for tagging content—an advantage over the rigid table structures of the relational model, and a necessary option over unstructure (e.g., a word processing document). This flexibility greatly aids the process of schema mapping; that is, converting the format of the original data source to that of the warehouse schema. XML's hierarchical nature supports nesting, giving further options for schema mapping. For example, a data source might specify "Metal" while another might specify "Metal" > "Bronze"; both can be accommodated naturally. XML's ordered elements allow the sequence of content in a document to be preserved even after the document has been marked up. XML comes with strict rules regarding the markup, allowing content to be designated as "well-formed" and therefore predictable to other computational processes.

The constellation of tools and services around XML as a technology, including XML Schema, XSLT, XPath, and XQuery, provide powerful mechanisms for querying and transforming data—features essential to data integration. Many Web services communicate using XML as their common language. In short, in the service of data integration XML provides a common format for database, document, and Web-based data alike. And for OCHRE, the ubiquity of XML and its suitability for heterogeneous, semi-structured, hierarchical data, proved to be compelling reasons for adopting an XML-based database strategy for the platform.

Furthermore, since XML is document-based it is well suited to represent the items created by OCHRE's item-based approach: for identifying structure in

[63] For justification of a graph database approach. see Harrison, G. (2015) who explains why "graph database systems shine" in comparison to relational systems or NoSQL databases.

[64] Doan et al. (2012, p. 31). See also Doan et al. Chap. 11 for a rigorous discussion of XML and its aptness for data integration.

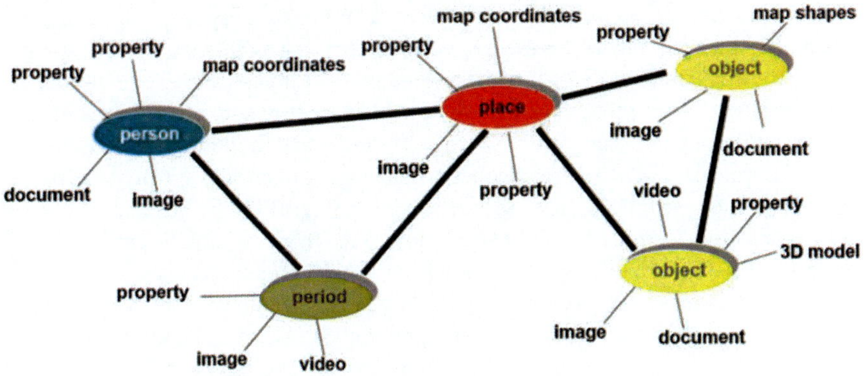

Fig. 2.13 Persons, places, things, and periods form a network of tagged database items

semi-structured data, allowing for the possibility of custom tags; for providing high-performance querying and transformation features; and for using a plain text format for data representation which encourages sharing and is suitable for archiving. Within the OCHRE implementation, the details of a single OCHRE item are delimited by markup in a single XML document, one document per item. OCHRE collects and organizes these item documents of all kinds within a common environment (e.g., as "nodes") letting them link to each other via references to their unique "key" identifiers (e.g., as edges or joins). The result is a unique database platform taking the best features of the hierarchical document model, the relational model, and the graph model and making them work together (Fig. 2.13).

The OCHRE Ontology

Even with XML-based, highly flexible underpinnings, one might wonder how it is that one database system can be used as a one-size-fits-all solution for representing widely disparate kinds of data from projects of all kinds in an easy and intuitive way. OCHRE is not a one-off, predefined data structure appropriate to some project then adapted or customized to meet the needs of other projects, nor is it a prepackaged collection of database fields and forms. Rather, it is a generic framework within which any project may implement its own more specific framework to represent the research data generated by that project.

In recent years, the term *ontology* has been borrowed from philosophy to define, broadly speaking, a formal conceptual or classification system that describes the knowledge being represented. For our purposes, we prefer a practical definition that focuses on the use of an ontology to help us think about and describe data within a database environment by addressing the question: "What kinds of things exist or can exist in the world, and what manner of relations can those things have to each other?" (Shirky 2008).

In the world of OCHRE, the ontology, or classification system, or warehouse schema, or data dictionary, or project vocabulary (pick your metaphor) is simple and high-level. Think of the "20 questions" game you played with your siblings on long road trips where you first tried to establish is it a person, place, or thing? Persons, places, and things form the basis of the OCHRE ontology. And that is it, almost. Because OCHRE was developed for managing historical and archaeological data, the notion of time is also treated as a meaningful "thing." Persons, places, things, and time periods are definable within OCHRE. A "thing" can be a flint blade, a Greek coin, a cooking pot, a letter written by Charles Darwin, a dry riverbed, a lion's tooth, a smudged cuneiform sign, a biological taxonomy, a questionnaire response, an audio file of a Marathi greeting, or an unusual grammatical form of a word. A "person" can be ancient or modern, dead or alive, an individual or a collective, imaginary or real. OCHRE does not care. Places are equally unrestricted but are managed as special *things* because they can often be situated spatially, either absolutely using coordinates within some universe (e.g., latitude/longitude) or relatively with respect to other items, making possible features such as mapping and geo-spatial analysis. Time periods, treated as special *things*, can be used to create a temporal frame of reference for other database items.

What a newly created, initially generic database item in OCHRE ultimately represents depends on which high-level category it is assigned to and how it is described in its particulars by the project. Each project uses its own terminology to define *properties*. A *property* is simply a *variable* representing a feature of interest along with a corresponding *value*. The constellation of properties, or variable-value pairs, defined by the project provides the descriptive framework used to identify its persons, places, and things of interest, that is, the database items (Fig. 2.14).[65]

Objects in OCHRE are thereby objects by description, not by definition; that is, an object in OCHRE has its identity and *is* something based on how it is *described* by an observer, not by how it is *defined*. This takes the pressure off the database system to get its definitions "right" and frees it from "the tyranny of small differences." That is, OCHRE does not attempt to prescribe any specific, or *local*, ontology. Rather, OCHRE is a *foundational* (or *global* or *upper*) ontology within which specific local ontologies can be defined. The power is in the hands of the scholar or researcher to adopt and implement their local ontology of choice and OCHRE provides tools to facilitate this.

There are many existing published ontologies that attempt to prescribe a standard to which scholarly expression and data description within a subject domain should conform. Some of these are popular and may be familiar, like the Text Encoding Initiative (TEI) specification for modeling texts in digital humanities circles, or the

[65] OCHRE's item-variable-value approach resonates with, and easily mapped to, the subject-predicate-object formulation (often described as "tuples") of the Resource Description Framework (RDF), an official specification of the W3C published in 1999. OCHRE and its predecessors, XSTAR and INFRA, were using the concept of an item with its set of variables and their values from the start, beginning with INFRA in 1989. The RDF specification served only later as a welcome validation of this highly compatible approach.

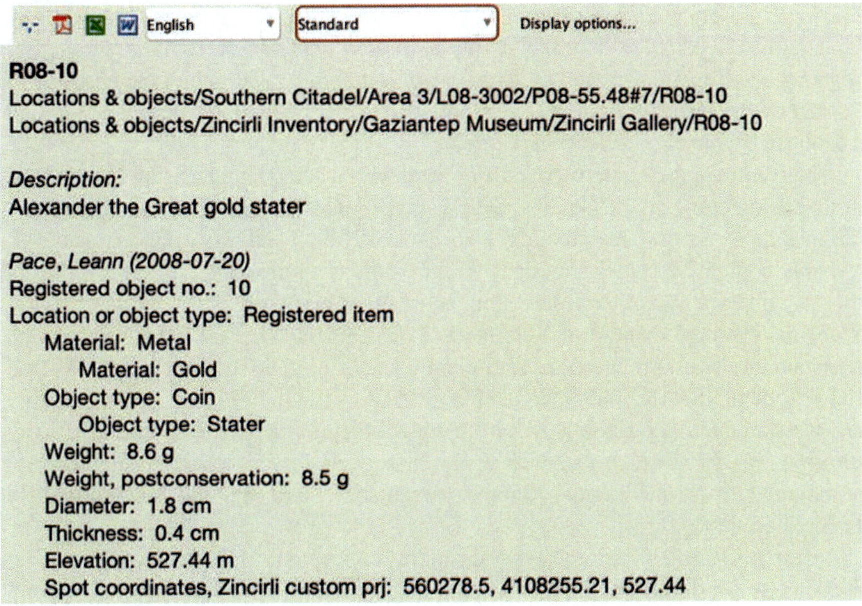

Fig. 2.14 A variety of properties describe a gold coin found at Zincirli in 2008

Europeana Data Model (EDM) for describing cultural heritage content. These are very specific formulations of a local ontology, the model for which could easily be implemented within OCHRE's upper ontology.[66] Equally, any completely custom description of people, places, things, and time periods could also be implemented within OCHRE, without regard for following "standards." Indeed, the invention of a new conceptual framework might constitute a work of scholarship in its own right. OCHRE, then, can be thought of as a tool for implementing an ontology of choice, whether a "standard" one or an idiosyncratic one and managing the data described by it.

OCHRE's item-based approach results in the proliferation of database items. Any individual item tends to be relatively small, easily represented by a single XML document, and for all intents and purposes, self-contained. These items are organized into **Categories** of data, where the categories correspond to the types of items allowed by the ontology. Collections of items within OCHRE's high-level categories can be further grouped into lists and trees, also referred to in OCHRE as **Sets** and **Hierarchies**, respectively. Trees, or hierarchies, are a natural and intuitive construct for organizing the world, the universe, and everything. If this seems like an exaggeration stop to consider the categorization of your iTunes albums and

[66] For TEI, see https://tei-c.org/; for EDM, see https://pro.europeana.eu/page/edm-documentation. OCHRE accommodates conformity with "standard" ontologies by providing tools to import from, or export to, formats based on the data models documented and encouraged by these specifications.

playlists, the organization of your laptop's hard drives, the generational levels of your family tree, your shopping list by store and department, the arrangement of seats by class on an airplane, the sections of a map or travel guide, the chapters of your favorite book, and so on, and notice the hierarchical organization implicit within such everyday collections of items.

The simple, generic, item-based approach with a heavy emphasis on hierarchical organization currently in use by OCHRE and originally intended to manage archaeological data was first described by D. Schloen (2001a) and was called ArchaeoML (Archaeological Markup Language). ArchaeoML as a schema definition was picked up early on by a few other systems, most notably Open Context[67] which provides a Web browser implementation of a subset of the ArchaeoML specification and which hosts and archives ArchaeoML-compliant data for participating projects.[68] As first INFRA, then XSTAR, and now OCHRE shifted from being *just* about archaeology and were adapted to represent data from many other domains, the ArchaeoML specification was left to take its place in the history of the development of the ideas pertaining to archaeological data representation and has not been actively maintained.

Instead, OCHRE's more generic, more conceptual, foundational ontology, appropriate for describing observations being made about a wide range of content, is documented under the name CHOIR which stands for "Comprehensive Hierarchical Ontology for Integrative Research." The CHOIR ontology "does not attempt to describe reality at all but simply prescribes a way of organizing scholarly statements about phenomena that makes it easier for scholars to do their work without limiting what they can say or how they may say it."[69] OCHRE represents one XML database implementation of the CHOIR ontology, but the ontology is documented separately so that other applications can be developed that are compatible with the OCHRE/CHOIR approach using different technologies. The CHOIR ontology, as a formal specification of concepts and relationships, remains independent of any implementation of it.

Conclusion

The flexible, upper ontology named CHOIR, appropriate for representing all kinds of data in the humanities, social sciences, and beyond, was developed and enhanced by a community of scholars working with archaeological, philological, and historical data over the past thirty years. Throughout this period of phenomenal technological progress and change, the ontology has been implemented first by INFRA, then XSTAR, and now OCHRE as a client-server application using Java and XML,

[67] https://opencontext.org/.

[68] The benefits of ArchaeoML are described by Eric Kansa et al. (2010, pp. 309–312).

[69] Schloen, D. 2023 https://digitalculture.uchicago.edu/platforms/ochre-ontology/.

successively refined with each major upgrade. The hybrid model implemented by OCHRE was motivated by the need to record the inherent complexity of research data. A research database platform should accommodate highly diverse data that is dispersed over space and time, that is characterized by various levels of details, that is semi-structured, and that contains uncertainty and disagreements. Integration of spatial, temporal, textual, lexical, and multi-media data should be supported naturally and intuitively. Not all computational approaches are well-suited to this task.

OCHRE is inspired by all the major database paradigms—the hierarchical, the relational, and the graph/network—taking advantage of the best features of each. As we examine the resultant OCHRE implementation in more detail and provide extended examples of its use by real-world research projects in the chapters that follow, the virtues of the generic ontology, the flexibility of the item-based approach, and the implications of hierarchies for database management in general, and for OCHRE more specifically, will become apparent. For now, suffice it to say that "OCHRE" might just as well stand for *Ontology Creation and the Hierarchical Representation of Everything*!

Chapter 3
OCHRE: An Item-Based Approach

Introduction

While walking to the commuter train station in the south suburban community of Homewood, Illinois, for the ride into the city of Chicago, S. Schloen would pass by a well-preserved "modern, attractive English home … with an exceptionally efficient floor plan" built in 1931. Based on the *Lewiston* design, this "happy combination of brick, tile and wood" could be ordered from page 44 of the Sears, Roebuck & Co. catalog, attic optional. The kit home would have been delivered in 12,000 pieces "already cut and fitted" and accompanied by a 75-page instruction book. Sears' post–World War II line of prefabricated homes came complete with pre-built walls, preinstalled windows, and preassembled stairs, taking the build time from 90 days down to three (Fig. 3.1).[1]

The expediency of a cookie–cutter approach to construction is hard for many to resist when it comes to building databases too. Designing a few simple tables with a few well-constructed columns and key fields makes it quick and easy to jump in and start collecting data. Sharing this pre-built structure with your colleague means they can get up and running quickly too—like with the *Lewiston*, 3 days instead of 90. But this one-size-fits-all approach has serious drawbacks as a strategy for managing research data.

Consider the following conceptual observations. This specific house at 18219 Riegel Road in Homewood, IL, is one instance of the *Lewiston* house plan; there were many others.[2] Apart from this specific house, there is the model of the *Lewiston* house. Beyond this house, beyond this plan, there is the idea of a house. A database created for the recording of a specific type of data by one specific project is the

[1] Sears, Roebuck & Co. catalog, Model No. P3287, http://www.sears-homes.com/2013/10/a-sears-home-in-homewood.html.

[2] See Thornton (2004) and Stevenson and Jandl (1986).

S. R. Schloen, M. C. Prosser, *Database Computing for Scholarly Research*, Quantitative Methods in the Humanities and Social Sciences,
https://doi.org/10.1007/978-3-031-46696-0_3

Fig. 3.1 18219 Riegel Road, Homewood, IL: The Lewiston model. (Photograph by S. Schloen)

equivalent of the exact *Lewiston* house in Homewood, IL. An internet search for "database of archaeological collections" returns thousands of examples—thousands of specific implementations of databases for specific projects—like the thousands of prefab houses built on the *Lewiston* plan. By analogy, not only is OCHRE more generalized than both the Homewood house, and the *Lewiston* plan; OCHRE is more abstract, even, than the idea of a house. OCHRE does not prescribe what materials can be used or what structures the researcher might build. This is intentional in the design of the database and critically important for research data in the humanities and social sciences so as not to put undue limitations on either the data or the scholar.

Research data tends to be highly variable, often semi-structured, typically fragmentary, and based on idiosyncratic designs specific to a scholar or project team. Forcing such data into preconfigured structures often compromises it in a number of ways: making it less authentic as it is translated to some other "standard" nomenclature; making it less granular as it is adapted for the prescribed fields; conflating qualities that are best retained as separate facets for analysis; resorting to free-form descriptions for data that does not fit, and so on. A pottery specialist might create three columns—"Class," "Ware," and "Type"—and will toss in "Notes" for good measure. Everything that can be said about any given potsherd will be recorded in one of these four table columns. A faunal expert might create columns for "Taxon," "Skeletal element 1," "Skeletal element 2," "Measurements," and, of course, the catch-all "Notes" and then start hammering away at the data entry. A textual scholar will create a list of documents of interest, identify some key features, choose some metadata elements, and then what?

OCHRE's item-based approach adopts a conceptually different strategy. Rather than building up uniform, predefined structures for data, OCHRE breaks data down into its most granular parts so that from these components, any number of appropriate structures and configurations can be assembled—"happy combinations of brick, tile, and wood"—as determined by the nature of the data itself or by the goals of the researcher. Having building blocks to work with as the primary structural units creates more flexibility in design, more potential for customization, and more options for fitting in with other structures. Whether constructing a composite view or a compelling argument, granular data prove to be more useful and flexible for addressing research questions.

What Is an Item?

The building blocks of any OCHRE project are *items*. Any physical or conceptual *thing* that can be observed, studied, and discussed can be represented by an OCHRE item. Breaking data down into its component parts, the building blocks, is a process we refer to as *atomization*. (Because database items are created in this process, we use the term *itemization* interchangeably.) Archaeologists study things like sites, temples, coins, pits, or pots. In most cases, each of these things is represented by a discrete item in OCHRE. An item can be a tangible thing like a Corinthian column, but it might just as well be a column of text on a manuscript of the Iliad. Philologists work with items like words, phrases, scripts, grammatical forms, and dictionary entries. Scientists work with items representing bryozoans, dinosaur bones, radiocarbon samples, or Linnaean taxonomies. Historians work with items that represent people, places, timelines, and ideas.

What are ***you*** studying? Pause for a moment to reflect on your own research. What are the *things* you study? Pottery? Texts? Coins? Inscriptions on coins (related texts and objects)? People and their social behavior? Places and their features? Trade networks (interactions between people and places)? Something else? Maybe you are studying a wide range of *different* things, like archaeological research projects which manage the entire, wide-ranging set of items they might find in an excavation. Maybe you are studying a vast collection of *similar* things, like the use of cuneiform on tens of thousands of ancient tablets. Maybe you are studying just *one* thing, like the world of Florence in 1427 as described by one of the earliest recorded censuses. What is it, specifically, that you are studying, recording, documenting, analyzing, publishing? What is the level of detail, the most minimal meaningful part, at which you make observations or interpretations?

All these things—these objects of study—are represented as items in OCHRE. Before going too much further, it seems important to reinforce that we are using the term "item" in a broad sense; do not think only of a physical object.

Rather, by "item," we mean anything about which an observation or interpretation can be made. Items can be tangible or conceptual, imaginary or real, singular or collective. The stone ramparts (or ruins thereof) that surround an ancient city will not be an object collected by the archaeology team, but there will be observations made about it; the rampart, as a whole, would be represented by an item. If, however, one of the individual stones at the base of the rampart was found to be carved with a commemorative inscription, that single stone would also, itself, be represented by an item. For another example, say there were 100 coins of interest collected with the intent of identifying and studying each one. Each coin should be represented by its own item to be observed and described. On the other hand, if a bucket of 100 unremarkable, non-diagnostic coins were collected, the entire collection could legitimately be treated as a single item of interest, noting only the combined count and weight of the collective.

The additional value of an item-based approach is that even semi-structured document content can be atomized—that is, broken down into the most minimal meaning parts as items to be identified and studied. The single lemma entry, "to cry out, shout for joy, cheer, …" in the Chicago Hittite Dictionary (eCHD) can be atomized into multiple meanings. Each "meaning," as an independent item, can be expounded upon, linked to exemplars from textual sources, cross-referenced, have bibliography attached, and otherwise interpreted (Fig. 3.2).

In a table-based approach, the research team creates tables, or linked tables, to collect the items of study. The structure of these tables defines how current and future things of interest are described. Some projects may adopt predefined structures for their data, based on some standard. Others will instinctively develop completely unique structures, but often without consideration for how their resulting data might interact with related scholarship beyond their own project. In an item-based approach, research data can be highly granular, or highly composite, with each item being atomized and described in as much detail, and only as much detail, as is required by the research questions. Data does not need to be described by a common, predefined set of metadata fields; it does not need to fit into predefined

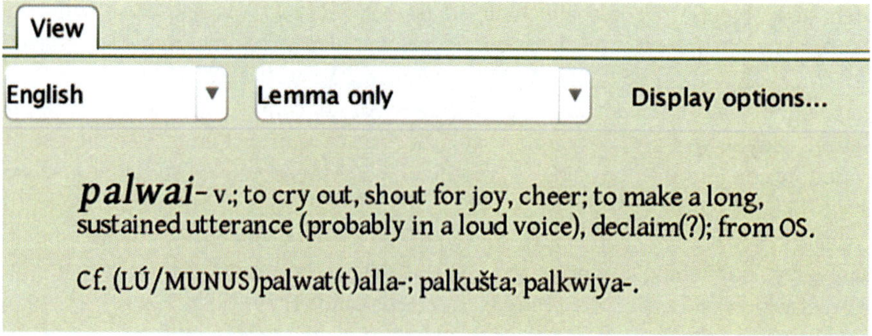

Fig. 3.2 A semi-structured dictionary unit is, in fact, highly structured; OCHRE makes the structure explicit

structures. In this model, the properties used to describe items are themselves items and can be mapped onto any number of metadata schemas like the Dublin Core schema, or SKOS (Simple Knowledge Organization System), for example. Follow along below as we explore the strategies of the item-based approach, the value of the flexibility it provides, and the way it resolves many of the conundrums that research data presents.

An Organic Approach to Data Management

In biology, the cell is the basic structural and functional unit of organic life. Like the "brick, tile, and wood" celebrated above, stem cells are the body's raw materials—undifferentiated cells from which all other cells with specialized functions are generated. Like a stem cell, each unit of data within OCHRE gets its start as an undifferentiated item capable of becoming the representation of *any* observable object, fact, or idea. Such items are the building blocks, the raw materials, of the OCHRE database.

Like most cells, items function more successfully as part of a larger entity. In OCHRE, every item comes into existence within the context of a research project. The item is given a name and is uniquely encoded by being assigned a universally unique identifier (UUID). Each item is discrete yet part of a larger organism—an OCHRE **Project** (Fig. 3.3).

Any unit of observation can be represented by an item and one full of possibility. A new item in OCHRE is generic, a stem cell so to speak, and has constituent characteristics that it shares with all other items. Along with the ability to be uniquely identified, these characteristics include the potential to be described by *properties*, related by *links*, tracked by *events*, annotated by *notes*, and situated within *space* and *time*. In the process of being thus analyzed, each item differentiates and becomes a unique representation of a distinct unit of data.

The first act of differentiation happens when the item is assigned to a high-level **Category** of data—one of the categories permitted by the CHOIR ontology.[3] Take, for example, the category of **Locations & objects**; items assigned to this category

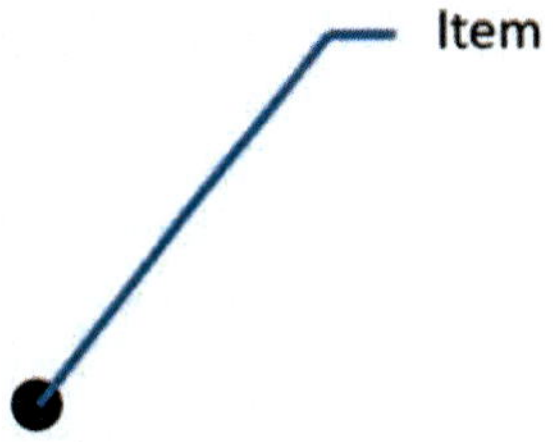

Fig. 3.3 Items: the building blocks of an effective data management strategy

[3] The CHOIR ontology was introduced in Chap. 2.

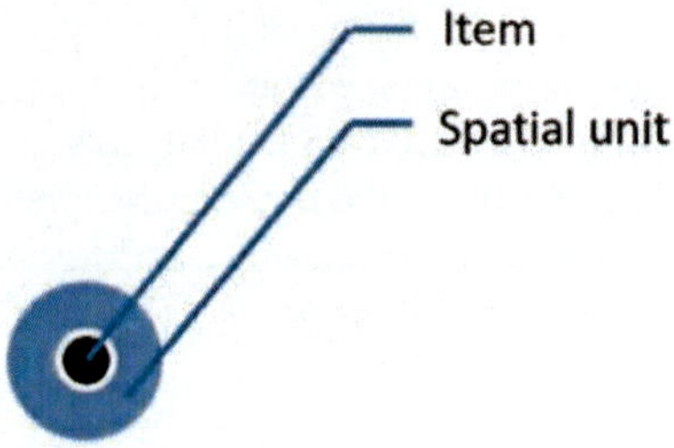

Fig. 3.4 Items are assigned to a Category of data to begin the process of differentiation

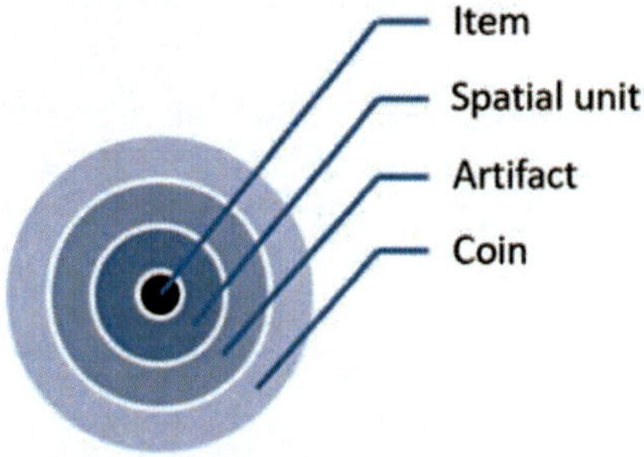

Fig. 3.5 Properties identify this thing as a Coin in the class of Artifacts

are called *spatial units*. Like all new items, a spatial unit is a generic item which needs further elaboration (Fig. 3.4).

As the next act of differentiation, *properties* are applied to make a spatial unit a meaningful representation of something—quite literally, some thing. The spatial unit illustrated below is described as an Artifact, then sub-classified as a Coin. By adding properties, the researcher continues the process of classifying the items in the Locations & objects category of this project (Fig. 3.5).

Oftentimes in archaeology, artifacts are discovered in such a poor state of preservation that very little can be said about them except at a very general level. Other times excavators get lucky and find objects about which they can say a great deal. With an item-based approach, the high variability of data description can be easily accommodated. Each item can be described, uniquely if necessary, and to the extent possible—no more, no less. OCHRE neither requires nor enforces any standardization of description (Fig. 3.6).

The process of differentiation is at the control of the scholar who, by necessity, is still the brains of the operation (although some artificial processes may well add intelligent behavior to aid in the collection or analysis of data under close supervision). OCHRE remains inherently neutral while providing enough structure for representing data of all kinds.

The backbone of the OCHRE environment is the set of **Categories** of data which enumerate the possibilities at the first stage of specialization (Fig. 3.7). An item might be assigned as a **Bibliography** item, a time **Period**, or an **Object**, to give a few examples. As the unit of data is modified and differentiated, other descriptive features, specific to the type of item, become available. A spatial unit may be pinpointed to a geographic coordinate. A time period might be assigned a range of dates. A bibliography item will be given an author and publication date.

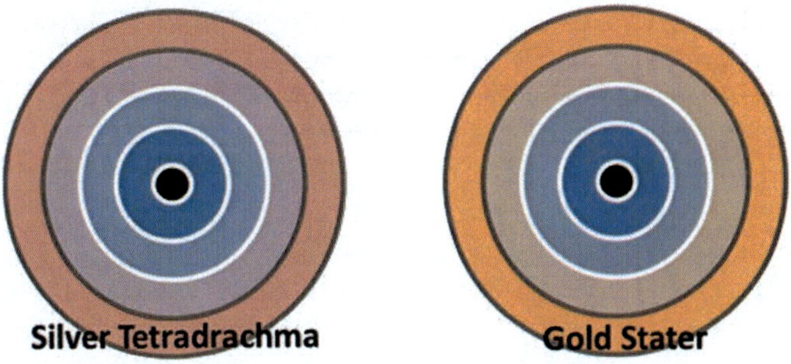

Fig. 3.6 Each item is described as its own thing, distinct from all other items

Fig. 3.7 OCHRE's high-level Categories provide a place for everything

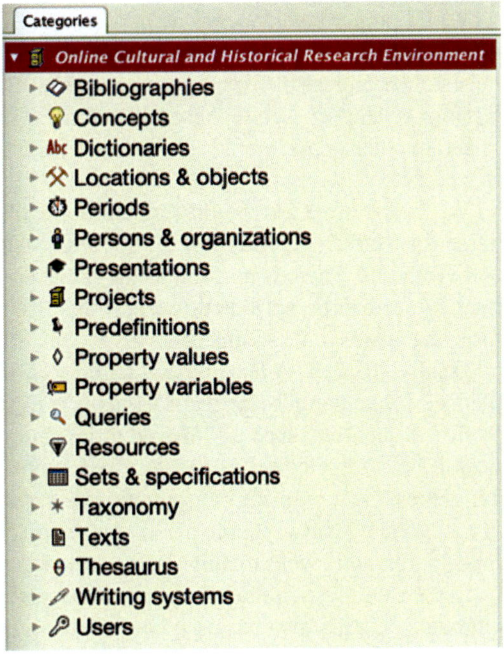

The bare bones framework offered by the initial list of categories is fleshed out by the creation of a project **Taxonomy**. The taxonomy defines the full set of properties available for describing database items, including constraints and dependencies. In effect, it represents the data dictionary, or ontology, for a specific project. Within the collaborative OCHRE environment, taxonomies can be adopted, or adapted, from other projects or from the OCHRE master project. An archaeological project that has collected coins, beads, bones, and pottery will have created properties to describe these as part of the recording process. Another archaeological project can benefit from the work that has already been done and which can be shared, as one project borrows from another a complete set of descriptors, taking the project's build time "from 90 days down to three," like with the *Lewiston*. There is no need to reinvent a database structure from the ground up. Where researchers do have differing descriptive schemes, say, for example, incompatible ways of classifying pottery, these differences can be customized by each project.

A property defined by the project taxonomy consists of a combination of a *variable* and a *value* that, together, ascribe a characteristic to an item: Artifact type is Coin, Diameter is 5.5 centimeters, Preservation is fragmentary, Excavation date is July 20th. Properties can be devised by the researcher to capture anything—features, qualities, measures, motifs, ideas.[4] There is no limit to the number of properties that can be defined, and there is a wide assortment of types of properties available like numeric, character string, logical (true/false), and date. Properties serve to classify individual items, allowing items with matching properties to be discovered by a query.

While properties give each item teeth, *links* add substance and bring it to life, allowing the item to interact with other relevant items. Images, audio clips, video, documents, and shapefiles, to name a few, are separate items managed by the **Resource** category. While these are cataloged in their own right, they are typically linked to other items in order to complete an item's identification and to illustrate it in whatever way is appropriate.

Where narrative text would add additional information to an item, *notes* provide a free-form text field for writing entries like catalog descriptions, processual records, and syntheses. There is no limit to the number of notes a researcher may add to an item. Notes can be attributed to **Persons** (also managed as items), current or historic, and can be date stamped.

Finally, if the item is to be compared to a living organism, its life history and planned future can also be recorded as part of the data. *Events* record moments in the life of the item, such as "Moved to laboratory." An event can also assign workflow to be completed by a team member, such as "To be photographed." Once this assignment is complete, an additional event can record that the item was "Photographed" by a specific person on a specific date. Combinations of properties, links, notes, and events distinguish each item from any other.

In the same vein, although data is often thought to be about tangible things and although OCHRE matured in the bosom of archaeology, a tool like OCHRE works as well for a wide range of scholarly species, including the philologist, historian, or scientist. OCHRE's categories of **Texts**, **Dictionaries**, and **Concepts** give scope to engage with scholarship of all kinds. Texts are decomposed into their atomic parts—*epigraphic units* representing signs or characters in a medieval manuscript or ancient tablet, and *discourse units* representing words, phrase, or poetic devices (Fig. 3.8). A *dictionary unit* will be ascribed a gloss or a meaning and given grammatical properties.

[4] We return to the idea of properties throughout the book. See Chap. 5 on how properties are implemented in OCHRE's item-based database model.

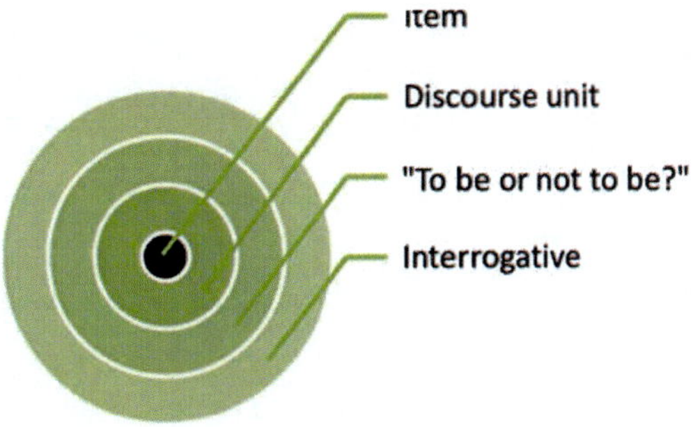

Fig. 3.8 OCHRE categories apply equally well to textual studies; here, the interrogative phrase "To be or not to be" starts life as a mere item before differentiating

Identifying Items

In addition to assigning an item to a high-level category to begin the process of differentiation, the researcher will give the item an identifying **Name** (or names). Upon creating an item, OCHRE generates and assigns to it a universally unique identifier (UUID). Because the UUID is unique, the name need not be. The coins in a collection of 100 coins could be itemized as "Coin 1," "Coin 2," and so on, or they could all be called simply "Coin"—OCHRE will not get them confused. OCHRE also uses the item's UUID as the basis for generating a unique **Citation URL** which is used to identify the item on the Semantic Web, in keeping with Berners-Lee's principle #1, that is, to "use URIs as names for things."[5]

One Item, Multiple Identities

Things often go by many different names. People have nicknames, married names, or various abbreviated names. Text editions might be numbered differently depending on the publication. Places might have historical names, modern names, or names based on different language traditions. In the Catasto project, the streets of Florence are spelled with many variations and often change names as they cross intersections (via del Ciriegio = via del Ciriagio = via de'Pepi = via del Pepi = via dei Bonfanti). Each OCHRE item has a primary **Name** field, but OCHRE also has the option to add any number of **Aliases** to the Name of an item. Aliases track all noted variations, treating them as stand-ins for the official Name and allowing them to be used interchangeably.[6] The **Person** item for the scientist "Siebold, Carl Theodor Ernst von" studied by the *Lives, Individuality, and Analysis* project has an Alias that lists a full set of spellings and abbreviations so that OCHRE can find him by matching on any combination of these.

[5] See Chaps. 2 and 9.

[6] See the section on Internationalization (Chap. 5) for a serendipitous use of Aliases.

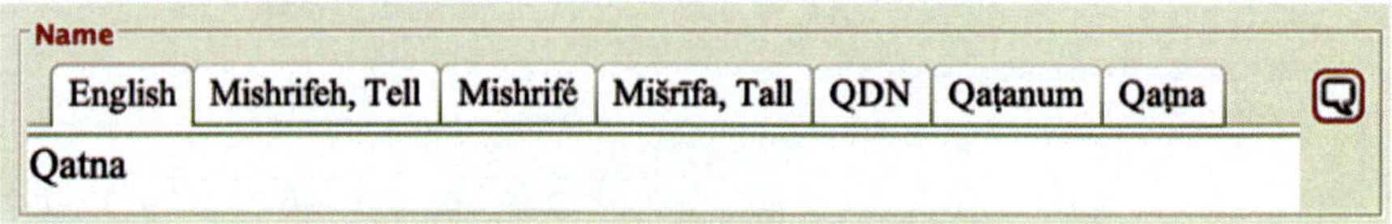

Fig. 3.9 A database lookup will match any of these variations of Qatna

C. (Carl) (Carolus) (Karl) Th. (Ernst) (Theodor) (Theodorus) (de) (von) E. (Ernestus) (Ernst) (de) (von) von (de) (v.) Siebold (Von Siebold), 1804–1885

The CRANE site database, which exhaustively catalogs thousands of historic sites surveyed throughout the Orontes watershed region (central Turkey and environs), illustrates another important use of Aliases. Because site locations are often speculative, and their identification sometimes tentative, different scholars may make different observations about the **Location** item. The CRANE strategy is to use the Alias mechanism to track all attested names for any given site as references are found in the publication record, shown here for the site of Qatna. The button designated with a speech bubble icon lets users add new variations to what might be a long list of options (Fig. 3.9).

One Item, Many Voices

One of the core principles of OCHRE is that as items proliferate, they do not become just more anonymous data in "the computer." With potentially many observations being supplied by many scholars, it is important to track who said what and when it was said.

A special feature of OCHRE is that items can have one or more *creators* (of Resources), *editors* (of Texts), *interpreters* (of Concepts), *observers* (of Spatial units), or *authors* (of Notes). Scholars, registered as Person items, are given appropriate credit where credit is due.

Consider the small find shown in Fig. 3.10 which was sent in from the field to the inexperienced registrar at Zincirli in July of 2010. After a cursory inspection of the still dirty, unimpressive artifact, she assigned the next available registration number, R10-119, listed it as a "Metal" object, checked the "Uncertain" box duly noting that she was unsure of her assessment, and then filed it away in long-term storage with other equally unimpressive objects.

Fully 3 years later, an enterprising student specializing in archaeometallurgy came to study the metal finds from this site. An OCHRE query identified all finds that were "Metal," or suspected to be metal, and the objects were pulled for her study. Under closer, expert analysis this formerly insignificant object was determined to be not only an unusual lead inlay of a writing tablet, but also inscribed by two lines of Luwian hieroglyphs. The item was fast-tracked through conservation and photography, with the conservator adding her own observation giving details of

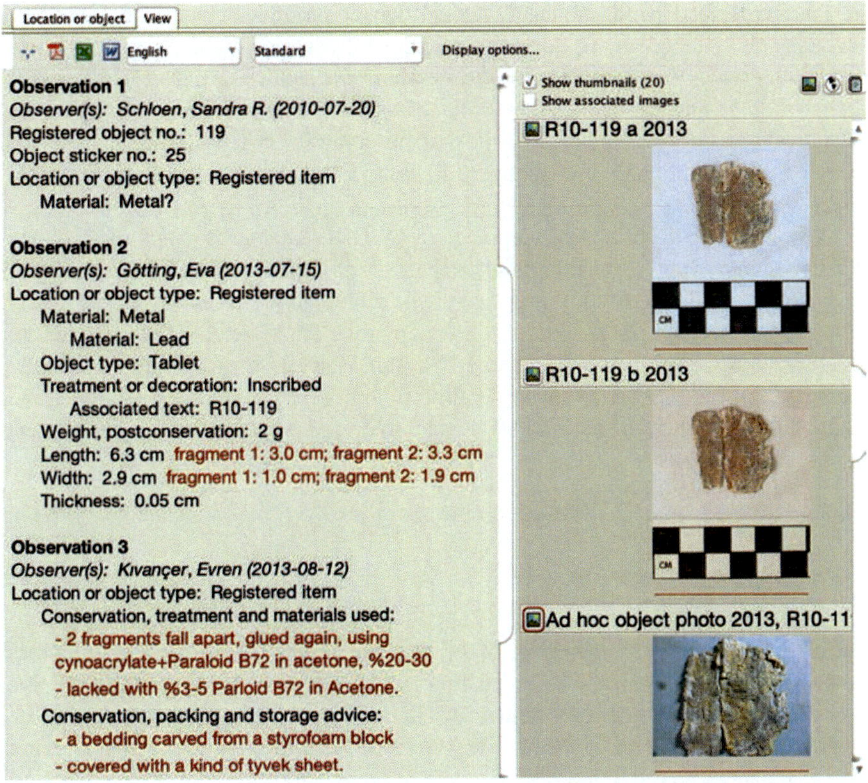

Fig. 3.10 A specialist is credited for her expert analysis of an artifact

its treatment, and the photographer getting credit for the high-quality photographs.[7] No doubt, this artifact had been overdue for a new observation by the specialist![8]

The ability to assign multiple observations to an item allows a project team to record the accumulated discussion pertaining to the item, track its movement through various stages of workflow, preserve the different voices that comment on it, and leave the conversation open. The final word on this Luwian inscription, of great interest to scholars, may not yet have been spoken.

There are many benefits of multiple observations in a research context. The CRANE initiative provides another example of using multiple observations to track the history of scholarship on a site. This avoids having to create potentially duplicate items to represent the same site, which would be awkward from a data

[7] M. Prosser, acting object photographer at Zincirli in 2013, produced a Polynomial Texture Mapping (PTM) image of this small object that allowed the project codirector Herrmann to identify the writing.

[8] S. Schloen, acting registrar at Zincirli that summer of 2010, is undeniably guilty of missing the importance of this special find.

perspective. It also avoids having to "agree" on a common understanding of the site. It is possible—one might argue even preferable—to document the differences without having to resolve them. Each **Observation** will credit the **Observer** (e.g., the archaeologist), and, typically, it will include a **Bibliography** reference, crediting the source of the information detailed in that observation. Individual notes, too, are ascribed to an author and time-stamped, allowing for further attributed discussion of an item.

This multivocality is a key component of OCHRE's item-based approach. There is no anonymous authority, no argument that "the computer says…" Rather, authorship and attribution are transparent, data contributions are tracked, and scholarly arguments are made possible as differing opinions are registered and attached to database items. The history of scholarly commentary is preserved as potentially many voices weigh in with an observation on any given item at a given date and time. This is the use of technology to facilitate collaboration, without requiring consensus, at its best.

Categorizing Items

OCHRE items fall into different, high-level categories, the full list of which is described below, organized as to their function, and ordered based on their relative proportions as represented by actual OCHRE projects.[9] These categories are the basis of the CHOIR ontology. After over 20 years of usage, we have yet to encounter data that cannot be fitted naturally into one of these categories.

Primary Categories

Locations & Objects

The category of Locations & objects represents places or things that have spatial context; that is, *spatial units*. A spatial unit is typically subordinate to another spatial unit (e.g., a coin is found within an excavation unit), or it has its own spatial context (e.g., its findspot). An item situated in space may be something as simple as a manuscript that has been in a museum or library collection for a century or a ceramic vessel that is being excavated after a millennium under a depositional layer. This category also includes geographic places—the "Locations" of "Locations & objects"—which are often assigned coordinates. Spatial units can be used for defining the scope of a query (e.g., "Find only coins from Zincirli"), and they can be visualized (e.g., plotted on a map) in OCHRE's built-in **Map View**.

[9] See also Schloen and Schloen (2012, chapter 2).

Resources

Resource items constitute one of the largest collections of items in the OCHRE database and are comprised of images, drawings, documents, video or audio files, or a variety of other representations of an item. Resources provide a catalog of files that are stored externally to OCHRE (e.g., on a remote server) but which link to database items like Objects, Persons, or Texts (as photographs), or to Dictionary units or Discourse units (as audio files representing spoken words). OCHRE provides built-in specialized viewers for files of common formats. Even for file formats that cannot be viewed directly within OCHRE, it is still helpful to use OCHRE to manage and organize sizable collections of external files as Resource items.[10]

Periods

Whether it is the birthdate of a nineteenth-century scientist, the date of the earliest manuscript of Genesis, the years during which a Pharaoh reigned, the radiocarbon-based date of a DNA sample, the cultural period of a certain style of pottery, or the date of a recording of a song, research data is often contextualized within time. Sometimes, this involves recording very specific dates; sometimes, it requires defining more general time periods. Because Periods are database items, the user can define them in whatever way is meaningful to their project. Analogous to the spatial contexts inherent in the Locations & objects category, Period items are characterized by temporal contexts. A broad historical period may contain periods that represent subperiods; for example, the Neolithic Period may contain Early Neolithic, Middle Neolithic, and Late Neolithic. Periods are sequential in nature, that is, organized in ordered lists so that questions about what is "before" and what is "after" can be asked and answered. Period items can be conceptual ("the Iron Age") or literal (the birthdate of Charles Darwin), relative ("Phase 1b"), or absolute ("604 BCE"). Periods are assigned as links wherever appropriate and can also be used to limit the scope of a query ("Find all fortifications from the Middle Bronze Age").

Persons & Organizations

Persons & organizations items, like Periods, can be conceptual ("the minting authority of ancient Athens") or literal ("Alexander the Great"), modern ("Prosser, Miller"), or historic ("Darwin, Charles"). This category includes organizations ("The University of Chicago") as well as individuals. Person items participate as nodes in the graph of knowledge of social and historical networks. More

[10]As of this writing, OCHRE is managing well over 100 terabytes of Resource data for over 80 projects.

prosaically, they may represent project staff that can be used in links that attribute the source of content, appropriately, on behalf of the project. The observer of the description of an object, the creator of a photograph, and the author of a bibliography item are all tracked as Person items.

Texts

Text items support the representation of any type of textual content: characters on a manuscript, words of a book, contents of a letter, etchings of an inscription. An OCHRE Text can (but need not) consist of both an *epigraphic* structure representing how the Text appears, including pages, columns, lines, and characters or signs, along with a *discourse* structure representing what the Text means, including words, phrase, sentences, and other grammatical or analytic constructs. As we shall see in sections to follow, OCHRE Texts are compound items that generally implicate many subordinate epigraphic and discourse units.

Dictionary Units

Dictionary items are complex structures, based loosely on the structure of the Oxford English Dictionary.[11] A Dictionary item organizes subordinate items that represent words having different grammatical forms and various spellings, and it also manages a hierarchy of multiple, nested, semantic meanings (Fig. 3.11). Each of these components can be richly annotated with properties, links, notes, and events, creating a comprehensive reference. In addition, OCHRE provides sophisticated tools ("wizards") to facilitate the construction of a corpus-based lexicon (see Chap. 8), linking words in a text to appropriate dictionary entries, or generating new dictionary entries if needed, as the scholar analyzes a Text.

Concepts

For things that are more intangible than tangible, the Concepts category serves as a place to record inventive, creative, or conceptual representations of data. In some ways, Concepts serve as a catch-all category for items that interact not in the world of space or time, but in the universe of ideas. Concepts can be described by means of properties assigned by multiple interpreters and enhanced with notes, links, and events as with other items. Examples include languages (Akkadian, Greek, etc.), measures (meter/metre, shekel, and more), motifs ("Hero controls bulls"), typologies ("Tell Ahmar Cooking Pot Ware"), or policies (Catasto census "declarations").

[11] The OCHRE dictionary model follows the Lexical Markup Framework (Francopoulo 2012), which is taken up in more detail in Chap. 4.

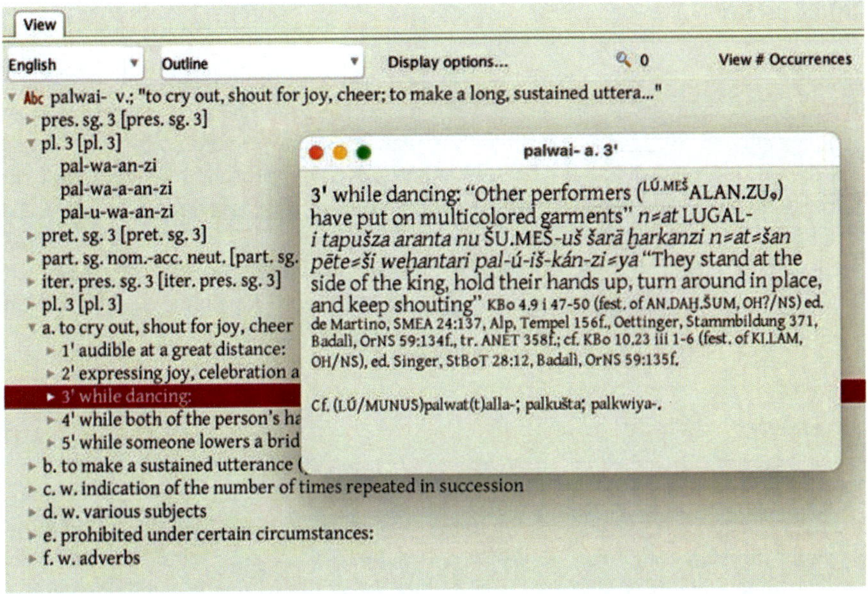

Fig. 3.11 The Hittite word "to cry out" is represented by a structured Dictionary unit

Concepts can be nested to create sub-concepts that share the features of the parent concept while adding unique sub-features.

Concepts are also valuable for combining individual things that, together, constitute a new whole. An event, say, an academic conference, will have participants (Persons), gathering in a place (Spatial unit), at a given time (Period), giving presentations (documents or video Resources). A psychology experiment will have subjects (Persons), questionnaires (document Resources), annotated video (Resources), and interpretation by the scholar (Description, Notes). A legal case will have a defendant, prosecutor, and jurors (Persons), briefs and affidavits (document Resources or Texts), trial dates (Periods), and venues (Spatial units). Concepts can collect, catalog, describe, link, and aggregate items that are related in any number of ways.

Specialized Categories

Projects

A Project is an organizational unit in OCHRE. A Project has an administrator, along with regular users. All data (items) belongs to some Project; a Project owns all of its data (items), although it may choose to share some of it, or make all or some of it public. Visibility, access rights, and publication options are all determined within the scope of a Project. From the perspective of a researcher, a Project is the part of the OCHRE environment to which they have access through credentials.

Bibliography

OCHRE allows the tracking and cataloging of bibliographic items via the Bibliography category. Although OCHRE provides its own basic means to organize bibliography, it also interacts with the popular Zotero bibliographic system,[12] so as not to reinvent the proverbial wheel. Hundreds of citation formats are supported via the Zotero API and OCHRE utilizes Zotero's styling capabilities. OCHRE's Bibliography items link naturally to Persons (as Authors, Editors, and Publishers) as well as to PDF files managed as OCHRE Resources. Bibliography can be assigned as links to items in the primary categories, to document the source of information about such items.

Taxonomy

Every project has one and only one Taxonomy which articulates the project's vocabulary. It is represented as a hierarchical list of properties, consisting of an alternating sequence of project-defined **Variables** and **Values**, which determine how the items of that project can be described. Hierarchical branches of any project's taxonomy can be borrowed from other projects. The OCHRE master project serves as a source of taxonomic descriptors that can be borrowed by new projects so that they do not have to start from scratch.

Thesaurus

An OCHRE Thesaurus provides a mechanism to link common terminology among projects. One project's "bucket" is another's "basket" or "lot" or "pail" or "goufa" or "cubo." The Thesaurus is also key to linking to the Semantic Web as we will see (Chap. 9), expanding the Web of knowledge available to a project's research data.

Writing Systems

Our history of working with ancient languages forced us to grapple with the complexity of Writing systems. In OCHRE, a Writing system is represented by a series of *script units*. Each script unit is a database item described by readings and allographs. Each script unit contains all the information needed to identify it in a text, including technical details such as its Unicode value and accounting for potential variations in its graphemic and allographic forms. To be clear, a Writing system accounts for the script and not specifically the language since the same script might be used for expressing multiple languages. Writing systems allow researchers to

[12] https://www.zotero.org/about/.

work with texts in native scripts or in Latin transcription. Individual projects do not normally create their own Writing systems. The OCHRE Data Service maintains highly articulated Writing systems for many of the world's various scripts that can be shared among projects. As of this writing, OCHRE has Writing systems available for Aramaic (including Hebrew and Phoenician scripts), Greek, Latin, Coptic, Syriac, Cuneiform (including Sumerian, Akkadian, and Ugaritic scripts), Devanagari, and Middle Egyptian Hieroglyphs. Writing systems perform validation for importing Texts and prescribe formatting for assorted Views of a Text based on its script(s) and/or language(s).

Supporting Categories

Presentations

The category of Presentations provides the means to create user interactions that showcase OCHRE data within the Java client graphical user interface (GUI) environment. While the trend is more toward creating pure Web-based interactions (not requiring Java), the Presentations feature still provides useful functionality for presenting OCHRE apps offline or for customized presentations.

Queries

The category of Queries gives a project the means to design queries to find and fetch data. Queries can target a variety of criteria, including matches on Properties, Events, Links, metadata, and full-text character strings. Queries can be scoped by space or by time and can be compounded; that is, multiple criteria can be used for any Query. A Query specification can be saved, and the resulting list of items generated by performing a Query can be saved and viewed using any number of export and visualization options. This is a powerful tool for data analysis.

Sets & Specifications

The category of Sets & specifications provides a bridge between an item-based approach and a table-based approach. At its most basic, a Set is a collection of database items that can be viewed together in a convenient structure, such as a table. A researcher may also page through items in a Set one at a time for the purpose of data entry or validation. Sets allow researchers to create and save structured collections of items to analyze, visualize, export, share, or publish. The specifications provide options for *how* the Set is to be analyzed, visualized, exported, shared, or published.

Property Values, Variables, and Predefinitions

While the taxonomy is the primary basis of a project's vocabulary, supporting categories give alternate access to its constituent items. Property Values and Variables alternate in a hierarchical structure to define a taxonomy, but both Variable and Value items are also managed separately in their respective supporting categories, allowing a project administrator to group and sort these descriptive elements as alphabetical lists for the purpose of staying organized. The taxonomy documents the full range of descriptive terminology, but a project may wish to enforce uniformity of data capture, for example, by a team of field members or laboratory assistants. OCHRE includes a mechanism for applying a template of variables whose values are to be filled in by the user. This template, called a Predefinition, allows a project administrator to preconfigure a select set of properties required for items of a given type, say Coins. So, even though OCHRE's item-based approach allows for heterogeneity of properties across items, the OCHRE application supports the recording of uniform properties where desired.

Users

OCHRE Users are Person items that have been granted access to an OCHRE project via a username and password on the authority of the project administrator. Users can be granted various levels of access (view-only, insert, insert-delete, etc.) to different categories of project data.

Complex Items

Surprisingly, it is not always self-evident how best to characterize items in OCHRE, even to the point of knowing in which high-level category they belong. Is the Institute for the Study of Ancient Cultures of the University of Chicago an *agent* (Persons & organizations, e.g., serving as a publisher or a sponsor of an excavation) or a *place* (Locations & objects, e.g., where King Tut is on display)?[13] It seems that it should be obvious into which category an item belongs, but sometimes it depends on the research purpose to which the item is subjected, and sometimes it reflects on how the scholar thinks of the data. The semantics are not absolute but are open to interpretation. In fact, an item may have qualities best represented by more than one category. Like with our stem cell analogy, sometimes it is necessary to divide in order to achieve the desired outcome.

[13] See also, for example, Chap. 12, where we struggle to decide whether the Mint at Athens is a Location or an Organization item. OCHRE addresses this in part by allowing geospatial metadata (e.g., coordinates) on Person/Organization items.

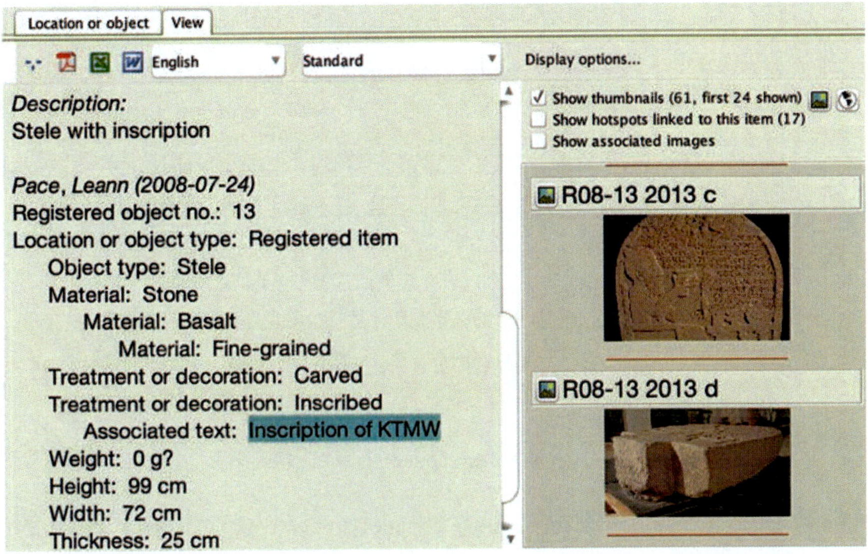

Fig. 3.12 The KTMW stele is an archaeological artifact with an inscribed text, represented by two OCHRE items

Conceptual Maneuver: Object Versus Text

Complex items pose interesting questions for atomization and categorization. What about the Katumuwa stele? Is it an **Object** (spatial unit) or it is a **Text**? Here, we pull a conceptual maneuver and answer … both are present!

In one respect, the stele is an archaeological artifact with tangible descriptive features like dimensions, material (basalt), and findspot. In other respects, it is a material support for a historical text, and we would weigh its interpretation rather than its mass. With the freedom to create items as needed, and without the rigid structures of tabular formats, we can create both a Spatial unit ("R08-13") to represent the stele as an artifact and describe its artifactual qualities *and* a Text item ("Inscription of KTMW") to represent its textual qualities, linking the items so as not to lose their relationship to each other. Archaeologists would make observations on the Spatial unit; the interpretations and discussions of the philologists would be documented as part of the Text item (Fig. 3.12).

Conceptual Maneuver: Epigraphic Versus Discourse

Textual data is characterized by other kinds of complexity that have implications for an item-based data model. What are the items? As Jerome McGann (2004, pp. 199–200) has observed, various digital approaches to addressing text follow a

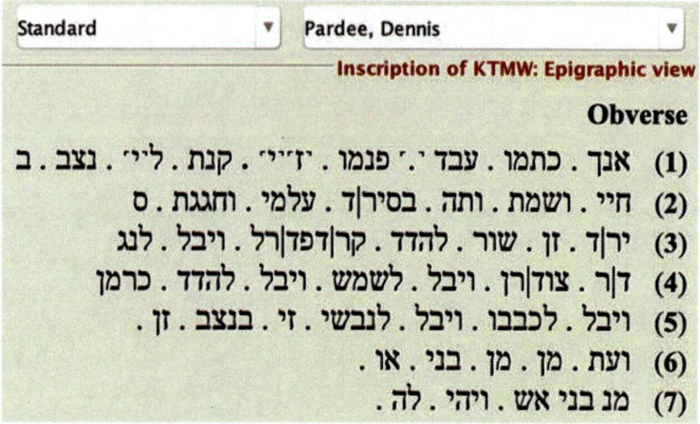

Fig. 3.13 Epigraphic representation of a Text captures its written structure

model similar to what print technology intended to achieve, namely to "constrain the shape shiftings of language." From SGML[14] to TEI, digital text has been forced to fit within the constraints of a schema developed by committee. In OCHRE, we embrace what McGann (ibid.) describes as the arbitrary units of natural language. OCHRE does not first impose words, then phrases, paragraphs, etc. Instead, OCHRE provides the undifferentiated stem cells, those items that can become whatever arbitrary units are appropriate to the text in question. Because there is "no obvious unit of language" (Hockey 2000, p. 20 cited in McGann 2004, p. 199), OCHRE neither seeks to impose one nor seeks for scholarly consensus on one. We return to this idea below in the section "Atomize: How Far Is Far Enough?"

OCHRE solves the problem of modeling textual data through generalization. In OCHRE, a text can be described in two ways, both of which record interpretations of the observer. First, the scholar inspects a text and asks, "*What can I see?*" In this case, we use **Epigraphic units** to describe the text—its structure, layout, and other "graphic" features. The KTMW inscription has 13 lines, uses dots as word dividers, and is written using a square script. Each line and each script character are itemized and detailed: this one is an aleph, this one is partially broken, this one is uncertain, and so on (Fig. 3.13).

Next, the scholar interprets the text and asks, "*What does it say?*". Here, we use **Discourse units** to itemize words, group them into higher-level, compound discourse units, and provide transliterations or translations. Each discourse unit, whether a word or collections of words like phrases, sentences, paragraphs, or passus, becomes a discrete item to which scholarly commentary can be attached (Fig. 3.14).

[14] SGML, the Standard Generalized Markup Language, was a more generalized markup format that preceded HTML which, in turn, was the predecessor of XML.

Inscription of KTMW: Discourse view

ʾnk ktmw ʿbd pnmw zy qnt ly nṣb bḥyy wšmt wth bsyr|d ʿlmy wḥggt syr|d zn
šwr lhdd qr|dpd|rl wybl lngd|r
ṣwd|rn wybl lšmš wybl lhdd krmn wybl lkbbw wybl lnbšy zy bnṣb zn wʿt mn
mn bny ʾw mn bny ʾš wyhy lh
nsyr|d znn wlw yqḥ mn ḥyl krm znn šʾ ywmn lywmn wyhrg bnbšy wyšwy ly šq

Notes

(1) ktmw

A personal name of Luwian origin, previously unattested. My informants in matters Anatolian have suggested two principal possibilities: (1) /kuttamuwa/, with the /kutta-/ element representing earlier /kuwatta/, as in Kuwattalla (for the latter name, see Laroche 1966: 102); (2) /katimuwa/, comparing the name Kati/Kate, king of Que, attested in the inscriptions of Shalmaneser III (see Hawkins 2007); here the /kati/ element might correspond to Luwian kat- having to do with fighting and hostility (see Morpurgo Davies 1986 with previous bibliography cited there). Because of the uncertainty regarding the precise form of the name {ktmw}, it appears best not to favor one form over another in scholarly discussions of the text.

Fig. 3.14 Project philologist provides a Discourse analysis along with commentary. See Pardee (2009)

It is worth emphasizing that the type and identification of Epigraphic units or Discourse units are not presented as constraints built into OCHRE. These observations are scholarly interpretations.

As part of the overall documentation of the stele, Bibliographic items are used to reference related scholarly works. Resource items like images and drawings that illustrate the stele are also linked. These items can be linked to either the Object item or to the Text item, depending on which seems most relevant (e.g., if the image is a close-up of a fragmentary phrase, it might be linked to the Discourse unit or the Text), or at the preference of the scholar. OCHRE makes it easy to traverse and expose the links among associated items from either direction.

In addition to the interpretation of the epigraphic and discourse nature of the text, a scholar may add any other interpretations that can be represented by properties, links, and notes. What if the research project were interested in pursuing the history of religious thought? The scholar may read the text and ask, "*What does it mean?*" Katumuwa's commemorative remarks on the stele famously make reference to his "soul"—an unusual comment for this time and place.[15] How would one identify the mention of the soul in this text, more than simply as the presence of the ancient word, but as the presence of a philosophical concept that pertains to the history of religion? The project could create an OCHRE Concept item for the notion of the "soul" and link it to the word or phrase (the Discourse unit) to research and track the uses of this idea at other times and places. Then, as other Concepts come to light in other texts, those Concepts would be described with the necessary properties.

[15] KTMW, lines 10–13: "He is also to perform the slaughter (prescribed above) in (proximity to) my 'soul' and is to apportion for me a leg-cut."

Eventually, the corpus of texts would be described by properties that identify the religious concepts identified by the scholars.

Practical Maneuver: Object Versus Text Versus Resource

Resource items typically represent external files like photographs, drawings, PDFs, or other types of documents and files that have an independent existence outside of OCHRE. Items like these are cataloged in OCHRE but are not loaded into the database. Rather, OCHRE records their metadata, knows where to find them on hard drives and servers, and presents them for viewing to users. But consider the letter written by Carl Theodor Ernst von Siebold to his fellow academic Rudolf Wagner on January 24, 1843, cataloged by the Lives, Individuality, and Analysis (LIA) project. Is this an **Object**, a **Text**, or a **Resource** item? (Fig. 3.15).

One valid option would be to follow the model as for the KTMW stele, treating the letter itself as an Object which, according to the Events listed for the item, the researcher has personally studied in the archive at Göttingen during 2011. But the research goals are not focused on the study of this document as an artifact (Object); it was enough to get some good photographs of it. The contents of the letter could be modeled as a Text—the character-by-character, line-by-line script covering two pages represented in epigraphic and discourse structures. But this would be overkill. The researchers do not care how it was laid out on the page; they are not interested in the variations of the long-hand script. They already understand the gist of the

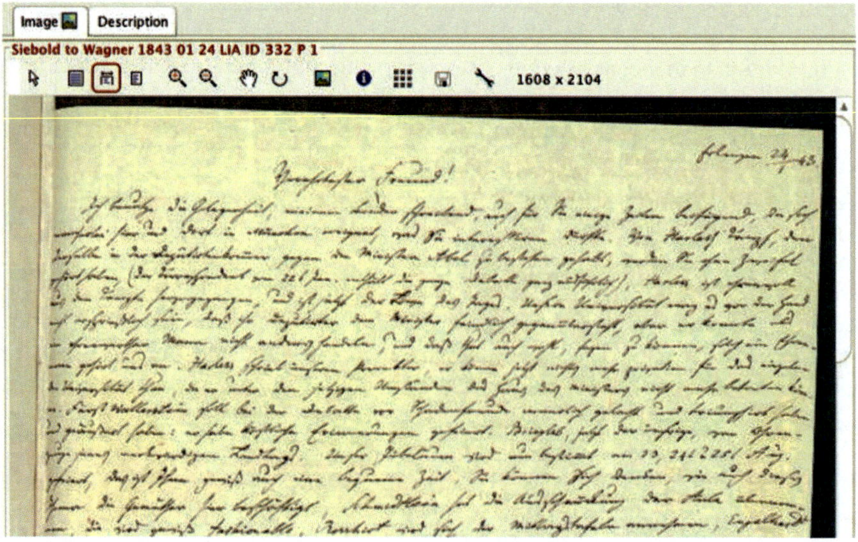

Fig. 3.15 What sort of item is this (image of a) letter exchanged between two scientists?

letter ("Complaining about Will, the zoologist, who does nothing"). It is the content of the letter that is important, and the ideas expressed therein.

In recognition of this common scenario, and without compromising the item-based nature of the data, we made a practical concession and built into OCHRE a variation of the Resource type: an "internal document" (in contrast to an external file). This letter from von Siebold is represented in OCHRE by such an "internal document"; a Resource item, but one that provides a special text field that allows the LIA team to transcribe the contents explicitly, thereby creating a digital representation of the letter without the unnecessary overhead of atomizing it as a Text item. The images of pages one and two of the letter (two Resources representing jpg files) are linked to the internal document Resource, making a natural association (Fig. 3.16).

An online database environment like OCHRE where each observable object has been itemized as its own database item facilitates collaboration when participating scholars have overlapping but distinct interests. Because items are highly granular, a user edits them one item at a time, thereby minimizing and localizing the possibility of data contention, allowing multiple hands to be at work. Each item is described

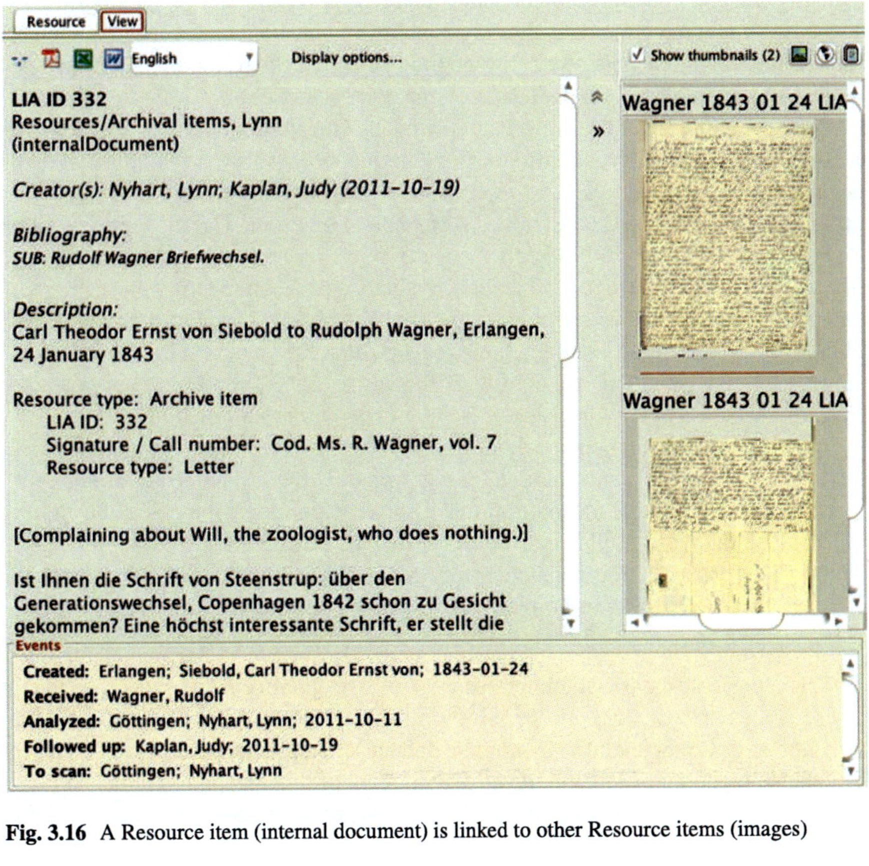

Fig. 3.16 A Resource item (internal document) is linked to other Resource items (images)

as fully as possible using properties, periods, notes, links, and events and is attributed to the scholar who is the authoritative source of the information. Related items are linked to each other: a coin (a Spatial unit) to its inscription (a Text) and vice versa. The coin specialist will query for just coins, dynamically creating a table of the items of interest, eliminating the need to sort through and filter out items not of interest. The textual scholar will query for just inscriptions, dynamically creating a much different table to support their research. A click-through link on the view of a coin leads to the supporting information on the linked inscription and vice versa. This strategy results in a comprehensive database environment that makes as much fully articulated data as possible, available to as many collaborating scholars as possible, for as many diverse purposes as possible.

Atomize: How Far Is Far Enough?

The example from the LIA project illustrates that the atomization and categorization of data depends very much on the project's research goals. As part of the project planning stage, and before project data is entered into the database, the question of how much to atomize the data should be carefully considered. A certain degree of atomization might be inadequate for one project but excessive for another. The flexibility of an item-based approach lets a project get it just right.

Consider some examples from textual studies. Our item-based approach to texts accommodates a high level of atomization, but just because we *can* atomize, it does not always mean that we *should*. We have spent years dealing with some of the most difficult languages: Hittite, Elamite, Akkadian, Sumerian, Ugaritic, and Middle Egyptian. In the study of these complex languages, it is typical to analyze the text down to the level of the sign or character, evaluating and commenting on each as the unit of observation and description. This has been the approach of many OCHRE philology projects because among their goals is the creation of reliable text editions. However, in a case where the edition of the text is not in question, it may not be necessary to use the individual letter as the most granular unit of study.

When approaching textual study in a database environment, it is important to ask the question, *How far is far enough?* Each project is free to define its atomic unit, that is, the most minimal meaningful unit of observation. In some cases, the atomic unit may be the word or phrase. In other cases, the scholar may want to drill more deeply. For example, the transliteration of a single phrase, "30 (measures) of emmer," from an Elamite text from the Persepolis Fortification Archive is:

ÙŠU ^{GIŠ}tar-mu^{MEŠ}

This represents the transliterated readings of five cuneiform signs, each of which is a separate database item (**Epigraphic unit**). They share a common context, Line 01 (another Epigraphic unit). As separate database items, each one can be described to indicate certainty of reading, type of sign, level of damage on the tablet surface, etc., thereby allowing the scholar to document the sign-by-sign interpretation of the textual content carefully and granularly.

A less complicated example will illustrate how many of the same principles are used, even if the text is not atomized down to the level of the individual sign or letter. To present Homer's Iliad for grammatical and literary analysis, the individual word serves as the atomic unit. Line one of the Iliad reads:

μῆνιν ἄειδε θεὰ Πηληϊάδεω Ἀχιλῆος
"SING, goddess, the anger of Peleus' son Achilleus"

Each Greek word represents an individual database item (**Discourse unit**). This allows the researcher to assign grammatical properties to the words. The first word, μῆνιν, links as an attested form to the **Dictionary item** μῆνις where it is parsed as a feminine singular noun in the accusative case. Because the word is the atomic unit, the researcher can also identify names in the text by matching the words to **Person** database items. These persons are identified as literary characters and described as to their literary role, sex, mortality, and age category.

The answer to the question *How far is far enough?* is entirely dependent on the goals of the research project. Over-atomize and the effort is disproportionate to the payoff. The Iliad does not need to be atomized c-h-a-r-a-c-t-e-r by c-h-a-r-a-c-t-e-r in order to discuss noun forms. But beware the risk of undue lumping. The KTMW inscription needs sign-by-sign granularity because some of the signs are ambiguous; if one sign is given a different interpretation by a different scholar, then that could change the meaning of the word. And if the meaning of the word is changed, that could precipitate other discussions. In this case, the signs serve as building blocks that could be used to reconstruct potentially diverging editions of the same text.

OCHRE does not prescribe any necessary level of granularity. Wallis et al. (2013) define "data" as "the objects—digital or physical—that researchers consider to be their sources of evidence for a given study." If your research is answering questions about brick, tile, and wood, then atomize fully. If prefabricated walls and preinstalled windows are sufficient to address your research questions, then do not break these down. The flexibility of an item-based approach gives the scholar options. The level at which an item becomes part of the scholarly discussion, at which it is argued about, about which articles are written and attributed—that is the appropriate degree of atomization.

Case Study: Fort. 1982-101

It might seem that the item-based approach proliferates items, the cells of our project organism rapidly splitting and multiplying. To this, we say—indeed! But that is why we use a database to manage them. What is the alternative? A spiderweb of linked tables? Free-form "Note" fields full of descriptive prose, fraught with all the errors and inconsistencies inherent in that? Much easier is to divide and conquer, making explicit every single thing about which observations are to be made, details are to be recorded, and relationships are to be specified (Table 3.1). Count along

Table 3.1 The variety of items that comprise Fort. 1982-101 are tallied

Item(s)	Running total
One spatial unit, a tablet found at the site of Persepolis.	1
One resource item, an external file of Polynomial Texture Mapping (PTM) format.	2
Six spatial units representing the six surfaces of the tablet: obverse, reverse, top/bottom/left/right edges; some are intact, others damaged.	8
Two spatial units representing two seal impressions, one quite legible the other very faint.	10
One spatial unit representing the cylinder seal, PFS 1633* (long since lost to history) responsible for making the two impressions (among others on other tablets).	11
One Aramaic inscription, a text item, written in faint ink.	12
One line (epigraphic unit) on one surface (another epigraphic unit), plus a controlling epigraphic hierarchy, providing context.	15
Three epigraphic units (one for each character) of the Aramaic text using alphabetic script.	18
One discourse unit, and a controlling discourse hierarchy, providing context.	20
One Aramaic word of the Aramaic text, a discourse unit.	21
One Elamite inscription, a text item, inscribed in cuneiform.	22
Twenty-one lines on three surfaces (obverse, lower edge and reverse, all epigraphic units), plus a controlling epigraphic hierarchy, providing context for cuneiform signs.	47
432 cuneiform signs (epigraphic units).	479
17 phrases (discourse units, each translated into English), plus a controlling discourse hierarchy, providing context.	496
226 Elamite words, organized into those 17 phrases.	**722**

with us as we press our point by itemizing this **Object** (or is it a **Text**?) from the Persepolis Fortification Archive (PFA) project (Figs. 3.17 and 3.18).

In all, over 700 items are implicated by this tablet, and that does not count other items linked to any of those—additional photographs of the tablet, a hand-drawing of the hero controlling winged lion creatures on the seal motif, the inscription on the seal (as evidenced by the impression), close-up photographs using special filters of the Aramaic inscription, the script units of the Hebrew and cuneiform writing systems that validate the epigraphic signs, etc.—thereby creating an extensive network of information pertaining to this single artifact. Each node of the network (each item) can be studied and described by the relevant specialist: the expert on seals, the Elamite specialist, the Aramaic scholar, and the photographer. The obverse surface of this tablet is beautiful too and is shown below as a visual accounting of the high number of cuneiform signs in our list (Fig. 3.19).

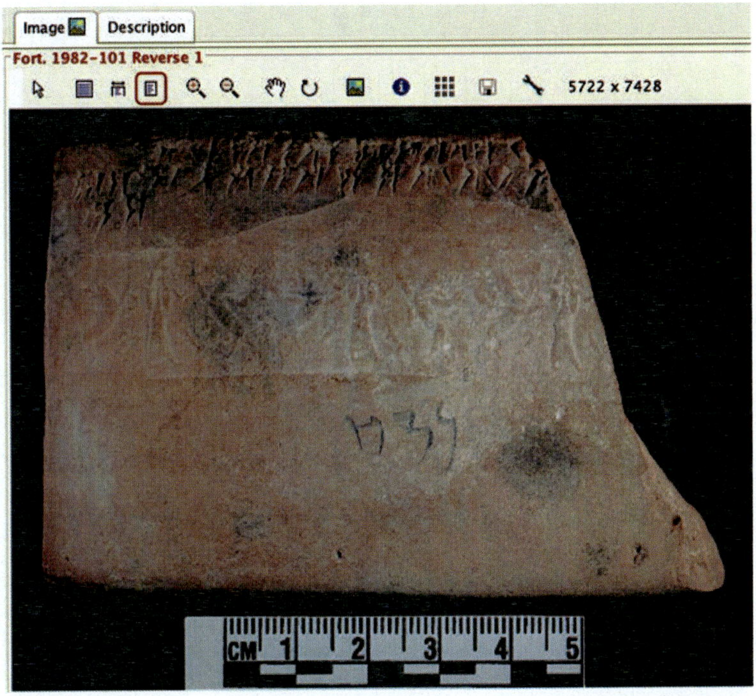

Fig. 3.17 Fort. 1982-101 is more easily studied and documented when it is itemized. (Photograph courtesy of the Persepolis Fortification Archive project)

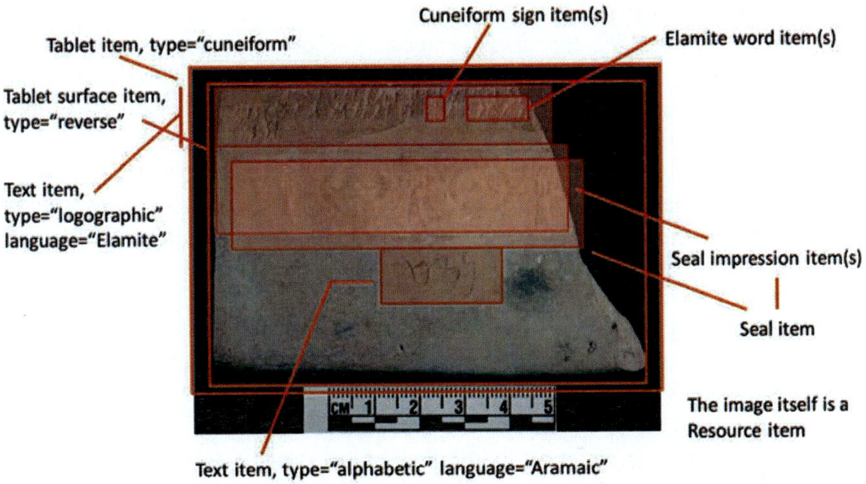

Fig. 3.18 The reverse surface of Fort. 1982-101 supports two Text items (one Elamite, the other Aramaic) along with seal impressions (Spatial units)

Fig. 3.19 The obverse surface of Fort. 1982-101 contains the bulk of the Elamite text. (Photograph courtesy of the Persepolis Fortification Archive project)

That's All Well and Good in Practice, but How Does It Work in Theory?

In this chapter, we began the discussion of how to represent research data within an item-based framework. We encourage the reader to pause and reflect upon how your own research data may be released from tabular structures like spreadsheets and reimagined as items, organized within the primary OCHRE categories. In the following chapters, we fill in important details. As a follow-up to *How far is far enough?* we consider how to organize items in OCHRE if not in tables. Using an item-based approach, the scholar needs to decide what the essential units of study are, the most minimal meaningful parts, and then proceed to atomize the data as a first step. Next steps are to organize these items into meaningful collections and structures, to annotate them with relevant tags and descriptors, and to analyze them in response to one's research questions. Ultimately, the goal is to publish one's scholarly interpretations and conclusions, along with the supporting evidence, and to archive the data to ensure its survival for future scholars.

Many scholars have an innate sense of how to organize data for the digital era in a natural way. Some do very well in practice; others struggle. But it is far too easy to create a mess when what we want is a masterpiece. A well-designed database system is a creative work, a thing of beauty. It has an unexpected elegance and a satisfying functionality which transforms it into a work of art. And so, we proceed

Fig. 3.20 T-shirts are designed to inspire and motivate incoming UChicago freshmen (http://uchicagoadmissions.tumblr.com/post/13123492245/thats-all-well-and-good-in-practice-but-how-does)

with the discussion of atomizing, organizing, describing, analyzing, publishing, and archiving with a view to motivating "best practice" and inspiring not mere digitization, but art. We also hope to provide rationale as to *why* one might choose a certain approach over another, specifically an item-based approach over a table-based approach, and what benefits might ensue. In keeping with our University of Chicago tradition, we expect that having a better understanding of how and why we do a thing allows us to do it better (Fig. 3.20).

Chapter 4
An Item-Based Approach: Organize

A Place for Every *Thing* … and Everything in Its Place

Pause for a moment to imagine the implications of an item-based approach—one that breaks knowledge down into small, highly atomic bits. You might wonder why it is a good idea to proliferate dozens, thousands, yes even millions of distinct items, each individually situated within a database context, independent of each of the others. Does this not lead to disorganization, to losing track of things?

The very notion of organizing suggests list-making: a grocery list, a to-do list, a passenger list, a watch list, or a wish list. In OCHRE, we start by making lists, the most basic of which is the list of Categories that we have already seen. This classification at the high level is the first cut at organizing a potentially huge number of database items. It is a simple and intuitive structure consisting of categories of persons, places, and assorted other things. As of this writing, the largest OCHRE project, the Persepolis Fortification Archive (PFA), manages 1,758,256[1] individually addressable items that include many complex objects, texts, spatial units, dictionary items, concepts, along with literally millions of interconnected relationships (Fig. 4.1).

Beyond this initial list, the second level of organizing extends the same simple list structure, creating lists within lists. Shown in Fig. 4.2, for example, is a partial outline of 15 years' worth of Locations & objects identified and itemized by the Zincirli team organized within a list of excavation areas, as of this writing a total of 120,922 items.[2] The third round, the fourth round, and so on simply propagate lists within lists: areas within the site; units of excavation within the areas; buckets, baskets, pails, or lots within the excavation units; and potsherds, artifacts, and

[1] This number is based on an OCHRE database query performed on 2023-07-20.

[2] As of 2023-07-20.

S. R. Schloen, M. C. Prosser, *Database Computing for Scholarly Research*, Quantitative Methods in the Humanities and Social Sciences,
https://doi.org/10.1007/978-3-031-46696-0_4

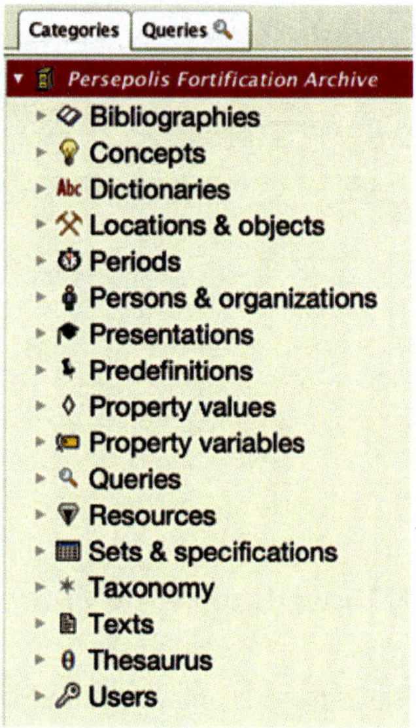

Fig. 4.1 The deceptively simple list of PFA Categories belies its depth and complexity

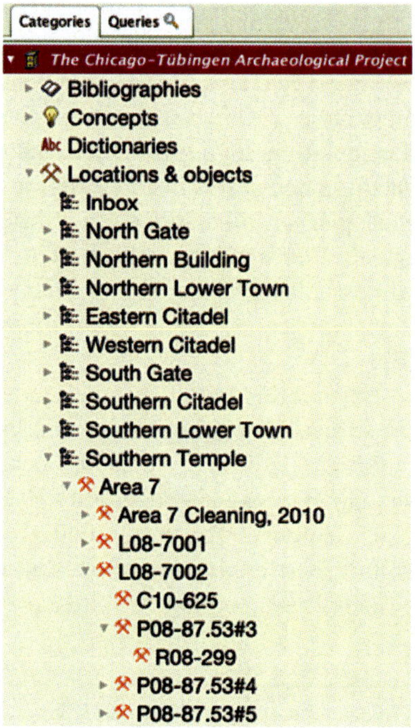

Fig. 4.2 Lists within lists naturally organize vast numbers of Locations & objects representing many years' worth of excavation

samples within the buckets. What we have in the end is a *tree* of information, or *hierarchy* as we call it in OCHRE, where each branch, and each subbranch, is a one-dimensional list.

The Uses of Hierarchies

A hierarchy is a powerful structure for organizing information of all kinds. You will recognize the implicit tree structure as you work with the folders and subfolders of documents in your file system; as you consider the management structure or chain of command at your place of employment; as you take your seat in economy class, row 26, seat A; as you find salsa in aisle 6 on the third shelf; as you shop online, filtering for Appliances, Refrigerators, Stainless steel, height of 70-inches-or-less.

It bears repeating: A hierarchical system of organization is a natural and intuitive mechanism for representing information of all kinds. Tasked with managing information of all kinds, OCHRE relies heavily on hierarchies as an organizational structure. Hierarchies are so central to the OCHRE system that a hierarchy is also, itself, an item in the database. A hierarchy item serves to collect and organize other database items, offering certain benefits or providing specific kinds of semantic value, which will be explored below. In the meantime, consider some cases of hierarchical structures, by way of illustration.

Organizational

Figure 4.3 illustrates a conceptually simple list of Persons & organizations, achieving nothing more than helping to organize the faculty, staff, students, and departments whom we serve at the University of Chicago, simply for practical purposes.

Collections of images or documents can be organized into hierarchies within the Resources category, just like you would organize them in file folders on a local hard drive or on a remote server. Group them by year, or type, or by year and type. Within the high-level categories that serve as the default system of organization in OCHRE, project users create these custom hierarchies, along with headings and subheadings, based on whatever system of classification makes sense for the project.

The electronic Chicago Hittite Dictionary (*eCHD*) team organizes its extensive Bibliography by nesting articles within journals, journals within series, creating a meaningful hierarchical structure. This strategy eliminates redundant entry of the higher-level items (series and journals). Subitems representing specific articles of interest are entered within the context provided by the items representing the series and journal volumes (Fig. 4.4).

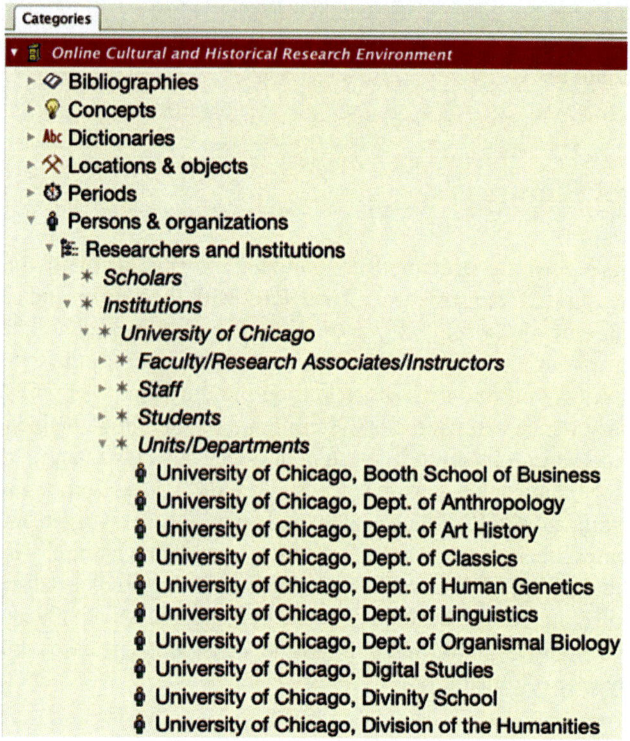

Fig. 4.3 Hierarchy items, followed by headings, neatly organize extensive lists of Persons & organizations

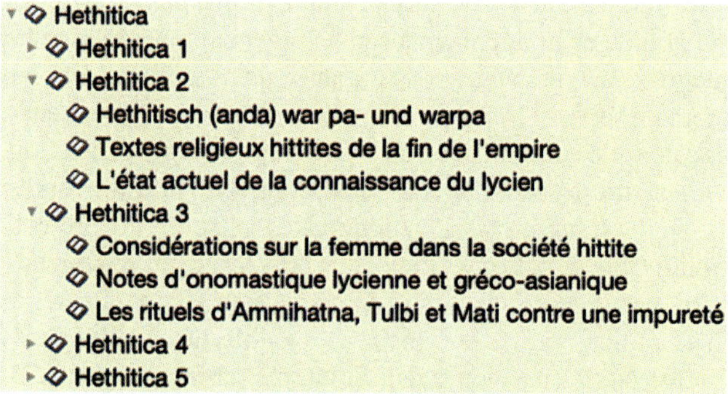

Fig. 4.4 Bibliographic entries fall naturally into logical hierarchical arrangements

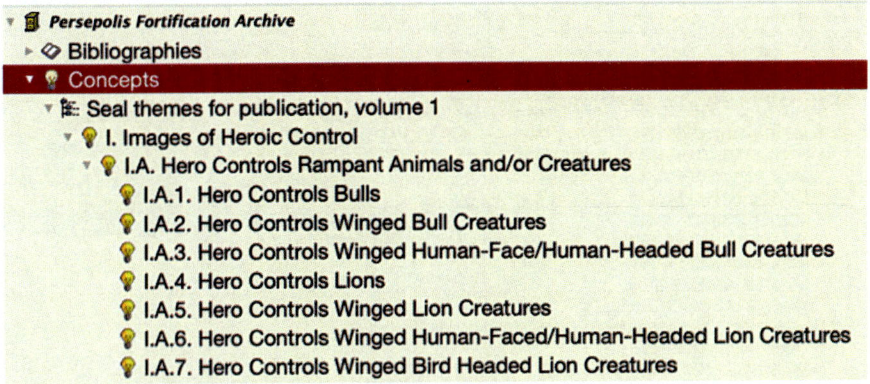

Fig. 4.5 A hierarchically organized inventory of seal motifs is used to describe seal impressions based on discernible details

Represent General to Specific

There are countless situations where a hierarchical structure is a logical way to represent high-level, more general items that break down into more detailed, specific items. This strategy is typical of dictionary entries, as we will illustrate later, but it is also commonly used for items in the Concepts category. In this example from the Persepolis Fortification Archive, artistic themes that describe imagery found on seal impressions are itemized starting off at a general level and becoming more specific as we drill-down through the levels in the hierarchy (Fig. 4.5).

The importance of a structure like this is that it allows tagging of the items at the appropriate level of detail. If an expert can see from a poorly preserved or fragmentary seal impression only the vague outline of a hero, the item's theme would be tagged as "I. Images of Heroic Control." A better-preserved specimen might reveal a hero controlling a rampant winged bull creature (theme I.A.2). Having been suitably tagged, the seals can be queried by theme, either specifically or broadly, for further study.

Represent Whole to Part

Much like general-to-specific relationships, hierarchies are useful for representing whole-to-part, or aggregate-to-individual, relationships. That is, a hierarchy can be used naturally to subsume a specific item, conceptual or real, contextually within an aggregate one. This next example shows a necklace found at the site of Ashkelon, "comprised of 30 glass beads, 1 carnelian bead and 4 amethyst beads"[3] and labeled as "MC 51323." Each of the individual beads from the necklace was registered with

[3] From OCHRE Notes on MC 51323; https://pi.lib.uchicago.edu/1001/org/ochre/c9e78907-34ef-53d5-9bc2-52240be2b130.

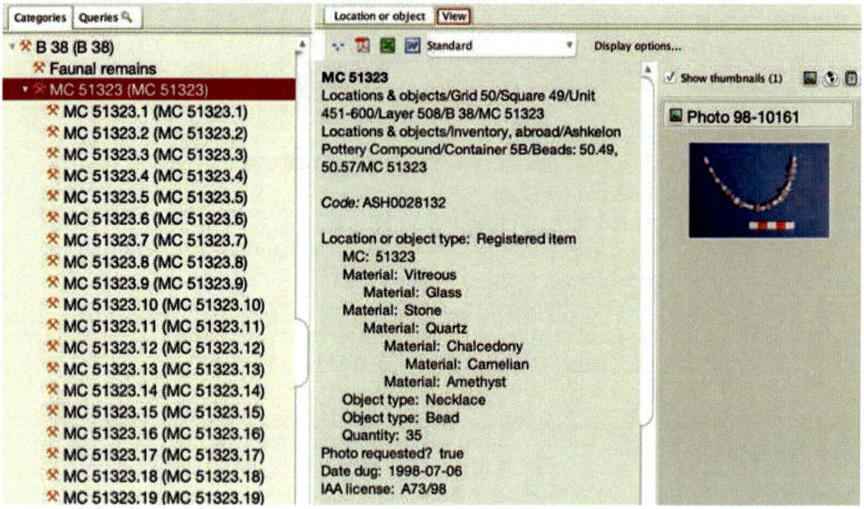

Fig. 4.6 Individual beads are contextualized within a (reconstructed) necklace

Fig. 4.7 Teeth are naturally organized within the mandible of this skeleton

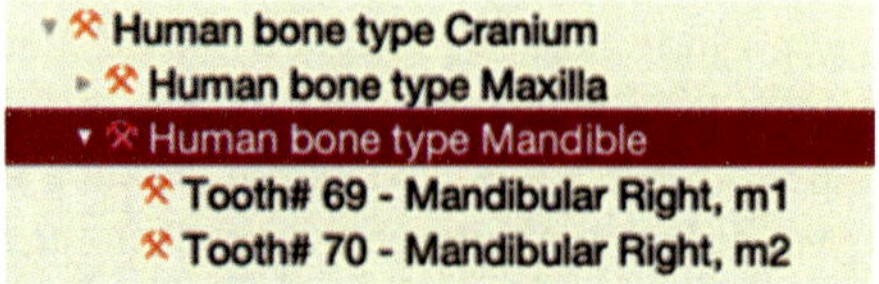

its own number: MC51323.1, MC51323.2, and so on. By arranging these bead items hierarchically within the aggregate necklace item, the relationship between the items, "A belongs to the collection B" is preserved. This data structure also allows a hierarchically sensitive query to "find all beads which were found in context as a necklace" (Fig. 4.6).

A variation on the theme is illustrated by the representation of excavated human remains, using a hierarchical framework to catalog individual bones within a skeleton. Notice how natural and familiar this seems—teeth within the mandible, the mandible within the cranium—as the body parts are articulated. There are many uses for contextualizing individual items within an aggregate—broken fragments joined to form a complete tablet or sculpture, an inscribed cornerstone within a rampart wall, an especially significant coin from a hoard—to list a few examples (Fig. 4.7).

Part-to-whole relationships need not be restricted to physical objects. Written language can be broken down into parts from wholes. Figure 4.8 shows a portion of the discourse hierarchy of the reading text from the CEDAR project's *Taming of the Shrew*, where acts and scenes are decomposed into lines and words. The hierarchy is simple and intuitive, yet captures a typical, well-understood, line-by-line format for reading a poetic work.

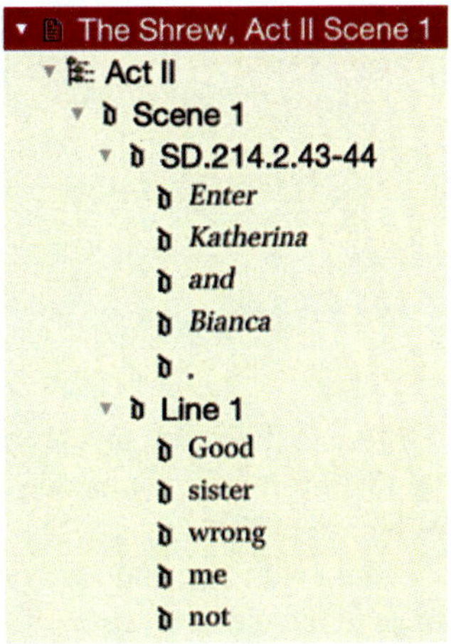

Fig. 4.8 Words naturally aggregate into stage directions and lines of poetry

Represent Context

Within OCHRE, the scholar has a great deal of freedom in representing their interpretation of the subject matter, whether tangible objects or interpreted texts. Whether a text is understood as a stable hierarchy, or as a fluid and overlapping series of hierarchical branches, hierarchy proves a useful structure. A poetic analysis of a work of Shakespeare's, for example, will not fall naturally into rows and columns of a table (relational model), but a carefully crafted hierarchy of such semi-structured data, comprised of tags, textual content, and metadata can expose a great deal of information that might otherwise remain elusive.

The first phrase of Hamlet's most famous soliloquy is shown "marked up" below using the *TEI simple* standard[4] of encoding (Shakespeare, n.d.). Although human-readable, it would take a careful eye to pick out "to be or not to be." But note the hierarchical structure: words (w) within lines (l), lines within speeches (sp). Not shown here are the speeches within scenes, scenes within acts, and so on.

```
<sp xml:id="sp-1762" who="#Hamlet_Ham">
    <speaker xml:id="spk-1762">
        <w xml:id="fs-ham-0271840">HAMLET</w>
    </speaker>
    <l xml:id="ftln-1762" n="3.1.64">
        <w xml:id="fs-ham-0271850" n="3.1.64" lemma="to" ana="#acp-cs">To</w>
        <c></c>
        <w xml:id="fs-ham-0271870" n="3.1.64" lemma="be" ana="#vvi">be</w>
        <c></c>
        <w xml:id="fs-ham-0271890" n="3.1.64" lemma="or" ana="#cc">or</w>
        <c></c>
```

[4] For TEI Simple, see https://tei-c.org/tag/tei-simple/.

```
        <w xml:id="fs-ham-0271910" n="3.1.64" lemma="not" ana="#xx">not</w>
        <c></c>
        <w xml:id="fs-ham-0271930" n="3.1.64" lemma="to" ana="#acp-cs">to</w>
        <c></c>
        <w xml:id="fs-ham-0271950" n="3.1.64" lemma="be" ana="#vvi">be</w>
        ...
    </l>
    ...
</sp>
```

More to the point, this is computer-readable in that a digital process can reliably use the information embedded in this structure to render the data for display on the Web or to make sense of it for analytical purposes (Fig. 4.9).

Along with the value provided by hierarchical structure comes an inherent challenge to the representation of texts—how to represent textual data that confounds a single strict hierarchical arrangement. To foreshadow the discussion to come, the item-based approach to textual data makes it possible to organize and reorganize textual data into multiple overlapping hierarchies.

While the hierarchical representation of Hamlet's speech sets it in context of Act 3, Scene 1, Line 64 (<l xml:id="ftln-1762" n="3.1.64">) this sort of hierarchical contextualization also applies to real-world objects in physical contexts. The Katumuwa stele excavated at Zincirli eventually found a permanent home in the Gaziantep Archaeological Museum (Fig. 4.10). Its current physical context can be represented hierarchically as:

Turkey ➔ Gaziantep ➔ Archaeological Museum ➔ Iron Age Gallery ➔ Zincirli Höyük Room

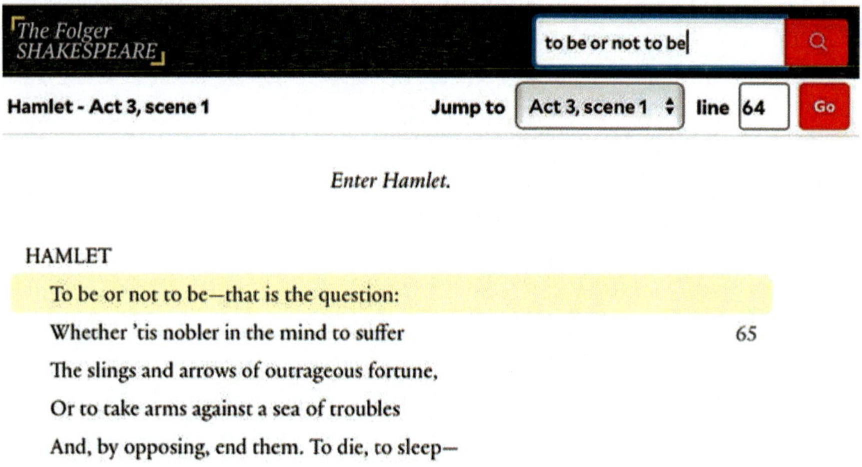

Fig. 4.9 Folger Digital Library's own stylesheet transforms this TEI-XML into HTML for viewing on their website (https://www.folger.edu/)

Fig. 4.10 KTMW's final context is in the Zincirli gallery in the Gaziantep museum in Turkey. (Photograph by S. Schloen)

Specific geographical locations can also be described hierarchically whether those locations are the excavation units on an archaeological site, the rooms in a library archive, or cities within counties and states. The Florentine Catasto project uses hierarchy to record the spatial representation of medieval Florence as evidenced in historical tax records. The complexity of this dense city—from the various quarters to the parishes and neighborhoods, down to specific workshops—is represented by a hierarchy built with highly atomized items that can be reorganized and cross-referenced in meaningful and flexible ways.

By further use of examples and case studies, we hope to provide a convincing argument that the easy and straightforward mechanism of organizing information as items in hierarchies is widely applicable to data being managed by a research project. Not only is it *possible* to use hierarchies for this purpose, but it is also highly *desirable*, and we invite you to consider the many benefits of doing so.

The Benefits of Hierarchies

Universality

The influential work by Hauser, Chomsky, and Fitch which explores the evolution of the human faculty of language begins with the premise:

> …life is arranged hierarchically with a foundation of discrete, unblendable units … capable of combining to create increasingly complex and virtually limitless varieties of both species and individual organisms. (Hauser et al. 2002, p. 1569)

The authors go on to "note that the human faculty of language appears to be organized like the genetic code—hierarchical, generative, recursive, and virtually limitless with respect to its scope of expression" (ibid.) Human language … life itself, modeled as discrete units arranged hierarchically? How can we go wrong?

In our earlier discussion of the OCHRE ontology (Chap. 2), we suggested that the acronym "OCHRE" might well stand for *Ontology Creation and the Hierarchical Representation of Everything*. We do mean everything! Herbert Simon, known for being an interdisciplinary scholar (computer science, business, philosophy, psychology, decision science) at Carnegie Mellon University, used the notion of hierarchy to describe complex systems ranging from astronomical galaxies to biological cellular structures, from social systems to spatial systems. Simon proposed that *any* complex system, by which he meant "one made up of a large number of parts that interact in a non-simple way" (Simon 1969, p. 86), could be modeled as a hierarchy.

Simon defines *hierarchy* as "a system that is composed of interrelated subsystems, each of the latter being, in turn, hierarchic in structure until we reach some lowest level of elementary subsystem" (ibid., p. 87). He explains how complexity can be modeled effectively by decomposing a complex system into successively simpler structures that relate to each other hierarchically. This is precisely the OCHRE way: atomize then hierarchize; divide and conquer!

Simplicity

A fundamental feature of hierarchical data structures is their simplicity. Lists within lists is such a simple concept that you do not need to be a technology expert or specially trained technical guru to understand it. There is no complex joining of linked tables, no tangled syntax within Web pages, no fiddly formatting of XML or JSON, no debugging of unruly scripts. This is not to say that building hierarchical data structures should be done without careful consideration or that it just comes naturally—there are many ways of organizing hierarchies of information that are less than ideal—but the basic tasks involved are inherently simple and accessible to everyone, without the need for specialized know-how or technical skills. Take, for example, this line of Hebrew from the first verse of Genesis, as represented by the CEDAR project; the collection of consonants, accents, and vowel markings is arguably a "complex system" in its own right.

בְּרֵאשִׁ֖ית בָּרָ֣א אֱלֹהִ֑ים אֵ֥ת הַשָּׁמַ֖יִם וְאֵ֥ת הָאָֽרֶץ

Reading right to left, we have a series of characters, some of which are themselves a complex interaction of consonants, vowels and accents. Scholars studying this verse could break this sentence into components and represent it as a hierarchy, the first word expanding as shown in Fig. 4.11. The text has been atomized, that is,

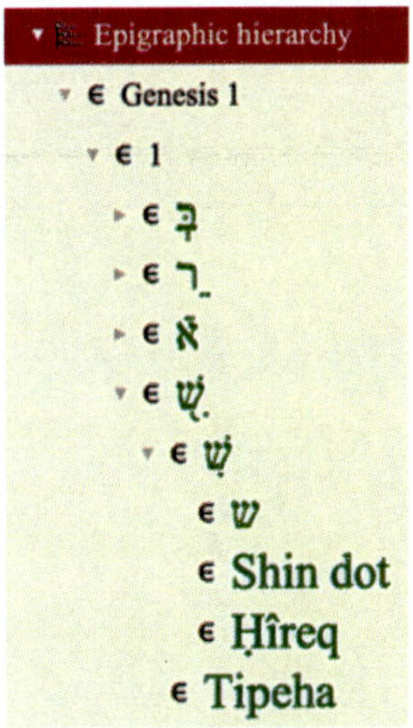

Fig. 4.11 "In the beginning" is shown as a hierarchy of Hebrew characters

decomposed into items which, themselves, are less complex. In OCHRE, each of these simpler units becomes its own item about which observations, or arguments, can be made.[5]

But how far is far enough? For the CEDAR-Bible project whose scholars study text-critical issues pertaining to the book of Genesis (among others), we started out, in the beginning, thinking it would be sufficient to capture the text chapter by chapter, verse by verse, word for word. But as we discussed the issues of interest to the biblical scholars and began to look at the relevant manuscript traditions, we ended up branching farther down, not only to the character-by-character level but even so far as to split the Hebrew and Greek characters into their consonants, vowel markings, and accents. Apparently, these are interesting and spark scholarly discussion and debate, and so they were atomized into database items in their own right. The vocalized and accented *SHIN*, broken into *its* constituent parts, is thereby simplified further, down to the smallest discrete unit that can be represented by a Unicode character.

In this way, we break down a problem, a question, or a data set into simpler problems, questions, and data structures, with the goal of simplifying a "complex system," making it more manageable as data and more accessible for research. The atomization of the textual contents of a Septuagint (Greek) manuscript that preserves a portion of Genesis 1 creates epigraphic units that can be linked to the image of the manuscript fragment, giving scholars an opportunity to document and study the text in granular detail (Fig. 4.12).

[5] For an overview of working with texts in OCHRE, see Schloen and Schloen (2012, pp. 167–184).

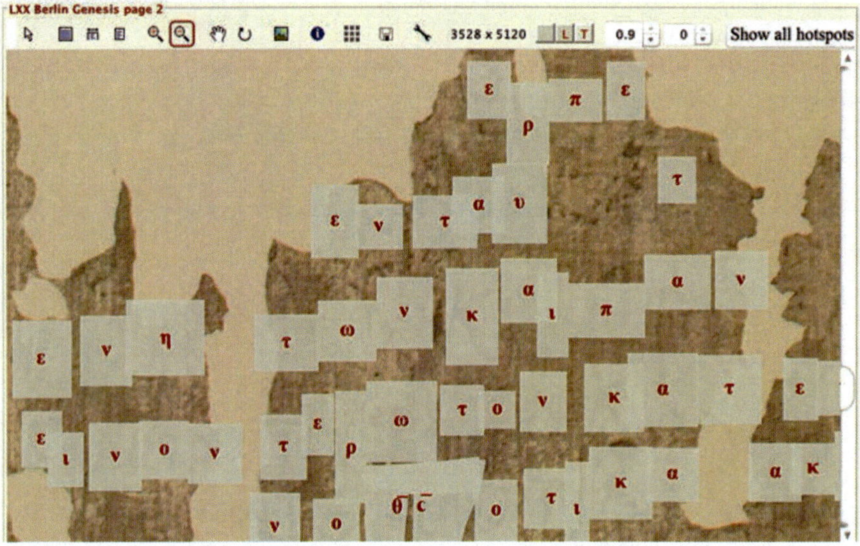

Fig. 4.12 A Text is atomized, with each character made individually accessible as an Epigraphic unit, shown here linked sign by sign to the (Resource) image of the Washington Manuscript. (From the Hannah Holborn Gray Special Collections Research Center, University of Chicago Library)

Flexibility

Notice from the example of a Hebrew script text that some of the characters were already simple, not needing further decomposition, others not. A hierarchy accommodates such variability easily, providing the flexibility to represent the data accurately. Items do not need to branch into subitems if the data does not merit it. Other items can branch again and again if needed. There are no limits to either the breadth or depth of a hierarchy, no requirement that the branches be of a consistent depth, no constraints on the number of lists that can be made—lists within lists. A hierarchy can take whatever shape is demanded by the information which it is modeling.

This feature of hierarchies is helpful in the field of archaeology where such flexibility is necessary to model the reality on the ground, and it provides a refreshing and liberating alternative to the rigid structures of tables and relational database systems. The recording of an archaeological survey, where data collection is done by field experts crossing mounds and ruins on foot, gathering whatever evidence they can glean from surface finds, would be represented by a hierarchical structure that is broad but shallow. Many sites would be visited, but each visit would require only a superficial investigation (literally and conceptually). The recording of a full-scale excavation of a single site, by comparison, would yield a narrow but deep hierarchical representation as the project team probed the site in their search for answers to research questions. Trying to represent both scenarios in a single, rigid, one-size-fits-all table-based system would force, and enforce, Procrustean uniformity and conformity, unnaturally and painfully.[6] In contrast, as an integration mechanism for data generated under different circumstances, for different reasons, and with different recording methods, hierarchies provide the structural flexibility to encompass them all.

Extensibility

Another benefit of hierarchies is their ability to expand or contract as needed, exposing or suppressing either levels of complexity or great quantities of data. Twenty-five years of excavation by the Leon Levy Expedition to Ashkelon are neatly encapsulated by a collection of hierarchies within the Locations & objects category, sparing the user from being overwhelmed by the sheer number of entries, well over 250,000 items in all.[7] The next season of excavation simply becomes a new branch of the existing tree. The Resources category of the Persepolis Fortification Archive project coherently organizes more than 178,000 images comprising over 100 terabytes of data.[8]

Efficiency

From a purely practical standpoint, a database that is organized hierarchically is efficient in that it need only fetch the items in the branches of the tree that have been opened for viewing or editing. As a user expands a branch of a tree, OCHRE fetches the items needed to display that branch. As any branch of the tree is collapsed, those items can either be cached or thrown away (from the computer memory). As items are edited and added, only the affected parts of the hierarchy need updating in the database. Even the manipulation of a huge tree can be managed efficiently.[9]

In addition, the XML-based Tamino database system used by OCHRE permits node-level updating of XML documents. This gives fine control over the editing of any document's element or attribute content. If a user changes the Name of an item, only the <name> element (node) of that single item's XML document needs to be updated. If a subitem is inserted as a leaf node on a tree branch, only its most

[6] See our previous discussion of Procrustes (Chap. 2).

[7] While the active excavations at Ashkelon have wrapped up, an OCHRE query revealed 252,668 items as of 2023-07-20.

[8] While photography of PFA tablets is winding down, an OCHRE query revealed 178,263 Resource items (of various kinds) as of 2023-07-20.

[9] Brachman and Levesque (2004, p. 172) assert that the use of a hierarchical structure (as a taxonomy) "will allow us to answer queries … much more efficiently, requiring time that in many cases grows linearly with the *depth* of the taxonomy, rather than its *size*. The net result: It becomes practical to consider extremely large knowledge bases, with thousands or even millions of concepts and constants."

immediate parent node needs posting. This avoids problems of loading, transferring, and saving potentially huge documents to or from the database.

Reusability

Another key benefit of using hierarchical structures in conjunction with an item-based approach is the option to reuse items in different contexts. The rather ordinary structure shown in Fig. 4.13 illustrates how Person items are organized in a hierarchy by the Zincirli archaeological project which tracks its personnel over the course of successive seasons of excavation. Many of the same staff members returned year after year to enjoy the charms of the neighboring local village of Fevzipaşa and to engage in the work on this impressive site. As this personnel list is updated each season, the same Person database item that represents a returning staff member is simply copied from one of its existing contexts and inserted within a new context representing the new season. Edits to a given item in one context automatically propagate to instances of that item in all contexts because there is only one database item reused, or reinstantiated, in multiple contexts. There is no redundancy. Unnecessary duplication of data is avoided by using—rather *reusing*—the same database item in potentially many new contexts.

Fig. 4.13 Person items are reused across many seasons at Zincirli

Fig. 4.14 Multiple contexts make explicit the reuse of a database item

The Contexts panel in OCHRE reflects the multiple instances of the selected database item, here indicating that the project archaeobotanist, Doğa Karakaya, participated in the 2015, 2016, 2017, 2018, 2021, and 2022 seasons at Zincirli, along with seasons at Tayinat (TAP), Tell Keisan (TK), and Cerro del Villar (CV). Atomize, hierarchize, economize! (Fig. 4.14).

Sharing

As it happens, the Zincirli project archaeobotanist works as a specialist on other archaeological projects throughout the Near East, some of which also use OCHRE for their data management. In a case like this, we simply extend the notion of reusability across multiple projects. Because OCHRE is a collaborative research environment, the same database item representing a Person can be shared among all of the projects for which he works. The project-based structure of OCHRE requires that one project "owns" the item, in this case the CRANE project, but other projects can "borrow" the item into their hierarchical structures as needed, simply by grafting the item into a project tree as a new leaf item.[10]

The level of project integration illustrated here is a boon to the researcher, too. In this case, the specialist can access all of his data via the same database environment and modeled in a similar way. Each project will, naturally, represent its data using its own specific recording methods, but the core representation of all botanical data, in this case, will be compatible.

Regional analyses or project comparisons are made easy in OCHRE's item-based, integrative environment. Research projects that agree to share data can reuse, and subsequently query, database items, or grafted hierarchical branches, across the projects, whether those represent Persons, Locations, Concepts, Resources, or Taxonomic items.

[10] For clarification and identification, the owning project's abbreviation is prefixed to uses of the item in the borrowing projects, for example, "CRANE: Karakaya, Doğa." Additionally, the borrowed item is shown in grey and is presented as read-only in all of the contexts in which it is borrowed. Only the owner of the database item can edit it.

The Power of Hierarchies

While we embrace hierarchies for their universality, their simplicity, and their flexibility, and while we have noted many of the benefits of using them in conjunction with an item-based approach, they provide much more than we might appreciate at first glance. Herbert Simon (1969, p. 87) explains that "hierarchic systems have some common properties that are independent of their specific content." This is what makes OCHRE a generic tool for a wide variety of research data, exploiting the common properties of hierarchic systems to provide common data structures and common data entry mechanisms. The tree structure is just that—a structure. It is data agnostic. It starts out empty. The content is up to the project or user.

Self-replication (Recursion)

That the notion of hierarchy is a natural way of thinking about the world is taken up by Michael Corballis in his book "*The Recursive Mind. The Origins of Human Language, Thought and Civilization.*" Introducing the idea of *recursion*, Corballis (2014, p. 3) gives several examples—mathematical, visual, and linguistic, some scholarly, some cheeky—our favorite of which is provided by the Victorian era mathematician Augustus De Morgan et al. (1915):

> Great fleas have little fleas upon their backs to bite 'em,
> And little fleas have lesser fleas, and so *ad infinitum*.
> And the great fleas themselves, in turn, have greater fleas to go on,
> While these again have greater still, and greater still, and so on.

Corballis goes on to call upon hierarchies as a mechanism for modeling recursion since "…one of the characteristics of recursion … is that it can take its own output as the next input, a loop that can be extended indefinitely to create sequences or structures of unbounded length or complexity" (Corballis 2014, p. 6). Another popularized analogy for recursion, "turtles all the way down,"[11] dates from as early as the 17th and 18th centuries, and includes usages by authors as varied as Stephen Hawking on theoretical cosmology, David Ambuel (2015) on Plato's Theaetetus, Antonin Scalia in rebuke of a self-referential argument,[12] and a Young Adult novel by John Green (2019). Hawking (1988, p. 1) opens his book, *A Brief History of Time*, with the anecdote of a well-known astronomer who, after a public lecture, got his comeuppance:

[11] See the Wikipedia article https://en.wikipedia.org/wiki/Turtles_all_the_way_down.

[12] Scalia used the saying in a June 2006 opinion Rapanos v. United States; https://www.law.cornell.edu/supct/html/04-1034.ZO.html. See also Cameron Ross (2018) in the Stanford Encyclopedia of Philosophy, "Infinite Regress Arguments."

> [A] little old lady at the back of the room got up and said:
>
> "What you have told us is rubbish. The world is really a flat plate supported on the back of a giant tortoise."
> The scientist gave a superior smile before replying, "What is the tortoise standing on?"
> "You're very clever, young man, very clever," said the old lady. "But it's turtles all the way down!"

OCHRE incorporates the notion of recursion, beginning with the process of data atomization which takes "greater" or more complex systems and makes them "lesser" simpler ones. Through supportive and compatible data entry practices, OCHRE enables the modeling of such data in tree structures that reflect the principle of self-replication: items within items, lists within lists, branching branches, fleas upon fleas, turtles all the way down.

Containment

Implicit in the nature of a hierarchy is the notion of *containment*. An item, represented by a *node* of the tree, contains those items that fall within it, either directly or through intermediate levels created by nesting items within other items, nodes within nodes. Naturally, this hierarchical mechanism is perfect for representing the spatial containment relationships among items uncovered within an archaeological excavation.

Archaeological data is primarily spatial data, and OCHRE uses the notion of a *spatial unit* to identify any tangible item of interest that is spatially situated. Excavators typically organize an archaeological site into defined fields, areas, or grids, within which they subdivide the space into trenches, squares, or other such subareas. Within these they identify units of activity by people of the past such as walls, pits, floors, rooms, and buildings. Excavated materials—the soil, the small finds, the bones, the potsherds, the samples, etc.—are typically removed in baskets, buckets, pails, or lots. Each of these items is a spatial unit represented by its own database item.

Collections of spatial units are recorded in hierarchies of spatial containment—across all scales of measure, the great fleas and the lessor fleas. From the highest level, representing the largest spatial unit such as the archaeological site, down to the smallest radiocarbon sample or speck of pollen, every item *is contained by* the items above it and *contain* the items below it in the hierarchy. Listing items together at the same level of a containment hierarchy indicates that they were discovered in the same context or that they occupy the same conceptual level of specificity. Every item is contextualized in relation to every other item.

An excavation might be based on a kilometer grid represented by a series of 100 grid units, each of which would contain 100 10 m x 10 m equal squares, or 400 5 m x 5 m squares. All grids are siblings to all other grids. All squares in a grid are child items of the containing grid. Below the level of square, some projects choose to use a fine-grid system that subdivides each square into 100 equal units. Others move from square directly to locus, pail, or small find. The flexibility of the OCHRE data model does not prescribe any part of this system; it is entirely at each project's discretion.

At Zincirli, for example, the site hierarchy of spatial units begins at the highest level with various excavation areas. In Area 5, the Northern Lower Town, one finds a Locus called L08-5006, a debris layer. This is one of 988 loci excavated in this area which are identified variously as debris layers, floors, pits, walls, and other types. In this specific locus, the team excavated four pails of soil. Contained in these pails are pottery sherds, small finds, and soil samples (Fig. 4.15).

In addition to the pails, this is the locus in which was discovered the stone monument, R08-13, commemorating the life of the important local figure named Katumuwa. Because the stele was not excavated within a pail (it is almost a meter tall), it falls directly below the Locus in the containment hierarchy, altogether skipping the "Pail" level.

This is a reminder that although every project will have a system of hierarchizing its spatial units, the system need not be applied uniformly at all levels of the hierarchy. At the topmost level of Area 5, for example, we find a range of items that include loci, pails, and other small finds. Whereas the Katumuwa stele (Fig. 4.16) is logically nested in a relatively deep containment context, the butchered bones found on the surface of the tell are assigned neither to a pail nor a locus. They are simply listed as a subitem of the area with no intervening levels of hierarchy.

Here again, OCHRE provides a level of flexibility that facilitates careful organization without requiring artificial uniformity like that which would be inherent in a more rigid data structure. Yet the hierarchy provides a unifying framework for all data so that, despite the lack of rigid structures, it does not feel disorganized and, in fact, is not disorganized. With hierarchies at its core, OCHRE supplies structure without enforcing content. Interestingly, we have noticed a positive side effect in

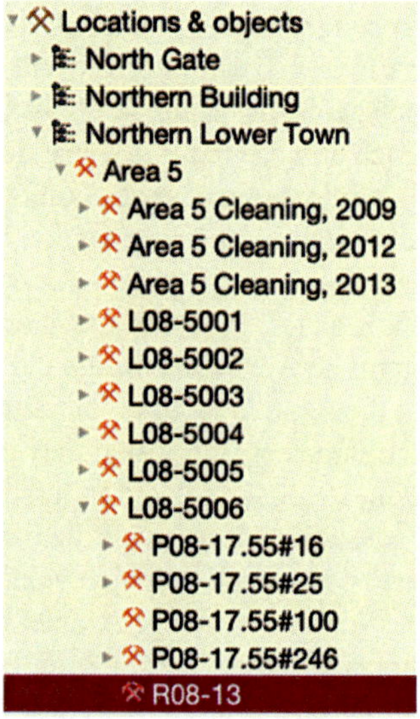

Fig. 4.15 Hierarchies model containment structures perfectly

Fig. 4.16 Katumuwa stele is shown in situ, Grid 17, Square 55. (Photograph by S. Schloen)

that the natural structure of a hierarchy encourages general conformity without requiring specific conformity (i.e., projects can opt-in at different levels of compatibility), and so it works well as an integrating device for a wide range of data. OCHRE is suggestive, not prescriptive, enabling, not enforcing.

Inheritance

One correlate of containment is the notion of *inheritance*. A subitem contained within higher-level items in the hierarchy is imbued, by logical implication, with characteristic information attributed to the parent item. Spatial items inherit spatial information. Temporal items inherit temporal information. Concepts may inherit properties as an implementation of the *Class:SubClassOf* in-kind relationship.[13] If a basket of pottery has its location tagged by a GPS coordinate, any individual potsherd of interest within that basket inherits this geo-location. This removes the burden, and the redundancy, of repeating details on subordinate items which can be derived from superordinate items in their hierarchical context. Items at each level of the hierarchy only need to record that which is new, since they inherit that which is already known about their context.

Inheritance is useful when the data is multi-tiered, partial, fragmentary, or uncertain, as is common in historical studies of all kinds. This is well illustrated by the way in which OCHRE uses hierarchies to represent time periods and the flexibility this gives for dating historical items (Fig. 4.17).

A hierarchy within the Periods category of OCHRE can be used to define both the breadth of relevant chronological sequences, and the depth of increasing levels of specificity within those higher-level timeframes. These *ordered* lists within lists may include historical, social, and cultural sequences. For an archaeological project, the researcher may use site-specific phases, broader cultural sequences, or

[13] Here, we use the terminology of the OWL Web Ontology Language (https://www.w3.org/TR/owl-primer/).

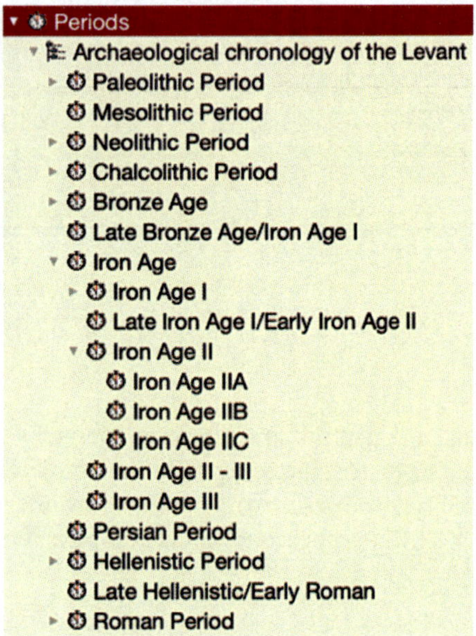

Fig. 4.17 Lower-level Period items inherit details from their parent items

specific references to years and months of political rulers or historical events. Time, itself, is represented as data within the OCHRE system.

Sometimes, we can precisely date an object of interest. Other times, we can only position it within a broad timeframe. The use of a hierarchical framework allows us to capture information at the most specific level available without forcing us, through the structural confines of an inflexible data structure, to commit to more than we can know. If we can determine a precise timeframe for an item of interest, we would tag it at a detailed level of specificity. If, however, we can only position it more broadly within a general timeframe, we would tag it at a higher level in the temporal framework.

The locus (L08-5006) in which the KTMW stele was found contained potsherds that help to provide temporal context for the locus. This unregistered sherd (Fig. 4.18), noted as two fragments of common ware pottery, was recognized by the ceramic specialist as being typical of the Iron Age II-III transition period. This dating information helpfully propagates *up* the hierarchy, providing temporal information to superordinate items for determining their chronological range based on their contents. The dating information also helpfully propagates *down* the hierarchy as the subitems, like the stele, naturally inherit their temporal context from the parent item.

Because the stele, like the potsherds, is hierarchically contained within this dated locus, it can be related to the Iron Age II–III transition period. Because the Iron Age II–III transition period is hierarchically contained within the Iron Age period, the stele inherits the knowledge that it belongs temporally to the Iron Age more generally. All of this is determined without having to specify any temporal information on the stele item explicitly. The containment and inheritance relationships demonstrate the power of a hierarchical structure.

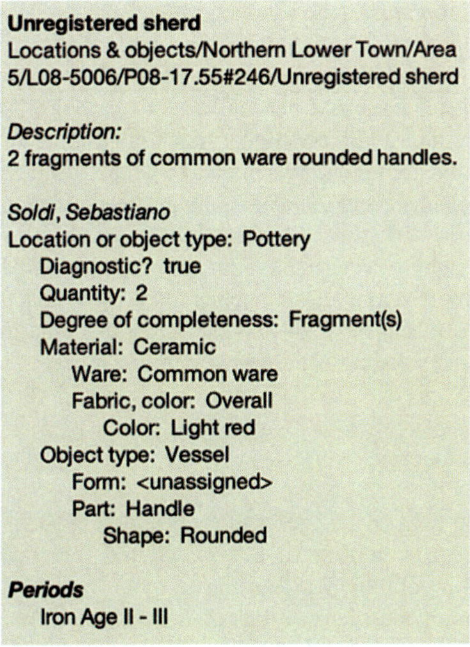
Unregistered sherd
Locations & objects/Northern Lower Town/Area 5/L08-5006/P08-17.55#246/Unregistered sherd

Description:
2 fragments of common ware rounded handles.

Soldi, Sebastiano
Location or object type: Pottery
Diagnostic? true
Quantity: 2
Degree of completeness: Fragment(s)
Material: Ceramic
Ware: Common ware
Fabric, color: Overall
Color: Light red
Object type: Vessel
Form: <unassigned>
Part: Handle
Shape: Rounded

Periods
Iron Age II - III

Fig. 4.18 Lower-level Spatial units inherit details from their parent items

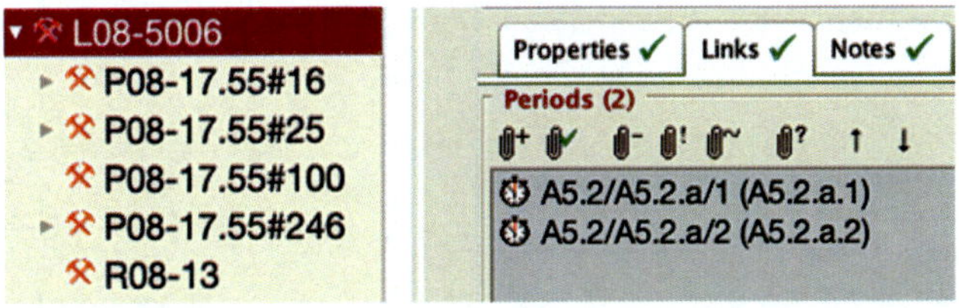

Fig. 4.19 Spatial units are assigned to temporal Periods using Links in the ordinary way

Multiple, Overlapping Polyhierarchies

The Katumuwa stele "can be dated quite precisely to around 735 BC, so it provides a chronological anchor for the investigation of the architectural phases in the lower town" (Schloen 2014, p. 34). This "quite precise" date correlates to a site-specific "phase" defined at Zincirli. This date also correlates to the broader chronological period of the Iron Age II–III transition period (Fig. 4.19).

Representing this assortment of temporal relationships would be a challenge were it not for another powerful benefit of hierarchies: any child item can have more than one parent. A tree structure where at least one child has more than one parent is called a *polyhierarchy*.[14] Many hierarchies can co-exist and even overlap as

[14] See the Wiktionary definition at https://en.wiktionary.org/wiki/polyhierarchy. Note, too, that when we speak of hierarchies in OCHRE we generally mean polyhierarchies.

subbranches are shared, grafted from one tree to another. This allows for a flexible mechanism to entwine related descriptive schemes without unintended entanglement.

OCHRE supports multiple, overlapping polyhierarchies where each hierarchy is itself a database item and can be treated as its own work of scholarship, representing a description or an interpretation attributed to a specific scholar. Scholarly attributions eliminate the impression that "the computer" wields the authority to make claims about the data. Scholars need not agree. Disagreement is common as scholars work out competing chronologies of historical events, explain complex stratigraphy of excavated areas, or propose conflicting readings of obscure texts. Items representing the component parts—the time periods, the excavated loci, the signs or words of the text—can be shared, but configured within specific, attributed hierarchies that reflect different interpretations.

For Time

Taking advantage of the tree structures of the Period hierarchies, the site-specific phases at Zincirli can be grafted into the "Archaeological chronology of the Levant"[15] which describes a more high-level, generally acceptable, outline of the temporal stages of this region of study. This situates project-based temporal units (Zincirli Area 5 Phase 2-c-2) within a broader context (Iron Age II-III), enabling interaction with relevant scholarship from other projects that share this general chronological framework. Period items shown in gray in Fig. 4.20 have been

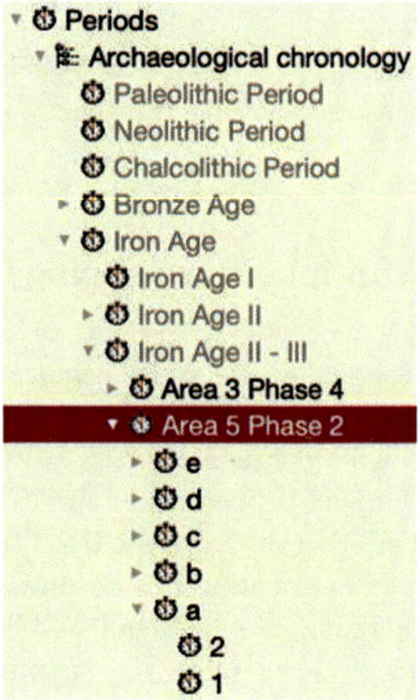

Fig. 4.20 Period items defined by a project are integrated within a broader chronological perspective

[15]The phasing of Zincirli Area 5 is attributed to codirector Virginia Rimmer Herrmann and is integrated within the broader chronology of the Levant as expressed by co-director David Schloen.

borrowed from the master OCHRE project and are shared with other archaeology project based in the Levant. Those Period items shown in black are project specific.

For Space

The spatial containment hierarchy that represents the excavation context of an item is only one of the possible hierarchical contexts. At a later stage of analysis, the researcher may choose to situate the spatial unit for a given locus in an interpretive hierarchy that represents a reconstructed view of the ancient architectural complex, with city quarters, administrative areas, buildings, rooms, and streets. The Katumuwa inscription, while found within Locus L08-5006, also falls into an architectural context, in Complex A, Building A/II, Room A3. The architectural context is a separate hierarchy that overlaps with the excavation context hierarchy, reusing the same subitems but organizing them for different analytical purposes (Fig. 4.21).

Furthermore, yet another spatial hierarchy is used to record the inventory location of registered objects using OCHRE's integrated inventory management system. Pottery, small finds, or other movable objects may be relocated from the archaeological site to storage rooms or scientific laboratories for conservation and analysis. When moved from the site to one of these locations, the user records an Event using the Moved-to action and specifying a link to the relevant destination (Fig. 4.22).

OCHRE then, in effect, inserts the item into the project's inventory hierarchy, reusing it in a new context. This system allows a team member to quickly identify the inventory location of all items or to ask questions like "Which items are at the

Fig. 4.21 Inscribed Katumuwa stele is shown in a digital reconstruction of the mortuary chapel, from T. Saul's artistic reconstruction in Rimmer Herrmann and Schloen (2014)

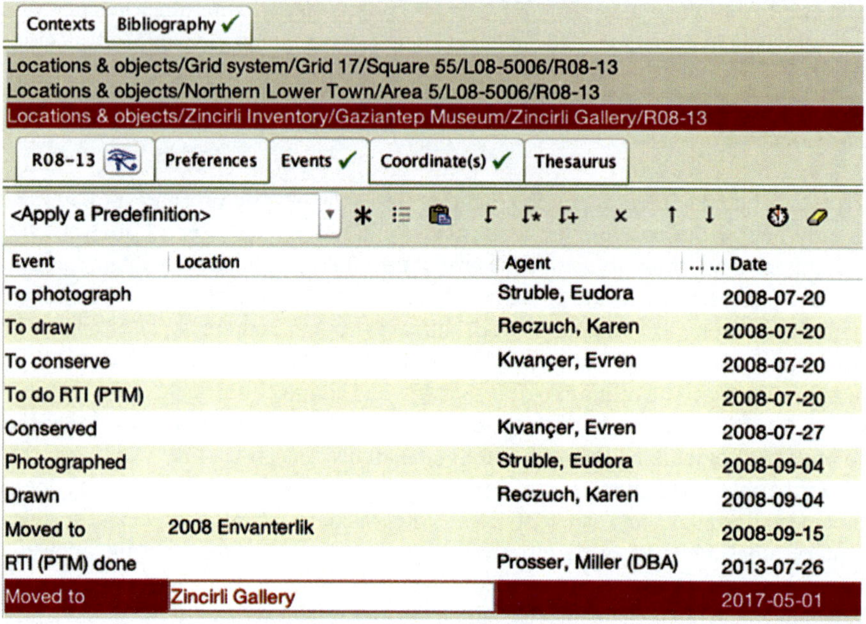

Fig. 4.22 Items are "Moved to" inventory locations, organized as a secondary hierarchy

radiocarbon laboratory?" or "Which items are on display in the Gaziantep Archaeological Museum gallery?"

To summarize, the Katumuwa stele exists only once in the OCHRE database as Spatial unit R08-13, but it participates in four distinct spatial hierarchies:

1. Original excavation context, Area 5, Locus L08-5006
2. Grid system context, Grid 17 Square 55
3. Reconstructed context, Complex A, Building A/II, Room A3
4. Inventory context, Gaziantep, Archaeological Museum, Iron Age Gallery, Zincirli Höyük Room

There is no duplication or redundancy, no standoff markup links, and no conflation of contexts—just a clean, clear set of hierarchies which, together with the Period hierarchies, richly situate this item in both time and space.

For Texts

Being mindful not to suggest that polyhierarchies are a feature whose power is limited to archaeology, consider again the use of hierarchies for textual analysis. Here, we need stray no further than the inscription on the Katumuwa stele. In keeping with the OCHRE strategy of divide and conquer, a text like this would be atomized into a sign-by-sign representation, where each sign is its own database item which can be described, contextualized, linked, annotated, and argued about like any other OCHRE item. But signs combine to form words, words combine to form phrases, and phrases combine to form sentences—lists within lists, fleas upon fleas, and turtles all the way down. So, we take a page out of Herbert Simon's book:

> A book is a hierarchy ... generally divided into chapters, the chapters into sections, the sections into paragraphs, the paragraphs into sentences, the sentences into clauses and phrases, the clauses and phrases into words. We may take the words as our elementary units, or further subdivide them, as the linguist often does, into smaller units. If the book is narrative in character, it may divide into "episodes" instead of sections but divisions there will be. (Simon 1969, p. 470)

Simon's description applies whether our "book" is a folio of Hamlet in inked English script, the Katumuwa inscription carved in stone using an Aramaic script, or a text from a tablet at Ras Shamra impressed in clay using cuneiform.

Our experience has shown that scholars using OCHRE represent both splitters and lumpers, but the level to which the units are divided and subdivided—that is, the answer to the question *How far is far enough?*—resides not with OCHRE, but with each researcher. What the quote from Simon does not consider is that the representation of text cannot be restricted to a single hierarchy. As McGann and Buzzetti (2006, p. 60) argue, textual relations cannot be constrained to a single ordered hierarchy. A text requires multiple overlapping hierarchies to be represented as the complex, dynamic, and multifaceted thing that it is.

For any Text item, OCHRE allows the articulation of both an epigraphic hierarchy and a discourse hierarchy, once again to allow entwining of content without unintended entanglement. As explained in the OCHRE manual (Schloen and Schloen 2012, pp. 22–23):

> The epigraphic hierarchy represents the physical structure of the text in terms of its division into epigraphic units at various levels of detail—usually sections, columns, lines, and individual graphic signs within a line. The discourse hierarchy represents the structure of the text in terms of its division into meaningful units of discourse at various levels of analysis; for example, paragraphs, sentences, clauses, phrases, words, and morphemes within words. Each epigraphic unit in a text's epigraphic hierarchy and each discourse unit in its discourse hierarchy is itself an OCHRE database item that can be described separately and linked to other OCHRE items. A text's epigraphic units are linked to its discourse units in a way that represents the relationship between physical graphic signs and their readings as meaningful linguistic expressions.

Beginning at the top line and reading right to left ("I am KTMW"), the Katumuwa inscription is itemized, sign by sign with signs grouped into lines, its Epigraphic hierarchy representing the sequence and structure of how it was written on the stele. The Text's Discourse hierarchy recombines these same signs into words. Words bubble up the hierarchy where they have been grouped into phrases, at which level the scholars have chosen to provide a translation. Each sign, each line, each word, and each phrase is a distinct database item about which scholarly discussion can be recorded (Fig. 4.23).

Taking the conceptual leap and splitting a text into separate epigraphic and discourse hierarchies cuts to the heart of a data representation problem commonly

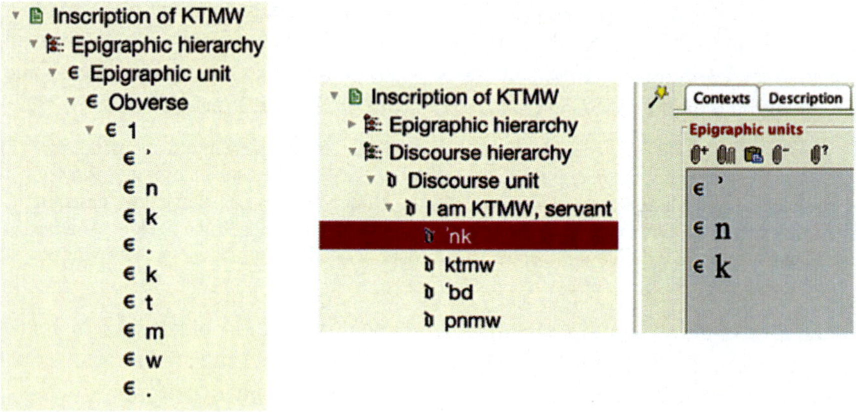

Fig. 4.23 Both an epigraphic hierarchy and a discourse hierarchy are needed to capture the complexity of a Text item

confronted by textual scholars in the digital humanities. As discussed in depth in the Schloen and Schloen (2014) article "Beyond Gutenberg: Transcending the Document Paradigm on Digital Humanities," the problem of representing multiple analyses of a single text without duplication and complication confounds most standard markup systems, even sophisticated schemes like the Text Encoding Initiative (TEI). But OCHRE's support for multiple, overlapping, polyhierarchies allows a scholar to create one hierarchy representing the dramatic structure of Hamlet, another hierarchy representing the metrical form, and yet another representing the grammatical structure, simply by reusing and reconfiguring the same pool of core content.

Another scholar could do the same, disagreeing with the first, by creating new hierarchies with the same reused content. That is, polyhierarchies provide the means to support multivocality for texts. Where a scholar's interpretation differs from that of the prevailing text edition, a new branch can be inserted—either epigraphic or discourse, either a single sign or an entire sentence—to represent a diverging opinion attributed to that scholar. That new text edition can graft existing content that is not in dispute or add original ideas altogether. In the world of scholarly research, we should do better than to let "the computer" serve as an anonymous authority requiring conformity and agreement. Polyhierarchies provide a mechanism for all voices to be heard.

Whether the core content is temporal, spatial, or textual, the use of overlapping hierarchies inspires data representation solutions in many areas of research. Schloen and Schloen (ibid., 107) justify the item-based approach of OCHRE, paired with its support for multiple, overlapping polyhierarchies, as they conclude:

> To achieve the full benefits of digitization, scholars need to be able to record multiple interpretations of the same entities in a predictable, reproducible digital form; and they need to be able to do so without error-prone duplication of data, without severing the complex interconnections among their various interpretations, and without being forced to adopt a standardized terminology that deprives them of semantic authority and limits the diversity of conceptualizations that motivates their scholarly work in the first place.

For Dictionaries

Like with Texts, Dictionary entries are highly structured documents, and while general-to-specific relationships are implicit in the (semi-)structure of any well-organized dictionary, OCHRE makes the structure explicit, atomizing a dictionary entry into multiple semantically meaningful hierarchies of database items. Thinking about the dictionary model from the top down, a dictionary begins with a list of lexical entries, or what we sometimes refer to as lemmas.[16] Each lemma represents gloss(es) and the part of speech and can be described by various metadata terms, including customized properties created by the researcher. In some cases, a researcher may wish to classify lemmas by semantic class or some other concept. For example, it may be useful to assign descriptive properties to all lemmas that deal with commodities, land transactions, animal husbandry, prayer, or other meaningful categories.

With the lemma as the root of the dictionary hierarchy, variations and nuances in the *senses* of the word are added as alternate or more detailed meanings, represented hierarchically from general categories of usage to more specific exemplars. The minimal, meaningful database item is a "meaning," with sub-meanings listed within meanings, sub-sub-meanings within sub-meanings, and so on. Along with the branching hierarchy of meanings within meanings is a second hierarchy of morphological and attested *forms* representing variations in grammar and spelling. The flexibility of a hierarchical model allows scholars to implement digital dictionaries with appropriate levels of complexity (if needed) or simplicity (if desired) (Fig. 4.24).

Some projects may not exploit the deeply nested possibilities of a hierarchical structure, not being concerned with recording every morphemic or orthographic form of a word. Other projects like the eCHD atomize highly, creating extensive branching into more and more detail as both the depth and breadth of a Dictionary unit are articulated digitally. The sample entry from the eCHD, *pai-*, "to go," starts with five explicitly numbered high-level meanings: **1.** to go, **2.** to pass/go past (something), **3.** to go by, pass (of time), **4.** to flow, and **5.** (idiomatic uses). Like hyperactive cells of a growing organism, the primary meaning (**1.**) immediately splits into **a.** an overview of subjects, **b.** method/means of locomotion, …, all the way to **j.**, **k.**, and **l.** In turn, **1.a.** splits immediately into **1′** gods and humans, **2′** animals, **3′** vehicles, **4′** concepts, and **5′** other. The section on the goings of gods and humans (1.a.1′) is extensive, that of animals (1.a.2′) much shorter, and that of vehicles (1.a.3′) a mere mention of a cart. Whatever level of description or atomization (subdivision) is needed, the use of a flexible hierarchy structure keeps these details organized and properly related.[17]

[16] In the literature of computational lexicography, there is a great deal of disagreement and discussion regarding the proper nomenclature for the various constituent elements of a dictionary. See Lipka (1992, pp. 130–134), Calzolari et al. (2012) and Francopoulo and George (2012).

[17] While the hierarchy of meanings (senses) is illustrated here, we return to this discussion to illustrate the hierarchy of forms for dictionary entries in Chap. 11.

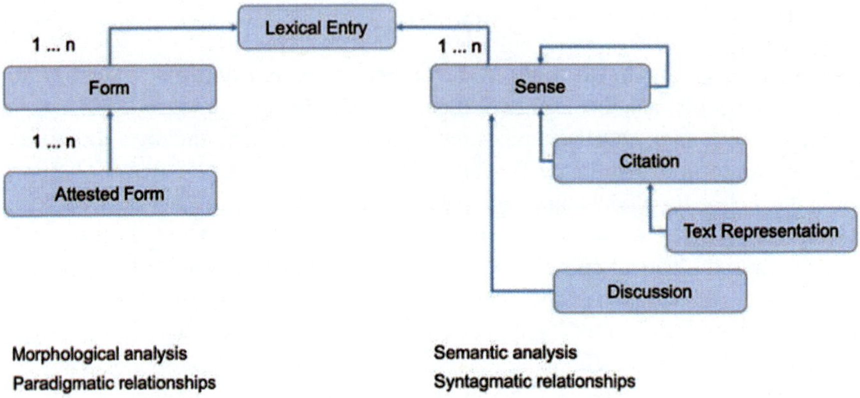

Fig. 4.24 OCHRE's hierarchical dictionary structure follows the Lexical Model Framework (LMF) and will feel familiar to users of the Oxford English Dictionary (See Francopoulo (2012) on the Lexical Model Framework. While the OCHRE dictionary model was not specifically based on this model, the similarity is due to the common structure of the OED)

The entries of the electronic Chicago Hittite Dictionary are presented by default as documents that mimic their pre-digital format. To reinforce visually that this document consists of highly *atomic* database items, Fig. 4.25 shows the standard **Document View** using display options that highlight links to textual and bibliographic sources and shows textual snippets colorized by their language (blue represents Hittite, red Akkadian, and magenta Sumerograms). To reinforce that this document consists of highly *structured* database items, OCHRE's **Outline View** presents the same database items in a tree structure, exposing the underlying hierarchy. Viewers can expand any level of the hierarchy to view the detailed branches below and can double-click any sub-meaning at any level to pop-up the default view of the detailed content of that sub-meaning. The tree-based display format is a concise, intuitive, and effective way of navigating a complex dictionary article that would otherwise go on for many dense printed pages (in the case of *pai*, 22 pages)[18] of detailed citations and commentary.

There is significant interplay between an OCHRE project's Texts and its Dictionaries. Not only do the respective hierarchies manage data within a category, but they allow for cross-cutting links across categories. OCHRE dictionaries are often based on a related text corpus, and the guided workflow wizards (described in Chap. 8) are used to identify words, link them (or add them) to the dictionary entries, add grammatical properties and provide a discourse transcription. This associates the words in texts with the appropriate lemmas in the dictionary, greatly speeding the process of building the dictionary entries.

[18] CHD Volume P (Güterbock and Hoffner 1997, pp. 18–40).

1. "to go" — **a.** an overview of subjects — **1'** gods and humans: *pa-i-ta-aš* ^{d}*Ḫapantaliyaš* "(the god) Ḫapantaliya went" KUB 28.4:22b (myth of the moon that fell, NS); ^{d}UTU-*uš aruni antaga=šša pa-it* "The Sungod went to the Sea(god) to his chamber" KUB 36.44 i! 12 (myth of missing deity, OH/MS?), translit. Myth 22; *nu* ^{URU}*Ḫattuša iyannaḫḫ[e]* LUGAL-*š=a* ^{URU}*Arinna pa-iz-zi* "I set out for Ḫattuša, but the king goes to Arinna" KBo 17.4 ii 8-9 (rit. for royal couple, OS); *n=aš kuedani* KUR-*ya pa-iz-zi* "To whatever land he (i.e., the one who escapes) goes" KBo 16.47:11 (treaty frag., MH/MS); *nu* ^{d}UTU-*ŠI ukila pa-i-mi* "I, My Majesty, will go myself" KBo 16.97 rev. 7-8 (liver oracle, MH/MS?); KÙ.BABBAR-*anza anda parna=šša pa-it* "Silver went into his house" KUB 17.4 obv. 8 (Song of Silver, NS); (When my grandfather heard about the disaster) "since my grandfather was still [si]ck, my grandfather (spoke) thus" [*kuiš=wa p*]*a-iz-zi UMMA ABU=YA=MA ammuk=wa pa-a-i-mi* "'Who will go?' My father replied: 'I will go'" KBo 14.3 iii 10 (DŠ frag. 14), ed. Güterbock, JCS 10:67; (If someone whom I or my father carried off flees to you, and you say to him) [*eḫ*]*u=wa i-it kuwapi=wa pa-i-ši* "'Come! Go wherever you go!'" KBo 5.9 ii 43-44 (treaty w. Duppi-Teššub), ed. SV 1:18f.

2' animals: *takku* GUD.ḪI.A A.ŠÀ-*ni pa-a-an-zi* "If cattle go onto a field (and the owner of the field finds them)" KBo 6.2 iv 12 (Law §79, OS), ed. HG 42f.; cf. *takku* ŠAḪ *šēliya našma* A.ŠÀ-*ni* ^{GIŠ}KIRI$_6$-*ni pa-i*[*z-zi*] "If a pig goes into a grain pile, field, or garden" KBo 6.3 iv 19 (Law §86, OH/NS), ed. HG 44f.; *ŠA* ^{d}*Mezzulla* UDU.ḪI.A *pa-iz-zi* "The sheep of Mezzulla go" KUB 10.28 ii 1-2 (fest. of winter, OH/NS), cf. ibid. ii 4, and KUB 9.38:4; *n=aš* 1 DANNA 20 IKU.ḪI.A *parḫanduš pa-a-an-zi* "They (the horses) go at a gallop for 1 DANNA and 20 IKU" KUB 1.11 iv 21-22 (MH/NS), ed. Hipp.heth. 120f.; for birds and bees see 1 b 4', below; for snakes see 1 l, below.

3' vehicles: *māḫḫan* ^{GIŠ}*ḫuluganniš parna=šša pa-iz-zi* "When the cart goes to its/his house" IBoT 1.36 iii 61 (instr. for the *MEŠEDI* guards, MH/MS), ed. AS 24:30f.

4' concepts (abstracts) — **a'** evils: *nu=wa kē kallar uttar apiya pa-id-du* "Let this evil matter go there" KBo 4.2 ii 22-23 (rit. of Ḫuwarlu, pre-NH/NS); *nu kī* <*i*>*nan ēšḫar NĪŠ* DINGIR-*LIM kuwapi pa-iz-zi zik šūrašūwaš* ^{MUŠEN}*apadda ītten* "Wherever this disease, blood, (or) oath goes, let you (sg.) *šūrašūwa*-bird go (pl.) there" KUB 30.34 iv 5-6 (rit. of Iriya, MH/NS), ed. Alp, Tempel 112f.; cf. personified evil KUB 15.39 + KUB 12.59 ii 19-20 (MH/NS), cited below, 5'.

Fig. 4.25 Complex, semi-structured eCHD entries break high-level general categories of meaning into increasingly more specific details

Conclusion

As we conclude this section, we do not want to leave the impression that hierarchies are the *only* means of organizing data within OCHRE. They are, indeed, a *primary* means but other derivative structures come into play. Lists, or Sets as they are called in OCHRE, manage collections of items, perhaps generated by a query or selected for some analytic purpose. But a list is simply a trivial, one-dimensional case of a hierarchy, so it falls naturally within an item-based, hierarchical model. Tables, maps, graphs, networks, simulations, and other specialized views or analyses can be modeled from items or derived from hierarchies, and so they are secondary structures rather than primary ones. We take up examples of these in illustrations and case studies to follow.

You may have wondered why the OCHRE icon is a tree (Fig. 4.26). It is a meaningful symbol of the hierarchical model at the core of OCHRE. Tree branches represent our multidisciplinary approach to data management. Squirrels and birds stand in for collaborators, working together, sharing the same research space, some to perch and sing, others to gather nuts. Squirrels of different sizes represent the diversity of scale accommodated by the OCHRE system. Individual leaves are denoted, many similar, many different, some unique, evoking our item-based approach. The maple leaves remind us of OCHRE's Canadian roots and its international reach. The browns, oranges, yellows, and golds, bring to mind the dirt colors of archaeology, from which we made our beginning.

Hierarchies provide a place for everything. Those *things* might be coins found within a coin hoard, tooth fragments of a skeleton, specific dates within a temporal

Fig. 4.26 It is no accident that the OCHRE icon is a tree

context, verb forms of words in a text, or sub-meanings of an expansive dictionary article. Each thing, in and of itself, is a relatively simple item but typically represents one part of a much more complex system. Divide and conquer. Atomize then hierarchize to be well on your way to a successful database strategy.

We are convinced of the importance of hierarchies for their role in modeling complex knowledge, but would like to add to our voices that of Herbert Simon who can hardly imagine being able to understand the world without them. Granted, his words from 1969 seem dated, and we suppose that modern technology's capacity for memory or calculation has far surpassed his imagination of it, but the sentiment still rings true:

> The fact, then, that many complex systems have a nearly decomposable, hierarchic structure is a major facilitating factor enabling us to understand, to describe, and even to "see" such systems and their parts. Or perhaps the proposition should be put the other way round. If there are important systems in the world that are complex without being hierarchic, they may to a considerable extent escape our observation and our understanding. Analysis of their behavior would involve such detailed knowledge and calculation of the interactions of their elementary parts that it would be beyond our capacities of memory or calculation. (Simon 1969, p. 108)

Chapter 5
An Item-Based Approach: Propertize

prop er tize \ˈprä-pər-tīz \ verb

the process of describing an OCHRE item with properties

OCHRE provides a mechanism to create descriptive elements called *Properties*, which are used to identify database items and ascribe qualities to them. We ask our readers' indulgence as we coin a new term to represent the process of using properties to describe database items. We refer to this process as *propertizing*, that is, as a shorthand for "imbuing an OCHRE item with descriptive properties." In short, the researcher assigns a series of properties to an item to classify it beyond the simple item category. For a Location, for example, we may add properties to describe the type of location (country, city, palace, library, etc.), the functional use of the location (civic, religious, private, etc.), or even custom typological classes (Settlement Ia, District 3, etc.). To Persons, we may add properties to identify intrinsic qualities like age or ethnicity, or familial or social relationships such as Father of, Mother of, Teacher of.

Propertizing is motivated by the goal of classifying OCHRE items based on their common features and relating items through user-defined (sometimes ad hoc), targeted links, bringing a degree of order to what might otherwise become an unruly collection of unrelated things. Merriam-Webster defines *classification* not only as "the act or process of classifying"[1] but also as a "systematic arrangement in groups or categories according to established criteria; *specifically*, TAXONOMY."[2] In OCHRE, a *Taxonomy* is the data structure that represents the systematic arrangement of descriptive elements organized according to some established criteria—the criteria being established by the scholar or the project, not prescribed by OCHRE. An OCHRE project's taxonomy is the foundation for the work of scholarship being

[1] https://www.merriam-webster.com/dictionary/classification; Definition 1.

[2] Ibid., Definition 2a.

S. R. Schloen, M. C. Prosser, *Database Computing for Scholarly Research*, Quantitative Methods in the Humanities and Social Sciences,
https://doi.org/10.1007/978-3-031-46696-0_5

constructed and the framework upon which any item's description is hung. Indeed, *all* project items will be described in accordance with the project taxonomy.

When an OCHRE item is first created using the item-based approach as discussed in Chap. 3, it remains an abstraction, an undifferentiated stem cell, and a nondescript brick from the pile, until it is described as something; literally, some *thing*. OCHRE represents it with a "**New ...**" label. A new what? That depends entirely on the Category to which the item is assigned, and the descriptive Properties assigned to the item. In Chap. 4, we discussed the use of hierarchy in OCHRE for organizing such *things*. In this chapter, we elaborate on the use of hierarchies for organizing *the description of* things. We then turn to a real-world case study from the world of zooarchaeology to illustrate the process of taxonomy building and propertization.

Data Versus Description

By "description," we do not mean a prose description like this for the Katumuwa stele and its dimensions: "Basalt stele; H: 1 m; W: 99 cm; TH: 50 cm." How would one use this information to find all steles less than or equal to a meter in height? How could one calculate the average thickness of the stones? Even searching for things like "basalt" or "Basalt" or for "stele" (or was that "stela"?) would be hit or miss, depending on the consistency of the data entry. Free-form text in table columns, typically called "Description" or "Notes" or "Comments," is just that—free-form information not generally useful as analytical data. Compare this to using specific data values for the attributes of Height, Width, and Thickness instead, where the type of stone was listed explicitly. Then, all steles where Height ≤ 1 meter could be found; the average Thickness of all steles found on the Acropolis could be calculated; and the proportion of basalt to limestone monuments could be studied.

Adam Rabinowitz (2016, p. 501) recounts the experience of the Chersonesos team recording the collection of its archaeological finds while allowing free-form descriptions:

> ...although we used digital data collectors ... we did not have preset vocabularies, with the result that we preserved an excellent record of human variability in the description of find types, but a rather less useful record for search and filtering (to map all the coins recovered from the excavation, e.g., one needs to filter the find layer in the geodatabase for not only "COIN" but "3.COINS," "BRONZE.COIN," "BROKEN.COIN," and so on).

Consistent data entry makes the data much more accessible. Even in a table-based system, there are simple strategies that can make the data more valuable for further analysis. Using a controlled vocabulary to restrict the valid values in any field goes a long way to improving the cleanliness of the data, removing inconsistency due to typographical errors, eliminating the use of obscure abbreviations, and minimizing variability in spellings. Using separate fields or columns for capturing different features is also worth the extra effort and is in keeping with the principle of atomization—breaking a descriptive comment into its component parts. The tendency to conflate descriptive properties is illustrated by even just the four examples of "COIN" above which include descriptive information about Quantity (3), Material (Bronze), and Preservation (Broken). None of the details regarding quantity, material, or preservation are useful as shown and barely an advantage over a paper-based system. The value of having predefined value lists, data validation tools, and a controlled vocabulary to capture data, so that it is useful for searching, filtering, and further analysis, cannot be overstated.

Data Versus Metadata: All Data Is Created Equal

Apart from properties, there are a limited number of fields built into OCHRE that are shared among all items, or among a subgroup of items. Every item, for example, has the possibility of being assigned a Name, an Abbreviation, a prose Description, and associated Notes. As new database objects differentiate into more specific types of items, other built-in qualities come into play. These might include, for example, the *author* of a Bibliography item, the *coordinates* of a Location item, or the *date* of an image Resource. These are features that are so well-accepted that we have chosen to provide built-in fields for these in OCHRE as a convenience. One might think of these as *metadata* fields.

Metadata is "best defined as the structured, encoded data that describe characteristics of information-bearing entities (i.e., *things*)" (Zeng and Qin 2016, p. 3), but the distinction between data and metadata is not always clear. The OCHRE project, *Lives, Individuality, and Analysis* (LIA), which studies the personal interactions and scholarly, influences among nineteenth-century scientists and catalogs the books authored by the scientists and the letters they have written, sent, and received. For this purpose, "Charles Darwin" might be mere metadata, used as the author tag on "*The Origin of Species by Means of Natural Selection*," represented in Dublin Core, but "Charles Darwin" as the node of a complex social network, with qualities, relationships, and other meaningful content, is needed as core research data for analytical purposes.

Using OCHRE's item-based approach, the same Person item representing Darwin can serve both functions, as core data and as metadata; there is no need to differentiate the two. In fact, OCHRE supports a minimal set of built-in metadata fields, choosing not to be overly prescriptive, preferring instead to leave it up to the user or project to determine what constitutes data and to create appropriate properties to represent it. One scholar's data is another's metadata. The computational platform should not be the one to make or enforce the distinction.

Taxonomies Are Data, Too

An OCHRE project can implement standard approaches to data representation—the Dublin Core, CIDOC-CRM, or TEI schemas, for example—but there is no requirement that a project conforms to any established standard.[3] In fact, this goes against the spirit of the generic and flexible OCHRE data model. A project is free to model data according to whatever method or standard is adopted by that project, whether a well-established standard or something completely idiosyncratic. We would only encourage and guide projects to model data well. This is not to be contrary or opposed to standards in principle. It is simply realistic because we should not assume a degree of ontological consensus that does not exist.

The title of this section, "Taxonomies Are Data, Too," is the name of a paper presented by David Schloen at the Chicago Colloquium on Digital Humanities and Computer Science at the University of Chicago, November 15, 2015, the subtitle of which, "*Dealing with Ontological Heterogeneity in Digital Humanities*," signaled his argument that

> …there is no external semantic authority who can impose a common ontology on individual researchers and there is no universally shared theory from which a common ontology can be expected to emerge. This is not a deficiency in the mode of research characteristic of the humanities. Ontological heterogeneity is not a vice to be eliminated but is actually a defining virtue of our mode of research … Indeed, we reward people who come up with new ways of seeing familiar objects of study.[4]

D. Schloen contrasts the use of predefined database schemas with the need for a more flexible ontology—a "formal specification of concepts and relationships within a given domain of knowledge…whether it is a simple controlled vocabulary, or a hierarchical taxonomy, or a more complex conceptual model." Schloen argues that "the high degree of ontological heterogeneity in many fields of the humanities … is not simply the result of egotism but reflects divergent interpretive paradigms and research questions." It is not for the software to dictate the descriptive schema of a research project. Rather "we simply need software that has been designed with our interests in mind and conforms to our research practices by allowing individual scholars as end-users to specify their own ontologies…but remaining responsible as end-users for their semantic choices."

If a data structure does not adequately capture the recording system, or the typology, or the system of categorization of a project's data, then the data will not be properly represented or well managed. Attempts to standardize, especially in the humanities and social sciences where data is less structured, more variable, highly subjective, and constrained by the needs of the research design, often fall far short of the supposed ideal. This is not the stuff of hard science, structured by laws of

---

[3] In order to play nicely with other computational systems, OCHRE can transform or export OCHRE data into other popular formats (e.g., CSV, PDF, Word, and Excel), or those needed by client projects (e.g., TEI-XML).

[4] D. Schloen, personal communication; from an unpublished conference paper.

motion or the periodic table. Who is to say that one's taxonomic scheme is correct, or not? Try telling a ceramicist how to define their pottery typology, or a linguist how to grammatically tag complex vocabulary, or a psychologist how to code their video, or a biologist how to classify an "individual." Humanities and social science research data demand a highly flexible data management system.

Rather than viewing this as repeated failure to standardize, we focus on capturing the descriptive schema as data, often as an attributed work of scholarship, modeling it effectively, and allowing it to integrate with the descriptive schemes of others. This allows overlap where possible but customization where desirable, without the pressure to conform to an approved "standard."

We were struck by Caraher's reflections on the ubiquity of the use of the term "bespoke" repeatedly used by speakers at the *Mobilizing the Past* workshop "to describe both applications and particular data structures made within those applications." In his review of the workshop on his blog post, he commented:

> The era of standardized data models is well and truly over and digital archaeologists have come to recognize that no matter how similar two data sets appear, comparing them in the most productive way remains a process best accomplished within the infinitely flexible context of the human mind.[5]

From our experience, there was never much uptake of standards by research communities, in archaeology at least. Perhaps in the world of Cultural Resource Management (CRM) archaeology a governmental agency can impose a data archiving standard that includes a core set of metadata fields, but in the domain of academic research, such homogenization is not realistic. The suggestion that a project use a database designed by someone else is often a non-starter.

To be clear, we are not arguing that all metadata schemas are to be discarded in favor of entirely idiosyncratic controlled vocabularies. Not at all. We are arguing that the data descriptors used as the primary and core vocabulary in the database software need not be limited to one or more approved schemas. A researcher must be free to record every valid observation, regardless of whether such an observation is allowed within a metadata schema. The item-based approach to a database taxonomy allows a researcher to use one or more established or customized metadata schemas to describe their data, while leaving open the option to map to unlimited standardized schemas later. That is, the primary step of data capture supports a secondary step of data integration.[6]

What makes possible an "infinitely flexible context" is an item-based approach to a controlled vocabulary, or data dictionary, or whatever your favorite term is for the allowable set of descriptors available to one's database for describing its content. In OCHRE, a *Property* is the use of a Variable representing some descriptive

---

[5] https://mediterraneanworld.wordpress.com/2015/03/02/mobilizing-the-past-workshop-review/.

[6] By treating the taxonomy as data composed of items, OCHRE allows for the mapping of multiple complex taxonomies onto each other. This approach answers the incorrect assertion that it is not possible to map complex multi-layer typologies onto controlled vocabularies. See the discussion in Lang et al. (2013), where the authors propose the use of SKOS for representing thesauri to map various classificatory typologies.

quality together with a Value to describe that aspect of a database item. For example, "Height" is a user-defined Variable with a Value of "1 meter" assigned to the stele, along with numeric values for "Width" and "Thickness." Each OCHRE Variable is defined to represent a certain type of data, whether numeric, date/time, logical (true/false), character string, coordinate, or a predefined list of named (nominal), or possibly ordered (ordinal) Values.[7] The stele's Material (the Variable) is Basalt (the Value), "Basalt" being one of the acceptable user-defined Values for "Material" chosen from the controlled vocabulary. Projects can borrow Variables and Values already available from a shared pool in the OCHRE master project, or they can invent their own. This gives a project the flexibility to use its own nomenclature and puts the process of defining the database vocabulary in the hands of the users. OCHRE is enabling, not enforcing.[8]

This granular approach to data definition and description is not unique to OCHRE. It underlies graph databases in general, including those based on the Resource Description Framework (RDF), "a standard model for data interchange on the Web" endorsed by the World Wide Web consortium (W3C) as the basis for the Semantic Web.

> RDF extends the linking structure of the Web to use URIs to name the relationship between things as well as the two ends of the link (this is usually referred to as a "triple"). Using this simple model, it allows structured and semi-structured data to be mixed, exposed, and shared across different applications.[9]

RDF triples are used to express *subject–predicate–object* relationships. In OCHRE terms, the triple is analogous to the *Item–Variable–Value* combination—a Property assigned to an item. Using the stele as an example, this would be expressed as follows: "the stele" (subject) "has-a-Height-of" (predicate) "1 meter" (object) or "the stele" (subject) "is-made-of-Material" (predicate) "Basalt" (object).[10]

This granular approach to data definition and description is also in the spirit of the longstanding *entity-attribute-value* (EAV) model,[11] where the *entity* is the item being described (the stele), the *attribute* is a quality or feature being identified (its Height), and the *value* is the value of the attribute as it applies to the entity (i.e., 1 meter). Hence, we find ourselves in good company, not just among other abstract data models, but with other systems that implement an EAV model like the

---

[7] See the OCHRE manual (Schloen and Schloen 2012) for details regarding the different types of variables and their values, Chapter 13, "*Organizing Terms in a Taxonomy or Thesaurus*," especially p. 247ff.

[8] For a good explanation of the differences between controlled vocabularies, taxonomies, thesauri, and ontologies, see the "Taxonomies & Controlled Vocabularies Special Interest Group of the American Society for Indexing" http://www.taxonomies-sig.org/about.htm.

[9] https://www.w3.org/RDF.

[10] While RDF relationships are analogous to our OCHRE properties, their implementation is quite different as they are based on URIs with the intent of modeling linked information for the Semantic Web.

[11] https://en.wikipedia.org/wiki/Entity-attribute-value_model See http://ark.lparchaeology.com/ and Dufton (2016).

Archaeological Recording Kit (ARK). This thoughtful and solution-oriented application, with a focus on data integration, starts out well using the EAV approach, playfully illustrated with sticky notes on a whiteboard, confirming just how natural it is to think about descriptive data in a granular, item-based way. The item "VM_2328" was "Excavated on" 14/9/2014, from "clay-ey silt with frequent pebble inclusions;" it is "Light brown" and "Friable" and has "Pottery type" of "African Red Slip" with "black glaze" (Dufton 2016, p. 374) (Fig. 5.1).

However, the ARK application then falls into the common assumption that tables are required to pull it all together.[12] OCHRE, instead, retains the natural item-ness of the data and reflects these items in its implementation, choosing to use a "graph view" instead of a table-based approach. The item-based approach treats the items (subjects) and objects (respectively, the entities and values) as nodes on a graph with a named link (the variable, predicate, or attribute) between them, which "is the easiest possible mental model for RDF"[13] and, by implication, also for OCHRE.

This is where OCHRE stands apart as a database application for scholarly research data. Having *atomized* the descriptive properties in an item-based way, we

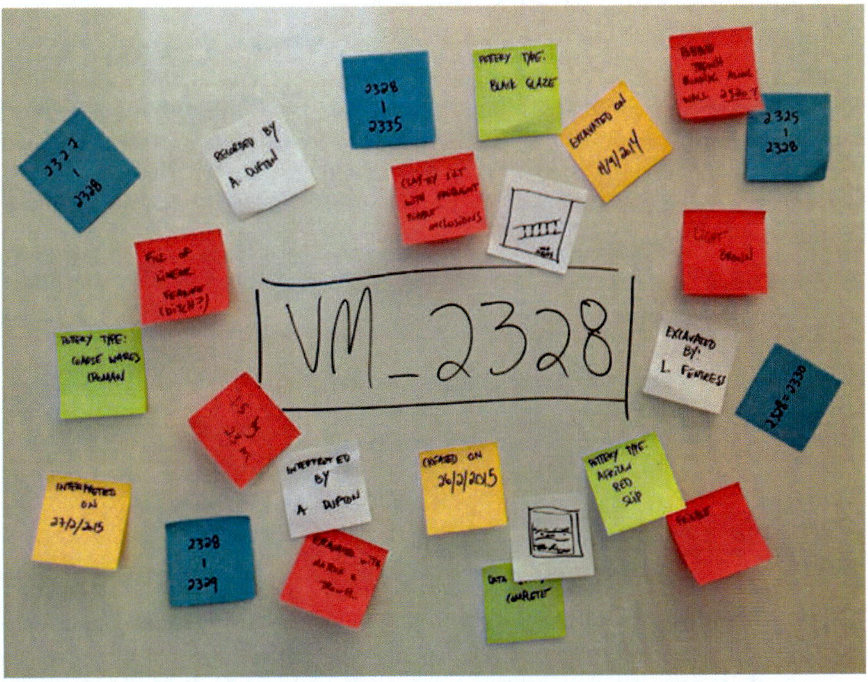

Fig. 5.1 A post-it note perspective on the EAV model supports an item-based approach (Dufton 2016, p. 374; CC BY 4.0)

[12] See, for example, "Figure 5-2: A simplified schematic representation of core and module-specific tables for ARK" (Dufton 2016, p. 376).

[13] https://www.w3.org/RDF.

then *organize*, but not using tables. As our readers already know, our favorite graph format is a hierarchy; technically, a directed acyclic graph. Brachman and Levesque, in their textbook on *Knowledge Representation and Reasoning*, use graph theory and formal logic to illustrate how "a taxonomy naturally falls out of any given set of concepts" and is effectively represented by a "special tree-like data structure" with "the most general [concepts] at the top and the more specialized ones further down" (Brachman and Levesque 2004, p. 172).

Despite all the examples of the uses of hierarchies we have seen already, it seems instructive, still, to consider the special advantages of a hierarchically organized taxonomy. Once again, we hope to illustrate that "taxonomies of kinds of objects are so fundamental to our thinking about the world that they are found everywhere, especially when it comes to organizing knowledge in a comprehensible form for human consumption, in encyclopedias, dictionaries, scientific classifications, and so on" (Brachman and Levesque 2004, p. 218)—and might we add databases.

Taxonomies Are Hierarchies, Too

An OCHRE Taxonomy, by definition, organizes properties hierarchically. The Properties pane of each OCHRE item specifies the arrangement of Variables and Values selected by the researcher to describe the item. Sometimes, these arrangements are unique, and the necessary descriptors are hand-picked. Sometimes, the properties are highly repetitive and can be applied all at once using a Predefinition, which serves as a template of preselected options.[14]

Inheritance

Notice the top-down progression from general to specific, represented by the "Location or object type" branch in Fig. 5.2. The stele is classified first as a Registered item (as defined by the Zincirli project), but more specifically, it is classified as a Stele, and here, the leaf node at the end of that branch is reached. For this project, there is no further subclassification of the Stele Value.

Notice, next, a different top-down progression from general to specific along the "Material" branch. The stele was carved from Basalt, but, moving up the tree to less specific Property Values, it *inherits* the fact that it is also Stone. Moving the other direction, down the tree, it is tagged more specifically as Fine-grained basalt. As instructed by Brachman and Levesque (2004, p. 172), each item "should be linked only to the most specific atomic concept" that is applicable, here, as fine-grained

[14] See the OCHRE manual (Schloen and Schloen 2012) for the use of Predefinitions, pp. 72–73. See also below for data entry strategies for faunal data based on Predefinitions.

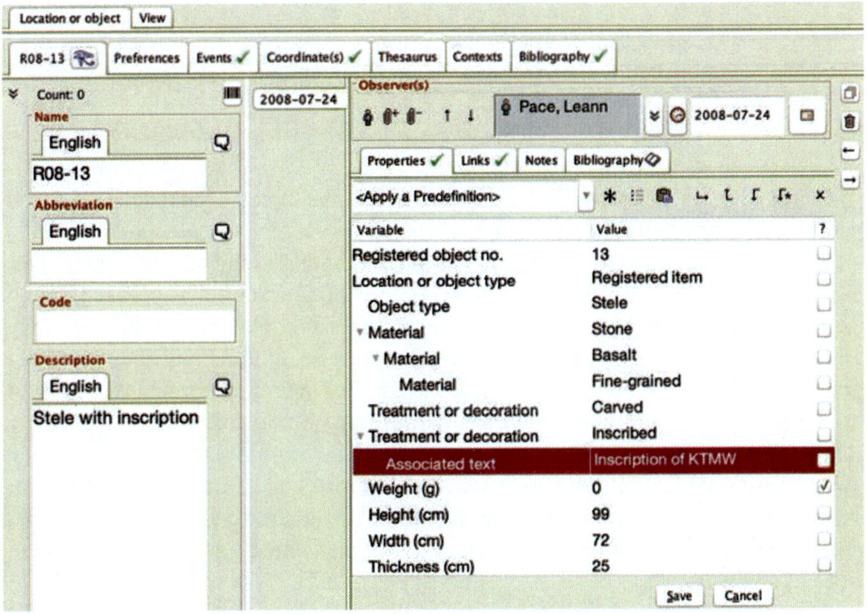

Fig. 5.2 Variables and Values are listed as Properties of the KTMW Stele, R08-13

basalt. Starting at the bottom, then it can be inferred by "logical consequence" (ibid., 25) that the stele is also basalt and also stone. In the typical arrangement of properties displayed for an item, OCHRE exposes explicitly the full inherited branch for any property, in this case Stone, then Basalt, and then Fine-grained basalt, allowing users to see the full context of the lowest, leafiest properties.

Consider the flexibility this provides for searching or filtering the items in the database. A search for all steles, or alternatively all registered items, will match this item (R08-13) in both cases. In a search for all basalt or all stone objects, R08-13 will also come up as a result. A search for all fine-grained basalt registered items would match on the stele along with spindle whorls and grindstones. A search for all stone steles would find those carved from basalt, limestone, or marble. A highly granular and hierarchical descriptive framework gives a high degree of flexibility along multiple dimensions.

Self-replication (Recursion)

If we were to model just this little bit of information about the basalt stele explicitly in a table structure, it would look something like the table shown in Fig. 5.3 with five fields needed to capture the same amount of information from these fully specified values. In the best case, the Material field (Stone) would need a sub-type

	A	B	C	D	E
1	**Material**	**Material sub-type**	**Material sub-sub-type**	**Object type**	**Object sub-type**
2	Stone	Basalt	Fine-grained basalt	Registered item	Stele

Fig. 5.3 Multiple fields are needed using a table scheme to describe a few features of the stele

(Basalt) and a sub-sub-type (Fine-grained basalt). The Object type field (Registered item) would need a sub-type (Stele).

In a relational database schema, it would be tempting to include only two fields, one for Material and one for Object type, but the limitations of this approach should be clear. How would one find all Stone items if the single Material field listed only "Fine-grained basalt"? No character-string search for "Stone" will match "Fine-grained basalt," but it would be unhelpful to list the Material as simply "Stone" if it were known to be fine-grained basalt. A properly normalized relational database schema would define a Values table for Material but would also require a second Values table for Materials that are a subclass of Stone and a further Values table for subclasses of Basalt. A tabular representation of hierarchical concepts becomes problematic, or unnecessarily complex, when implemented across multiple dimensions of analysis.

A natively hierarchical schema captures all the nuances of this description while requiring only two Variables: *Material* and *Object type*. The tree structure of a hierarchical taxonomy has the capacity to nest each of these Variables recursively, each instance reused and recontextualized within its higher-level self at the next level down, representing another level of specificity. The economies provided by this strategy are significant, as the number of Variables needed to provide the required descriptive structure is reduced overall, simply by reusing existing ones in multiple contexts at different levels of the hierarchy.[15]

Material (Stone)

    Material (Basalt)

        Material (Fine-grained basalt)

Containment

Within the context of a taxonomic hierarchy, containment takes on a new purpose, that of constrainment. Variables and Values alternate as they are organized in the hierarchy. Subsumed within each Variable are only the Values that are valid for that Variable. Subsumed within each Value are only valid Variables. The hierarchy represents, then, the full list of valid relationships permitted in the project vocabulary; the "authority file" so to speak.

[15] To see how this works itself out for philology, see the RSTI Case Study in Chap. 11.

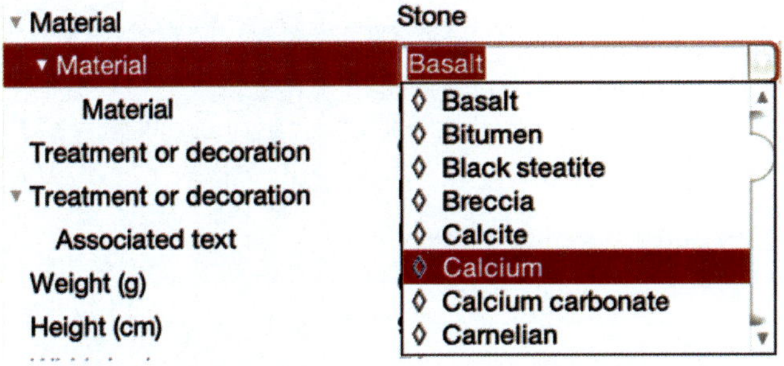

Fig. 5.4 Only valid options, based on the Taxonomy, are available for data entry picklists

The structure of the Taxonomy tree defines a set of constraints that are utilized by the Properties data entry mechanism to populate picklists with valid options. By limiting the available choices only to those prescribed by the hierarchical containment relationships, OCHRE can constrain data entry appropriately, in this case enforcing valid options, by consulting the taxonomy (Fig. 5.4).

Constrainment pertains both to recursive and non-recursive properties. The Material property is a recursive property because the same Variable is used in a repeated nested structure to record in-kind observations. Any kind of Material nested within Stone is therefore a kind of Stone. However, non-recursive nested Variables also helpfully constrain data entry. If a specific measurement applies to a specific part of a ceramic vessel, the Diameter of a jug Rim for example, the Diameter Variable may be nested as a child of the Rim Value in the taxonomy. Notice that the measurement is not a more specific kind of jug Rim, but rather an aspect of that Rim. In this arrangement, we achieve two results. First, on a practical level, this serves as a data entry cue that this specific part (Rim) can be described with a Diameter measurement. Second, this allows for querying and analysis of measurements associated with specific vessel parts. This type of non-recursive nesting can apply wherever needed to achieve these two outcomes. In the end, a hierarchical taxonomy in OCHRE is a combination of recursively constrained in-kind properties and non-recursive contextualized properties.

Reusability

A striking feature of the use of basalt at Zincirli was the way in which the ancient artisans mimicked their ceramic forms in stone. Beautiful basalt vessels at Zincirli attest to the same graceful lines and smooth profiles as familiar ceramic vessels, but because the pottery is typically managed by the ceramic specialist and the stone items are managed with other artifacts by the registrar, or by the geologist, the stone and ceramic vessels would not likely coexist in the same database table. However, with an item-based approach, and with a hierarchy that diverges near the top,

Fig. 5.5 A basalt vessel (R12-441) from Zincirli with a Footed Base and Carinated Shape is modeled after a common ceramic form. (Photograph by S. Soldi, courtesy of the University of Chicago Zincirli Excavations)

defining one taxonomic branch for Vessel form (regardless of the material), and another taxonomic branch for Material (regardless of the vessel form), we can use—rather, *reuse*—the same descriptive properties to describe quite different kinds of items (Fig. 5.5).

Once again, the efficiencies gained are significant, and the overall complexity of our descriptive scheme is reduced. Furthermore, a show-me-more-like-this query might well fetch similar items from a broader range of options, producing sometimes unexpected but interesting comparisons, in this case mixing stone and ceramic vessels in the same set of results. Whether it is stone vessels mimicking ceramic ones, or ceramic vessels mimicking metal ones, or some other form of *skeuomorphism*,[16] this is a perfect opportunity to reuse branches of the taxonomy in different contexts.

Taxonomy Building ABCs

Constructing the Taxonomy is one of the first and most important steps involved in configuring an OCHRE project. Not only is this necessary, practically speaking, in order to begin entering data but the planning process can reap unexpected rewards and should be done thoughtfully.

[16] One definition given by Wikipedia (https://en.wikipedia.org/wiki/Skeuomorph) describes the phenomenon of skeuomorphism as "a physical ornament or design on an object made to resemble another material or technique".

Clarification

With more of an emphasis on propertizing items, and less tolerance for the use of free-form notes, the process of building an OCHRE taxonomy encourages scholars to pinpoint what, exactly, they wish to capture, and for what purpose. The researcher must take a clear and critical look at the nature of the data, resolve issues of fuzziness, and itemize descriptive concepts and values. This is not to say that OCHRE cannot accommodate fuzzy thinking; rather, it is to suggest that the scholar be intentional about noting it. Properties called "Degree of certainty," "Confidence level," "Stage of analysis," or "Noteworthy?" with assorted alphabetic or numeric scales assigned as values could be used to track data that might need to be revisited or evaluated by an expert.

The process of building the taxonomy also forces the issue *How far is far enough?* What level of detail should be recorded as properties? For the Katumuwa stele, is it enough to record that it is made from stone? The Zincirli team uses the highest level of specificity possible, recording the stele as Stone > Basalt > Fine-grained basalt. This nesting of more detailed specifications can be applied to any property where the Variable gives as options a list of Values, any of which could be further qualified. Any text genre can be further classified into a system of subgenres. Any linguistic or grammatical property, like Verb, can be further specified through the recursive use of a property like Part of speech.

Construction

Building a project's Taxonomy in OCHRE is a matter of creating a tree, as simple as A, B, C. The same user interface mechanism used to build other hierarchies in OCHRE, like excavation contexts or discourse hierarchies, is available to the user to add new descriptive properties or create new "fields" without needing "technical support," but there are additional nuances that come into play for taxonomy construction.

A Is for Adopt

In the spirit of not reinventing the wheel, OCHRE makes it easy to adopt, wholesale, branches of taxonomies that already exist, either from other projects that have made their taxonomy public, or from the OCHRE master project, which maintains a master taxonomy tree that has been derived from many project's contributions. Archaeology projects have stones and bones, walls and floors, coins, and pots to describe. Philology projects have nouns and verbs, phrases and folios, authors, and genres to identify. All projects have images and documents, dates and places, and

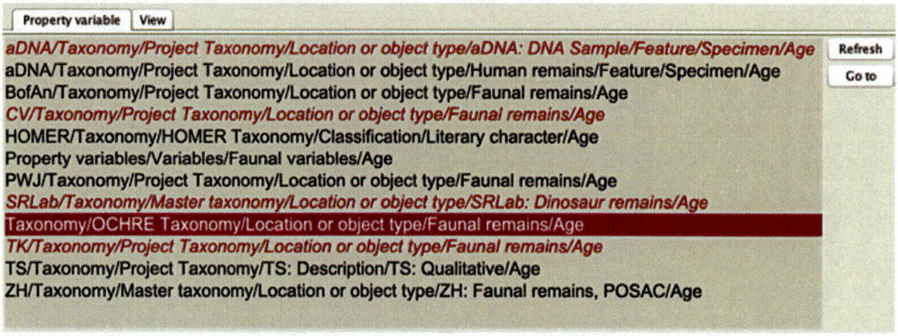

Fig. 5.6 The "Age" property is used by several projects in widely different contexts

counts and measures to tag. In these cases, a new project may choose to adopt an entire taxonomy branch. As a helpful visual aid, these taxonomy branches are displayed in red text, denoting that the copied branch cannot be changed in any way by the adopting project (Fig. 5.6). It is taken as is. In fact, OCHRE just points to the source branch without actually copying it (we sometimes refer to this as a *clone*). The positive effect of this is that any changes made to the source branch are automatically picked up by the adopting project. This option is typically used for branches that are universally applicable, like faunal, botanical, or geological taxa, rather than project-specific, or more interpretive content.

B Is for Borrow

In other cases, a project may wish to adopt a taxonomy branch, but then manipulate or rearrange it. In this scenario, a project can borrow a branch, which OCHRE displays in gray text. The gray-copied Variables and Values are reused but can be reconfigured within the taxonomy tree. This is sharing more broadly, without being bound to another's exact usage.

C Is for Customize

Every project requires custom properties. Once pre-existing Variables and Values have been adopted or borrowed, a project fills in the rest of its taxonomy with customized vocabulary. This alleviates the pressure on OCHRE to provide options for "standard" metadata. If a user needs a "field" not built into OCHRE, it can be created as a custom property, entirely at the discretion of the project. In addition, each project will have its own system of registration numbers or identifying items using codes or conventions. OCHRE cannot predict what else a research team might need but enables users to build up the project vocabulary: Time-of-sunrise, Distance-from-water-source, Date-treaty-was-signed, Number-of-wedges-in-sign, Color-of-ink-on-manuscript, Number-of-occurrences-of-word, and Whatever-else-is-needed.

Integration

What we had not anticipated was the degree to which scholars had more in common than they might have thought. Tools that allow for sharing and reuse of taxonomic branches in highly selective ways actively encourage sharing and reuse. When the director of the Tel Shimron excavation implemented a branch for describing and analyzing phytoliths, this ready-made, prefabricated structure was picked up eagerly by the archaeobotanist at Zincirli. Similarly, as the CRANE collaboration got underway the OCHRE Data Service had prepared for a high degree of customization as data from contributing sub-projects were integrated into the generic research framework provided by OCHRE, but it became more and more apparent that much could be shared, either at the level of subbranches or of individual Variables and Values, resulting in a great deal of automatic alignment of common features, thereby naturally integrating data from diverse sources. A stone is a stone is a stone. Note, however, that even between archaeological projects working in the same region, there often exists enough variation, for any number of reasons, to prevent the adoption of a uniform project taxonomy, but where terms are common and well-defined, a new project can adopt and borrow, leveraging the item-based structure of the OCHRE taxonomy, before turning to customization (Fig. 5.7).

The adoption and borrowing of taxonomic branches are notably helpful for describing the natural world or the representation of general knowledge or historical events. The sequence of major rulers of the seventeenth century does not need to be redefined by each historical project, neither do bird, fish, and mammal taxa when analyzed by faunal specialists, or grapes, olives, and pistachios, when studied by archaeobotanists. Each project does not need its own Quantity Variable. The OCHRE Data Service maintains master lists of commonly used measurements and other properties, updating them as needed for new projects.

The *natural* integration that falls out of adopting and borrowing common terminology can be augmented by *intentional* integration as sub-projects realize and concede their slight differences or as they choose to adopt the systems of their collaborators. Pottery typologies and botanical analyses, having already been articulated in one taxonomy, are often irresistibly reused in another project while retaining the authorship of the typology creators. When D. Schloen started a new archaeological project at Tell Keisan in Israel, for example, after adopting and borrowing existing branches from the Zincirli taxonomy, and adding a few customizations, the new project's taxonomy was essentially done.

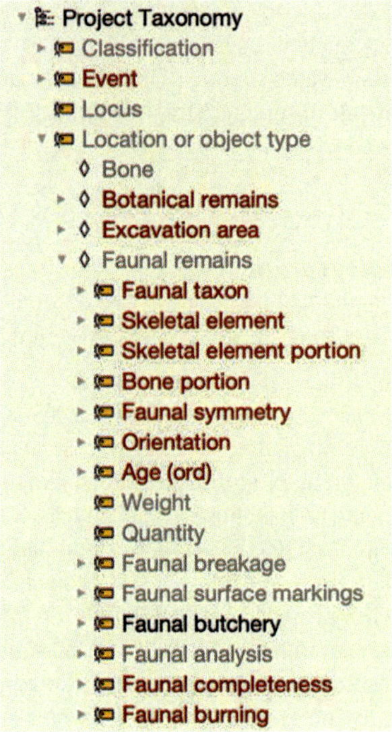

Fig. 5.7 The color-coded project Taxonomy indicates which items are adopted (red), borrowed (gray), or completely custom (black)

Internationalization

Another significant outcome of an item-based approach to defining a controlled vocabulary is the ease by which it can be internationalized. Since each descriptive term exists only once as a database item, and is used *by reference* everywhere else, each term can be translated, just once, and then displayed in any of its available translations, on demand. OCHRE includes an **Alias** mechanism to indicate that a term is *also-known-as* its Latin name, or its French counterpart, or the Turkish equivalent. Because of this flexibility, there is no necessity for using English as the default language in OCHRE. In fact, an OCHRE project can select which language is to be considered the default and then provide its content in that language.[17] Each project can also choose to support additional languages. Then, if a user asks for a view in, say, French, any vocabulary that is available in that language will be

[17]Translation of the OCHRE taxonomy into other languages is happening organically, time and energy permitting, often by end-users of OCHRE who have an interest in representing data in their native language. The Google Translation API has been integrated into OCHRE, providing built-in, automated help with translation.

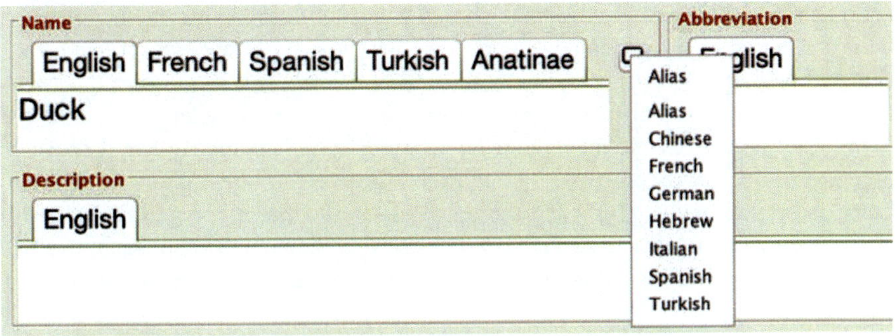

Fig. 5.8 Multi-lingual features are easy to support when the vocabulary is item-based

presented in that language; terms that have not yet been translated will display in the project's default language (Fig. 5.8).

Inspiration

There is an odd sense of gratification that comes with building a comprehensive taxonomy to support one's research. It is satisfying, even inspirational, to have a place for every *thing*, and the means to put everything in its place, itemizing, classifying, and propertizing. Using OCHRE, if something is lacking in the descriptive scheme the scholar is empowered to supply it and has the tools to do so. No data need fall through the cracks. Furthermore, there is not necessarily a "right" way to build a taxonomy (although there are some wrong ways which we help to guard against). In our role as project consultants, we have learned to keep an open mind as we watch project administrators do things their own way taxonomically. It is often not the way that *we* would do it, but that is the point! Granted, there is a science to it, and some math if one considers the logic involved, but it is also an art. Consider the sentiment of Michael Daconta, chief architect of the US government Department of Defense XML-based Virtual Knowledge Base, who says of building ontologies:

> People intuitively know an elegant design. Sometimes it is efficiency. Sometimes it is simplicity. You just say, "That is the right way to go." You sense the elegance of the design. You see how things smoothly fit together with few moving parts so that it does not get into a morass by being too complex. (Jackson 2004)

Case Study: Faunal Data

We conclude this section with an extensive, targeted case study that illustrates a wide range of issues to be considered, and innumerable decisions to be made, when building a project taxonomy to model and manage data using an item-based approach. For this example, we have chosen a category of data that we have found to be problematic on multiple levels but is well-attested by all the archaeology projects with which we work: faunal data. Even if faunal data is not your area of expertise, we invite you to follow along as we illustrate in more detail the use of an item-based approach (atomize!) and an OCHRE-style **Taxonomy** (organize!) to describe project data (propertize!), highlighting both the range of options that a hierarchical strategy supports and the range of pitfalls that it helps to resolve. We also consider practical issues related to data entry, both manually and through automated import processes, that make concrete the idea of data as items instead of tables.

Faunal data is complex and fraught with data representation challenges. There are a variety of relationships, including parts to wholes, general to specific, and collective to individual. Faunal objects are typically highly fragmentary comprising many shades of knowing and not knowing. A specialist may be able to determine that a sample is a mammal bone and may wish to record, with uncertainty, that it may be from a bovid. They may be able to determine that it is a long bone but only uncertainly that it is a femur. There are many different kinds of things to say about many different kinds of things. Present or not present? Female or male? Distal or proximal? Left or right? Molar or incisor? Fused or unfused? Juvenile or adult?

Like the entity-attribute-value model, OCHRE's granular approach to describing items with properties suits the scenario where there is scope for encoding "in a space-efficient manner, entities where the number of attributes (properties, parameters) that can be used to describe them is potentially vast, but the number that will actually apply to a given entity is relatively modest."[18] Each faunal item will typically be described with only a few properties, but selectively from of pool of a "potentially vast" number of things that *might* be said about any given bone.

Sparse Data

When a faunal expert processes a collection of faunal specimens, they will often take measurements of common features of the bones like "Greatest Length (GL)" or "Greatest Breadth (GB)," but also of highly specific features like "Smallest breadth of the shaft of the ilium (SB)," or of obscure elements like "Greatest length of the arch including the *Processus articulares caudales* (LAPa)." As data consultants at the OCHRE Data Service, we help ensure that the metrics captured by the faunal expert are processed correctly, *as data*, as it is imported into OCHRE. That is, we do not merely want to capture the recorded measurements, as in a digitized version of the paper record, but we hope to make it useful for calculating averages or plotting on a graph. In one sample spreadsheet of faunal data, the columns ranged from A, B, C, … AA, AB, … EU, EV; that is, 126 columns in all. The measurements had

[18] https://en.wikipedia.org/wiki/Entity-attribute-value_model#The_attribute.

cryptic abbreviations which encouraged all manner of typographical errors and inconsistencies. There were almost 15,000 bones described in this data set, most having only one or two relevant measurements if any at all—that is a lot of blank cells in a table! Another OCHRE project exhibited a vastly different approach to measurement taking. A single table column tagged as "Measurement" captured the relevant details: "GL:26.2 cm; Glpe:22.5 cm; SC:3.5 mm." How would it be possible to perform statistical analysis on measurements such as these? This is data as mere record-keeping, not data for research.

Faunal data is a good example of what is called *sparse data*. To represent these metrics responsibly and numerically for analysis would require an unwieldy number of table columns, most of which would be empty for any given row (representing an individual faunal specimen). The temptation to take shortcuts is practically irresistible—like combining different values in the same column to minimize the total number of columns needed or using mysterious abbreviations—sending the user down a slippery slope toward data of compromised quality. Even if this temptation is resisted and a reliable, "normalized," relational data structure is configured, the tables would be highly sparse. By using an item-based data model such as OCHRE's instead, any given faunal specimen can be described with *only* the details that are relevant to it. If the circumference of the bone cannot be measured due to partial damage, then this property need not be present; it does not need to be represented by an empty cell. If a feature or property, say "Bone modification," requires multiple notations, the variable can be recorded more than once, each time with a relevant value:

Bone modification = Rodent chew
Bone modification = Weathering
Bone modification = Butchery

Data Classification

Frankly, we used to shudder at the prospect of handling a spreadsheet of faunal data, but faunal data is amenable to a divide-and-conquer, atomize-then-organize strategy. We start by identifying every *thing* insofar as it is possible, sometimes pushing atomization to the extreme, yet always evaluating *How far is far enough?* This organizational step results in highly articulated hierarchies as everything is put in its place: biologically, anatomically, and categorically.

Biological Classification

Some OCHRE projects use a single property recursively, shown in Fig. 5.9 as *Faunal taxon*, to express the general-to-specific nature of nature. This is an approach often used with both faunal and botanical samples, and it is an economical way to

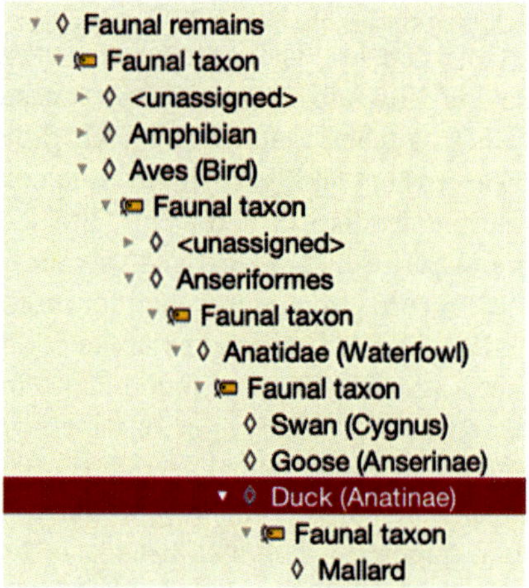

Fig. 5.9 The Variable "Faunal taxon" is used recursively to narrow down the species identification

propertize with a minimal number of Variables. In this case, like with the Fine-grained basalt example, each item is linked to the most specific value that applies (Brachman and Levesque 2004, p. 172). If we can identify a bone as that of a duck, then *Duck* is assigned as its Faunal taxon, but if we only know that it is part of some bird, then we assign the value *Bird* from higher up in the taxonomy. As Brachman and Levesque (2004, p. 218) remind us: "hierarchies allow us to avoid repeating representations—it is sufficient to say that 'elephants are mammals' to immediately know a great deal about them." In our example, if we can say a bone sample is from a Duck then we can safely infer that it is from a Bird.[19]

OCHRE tracks an item's usages, and reusages, in potentially multiple hierarchical branches, sometimes listing property values in unexpected contexts. The value *Duck*, used to describe bones found in an ancient pit, might also be used as a value of the *Motif* property describing the artistic elements of the elegant carving of the KTMW stele. As they say, if it looks like a duck…

Anatomical Classification

Any given bone can be classified both within its context in the tree of life (a Duck), *and* within its skeletal context. A recursive, hierarchically organized descriptive scheme details general-to-specific anatomical relationships using the property *Skeletal element*. This property is used and reused in a wide range of contexts, itemizing the skeletal components of a pelvis, or a skull, or a mandible, effectively simplifying complex systems into their atomic parts. *How far is far enough?* depends on the goals, and patience, of the researcher (Fig. 5.10).

[19] On the botanical front, by comparison, some OCHRE projects have chosen to be explicit about *Family*, *Genus*, and *Species*, re-using this trio of properties (hierarchically, but non-recursively) to flesh out the relevant branches of the tree of life.

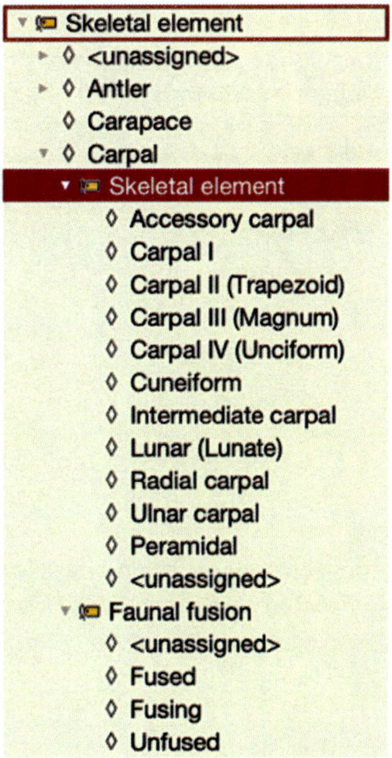

Fig. 5.10 Faunal Skeletal elements are organized anatomically

Other (non-recursive) properties are featured, as needed, to describe aspects that are specific to a subbranch. Sometimes these too, like *Faunal fusion* (the degree of which helps determine the age of the specimen, e.g., whether a juvenile or adult), which can apply to tarsals, the skull, vertebrae, and many other kinds of bones, are reused in a variety of appropriate contexts.

The result is a branch of the Taxonomy, which is valuable as an end in itself in that it itemizes and documents the analytical framework used for studying the bones. It also serves to constrain data entry appropriately, presenting as options only the relevant Variables and Values allowed by the Taxonomy at each juncture. If the item in question is a Vertebra the taxonomy allows the researcher to further specify *which one?* If it is a Tooth, then is it a Molar or Premolar? By using hierarchical contextualization, only relevant options are made available by the taxonomy. Furthermore, if we cannot identify *which vertebra?* or *which tooth?* we simply stop, going no further down the hierarchy once we run out of things to say.

Handling Uncertainty

If we are *uncertain* about something that we want to say, but do not wish to leave it unsaid altogether, we can mark uncertainty at the level of any property, as metadata. The OCHRE interface captures the uncertainty option using a check box. The highly

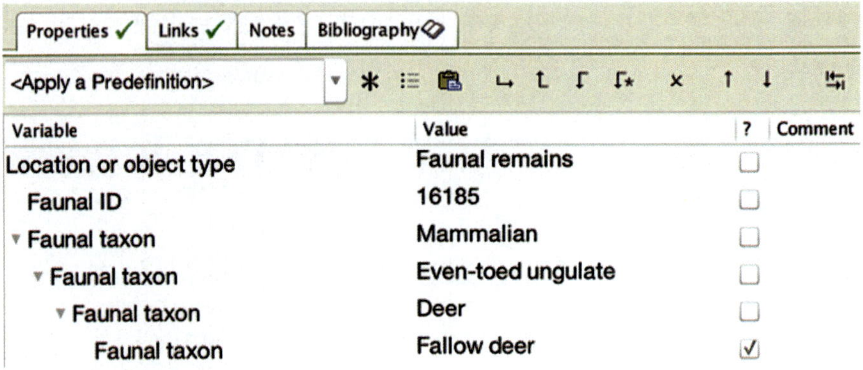

Fig. 5.11 This item is probably a Fallow deer, but uncertainty is noted as metadata

atomized approach to descriptive properties also allows a Comment to be noted at the level of a property. In this way, a user can be precise about what is uncertain and can use targeted annotations for clarification (Fig. 5.11).

Handling Multiplicity

A different issue is raised when we have *multiple* things to say about a bone. In a relational model, the database schema must be configured to allow for multiple attestations of the same metadata field for any given record. While this is not impossible, it becomes cumbersome to update the data schema each time another instance of a property is needed. This is no problem for an item-based approach. If a Tibia has both its Distal shaft and Distal end preserved, we list the Skeletal element portion property twice, once for each value. Furthermore, the hierarchically organized taxonomy allows the nesting of other relevant metrics within each value, noting the Percentage preserved of each portion. This clear, untangled approach is possible when items are freed from the constraints of the rigid table structure.

Handling Contextuality

Metrics can be subsumed within their relevant contexts (e.g., the "Smallest breadth of the shaft of the ilium" nested within the Skeletal element Ilium), but some projects like to list them all together, collecting the full set of measures as a flat list for easy access analytically. This strategy also lets the user survey the range of options while considering a bone and determining which measures might be relevant.

Handling Variability

While there are almost 100 properties related to faunal measurements already in OCHRE, only a handful would apply to any given bone. In contrast to a highly sparse tabular format that would result if each metric were to be represented by a table column, the item-based approach is a compact and readable format where each item captures only its relevant properties. Each specimen can be uniquely described within a unifying framework that imposes order without rigidity and that is compact yet comprehensive. An unremarkable skull fragment of an unknown type of medium-sized mammal will have a minimal set of properties, as will a nondescript vertebra of a fish. A tooth of a bear, a turtle's shell, an elephant's tusk reworked as a tool, the astragalus of a sheep/goat polished by use, a cowrie shell reused as a bead—an endless assortment of samples can be itemized and described to whatever extent is possible in a systematic way. Supporting notes, and illustrative photographs, can be attached to any item, providing a more complete picture.

Along both the biological and anatomical branches, the flexibility afforded by a hierarchical taxonomy allows the specialist to identify what is known, without overspecifying—no more, no less—by tagging an item with descriptive values at the appropriate level of the hierarchy. At the more general end of the spectrum, "mammal shaft fragment" might be all that can be said, but sometimes enough information is preserved so that the identification can be more specific, for example, "the proximal end of the tibia of a fallow deer." This degree of flexibility is invaluable when working with highly disparate and highly fragmentary data (Fig. 5.12).

When dinosaur bones from all over the world were added to the OCHRE repertoire by the Sereno Research Lab of the University of Chicago, it was only a matter of adding the *Dinosauria* branch of the biological taxonomy (Faunal taxon), and a few additional Skeletal elements (e.g., "Scute," to identify the bony plate of a stegosaurus). It was interesting to observe how the same anatomical taxonomic data structure could apply to dinosaur fossil and human bone analysis just as well as it supported the description of other animal bones. Humans, like sheep and dinosaurs, have Carpals, Tibias, a Pelvis, a Skull, Vertebrae, and Teeth. But analysts of human bones—where samples often come from burials as full, partial, or commingled skeletons rather than from refuse pits where ancient diners discarded their fish bones after dinner—seem to have a completely different system of describing and recording their material. As a result, OCHRE's Variables and Values are typically borrowed and customized in idiosyncratic configurations, rather than adopted, allowing each researcher to implement their own preferred system of analysis. OCHRE is enabling, not enforcing.

Reclassification

There are many other kinds of classifications of bones that might be useful, depending on the research questions. What are the percentages of carnivores, herbivores, and omnivores? Where do we find domesticated animals? What proportion of

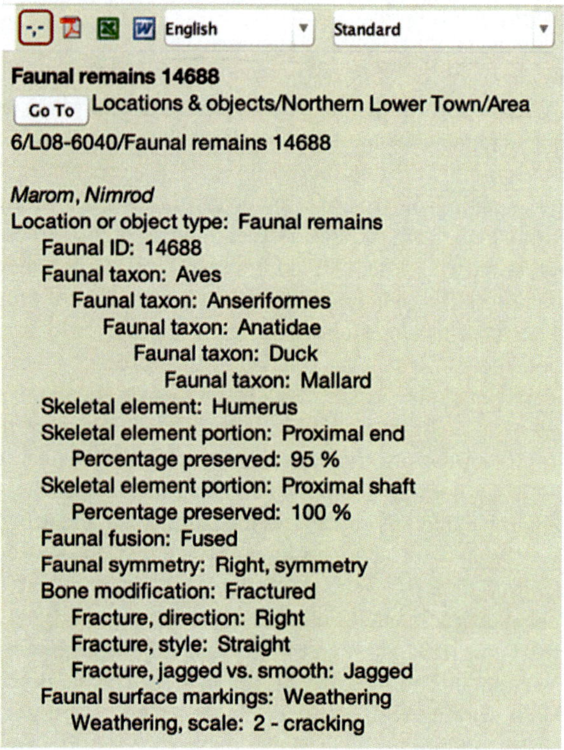

Fig. 5.12 Of more than 18,000 faunal specimens collected over 15 years of excavation at Zincirli, there is only a single example of a duck bone—a fractured humerus, described uniquely

astragali are from large artiodactyls versus small ones? We think of these as *secondary* classifications, rather than primary ones, since we would not likely classify an animal as Wild without first knowing that it is an Elephant, but that is beside the point—the real point being that having a hierarchical taxonomy makes it almost trivial to *reclassify* those same items in other meaningful configurations. This will happen in any domain of knowledge, like the botanical world where grains might be classified as crops or weeds, or in the literary world where texts might be classified by genre, as legal, ritual, or economic. Having the ability to use polyhierarchies, that is, multiple, overlapping hierarchies, where any given item (in this case, a property value) is permitted to have more than one parent context, gives the ultimate freedom to classify and reclassify at will, without changing any of the core data.

Practically speaking, reclassification of Property Values entails these steps: adding a new branch to the taxonomy (here, *Faunal analysis, domestic* vs. *wild*); adding the classes to be tracked (here, *Domestic* and *Wild*); borrowing the existing Values from the appropriate classes … *Aurochs*, *Bat*, *Bear*, *Beaver*, as *Wild*, and so on. These terminal Values will be a flat list because no further branching is needed to capture the distinction being recorded in this context. Each reclassification can be its own branch of the hierarchy, reusing the same pool of Values, thereby avoiding the creation of a muddle of cross-cutting links, and preventing redundancy (Fig. 5.13).

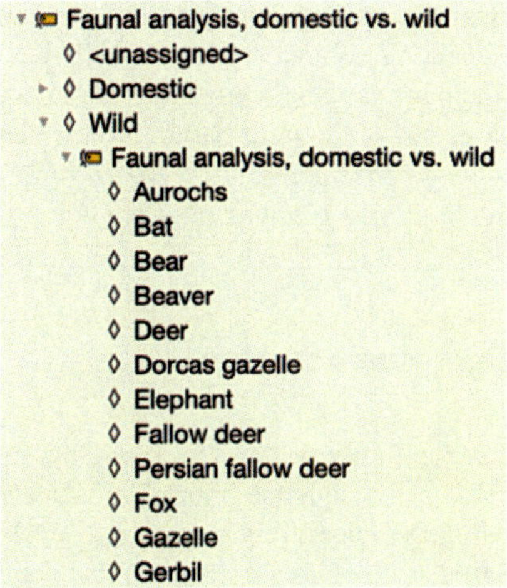

Fig. 5.13 Animals are easily re-classified using an item-based, hierarchical organization

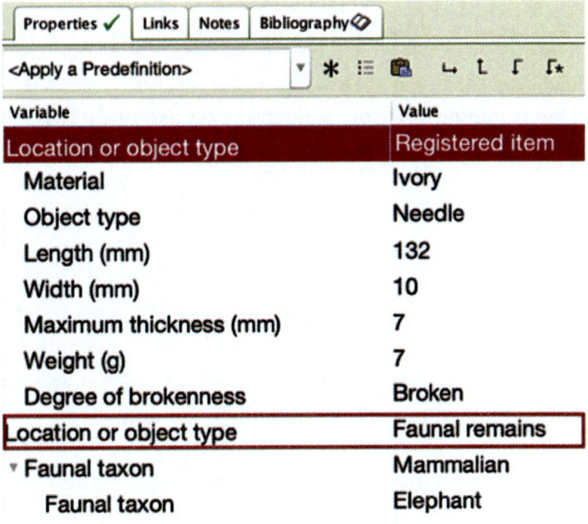

Fig. 5.14 Worked bones are classified as *both* Faunal remains and Registered items

Keep in mind that none of the underlying primary data needs to change. An ivory tool, by virtue of having been identified as Elephant ivory, is also classified, by logical consequence, as coming from a *Large*, *Wild*, and *Herbivore* animal (Brachman and Levesque 2004, p. 25). If, in the context of the relevant research, elephants are considered to be domesticated, the *Elephant* value is reclassified in the secondary branch (simply drag-drop) before the analysis is done. The Web of knowledge expands and adapts without needing to adjust the core data.

On the same theme, but with a slight difference, having access to multiple, overlapping hierarchies is useful even when the hierarchies hardly overlap, in effect allowing an item to be assigned to *multiple* classes. In Fig. 5.14, an ivory needle is classified as *both* a Registered item and as Faunal remains, simply by applying the Location or object type property twice. This item will match on queries looking for Elephant remains while still being managed as a Registered item in the usual way. Once again, the item-based, hierarchically organized system of properties is shown to be a convenient, unforced, uncomplicated mechanism to represent multiple distinctions with clarity and efficiency.

Data Entry Strategies

The flexibility of the item-based approach has implications for the data entry process. A consequence of breaking data free from the rigid structure of a table, and of building in flexibility on multiple levels, is the loss of the traditional, familiar table-based style of data entry with its explicit and reassuring configuration of rows and columns. Initially, the myriad of options permitted by extensively branching hierarchically linked descriptors can be overwhelming. OCHRE addresses this practical issue by providing a variety of input mechanisms to aid and simplify the data entry of highly variable data. Having watched assorted users make peace with this process, we offer the following strategies for describing items that are either highly regular and compatible descriptively, or highly fragmentary and disparate as a collection, or both.

Pool of Predefinitions

Any collection of **Properties** can be saved as an OCHRE **Predefinition,** which then serves as a template for data entry. This prefabricated set of descriptors can be applied to new items, over and over, with just a few keystrokes. As users work with their data and get a sense of what the commonly encountered items will need as properties, predefinitions can be defined to cover these—a sheep/goat astragalus, a mammal shaft fragment, or a tooth. Predefinitions can be created using any valid combination of properties and can be applied to any type of item: common ware pottery fragments; coins; excavated walls; and first-person singular verbs.

Predefinitions are prescriptive. They collect a potentially long list of properties in a single template and are useful in standardizing the implementation of a project's metadata. What constitutes appropriate tagging of a Coin? A project administrator simply creates a collection of properties that represent the preferred descriptive qualities and saves it as a Predefinition. Data entry personnel then apply the Coin Predefinition and customize the values of the predefined properties, as needed, for any given instance.

Predefinitions are also suggestive. We watched as one faunal specialist started by applying to the Properties sheet of each bone item a full-featured predefinition where the values were all <unassigned>. As she studied each bone or fragment, the predefinition would remind her which features to consider. "Hmmm, does it have the distinguishing characteristic of the sub species?" "Is the distal end fused?" "Are there any butchery marks?" "What is the greatest length?" By systematically considering each descriptive option and filling in the blanks, upon clicking **Save** the item was richly described to the fullest extent possible. While this may seem time-consuming, it was time well invested and resulted in a clean and clear data set ready to take into the next stage of analysis.

Having a pool of predefinitions to kick-start data entry is not just a consolation for the lack of a tabular format. Effective use of a carefully considered collection of templates can speed up data entry since a full set of properties can be applied quickly, then tweaked if necessary. Additional shortcuts are built into the OCHRE app, like copy-paste of properties, and a "ditto" feature, which repeats the previous action, to facilitate data entry.

Concession to Tables

Still, there is no arguing that a well-organized tabular format is a streamlined and efficient way to capture data. OCHRE can display data in a **Tabular View** without compromising the item-based data model. For any given **Set** of items, OCHRE can create a table with one item per row and make it available to qualified users for editing. The table will have a fixed structure, which, by definition, may well be sparse and will necessarily nullify some of the flexibility of the item-based approach. OCHRE compensates for this, however, by allowing the user to double-click on any row of the table to pop up the item represented by that row along with its Properties sheet. New properties not included in the table format, or multiple instances of a property, or multiple Notes, and so on, can be applied in this item view. When the pop-up window is closed, the table cells are updated, but any data not exposed by the table format remain intact.

Having conceded that a tabular option can be a helpful aid to data entry, a Predefinition is used to define which properties the table columns should represent, and the user is allowed to select from a range of **Format Specifications** on the Set, for example, whether to include built-in fields like the Description. Furthermore, and importantly, the table retains taxonomic awareness of the constraints made explicit by the taxonomic hierarchy. This lets OCHRE ensure that only valid values are entered into any cell, thereby maintaining data integrity. Keyboard shortcuts, and the use of default values built into the controlling predefinition, add value to these data entry options (Fig. 5.15).

Since a tabular format is effective for collections of items that are similar, OCHRE lets a project opt-in to the use of tables, by default, for items that share a common **Property value**; for example, *Faunal remains*, *Pottery*, or *Chipped stone*. Tabular views are generated selectively for these specified items and are integrated fully within the hierarchical framework, ensuring that the items remain properly contextualized.

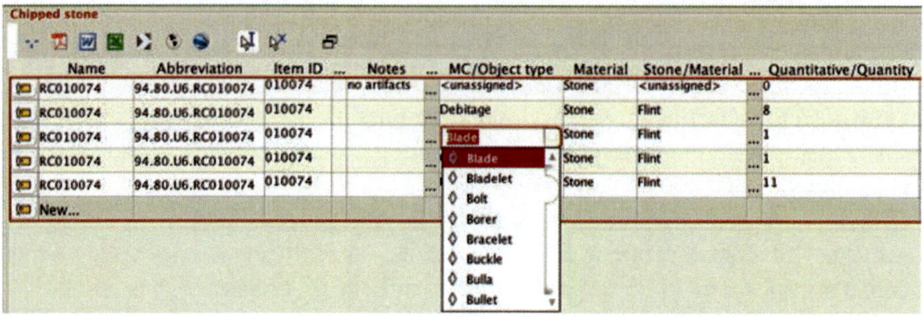

Fig. 5.15 A taxonomically aware Tabular View provides an alternate data entry option

Importing from Tables

Many projects already have extensive data in tabular formats, either in simple spreadsheets (like Microsoft Excel) or in relational database systems (like Microsoft Access or FileMaker). The OCHRE Data Service has developed sophisticated tools to import such data *en masse* to ease the transition to an item-based model such as OCHREs, and its staff are available to consult on this process. Yet, it seems worthwhile to work through an example to illustrate the process of moving from a table-based organization to thinking about data as items. That is, how do we make the leap from tables to items? This process will also reinforce the need for clean and consistent data to feed the import process. The source data for this exercise is "a Microsoft Excel file of 31,143 faunal remains from the 1972–1978 seasons" of the site Chogha Mish in Southwestern Iran, made available as a companion file to the Oriental Institute Publication volume.[20] Let us be clear that this is not a critique of this specific data set. Our critique is of the table model itself. Rather, we use this file as a good example of well-organized, clean data. It is typical of (or better than!) the kind of data we see on a regular basis, and which will seem familiar to our readers, in format and spirit if not in content (Fig. 5.16).

As an initial observation allow us to point out how sparse this data is. At first glance, there do not appear to be many empty cells, but this is because the term "Not applicable" was used in the cases where the cell would otherwise be empty. In addition, the null or negative case—Indeterminate, Unburnt, Not diseased, Unmodified, Not marked, etc.—was noted explicitly, masking the true sparseness of the data.[21] If

[20] https://isac.uchicago.edu/sites/oi.uchicago.edu/files/uploads/shared/docs/oip130.xls; see also *Lessons in Data Reuse: A Blind Analysis of Faunal Data from Iran* for more information about this data set and some examples of its re-use (http://visiblepast.net/see/antiquity/lessons-in-data-reuse-a-blind-analysis-of-faunal-data-from-iran/).

[21] In OCHRE, we would not normally be explicit regarding the absence of a feature, tagging only those properties that *do* apply to an item, and ignoring those that are not relevant. This gives a concise and uncluttered description of an item. We appreciate, however, that this might be different from "we checked but could not tell," so the use of an explicit property like *Indeterminate* might be valuable information, not just the null case.

L	M	N	O	P	Q	R	S	T	U	V	W	X	Y	Z
Identification	**Element**	**Symmetry**	**Condition**	**ProximalDista**	**LateralMedial**	**AnteriorPosterior**	**DorsalVentral**	**Fusion**	**Burning**	**Disease**	**Modification**	**Butchered**	**Domesticated**	**ToothType**
Sheep-Goat	Tibial tarsal (Astragalu	Left (sinster)	Complete (wit	Complete (wit	Complete	Complete		Fused	Burnt (bla					
Gazelle	Horn core (Antler)		Portion of		Complete	Complete	Ventral (centrur						Wild	
Sus scrota	Maxilla with teeth	Left (sinster)	Portion of		Complete	Middle portion	Complete						Wild	
Sus scrota	Tooth (Isolated)	Right (dexter)	Portion of		Complete	Complete	Dorsal (arch) (cr						Wild	Permanent
Bos	Mandible with teeth	Left (sinster)	Portion of		Complete	Middle portion	Dorsal (arch) (cr							
Medium Mammal			Fragment of	Shaft (body)										
Medium Mammal			Fragment of	Shaft (body)										
Sheep-Goat	Humerus	Right (dexter)	Portion of	Distal end (Ar	Complete	Complete		Fused	Partially al					
Medium Mammal			Fragment of	Shaft (body)										
Medium Mammal	Rib		Fragment of		Complete	Complete	Middle portion							
Sheep-Goat-Gazell	Maxilla with teeth	Left (sinster)	Fragment of		Lateral (buccal)	Middle portion	Ventral (centrur							
Sheep-Goat-Gazell	Tooth in association	Left (sinster)	Complete (wit		Complete	Complete	Complete							Permanent
Sheep-Goat-Gazell	Tooth (Isolated)	Left (sinster)	Portion of		Complete	Anterior (mesial)	Complete							Permanent
Sheep-Goat-Gazell	Tooth (Isolated)		Fragment of		Lateral (buccal)	Middle portion	Middle portion							Permanent
Medium Mammal			Fragment of	Shaft (body)										
Medium Mammal			Fragment of	Shaft (body)										
Medium Mammal			Fragment of											
Medium Mammal			Complete shaf	Shaft (body)	Complete	Complete		Foetal or						
Medium Mammal			Fragment of											
Medium Mammal			Fragment of											
Sheep-Goat	Ulna	Left (sinster)	Epiphysis only	Proximal artic	Complete	Complete		Unfused						
Medium Mammal	Rib		Fragment of			Complete	Middle portion							
Rodent	Femur	Left (sinster)	Complete shaf	Shaft (body)	Complete	Complete		Unfused						
Sheep-Goat-Gazell	Mandible with teeth	Left (sinster)	Portion of		Complete	Middle portion	Complete							
Sheep-Goat-Gazell	Tooth in association	Left (sinster)	Complete (wit		Complete	Complete	Complete							Permanent
Sheep-Goat-Gazell	Tooth in association	Left (sinster)	Complete (wit		Complete	Complete	Complete							Permanent
Sheep-Goat-Gazell	Tooth in association	Left (sinster)	Fragment of		Complete	Anterior (mesial)	Ventral (centrur							
Bos	Mandible without tee	Right (dexter)	Fragment of		Complete	Posterior (posterio	Dorsal (arch) (cr							

Fig. 5.16 An impressionistic view of this table of faunal data illustrates its sparseness

L	M	N	O	P
Identification	**Element**	**Symmetry**	**Condition**	**ProximalDistal**
Sheep-Goat	Tibial tarsal (Astragalus)	Left (sinster)	Complete (with	Complete (with
Gazelle	Horn core (Antler)		Portion of	
Sus scrota	Maxilla with teeth	Left (sinster)	Portion of	
Sus scrota	Tooth (Isolated)	Right (dexter)	Portion of	
Bos	Mandible with teeth	Left (sinster)	Portion of	
Medium Mammal			Fragment of	Shaft (body)
Medium Mammal			Fragment of	Shaft (body)
Sheep-Goat	Humerus	Right (dexter)	Portion of	Distal end (Art.
Medium Mammal			Fragment of	Shaft (body)
Medium Mammal	Rib		Fragment of	
Sheep-Goat-Gazelle	Maxilla with teeth	Left (sinster)	Fragment of	
Sheep-Goat-Gazelle	Tooth in association	Left (sinster)	Complete (with	
Sheep-Goat-Gazelle	Tooth (Isolated)	Left (sinster)	Portion of	
Sheep-Goat-Gazelle	Tooth (Isolated)		Fragment of	

Fig. 5.17 Features of interest are reflected in the column headings of a table; these are converted to OCHRE Variables

we assume the null case, and take *Not applicable* and *Indeterminate* for granted, we see the sparseness of the data set.

Atomize

The first step in this process is to *atomize* by asking *what are the items?* What are the things being observed and described? Bones, for starters, one specimen per row, identified by taxon (*Identification*) and skeletal *Element*; also, evaluated based on other features such as *Symmetry*, *Condition*, etc. (from column L on) (Fig. 5.17).

A	B	D	E	F	G	H	I	J
ModernName	**PlaceID**	**Area**	**Unit**	**Locus**	**Locus2**	**Context**	**TopElev**	**Bottom**
Chogha Mish	KS0001.EI0.00						0.00	0.00
Chogha Mish	KS0001.EI0.01-0.30	Trench V				Vic. of Protolit. Pits and Wall	0.30	0.01
Chogha Mish	KS0001.LcG26-27.EI80.25	Trench X	G26-27		Middle	Vicinity of BRB Deposit	80.25	80.25
Chogha Mish	KS0001.LcG26-27.EI80.25	Trench X	G26-27		Middle	Vicinity of BRB Deposit	80.25	80.25
Chogha Mish	KS0001.LcG26-27.EI80.25	Trench X	G26-27		Middle	Vicinity of BRB Deposit	80.25	80.25
Chogha Mish	KS0001.LcG27.701.EI81.26	Trench XXXVI	G27	701	E part of	Inside Kiln+Kiln+Kiln Area	0.00	81.26
Chogha Mish	KS0001.LcG27.701.EI81.26	Trench XXXVI	G27	701	E part of	Inside Kiln+Kiln+Kiln Area	0.00	81.26
Chogha Mish	KS0001.LcG27.701.EI81.62	Trench XXXVI	G27	701		Inside Kiln+Kiln+Kiln Area	0.00	81.62
Chogha Mish	KS0001.LcG27.701.EI81.62	Trench XXXVI	G27	701		Inside Kiln+Kiln+Kiln Area	0.00	81.62
Chogha Mish	KS0001.LcG27.701.EI81.62	Trench XXXVI	G27	701		Inside Kiln+Kiln+Kiln Area	0.00	81.62
Chogha Mish	KS0001.LcG27.701.EI81.71	Trench XXXVI	G27	701	E part of	Occupational Debris	0.00	81.71
Chogha Mish	KS0001.LcG27.701.EI81.71	Trench XXXVI	G27	701	E part of	Occupational Debris	0.00	81.71
Chogha Mish	KS0001.LcG27.701.EI81.71	Trench XXXVI	G27	701	E part of	Occupational Debris	0.00	81.71
Chogha Mish	KS0001.LcG27.701.EI81.71	Trench XXXVI	G27	701	E part of	Occupational Debris	0.00	81.71

Fig. 5.18 Along with bone data, this table contains details of the locus items (organized as hierarchical contexts)

Notice that there is also locus information (Fig. 5.18). The *Locus* column provides the immediate context of the bones, but there are several columns in all (F–J) that pertain to the *Locus* (shown in blue) instead of the bones, including its description (*Context*) and elevations. Because many bone items may be contained within any given locus, the *Locus* item (*701*) is repeated. Because the locus details are in the same table as the bone details, the locus details (*Inside Kiln…*) are *also* repeated. When this data is transformed from this table format into an item-based format, the data relevant to the bones will be applied to the bone items, while the data relevant to the loci will be applied to the Locus items.

Organize

Step two is to *organize*. Bones are intuitively contextualized within loci. Working back toward the left-most end of the spreadsheet we find that loci are subsumed within *Units*, which themselves are contained within *Areas*. Front-loaded into most tables are at least a few columns such as those that define the spatial context for the core items. Values of *PlaceID*, an apparent hash of the Area, Unit, Locus, and Elevation, will be captured by an idiosyncratic alphanumeric property, specific to just this project, and applied to the Locus item. This generates as **Locations & Objects** the following: a few levels of high-level excavation contexts (the pink columns of Fig. 5.18), which situate loci (the blue columns of Fig. 5.18) in which are found bones and teeth (the yellow columns, and others, of Fig. 5.17).

Propertize

Step three is to *propertize* by setting up a project taxonomy. Most of the descriptive properties are ones commonly used by faunal specialists and which would already exist in OCHRE. A few adopted and borrowed branches from the OCHRE master taxonomy provide a satisfying selection of descriptive options.

It is helpful to apply Excel's **Data > Filter** option to examine the values in each column. Undoubtedly, there will be data cleanup to do, eliminating conflated values, resolving abbreviations, confirming that we understand nuances of terminology, and ensuring that the set of values in each column resolves to match the controlled vocabulary defined by the taxonomy. It seems clear that picklists were used to do the data entry since there is good consistency throughout this table. Nevertheless, we would examine each column, resolving its values to a clean, consistent, minimum set of unique values that will become **Property values** in OCHRE.

We take time to make explicit the hierarchical relationships implicit in these sets of values, for make no mistake, hierarchies lurk beneath the supposedly flat lists of values provided. The *Identification* column lists genus values of Canis and Equus, which are further qualified to identify species. Nesting the species values within the genus values makes it much easier to find all horses, donkeys, and zebras by querying for a single term (Equus) while getting matches on all the subordinate values too (Fig. 5.19).

The *ToothClass* column, containing the values "Molar," "Premolar," and "Premolar or molar," is a good example of why we do not want to rely on string matching for querying. A search for "Molar" gives us more than we bargained for, picking up "Premolar" too, as well as the conflated combination of "Premolar or molar." Certainly, a database developer could devise a string-matching formula

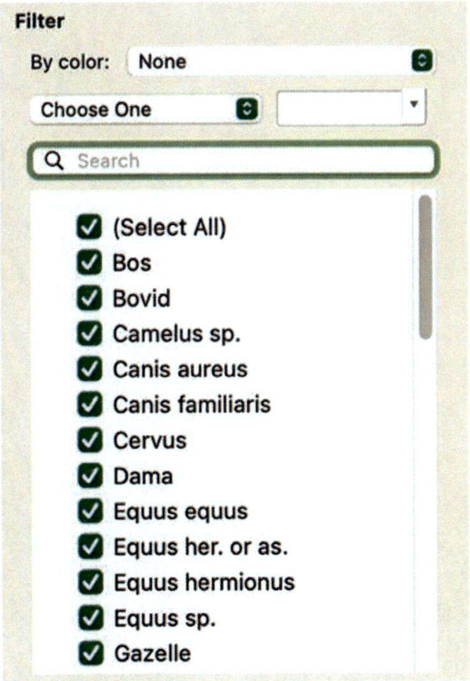

Fig. 5.19 When we use OCHRE to expose hierarchical structures, we do so because they are already there

using a regular expression sequence[22] or some other strategy, but this is precisely the type of manual effort that is not needed when using a controlled vocabulary. In OCHRE, the Molar Value is a unique database item for which we can unambiguously query to find only the teeth described as molars.

Next, notice the number of permutations and combinations needed to capture distal and proximal fusion in the *Fusion* column. Hierarchically organized properties can achieve this with just three values—Unfused, Fusing, and Fused—contextualized within the two values Proximal end and Distal end. The fusion properties in OCHRE also do double duty in other contexts like Pelvis and Skull (Fig. 5.20).

If it seemed that there would be a lot of cleanup needed, we would be tempted to run the data set through Open Refine[23] to resolve inconsistencies in spelling and abbreviations. Keep in mind, too, that not all data values need to be propertized, which reminds us to ask, *How far is far enough?* Researchers should ask themselves: Will I ever want to search or filter faunal items based on whether both their proximal and distal ends are unfused ("Proximal unfused/distal unfused")? If it would ever be useful to query for one of these properties, then the spreadsheet values should be split into discrete fields to be imported into OCHRE as separate properties. If not, then the data may be imported as either an alphanumeric property or a

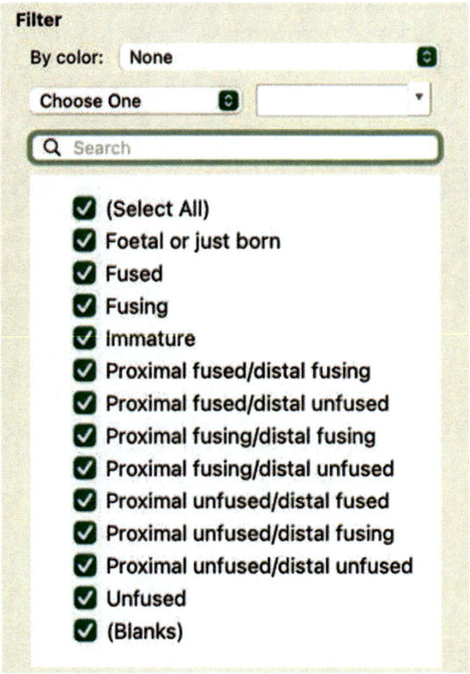

Fig. 5.20 Conflation of descriptive values runs amok

[22]Regular expression is a commonly used pattern-matching syntax for matching string text (see https://en.wikipedia.org/wiki/Regular_expression).

[23]OpenRefine is a useful tool to rationalize tabular data (see https://openrefine.org/).

labeled note. Searching an alphanumeric property or a string note in the OCHRE app is possible, even using regular expressions; however, more rigorous and accurate queries can be composed to match against values of nominal property variables. In any case, "the computer" does not decide how data should be modeled (e.g., based on which fields are pre-defined by the software); the scholar does.

Itemize

With a containment hierarchy in place, and a taxonomic hierarchy available for description, we are ready to create items using OCHRE's automated mechanisms. Each bone item is represented by a row in the spreadsheet, with everything needed to describe the item available in that row. Structurally, the **Locations & objects** hierarchy of items would look like the outline shown in Fig. 5.21.

Chogha Mish, Trench XXXVI, and G27 would be named items, minimally described by a property designating them as excavation areas (lacking any other information about them in this file). Locus 701 would be a named item described with properties:

- Locus type = Occupational debris
- Bottom elevation = 82.19 m

As we peruse additional records in the file, we notice that Locus 701 has been subdivided into the "E part of" and its north, south, and west parts. This is no problem, but it becomes a narrower, more specific, context for the faunal specimen represented by an extra level of nesting in the contextual hierarchy. Some specimens will have specific contexts, others not. The flexibility of OCHRE's hierarchical structure can accommodate this easily and naturally.

As for the bone and teeth items, what do we name these? It does not really matter, especially if it did not matter to the original excavators to identify and label them uniquely. OCHRE will give them a unique identifier (UUID), but in order to have a

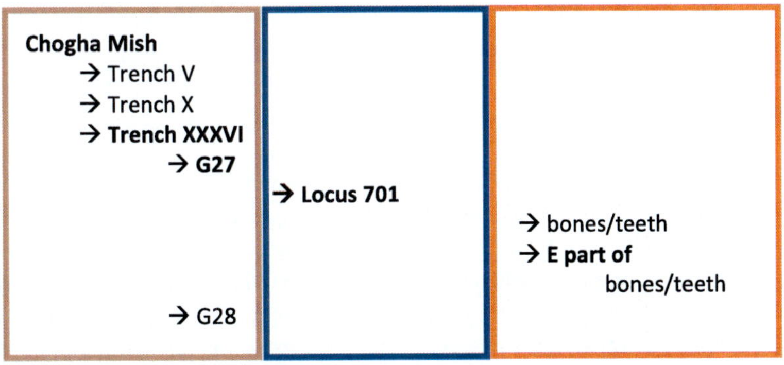

Fig. 5.21 Spreadsheet column values are mapped to properties on either the appropriate high-level context items or the detailed faunal items

more readable name we might give each item a generic name such as "Bone" or "Faunal remains." If having thousands of items all named the same does not appeal to the researcher, an arbitrary name could be assigned based on, say, the record number in the file ("Faunal remains 1," etc.). Within Locus 701, then, we would find, among others:

Locus 701

- ➔ E part of
  - ➔ Faunal remains 18
  - ➔ Faunal remains 19
  - ➔ Faunal remains …
- ➔ **Faunal remains 20**
- ➔ Faunal remains 21
- ➔ Faunal remains

Faunal remains 20 would be described with properties such as:

- Faunal taxon = Medium mammal
- Skeletal element portion = Shaft
- Condition = Fragment

With over 30,000 items to import, we reach out to the OCHRE Data Service, which runs the data set through its error-checking tools. Matching the input file against the project's new taxonomy, OCHRE will find any remaining inconsistencies. OCHRE requires exact matches against values in the Taxonomy and so there will, no doubt, be further rounds of cleanup and adjustments needed. There will be decisions to make, fuzziness to clarify, and consideration of ways to do things better given a new start. In the end, there will be 31,143 bone/teeth items, contextualized within a couple of dozen excavation units, which together contain fewer than 100 separate loci. Each bone or tooth will have been uniquely identified and a large percentage of them will be uniquely described, but all within a comprehensive and structured framework that leaves them exquisitely organized.

Conclusion

When the item-based approach is combined with hierarchical structure to create a custom-controlled vocabulary, a **Taxonomy**, we transcend the restrictions of any single metadata schema. OCHRE allows for the implementation of multiple, overlapping metadata schemas, either directly as expressed as a Taxonomy or mapped for export from OCHRE to any number of new structures. When research data is described uniquely on an item-by-item basis, we escape the limitations of the tabular approach.

An OCHRE Taxonomy is a work of scholarship that can be attributed to a scholar or team of scholars. The structure and terms are entirely customizable but can be based in part on other existing project taxonomies. The Taxonomy defines what can be said about any given item in the database. As such, the planning and creation of the project taxonomy is an important part of the project startup stage, and it is good practice to take time upfront to consider carefully how best to describe one's project data and build an appropriate framework. Keep in mind that the Taxonomy, itself, is a database item composed of Variables and Values, so that its structure can be tweaked and adjusted even after the project is well underway.

When the item-based approach to properties is combined with the item-based approach to other project data, the result is an infinitely flexible system for recording and describing research data. When thinking about the complex and nuanced topics that characterize research in the humanities and social sciences, software should not place limitations on what the researcher may ask. The researcher must be allowed to make and record any meaningful observation or statement about the data. The database must not only capture these observations, it must do so in a way that is efficient, flexible, and customizable.

Chapter 6
An Item-Based Approach: Rationalize

Database Design Mirrored in Software Design

The data management strategies implemented by the OCHRE database platform were motivated, in part, by software engineering principles, and there are many parallels between the data structures built into OCHRE and the structures and techniques commonly used by software developers, resulting in a happy confluence of theory and practice. For our readers interested in a glimpse behind the scenes, we present the rationale behind OCHRE's data model and offer some reflections on the interplay between the process and the product; that is, the process of OCHRE development itself and the products that result from OCHRE data management. To appreciate what puts OCHRE in good company computationally, solidly in the mainstream while standing apart from the crowd, stick with us as we examine these principles and practices that guide and inspire our non-tabular database design.

The Object-Oriented Approach

OCHRE was developed in Java, which is an object-oriented programming (OOP) language.[1] From a software perspective, an object-oriented approach is one based on the use of software objects—programmed entities that have a defined *state* and a list of possible *behaviors*. As explained in the Oracle Java tutorial[2]:

> An object stores its state in *fields* (variables in some programming languages) and exposes its behavior through *methods* (functions in some programming languages). Methods oper-

[1] Other popular modern programming languages like C++ and Python are based on the object-oriented programming paradigm.

[2] https://docs.oracle.com/javase/tutorial/java/concepts/object.html.

S. R. Schloen, M. C. Prosser, *Database Computing for Scholarly Research*, Quantitative Methods in the Humanities and Social Sciences,
https://doi.org/10.1007/978-3-031-46696-0_6

ate on an object's internal state and serve as the primary mechanism for object-to-object communication. Hiding internal state and requiring all interaction to be performed through an object's methods is known as *data encapsulation*—a fundamental principle of object-oriented programming.

Dr. Alan Kay, the computer scientist widely regarded as the father of object-oriented programming, was inspired by his training in biology which led him to reflect on "both cell metabolism and larger-scale morphogenesis with its notions of simple mechanisms controlling complex processes and one kind of building block able to differentiate into all needed building blocks."[3] Kay arrived at the notion that "everything is an object," essentially self-sufficient, and with the means to interact with other objects. This was thinking outside the box in a time of linear and procedural "structured programming."[4] One of the first object-oriented programming languages, Smalltalk, was designed by Kay based on the "insight that everything we can describe can be represented by the recursive composition of a single kind of behavioral building block that hides its combination of state and process inside itself and can be dealt with only through the exchange of messages" (ibid.).

The item-based OCHRE system is essentially object-oriented, where everything (every *thing*) is an item (object)—a hierarchy, location, person, concept, dictionary lemma, text, or even a taxonomic variable or value. Like stem cells and "behavioral building blocks," OCHRE items start off generic but differentiate into whatever is needed to describe research data. Items with properties, links, notes, and events—self-contained to varying degrees of complexity, self-describing to varying degrees of differentiation, recursively organized to manage complexity—interact in predictable ways with other items. An OCHRE Resource item, for example, will have "fields" which include a file name or URI, "methods" which include the ability to display itself on a View, and will be linked in expected (or unexpected) ways to illustrate other items.

This is not to suggest that the use of object-oriented programming necessitates an item-based approach, nor the converse, that an item-based approach requires the use of object-oriented programming. Object-oriented programming strategies can be used to implement any number of data structures. But an object-oriented paradigm is well suited to modeling and implementing OCHRE's item-based approach, so much so that object-oriented software engineering principles have inspired and guided OCHRE's overall design and development.

---

[3] Kay (1993).

[4] The OOP model contrasts with traditional "structured programming" (e.g., languages like C, Fortran, Pascal, and PL/1) where imperative statements determine logical control flow; see *An Introduction to Structured Programming* (https://link.springer.com/article/10.3758/BF03205654). Structured programming, itself, was in reaction to "spaghetti code" (yes, what you would imagine), where the "goto" statement is used freely; see https://www.geeksforgeeks.org/spaghetti-code. OOP also contrasts with "functional programming" (e.g., languages like LISP), a style in which computation is broken down into single-purpose functions that act on the data; see https://github.com/readme/guides/functional-programming-basics.

Encapsulation

One of the core tenets of object-oriented programming is that of *encapsulation*. This is the bundling together of state and behavior, fields and methods, into a software object.[5] Encapsulation can have the helpful side effect of hiding the inner workings of the object from outside processes. Inspired by this principle, OCHRE goes to some trouble, where it is helpful, to encapsulate data components within a single item, both to mask its complexity from the user, making it seem simpler than it really is, and additionally to hide detailed parts of the item from the user in order to protect its integrity.

Take, for example, image files in the Polynomial Texture Map (PTM) format.[6] The Persepolis Fortification Archive project has produced tens of thousands of PTM images of the seals and inscriptions on the clay tablets in this archive, amounting to over 100 terabytes of image data. Each PTM object is packaged within a single Resource item in OCHRE, having the usual fields that include a Name, Description, and File URI.[7] But behind this single item stands up to 32 separate digital images with different lighting angles, high-resolution TIF files created during the processing of the PTM, one high and one low-resolution PTM file, and a small JPEG thumbnail. This assemblage of files is encapsulated into a single OCHRE item. The user is mostly unaware of the complexity of the components behind the scenes, which need not be curated manually. The PTM Resource item is attributed to its Creator, described with camera metadata Properties, linked to the Text item that corresponds to its cuneiform inscription, and tracked by Events that list its processing history. Most importantly, it also knows how to display itself in a View (Fig. 6.1).

Inheritance

In object-oriented terms, objects are instances of a *class* of objects—the class being the "blueprint from which individual objects are created."[8] In much the same way, OCHRE items are instances of the categories within which they are instantiated. With instantiation comes *inheritance* as instances take on the properties and procedures of the classes from which they derive. And just as Kay's software building blocks recurse, creating hierarchies conducive to inheritance, so too do OCHRE's

---

[5] https://www.javaworld.com/article/2075271/core-java/encapsulation-is-not-information-hiding.html.

[6] The PTM format, also known as Reflectance Transformation Imaging (RTI) was developed at the Hewlett Packard Laboratory and published by Tom Malzbender, Dan Gelb, and Hans Wolters in November 2001.

[7] See "Fort.0117-002Reverse2,ptm" at https://pi.lib.uchicago.edu/1001/org/ochre/624d183a-08c2-4649-99b1-588581ea9d86.

[8] https://docs.oracle.com/javase/tutorial /java/concepts/class.html.

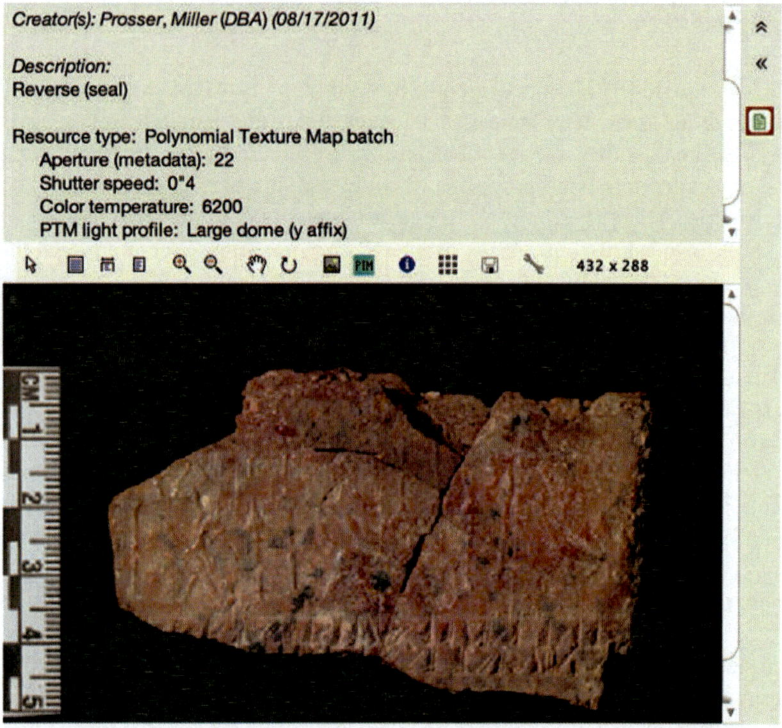

Fig. 6.1 Everything this image *is* and *does* is encapsulated within a single database item. (Photograph courtesy of the Persepolis Fortification Archive project)

items recurse, creating meaningful relationships of inheritance and containment that make for efficient, nonredundant data structures.

Inserting a new photograph into a list of OCHRE Resources instantiates a new Resource item. The photograph item will have *fields* that correspond to camera metadata values (i.e., that describe its state) and *methods* that include its ability to be hotspotted. These are features that are true of all instances of OCHRE image Resources.

Traversing *up* the OCHRE class hierarchy, the photograph will inherit, from its Resource parent class, the field representing its file name or URI. We also learn that the Resource class is a subclass of the Geo-item class, instances of which have fields for spatial information and behaviors that include the ability to draw themselves on a map. A Geo-item, in turn, inherits from OCHRE's Item superclass which contains core information like Name and Description and which has basic functionality like the ability to insert itself into (or delete itself from) a hierarchy. All of this is possible by way of inheritance (Fig. 6.2).

Fig. 6.2 OCHRE items are organized as a hierarchy of classes

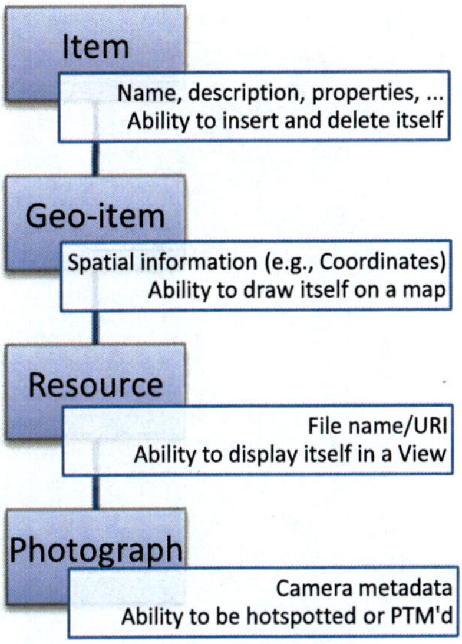

Polymorphism

We have seen already how the item-based approach of the *Lives, Individuality, and Analysis* project uses the Person item of "Charles Darwin" to reference him as the author of a book, in one context, the teacher of a student, in another, and the subject of correspondence in letters circulated among nineteenth-century scientists. *Polymorphism* represents the ability of an item to take different forms or roles in different instances. The behavior or characteristic exhibited by an item will vary, depending on whether it is performing a method inherited from its parent class or demonstrating more specialized behavior from its own (child) class.

Propagating *down* the OCHRE class hierarchy we note that it is highly economical to add new subclasses of items in the spirit of *extensibility* (to use the object-oriented term). If we add a new Resource type, say a shapefile or a PTM file, each type will be represented by a new class with new fields and methods specific to its requirements. For example, given its unique format, a PTM file will need its own special method, one that *overrides* its inherited method, to draw itself (Fig. 6.3). Otherwise, it will *already* have fields for its Name, Description, File URI, and spatial information and will *already* have the ability to be plotted on a map or inserted into (or deleted from) a hierarchy. Instances of subclasses receive the full range of properties and methods from inherited superclasses. Being able to "add or extend the functionality of any pre-existing package without re-writing the entire definition of the whole class again and again … [makes] it easy for the programmer" (Fig. 6.4).[9]

[9] https://www.geeksforgeeks.org/perl-polymorphism-in-oops/.

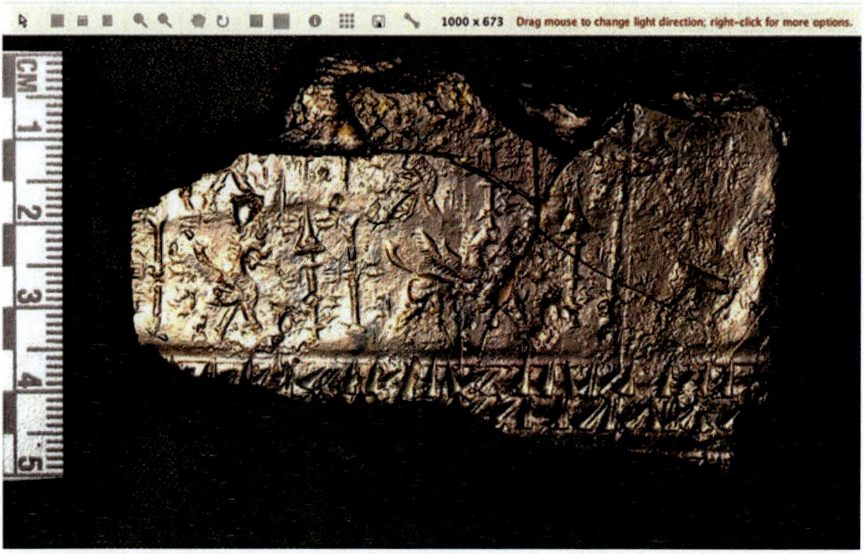

Fig. 6.3 Specular enhancement, a feature of a specialized PTM View, makes the seal impression pop. (Photograph courtesy of the Persepolis Fortification Archive project)

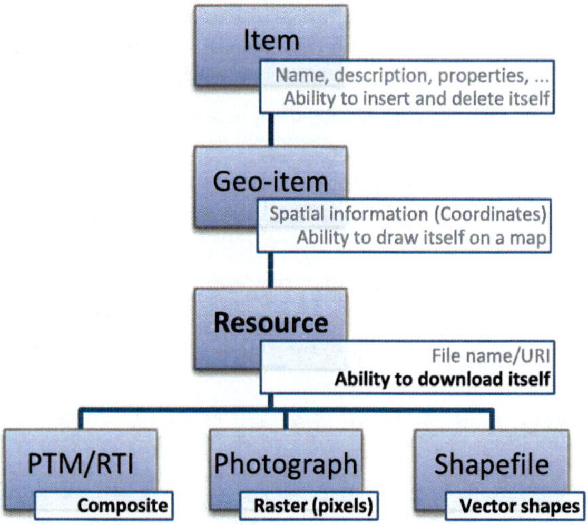

Fig. 6.4 Download functionality, added to a superclass, is accessible to all subclasses

Extensibility can apply at the higher branches of the hierarchy too. Imagine that we want to add a behavior to download a file from the cloud to a local computer. What type of file? A PTM file? A photograph? A shapefile? Well, … all of them. Rather than adding the method to each of the classes of the different file types, we simply add the method at the level of the Resource superclass and expose the

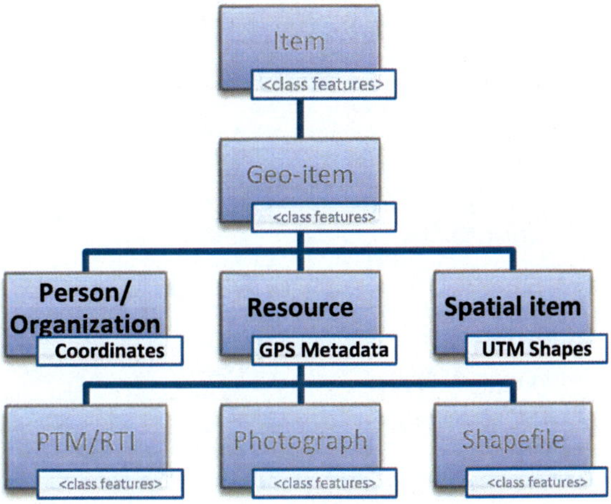

Fig. 6.5 Hierarchies provide the ultimate flexibility—branching can occur anywhere

behavior so that all the subclasses can take advantage of it. This extends the functionality of each subclass in an efficient, economical, and object-oriented way.

Figure 6.5 illustrates the subclassing of Geo-items: Resource items are often tagged with GPS data, and so they can be spatially situated; Organization items have fields to capture geographic location as latitude and longitude values; Spatial units are often situated in coordinate systems (e.g., UTM) and/or represented as shapes. Each Geo-item subclass will have fields for representing its type of spatial information and its own methods for drawing itself on a map. And so it goes, objects within objects, branching branches, fleas upon fleas, and turtles all the way down.

Reusability

We have already seen how OCHRE items are available for extensive reuse *within* a project and for extensive sharing *across* projects. But when everything is an item, and when all items are managed hierarchically, and when hierarchies are themselves items, and when subitems extend and inherit from common super-items, there is also tremendous scope for extensive reusability of the software components themselves. Reuse of the same, inherited item–management interface components, say the Properties sheet, can accommodate an artifact, a tooth, a pottery pail, an author, an image, a dictionary lemma, a noun, or indeed any *thing* (Fig. 6.6).

The same hierarchy management components can manage site excavation zones, the skeletal structure of a skull, a system of inventory, articles within journals within series, folders of photographs, the meanings and sub-meanings of a Hittite dictionary article, or the metrical structure of a Shakespearian play. Whether we are inserting a verb into a sentence or a coin into an excavation context, we do it the same way using the same multipurpose tools into the same kind of hierarchy, regardless of its branching structure or its item content (Fig. 6.7).

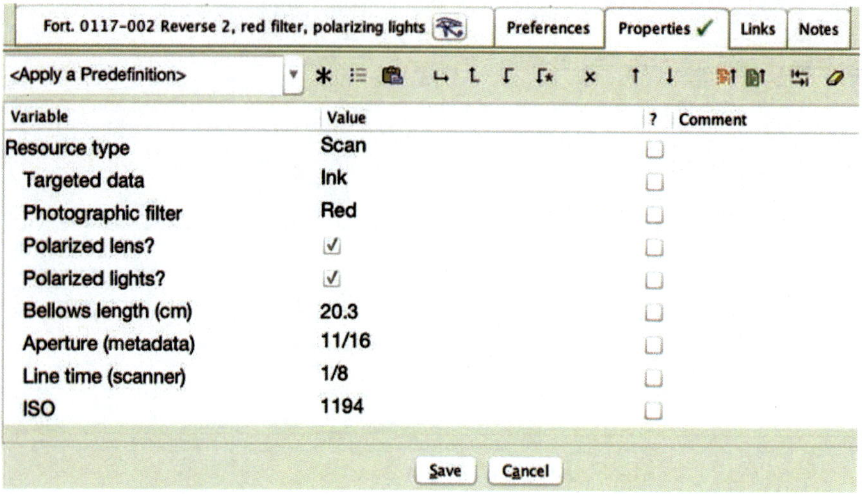

Fig. 6.6 A typical Properties sheet captures photographic details of an image Resource

Fig. 6.7 Core set of buttons on the toolbar manages structures for all kinds of items

Throughout the development process, OCHRE builds on the functionality of its underlying enterprise-scale database system, Tamino from Software AG, which in turn builds on Java functionality since "after all," the Tamino documentation declares, "object-oriented programming is about reuse."[10]

XML Justified

Tamino was originally chosen as the database for implementing the OCHRE design because it was based on XML and had a corresponding suite of tools for manipulating, querying, and transforming XML. Other industry standards based on XML—XQuery, XPath, and XSLT (eXtensible Stylesheet Language Transformations)—are specifically designed to work with hierarchically organized data. Having explained the OCHRE way, that of creating hierarchies of self-replicating items, it is easy to appreciate how the nesting of elements within elements, made possible by XML, is a natural fit for representing the OCHRE data model.

[10] http://documentation.softwareag.com/webmethods/tamino/ins97/print/advconc.pdf.

Normalization

XML is a structured, self-describing, human-readable format. But this can lead to redundancy and verbosity in XML documents as descriptive elements are used over and over, say, for example, every time we need to tag a "verb" in the text of Hamlet. When used as a core data format for OCHRE, it is less important that the XML be *human*-readable (since most of the processing is happening behind the scenes), and more important that it be efficiently modeled. Hence, we take inspiration from the relational database approach and apply the principle of *normalization*.

In proposing the structure of the "relational model and normal form," E. F. Codd of the IBM Research Laboratory borrowed from the field of formal logic to describe a new method for representing data, one that permitted independence from any specific implementation, and which formed a "sound basis for treating derivability, redundancy, and consistency of relations" (Codd 1970, p. 377). Without going into the mathematics behind a specific concept like the "3rd normal form," allow us to explain how we apply the principle of normalization in OCHRE.

Recall that every item in an OCHRE database is assigned a universally unique identifier (UUID), which serves as a rough equivalent to a "primary key" in the relational model.[11] Whenever OCHRE needs to tag an item as a verb, rather than using the human-readable form "Verb," OCHRE uses the primary key that represents the verb item instead, here "5976855b-fb44-c09e-8b05-2eee47b52d90." Subsequently, whenever such references to a verb are retrieved by queries or for display, a quick lookup of the verb item using the primary key allows OCHRE to substitute in the label "Verb."

```
<value uuid="5976855b-fb44-c09e-8b05-2eee47b52d90">
        <identification>
                 <label>Verb</label>
                 <abbreviation>v.</abbreviation>
        </identification>
</value>
```

In the spirit of reusability, this verb item can be used to tag all the verbs in Hamlet, the Iliad, the Epic of Gilgamesh, and Genesis, as the case may be. In the spirit of flexibility, say we wanted to rename this verb item to "Finite verb" or to translate it into the French "Verbe." We do this just once, updating the item's label. The change will propagate to all instances of its uses everywhere, instantly, because it is the same item in every instance.

Alternatively, a user might request a different View format or ask to see the View displayed in French. The lookup mechanism might return the <abbreviation> or the <alias> instead. While there will be a slight performance penalty paid for the

[11] A primary key is the unique identifier of a record in a table (ibid., p. 380). Of course, in OCHRE, items are not stored in tables.

additional lookup time, this is more than compensated for by the efficiency and flexibility of having content that is not hard-coded throughout the database.[12]

```
<value uuid="5976855b-fb44-c09e-8b05-2eee47b52d90">
        <identification>
                <label>Finite verb</label>
                <alias language="fre">Verbe</alias>
                <abbreviation>v.</abbreviation>
        </identification>
</value>
```

By applying normalization to the implementation of the item-based data model, we avoid data redundancy while maintaining *referential integrity*, that is, ensuring that a primary key is not deleted if it is being cross-referenced. OCHRE will deny a request to delete an item if there are *any* references to it from any items anywhere in the database, thus preventing broken links.

Any downside to the trade-off we have made by sacrificing human readability on the altar of efficiency is redeemed by having the option to publish or export any OCHRE data in a denormalized format using a process that substitutes back into the XML the human-readable labels in place of the computer-readable UUIDs. This transforms the XML into a document better suited to human consumption and appropriate for further manipulation and publication.

Recursion

In "*The faculty of language: what's special about it?*" cognitive psychologists Steven Pinker and Ray Jackendoff define recursion as "a procedure that calls itself, or ... a constituent that contains a constituent of the same kind," thereby defining recursion as both a *process* and a *structure* (Pinker and Jackendoff 2005, p. 203). What is special about XML? It supports recursion as both a process and a structure.

As we have seen, the extensive Chicago Hittite Dictionary (CHD) entry for the verb "to go" runs over 20 pages of dense text,[13] its headers leaving bread crumb trails such as **pai- A I d I' a' 2"**[14] for its readers' reference. But its inherent, deeply hierarchical, recursive structure is simple in OCHRE as we use XML to nest

---

[12] By way of comparison, Microsoft Excel uses a strategy similar in spirit. A table column "Part of speech" in which the word "Verb" was listed 800 times would represent the character string "Verb" only once, but would point to it from 800 instances. This is clearly seen in the XML structure of the .xslx format. The difference, however, is that Excel is a table-based format, not an item-based format. Changing "Verb" to "Verbe" will change only the affected table cell (instantiating a new character string), not every instance of it.

[13] CHD Volume P (Güterbock and Hoffner 1997, pp. 18–40).

[14] Ibid., p. 23.

<meaning> elements within <meaning> elements, creating branching branches, fleas upon fleas, and turtles all the way down. Part of the simplified XML structure of the entry "to go" is shown below:

```
<meaning meaningID="1.">
     <gloss>"to go"</gloss>
     <meaning meaningID="a.">
          <gloss>an overview of subjects</gloss>
          <meaning meaningID="1'">
               <gloss>gods and humans:</gloss>
               <citation>...</citation><citation>...</citation>
          </meaning>
          <meaning meaningID="2'">
               <gloss>animals:</gloss>
               <citation>...</citation><citation>...</citation>
          </meaning>
          <meaning meaningID="3'">
               <gloss>vehicles:</gloss>
               <citation>...</citation><citation>...</citation>
          </meaning>
          <meaning meaningID="4'">
               <gloss>concepts (abstracts)</gloss>
               <meaning meaningID="a'">
                    <gloss>evils:</gloss>
                    <citation>...</citation><citation>...</citation>
               </meaning>
               <meaning meaningID="b'">
                    <gloss>news (personified):</gloss>
                    <citation>...</citation><citation>...</citation>
               </meaning>
          </meaning>
          <meaning meaningID="5'">
               <gloss>(other)</gloss>
               <citation>...</citation><citation>...</citation>
          </meaning>
     </meaning>
</meaning>
```

Consistent use of the same recursive structure for each <meaning>, regardless of its depth in the hierarchy, has profound implications for the *process* of creating and using such data. The same behaviors for accessing, manipulating, and formatting the data can be used at all levels of the hierarchy, traversing only to the required depth or breadth, recursively calling themselves to be reapplied at the next level. To create new meanings in a dictionary entry, a new item (e.g., "1") is simply inserted, then inserted again for a subitem ("1.a"), then again for a sub-subitem (1.a.1'), and so on, as needed. The same process can apply recursively, indefinitely, and simply along both the depth and breadth dimensions.

Transformation

Originally conceived as a data exchange format among systems that did not have other practical means of sharing data, XML was designed to be easily composed or transformed into formats needed by collaborating applications. Because of this, OCHRE can readily reformat its core normalized data into other standards formats for export (e.g., as TEI-XML) or for display (e.g., as HTML).

XSLT, the native tool for transforming and formatting XML, is built to traverse hierarchically structured XML recursively, applying its styling templates to XML elements, at whatever level of the hierarchy they might be found. Calling an XSLT stylesheet to <apply-templates> only to the root-level <meaning> elements, without traversing any hierarchical depth, results in a display of a high-level summary (Fig. 6.8).

A second XSLT stylesheet might traverse the entire hierarchy of the same XML document, along both its depth and its breadth, but suppressing all the <citation> detail while exposing only the <meaning> and <gloss> elements. The resulting display is a simplified outline of the dictionary entry (Fig. 6.9).

Yet another, third, XSLT stylesheet might act against the same XML document, but this time formatting all elements at all levels of detail throughout the hierarchy. The result is the full dictionary entry, displayed in a format that mimics in its entirety the printed version (Fig. 6.10).

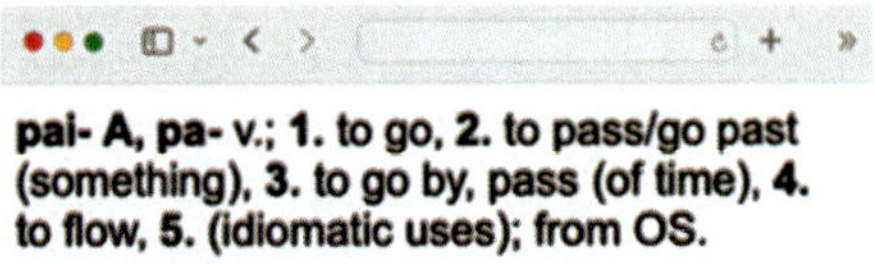

Fig. 6.8 A concise lemma view is created using XSLT

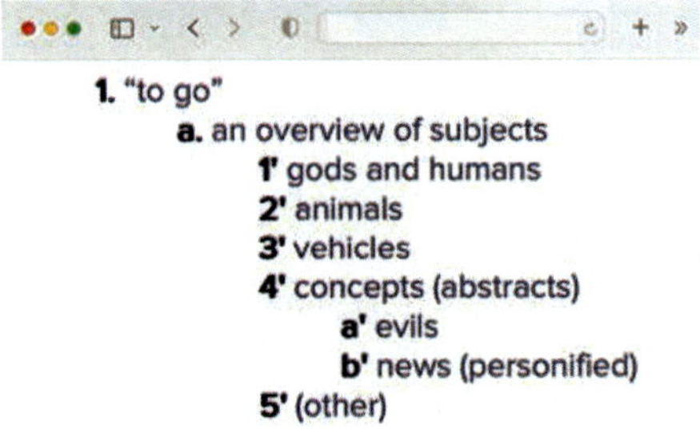

Fig. 6.9 Meanings and sub-meanings are styled into a simplified view

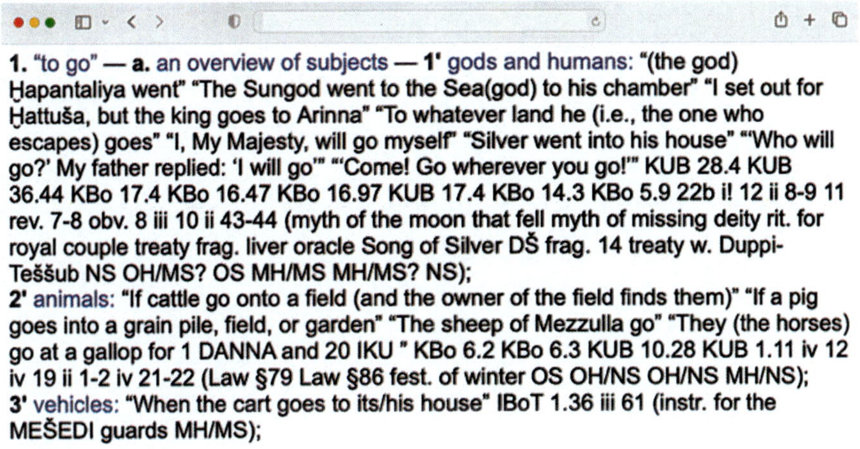

1. "to go" — **a.** an overview of subjects — **1'** gods and humans: **"(the god) Ḫapantaliya went" "The Sungod went to the Sea(god) to his chamber" "I set out for Ḫattuša, but the king goes to Arinna" "To whatever land he (i.e., the one who escapes) goes" "I, My Majesty, will go myself" "Silver went into his house" "'Who will go?' My father replied: 'I will go'" "'Come! Go wherever you go!'" KUB 28.4 KUB 36.44 KBo 17.4 KBo 16.47 KBo 16.97 KUB 17.4 KBo 14.3 KBo 5.9 22b i! 12 ii 8-9 11 rev. 7-8 obv. 8 iii 10 ii 43-44 (myth of the moon that fell myth of missing deity rit. for royal couple treaty frag. liver oracle Song of Silver DŠ frag. 14 treaty w. Duppi-Teššub NS OH/MS? OS MH/MS MH/MS? NS);**
2' animals: **"If cattle go onto a field (and the owner of the field finds them)" "If a pig goes into a grain pile, field, or garden" "The sheep of Mezzulla go" "They (the horses) go at a gallop for 1 DANNA and 20 IKU " KBo 6.2 KBo 6.3 KUB 10.28 KUB 1.11 iv 12 iv 19 ii 1-2 iv 21-22 (Law §79 Law §86 fest. of winter OS OH/NS OH/NS MH/NS);**
3' vehicles: **"When the cart goes to its/his house" IBoT 1.36 iii 61 (instr. for the MEŠEDI guards MH/MS);**

Fig. 6.10 An XSLT stylesheet formats an eCHD entry to mimic the printed version

The beauty of recursion as a structure, and its usefulness as a process for transformation, manifests in cases such as this to be concise syntactically, infinite in its reach, and elegant in its simplicity. So universal and powerful, too, it inspires even the poets:

> here is the deepest secret nobody knows
> (here is the root of the root and the bud of the bud
> and the sky of the sky of a tree called life[15]; which grows
> higher than soul can hope or mind can hide)
> and this is the wonder that's keeping the stars apart
>
> e e cummings

Conclusion

The item-based strategy described in this book resonates with the strategic value of object-oriented thinking which informs Java (and other programming languages), XML, and the OCHRE implementation. This extensible, flexible, and reusable paradigm proves to be a natural fit with the way researchers in the humanities and social sciences order their thinking into complex and nuanced instances of classes and subclasses that at times encapsulate and inherit and at other times resist simple classification. OCHRE, as a database, respects these complexities.

---

[15] E. E. Cummings has been noted elsewhere as having used recursion as a "para-grammatical device" to "signal the idea of juxtaposition of parts so as to bring about continuous increment toward a remote whole" (p. 68 John B. Lord, Para-Grammatical Structure in a Poem of E. E. Cummings) but we find it striking in this poem, "i carry your heart with me," where he uses recursive structures in conjunction with a reference to a tree. https://www.jstor.org/stable/1316795.

Chapter 7
Data Integration and Analysis

Introduction

Every once in a while, we come across an old paper record with a black-and-white photograph paperclipped, glued, or taped to it, harkening back to a pre-digital strategy of making a connection between two things. Using the paperclip as a metaphor for making connections, OCHRE tackles the challenge of data integration (Fig. 7.1).

Our discussion thus far has been focused on strategies implemented in OCHRE to create highly atomized items that represent meaningful *things*, to organize those things into useful data structures, and to describe, annotate, and illustrate them extensively in ways that suit research goals, at the discretion of the scholar, and in opposition to alternative options. We have considered the virtues of hierarchies as an organizational principle, but are reminded that an overly rigid hierarchical database structure was one of the problems that E. F. Codd sought to address when developing the principles of a relational database system (Codd 1970, pp. 377–379). However, relational tables, too, are controlling and constricting. We have touted the value that can be gained from semi-structured data, while recognizing that when hierarchy is used to model a textual document, as is common in the TEI-XML schema, for example, the result is, again, an overly rigid structure that limits the potential for what can be done with the data. An item-based approach stands in stark contrast to a document model, a hierarchical structure, or a relational table. The graph data model, in which millions of OCHRE database items are organized, frees those items to be instantiated, and reinstantiated, in as many contexts as necessary, whether those be lists, tables, hierarchies, maps, graphs, or networks. They can be related to each other in any number of ways, reaching across categories to relate people to places, images to objects, dictionary lemmas to texts, and any *thing* to any *thing*.

In this chapter, we turn our attention to the manipulation of the *things* in an item-based database. We show how to relate items with links to enhance integration, how

S. R. Schloen, M. C. Prosser, *Database Computing for Scholarly Research*, Quantitative Methods in the Humanities and Social Sciences,
https://doi.org/10.1007/978-3-031-46696-0_7

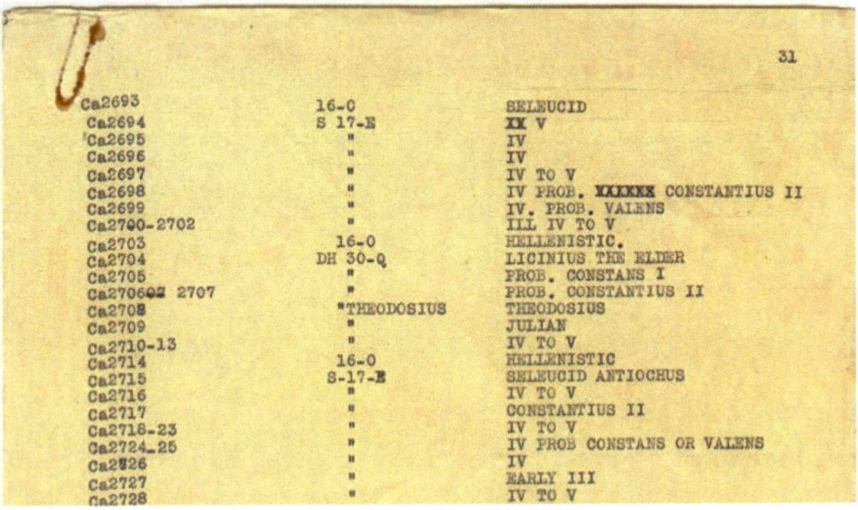

31

Ca2693	16-0	SELEUCID
Ca2694	S 17-E	IX V
Ca2695	"	IV
Ca2696	"	IV
Ca2697	"	IV TO V
Ca2698	"	IV PROB. XXXXXX CONSTANTIUS II
Ca2699	"	IV. PROB. VALENS
Ca2700-2702	"	ILL IV TO V
Ca2703	16-0	HELLENISTIC.
Ca2704	DH 30-Q	LICINIUS THE ELDER
Ca2705	"	PROB. CONSTANS I
Ca2706 2707	"	PROB. CONSTANTIUS II
Ca2708	"THEODOSIUS	THEODOSIUS
Ca2709	"	JULIAN
Ca2710-13	"	IV TO V
Ca2714	16-0	HELLENISTIC
Ca2715	S-17-E	SELEUCID ANTIOCHUS
Ca2716	"	IV TO V
Ca2717	"	CONSTANTIUS II
Ca2718-23	"	IV TO V
Ca2724-25	"	IV PROB CONSTANS OR VALENS
Ca2726	"	IV
Ca2727	"	EARLY III
Ca2728	"	IV TO V

Fig. 7.1 Evidence left by a rusty paperclip speaks to pre-digital "linked data." (ANT_COR_CL-33.jpg, courtesy of the Antioch Expedition Archives, Department of Art and Archaeology, Princeton University)

to find items with queries, how to collect items in sets, how to track items with events, and how to analyze *things* statistically and visually. In the chapters to come, we demonstrate further how an item-based approach to data makes possible a wide variety of computational methods and publication options. Then, in the later case studies, we follow along with specific research projects, from beginning to end, to show how the entire system works together, enabling and motivating scholars to make the most of their data, and inspiring new research possibilities. First, consider various strategies for integrating, finding, and leveraging data in OCHRE.

Relating Things: Links

OCHRE provides various mechanisms for making digital connections between items, that is, creating *links*, to use OCHRE's terminology. Given that data in OCHRE is organized as items, *any* OCHRE item can be linked to *any other* OCHRE item, thereby establishing a relationship between them.[1] In practice, only certain types of links make sense, but one could argue that it is not up to the software to determine what makes sense and what does not. OCHRE gives scholars the latitude

[1] As a comprehensive data integration platform, OCHRE can link to content external to the OCHRE database too. See the discussions on creating links using the Zotero API in the case studies (Chaps. 10, 11, and 12), along with the example of linking to published Semantic Web content in Chap. 9.

to define this for themselves and in ways that reflect their data-driven research. Computationally, creating links is a very simple process when using an item-based approach. Because we are dealing with simple items—rather than with tables, documents, or other more complex structures—small, granular, self-contained units of information can be related easily to other small, granular, self-contained units of information. If we call the small, granular, self-contained units of information "nodes" and if we call the relationships between them "edges," we have described the *graph data model* on which OCHRE has always been structured,[2] providing projects with the means to create countless nodes connected by unlimited numbers of edges representing meaningful relationships between them. Serious research demands the creation of "rich networks of research data: more data, more agility, more speed and—most importantly—more connections."[3]

Note that there is no need to choose between a graph of items and a hierarchy of items. A hierarchy *is* a graph.[4] OCHRE exploits the advantages of graphs, in general, and hierarchies more specifically.[5] Whereas a hierarchy can be thought of as a set of links that captures items within recursively nested contexts, it is also important to consider other kinds of links that represent non-hierarchical relationships. Links, and the mechanisms to create them, are covered in detail in the OCHRE manual,[6] but after a brief summary here we will look at links that go beyond ordinary use cases or that exemplify the analytical value of a rich network of linked data.

General Links

"…[D]ata exists as objects and the relationships between those different objects,"[7] and there are any number of common and expected reasons to want to connect items, creating links between them. Take, for example, the simple case where we relate a photograph to the object of which it is a representation. This is an example in OCHRE of a *general link*, that is, an obvious one, in the normal sense of a relationship between two items. There are hundreds of thousands of such links in the OCHRE database, relating photographs of objects to the objects of which they are

[2] The future is just now catching up to OCHRE: https://neo4j.com/blog/why-graph-databases-are-the-future/. See also Robinson et al. (2015, p. ix) where the co-founder of Neo4j effuses about the "wonderful emerging world of graph technologies."

[3] Hunger et al. (2021, p. 2).

[4] According to Robinson et al. (2015, p. 109) "A graph database's structured yet schema-free data model" makes it "ideally applied to the modeling, storing, and querying of hierarchies…" Examples are given of how to represent "cross domain models" (ibid., p. 41ff) which is analogous to how OCHRE manages multiple overlapping hierarchies without difficulty using a graph approach.

[5] Prosser and Schloen (2021, p. 4).

[6] Schloen and Schloen (2012, Chap. 6).

[7] Hunger et al. (2021, p. 1).

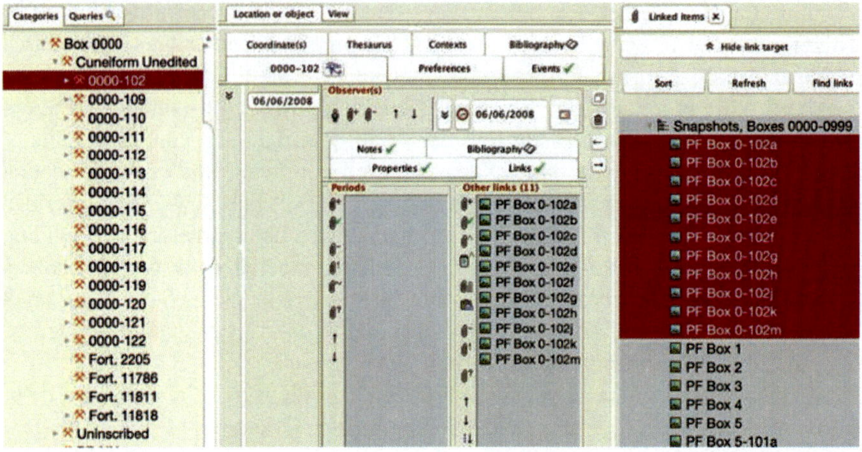

Fig. 7.2 Buttons with paperclip icons are used to link selected image Resources to a selected Tablet

an image. These are simply one-dimensional links between two items and are examples of how the network of data is enhanced in ways that are non-hierarchical.

Since any OCHRE item can link to any other OCHRE item, OCHRE provides the **Linked items** tab on the reference pane to assist with making links. The user will navigate to the source item in the navigation pane on the left-hand side of the screen, then use the Linked items tab to select the Category, the hierarchy, and the item(s) to be linked from the panel on the right-hand side of the screen. Buttons identified with paperclip icons can be used to make the link between the selected items. When viewing or editing any given item, all the images that are linked to it as general links are on display (Fig. 7.2).

Named Links

Sometimes, it is not enough that a relationship specified by a general link be implicit, preferring instead to assign explicit semantic meaning to it. The *author* of a Bibliography item or a Note, the *creator* of a photograph, the *editor* of a Text, the *observer* of an observation: these are all examples of semantic meaning ascribed in the assignment of a *named link* to an appropriate target item (Fig. 7.3). Named links may be thought of as "metadata" and very often align with published metadata schemas such as Dublin Core.

Fig. 7.3 A Person item is assigned as the creator of this image Resource item

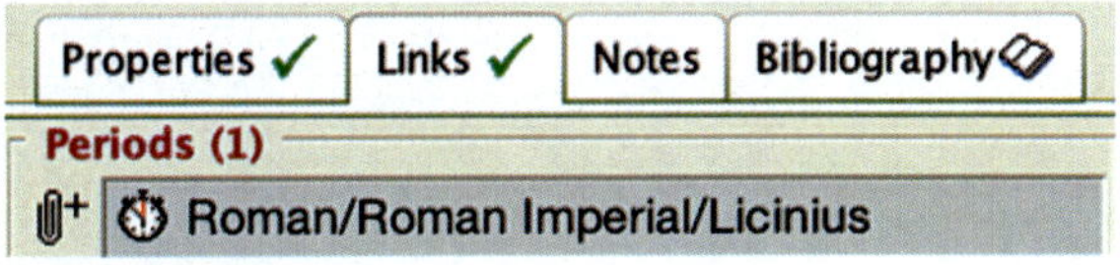

Fig. 7.4 The date of a Roman coin is documented using Period links

Period Links

General links between items, along with named links, can be used to specify metadata fields. However, links may also implicate time periods. Seals, ceramics, coins, excavation units, texts, or any other person, place, or thing, are situated in time as much as in space. As explained already (Chap. 4), time periods are treated as user-defined data, organized into hierarchies of any needed breadth or depth. Individual items are assigned to a period via *Period links*, to whatever level of specificity is discernable (Fig. 7.4).

Many of the coins from the excavations at Hippos–Sussita, an ancient city of the Decapolis near the Sea of Galilee in Northern Israel excavated by co-directors Michael Eisenberg and Arleta Kowalewska of the Zinman Institute of Archaeology (University of Haifa), can be dated to a specific political ruler. The paperclip buttons together with the Linked Items pane are used to make this association. By creating this link between a time period and a coin, the researcher leverages the item-based data model to associate data in two discrete hierarchies: the Locations & objects hierarchy that represents the excavation context of the coin and the Periods hierarchy that represents the recursively nested configuration of this historical period.

The OCHRE View of Coin #12865 shows other linked items, along with the linked Period. The coin's Denomination property links it to a Concept item. Its Mint property links it to an item in the Persons & organizations category. The artistic motifs on the coin's obverse and reverse link multiple times to the motifs also cataloged as Concepts. The Associated text relational property links to the text item that represents the coin's inscription. These observations are attributed to the excavator, linked by her Person item.

Fig. 7.5 A Hippos Excavations Project coin is shown with its many relational properties

Kowalewska, Arleta (12/07/2018)
ITM Coordinate: 262085.43, 742682.64, 115
Location or object type: Basket
- Basket: 12865
- Basket opening date: 12/07/2018
- Elevation: 114.95 m
- Material: Metal
  - Material: Bronze
- Object type: Coin
  - Diameter, minimum: 19 mm
  - Diameter, maximum: 21.2 mm
  - Weight: 2.39 g
  - Date (year), earliest (TPQ): 321
  - Date (year), latest (TAQ): 324
  - Denomination: Follis
  - Mint: Heraclea
  - Coin face type, obverse: Bust
  - Coin face type, obverse: Radiate
  - Coin face type, obverse: Cuirass
  - Coin face type, reverse: Jupiter
  - Coin face type, reverse: Victory
  - Coin face type, reverse: Sceptre
  - Coin face type, reverse: Globe
  - Coin face type, reverse: Eagle
  - Coin face type, reverse: Captive
- Associated text: Coin 12865

Relational Properties

OCHRE does not limit the user to a predefined schema of general, named, and period links. Because OCHRE is designed to be generic, flexible, and customizable, it supports the creation of customized *relational properties*—that is, Variables that target other items as their Values, thereby creating user-defined links. The user can create these for any purpose relevant to data collection or analysis simply by giving the property a meaningful name that indicates its semantic value and designating one of the OCHRE categories as the source of the target values. Some examples will illustrate the range of uses of relational properties (Fig. 7.5).[8]

OCHRE tracks certain metadata fields that involve people—authors, editors, photographers, and so on. But what of recording the identification of the Person who served as the supervisor of a given excavation square, or the senior supervisor of an entire excavation area, or specialists serving staff roles? Relational properties, targeting items in the Person category, achieve this goal. An archaeology project

[8] The reader would be correct to wonder at this point if this system has the potential to lead to chaos. While it may be in the best interests of a project to follow a published ontology of a metadata schema when creating customized relational links, this decision remains entirely in the hands of the researcher. The OCHRE interface does not enforce adherence to any specific metadata schema. OCHRE has been applied in too many domain areas to prescribe any predefined schemas.

JGt 9
Pinched Mouth Juglet: flaring rim; thickened on both int./ext.; out-beveled top of rim, flattened-to-slightly convex; no slip; abraded & poorly preserved (especially on int.)

Location or object type: Registered Pottery
Excavation & Recording: Identification
Date excavated: 2011-06-23
Registered by: Johnson, Barbara
Analyst: Johnson, Barbara
Area supervisor: Tappy, Ron
Area supervisor: Barkay, Gabriel
Square supervisor: Lowmaster, Nancy
Square supervisor: Tappy, Madeleine

Fig. 7.6 A pottery analysis is credited to the pottery specialist of the Zeitah Excavations, along with identification of other supervisory roles, using custom relational properties

may create Variables like "Area supervisor" or "Registered by." Values that complete these properties will be database items that represent appropriate Persons (Fig. 7.6).

Another example of relational properties identifies the Person to whom, or by whom, letters were addressed in the ancient kingdom of Ugarit. The user-defined Addressor and Addressee properties, both targeting Person items, describe the letter written upon a clay tablet and sent from the King of Ugarit to the Queen. Figure 7.7 shows how the value of a relational property is assigned using the buttons with paperclip icon(s) in conjunction with the currently selected item in the Linked Items pane. Only valid items in the designated Category (here Persons) are allowed. One could imagine identifying multiple Addressees, in which case the property can be repeated as many times as needed, each time targeting a different Person value.

A relational Variable can be configured to document any identifiable person in the data. So, whether a project is dealing with manuscript copyists, Shakespearean characters, property owners, fathers and sons, or contract witnesses, to name just a few examples, these persons—database items in their own right—are linked to the text, document, or other object where they are mentioned.

Relational Properties with Auto-generated Bidirectional Links

Relations, by definition, involve two items, the source item and the target item. Practically speaking, a link is created from one item to the other. Sometimes, though, it is helpful to expose the link in both directions, explicitly, so that the target item also reflects the inverse relation that links to the source item. When creating a new relational property, the user may specify that OCHRE should create the inverse property *automatically* and *explicitly* on the linked item. In doing so, the relationship is available from either direction from either item.

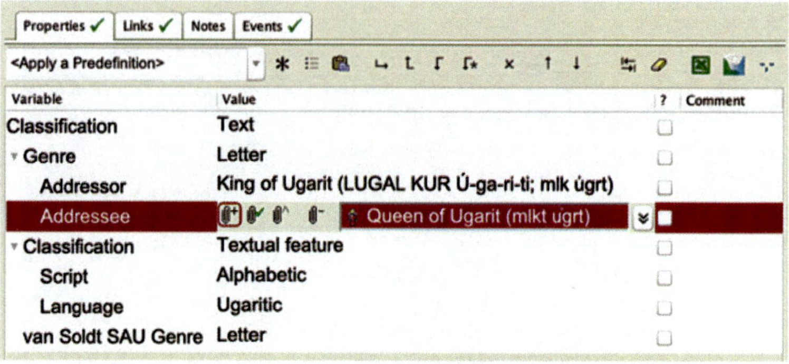

Fig. 7.7 Links document the correspondence between the King and Queen of Ugarit

Archaeologists use this feature to capture numerous stratigraphic relationships among the units of excavation. If an excavator indicates that Lot A "is over" Lot B, then that logically implies and makes necessary that Lot B "is below" Lot A. OCHRE will, on request, automatically create the relationship explicitly in both directions, allowing the user to access them from either direction whether doing data entry or querying for the presence of this property.[9] Due to the resulting dependency between the two items, data entry is constrained appropriately to maintain the integrity of the links (Fig. 7.8).

Any of the primary OCHRE categories can support relational properties. One of the categories that we have not discussed much, the **Concepts** category, often comes into play at the analysis stage. As a category for content that is not a person, place, or thing, **Concepts** can be used to describe complex or intangible notions like currency,[10] systems of measures, artistic motifs, literary themes, and ceramic typologies. The thousands of seals preserved only as impressions on the tablets in the Persepolis Fortification Archive collection are cataloged using an extensive, hierarchically organized typology of image themes. Individual seals are linked using a relational property to the theme that most closely matches the style and content of the seal image at whatever level of specificity is discernible. For example, the Image theme Variable links seal PFS 0002 to theme I.A.2 Hero Controls Winged Bull Creatures (Fig. 7.9).

Relational Properties Across Categories

The Florentine Catasto project organizes its data more as a graph (network) rather than by hierarchies. Relational properties are used extensively to relate individuals to families, properties to parishes, streets to districts, and so on. A Catasto

[9] For more details, see the Harris Matrix example in the Tell Keisan case study (Chap. 10).

[10] See the Greek Coin Hoard case study (Chap. 12) for a further example.

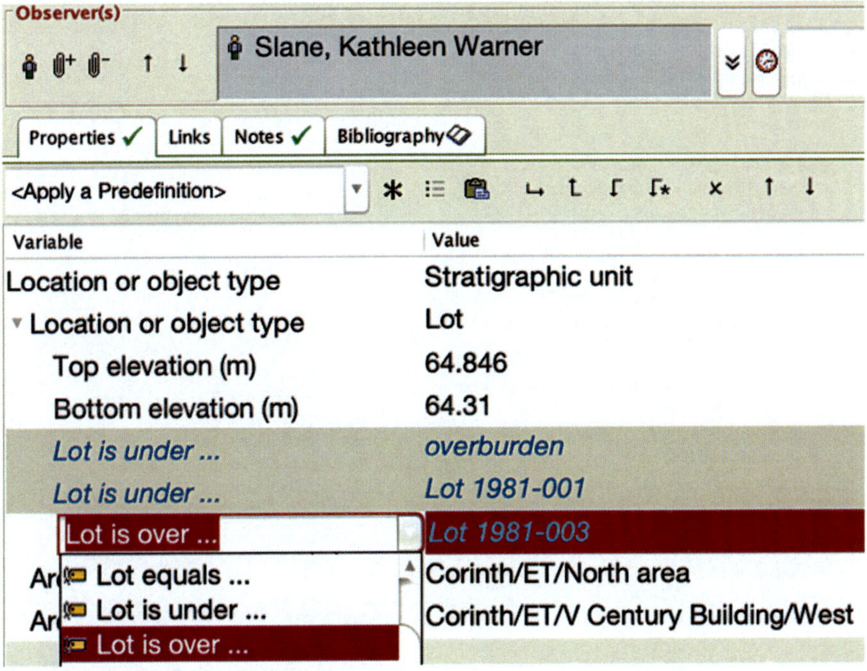

Fig. 7.8 Bidirectional relational property links are accessible from either direction

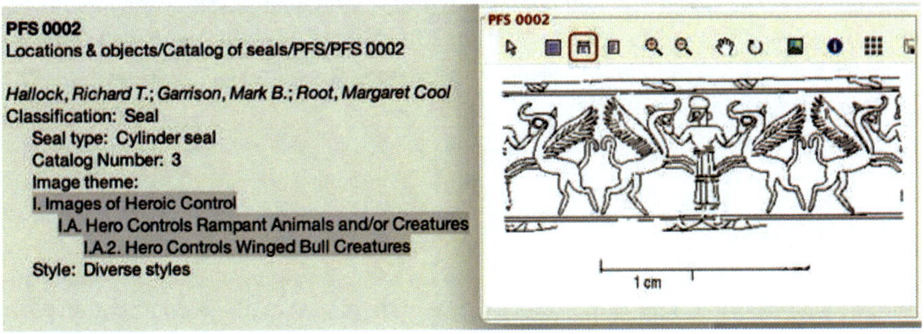

Fig. 7.9 A Seal (Object) is linked via the "Image theme" relational property to a Concept

declaration, itself a Concept item, elaborately details the declarer, owner(s), renter(s), and *confine* (neighbors) as links to Person items, along with links to houses/workshops (defined as Location items). In declaration AV1184 (Fig. 7.10), the Santa Croce dei Frati Minori convent (the declarer) declares itself to be the owner of a house (property 2-C-3), on the street Arno, rented by Giovanni the locksmith (chiavaiuolo), and having assorted other neighbors. Each of these linked items link back to the original declaration. For example, the pop-up window triggered by

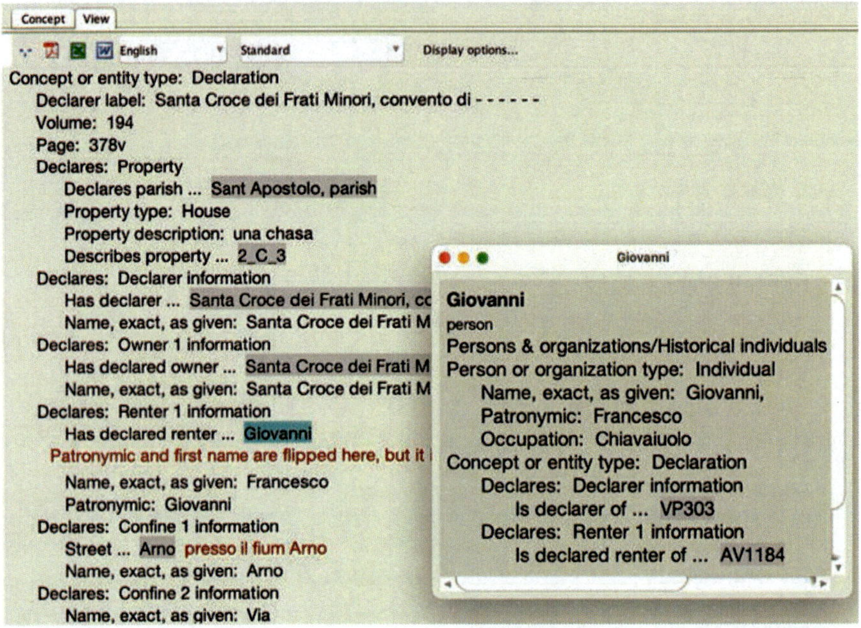

Fig. 7.10 Linking items from different categories allows for building a rich network of relationships

the reverse link, illustrates that Giovanni is known to be the declared renter of declaration AV1184. Data that had previously been stored in a spreadsheet with an unmanageable number of columns was greatly enhanced by the auto-inverse links. Now with a network of data, the project leverages these inverse properties to untangle this dense archive.

Hotspot Links

Image data offers a unique opportunity to integrate data visually in conjunction with OCHRE's hotspot feature. Pixel regions on an image can be outlined and associated with any OCHRE item using *hotspot links*. Many creative uses have been made of this feature. In Fig. 7.11, the individual vessels of a ceramic assemblage are identified using hotspot links. Each of these ceramic vessels is represented by an item in the Locations & objects category. A researcher uses the OCHRE hotspot feature to outline an item in the photograph and associate the vessel item with that outline. Options on the OCHRE View allow the hotspots to be toggled on or off, or to show the labels only, for example. Color and transparency options control the display of the hotspots.

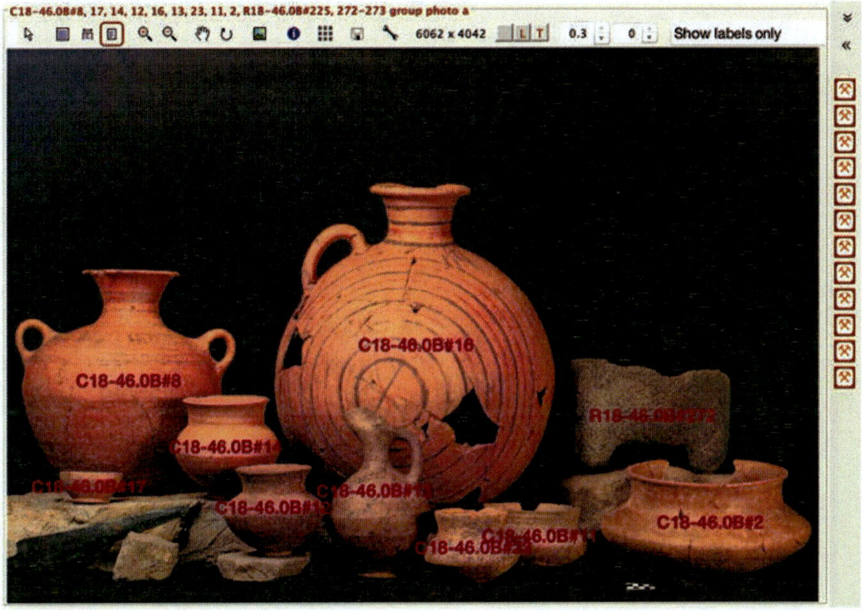

Fig. 7.11 Archaeologists use OCHRE's hotspot-link feature to annotate a ceramic assemblage from Zincirli. (Photograph by R. Ceccacci, courtesy of the University of Chicago Zincirli Excavations)

Archaeologists use OCHRE's hotspot-link feature extensively to annotate field photographs. Figure 7.12 illustrates how field photographs were annotated using pre-digital methods by the Zeitah Excavations. Figure 7.13 shows how this is achieved using hotspot links. Each polygon demarcates a locus of excavation and serves as a link to the database item that represents the locus. Clicking on the hotspot pops up the related locus information, creating an interactive, annotated image.

Image tagging, made ubiquitous by Facebook and other social media platforms, is a simple concept but often absent from typical database systems. It is the item-based approach, where every item is separable from all others and individually addressable as the target of a link, that makes the implementation of this feature by OCHRE easy and intuitive.

Integration of Texts, Writing Systems, Dictionaries, and Bibliography

Text processing using the OCHRE platform is a complex topic due to the high level of data granularity and the preferred use of a database model over a document model.[11] While this topic is discussed in detail in other sections of this book, it is

[11] See Schloen and Schloen (2014).

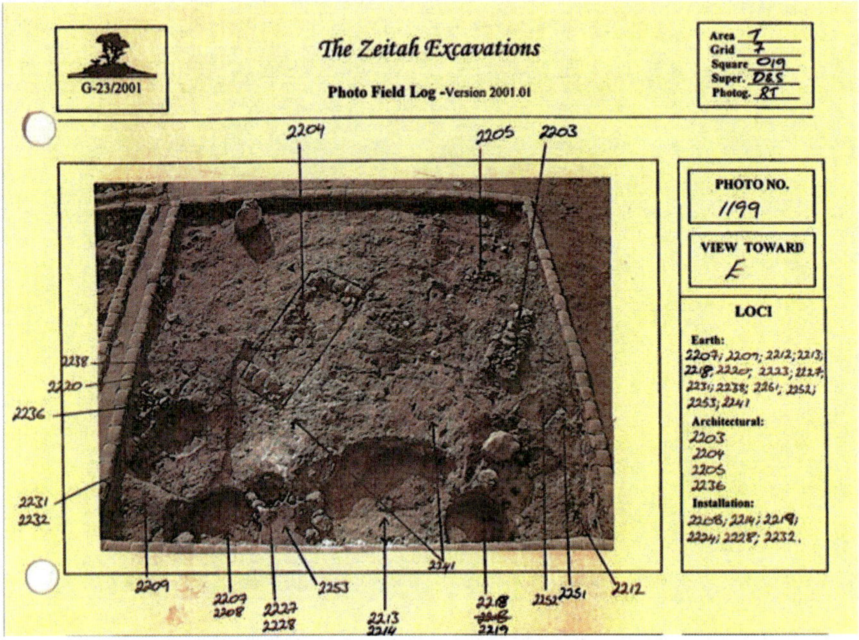

Fig. 7.12 Archaeological field photographs were annotated using pre-digital methods which required a felt-tipped pen. (Image courtesy of R. E. Tappy, The Zeitah Excavations)

Fig. 7.13 Archaeological field photographs are annotated digitally using hotspot links

worth highlighting the extensive integration and the rich network of links created when texts are modeled using an item-based, hierarchically organized approach.

Textual content is normally imported into OCHRE from a prepared document. OCHRE's sophisticated import facility atomizes that document into database items, first sign by sign (character by character) into epigraphic units organized by an epigraphic hierarchy, and simultaneously word by word into discourse units organized by a discourse hierarchy. The epigraphic units and discourse units are mutually related by links so that each word knows which characters it is comprised of, and each character knows to which word it belongs.

Furthermore, each epigraphic unit (sign or character) is validated against, and linked to, its matching sign in a master list represented as a Writing System which serves as a complete catalog of valid signs or characters for that script or language. Similarly, each discourse unit (word) is matched against the project Glossary and is linked to the word in the glossary that matches the spelling of the word being imported.

On line 02 of the Persepolis Fortification Archive text, PF 0001, shown in Fig. 7.14, the first two epigraphic units, "be" and "ul," each linked to their corresponding sign in the Cuneiform Writing System, are also linked together to form the word "bel" which, itself, is linked to the Glossary entry "bel" meaning "year."

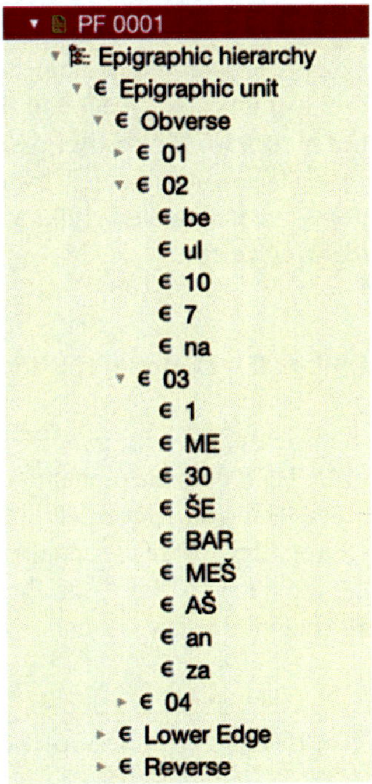

Fig. 7.14 The sign-by-sign representation of a text is captured by its Epigraphic hierarchy

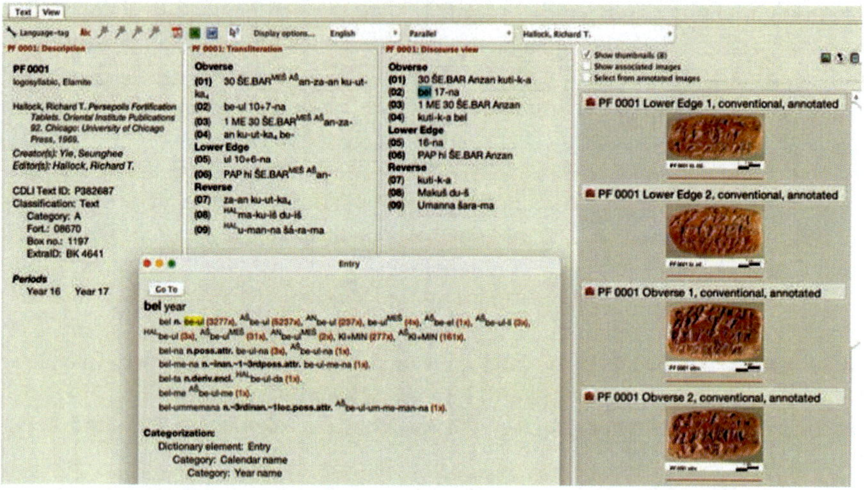

Fig. 7.15 Integrated Text and Glossary items are shown in OCHRE's Dictionary View

A View of this Text shows the sign-by-sign epigraphic view (here **Transliteration**) alongside the word-based **Discourse view**. Clicking on "bel" using the Glossary-lookup button pops up the glossary entry which shows that this word means "year" and that there are over 2800 other attestations of this spelling of this word already linked in this text corpus (Fig. 7.15).

Texts are represented by extensive collections of (epigraphic and discourse) items that may include links to many other items. Other links that may be at play are itemized below.

Link to the Editor of the Text

In this case, the edition of PF 0001 was edited by Richard Hallock.[12] The Text item in OCHRE uses the preconfigured Editors field to link to the Person item that represents "Hallock, Richard T." If the Persepolis project decided to record an alternate edition, the differences could be recorded as part of the same Text item, but attributed to a new editor. Even the difference of a single line or single character can be attributed to a new editor.

[12] See Hallock (1969, 87), available online at https://isac.uchicago.edu/research/publications/oip/persepolis-fortification-tablets.

Link to the Item on Which the Text Is Written

OCHRE keeps separate the idea of the Text and the Object on which the text is recorded. In this case, there is a bidirectional link using the relational property "Associated text." The object representing the tablet links to the text. From the perspective of the text, the inverse of that same link displays as "Associated item," referring back to the tablet.

Link to Resources That Are Photographs or Drawings of the Text

There are several high-quality images of this text. These are Resource links on the Text item. In this context, resources can be any standard image format. Some of these may be photographs. Others may be black-and-white line drawings that researchers produce as another interpretation of the object and text.

Link to Bibliography

The original publication by Hallock (OIP 92, 1969) is included as a bibliography link from the integrated Zotero library. The link displays the volume information formatted according to project specifications, choosing from any of the thousands of preconfigured Zotero bibliography citation formats. The inverse relationships allow users to find all places where a specific bibliography item is cited in the database.

Link to Persons or Locations Represented in the Textual Content

Names of people and places mentioned in the text are linked to **Person** and **Location** items, respectively. Any discourse unit (word or phrase) that represents the name of a Person can be linked to that Person item using a relational property. A list of the most common types of relational properties relevant to texts and the proper names found therein is available to all projects by borrowing from the taxonomy of the OCHRE master project. As with all taxonomic properties, a project may define a new relational property to capture the specific semantic force of the relationship in its specific texts.

Case Study: Digital Paleography

With highly granular textual content at hand, philologists can use OCHRE's hotspot-link feature to identify and annotate often difficult-to-read characters on a manuscript. Sign by sign, each hotspot can be linked to the corresponding epigraphic unit in the epigraphic hierarchy of the corresponding text, providing careful and detailed documentation of a high-resolution image. This rigorous inspection and markup of a text's image helps the scholar grapple with the identification of each unit of writing. The result is a highly annotated image useful for communicating a scholarly interpretation and for training students on reading the script. If enough characters from a corpus are identified, the scholar can produce character charts by period, genre, findspot, or other criteria.[13]

OCHRE projects that deal with text-critical issues, primarily those associated with the Critical Editions for Digital Analysis and Research (CEDAR) initiative,[14] extensively hotspot problematic manuscripts. As part of this effort, CEDAR team members utilize OCHRE's **Reconstruction tool**. This feature enables a scholar to use exemplars of signs *in the scribe's own handwriting* to compare with broken or fragmentary bits or to experimentally fill in the gaps on the image of the annotated manuscript. This interactive, digital paleography tool greatly enhances the study and decipherment of historical manuscripts.

The CEDAR project has hotspotted the Dead Sea Scroll fragments that represent portions of the Book of Samuel. Using the wrench-icon button to toggle on the Reconstruction tool, OCHRE populates the Sign Gallery—a scrollable, filterable list of all the characters of the manuscript with each character represented by its hotspot cutout. Sorting this list by sign, a scholar can see all exemplars of any sign written by that scribe. When studying small fragments for which there are few exemplars, the scholar can add the hotspot exemplars from some other manuscript, presumably one with comparable paleographic characteristics.

Say, for example, you wanted to argue for the presence of a *mêm* along the bottom, broken edge of this fragment, following the partial *ʾaleph*. While viewing the high-resolution image, you zoom in and pan to the area in question. Filter the Sign Gallery to the list of all *mêm* exemplars in the scribe's own handwriting using the Gallery picklist. Drag and drop selected exemplars from the Gallery onto the image, testing them in context relative to the visible bits of the fragmentary character or in proximity to neighboring characters. Change the transparency of the inserted character to see if it properly overlaps with the ink traces. Rotate as needed. Remove an exemplar from consideration by dragging it off the image canvas. Filter for *ʾalephs* and select an unbroken exemplar, positioning it alongside the suggested *mêm* to

---

[13] On the use of OCHRE and hotspotting for paleography, see Yardney et al. (2020). See also the Ras Shamra case study (Chap. 11) and Prosser (unpublished), "Generating epigraphic letter charts in a database environment: a case-study in alphabetic Ugaritic mythological and administrative texts," April 24–25, 2014. Computer Applications and Quantitative Methods in Archaeology Conference, Paris; slides available at https://www.academia.edu/12465628.

[14] https://cedar.uchicago.edu.

Fig. 7.16 OCHRE's Reconstruction tool is digital paleography in action

determine whether the character combination would work together. Repeat, explore, experiment, discover, and make a convincing argument! (Fig. 7.16).[15]

Finding Things: Queries

One of the biggest challenges faced when managing highly integrated data within a common framework is the sheer amount of possibility. The scope and complexity of the data can seem overwhelming. With so many research questions to be investigated, and so many relationships to be explored, it is *hard* to make it *easy* to ask meaningful questions. To address this challenge, a variety of strategies for searching, exploring, and otherwise interacting with the data have been developed. This section will review these strategies, hopefully without losing our readers in the weeds of syntax or in the bog of arcane details.[16]

[15] For a more in-depth explanation of the use of this reconstruction tool for biblical text criticism, see Yardney et al. (2020).

[16] This section is intended as an overview of strategies, not a how-to guide for designing specific queries. For more information, refer to the OCHRE manual (Schloen and Schloen 2012, pp. 265–296).

Fig. 7.17 A search for "year" in the Elamite dictionary checks all possibilities

Finding Things Based on Properties and Metadata

The advantage of an item-based approach is that *things* can be found, and other things like it, based on the characteristics of the thing. Remember that items in OCHRE take on identity based on the data category into which they are added, by the names and aliases given to them, and by the properties, notes, and links assigned by the researcher. Any aspect of these characteristics is available as search criteria—everything from specific property values to complex text string searches. Querying in OCHRE is essentially a process of finding items that match search criteria. Just tell OCHRE which **Project** is of interest (by default, the one in which the user is currently logged in) and which **Category** of things you want to search, and on what basis, and OCHRE will return a list of matching items.

The simplest way to find anything in OCHRE is the quick-find option on the Linked Items pane which uses standard string matching to find the requested item(s) based on the item Name (Fig. 7.17).[17] In this interface, the search also considers the

[17] A find-by-barcode option is also available and is useful for any project managing an inventory of objects. By connecting a scanner to a computer running OCHRE, a researcher can scan a barcode to quickly locate individual items in the database. This is useful for specialists working through objects to perform analysis after the object has been stored, or for a photographer working in an imaging laboratory.

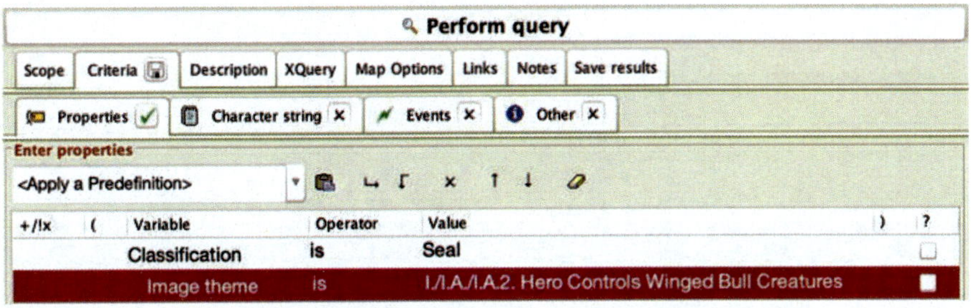

Fig. 7.18 The Query Criteria, with lots of possibility, targets the items' properties

Abbreviation and Aliases of items when looking for matches. When looking for Dictionary items, OCHRE considers any form of the word including the native language, the translation, the transcription, and any assorted spellings. For example, the **Find item by name** values of "year," "bel," and "be-ul" in the PFA project will all result in the lemma for "year." In fact, a search for "year" will yield two results: one in Elamite and another in Aramaic.

By default, the result of a query is simply a list of items—not tables, not documents, not pages, simply items. OCHRE provides a quick-view toolbar on the **Query Results** pane with several default options for viewing these items: as a List, a Table, an Event-list, an Image Gallery, a Graph, a Map, or as XML objects. The default views make many formatting assumptions and provide merely a quick and basic view of the results. A list of items sorted alphabetically or numerically is often enough to go on, for a start. Simply click an item in the list to see its details.

When a simple search by name, alias, or other basic information is not enough, OCHRE provides an alternative interface for building queries. Even queries are items in OCHRE, complete with the ability to add notes and scholarly attribution, as with other OCHRE items. However, instead of being described by properties, a query item is configured with properties and other specifications to serve as the match criteria against other items in the database. Because there are so many ways in which we can describe items—by properties, by metadata, by events, by prose descriptions, and by notes—there are many options available to find items. The **Criteria** tab of the Query specification interface, shown in Fig. 7.18, suggests these possibilities, allowing us to search by **Properties**, **Character string** (for full-text search), **Events**, or **Other** criteria. To start with a simple example from the PFA project, let us find those seals that attest the concept called *Hero Controls Winged Bull Creatures*. Here, we search by Properties, replicating in the query criteria the structure of the properties that were assigned to the seal items.

Clicking the **Perform query** button runs the query, fetching matching items from the database, and displaying the **Query Results** list. The Table View option of the quick-view toolbar constructs a reassuringly familiar table-style presentation of the items (Fig. 7.19). This is an interactive table. Double-clicking any row of the table pops up the full details of the item listed in that table row for viewing or editing.

Seal, all-purpose: Default table

Show table formatting

Name	...	...	Obs. Date	Observer	...	Classification	/Seal type	...	/Image theme	/Style
PFS 0002	..	..		Hallock, Richard T.; Garriso...		Seal	Cylinder seal	..	I./I.A./I.A.2. Hero Controls Winged...	Diverse styles
PFS 0007*	..	..		Hallock, Richard T.; Garriso...		Seal	Cylinder seal	..	I./I.A./I.A.2. Hero Controls Winged...	Court style
PFS 0036*	..	..		Hallock, Richard T.; Garriso...		Seal	Cylinder seal	..	I./I.A./I.A.2. Hero Controls Winged...	Fortification style
PFS 0429	..	..	11/13/2008	Garrison, Mark B.; Root, M...		Seal	Cylinder seal	..	I./I.A./I.A.2. Hero Controls Winged...	Modeled style
PFS 0524	..	..	11/17/2008	Garrison, Mark B.; Root, M...		Seal	Cylinder seal	..	I./I.A./I.A.2. Hero Controls Winged...	Mixed styles II
PFS 0778	..	..	12/02/2008	Garrison, Mark B.; Root, M...		Seal	Cylinder seal	..	I./I.A./I.A.2. Hero Controls Winged...	Fortification style
PFS 0841	..	..	12/02/2008	Garrison, Mark B.; Root, M...		Seal	Cylinder seal	..	I./I.A./I.A.2. Hero Controls Winged...	Mixed styles I
PFS 0970	..	..	01/28/2009	Garrison, Mark B.; Root, M...		Seal	Cylinder seal	..	I./I.A./I.A.2. Hero Controls Winged...	Court style
PFS 1189	..	..	02/18/2009	Garrison, Mark B.; Root, M...		Seal	Cylinder seal	..	I./I.A./I.A.2. Hero Controls Winged...	Diverse styles
PFS 1460	..	..	02/20/2009	Garrison, Mark B.; Root, M...		Seal	Cylinder seal	..	I./I.A./I.A.2. Hero Controls Winged...	Fortification style
PFS 1467	..	..	02/20/2009	Garrison, Mark B.; Root, M...		Seal	Cylinder seal	..	I./I.A./I.A.2. Hero Controls Winged...	Fortification style
PFS 1499	..	..	02/20/2009	Garrison, Mark B.; Root, M...		Seal	Cylinder seal	..	I./I.A./I.A.2. Hero Controls Winged...	Fortification style
PFS 1550	..	..	02/23/2009	Garrison, Mark B.; Root, M...		Seal	Cylinder seal	..	I./I.A./I.A.2. Hero Controls Winged...	Modeled style
PFS 2082	..	..	08/07/2013	Kruse, Megan		Seal	Cylinder seal	..	I./I.A./I.A.2. Hero Controls Winged...	<unassigned>
PFS 2100	..	..	08/07/2013	Kruse, Megan		Seal	Cylinder seal	..	I./I.A./I.A.2. Hero Controls Winged...	<unassigned>
PFS 2104	..	..	08/07/2013	Garrison, Mark B.; Kruse, ...		Seal	Cylinder seal	..	I./I.A./I.A.2. Hero Controls Winged...	<unassigned>
PFS 2273	..	..	08/07/2013	Garrison, Mark B.; Kruse, ...		Seal	Cylinder seal	..	I./I.A./I.A.2. Hero Controls Winged...	<unassigned>
PFS 2278	..	..	08/07/2013	Garrison, Mark B.; Kruse, ...		Seal	Cylinder seal	..	I./I.A./I.A.2. Hero Controls Winged...	<unassigned>
PFS 2324	..	..	08/07/2013	Garrison, Mark B.; Kruse, ...		Seal	Cylinder seal	..	I./I.A./I.A.2. Hero Controls Winged...	<unassigned>
PFS 2480	..	..	08/07/2013	Kruse, Megan		Seal	Cylinder seal	..	I./I.A./I.A.2. Hero Controls Winged...	<unassigned>

Fig. 7.19 The Table View of Query Results shows the details of the matching items

Finding Things in Context

We have made much of the use of hierarchies as an organizational principle. Hierarchical structures come into play in several helpful ways when searching for items in the database.

Is or Is Contained By

Imagine that we want to broaden our search to seals that contain images of heroes controlling rampant animals of all kinds, not just winged bull creatures. We broaden the matching **Concept** property to I.A. *Hero Controls Rampant Animals and/or Creatures,* the *parent* item of I.A.2 *Hero Controls Winged Bull Creatures* in the conceptual typology that classifies the seals. Then, instead of using the query operator "is" to find an exact match, we use the operator "*is or is contained by*." This option expands the range of matching items to include *any* of the subitems within the context of the requested matching criteria. This is a *hierarchically aware* query that will find the winged bull seals, not because they are tagged explicitly with the requested matching property, but because they *inherit* the matching property from their context. The query results will also include images of heroes controlling lions, winged lions, winged horn animals, and birds, among a wide range of other subcriteria that fall *within the context of* the requested matching property (Fig. 7.20).

Consider an example from a different angle to illustrate the wide applicability of this option. After many seasons of excavation at the site of Zincirli in south-central Turkey, the architectural layout of the Northern Lower Town in Area 5 began to come into focus. The archaeologists there captured the arrangement of Complexes,

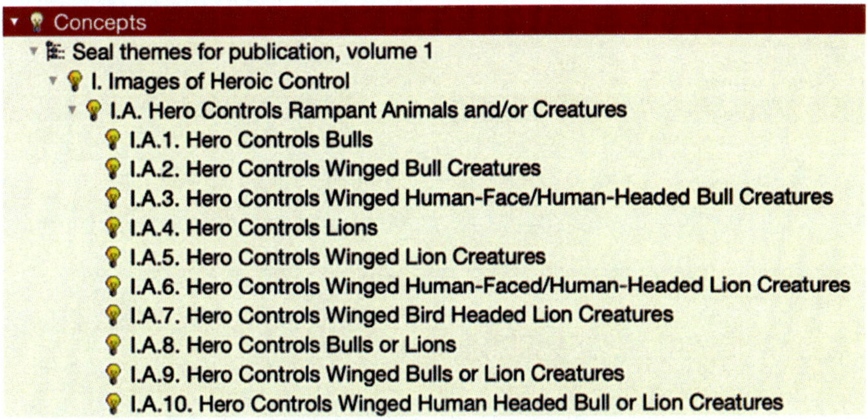

Fig. 7.20 Hierarchically aware queries inherit matching properties

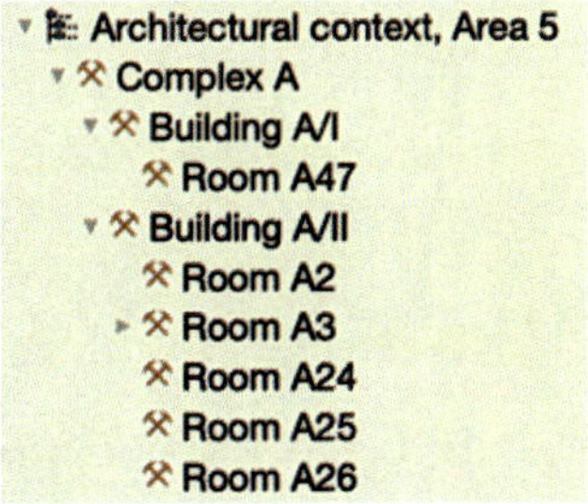

Fig. 7.21 The Architectural context at Zincirli provides an analytical perspective

Buildings, Rooms, and Courtyards in a carefully outlined *secondary* spatial hierarchy, separate from the excavation spatial hierarchy that represents the layout of the excavation site. Notice in Fig. 7.21 that the excavated loci and objects do not appear in the Architectural context hierarchy, that is, most Rooms have no child items in the hierarchy. Instead, individual loci from the contexts in the excavation spatial hierarchy were assigned to these rooms or buildings in the Architectural context using a relational property (aptly named Architectural context) to make a relational link.

It seems obvious that a Query could find all loci associated with a selected Room, using criteria based on the explicit intrinsic properties of the tagged loci, for example, "Architectural context is Room A3." Less obvious is that even if none of the loci had been explicitly tagged as being associated with Building A/II, the query criterion "Architectural context *is or is contained by* Building A/II" will find all the loci associated with any of the Rooms within the context of Building A/II by virtue of *inheritance*. That is, a locus assigned to Room A3 is also aware that it is located contextually within Building A/II, and within Complex A, making that locus findable by either the room or the building. The hierarchically aware *is or is contained by* query operator capitalizes on this inherited relationship (Fig. 7.22).

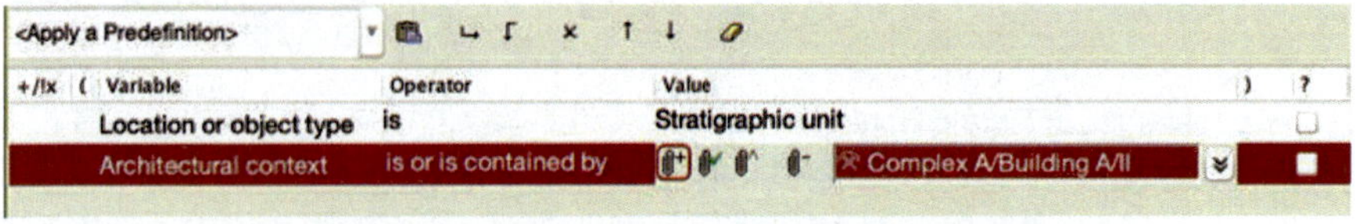

Fig. 7.22 The notion of inheritance enables hierarchically aware query criteria

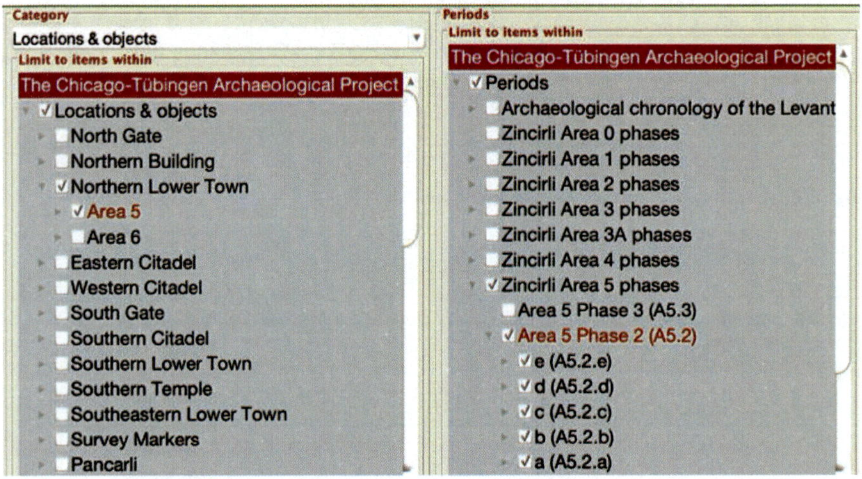

Fig. 7.23 The use of Scope criteria limits the range of an OCHRE Query in space and time

Scoping: Containment as Constrainment

With the extensive use of hierarchy as a primary organizing principle throughout OCHRE, it makes sense to make it as natural as possible to use hierarchical containment as constrainment for a query. Recall the Katumuwa stele found at Zincirli, carved on a dense basalt stone. The relief scene shows a figure seated at a banquet table, upon which are some vessels containing food, presumably.[18] Given the preponderance of basaltic rock in the region, imagine that we are interested in studying basalt vessels found at the site, but we want to restrict our search to the excavation area and the time period that correspond to the stele's context. The **Scope** tab of the Query specification allows us to choose the hierarchical context of both space (Locations & objects) and time (Periods). Selecting "Area 5" of the Northern Lower Town and "Phase 2" of the Area 5 phases restricts our search to items that fall within the scope of those hierarchical contexts, that is, to items that are descendants, at any level of the tree, of those parent items (Fig. 7.23).

[18] See Struble and Herrmann (2009, p. 28).

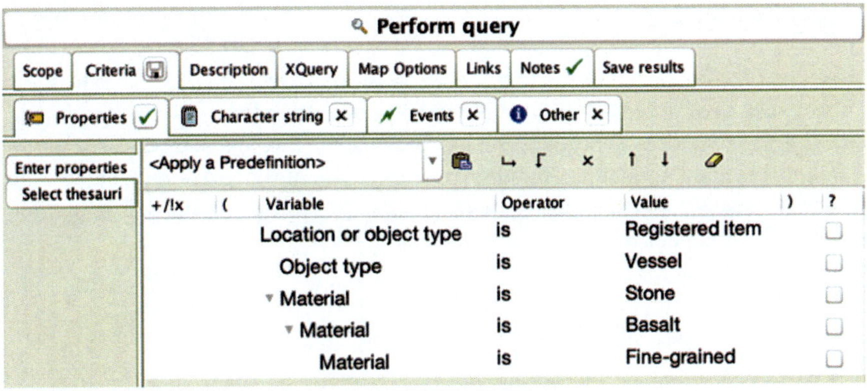

Fig. 7.24 Intrinsic item properties are used to limit the Query criteria

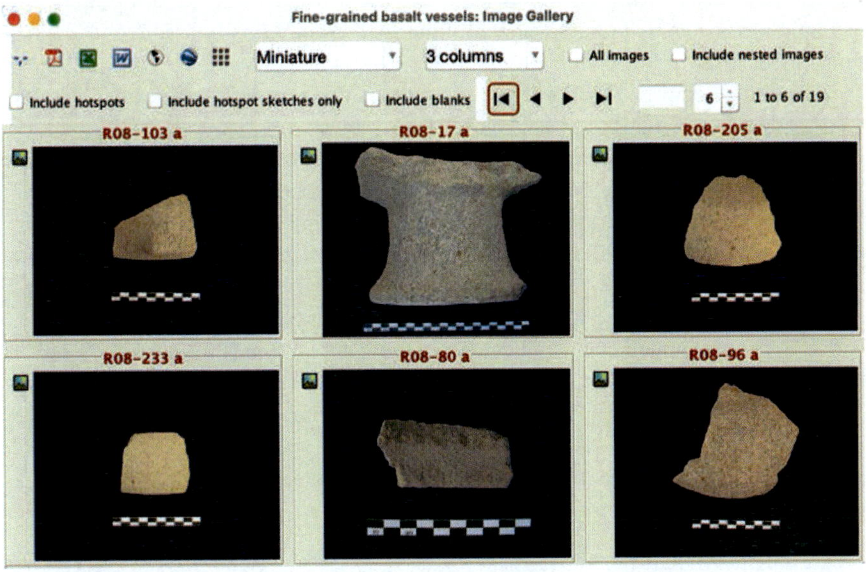

Fig. 7.25 Clicking the Image button on the quick-view toolbar pops up the Image Gallery for the Query Results

To find all finely made dense basalt vessels, we target the Properties of the items, using the hierarchical structure of the taxonomy to restrict to the "Fine-grained basalt" subtype of Basalt Stone (Fig. 7.24).

Performing this highly targeted query finds the individual items that satisfy all the conditions of the criteria, that is, the intersection set of items that match the properties, the spatial scope, and the period scope (Fig. 7.25).

Using Compound Queries

To address the challenge of making it easy to ask hard questions, OCHRE features a **Query-by-example** mode where a high-end power user (in consultation with the OCHRE Data Service, as needed) can pre-package queries so that more casual users can fill in the blanks and run common types of searches through a more user-friendly frontend interface. In this mode, there are also **Advanced options** that provide methods for compounding queries in interesting ways.

Sequential Queries: Combine, Intersect, Exclude

Every Query is a database item having a Name, perhaps a Description, and Notes, along with Properties and/or Events that specify its criteria. If we apply the item-based approach to queries-as-database item, we can set up a library of queries, in effect, where each query has a specialized task in a chain of queries. Query-by-example mode lets us mix and match individual query items in assorted combinations for maximum flexibility.

As a simple example of how multiple queries can be combined, let us pick two queries that we would like to apply together: a query that lets us choose **Items by Object type** where we will choose the Object type "Bead," and another query that lets us choose **Items by Material** where we will choose the Material "Glass." Performing the compound query runs both individual queries and combines the result: all Beads along with all Glass objects. Note that in this mode, each query can be performed individually using the **Perform** button on each query's own tab, and each query's result can be listed separately by clicking the related "count" button. Running the compound query indicates that there are 98 Beads whose results can be listed separately and 33 all things Glass whose results can also be listed separately. In total, 120 objects match the compound query criteria, with some items matching on both criteria. While a search for glass beads could be run directly in the OCHRE backend Query facility using Boolean operators (namely, "and," "or," and "not"), the Query-by-example mode is more exploratory and user-friendly, allowing the user to consider all things Glass, all types of Beads, or combinations thereof.

By default, the results of queries in this mode are joined using the **COMBINE** operator. Users can click to toggle between COMBINE ("or"), INTERSECT ("and"), and EXCLUDE ("not") operations. Figure 7.26 shows the specification of the combination of the two queries: all Beads along with all Glass items.

Toggling to choose the INTERSECT operator instead, the Query Results adjust to list only the Glass Beads, since the conditions of *all* queries must be satisfied. Toggling to choose the EXCLUDE option instead, only those Beads that are *not* Glass will be matched (Fig. 7.27).

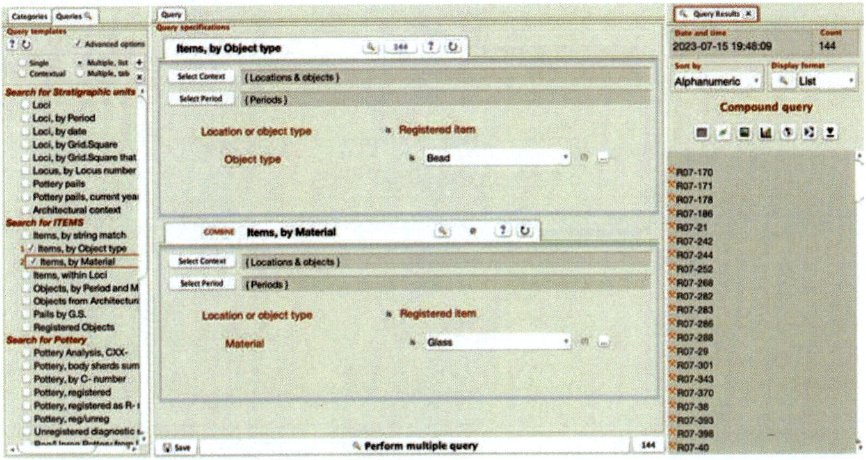

Fig. 7.26 Query-by-example mode shows the use of compound queries whose results are joined using the COMBINE operator

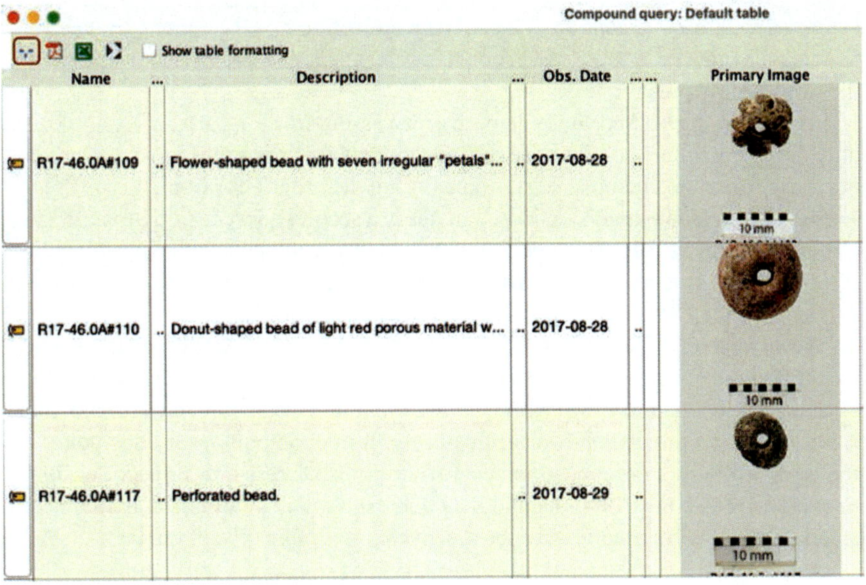

Fig. 7.27 Query Results are shown in Table View with the "Show thumbnails" option turned on

Nested Queries: From Which; That Contain

We have demonstrated how compound queries can work either individually or together in various combinations. But by now it must be clear that one of the core qualities of OCHRE is its extensive use of hierarchical arrangements of its items.

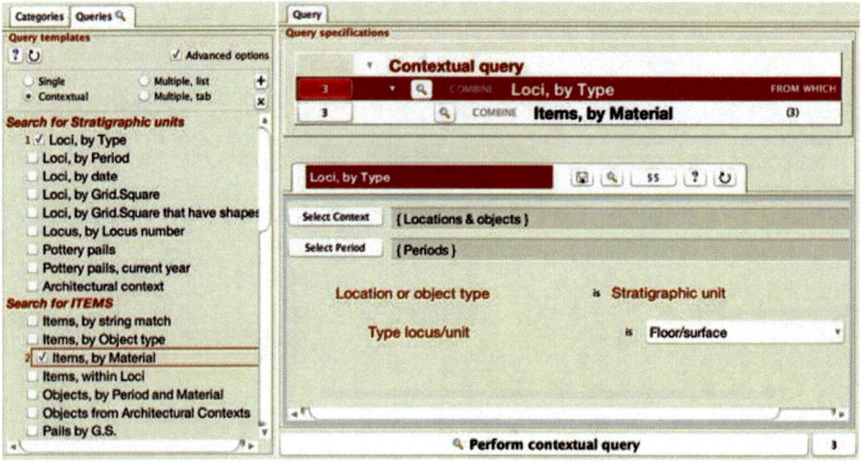

Fig. 7.28 Query results establish scope FROM WHICH other results are determined

Query items are no exception. The **Advanced options** of the **Query-by-example** feature allow *nested queries* which constrain the result of a subordinate query within the results of its parent query.

Imagine trying to find those same basalt vessels from our earlier example, but only those from more relevant excavation contexts that represent floors or surfaces, not those from fills and pits. Start by specifying the criteria for Loci of type "Floor/surface." Then, contextualize within that query a second query to find Stone Vessels. Using the "FROM WHICH" operator narrows the scope first to the matching Loci (Floors/surfaces), then finds the matching Stone Vessels located *within* those spatial contexts (Fig. 7.28).

The inverse of "FROM WHICH" is the "THAT CONTAINS" operator which would find the Floor/surface Loci that contain the matching Stone Vessels instead. Note that even when working with Queries, an item-based approach with hierarchical organization provides powerful flexibility. It may be obvious by this point, but this sort of query can be customized for any type of research project and is not restricted for use only for archaeological context. Any item arranged hierarchically and described with properties can be discovered with this type of query.

Querying Multiple Hierarchies: Select from

Recall the faunal remains case study in Chap. 5 where excavated bones, originally classified based on faunal taxon—sheep/goat, rodent, bear, and bird—were reclassified into secondary hierarchical categories based on size (small, medium, large, etc.), domesticity (domestic and wild), and dietary habits (herbivore, carnivore, and omnivore). The "Select from" query operator identifies which of the categories of

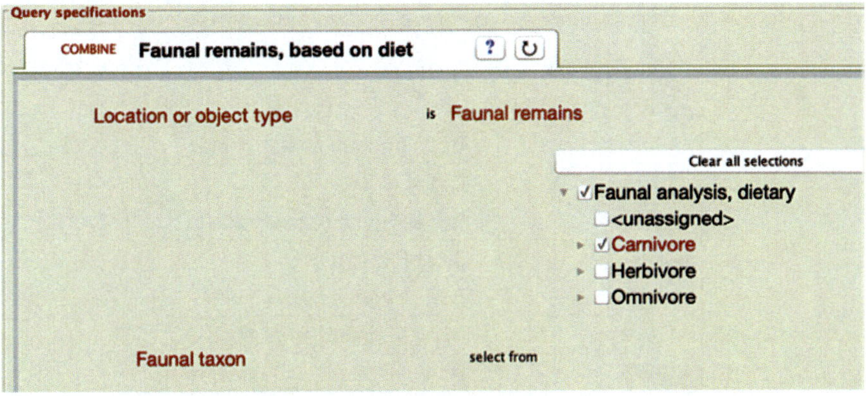

Fig. 7.29 Faunal remains are queried based on dietary habits of the species in question

analysis is to be used for the query. This query looks for matches using a secondary hierarchy of Variables and Values to return items that have not, themselves, been described with the Variables and Values from this specific taxonomic branch. Instead, the matching items share a Variable–Value property that has reorganized the items into a second taxonomic hierarchy. The query in Fig. 7.29 is based on the dietary habits of the mammals whose bone fragments have been excavated, rather than based on the original classification scheme of faunal taxon (Cattle, Equid, etc.).

Choosing "Carnivore" results in an interesting list of bear, lion, and other less commonly found non-sheep/goat species. Remember that this did not require the 17,000 individual faunal remains items to be described using properties for dietary habit. Rather, faunal taxon values were categorized into dietary groups: Bear = Carnivore; Sheep/goat = Herbivore, etc. The faunal remains, explicitly tagged as to taxon, determine their size, domesticity, and dietary habits based on the *reclassifications* of their *original* Variables and Values. That is, every bone fragment tagged only as sheep/goat inherits the information that it is part of an herbivorous, domestic, medium-sized mammal (Fig. 7.30).

Finding Things in Other Projects

Noticing lions in the Query Results piques our interest in other places that might attest lions, or *felids* more generally. The advantage of a comprehensive warehouse-style database is that it is simple to broaden the scope of a search to include data from other projects. From our vantage point as database administrators, we are able to see all the data from all OCHRE projects, even though user credentials prevent

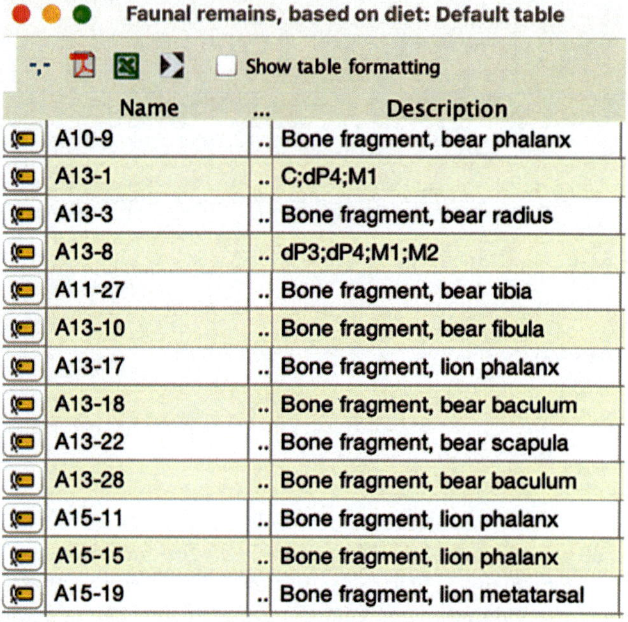

Faunal remains, based on diet: Default table

Show table formatting

Name	...	Description
A10-9	..	Bone fragment, bear phalanx
A13-1	..	C;dP4;M1
A13-3	..	Bone fragment, bear radius
A13-8	..	dP3;dP4;M1;M2
A11-27	..	Bone fragment, bear tibia
A13-10	..	Bone fragment, bear fibula
A13-17	..	Bone fragment, lion phalanx
A13-18	..	Bone fragment, bear baculum
A13-22	..	Bone fragment, bear scapula
A13-28	..	Bone fragment, bear baculum
A15-11	..	Bone fragment, lion phalanx
A15-15	..	Bone fragment, lion phalanx
A15-19	..	Bone fragment, lion metatarsal

Fig. 7.30 OCHRE allows re-classification of items based on secondary characteristics

other projects from seeing each other's data (except by explicit agreement among collaborating projects, or by virtue of having made such data public) (Fig. 7.31).[19]

A search of all OCHRE projects for *felids* yields many lions represented at the aptly named "Lion Temple" at Jaffa (on the coast of Israel), and a lone exemplar at neighboring Ashkelon (which appears to have generated some excitement based on the note "FIRST LION BONE FOUND" entered on the registered item MC 49064 in 1997). Given the lions represented at Zincirli Höyük (ZH), it is no surprise to find big cats also at the sister site of Tayinat (TAP), both situated in the Amuq Valley of south-central Turkey. Farther afield, several wildcats were tentatively identified by the Sereno research (SRLab) team at Gobero (central Sahara).

[19] Data access is a decision made by each project, not determined by the OCHRE platform or the OCHRE Data Service. The OCHRE platform will support entirely "open" data, or it will keep data completely private, depending on the project's preferences. The CRANE consortium of projects, for example, has agreed to share access among all the CRANE members, and so, this is permitted within the OCHRE environment. We do not view this as a technical issue; rather, it is a challenge for scholarly collaboration.

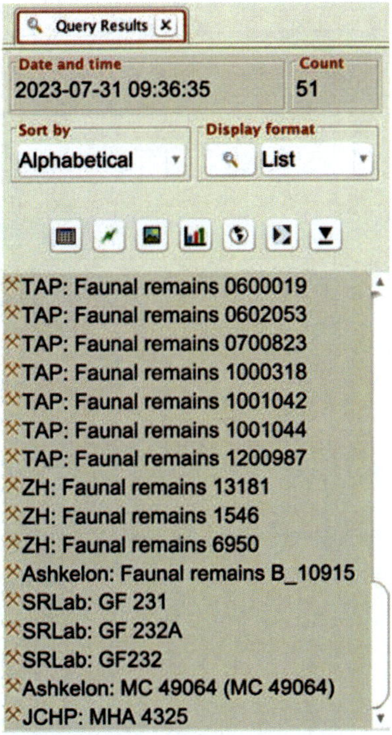

Fig. 7.31 Evidence of felids has been tagged by OCHRE projects working across the Middle East and northern Africa

The **Chart** option of the quick-view toolbar provides a helpful pie chart showing the distribution of attestations by faunal taxon and also gives a clue as to what proportion of the species could be identified, or not (Fig. 7.32).[20]

The scientific standardization of faunal taxonomy, and the regular modeling of this in the OCHRE taxonomy—by class, family, genus, and species description—makes it convenient for projects to borrow an entire taxonomic branch for use within their own projects. This allows querying across projects for faunal items since their descriptive properties will conform to a shared descriptive taxonomy. But the spirit of OCHRE is that projects are not forced to share and standardize. Faunal remains might be found within baskets or pails or buckets or lots; those might be found within loci or units or features or contexts. There are valid reasons why a project will want to use its own recording system and nomenclature, and not have to borrow or share. In the next section, we describe how to find items across projects even when they are described with different properties.

[20] The OCHRE approach intentionally accommodates a wide range of users, from casual assistants to highly specialized experts. Often data remains somewhat high level until a specialist studies the material, at which point a specimen might go from being tagged as a "Mammal" (generally) to "*Felix sylvestris*" (species-level identification). The hierarchical descriptive taxonomy of OCHRE makes it easy to make these adjustments, in this case, by inserting one or two additional levels of detail to the property that has already been assigned.

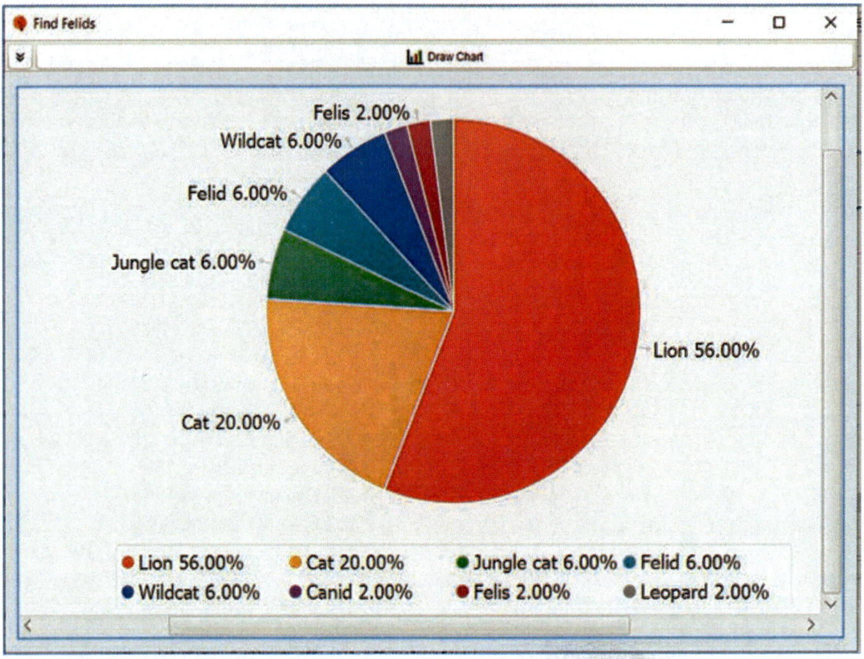

Fig. 7.32 A pie chart summarizes the proportion of felids from many OCHRE projects

Skip Operator

OCHRE includes mechanisms to find items across projects when those items have been described using different taxonomic branches. One such technique is the use of the **Skip** query operator which tells the query to ignore the intervening structure of the taxonomic branch and target just the leaf nodes of the branch. There is no need to create a new property value for "Coin" and "Lion" and "Bowl" and "Basalt" in each project, because generally the leaf items that represent common vocabulary are shared among projects. It is the organization of these items within a descriptive hierarchical taxonomy that can vary greatly. By skipping over the variations in project-specific taxonomic branches and focusing on the values in common, the query in Fig. 7.33 can find all Basalt Vessels, regardless of whether they were called "Registered item" or "Small find" or "Object" or "Material culture" etc. Those higher level descriptors need not match, either by name or by nested level within the hierarchy, because they are skipped.[21]

[21] Those familiar with XQuery and its use of XPath will recognize the use of the search directive "//" which targets descendant-or-self nodes (versus "/" which targets only immediate child nodes) to skip the intervening parent nodes.

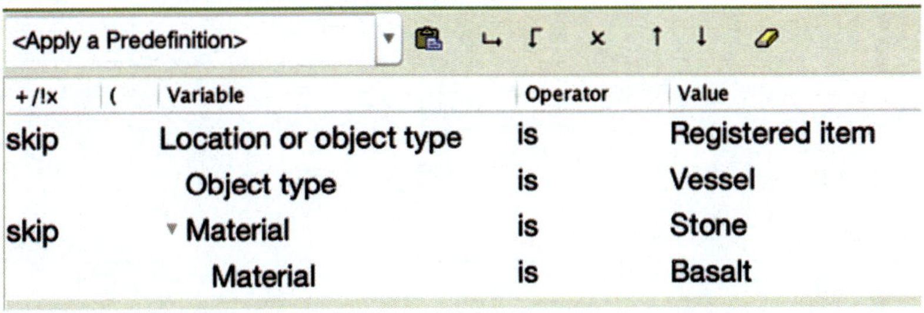

Fig. 7.33 OCHRE accommodates varying descriptive hierarchies using the skip operator

Setting the Project Scope to include several participating projects of the CRANE collaboration is as simple as checking on the checkboxes of the projects to include from the full list of projects to which the user has access. Using the skip operator to ignore differences of description yields almost 500 basalt vessels from the basalt-rich regions of Zincirli, Tayinat, and Tell al-Judaidah.

Queries Related to Texts

To avoid giving the wrong impression that only Locations & objects can be found, and only by querying Properties, consider a few examples that apply to textual data.

Character-String Matching

Imagine a biblical scholar performing text-critical analysis to reconstruct a Dead Sea Scroll (DSS) fragment from the Book of Samuel. Say, for example, an *ʾaleph* and a *lamed* are preserved on the fragment and the goal is to find all other words attested in the content of the Samuel DSSs that contain this sequence of characters, in the hope that one of those words would fit in the fragmentary gap. This can be achieved using Query settings:

- On the Project Scope tab, restrict to the CEDAR-Samuel project
- On the Category Scope tab, restrict to Discourse units
- On the Criteria tab, choose the Character-string option
- On the Search field, specify the required sequence of characters, surrounded by the match-any-character wildcard (*אל*)
- restrict the search to Phonemic content only, so that the query does not inefficiently consider other text fields like description and notes (Fig. 7.34).

Performing the query matches all the conditions and produces a set of words for further consideration which can be viewed in Table View. Double-clicking any table

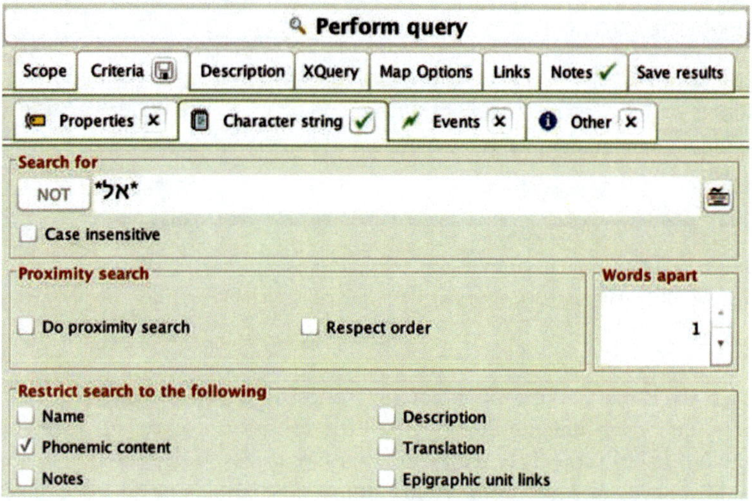

Fig. 7.34 Textual content can be found by querying for character-string matches

row will pop up that item and all its details for review (or editing), including information identifying the locations of the attested words on the other Samuel manuscripts. The table is just another view of items that already exist independently in the database and which can be accessed individually.

A character-string query can be supplemented by limiting the search to discourse units (words) with specific properties. To achieve this end, the Character-string settings would be configured; then, the properties to match (e.g., Part of speech is a Verb) would be assigned on the Properties tab (which would be checked "on" so that it is made active). As such, the query would return only the words with both the requested text string and the custom properties.

Co-occurrence Queries

Another common text-based research question involves finding sequences or co-occurrences of words. In the Persepolis Fortification Archive, for example, many of the texts are formulaic: lists of rations or personnel and receipts for transactions. Finding recurring phrases can shed light on social networks or economic practices. Traditional Digital Humanities text-based analysis typically uses natural language processing (NLP) strategies to "scrape" the text for certain types of content, "mine" the data for patterns, or search for "n-grams" (some number of words in sequence). The complexity of many of the ancient languages with which we work thwarts the effectiveness of NLP and leaves too many potential matches behind. When the sample of textual content is already finite and fragmentary, we need more intentional and specialized strategies to make the most of the data.

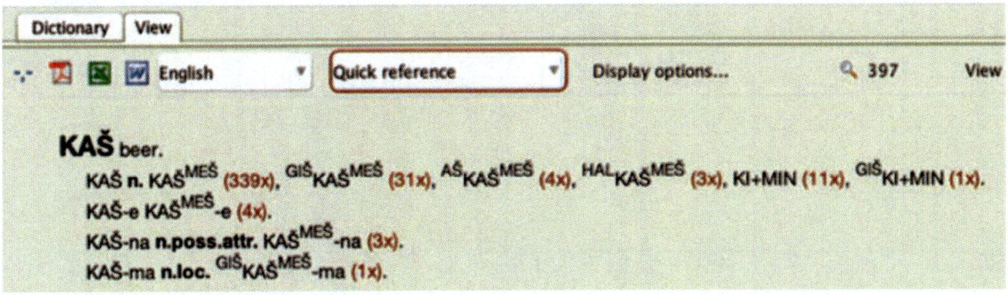

Fig. 7.35 "Beer" is spelled many different ways in the Elamite Glossary of the PFA

Follow along with this demonstration of the OCHRE strategy to make it easy to ask a hard question like: *Find all texts that record an allotment of any measure of beer*. Admittedly, an ordinary character-string search on the word for "beer" (KAŠ) would be a decent start. But the PFA Elamite Glossary compiled in OCHRE identifies seven known spellings of "beer" along with at least twelve instances where scholars have determined that beer is being referred to using a "ditto" notation (KI + MIN) to a previous attestation. Already, a string-based search becomes complicated as it would need to account for these variations. The item-based glossary organizes and describes all variations in form and grammar and can pinpoint all 397 references to any instance of the word "beer" attested in the current corpus (Fig. 7.35).

Similarly, the Elamite word for "allotment, by the hand" (kurmin) is attested by the spellings: kur-ma-n, kur-mín, kur-man, mín-kur, kur-mín^{MEŠ}, kur-me-in, ^{HAL}kur-mín, kur-ma, and kur-mi. Again, a string-based search on "kur" would be a start, but in this case, it would pick up thousands of unwanted matches based on hundreds of other words that start with the common sequence of letters "kur."[22]

Beyond targeting the keywords for "beer" and "allotment," the research question requires the inclusion of a measured amount. The PFA team has categorized the words in the Elamite glossary, using OCHRE properties in the usual way, to identify personal or geographic names, commodities, occupations, calendar entities (months, days, or years), and for this purpose, units of measure. A simple property-based query finds thirty different lemma entries in the glossary that represent units of measure, each with any number of variations of form and spelling. In addition, PFA researchers have transliterated numbers as ordinary numerals which OCHRE can recognize as such.

With that background, we turn to the category of OCHRE Concepts to express the meaning of the original question: *Find all texts that record an allotment of any measure of beer*. An ordered list of links called **Component(s)** on a Concept lets the user specify the sequence of things to be found (Fig. 7.36). In this example, the user has specified the structure of the formulaic phrase of interest:

[22] The underlying core database, Tamino, provides full-text search capabilities with proximity constraints (e.g., "within 3 words"), and OCHRE exposes this for the character-string criteria, but it is of limited value in cases such as this where string matching is insufficient.

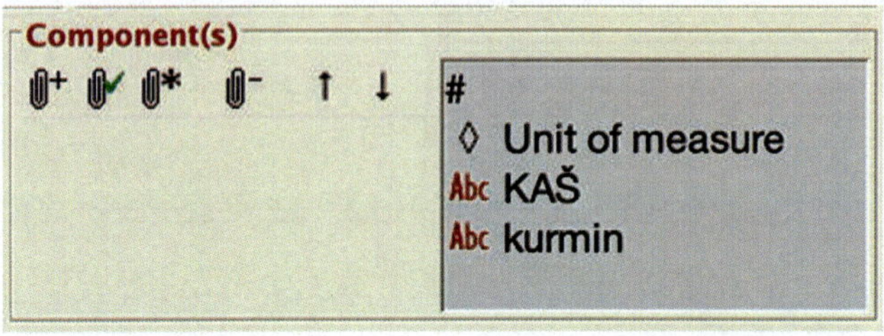

Fig. 7.36 An OCHRE Concept itemizes the elements of the co-occurrence criteria

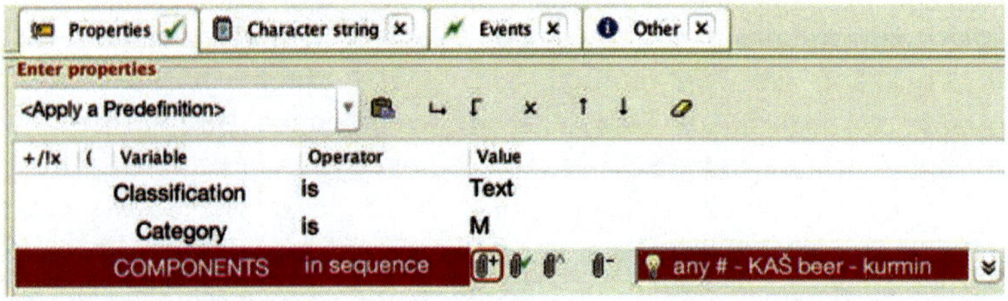

Fig. 7.37 This co-occurrence query will find any allotments of beer in ration texts

- Any number (using a special-purpose built-in option represented by "#").
- Followed by any unit of measure (targeting the required Property Value).
- Followed by any form of the word for "beer" (linking in the appropriate Dictionary lemma).
- Followed by any form of the word for "allotment."

On the Query specification form, we Scope the query to the Texts category and activate the Properties criteria tab. The metadata Variable **COMPONENTS** is available as a built-in option for Text queries and comes with two operators: "that occur" (for simple co-occurrence) or "in sequence" (to require that the targeted words appear in the prescribed order). The COMPONENTS Variable takes as its Value the Concept that lists the elements to be found co-occurring. To constrain the query further, the texts to be considered are restricted to those tagged as Category M (Special Rations) (Fig. 7.37).

Upon performing the Query, OCHRE reports preliminary results for each of the components we defined as part of the Concept. This first stage of the query reports how many texts are attested in the junction of these classes. In other words, when these preliminary results overlap in all four cases, how many texts do we find in this subset? A somewhat complex XQuery reports that there are 44 Special Ration texts in which matching elements co-occur. When the "in sequence" operator is used, another step determines how many of these 44 texts attest the components *in the desired sequence*. Because it is possible to create unreasonable queries that will be computationally very expensive for examining sequences, OCHRE performs an initial analysis and gives the user a chance to opt-out in order to further refine the search. If the initial search had resulted in thousands of texts with the components,

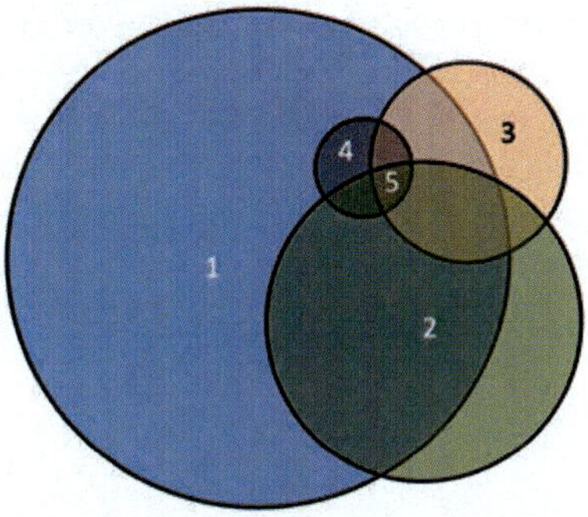

Fig. 7.38 The intersection of co-occurring query COMPONENTS is illustrated. As of 2021, the results are as follows: (1) 52,650 instances of any number, (2) 11,337 instances of units of measure, (3) 4080 references to kurmin (allotment), (4) 394 references to KAŠ (beer), and (5) the in-sequence co-occurrence of all four components of the Concept in 37 texts

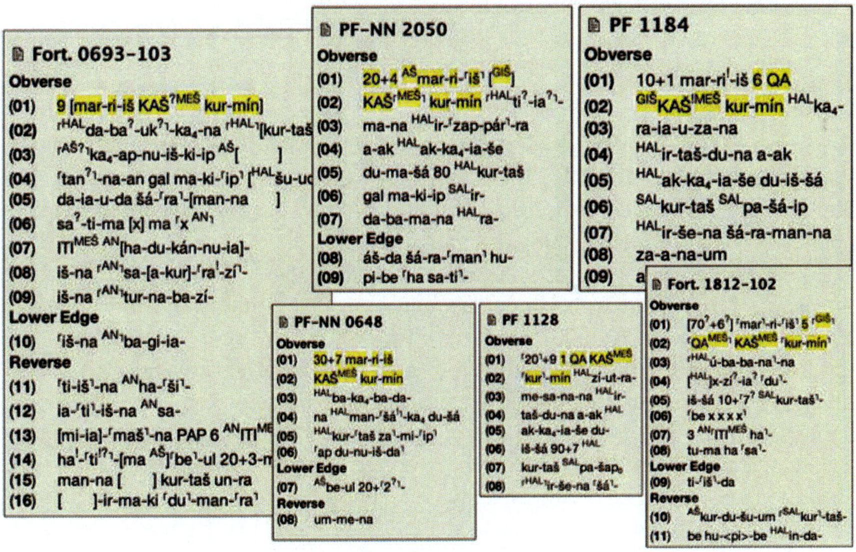

Fig. 7.39 Matches for co-occurrence, in sequence, of allotments of beer are highlighted

it would be prudent to refine the criteria to be more selective. However, 44 is a reasonable set to consider, so we confirm that OCHRE should continue with the next phase of the query. Of these, we learn that 37 texts attest the elements in sequence (Fig. 7.38).

The Text option of the quick-view toolbar displays the results with matching elements highlighted for easy identification (Fig. 7.39). It is often striking to view these results, noting the variations in spelling, the different ways in which numbers are composed, the variety of words fulfilling criteria (here "QA" and "marriš" as the most common units of measure), and the inclusion of content reconstructed from damaged tablets (marked here within full or half-square brackets). Without a richly tagged, comprehensively linked database organization of textual and lexical content, such a query would be, quite literally, impossible.

Specialized Views

With so many kinds of things to find and so many ways to find them, we reiterate our earlier point that it is hard to make it easy to find the data of interest. However, in many cases, items in OCHRE are related in predictable and regular ways using the common and customary methods built into OCHRE. In these cases, instead of requiring the user to compose a query to join the data in a table or map, OCHRE can produce some highly detailed and specialized views on demand.

Comprehensive View

To generate a Comprehensive View, the user selects an item of interest, and from its graph of knowledge, OCHRE gathers *everything* that is known about that item, and all the other items related to it, listing and summarizing the collected information in a helpful format for further study and analysis.

For example, many projects begin with observations about objects. To these objects, they link images, bibliography, and even text editions. There is much to learn about the seal PFS 0002 from the PFA collection, one of those illustrating heroic control over animals found by the query shown earlier. It is attested on 101 tablets by 203 impressions, in a few cases multiple times on the same surface. In Comprehensive View, a detailed table of the seal impressions, tablets, and surfaces is shown, and this table is available to be exported as a Microsoft Excel spreadsheet. The Text items associated with the textual content on those tablets are also listed as links. Bibliography, with the associated PDF linked as a live resource, directs the viewer to the truly comprehensive and authoritative commentary on this seal. Over forty image hotspot cutouts are shown at-a-glance, providing a visual array of exemplars. With an item-based, richly linked database, items of all kinds can be mixed and matched in any assortment that is helpful to the scholar (Fig. 7.40).

Illustrated View

For an example of a specialized view for a text-based project, consider Act 1 Scene 1 of Shakespeare's *Taming of the Shrew* in OCHRE. Although typically presented as a line-by-line rendition of the play in Standard View, behind the scenes OCHRE

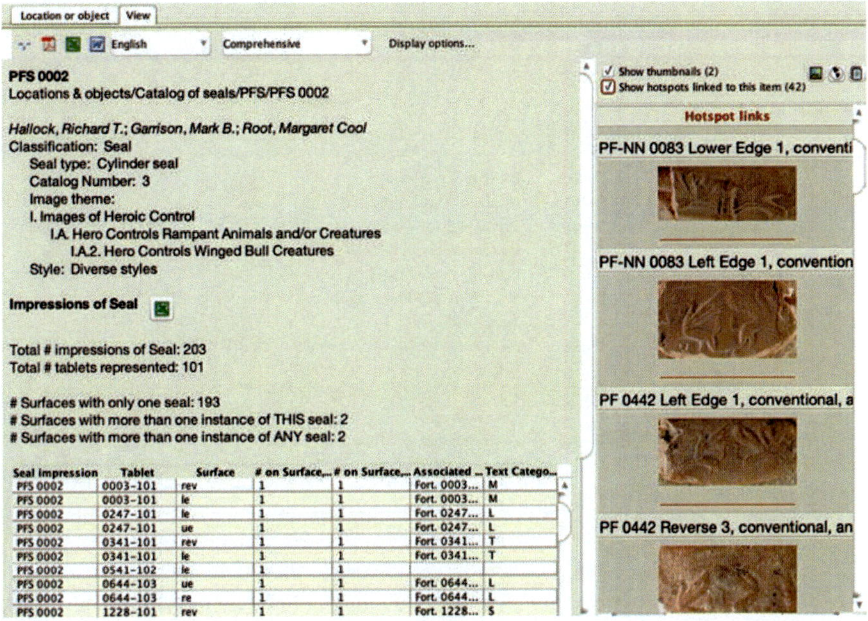

Fig. 7.40 A Comprehensive View of a Seal item provides a detailed summary of all its relevant links, images, and other associated information

has atomized and itemized the word-by-word (indeed, character-string-by-character-string) content of the entire play. The "*glaſſes*" which the Beggar has "*burſt*" and which he is entreated by the Lord to pay for is linked to the "Glass" Value in an illustrated Ontology of Things, which has been designed by the scholars, and implemented as part of the OCHRE Taxonomy, to document both the tangible props and the ephemeral ideas that they wish to tag and track. The "Glass" Value, in turn, has linked to it images (OCHRE Resource items) of assorted cups that illustrate the type of glasses being referenced.

For the Illustrated View, a click on a relevant word item (a Discourse unit) triggers the traversal of links that lead to a property Value, which is illustrated by links to a Resource item. OCHRE makes it easy to follow the network of knowledge to enrich the experience of the user by illustrating the content of an otherwise plain text view. And while this example may seem rather idiosyncratic and specific to the CEDAR-Shrew project, the underlying strategy of linking discourse units to images and presenting them in an Illustrated View is generalizable to any text project (Fig. 7.41).

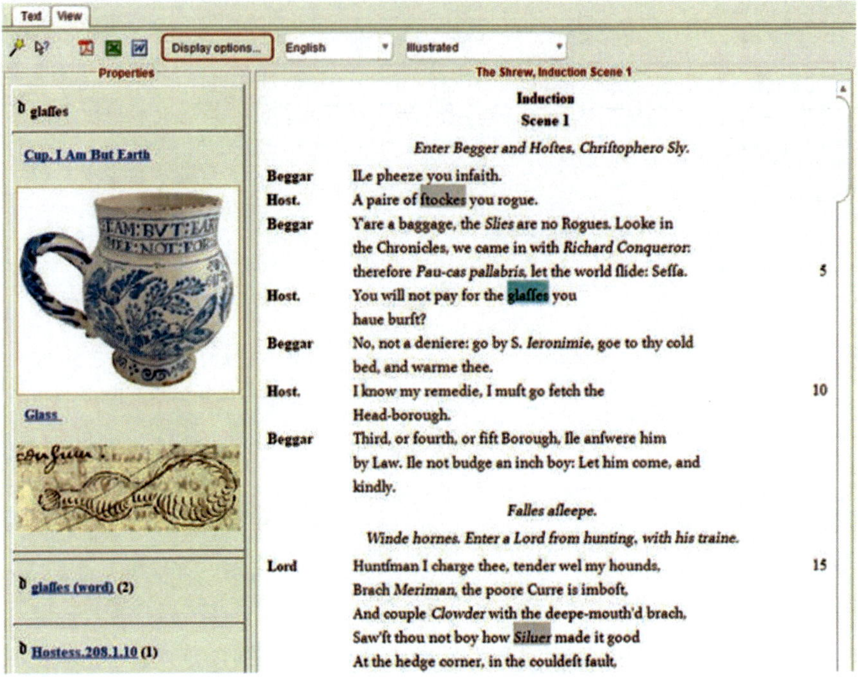

Fig. 7.41 *Taming of the Shrew* is itemized word by word and illustrated by linked images

Collecting Things: Sets

Once *things* have been found by a query, it is often helpful to keep that collection of things—to come back to it, to assign a student to work on it, to send it to a colleague, or to export it to other formats for further analysis. In OCHRE, any collection of items, whether generated by a Query or by selecting manually from the Linked Items pane, can be saved as a Set—a one-dimensional list of items. Note that a Set does not introduce a new burden on the data model, as it is the trivial case of a hierarchy, that is, a hierarchy with no branches. But the use of Sets gives users the ability to find and save items as an alternative way to organize the data. An archaeologist can find all coins, originally entered within an excavation hierarchy, and save them to a Set, creating a new collection, or class, of coin items. A historian can find and save a collection of personal names, originally entered via the discourse hierarchy of a text, creating a node list of person items to use for social network analysis. A geographer can find and save a collection of places to form the basis for a gazetteer. Collections of items saved in Sets are also useful for sharing with other applications, or for sharing among collaborators.

Items in a set are not duplicates of other items. In creating a Set, items that *already exist* in the database are *reused* in a new context; there is no duplication or redundancy of data. Existing items identified by their universally unique identifiers (UUIDs) are reassembled as components of a new item—a Set item. Such Sets are also uniquely identified and can be configured or displayed in many ways. A Set works much like the Query Results list and can be formatted to display as a Table, Graph, Map, Gallery, and so on. In fact, a specific Set can be associated with a Query by using a simple link. This identifies the destination where the results of the query can be saved when the Query is performed or updated against new data. Results can be added, removed, or joined with data in the corresponding Set.

Using Sets to Constrain Queries

A Set may also be used to constrain a query by restricting its scope. In one scenario, the Set will define the subset of data within which to search. Instead of searching all items in the project, the query will consider only those items contained in the Set. In another scenario, a query can be configured to return only results that are linked to items in the constraining Set, for example, to find images, but only those that are linked to the pottery items that have been collected in a Set.

Using Sets to Create Classes

Typically, OCHRE users run Queries to create Sets to view data as a table—a familiar presentation of rows and columns that is intuitive, flexible, and portable. This has the effect of transforming the network of item-based data into more specific classes of data that resemble relational tables in the usual sense—all coins, all bones, all kings, all proper nouns, and so on—which comes as a relief to users who are wary of the item-based approach. In this way, OCHRE provides the benefits of tabular presentation as a *secondary* format for viewing and exchange, without being restricted by its limitations as a *primary* format for data representation.

OCHRE provides a tool for defining the columns of the table to be created based on the properties of the items in the Set, and to configure many other formatting options. The quick-view tables already shown presume some default settings over which the user has ultimate control. In addition, a Set can be used to join data from items associated with the items in the Set.[23] For example, suppose a Set contains a list of inscribed metal objects. Using OCHRE's item-based approach to data, each inscription is represented as a separate Text database item distinct from, but linked to, its associated object. Information about the language and script of each inscription is stored as a property on the Text, not as a property on the Object. However, the Set of inscribed objects can be configured to include a column that lists the language property from the related texts. When viewed, OCHRE joins the inscribed Object

[23] More technical readers may recognize the principle of a "join" (like that of SQL) which allows content to be added to a table from items that are *linked-to* the items in the table and not being restricted to the intrinsic qualities of the primary items themselves.

and the Text by following the relational link between these two ("Associated text") and returns the value of the language property from the Text as an extra column in the resulting table generated by the Set.

Just as OCHRE uses links to join data in a table, it takes advantage of its other primary organizing structure, hierarchies, to *inherit* data for a tabular view. For example, the items listed in a table of Pottery by Ware can inherit the Period assignment of the excavation unit (e.g., the Locus) in which it was found thereby including the relevant temporal context of the items as a column in the tabular view of the Set of pottery. Similarly, words representing proper names of people or places can inherit properties from the phrase ("Economic transaction") or from the Text ("Administrative genre") in which they are contextualized and include these details as additional columns in the table derived based on the configuration of the Set.

Using Sets to Design Views

While hierarchies and tables typically organize items of a similar type, an OCHRE Set, freed from the constraints of table structures, can organize items of different types. This is a boon to the Florentine Catasto project with its mixture of social and geographic networks. Workshops and houses in adjoining blocks of the Unicorno and Vipera districts are added to a Set (based on the result of a Query). Workshops, houses, palaces, streets, blocks, and districts do not share any table columns or characteristics. But viewed together on OCHRE's Map View, they paint an interesting picture of the Piazza Santa Trinita neighborhood in 1427 (Fig. 7.42).

Using Sets to Specify Outputs

The simple structure of a Set gives a starting point for anticipating the ways in which users will want to combine data and for facilitating the traversal of links to find related items and their properties. In the same way that OCHRE provides specialized views (e.g., the Comprehensive View) to gather all the pertinent information related to an item or class of items, it also provides specialized exports to reformat items as tables and save them on export to be used as input to other programs or processes. While OCHRE could not possibly compete with more specialized software to do advanced analysis, it can certainly facilitate the reuse of clean, well-formatted data extracted from the OCHRE repository for other purposes.

Consider again the seals from the PFA, many of which attest personal names of persons of significance. These important people are represented by Person items in the OCHRE database. The names of these persons are attested in the text corpus (as words, i.e., discourse units) in many different forms and with many different spellings, all of which are grouped and rationalized by the OCHRE glossary. Such words (representing the personal names) appear in texts on tablets whose potentially

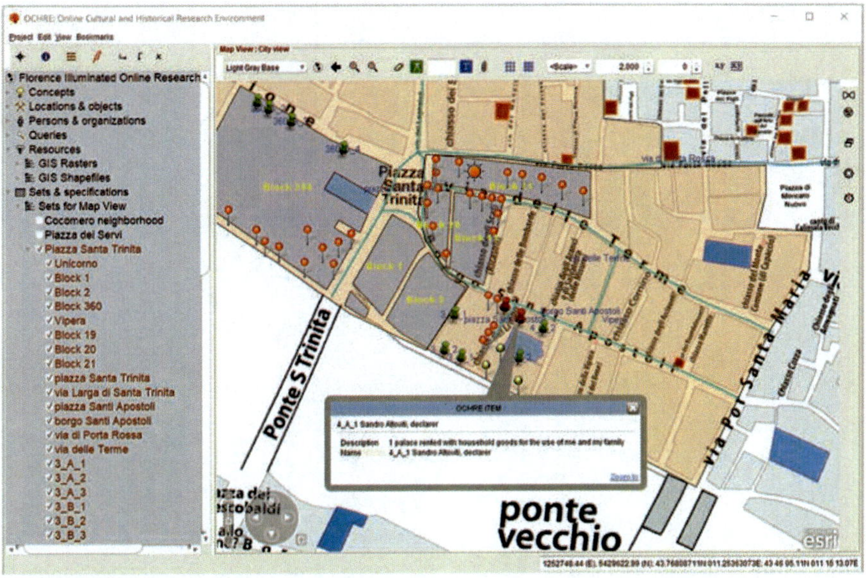

Fig. 7.42 Items with different characteristics can be collected in a Set for a Map View (geospatial analysis by analyst C. Caswell)

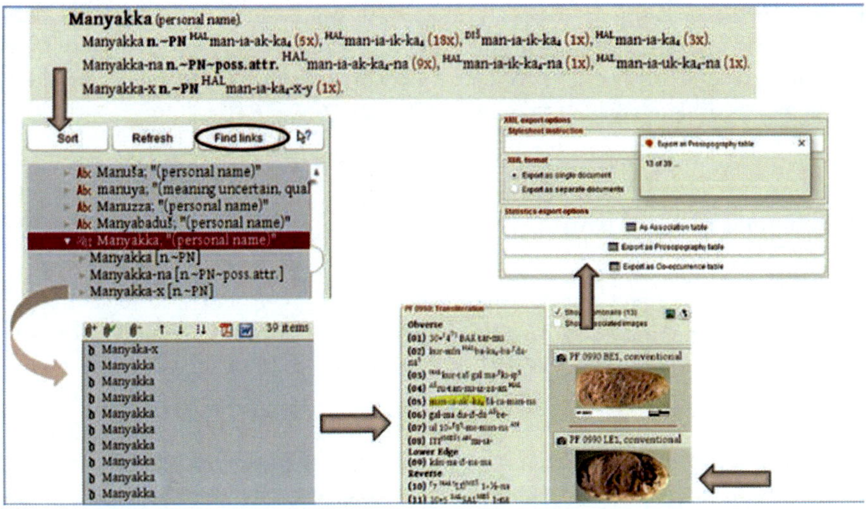

Fig. 7.43 Extensive linking among items of different types creates a vast network of data

multiple surfaces have been impressed upon by potentially multiple seals. Complex routes based on traversal of links—from Person to Dictionary to Discourse unit to Texts to Seals to impressions of those Seals made on surfaces of real tablets—result in a rich network of associations (Fig. 7.43).

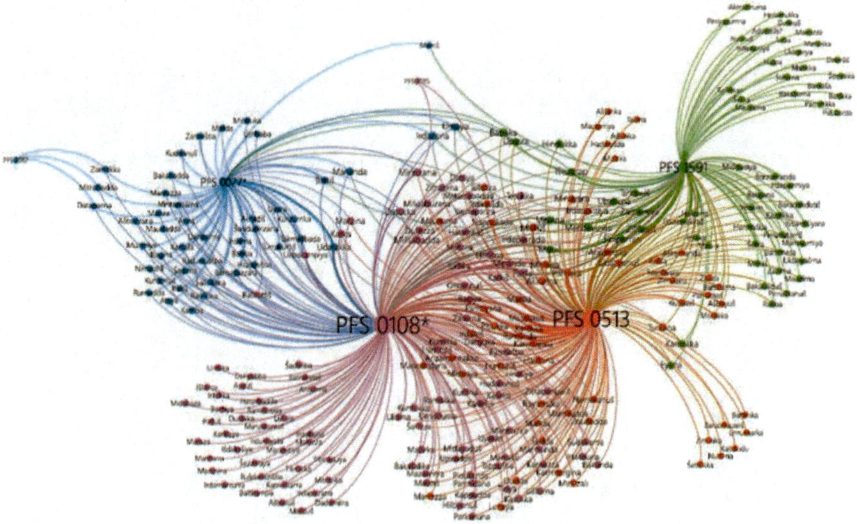

Fig. 7.44 A node-edge list exported from OCHRE can be visualized in Gephi, illustrating the networks among people and places as evidenced from the accounting seals of PFA. (Image courtesy of Tytus Mikolajczak, Mikołajczak, 2018, p. 86)

Recognizing the importance of this network of links, OCHRE can export the full set of related data as a node-edge list, suitable for import into a specialized package for network analysis. From there, meaningful visualizations can be made, along with analysis and implications for social networks, family organization, political and economic influence, trade relations, and so on (Fig. 7.44).

Tracking Things: Events

It is not enough to find things, collect things, and relate things to other things. Things happen to things, and those things need to be tracked as well. OCHRE provides the means to observe, comment on, and otherwise track the various events in the life of the item. We may be observing the lives of nineteenth-century scientists, which can be described with processes common to life histories: born, died, moved to, studied at, etc. We may be observing the process of discovering, conserving, storing, or displaying an artifact. OCHRE provides a special purpose-built mechanism for purposefully recording the Events that constitute the sequential process of observations for an item.[24] The need for events was initially a pragmatic one—tracking what was being done to an item, by whom, and when.

[24] Events are described in detail in the OCHRE manual (Schloen and Schloen 2012), *Chap. 7, Recording Events that Affect an Item*, pp. 97–103.

Adding an Event creates an assortment of links on the current item:

- *What* action is being tracked? This is designated by a link to a Property Value item representing the outcome of the Property Variable "Event," for example, "Photographed."
- *Who* is doing the action? This is noted by a link to an agent, a Person item.
- *Where* is the action implicated? For example, an item is "Moved to" the "Gaziantep Museum," a Location item, triggering Inventory analysis.[25]
- *When* was the action performed? This is identified by a link to a Period item, or, alternatively, by an explicit date.
- Each Event also allows a specific Comment to explain *Why?*
- Optionally, an Event may have a link to another Property Value that represents the *fulfillment* of that Event.[26]

Managing Workflow

Our favorite Canadian archaeological object illustrator, Karen Reczuch, regularly takes time off from her day job as a well-known children's book illustrator to labor next to a blowing fan, under a dubious table lamp bought in the local market, meticulously creating detailed stippled drawings of artifacts ranging from exotic scarabs and coins to mundane flint blades, clay loom weights, and grindstones. Her first and most unexpected assignment was to draw the Katumuwa stele on her first archaeological trip abroad in 2008, a case of "beginner's luck" if ever there was! Karen generates hundreds of drawings every summer, using OCHRE Events to manage the task. As artifacts are processed by the registrar, and reviewed by the dig director, those deemed worthy of the attention of a professional illustrator are flagged with the event "To draw."

Events are simply OCHRE Property values of the special-purpose Variable "Event." But Event values are imbued with an extra feature whereby they can link to a related event that represents the fulfillment of the event, in this case, "Drawn." Once the task has been completed, Karen adds the fulfillment event, tagging herself as the Agent, setting the Date, and supplying any additional details via the Comment field. The Agent field is not just a string field, but a link to Karen's Person item, adding to the growing graph of relationships among database items (Figs. 7.45 and 7.46).

As she completes each drawing—and as the row of artifacts lined up on her drawing table dwindles—Karen turns to an OCHRE Query for her to-do list. The query is based on the **Events Criteria** and is set to find all the items assigned a "To draw" event that *have not yet been fulfilled* by the "Drawn" event. The query provides the updated list of items remaining to be drawn. Restricting instead to the

---

[25] On the use of Events for Inventory Management, see the Tell Keisan case study (Chap. 10) and the OCHRE manual (Schloen and Schloen 2012, pp. 101–103).

[26] For another example of event fulfillment, see the Ras Shamra case study (Chap. 11).

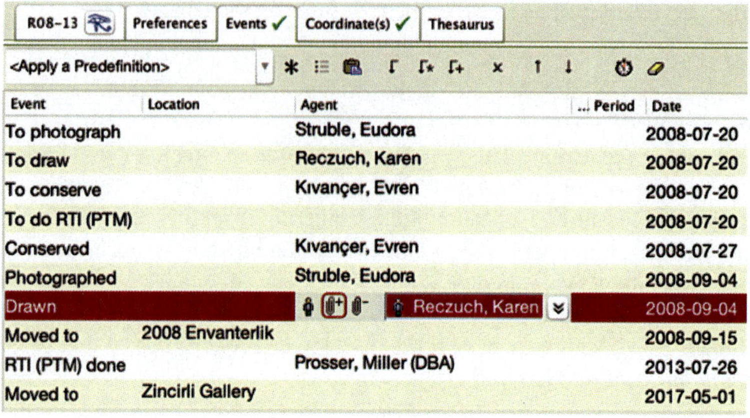

Event	Location	Agent	... Period	Date
To photograph		Struble, Eudora		2008-07-20
To draw		Reczuch, Karen		2008-07-20
To conserve		Kıvançer, Evren		2008-07-20
To do RTI (PTM)				2008-07-20
Conserved		Kıvançer, Evren		2008-07-27
Photographed		Struble, Eudora		2008-09-04
Drawn		Reczuch, Karen		2008-09-04
Moved to	2008 Envanterlik			2008-09-15
RTI (PTM) done		Prosser, Miller (DBA)		2013-07-26
Moved to	Zincirli Gallery			2017-05-01

Fig. 7.45 Processing of the Katumuwa stele is tracked by Events performed by specialists

Fig. 7.46 The Katumuwa stele is drawn Reczuch style. (Image courtesy of the University of Chicago Zincirli Excavations)

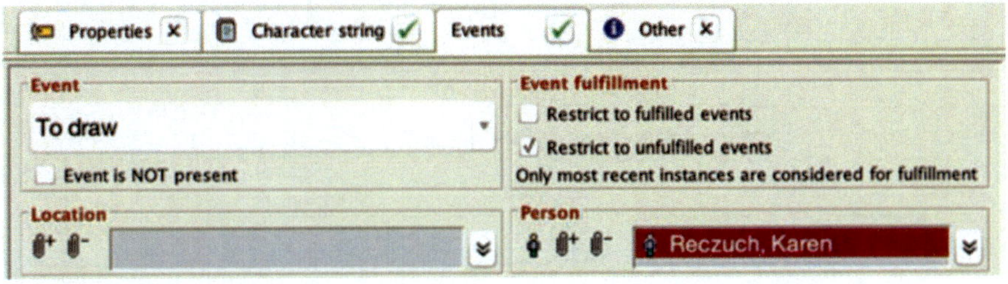

Fig. 7.47 Events are analyzed in conjunction with a Query to create a to-do list

events that *have been fulfilled* shows which items have been drawn and provides a sense of accomplishment! (Fig. 7.47).

Given the number of specialists that participate in an excavation and the vast quantity of items being worked on in various ways, the Events provide an invaluable mechanism for managing workflow. Repeat the above process for the photographer, the conservator, the ceramic illustrator, the assistant creating 3D sherd profiles, the botanist processing samples for radio-carbon analysis, and the scientist performing petrographic analysis. And note that in a completely customizable platform like OCHRE, the event Values can be created as needed to manage whatever types of events are needed by the project staff: "To pick up from airport;" "To prepare meat for barbeque night." The list goes on.

Case Study: History and Life Histories

While originally intended for tracking workflow of staff and movement of objects, the Event feature was put to creative use by the Lives, Individuality, and Analysis (LIA) project as they studied the life histories of nineteenth-century scientists and tracked their interactions with each other. Using relational properties to link parents, children, and siblings via Person items, an extensive network of family relationships was developed. Events were then used to track personal events such as births, deaths, and marriages; academic studies, from kindergarten through graduate school, noting specializations, awards, and publications; employment over time and in various places; travels to and from cities or universities, and the purposes of such; and communications among individuals as letters were sent to and fro, among Persons, in Locations, during Periods.

Furthermore, to fill in the details of the historical picture, copies of the actual correspondence were scanned, transcribed, and linked to the relevant person items. These letters, some written in German or French, all using flowery cursive typical of the day, sometimes including the original envelopes with postmarks, are fascinating historical artifacts now preserved digitally (Fig. 7.48).

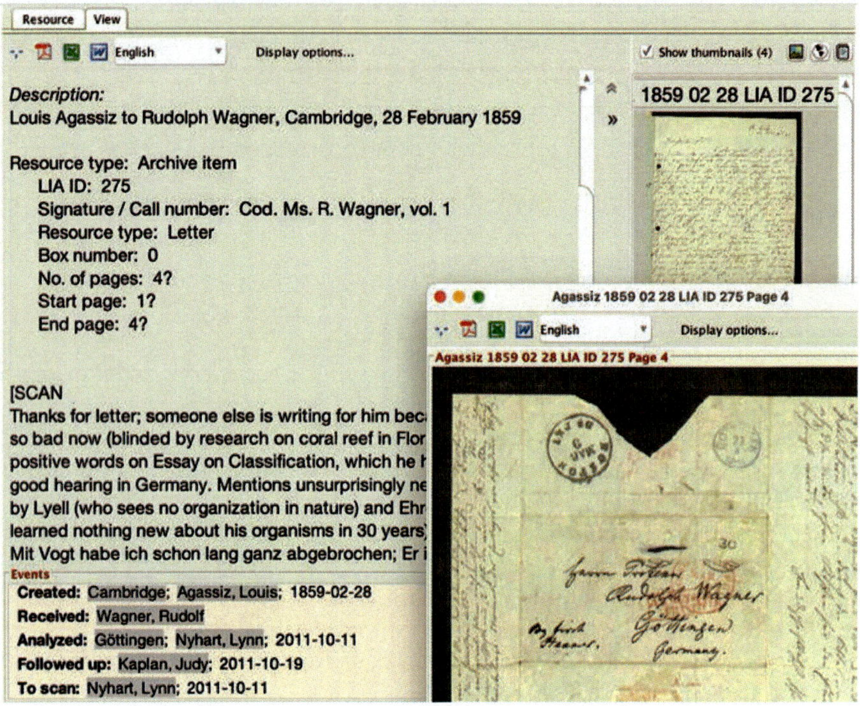

Fig. 7.48 Events are used to record life histories of historical characters. Linked images fill in the picture of historical relationships

As a final comment on the utility of Events, notice the range of events captured on this letter:

- Written (created) by Louis Agassiz on February 28, 1859, and who, although born in Switzerland and studied in Germany, was at the time establishing Harvard's Museum of Comparative Zoology in Cambridge, Massachusetts (as we learn from his life history documented in OCHRE).
- Received by Rudolf Wagner at some unknown point during that historical period who, if we follow the graph of links, we find was a Professor of Physiology, Comparative Anatomy & Zoology of the University of Göttingen, where he later died.
- Visited, and revisited, in Göttingen over 150 years later (October 11, 2011) by a modern-day scholar.
- Followed up on for further processing by the project team in modern time.

In an organized, comprehensive, and item-based digital environment, the network of knowledge and the tracking of progress need reach no bounds, ever-expanding across space and time.

Analyzing Things: Statistics and Visualization

There are already many tools available for sophisticated statistical analysis and data visualization. OCHRE makes no attempt to rise to the level of dedicated tools, or to reinvent the proverbial wheel by copying, in rough measure, what other more specialized software does very well. But there is often a great deal of the time and effort expended transforming data from one input format to another—exporting to CSV files, to XML, to a spreadsheet, only to edit and adjust then turn around and import the same data back into another software package, first for a table, then for a chart, next for a map, again for a graph.[27] It is helpful to have built-in access to analytics and visualization to gain otherwise unseen, or difficult to see, perspectives on one's data. Basic sorting of a table by different columns is an effective way to find outliers that may represent errors. A simple pie chart whose biggest slice is "<unassigned>" might be a sign that data was overlooked or is incomplete. As an *item-based* environment, where data is not primarily constrained to predefined table structures, OCHRE provides unparalleled flexibility for analysis. Within such an *integrated* environment, where items co-exist with related items, users can perform preliminary analysis, gain meaningful feedback, and determine more fruitful and specialized pursuits. As a *comprehensive* environment with an extensive feature set, OCHRE provides practically instant gratification.

OCHRE is able to support a wide range of projects—archaeological, textual, lexical, historical, scientific—because its item-based approach is agnostic as to the type of data being managed and its data structures (items and hierarchies) are generic. By abstracting data to the level of items, to any kind of items—each one potentially unique by virtue of how it is described, annotated, and tracked, but each also sharing the essence of all other items—the same tools, views, and strategies can be applied broadly in many different contexts. What follows is a presentation of two case studies, each of which will be presented with an initial set of data; then, the same scenario will be replayed, only with data from a different time, a different space, and a different content domain. This exercise will demonstrate that an item-based approach, appropriately neutral as to time, space, and domain, may use the same tools to serve different scenarios while yielding meaningful results.

Case Study with Replay: Basic Statistics

Charting, for Pottery Analysis

We begin with an analysis of pottery from the area of the Southern Citadel at the archaeological site of Zincirli in south-central Turkey. The archaeological team there collected thousands of broken fragments of pottery from the site over many

[27] Many research projects will use different software tools for a core database, a GIS database for geospatial data, network-analysis visualizations, and a publication platform, for example.

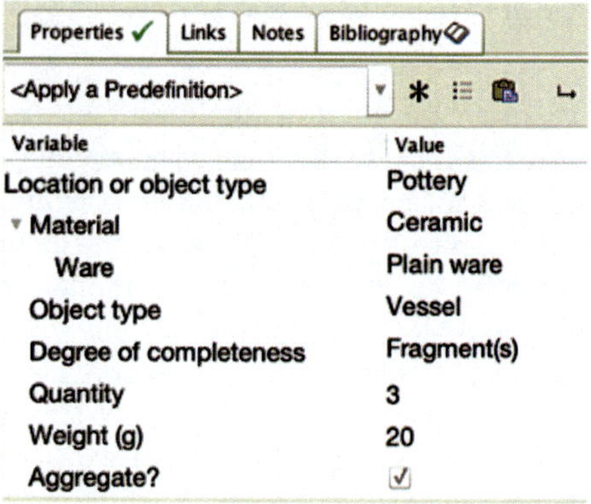

Fig. 7.49 Counts of pottery types provide quantitative data for statistical analysis

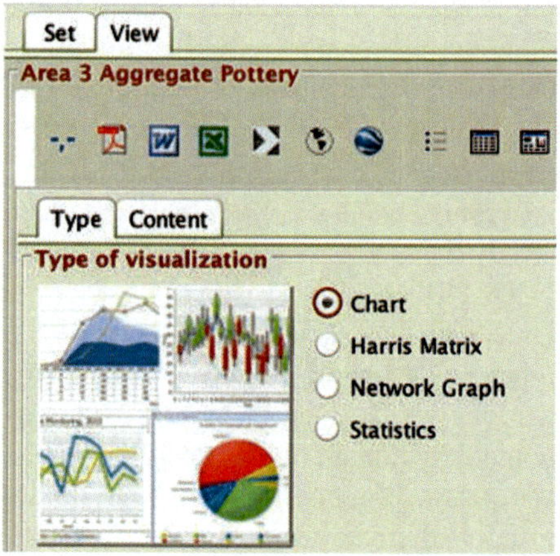

Fig. 7.50 The OCHRE Visualization Wizard provides many options for data analysis

years of ongoing excavations, sorting and classifying these potsherds broadly by type (Ware) and using volunteer assistants to count and weigh them during scorching hot Turkish summer afternoon work sessions. These groups of pottery were logged in the aggregate and in context—within the locus in which they were collected—by Ware types and represented in OCHRE as database items with a given Quantity and Weight (g) (Fig. 7.49).[28]

An OCHRE Query finds all the aggregate Pottery in Area 3, the Southern Citadel. A total of 4954 collections of broken potsherds from this area have been counted and weighed. Collecting these query results as a Set and selecting the **Chart** option of the **Visualization Wizard** built into OCHRE let us specify the details of a View (Fig. 7.50).

[28]Note that we use "Quantity" as a rough measure, assuming vessels are broken in approximate proportionate measure. "Weight" is skewed by vessel type, that is, the delicate "Fine ware" vessels will weigh disproportionately less than the heavy utilitarian "Storage jar ware." Researchers could create a derived, calculated property to devise some appropriate ratio that factors in the differences, but we will leave that to them.

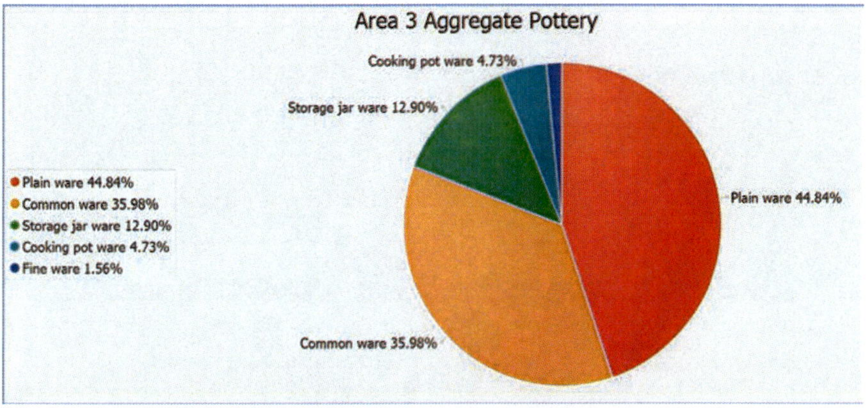

Fig. 7.51 A pie chart shows the proportions of potsherds by Ware type

In this case, we request a default pie chart showing the proportions of the Quantity of sherds, broken out by Ware type. Unsurprisingly, a casual observer will note that the Plain ware and the Common ware are notably common, while the Fine ware appears somewhat rarely (Fig. 7.51).

Furthermore, through a careful analysis of the pottery of Area 3, in conjunction with observations of the excavated loci, the researchers have identified ten separate phases of occupation of the Southern Citadel. The temporal sequence represented by these phases is organized hierarchically using Period items in OCHRE. Items at the same level of the hierarchy are listed in sequence, that is, each sub-list is an ordered list representing temporal progression.

Each excavated locus is assigned, via a Period link, to the temporal phase in which it is determined to have been historically relevant. All of the hierarchically organized subitems of each locus—the small finds, the pottery, the bones, and so on—*inherit* that temporal information. This means that each of the aggregate pottery groups that were counted and weighed has temporal context as well as spatial context.

This time for our chart, we ask for the counts of pottery by ware (Spatial units) to be broken out over time (Periods). Adding the extra analytic dimension of time to the visualization as a "group-by" option and choosing a two-dimensional chart type that supports an additional vector of analysis, in this example a stacked bar chart, allows us to compare trends over time (Fig. 7.52).

Replay: Charting for Character Analysis

Allow us to replay now the process of building a chart of hierarchically organized counted items (Pottery groups as Spatial units), having a certain quality (assigned to a Ware type via a Property), and showing progression over time (Phases as Period items). This time we will use a case study based on textual content rather than

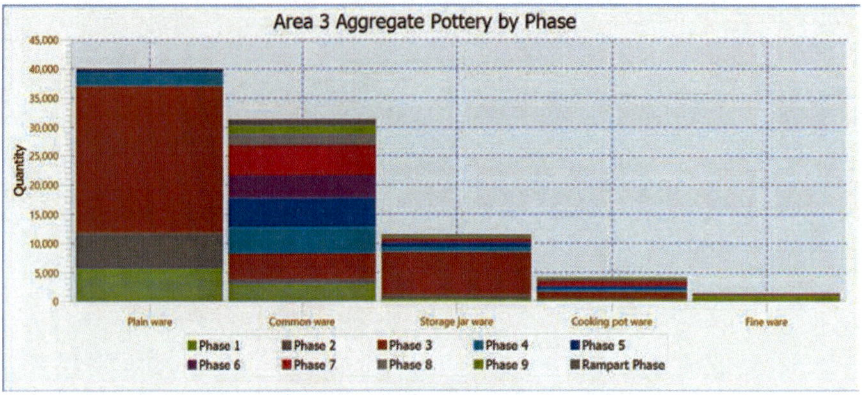

Fig. 7.52 A stacked bar graph in Chart View shows Aggregate Pottery by Phase

spatial content to highlight how an item-based approach can be effectively agnostic as to the type of item, thereby maximizing the reusability of the data structures and the tool set.

Consider the cast of Shakespeare's *Taming of the Shrew*. Which character has the largest speaking role? In which scenes do different characters dominate? Recall that a Text in OCHRE is organized into an epigraphic hierarchy (in this case, the organization of the characters on a manuscript page) and a discourse hierarchy, in this case a representation of the words of the play. The CEDAR Shakespeare project team has chosen to organize the discourse hierarchy based on the speakers and their speeches, grouping each set of words representing a spoken unit within a parent Discourse unit tagged with a Person item that identifies the speaker (Fig. 7.53).[29]

While textual context is not often considered quantitatively for statistical analysis, OCHRE makes it easy to quantify the contents of each speech using *derived properties*.[30] In this case, "Word count" is a simple integer Variable assigned to use the built-in **Count** option to count the items of the specified category, in this case Discourse units.

Applying a Count-based derived property to a hierarchical parent item will count all the qualifying subitems and will assign and save the result as the corresponding property Value. Notice in Fig. 7.54 that the value is styled as read-only since it is a computed value.

On the replay, there is enough information to create a chart of hierarchically organized counted items (words of a speech unit as Discourse units), having a certain quality (belonging to a speaker, as assigned by a Property). A simple pie chart shows that Petruchio is the most voluble, arranging the remaining speaking roles in

[29] The remaining content is tagged as scene identifications, headers and footers, stage directions, and so on, thereby accounting for all the textual content of the play.

[30] For more on derived properties, see Chap. 8 on Computational Wizardry.

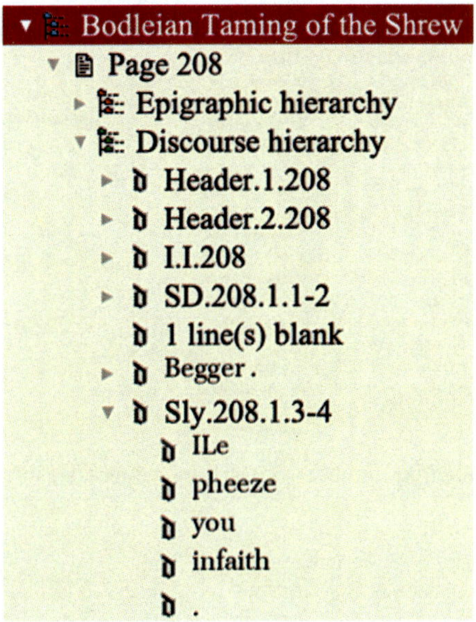

Fig. 7.53 Words in the *Taming of the Shrew* are organized hierarchically into speeches

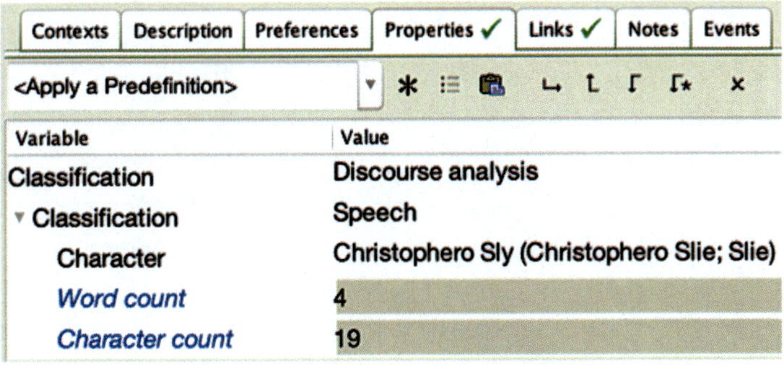

Fig. 7.54 Word and character counts transform textual data for quantitative analysis

descending sorted order, based on the quantification (percentage) of the words each character speaks (Fig. 7.55).

In the pottery example above, the temporal sequence of the Phases in which the pottery was contextualized was used as an additional dimension of analysis. Is there a correlate here on the replay? Certainly! The Acts and Scenes of the Shakespearian play define a temporal sequence. One would not want to read Scene 1 of Act 5 before the Induction at the start of the play. The Periods category is used to describe a temporal sequence, each Period item tagged with a property that indicates its Scene. Each speech in the discourse hierarchy is assigned in the usual way, via a Period link, to its temporal phase, that is, its Act-Scene (Fig. 7.56).

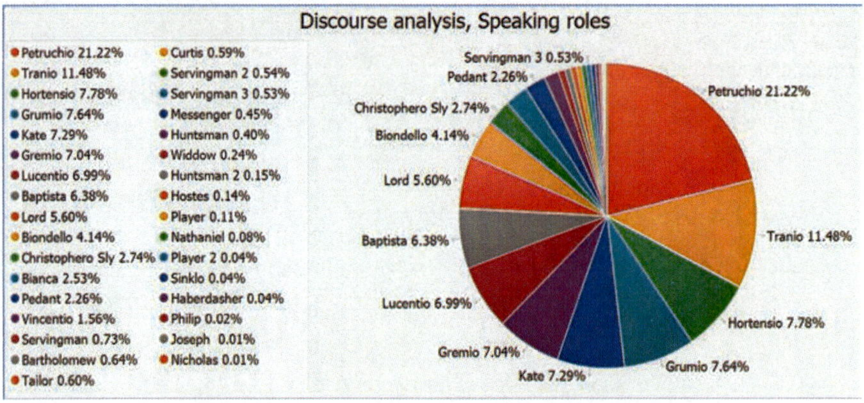

Fig. 7.55 A pie chart quantifies the speaking roles of *Taming of the Shrew*

Fig. 7.56 Period items organize Acts and Scenes of *Taming of the Shrew* in sequential order

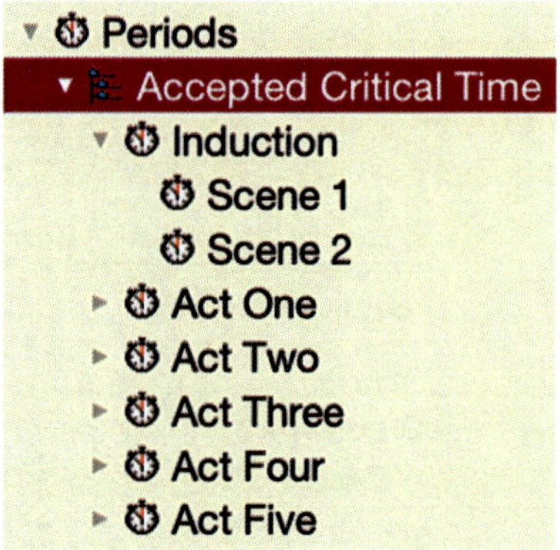

Adding the extra analytic dimension of time to the visualization as a "group-by" option and choosing a two-dimensional chart type, in this example a stacked bar chart, provide a view of the trend over time, charting the speaking parts over the course of the play. The result is analogous to the pottery chart by Ware type broken out by phases. Given the large number of characters, many of whom have limited roles, the chart is additionally limited to show only the "top 10" speaking roles, helpfully decluttering the visualization. In addition, the y-axis shows the absolute word count rather than the percentages, with the bar segments breaking out the count by scene (Fig. 7.57).

The replay had a successful outcome, charting hierarchically organized counted items (words in a speech), having a certain quality (ascribed to a Speaker), and showing progression over time (Acts and Scenes). Whether potsherds or words, whether wares or persons, and whether long or short *durées*, the same data structures and tool set proved to be effective. The flexibility and utility of an item-based approach combined with hierarchical structures, and the applicability of a generic framework to support any kind of data over space, time, and discourse, is striking.

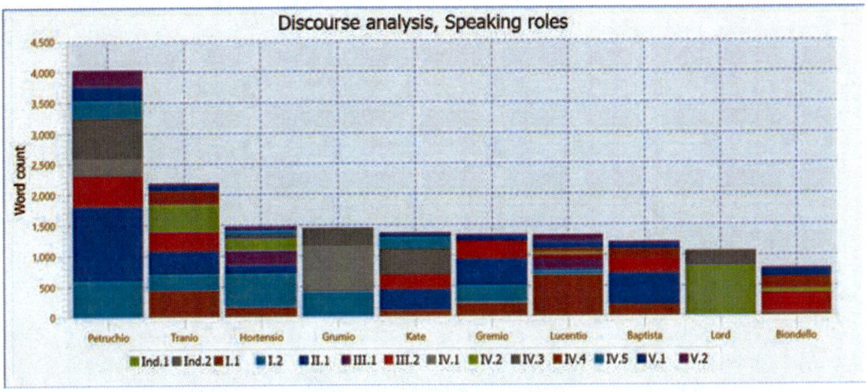

Fig. 7.57 Speaking roles by character and by scene are visualized in a stacked bar chart

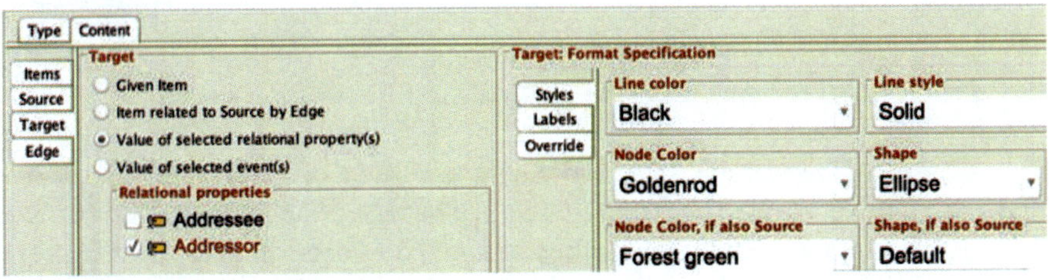

Fig. 7.58 Content and styling of a node-edge graph are specified using the Visualization Wizard

Case Study with Replay: Network Graphs

Correspondence Analysis[31] (Ancient)

Consider once again the letter previously discussed, from the King of Ugarit addressed to the Queen of Ugarit, in which the King asks after the well-being of his mother and wishes her well. The Addressor and the Addressee are noted as relational Properties, in the usual way, on the Text item that represents the contents of the letter. The targets of the relational properties are Person items (the King and Queen, here) who, along with other Person items engaged in correspondence, define the nodes in a node-edge graph. If correspondence was sent from the Addressor-person to the Addressee-person, an edge exists between their respective nodes (Fig. 7.58).

The OCHRE Visualization Wizard lets the user specify which relational properties or events to use to identify the value of the nodes for the Source (the value of

[31] Pun intended; here, we mean analysis of the correspondence (e.g., letters) sent between individuals, not the statistical technique known as "correspondence analysis."

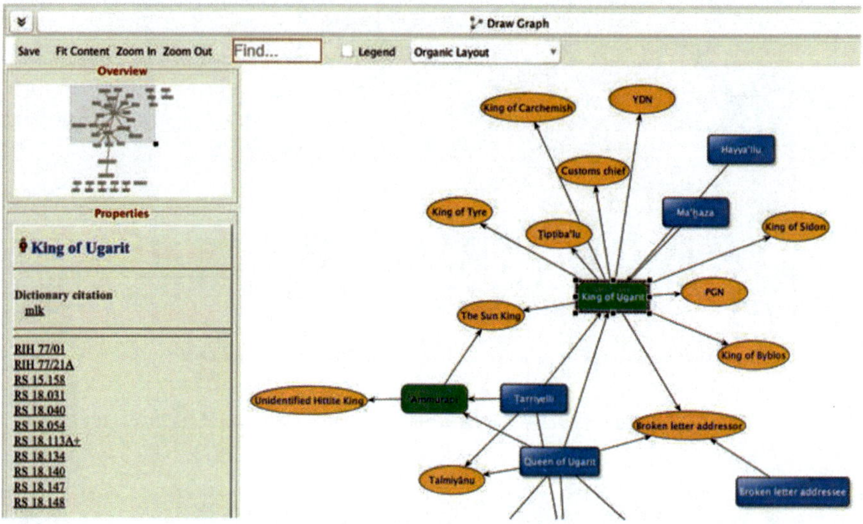

Fig. 7.59 The King's correspondence from the Royal Archive is visualized as a network

the relational property Addressor) and Target (the value of the relational property Addressee), respectively. The edges are implicit in these relational properties which link the two (Person) items—the Addressor and the Addressee. Selecting the project's Phonemic font to accommodate the special diacritical characters in the ancient names, choosing the **Fit Node to Label option** to adjust for the long names, and opting for the **Organic** layout of the graph yield a clickable, interactive display, illustrating the range of correspondence received by the King of Ugarit, including letters from the heads of neighboring kingdoms. Selecting the King of Ugarit's node lists the text references in which he is implicated. Using assorted colors and/or shapes to style the graph makes it immediately clear who are the senders and recipients of the correspondence, and which persons are both senders and recipients. Arrows are turned on for the Target node to indicate the direction of the correspondence, from Addressor to Addressee (Fig. 7.59).

Replay: Correspondence Analysis (Historical)

On the replay, the correspondence being tracked among individuals jumps forward in time by several millennia. The medium changes from stylus impressions on clay tablets to elegant cursive ink on writing paper. The persons involved are not ancient kings and their contemporaries asking after their mutual well-being, but nineteenth-century scientists exploring new ideas. We turn to the letters sent among Charles Darwin and his associates as they contemplated and discussed the scientific discoveries of *their* day. The correspondence among these scientists and their peers was tracked by the project Lives, Individuality, and Analysis (LIA) using OCHRE's

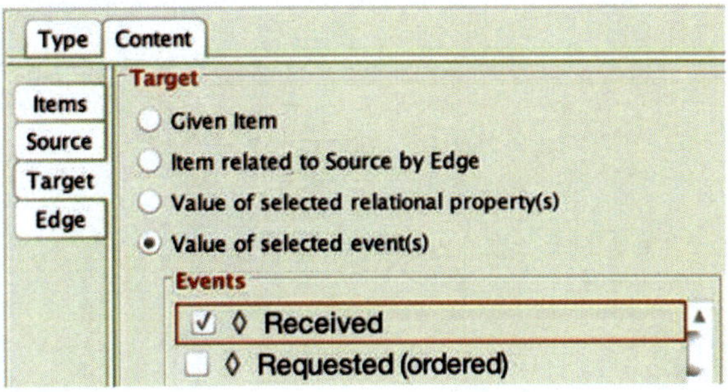

Fig. 7.60 Events, rather than relational Properties, identify network edges between items

Events mechanism instead of Properties. The letter LIA ID 275 from Louis Agassiz to Richard Wagner in February of 1859 "mentions unsurprisingly negative reception by Lyell (who sees no organization in nature) and Ehrenberg (who has learned nothing new about his organisms in 30 years)." This letter is described as **Created** (an Event), by the Agent (a Person item) Agassiz, and **Received** (another Event) by the Agent (a Person item) Wagner. The Person items, Agassiz and Wagner, become *nodes* in the network graph, and the existence of a letter that passed between them (LIA ID 275) becomes an *edge* (link) (Fig. 7.60).

Events are simply links among Location items and/or Agents (Person items). The implicated Locations or Persons thereby qualify as nodes in a network graph. The Visualization Wizard provides options to specify which events or relational properties to use to identify the value of the nodes for the Source (value of the selected Event Created) and Target (value of the selected Event Received) nodes, respectively.

Formatting options of the Visualization Wizard allow the user to make some judicious selections—black text on white for the Source nodes, white text on dark gray for the Target nodes, and white text on dim gray for nodes that are both Source and Target nodes (i.e., Persons who both Created and Received letters). Furthermore, so as not to depend entirely on color to differentiate nodes, the shape of the nodes that represent items that are both Source and Target nodes (otherwise all rectangular) is changed to octagonal.

On the replay, these choices result in a visualization that immediately exposes the scientists at the heart of the discussions and reveal who were senders, who were receivers, and who were both senders and receivers of the correspondence (Fig. 7.61).

Whether the letters that passed among assorted Person items represent ancient correspondence among neighboring kings, or stimulating arguments among modern-day competing scientists, they can be described in detail regardless of their specific contexts in space and time.

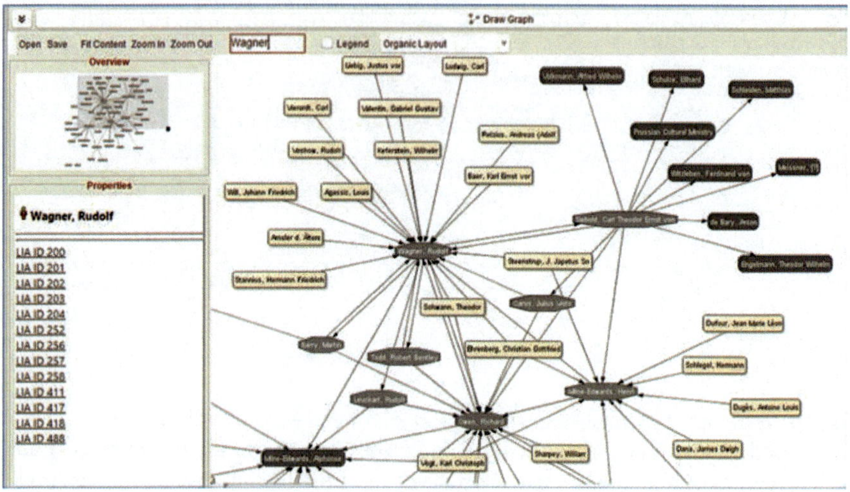

Fig. 7.61 Correspondence among nineteenth-century scholars is visualized as a network

Conclusion: Visualizing OCHRE

In this chapter, we cover a wide range of OCHRE features related to data integration and analysis. We maintain that a prerequisite for accurate and reproducible analysis is a data set that is clean and curated. As a matter of best practice, at the data analysis stage, issues of data inconsistency or formatting should have been resolved already. To achieve integration, data should not be dispersed across single purpose databases or siloed in custom one-off applications. A comprehensive warehouse is ideal, one poised to interact with compatible, item-based data from other sources. OCHRE is designed as a single platform for all research data. As such, the data becomes integrated through linking and organizing, making it available for robust analysis (Fig. 7.62).

Integrating and enriching data for analysis begins, in OCHRE, by creating semantically meaningful links between items. Some of these links are built into the OCHRE system, such as the link between an image and an object. Other links are created as needed by projects. These types of links replace the rigid and non-intuitive links between normalized tables in a relational database. As illustrated in this chapter, the goal in OCHRE is to leverage data about time, space, agents, text, and images in the same analysis. Time is data, recorded as Periods in OCHRE. Text is data, atomized as individual signs if required. Images are data, ranging from common digital photographs to 3D scans to spatially referenced maps (Fig. 7.63).

Analysis of this complex graph of data is made possible through OCHRE's intuitive query interface where data can be retrieved as simple matches against properties or by complex sequences of containment and linking. Any type of data can be queried and retrieved for analysis. The results can be visualized as a table, chart, on

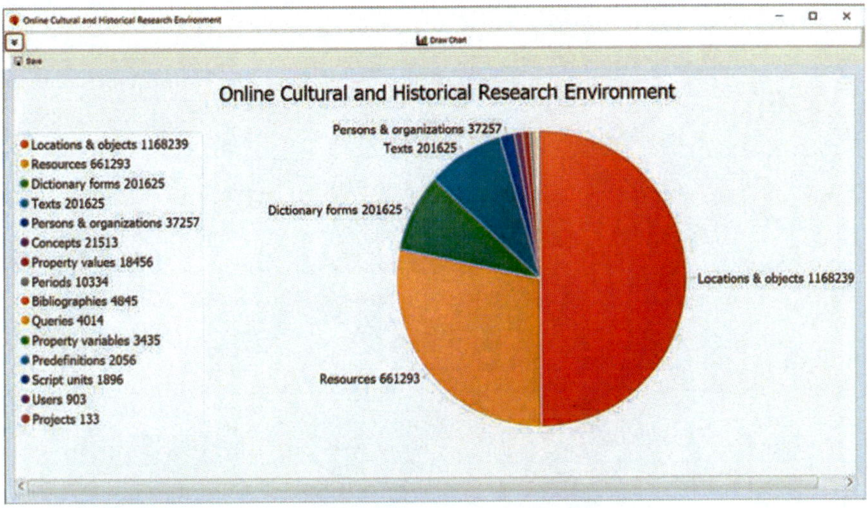

Fig. 7.62 A pie chart, visualizing the proportions of OCHRE items by Category, testifies to the comprehensiveness of the OCHRE platform (as of January 01, 2023)

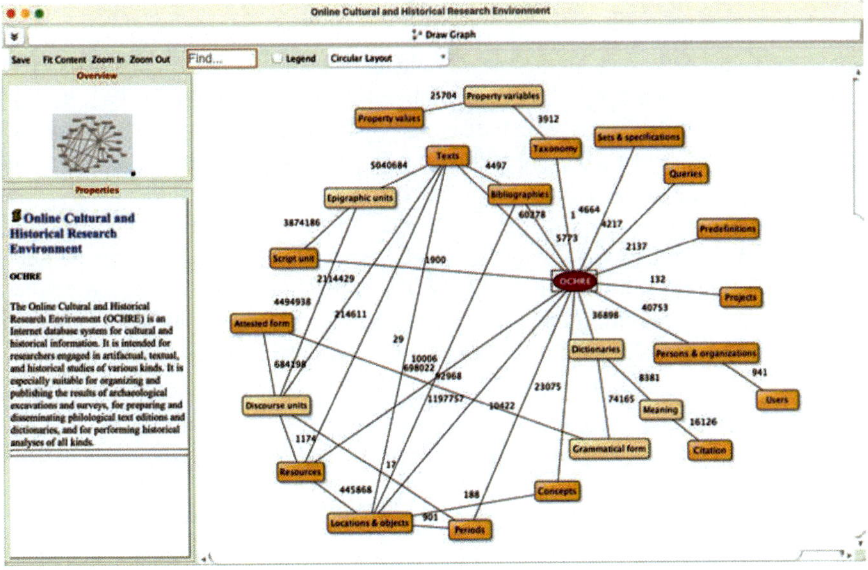

Fig. 7.63 A self-describing graph attests to the extensive linking among OCHRE items

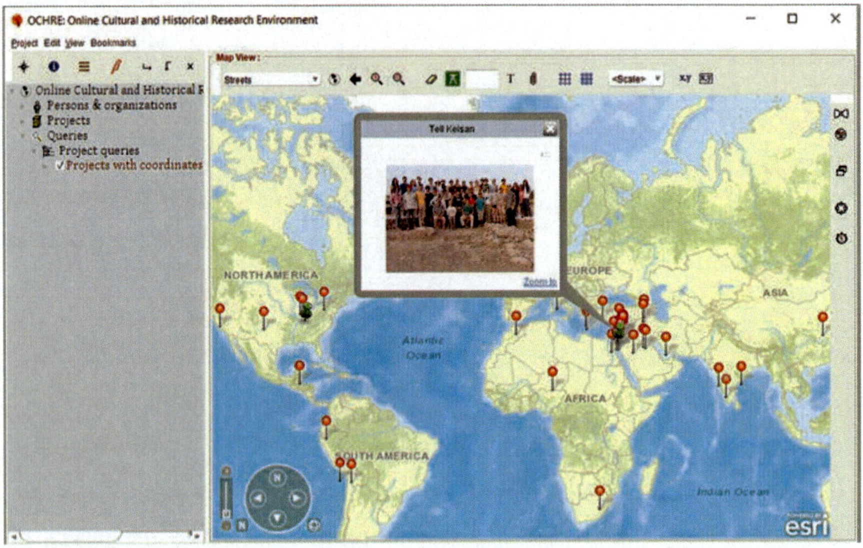

Fig. 7.64 OCHRE's Map View of its own projects reinforces that OCHRE makes no assumptions regarding spatial location

a map, with linked images, in the context of a dictionary, as a set of matching texts, or even in a Comprehensive View that combines a variety of these. In other words, the principle of integration is leveraged as part of the visualization stage of analysis. A query result or a manually compiled set of items can be saved for a variety of uses: to reproduce an analysis or visualization (the specifications of the query being saved with the matching list of items); to share data with team members or colleagues; and to publish for viewing on the web as appendices, maps, or any number of other meaningful forms (Fig. 7.64). While OCHRE does not presuppose what type of analytical questions a research project may ask, it was created according to basic principles that allow for investigation of a wide variety of research questions.

Chapter 8
Computational Wizardry

Introduction

The welcoming remarks to the 2015 Chicago Colloquium on Digital Humanities and Computer Science took a turn from technical to inspirational when Birali Runesha, Associate Vice-President for Research Computing at the University of Chicago stated, "magic happens when science is paired with humanities."[1] We have all had those moments when we signed into Amazon to buy something only to find that the item we intended to buy was presciently displayed on the welcome screen, or when Google offered a helpful, specific, traffic warning as we ventured out on our commute. Huge databases capturing our purchasing history or travel patterns, paired with clever algorithms, make technology seem "practically magic" as corporate Apple has claimed.[2]

In recent years, the field of artificial intelligence (AI) has been transformed by a new paradigm based on *machine learning*, powered by incredible advances in super-computing (advanced hardware), the availability of large, annotated data sets,[3] and software algorithms ("neural networks") that can reach conclusions or make predictions by examining vast amounts of data and "learning" from it. This is in stark contrast to the early days of AI research—what has since come to be known as good old-fashioned artificial intelligence (GOFAI)[4]—the aim of which was to program computers with enough rules and facts so that they could "reason" and

[1] November 14, 2015, Regenstein Library.

[2] See Burns (2016), "Apple's 'Practically Magic' Advertising Campaign Feels More Like A Sleight Of Hand."

[3] The MNIST (National Institute of Standards and Technology) database of 60,000 images of handwritten digits, and its extended version (EMNIST) of 240,000 images, are commonly used by students and researchers to train machine-learning algorithms, as is the ImageNet image database with over 14 million annotated images.

[4] The acronym was coined by Haugeland, John. "Artificial intelligence: the very idea." (1985).

S. R. Schloen, M. C. Prosser, *Database Computing for Scholarly Research*,
Quantitative Methods in the Humanities and Social Sciences,
https://doi.org/10.1007/978-3-031-46696-0_8

exhibit intelligent behavior. Hubert Dreyfus, the late Professor of Philosophy at University of California, Berkeley, and author of 1972's "What Computers Can't Do" was an outspoken critic of early AI research, arguing that beyond representing "knowledge" there was an "everyday commonsense background understanding … a kind of *know-how* … which would have had to be conveyed to the computer as knowledge"—to Dreyfus this seemed "a hopeless task" (Dreyfus 1992, p. xii). By the time of his revised 1992 edition, "What Computers *Still* Can't Do," he declared that "it is now clear to all but a few diehards that … the research program based on the assumption that human beings produce intelligence using facts and rules has reached a dead end" (ibid., p. ix). Fifty years on, a new "gold rush" of AI[5] grips the imagination of the world with the emergence of DALL-E and ChatGPT[6]—generative systems, trained on huge amounts of data, that can create art and literature indistinguishable from human-generated works. The "neural-net revolution" in AI has shifted the research strategy to "creating artificial intelligence by modeling the brain's learning power rather than the mind's symbolic representation of the world" (Dreyfus 1997, p. xiv).

But Dreyfus conceded that while the AI theorists had given up on "making generally intelligent machines that model the whole range of human intelligent behavior," the engineers who focused instead on building "special-purpose programs tailored to narrowly restricted domains" might have reasonable success (ibid., p. 3). So, without making overly grand claims for representing the knowledge of the world, we are inspired by lessons learned from GOFAI that highlight the value of knowledge representation and reasoning when applied within an appropriately constrained domain using a carefully crafted database system. Indeed, as the new generative AI models pronounce falsehoods as truth and deliver misinformation with absolute certainty and without qualification—a phenomenon so prevalent it has been dubbed "hallucination"—one wonders whether a backlash or, at least, a correction grounded in facts and knowledge representation, isn't called for.[7]

Our goal as researchers is to represent research data in a way that supports automated reasoning or that can be used to train a machine learning algorithm, even if only in a narrowly focused domain. Built into OCHRE are a variety of special-purpose features, utilities, and workflow wizards that exploit the rules and relationships defined by the database structures to assist the user in explicating and exploring their data. In this chapter, we examine ways in which OCHRE's item-based data model, its use of hierarchical organizational structures, and its possibilities for building intelligent relationships among items within a limited domain of knowledge, can create conditions under which the work of scholarly research might appear to happen as if by magic.

---

[5] From Griffith and Metz (2023), *A New Area of A.I. Booms, Even Amid the Tech Gloom*, "no area has created more excitement than generative artificial intelligence, the term for technology that can generate text, images, sounds and other media in response to short prompts."

[6] See https://openai.com/dall-e-2/ and https://openai.com/blog/chatgpt.

[7] The industry is struggling with how to mitigate hallucinations by AI models; see, for example, https://openai.com/research/improving-mathematical-reasoning-with-process-supervision.

Knowledge Representation

In the preface to *Knowledge Representation and Reasoning,* Brachman and Levesque define knowledge representation and reasoning as "the area of Artificial Intelligence (AI) concerned with how knowledge can be represented symbolically and manipulated in an automated way by reasoning programs" (2004, p. xvii).[8] Their approach to knowledge representation resonates with the OCHRE strategy of building a computational platform that properly models data in a way that supports and enables intelligent scholarly research:

> It is taken as a given that what allows humans to behave intelligently is that they know a lot of things about a lot of things and are able to apply this knowledge as appropriate to adapt to their environment and achieve their goals. So in the field of knowledge representation and reasoning we focus on the knowledge, not on the knower. We ask what *any* agent—human, animal, electronic, mechanical—would need to know to behave intelligently, and what sorts of computational mechanisms might allow its knowledge to be made available to the agent as required (ibid.).

In doing the work of engineering the knowledge base, Brachman and Levesque underscore the importance of staking out "an ontology—the kinds of *objects* that will be important to the agent, the *properties* those objects will be thought to have, and the *relationships* among them" (ibid., p. 32). They also make much of the utility and efficiency of taxonomic hierarchy to create structured descriptions that "exploit the fact that concepts are naturally thought of as organized hierarchically" and to capture "subsumptive relationships" (ibid. p. 172).

> In representing commonsense information like this we also find that we need individuals for numbers, dates, times, addresses, and so on. Basically, any 'object' about which we can ask a *wh*-question [who? what? when? where? how? why?] should have an individual standing for it in the KB [knowledge base] so it can be returned as the result of a query (ibid. p. 42).[9]

As should be apparent at this point, an object-centered approach, the use of properties, and hierarchical relationships are at the heart of the OCHRE data model. When tested against the guiding strategies provided by Brachman and Levesque, OCHRE's mechanisms for defining a well-structured knowledge base make it well-suited as a platform for knowledge representation and provide a research environment equipped for computational wizardry. To make this discussion less theoretical, consider some simple problems commonly faced by archaeologists and other scholars but easily addressed by careful knowledge representation.

---

[8] *Knowledge Representation and Reasoning* is an excellent and extensive, yet accessible, treatment, widely used as the textbook for an introductory course in this field of study.

[9] The *wh*-questions are itemized on p. 39.

Intelligent Properties: "Aware" Variables

Managing Measures: Units-Aware

Often there is inconsistency in the capture of numeric data such that some measures are expressed in centimeters, some in millimeters, and some perhaps in inches. Data from earlier historical excavations at the same site, data from collaborating specialists, or data collected using specialized tools (e.g., digital calipers) is captured under different scenarios and to differing standards. How then does one find all vessels with a rim diameter greater than 20 centimeters for a study of ceramic bowls when some diameters are recorded in centimeters, some in millimeters, and others in inches?

OCHRE employs the principle of abstraction and includes intelligent handling of numeric property values so data that may have been collected using differing units of measure can be evaluated and compared, saving the scholar potentially a great deal of trouble. The **Concepts** category in the OCHRE master project is used to define concept-items available system wide that represent the units described by the International System of Units (SI)—meter for length, kilogram for mass, etc.—along with other commonly used non-SI units (like liter for volume). The standard units, and other arbitrarily chosen base units, are defined as concepts and assigned a value of 1. Related units are then organized within the base units and are assigned a Conversion factor property to represent the mathematical relationship between the base unit and the related unit. As shown in Fig. 8.1, the base unit Meter (with a value of 1) has as a related unit Kilometer which is assigned a value of 1000. This captures the fact that a kilometer represents 1000 meters.

With these relationships defined behind the scenes, the user can record the diameter of a pottery rim using whichever length unit is appropriate. The property that

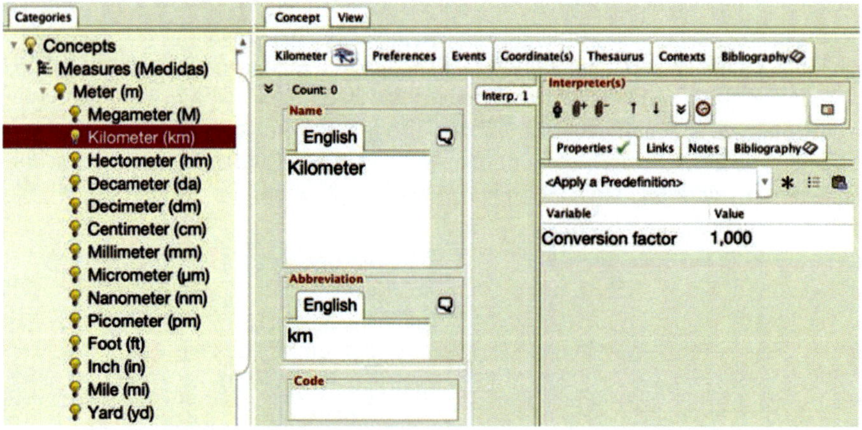

Fig. 8.1 Units of measure are represented as items and related to each other

records the measurement (e.g., Rim diameter) is associated with the appropriate category of measurement in this hierarchy of concepts (Meter), allowing OCHRE to recalculate and present the measurement in any of the available units. Relating a measurement property to a standard unit of measure gives OCHRE the knowledge needed to perform automatic units-conversion processing. In effect, OCHRE captures the measure's value as entered by the user (e.g., "4 cm") and retains this as the original form of the data value. But it also calculates on-the-fly an appropriately converted value using the Conversion factor associated with the standard unit on which the variable is based and saves this converted value as a parallel value along with the original value. All the parallel values are thus represented and stored based on a common unit appropriate for compatible comparisons. That is, all length-related units of measure—(1) Rim diameter, (2) Length at the occlusal surface of the tooth, (3) Height of the wall, (4) Distance from the sea—will be captured as millimeters, centimeters, meters, or kilometers but calculated and stored automatically in the standard unit of meters. When a query searches for all sites within 2 kilometers of the sea, or all ceramic bowls with a rim diameter greater than 20 centimeters, standardized values are used, thereby returning all valid matches no matter the unit in which the original measure was recorded. Simple arithmetic makes OCHRE seem intelligent when handling numeric values provided in disparate units of measures.

By a happy synergy, the use of Concepts to model relationships between items is sufficiently generic to apply to any type of measure. In a study of coin hoards from ancient Greece, it was important to be able to record the monetary value of each hoard in the cases where sufficient data was available. A jumble of staters, hemistaters, drachmas, and tetradrachms can be evaluated intelligently by selecting one type of coinage as the "standard" unit of valuation (the HARP project used the tetradrachm; see Chap. 12) then relating the others using appropriate conversion factors and letting OCHRE do the math. If the value of a currency changes over time, these temporally specific values can be captured in the **Concepts** hierarchy and applied as needed. This is a common problem for the study of ancient values. A stater minted in one place in a given year is not the exact weight or value as a stater minted elsewhere. As another example of this strategy, an OCHRE-based analysis of the valuation of looted artifacts sold in modern-day auctions easily compares monetary values listed in Euros, US dollars, or British pounds.

Coordinate Variables: Spatially Aware

Numeric variables that are assigned to a specific category of units of measure, and are thereby units-aware, are just one of the types of "aware" variables available in OCHRE that allow more intelligent handling of data. Variables of the coordinate type are spatially aware, providing the means to specify x- and y- and optionally z-values within a predefined or standard coordinate system such as the WGS84 system, or the UTM system.[10] Archaeologists can assign a "find spot variable" to artifacts which records the exact find spot location (x, y) and elevation (z) on the excavation site. In fact, such data is commonly captured by a GPS-enabled instrument to a high level of precision. This machine-generated data is easily entered into OCHRE (via export-import, or Bluetooth interaction). Each OCHRE item that represents an artifact thus knows its exact location, allowing objects to be plotted on interactive maps or to have their findspots used as criteria in queries.

Aggregate (Derived) Variables: Hierarchically Aware

A special category of *derived* variables is built into OCHRE. Variables derived using an *Aggregation* method are hierarchically aware, supplying a mechanism for summing up the values of numeric properties assigned to items nested within hierarchies. Say, for example, that seeds, bones, or potsherds, found within samples of soil from hierarchically organized excavation contexts, are being counted. The quantities assigned to deeply nested individual samples bubble up the hierarchy as they are summed by an aggregation variable, providing a locus or other higher-level context with totaled values for analysis. Weights or valuations of coins can be tagged first at the level of the individual coin then aggregated at the level of the hoard, providing the means of usefully and efficiently capturing both the detailed and the summarized data.

Hierarchically aware variables are applicable to textual analysis too. OCHRE's CEDAR project based on the Taming of the Shrew organizes discourse units hierarchically. Words are grouped into speeches, attributed to the speakers, and organized as Scenes and Acts. A hierarchically aware property, say "Word count," uses simple math to aggregate the words within each speech and report the totals.

Calculated (Derived) Variables: Arithmetically Aware

Another category of *derived* variables, based on the *Calculation* derivation method, are arithmetically aware, providing the option of using basic arithmetic to derive a new value from existing numeric values. The East of Theater, Corinth OCHRE project has classified and analyzed twelve tons of pottery at Corinth counting the number of Rims, Bases, Handles, Nozzles, and other non-diagnostic Sherds contained within a given Lot of pottery. But the researcher's analysis requires that she also compute the total number of sherds within that Lot. By creating a derived variable, "Total RBHNS" that is defined as the number of Rims plus Bases plus Handles plus Nozzles plus Sherds (R + B + H + N + S), OCHRE can calculate the total number

[10] See the World Geodetic System at https://en.wikipedia.org/wiki/World_Geodetic_System and the Universal Transverse Mercator system at https://en.wikipedia.org/wiki/Universal_Transverse_Mercator_coordinate_system.

of sherds automatically. If the base numbers change then the computed values will also automatically adjust, as would be expected.

While simple, the use of aware variables can significantly enhance the value of data, transforming it from raw numbers and characters to meaningful information. The computational work involved is almost trivial, requiring merely addition and multiplication, but when used with care and intent, these strategies greatly ease some common problems of data capture and reap disproportionately useful benefits for further quantitative analysis.

Domain Representation

As already established, an OCHRE taxonomy is used to define the vocabulary of a project, prescribing the terminology and the sets of properties available for describing project items and the relationships between them. But sometimes there is core data—simple, basic well-established facts—that delineate the scope and substance of a specific domain of knowledge and provide the building blocks with which more complex knowledge is created.

We have already shown (Chap. 3) how OCHRE's granular data model and hierarchical structures can represent the content of a **Text** with a view to both epigraphic analysis (an interpretation of how it is written) and discourse analysis (a scholarly interpretation of form, structure, or translation). But OCHRE takes this a step further— the representation of the system of writing itself. The **Writing system** category of OCHRE provides a mechanism for describing simple alphabetic writing systems like English, Hebrew, Greek, or Ugaritic, but also for capturing the complexity of systems like logosyllabic cuneiform or hieroglyphic Egyptian. Take the example of the Sumero-Akkadian logosyllabic writing system; OCHRE's integrated signary[11] represents the signs used in this writing system and the values each sign is used to express. OCHRE provides the means of studying the writing system asking research questions like which are the most productive signs, which signs came in and out of use during different periods, and so on. A careful and comprehensive articulation of the writing system, specifying what is known within this highly circumscribed domain of knowledge, provides the foundation for a more informed study of the textual content.

The signary serves to validate the accuracy of any logosyllabic text added to OCHRE, to avoid typographical errors, and to impose desired consistency. Content given on import can be matched against the signary and flagged if no match is found, thereby catching typographical or other errors. And because each sign is represented by an OCHRE item known as a *script unit*, other relevant information about a sign can be captured by using Properties in the usual way. Figure 8.2

[11] A signary, in the case of the Sumero-Akkadian logosyllabic writing system, is a detailed list of signs, with information about reading values, allograph values, and other meaningful information. The signary is exemplified in publications like Borger (2004), *Mesopotamisches Zeichenlexikon*.

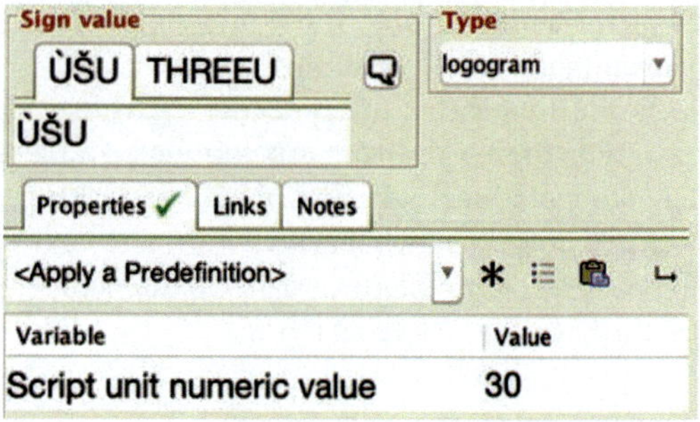

Fig. 8.2 A logographic sign represents the number "30"

Fig. 8.3 The top-left cuneiform sign having 3 vertical wedges represents the number 30. (Photograph courtesy of the Persepolis Fortification Archive project)

illustrates how a property called "Script unit numeric value" is assigned to logographic signs that are used to represent numbers. As OCHRE matches given data to sign list entries that have been identified as numbers it can ascribe the numeric value to these signs in preparation for intelligent analysis.

Look closely at the following tablet from the Persepolis Fortification archive in Fig. 8.3. Can you spot the sets of 3 elongated vertical wedges that represent the number "30"?

The transliteration of this tablet (Fig. 8.4) indicates that "30" is used as part of a compound number at the beginning of both line 1 and line 2 of this text. When OCHRE is given the sign UŠÙ (e.g., in an import document or via data entry), it

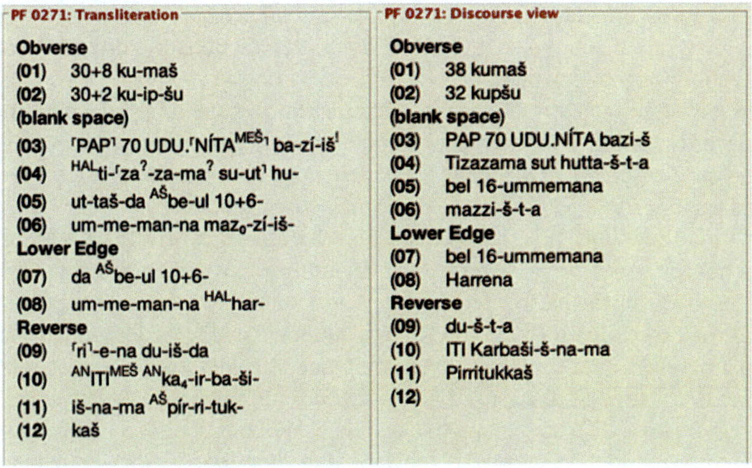

Fig. 8.4 Knowledge of numeric signs, represented as properties, adds value to the data

looks for a match in the signary, creates a link to the matching sign, and substitutes the matching sign's numeric value of 30.[12]

Individual signs represented by numeric values that are compounded into words are expressed in the **Discourse view** as the sum of their numeric values, here 38 (30 + 8) and 32 (30 + 2) in lines 1 and 2, respectively. Transforming otherwise raw textual content into numeric data readies it to inform research questions using quantitative methods.

For scholars who work with modern languages or simple alphabetic systems of writing this example might seem bizarre, but we hope you can appreciate that when scholars who deal with complex writing systems of this sort provide OCHRE with the transliteration "1GÉŠU.1UŠÙ.8DIŠ" and get back "638" automatically, it feels like magic!

Intelligent Relationships

Relationships, Dictionary-Based

When using an item-based data model, intrinsic information about potentially highly atomized textual components is supplemented by recognizing and representing relationships between them. Working from the ground up, characters (signs) in

[12] To provide more context for the interested computational philologist, the process is slightly more nuanced. The user provides the transliteration 1UŠÙ, the sign with a number prefixed to indicate to OCHRE that this sign is being used in the text as a numerical logogram and that the numeric value is 1 x the value of the sign. It is theoretically possible that a scribe may use three consecutive signs to record a multiple of the number. In this case, the import text reads 3UŠÙ. We acknowledge that these details are very specific to this writing system, but we mention it here to demonstrate the extremes to which the OCHRE platform has been used for knowledge representation and analysis.

the texts are used as building blocks to create words which then buttress further textual analysis by being linked to carefully crafted dictionary entries that capture the relationships between them.

Any language typically has many variations in the spellings and meanings of related words. OCHRE's hierarchical architecture of a complex dictionary or a simpler glossary ensures that all roads lead back from specific grammatical forms or attested spellings to a parent lemma. A corpus-based dictionary that documents all word forms allows OCHRE to match attested spellings of words in texts to the correct dictionary entry, even when the character strings are vastly different. This is a powerful mechanism that overcomes the shortcomings of basic string-matching operations, especially for complex or uncommon languages for which part-of-speech processors or other natural language processing algorithms are not effective. This, in effect, provides the step of *lemmatization* for languages where natural language processes (NLP) are not readily available. While artificial intelligence strategies have created sophisticated NLP tools for languages like English, French, Greek, or Chinese, as might be expected, these tools are often ineffective for complex ancient languages such as Elamite, Ugaritic, and Demotic.

Returning to the sample Elamite administrative text, PF 0271, the second word in line 2 turns out to be one of half dozen or so spellings of the word for she-goat—the most common spelling of the nominal form, in fact. Because the PFA project has *already* documented 309 examples in other texts, OCHRE can use built-in logic to associate the word in the text with this form in the dictionary (Fig. 8.5).

The underlying database captures the relationships between the different spellings and grammatical forms of these words hierarchically, and displays them in a hierarchical, tabular format, providing tools to count, edit, find, and tag these **Dictionary units** (Fig. 8.6). Furthermore, the dictionary entry, as its own database item, is described with properties that identify this lemmatized entry as referring to a Commodity, and more specifically, an Animal. A study pertaining to the involvement of animals in trade or transport would have a rich set of information available for analysis.

kupšu she-goat

kupšu **n.** ku-ip-šu (309x), ku-ip-ši (2x), ki-ip-ši (1x), ki-ip-šu (1x).

kupšu-na **n.poss.attr.** ku-ip-šu-na (42x), ki-ip-ši-na (1x), KI+MIN-na (4x).

Categorization:

Dictionary element: Entry

Category: Commodity

Category: Animal

Fig. 8.5 A Dictionary unit itemizes and relates various forms and spellings of a word

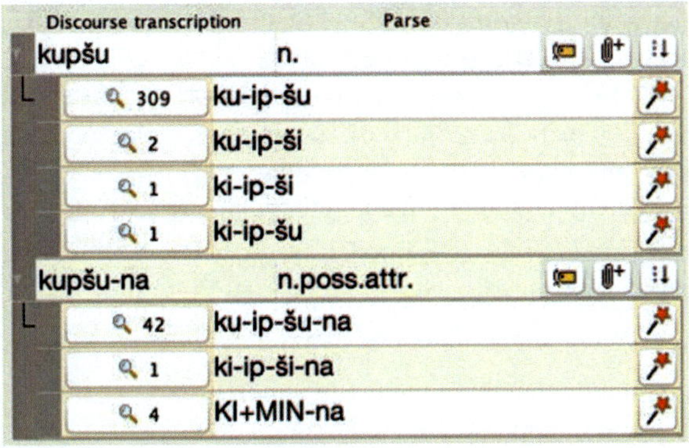

Fig. 8.6 Various spellings and forms of an Elamite word are itemized, organized hierarchically, described by properties, and related to actual instances in the text corpus

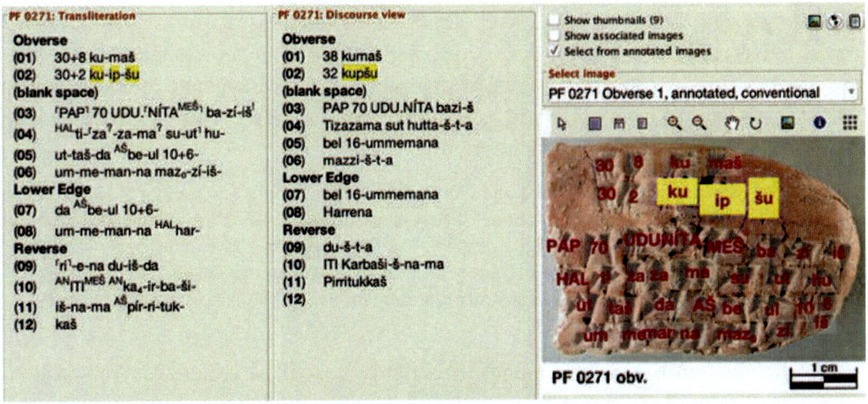

Fig. 8.7 OCHRE's Synchronized view highlights related (linked) components of a Text

Relationships, Text-Based

As previously discussed (Chap. 4), the **Text** represented in OCHRE can be organized via multiple, overlapping hierarchical structures. Specifically, an epigraphic hierarchy captures the sign-by-sign analysis of the text and its orthographical arrangement on the clay tablet in this case. Hotspot links itemize and identify individual signs on images of the tablet. The discourse hierarchy reorganizes the signs into words, phrases, clauses, and so on, elucidating the actual meaning of the text. Translation options provide another analysis of the text's meaning.

The atomic database items and their relationships to each other form a web of meaning and analysis that can be presented in a variety of recomposed views. The **Synchronized View** shown in Fig. 8.7, which highlights the related components in *all* of the views when *any* one of the components is clicked, is a visual reminder of the underlying relationships that make possible richly linked presentations of the textual content. This is achieved without the brute-force mechanism of string matching which would be inadequate and unreliable given the complexity of the textual corpus and writing system.

A library of signs, a dictionary of words, an annotated image, an analysis of a text, each its own work of scholarship, together comprise a whole that is greater than the sum of its parts. A dynamic knowledge base such as the one we have described here will grow and be enhanced as additional textual sources are studied, feeding the hope that intelligent processes will increasingly be enabled to perform wizardry against such data to bring to light new insights.

Reasoning

Knowledge representation only takes us so far down the path to artificial intelligence. What can we learn from our explicitly represented knowledge base? What new information can become known? For Brachman and Levesque "the reasoning side of the equation is as important as the representation side" and we turn again to them for an explanation of reasoning in this context.

> In general, it is the formal manipulation of the symbols representing a collection of believed propositions to produce representations of new ones. It is here that we use the fact that symbols are more accessible than the propositions they represent: They must be concrete enough that we can manipulate them (move them around, take them apart, copy them, string them together) in such a way as to construct representations of new propositions (Brachman and Levesque 2004, p. 7).

OCHRE's item-based data model uses richly described concrete symbols that can be manipulated in a quest to learn something new. OCHRE's hierarchical structures support logical inference—the ability to draw logical conclusions from initial propositions. "If Fido is a Dog and a Dog is a Mammal then Fido is a Mammal" (ibid. p, 25). Reasoning "bridges the gap between what is represented and what is believed" (ibid. p. 4) and from our explicitly represented knowledge we expect to draw logical—that is, *reasonable*—implicit conclusions.

Case Study: Intelligently Representing a Text

A carefully represented signary, together with a well-modeled, hierarchically organized, corpus-based dictionary facilitates a special sort of wizardry—one that intelligently guides a scholar through the process of representing, linking, and documenting the careful analysis of a text. The stages of this process are as follows: (1) import the text into the database, (2) link the words in the text to the project dictionary, (3) parse the words for grammatical properties, and (4) identify persons and places in the text to use in social network graphs and other forms of analysis. Can we construct a persuasive argument that some sort of reasoning is happening in this process, where *logical inference* is used as the primary tool?

Workflow Wizards

Guided workflow wizards built into OCHRE and available to qualified editors, help the user import a Text, identify words in a Text, make associations with Dictionary items, and add missing dictionary entries when necessary. Wizards are also available to help enrich both Texts and Dictionary items by making it easy to find and propertize content.

Text Import Wizard

Converting text editions from word processing documents—typically the form in which they exist before being added to OCHRE—to highly atomized XML is the first step in the process of representing a Text in OCHRE. The Text import wizard allows the user to select a document from a local computer to load into a pending-import field in the database. The import wizard has been taught to understand a document that has been carefully formatted to the import specification. Such a document typically contains only a transliteration of the text arranged into sections such as *recto/verso, folio/chapter/page*. The user will:

- Define project-level epigraphic sigla so that the import wizard knows how to identify signs and words, and how to interpret special markings for damaged signs, missing signs, etc. For example, a dash might be used as a syllable-separator; an illegible sign might be surrounded by square brackets; a missing sign might be noted by an "x."
- Describe the formatting conventions used in the document so that OCHRE can tag the content appropriately. For example, a lowercase, italicized sign might be interpreted and tagged as being written in the Ugaritic language.
- Indicate which features the wizard should provide: Are both epigraphic and discourse processing desired? How should numerals be formatted? Should alphabetic words be broken down character by character?
- Identify the Writing system relevant to the text (Greek? Hebrew? Cuneiform? Devanagari?).

The wizard will:

- Parse the text, section by section, line by line, word by word, character by character (if needed), creating a new database item for each component.
- Match the signs/characters against the specified Writing system, reporting on items that do not match (presumably either errors or new instances).
- Assign language tagging and other metadata features like damage or uncertainty.
- Build the epigraphic hierarchy representing the layout of the text, based on the formatted import document.
- Build the discourse hierarchy representing the semantics of the text, based on the interpretation of signs/characters into words.
- Allow the user to Preview the resulting Text, prior to Accepting it to complete the import process.

The result will be a highly granular representation of a Text ready for further analysis.[13] Once defined, the user rarely needs to tweak the settings. Texts simply import magically.

Text Lexicography Wizard (TLex)

The *Text Lexicography Wizard* guides the user through the elements of a Text, represented as database items, and provides a means for linking every word to an entry in the project dictionary. To illustrate the intelligence of this wizard, we will use the example of a text from the Assyrian trading colony of Kültepe Kanesh.[14] This short text is a letter regarding the payment of silver. It is written in logosyllabic cuneiform, the same Writing system defined by the OCHRE Sumero-Akkadian cuneiform signary. We pick up the process below after the text has been imported and linked to values in the signary.

TLex is available from the View of a Text for an authorized editor. When activated by clicking the orange wizard wand button on the toolbar, TLex finds the first word in the text that has not yet been linked to the dictionary. If none of the words has yet been linked, the wizard finds the first word in the text, here um-ma. The wizard searches the project dictionary for all words spelled um-ma. Only one word is found, so the user can instruct the wizard to Accept the identification and move on to the next word. Had the wizard found two words in the dictionary with the same spelling, it would have presented the user with the two valid options. This is the case for the word a-šu-mì in line 5. This spelling could represent either a preposition or a conjunction. TLex presents both options in a picklist, allowing the user to make the appropriate selection. The process continues until every word in the Text is matched to an attested spelling in a Dictionary item (Fig. 8.8).

If a word is not yet attested in the dictionary the TLex wizard will return zero matches. However, the wizard provides a convenient method for adding the newly discovered word to the dictionary without leaving the guided workflow. Additionally, tools are provided to add properties to both the words in the dictionary and to the specific attestations of the words in the texts. These properties may include parse or declension details, or they may identify a word as a personal or geographical name, for example. So, in addition to linking texts to the dictionary, TLex provides an interactive and user-friendly method for populating and tagging the project dictionary, thereby assisting with the building of a corpus-based lexicon.

It is often the case when dealing with clay tablets that the text is not well preserved, especially at either the beginning or the end of the line. When a word in the text is only partially preserved, the TLex wizard will search for near matches in the

[13] See the Ras Shamra Tablet Inventory case study (Chap. 11) for a step-by-step explanation of the import process.

[14] This text is part of a research project funded by the Neubauer Collegium at the University of Chicago: Economic Analysis of Ancient Trade: The Case of the Old Assyrian Merchants of the 19th Century BCE. https://neubauercollegium.uchicago.edu/faculty/ancient_trade/.

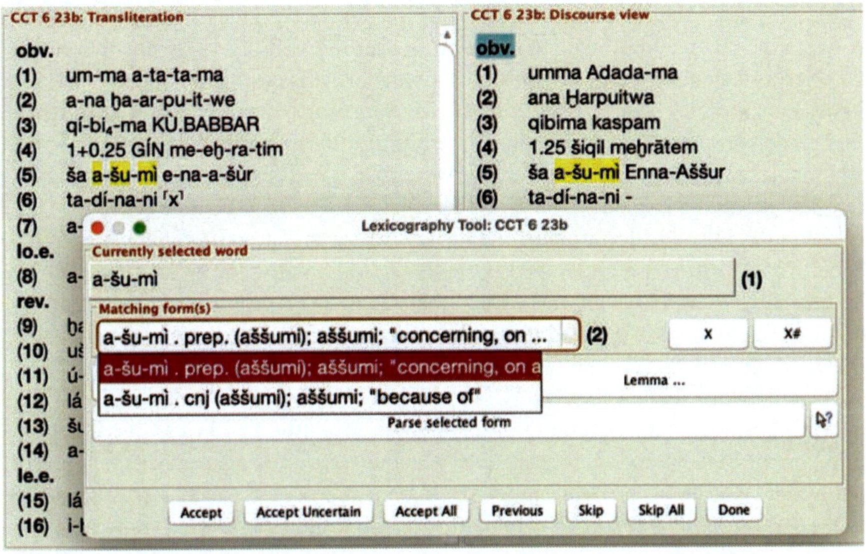

Fig. 8.8 The Text Lexicography Wizard walks the scholar through linking and studying a Text

project dictionary, sometimes coming up with unexpected suggestions. By using string matching, logical inference drawn from a knowledge base represented by links and hierarchies, and human interaction, TLex serves as a supervised workflow wizard.

Prosopography Tool (ProTo)

Once all valid words are linked to entries in the dictionary, the user can use another set of workflow wizards to associate these words with specific persons and places. The *Prosopography*[15] *Tool* (or ProTo) addresses each proper name in the text, giving the user the opportunity to associate a name with a specific agent. To review, OCHRE's item-based approach keeps separate the Dictionary item that manages different spellings and forms for a name as a lemma, the specific attestation of the name in the Text (a Discourse unit), and the identification of the Person of that name. This model allows the database to keep separate the etymology of a specific name and the various Persons who share that name. The orthography and etymology are described on the Dictionary item. But the identifiable individuals are modeled as Persons. Properties that would apply to discrete individuals, like vocation or family relations, do not get mixed up with properties that apply to the Dictionary item.

[15] For those not familiar with *prosopography*, this type of investigation attempts to identify individuals and their relationships with other individuals, commonly in a historical or literary context.

ProTo guides the user in much the same way as TLex. The wizard finds the first name in the text not yet linked to a Person. It uses the spelling of the name to search the Persons category for all possible string matches. Not surprisingly, there could be many Person items with the same name. If the text specifies a'rtn, the wizard will find all persons named a'rtn. The user is presented with a picklist containing all possible matches. If the user can identify which a'rtn is attested in the text, then the relevant selection can be made from the picklist. ProTo adds the necessary link between the Discourse unit and the Person. Again, this process uses logical inference: if the word (Discourse unit) is spelled "a'rtn" and if "a'rtn" is a match for a lemma in the dictionary, and if the Dictionary item has been propertized as a proper noun and a personal name, and if there is a Person item with a matching name, then the word represents a person (Fig. 8.9).

This network of links may serve as the basis for social network analysis. The analysis has access to everything that is known about the word (it is in the context of a "list of herders and their assistants"), about the dictionary entry (it is a proper noun representing a personal name), and about the person (he is a servant of the king). After linking a reliable sample of texts, the result is a network of persons and places in texts that would be difficult to manage in printed, tabular, or nearly any other format. The graph data model implemented by the item-based approach represents this knowledge naturally and intuitively. Further, each person in the social network can be traced back to their specific attestations in the text corpus. This lets

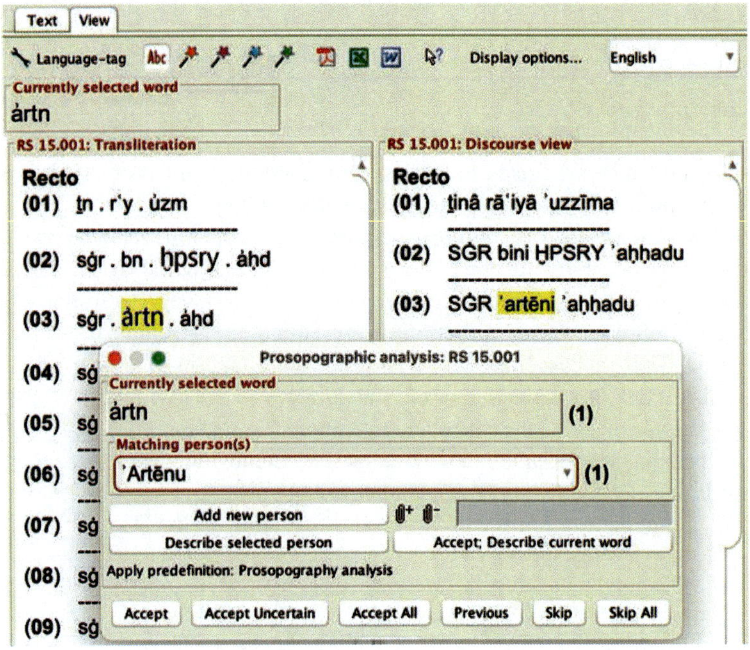

Fig. 8.9 The Prosopography tool facilitates matching and linking Words to Persons

the researcher easily track down a specific person to verify their identification or add further properties.

Like ProTo, but processing Locations instead of Persons, is OCHRE's geographic *Gazetteer Tool* (abbreviated GeoTo), which aids the scholar in relating words (Discourse units) and Locations. Using an item-based approach, the Location is modeled as a separate item from the Dictionary item, again because it requires properties that are appropriate only for a Spatial unit, including geospatial data such as longitude and latitude coordinates. Attestations of geographic places in the text (Discourse units) link to both the Dictionary item and the Location (a Spatial unit) creating a network of relationships. By integrating textual and spatial data, a project opens many avenues of analysis and visualization, from transport cost analysis to distribution analysis.

An Interlinear View

Once a Text is fully analyzed using the text analysis tools, the linked lexical and morphological data becomes available to specialized views of the Text. Consider, for example, the **Interlinear View** shown in Fig. 8.10, generated as OCHRE navigates its knowledge base, following links to extract and expose the lexical and morphological properties of each word. This view summarizes the textual data from the database in a more natural format as a document, in effect providing a rough-and-ready translation. In this text from the Persepolis Fortification Archive, we can

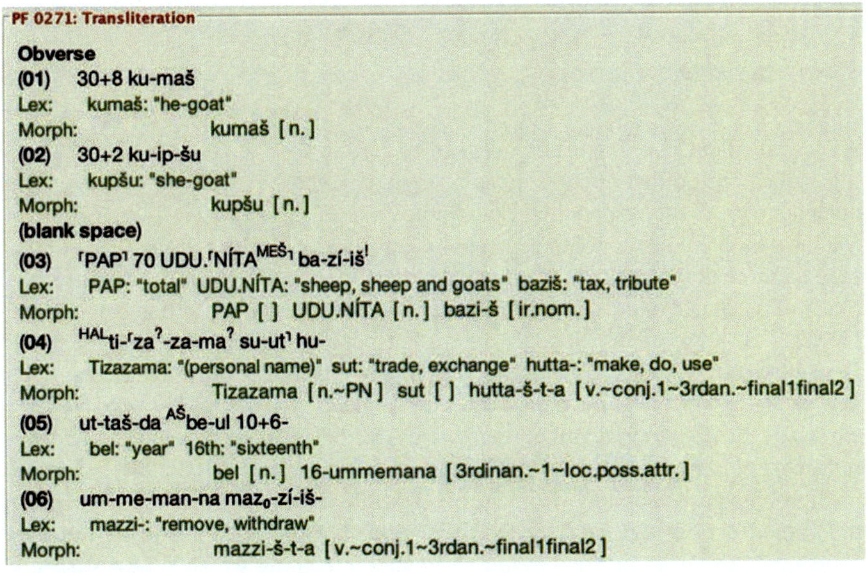

Fig. 8.10 The Interlinear View of PF 0271 combines textual, lexical, and morphological information

understand the essence of the content: "38 he-goats and 32 she-goats for a total of 70 sheep and goats, given as tax/tribute to Tizazama in the 16th year…"

In Support of Machine Learning (ML)

Transforming a Text from a semi-structured document representation to a database representation, then back again to a composite, coherent document, is relatively straightforward with an item-based system like OCHRE that uses a graph data model. Atomizing a text to its individual signs, validating them against a carefully articulated writing system, organizing the signs into words, and integrating those words within a carefully articulated glossary requires highly granular elements collected into highly organized hierarchies.

Having an intelligent import process and several user-supervised workflow wizards was a big step forward in the scholarly preparation of text editions for publication. But these steps started with a document as the source input—a document prepared manually by an expert scholar carefully examining and transcribing, sign by sign, character by character, the content of a tablet, or some other type of manuscript. This is a time-consuming and tedious task. While following the trends in the technology industry, watching optical character recognition improve, getting caught up in the promise of expert systems based on rapidly improving machine learning strategies, and inspired by a variety of advances in AI, we paused to wonder whether such a task could be handed over to a computational process.

Case Study: DeepScribe

As described in Chap. 7, hotspot links can be used to annotate images of texts, linking a pixel region that circumscribes a single character or sign on an image of a document to its corresponding Epigraphic unit in its itemized Text. Professor Matthew Stolper, director of the Persepolis Fortification Archive project, was a keen proponent of this technique. Graduate students who came to the Institute for the Study of Ancient Cultures to study Elamite with him were pressed into service over the years as "hotspotters." Not only did the hotspot annotations document the scholar's authorized readings of the Elamite texts, but hotspotting proved to be an excellent pedagogic exercise for the students. A targeted OCHRE query one day by a curious S. Schloen revealed that there were over 6000 annotated images. A determined effort to extract the annotations exposed an astonishing 100,000+ hotspots!

Sign-by-sign hotspotting of images is possible because of the highly granular, item-based data model used by OCHRE. Each hotspot is a link to the relevant Epigraphic unit from the Text item's epigraphic hierarchy which itemizes the text line by line, sign by sign (Fig. 8.11).

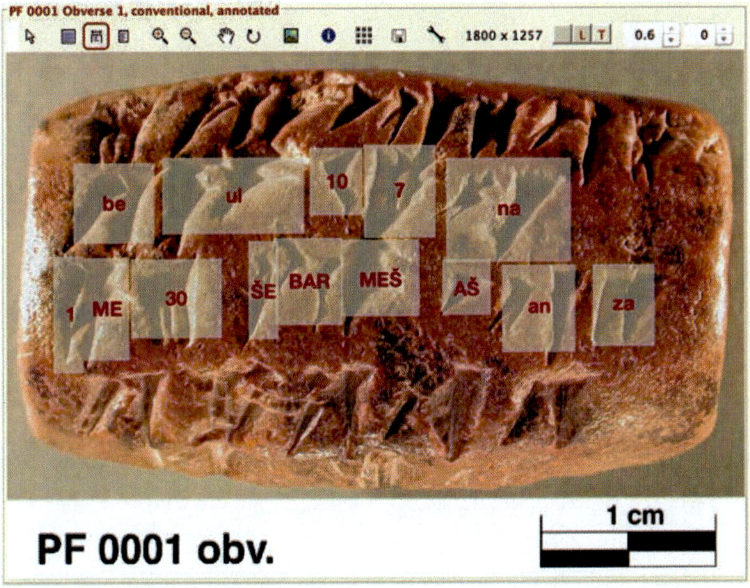

Fig. 8.11 Hotspot links annotate images of cuneiform tablets, sign by sign. (Photograph courtesy of the Persepolis Fortification Archive project)

In the hope that this unique collection of annotated images had the potential to serve as a training set for a machine learning classifier, we set about doing image processing. Creating a special-purpose utility we extracted image cutouts of the individual hotspots. The label of each miniature image was based on the UUID (universally unique identifier) of the single database item that was represented by the pictured sign, and qualified by the UUID of the database item that represented the source image of the tablet. This allowed us to label each hotspot cutout uniquely while retaining knowledge of the context of each individual pictured sign. We also prefixed the hotspot cutout label by the name of the sign itself so that instances of the same sign would sort together.

Take a look at the gallery of images in Fig. 8.12. Even a non-specialist could guess that these images represented the number "3" and would be able to recognize additional instances of this cuneiform sign in other images. How much more could a computer do? If a machine learning algorithm could be taught to "read" an image of a tablet, determine what the signs were, and create a preliminary transcription, this "document" could be given to OCHRE as its initial input. The rich knowledge base already available in OCHRE could provide valuable additional input. OCHRE has information about the context for each sign—what sign comes before, which sign comes after—and could recognize improbable sequences of signs or suggest valid combinations of signs. OCHRE could generate probabilities based on currently known sign usage; if the algorithm had alternative possibilities, it could factor in the likelihood of a common sign over a rarely used one. OCHRE's extensive

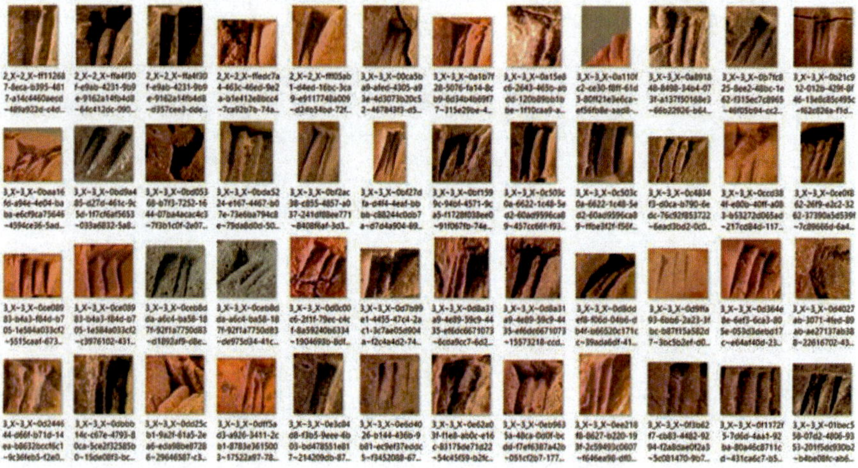

Fig. 8.12 Hotspot cutouts represent the number "3" in cuneiform script

dictionary could serve as a master list of possible legitimate words—if a combination of signs was being considered that did not already exist as a word, perhaps a different combination matching a known word is more likely.

Image Classification

With this unparalleled set of over 100,000 tagged images of cuneiform signs in hand we ventured from our ivy-covered tower to broach the question with machine learning experts as to whether this collection of images could be used as a training set for teaching computers to read cuneiform. After ad hoc experimentation showed promise, we began the *DeepScribe* project—a collaboration between the Institute for the Study of Ancient Cultures and the University of Chicago's Computer Science department to pursue this question in depth.[16]

Early efforts by Edward Williams, an engineer with formal training in machine learning and an interest in cuneiform, using hotspot cutouts from OCHRE prepared by S. Schloen, showed better than 80% success identifying a selected set of signs using a convolutional neural network (CNN) algorithm.[17] The process involved *training* the neural network using 20% of the hotspot collection, teaching it to recognize the "classes" of items, then *testing* it to see how well it could classify the remaining 80% of the hotspot images. Each cuneiform sign represents a "class" in

[16]The DeepScribe project team is grateful to Matthew W. Stolper, Professor of Assyriology Emeritus at the Institute for the Study of Ancient Cultures, for access to the rich data set of the Persepolis Fortification Archive. DeepScribe was formally established with funding provided by the Data Science Institute at the University of Chicago; https://datascience.uchicago.edu.

[17]Results were based on the use of a ResNet18 convolutional neural network trained on the OCHRE collection of image hotspots.

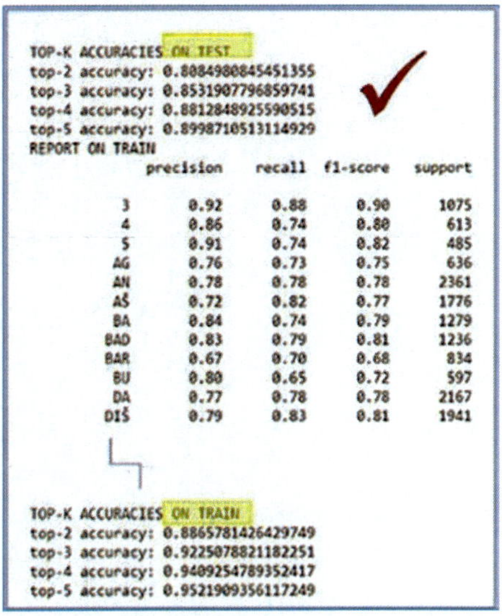

TOP-K ACCURACIES ON TEST
top-2 accuracy: 0.8084980845451355
top-3 accuracy: 0.8531907796859741
top-4 accuracy: 0.8812848925590515
top-5 accuracy: 0.8998710513114929
REPORT ON TRAIN

	precision	recall	f1-score	support
3	0.92	0.88	0.90	1075
4	0.86	0.74	0.80	613
5	0.91	0.74	0.82	485
AG	0.76	0.73	0.75	636
AN	0.78	0.78	0.78	2361
AŠ	0.72	0.82	0.77	1776
BA	0.84	0.74	0.79	1279
BAD	0.83	0.79	0.81	1236
BAR	0.67	0.70	0.68	834
BU	0.80	0.65	0.72	597
DA	0.77	0.78	0.78	2167
DIŠ	0.79	0.83	0.81	1941

TOP-K ACCURACIES ON TRAIN
top-2 accuracy: 0.8865781426429749
top-3 accuracy: 0.9225078821182251
top-4 accuracy: 0.9409254789352417
top-5 accuracy: 0.9521909356117249

Fig. 8.13 Experiments with supervised deep learning showed promising results and inspired further efforts based on machine learning

this scheme, and it became clear that the hotspot collection is marred by what is called *skew*: a few of the signs (classes) are extensively represented while many are quite rare having only one or two exemplars. Despite the challenges, *DeepScribe* principal investigator, Professor Sanjay Krishnan of the University of Chicago computer science department, is leading an effort to improve on the early results.[18] Certain to help is the extensive collection of transliterated texts in the Elamite language that have been processed by the PFA project. Pairing the image classification process with a model of the Elamite language (e.g., which signs typically come before or after other signs; which signs typically start or end words) informs the process of predicting valid sign classifications and is expected to improve the neural network's performance overall. Valid words can be matched against the project dictionary to derive a preliminary "reading" of the text. The tight integration of textual, lexical, and image data in OCHRE's highly granular knowledge base is reaping rich rewards for research (Fig. 8.13).

Object Detection

Ultimately, the hope is that the image classification strategies developed by *DeepScribe* will be effective for reading texts from images not previously seen by the machine learning model, and indeed, for reading other sets of images of other texts written in other languages that use the cuneiform script. But obviously it will do no good if another corpus of texts would require another 100,000 hotspots in

[18] At this writing, the project is publishing a report on our initial findings in the Journal on Computing and Cultural Heritage, Williams et al. (forthcoming).

Fig. 8.14 Predicted hotspots shown in yellow, compared to actual hotspots shown in red, illustrate the success of computer vision techniques to detect hotspots boundaries. Analysis was produced by Edward Williams, November 2022, for the DeepScribe project using a RetinaNet Object Detector against the OCHRE image of tablet PF-0339

order for the sign classification to be effective. To this end the *DeepScribe* team has turned to AI-based deep learning object detection algorithms, drawing on advances in computer vision, like those commonly used to help robots "see" and to help self-driving cars navigate their surroundings.

This time, the thousands of images which had been hotspotted were serialized from OCHRE into a JSON-formatted text file that itemized each image's hotpots listed in reading order from top-left to bottom-right. The rectangular pixel coordinates and the label of the cuneiform sign circumscribed by the hotspot bounding box were also given. Preprocessing was done to automatically crop the source images to include only the annotated regions, as it became clear that the neural network being trained was penalized for finding sign boundaries where none had been provided. (In the example of PF 0001 shown in Fig. 8.11, lines 1 and 4 of the script would be cropped from the image, leaving only lines 2 and 3 which had been hotspotted.) Most of the images, with their lists of *ground-truth*,[19] labeled, bounding box coordinates, were used to train a convolutional image classifier network, with the rest set aside to test the resulting model. Success of the model was measured by comparing the predicted object bounding boxes with the actual ones and seeing how well they overlapped (Fig. 8.14).[20]

[19] In this context, ground truth represents the hoped-for result, the "right answer" as defined by the researcher. This term typically describes real-world data used to train a ML model. For more on the subjective nature of AI, see "Why AI and decision-making are two sides of the same coin" (https://towardsdatascience.com/in-ai-the-objective-is-subjective-4614795d179b).

[20] This is measured mathematically using the ratio of the intersection of the predicated and actual boxes relative to their *union* (IoU). For best matches, this ratio will be close to 1.

Given a set of images of texts written in cuneiform, we envision the following pipeline. Step 1 would involve detecting the boundaries of cuneiform signs using a trained object detection model. In Step 2, the predicted image bounding boxes would be fed as input to an image classifier which would categorize these into predicted cuneiform signs. Step 3 would involve evaluating predictions against an appropriate language model of the texts, validating and improving on, and selecting from the predicted options from Step 2, in the hope of deducing words. The final step would involve matching words against the lexical information in OCHRE to create a provisional translation. While many challenges remain in creating this processing pipeline, the value of a highly organized, extensively labeled, data set in support of exciting research is undeniable.

Conclusion

This chapter began with a statement from an address at the annual Research Computing Expo and Symposium, Mind Bytes, at the University of Chicago; so too would we like to end it. Runesha, the Research Computing Center's director, has made a practice of scheduling a keynote speaker from industry to add substance and interest to the event as well as a perspective from outside academia. The 2017 keynote speaker was Alfio M. Gliozzo, a Research Manager on the IBM T. J. Watson Research team responsible for "knowledge induction."[21] After capturing the attention of the crowd with a video clip showing the much-hyped event where Watson, IBM's artificial intelligence masterpiece, bested Ken Jennings, the reigning grand champion of the game show Jeopardy, the audience was primed to expect the usual rah-rah cheerleader-style enthusiasm for the promise of artificial intelligence to follow.

Instead, Gliozzo's talk took a surprising turn. He confessed that despite all of the effort and progress made in programming AI systems to become expert in a given domain—by training systems with source material, extracting keywords, matching terms, building concepts and concept hierarchies, finding relations and relation hierarchies, deriving axioms, etc.—despite all of the progress, we are still "very, very far" from matching expert human performance in any field of knowledge.[22] It is not more clever algorithms and more sophisticated natural language processors, like those developed in the "programmable era," that are going to usher in the new "cognitive era" of computing, said Gliozzo. Rather, with an optimism that called to mind the original aspirations of GOFAI, Gliozzo proposed that rich knowledge bases, and

[21] Knowledge and Reasoning in Cognitive Computing, Alfio M. Gliozzo, Research Manager, Knowledge Induction IBM T.J. Watson (Keynote Speaker, Mind Bytes, Research Computing Expo and Symposium, May 2, 2017).

[22] In February 2021, there came a reality check on the promise of AI expert systems with the announcement that "IBM prepares to 'throw in the towel' as they look for a buyer for Watson Health ... it didn't live up to the hype" (Hernandez and Fitch 2021).

processes capable of making inferences and thereby "reasoning," will enable the "deep learning" needed to truly advance the intelligence of artificial systems.

The rich, carefully curated, painstakingly labeled image data set of the Persepolis Fortification Archive made the innovative deep learning processes of *DeepScribe* possible in a field of research where AI is only just beginning to take root. Much remains to be seen as a new age of generative AI fans the flames of progress, supercharging the field, raising afresh debates regarding sentient machines and the line between human and artificial intelligence (Metz 2022). Although we are not qualified to weigh in on such questions, the conversation is nonetheless inspirational, and we remain motivated to build rich knowledge bases from research data with which intelligent machines of the future will surprise us with the means to "enhance, scale, and accelerate human expertise."[23]

[23] Gliozzo, public comments.

Chapter 9
Publication: Where Data Comes to Life!

Data Sharing and Reuse

> By the authority vested in me as President by the Constitution and the laws of the United States of America, it is hereby ordered as follows: …

That an executive order by a President of the United States of America has anything to do with this book is a testament to the high-level awareness of, and an appreciation of the importance of, managing and making available digital data. President Barack Obama's executive order titled "Making Open and Machine Readable the New Default for Government Information" affirms that "as one vital benefit of open government, making information resources easy to find, accessible, and usable can fuel entrepreneurship, innovation, and scientific discovery that improves Americans' lives and contributes significantly to job creation."[1] This document, formally written using boilerplate legalese, is nonetheless inspirational and goes on to state as a case in point the achievements that ensued when the U.S. government made weather data and the Global Positioning System (GPS) data freely available. From the U.S. Department of Defense (DoD) website: "The Global Positioning System (GPS) is a space-based satellite navigation system built and maintained by DoD and is freely available to anyone in the world with a GPS receiver. In addition to navigation, uses of GPS include precise timing for financial transactions, search and rescue, communications, farming, recreation and both military and commercial

[1] The White House, Office of the Press Secretary, May 09, 2013. https://obamawhitehouse.archives.gov/the-press-office/2013/05/09/executive-order-making-open-and-machine-readable-new-default-government-.

S. R. Schloen, M. C. Prosser, *Database Computing for Scholarly Research*, Quantitative Methods in the Humanities and Social Sciences,
https://doi.org/10.1007/978-3-031-46696-0_9

aviation."[2] Without GPS data, hundreds of millions of people of all ages in the world over would not be enjoying Pokémon GO![3]

The move to open government data long predates the executive order. A 2007 workshop of technology leaders from industry, government, and academia established eight guiding principles for "open government data." As the workshop participants were careful to note, it is important to distinguish between "open" and "public," a distinction that is often muddied in the discussion of this topic.[4] The Open Government Data principles do not address what data should be public and open. Privacy, security, and other concerns may legally (and rightly) prevent data sets from being shared with the public. Rather, these principles specify the conditions public data should meet to be considered "open."

As true as this is for government data, so too is it important for academic research data, where concerns regarding publication rights, credit for tenure consideration, cultural sensitivity of the collected data, and other matters, might provide legitimate justification for data to remain private. Our discussion here, then, is not whether private data should be made public, but rather, how public data should be made open.[5] Furthermore, although these eight principles were developed specifically with government data in mind, they provide a useful rubric with which to consider digital information generated by academic research. Our brief review here is both to appreciate the spirit and substance of these principles, and to consider how a comprehensive, item-based platform such as OCHRE can support such ideals.

OCHRE and Open Data

1. **Complete**: All public data is made available. Public data is data that is not subject to valid privacy, security, or privilege limitations.

With this first principle, the researcher is faced with a technical challenge. Given that we wish to make available all public data, how do we disentangle this public data from the data that is subject to valid privacy restrictions? In some cases, for certain projects, perhaps the entire data set is created for eventual publication as open data. However, we cannot insist that this be the case for every research project. We must have tools that allow for some subsets of data to be subject to privacy concerns and others not. When these two tranches of data are tightly intertwined, the

[2] https://data.defense.gov/.

[3] Released in 2016, the Pokémon GO app reached over a billion downloads as of early 2019. Authors Schloen and Prosser have both participated in the thriving Pokémon community at the University of Chicago. https://en.wikipedia.org/wiki/Pokémon_Go.

[4] From "Definitions" at https://opengovdata.org/.

[5] A collaborative document which discusses this topic as it relates to the field of archaeology, and which poses a challenge, "to support open, transparent, and reproducible science in archaeology," was written by the Open Science Interest Group of the Society of American Archaeology (SAA) (Marwick, et al. The SAA Archaeological Record 17(4): 8–14.

technical challenge is how to share one subset without compromising the private subset. OCHRE's item-based design essentially makes this problem moot, allowing the scholar to choose, item by item if needed, which items remain private and which are made public. By contrast, a relational database often lacks the necessary level of granularity to make this sort of discrete sharing possible.

As we have seen in the OCHRE environment, with an item-based approach all data is created equal. Whether the impressive Katumuwa stele, or a damaged Aramaic sign carved upon it, each item worthy of observation has all the rights, privileges, and honors pertaining thereunto: the right to be universally unique and addressable; the right to be timestamped and attributed upon its creation; the right to have Properties, Links, Notes, and Events; the right to have access to it be controlled; the right to be publishable and safeguarded. There is no second-class data. The raw, attributed observations that make up the details can be made available as easily as the summary tables or insightful analyses. Hierarchies and lists provide useful and familiar structures with which to organize the data, while links expose the relationships between items to fill in the complete picture. There is a place for everything, and in a comprehensive platform like OCHRE, everything is put in its place.

Furthermore, *any* highly atomic unit in OCHRE can be published apart from any other item; the data model does not need to be adjusted to accommodate the need to assign "private" or "public" status to an item. Items are not tangled up together in tabular subsets of data or in highly intertwined normalized tables. Quite simply, any item can be marked as private, preventing it from being published; conversely, any item not marked as private can be published individually. In fact, an item, like an inscribed stone, can be logged, described, and published, yet the photograph to which it is linked can remain private, until such time as the scholar can decipher and report on the inscription. To satisfy the ***complete*** requirement of this first principle, it is practical to use OCHRE's system of sets and hierarchies as publication units. Any hierarchy of resources (PDFs, images, etc.) or set of items can be published as a unit and accessed by its universally unique identifier (UUID). Complete, yet carefully controlled, publication of data is easy to achieve and manage using an item-based approach.

2. **Primary**: Data is collected at the source, with the highest possible level of granularity, not in aggregate or modified forms.

We find it interesting that the issue of granularity is addressed in these principles. While some consumers of research data will want just the highlights, it is the carefully collected atomic bits that provide the basis for conclusions and summaries. These are the real stuff of research data. We demonstrate throughout this book the value of the item-based approach for capturing data at all levels of detail as we constantly evaluate *How far is far enough?* And we illustrate how technology has developed to the point that data can effectively be "born digital" by the primary observers, for example, in real time by field supervisors on an archaeological expedition.[6] The

[6] See the Tell Keisan case study (Chap. 10).

mantra from the 1980s, when S. Schloen was studying computer science—get it once, get it early, get it right—is still sound counsel.

3. **Timely**: Data is made available as quickly as necessary to preserve the value of the data.

Too often, data once captured is incarcerated in some local database system, sentenced to an extended confinement. Years, even decades, might pass before it ever sees the light of day. It is one thing for a scholar to make the intentional choice of withholding valuable information from the public—one is reminded of the slow pace with which the Dead Sea Scrolls were published.[7] It is another thing entirely if the scholar has every intention of sharing the data with the world but lacks the tools to achieve this goal. An effective database platform can greatly reduce the elapsed time between data capture and data publication. As we argue, what is often thought of as a data "life cycle"—a useful and fashionable metaphor which suggests a progression from data creation through to curation, analysis, publication, and archiving—can now happen in a moment. Research data is no longer condemned to obscurity but can be freed to participate in the wider scholarly discussion. The degree to which the timeframe can be compressed, from data capture to data publication, is limited by the scholar, not by the technology.

4. **Accessible**: Data is available to the widest range of users for the widest range of purposes.

A 2019 policy paper commissioned by the Organization for Economic Cooperation and Development (OECD) revisited the "open government data" principles set forth by the 2007 workshop. The result was the Open, Useful, and Re-usable data (OURdata) Index, promoting "transparency, accountability, and value creation by making government data available to all with no restriction for its re-use," thereby also promoting collaboration and innovation.[8] The OURdata Index helpfully underscores the need for data providers to make it easy for users to *consume* open data, for example, by providing data in appropriate file formats, making tools and procedures for data publication available, and ensuring high levels of data quality and interoperability.[9] Data provided as "open" data but trapped in proprietary formats or plagued by idiosyncratic coding schemes cannot be considered "accessible."[10]

Having been implemented as a client-server application from the start, OCHRE's database platform is already available to the Internet, and so it is easy to make data

[7] On the publication of the Dead Sea Scrolls, see the Leon Levy Dead Sea Scrolls Digital Library of the Israel Antiquities Authority https://www.deadseascrolls.org.il/learn-about-the-scrolls/discovery-and-publication. Any number of newspaper articles covered the controversy.

[8] https://www.oecd.org/governance/digital-government/ourdata-index-policy-paper-2020.pdf. See especially pp. 4, 14.

[9] Ibid., p. 34.

[10] Ibid., p. 39. Listed as examples of potentially "open" data that make reuse difficult are the popular non-machine-readable PDF format, and the proprietary Excel format.

public at large, or made accessible to credentialed users, at the discretion of the project team which owns the data. Once public, OCHRE data is available around the world. The high-resolution photograph linked to the OCHRE item representing the Luwian inscription found on a remote site in central Turkey can be studied moments later, 8000 miles and eight time-zones away, by one of the world's leading Luwian experts at the University of Chicago. Collaborating team members, wherever they are geographically, have access to all project data, contributed by all the other members of the research project.

But how do we address the issue of usability for the widest range of purposes? This recommendation places a heavy burden on the data. Sharing data often requires reformatting or decoding the data, but here the item-based approach shines. Items-as-bricks can be used to build new structures in ways that more rigid tabular formats cannot. Aliases and thesaurus mappings of individual items can accommodate different terminologies. Data as richly documented, highly granular units has practically no limits for how it can be used. A given data set can be used for multiple purposes: to create appendix-style tabular webpages that allow for human-accessible browsing; to populate highly specialized matrices, vectors, or lists for analysis using statistics in R; to visualize spatially as the basis of an online GIS map. Data that exists in a form that can be recombined and reformatted for various purposes satisfies the spirit and practice of this fourth principle.

5. **Machine processable**: Data is reasonably structured to allow automatic processing.

The fourth principle anticipates this fifth principle. It is one thing for public data to be "open"; it is another thing entirely to have "high quality, timely and disaggregated data in machine-readable, structured, and non-proprietary formats (e.g., CSV and JSON) … that are easy and open to re-use by both humans and machines towards greater re-use, value and integration."[11] On this point, XML proves to be reasonable, self-documenting, naturally structured, and both human- and machine-readable. As an industry standard, XML puts OCHRE on solid ground and is a viable option for many data management systems. XML can also be easily transformed into other formats, typically by using Extensible Stylesheet Language Transformations (XSLT). From the World Wide Web Consortium: "XSLT is a language for transforming XML documents into other XML documents, or other formats such as HTML for web pages, plain text or XSL Formatting Objects, which may subsequently be converted to other formats, such as PDF, PostScript and PNG."[12] Furthermore, OCHRE specifically, and the item-based approach more generally, is highly compatible with linked data (LD) mechanisms used across the Internet to publish data in ways that are programmatically accessible to other applications in a standards-compliant way. We will demonstrate this in more detail as we discuss the Semantic Web later in this chapter.

---

[11] OURIndex, p.39. The term "openwashing" has been coined for "the release of 'open data' in formats and procedures that make re-use extremely difficult, or impossible" (p. 34).

[12] https://www.w3.org/TR/xslt-30/.

6. **Non-discriminatory**: Data is available to anyone, with no requirement of registration.

This principle falls under the umbrella of data policy and is not so much a technical matter. The OCHRE platform does not place any limits on what a project can make available to its users or publish online. It is also worth noting, again, that all OCHRE data belongs to a specific project; OCHRE makes no claim on it. Each project decides whether and when any or all its data should become public and made accessible, and to determine how its data is presented for use. The OCHRE software includes tools and options to publish data selectively or *en masse*, so that project administrators can control the timing and scope of data publication. We encourage and support reducing barriers to access and making as much data as possible available to as many people as possible for as many purposes as possible.

7. **Non-proprietary**: Data is available in a format over which no entity has exclusive control.

As a human-readable, industry-standard format, XML satisfies this principle in the case of OCHRE and is a popular, flexible, and powerful option for other data management systems. It is also easily transformed into other useful, non-proprietary formats such as JSON or HTML.

8. **License-free**: Data is not subject to any copyright, patent, trademark, or trade secret regulation. Reasonable privacy, security, and privilege restrictions may be allowed.

Also in 2019, the summit of 9 "digital nations" (D9) promoted the principle of *openness by default*, which aims to "make data easily accessible and available […] under an open license, unless there is a specific, legitimate reason why that data cannot be made open, and that reason is clearly communicated to the public as needed."[13] Academia, like government, might have specific, legitimate reasons why data cannot be made open, but openness by default is, perhaps, a good place to start. Prior to publishing data through OCHRE, the project administrator can apply a license to the data to be published. The license terms are embedded in the metadata of the published items and made available to stylesheets for display on webpages (Fig. 9.1).

FAIR Data Principles

In the wake of "big data," which has overwhelmed the capacity of the human mind to process, and which has left humans depending more on computational strategies for finding and using information, a new rubric for thinking about data, FAIR, both in the short term and for the long term, has gained some traction.

---

[13] Digital Nations (D9), 2019[3].

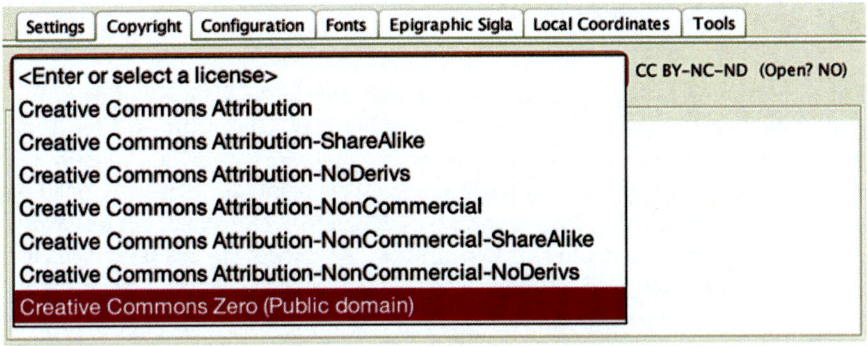

Fig. 9.1 OCHRE has built-in support for the Creative Commons licenses which, after 20 years, are advocating "Better Sharing – advancing universal access to knowledge and culture, and fostering creativity, innovation, and collaboration for a brighter future" (https://creativecommons.org)

In 2016, yet another "diverse set of stakeholders—representing academia, industry, funding agencies, and scholarly publishers" held a workshop "to design and jointly endorse a concise and measurable set of principles" for the purpose of "bringing some clarity around the goals and *desiderata* of good data management and stewardship, and defining simple guideposts to inform those who publish and/or preserve scholarly data" (Wilkinson et al. 2016). Although motivated by research in the life sciences, once again the "FAIR Guiding Principles for scientific data management and stewardship" are sufficiently useful and generic to apply to scholarly research data of all kinds.

FAIR is an acronym that represents four principles: Findability, Accessibility, Interoperability, and Reusability. Rightly, this group applies these principles not just to the data but to the tools, algorithms, and workflows that produced the data. For anyone involved in data management, or making decisions regarding data management, the FAIR principles document is worth a careful read (Wilkinson et al. 2016). There is little to argue with the recommendation that all digital research objects should be findable, accessible, interoperable, and reusable. But this raises the question, how do we make this possible?

In posing a scenario from the domain of biomedical research, the FAIR proponents identify many obstacles to effective data management and integration and ask: "Where does the researcher begin?" To this we answer: with an item-based data model supported by a sufficiently generic ontology implemented and managed from a central, ubiquitously accessible platform. In our view, a comprehensive platform that manages item-based data, using a consistent set of tools, with an upper ontology that accommodates various domain-specific taxonomies, is a prerequisite for addressing FAIR principles. The more granular the data, the more flexible it is for publication in various forms. A generic yet self-describing data model promotes both accessibility and reusability. Further, the need to share data requires that it be accessible, long term.

Preservation as Publication

Data preservation is often conceived of as a late stage in the life cycle of data. This is a fundamental misconception. The distance between data capture and preservation should be minimal, conceptually and practically, with data passing quickly and easily from capture to preservation without intervening hurdles. The coin found on the surface of the tell, once logged as an OCHRE item within minutes of discovery, has a unique identity that allows it to be tracked, described, plotted, preserved, and shared. The new reading of a sign on a broken tablet, or the almost indecipherable writing on the faded parchment, is recorded, attributed, and appropriately contextualized the moment it is entered into OCHRE, already available to be published and shared.

Rather than thinking of data as progressing through a life cycle we like to imagine each item as simply existing in an ontological sense—ontological, as used before the term was appropriated by data scientists. When data is "born digital," finding its home in an item-based context like the OCHRE database, it accomplishes all stages of the life cycle in an instant. It becomes, it is, and it remains, all at the same time. Legacy data—that which was created before the adoption of digital methods—enters the repository as facsimile images, transcriptions, maps, or links, becoming viable, vital, and integrated. Identified uniquely from the start, each OCHRE item is already represented in a human-readable, self-documenting, highly structured, XML document that could stand alone or with others, remain private or become public.

Each database item, thus created, becomes a part of the project repository, but that is just a beginning, not an end. In the company of other project items—excavation strata, artifacts, pottery, bones, in the case of archaeology projects; or characters, words, phrases, and documents as befits a philology project; or images, commentary, bibliography, and analysis of the historians; or measurements, findings, hypotheses, statistics, and conjectures of the scientists—each item finds its contexts within the project as a whole and makes its mark on the research enterprise.

A high degree of intentionality is needed to ensure that data remains useful, usable, and reusable throughout its life cycle. Data management and integration are critical prerequisites to stable data publication and should support a wide range of presentation, analysis, and archival strategies.

Data Silo: Where Data Goes to Die

Most researchers would agree that storing data on personal computers or external hard drives would not meet FAIR standards, but alternatives are not always easy to implement. Managing one's own data, much less trying to share it, has always been a challenge, especially for those of us who grew up through the early days of computing and who rode the wave of the technological revolution.[14] What we are dealing with now is a vast amount of data locked into separate silos, each with its own bespoke organization.

Are you one of those who has old files in old formats on old computers that you are loath to toss in case there is something good there that will be salvaged some day? Do you know why the hard drive on your laptop is called **C:**?[15] The breakneck speed of progress toward the next greatest idea, the search for new problems to give merit to our new solutions, the pressure to keep up with technological advances in hardware, software and "apps," and the haste, pressure, and compulsion to upgrade, has left in its wake a vast detritus of old technologies and, more regrettably, old data.

There are all too many ways of losing data or losing track of data. World Backup Day, inaugurated in 2011, invites users to take its pledge: "I solemnly swear to backup my important documents and precious memories on March 31st"[16]—sound advice on the eve of a day known for jokes and hoaxes. Statistics abound on estimated amounts of data loss by individual users, small businesses, or major corporations due to neglect, accident, or malice.[17] Other factors, like software, file format, and hardware obsolescence, are not to be underestimated. Legacy data, stuck in old or obsolete formats or on old or obsolete systems, may no longer be supported, may be difficult to access, and may be impossible to salvage if anything should break.

Despite a growing awareness of the risks, and despite an increased use of web-based resources—storing photographs in online services like Flickr or sharing documents via online tools like Google Drive—it is certain that there is a great deal of research data exposed to great risk, especially data captured before the advent of cloud storage.[18] Traditional research data sets may be simply collections of old files in outdated formats, or based on proprietary, now-defunct, software, or encoded using no-longer-supported fonts, or developed by long-lost IT personnel. A one-off, bespoke database, such as those common in archaeology circles, is especially vulnerable, leaving a project at the mercy of its creator. It would have required a dedicated effort over the past, say, 40 years of technological advances *not* to lose data

---

[14] The technological revolution is variously thought to have begun in the 1950s with the space race (https://www.space.com/space-race.html) or with the invention of the semiconductor (https://www.britannica.com/technology/electronics/The-semiconductor-revolution), with the introduction of the personal computer in the late 1970s (https://www.britannica.com/technology/personal-computer), or with the dotcom boom in the 1990s (https://en.wikipedia.org/wiki/Dot-com_bubble). What is certain is that it is not over.

[15] Some of us might still have some 3½-inch disks or even some 5¼-inch "floppies" in boxes or desk drawers, the slots for which were **B:** and **A:** respectively.

[16] https://www.worldbackupday.com.

[17] For example, Small Business Trends tells us that "58 percent of small businesses are not prepared for data loss" https://smallbiztrends.com/2017/04/not-prepared-for-data-loss.html.

[18] Users of free services from companies like Flickr or Google must beware that the terms for these free services are likely to change, making the service no longer free, or at best a freemium service in which service beyond a certain threshold is no longer free. Even worse, Google is somewhat notorious for sundowning support for its products, the point being that none of these tools is necessarily a secure long-term solution.

collected along the way. In our work at the OCHRE Data Service at the University of Chicago we find ourselves increasingly performing rescue operations, salvaging research data from the past as professors reach retirement and wonder about the future of their life's work, or as hardware is retired and a new home for project data is needed.

But even data added to a spreadsheet last week, or to a document this morning, is at risk if there is not an intentional plan in place to care for it. OCHRE serves as such a place—a database system for representing and storing data generated by a research project.

We hope we have given you a taste of how and why OCHRE is not an isolated or inaccessible data silo. Its item-based approach provides the opportunity for rich articulation and diversity of description of all kinds of data. The flexibility and simplicity of its intuitive hierarchical structures can mask great complexity and have wide application. Its Web-accessible architecture and core XML format protect against obsolescence and promote open data. There is practically no limit to the scope and substance of what OCHRE can represent and store, which makes it perfect as an integrated data warehouse, not an isolated data silo, that allows the researcher to publish digital data according to FAIR principles.

Data Warehouse: Where Data Goes to Live

To use Wikipedia's simple definition, "data warehouses are central repositories of integrated data from one or more disparate sources."[19] The key word here is "integrated." Kintigh et al. (2018) rightly emphasize the importance of "Data Integration in the Service of Synthetic Research." They describe how data integration greatly facilitates data reuse, listing a number of factors that affect the reusability of the data (i.e., its relevance, discoverability, accessibility, adequacy of metadata, availability of contextual information, and ease of use). The data repository endorsed by Kintigh is the Digital Archaeological Record (tDAR),[20] which uses "query-driven, on-the-fly data integration." While we prefer the data warehouse approach, which entails integrating data ahead of time, we agree:

> To answer many of the most pressing questions of concern to archaeologists, to scientists more generally, to policy makers, and to the broader publics to which we are responsible, archaeology needs to conduct synthetic research. That synthetic research requires that we integrate primary data from multiple projects that do not typically collect data in completely consistent ways. As a result, we must have means of integrating observations across datasets in ways that maintain their semantic integrity (Kintigh et al. 2018 p. 39).

[19] https://en.wikipedia.org/wiki/Data_warehouse. For a detailed discussion of data warehouses, and data integration more generally, see Doan et al. 2012.

[20] https://core.tdar.org/.

In reality, data integration of diverse data sets from diverse sources remains a key challenge. This is the problem of ontology alignment—one project will record and describe data one way; another project will describe similar data differently. Small differences that prevent a "match" can be as problematic as big differences. Such "local," domain-specific ontologies will not mesh well as different data sets attempt to coexist in a common data warehouse.

OCHRE embraces its role as a data warehouse. The recent advance of cloud computing, and corresponding services for managing "big data," has been a boon for the development and support of data warehouses. In fact, data warehouses are not just places to park data but are central repositories of "information that can be analyzed to make better informed decisions."[21] Amazon Web Services, for example, gives its customers the option of a data warehouse (highly integrated data for business analytics), or, using more recent metaphors, a "data lake" (for un-curated, raw data of all kinds, structured, and unstructured) or a "data mart" (a boutique collection of pre-digested data for targeted users) or a "data mesh" (unites disparate data sources), and so on. But for massive collections of data to be usable, especially when data have come from diverse sources (e.g., multiple research projects), they must be compatible at some basic level for comparison, aggregation, and other forms of analysis.[22]

But in constructing a data warehouse, the key problem is ontology alignment. This has been expressed as follows by David Schloen, the co-inventor of OCHRE:

> A data warehouse is a database that relies on a generic global ontology within which heterogeneous tables and documents and other data can be merged without loss of information, while preserving all of the terms and conceptual distinctions in the local ontologies that these datasets reflect. A warehouse has a single logical schema that conforms to the global ontology and permits efficient, semantically reliable queries. Single-schema data warehouses should not be confused with multi-schema data repositories in which there is no global ontology to facilitate large-scale querying, but just a collection of heterogeneous datasets, each with its own ontology.[23]

FAIR advocates, Wilkinson et al. (2016), appreciate the value of repositories but find themselves with a conundrum, nonetheless. On the one hand, they laud data repositories as "foundational and critical core resources [which] are continuously curating and capturing high-value reference datasets and fine-tuning them to enhance scholarly output, provide support for both human and mechanical users, and provide extensive tooling to access their content in rich, dynamic ways" (Wilkinson et al. 2016). On the other hand, they recognize that often such repositories can only accommodate the special-purpose data for which they were designed.

[21] See https://aws.amazon.com/data-warehouse and https://aws.amazon.com/what-is/data-mesh.

[22] Given the rise of cloud computing, it should also be noted that a "warehouse" does not suggest that all data lives in a single database. A virtual database, or warehouse, can be distributed across multiple, actual, databases residing on physical servers anywhere. Similarly, a data warehouse like OCHRE might reference thousands of documents or images housed on many different servers, potentially in far-flung places.

[23] D. Schloen personal communication; from an unpublished conference paper.

As a general-purpose data repository, but one based on a global ontology, OCHRE supports integration but avoids the pitfalls described here:

> [G]eneral-purpose data repositories … accept a wide range of data types in a wide variety of formats, [but] generally do not attempt to integrate or harmonize the deposited data, and place few restrictions (or requirements) on the descriptors of the data deposition. The resulting data ecosystem, therefore, appears to be moving away from centralization, is becoming more diverse, and less integrated, thereby ***exacerbating the discovery and re-usability problem for both human and computational stakeholders*** (Ibid., emphasis added).

In Chap. 2, we nicknamed OCHRE "Ontology Creation and the Hierarchical Representation of Everything" and we will not repeat that discussion here. But allow us to emphasize that an item-based approach, in tandem with a generic, upper ontology, as implemented in a platform like OCHRE, provides both the conceptual framework and the computational tools for facilitating data integration and preservation.

Data Archive: Where Data Goes to Live … Forever

A digital archive shares many of the same goals as a data warehouse, but, typically, with a greater emphasis on data preservation. Indeed, the lines are blurring between a warehouse and an archive, as data warehouses ensure that they are secure and sustainable, and as archives provide greater accessibility to the data in their care. The Archaeology Data Service, based in the UK, which has specialized in the digital archiving of archaeological data for over 20 years, exemplifies these twin goals in their "Guides to Good Practice," which state that "the overall goals of digital archiving are simple: permit easy and wide access to digital archaeological data for cultural, educational, and scientific purposes; ensure the long-term preservation of digital data so that it remains accessible for appropriate uses in the future."[24]

Furthermore, today's research projects are generally required to have a data management plan, either by the grant agency providing funds for research, by the supporting institution which has a stake in the ownership or outcomes of the research, or, at the very least, by a modicum of common sense within which the research is presumably framed. Why bother collecting data but to use it, learn from it, guard it, preserve it? One hopes that sloppy curation habits become things of the past, giving way to carefully provenanced data, reproducible experimentation, and responsible curation of both inputs and outputs. Organizations like the Digital Curation Center (DCC), also based in the UK, provide advice, support, and helpful guidelines for digital curation. Their "Checklist for a Data Management Plan," for example, is a

[24] http://guides.archaeologydataservice.ac.uk/g2gp/ArchivalStrat_1-0. Included are useful guides for best practice in archiving archaeological data.

well-considered resource for research projects seeking to do responsible data management and curation.[25]

OCHRE supports responsible data management and curation by providing a secure platform and requisite tools for effectively performing the activities listed in the DCC's Checklist: "data capture, metadata production, data quality, storage and backup, data archiving & data sharing." Specifically, the University of Chicago's Digital Library Development Center (DLDC) is an active partner with the OCHRE Data Service. We rely on its professional staff[26] which has provided system administration in support of OCHRE for over 20 years.

OCHRE: Where Data Comes to Life!

OCHRE *is* a database appropriate for managing legacy data salvaged from the past. OCHRE *is* a data warehouse well suited to data integration where data is redeemed in the present and made available and accessible for analysis and publication. OCHRE *is* an archive where data is preserved and safeguarded for the future. But more than each of these, OCHRE is a platform where data comes to life!

From the outset, data collected by OCHRE is repository-ready, but also publication-ready, and can be fully leveraged for use in analysis, in publication, or as linked data on the web. That is, every item created in OCHRE has a unique identifier and persistent **Citation URL** from the moment of its creation and can be targeted by a linked reference, viewed by a web browser, and accessed by the community of users for which it was intended. Data can be organized and reorganized in OCHRE, then published with a single click, making it accessible from outside the database.

Once published, the Citation URL of each OCHRE item, whether a Hierarchy, Set, or individual database item, serves as its stable, citable, durable, and unique (based on its UUID) identifier. The Citation URL is displayed across the bottom of the View of any item in OCHRE, along with its Publication Date. A copy button makes it quick to copy the Citation URL to the system clipboard so that it can be pasted into other documents or webpages. Figure 9.2 shows the Citation URL for Feature 777, a wine press or plaster basin of some kind, from the Leon Levy Expedition to Ashkelon.[27]

Fig. 9.2 An item's Citation URL exposes its published format, revealing it to the world

[25] http://www.dcc.ac.uk/sites/default/files/documents/resource/DMP/DMP_Checklist_2013.pdf.

[26] https://dldc.lib.uchicago.edu; with thanks to Charles Blair and the DLDC staff.

[27] https://pi.lib.uchicago.edu/1001/org/ochre/33614d92-8c89-f68b-cb4a-73aaef8aa9b0.

This degree of flexibility leaves the choice of *when* to publish and *what* to publish entirely in the hands of the researcher who decides which collections of data are to be published in which formats and with what copyright, properties, and metadata. Neither the software (OCHRE) nor the technical consultants (the OCHRE Data Service) should determine these choices. As researchers, we all must wrestle with the requirements or obligations for making data open, while on the other hand balancing an acceptable and reasonable level of scholarly privacy. OCHRE supports as much data sharing and reuse as is desired by the research project and tries to minimize the leap from data capture to data sharing and publication. It should be a simple process to turn research data into open data.

Approaches to Digital Publishing with OCHRE

Digital publication from the OCHRE database can mean many things. In most cases, a researcher will make published data accessible through a web browser, but a Citation URL can be accessed by any method that can open a link and process data. Typical publications may represent digital catalogs, appendices, spatial data for use in GIS analysis and visualization, digital lexicons, text editions, or even data archives. However, because individual items can be published with unique Citation URLs, one could imagine new horizons for digital publication. Citation URLs can be embedded in PDFs or other digital book editions to present the reader with unlimited resources that supplement the text of the book. A large collection of data can be accessed by its Citation URL as the source for a machine learning or natural language processing analysis. In short, when we use the term digital publication, we do not simply mean the production of a PDF that reproduces the page layout of a printed book. Nor do we mean data published solely to be presented as a browsable webpage. We mean digital scholarly communication in the broadest possible sense, for archiving, computational analysis, interoperability, and reuse.

Note that we do not identify digital publication, itself, as a challenge. Any modern platform can export data in a format appropriate for presentation on the World Wide Web. No, the challenge is to provide a platform where the data can be easily changed in the backend then republished in multiple formats for multiple uses on the frontend; a platform that requires little technical expertise from the scholar while allowing for customization by a trained web developer; a publication system that is not so fragile that the website becomes a dead link mere months after initial launch. An item-based approach with reuse of items in various contexts, integration of all types of data, and strong institutional support—these concepts are leveraged to create a data publication component that integrates tightly with the database backend and allows for a wide variety of publication options on the frontend.

So what format is used for publication? What standard is adopted? In response to this, we say ... any. Having captured *items*—not tables, not triples, not documents, not webpages of data—OCHRE has the flexibility to restructure the data in whatever format is needed. Already atomic, the highly granular items can be repackaged at will. In principle, any format is possible. If data is already constrained by data structures, it is much more difficult to restructure.

We also acknowledge the ephemeral and evolving nature of the Web. Even when W3C standards[28] are followed, digital publications will evolve over time, sometimes significantly, requiring ongoing maintenance. Web browsers change, accessibility standards improve, and quite naturally the styles for look-and-feel need to remain fresh. This constant state of flux is further reason for storing the data separate from its presentation, allowing the frontend tools to be upgraded without compromising the supply of secure and stable data on the backend. Unlike with some content management systems, OCHRE data is not trapped within a custom app, embedded within a static frontend framework. Rather, a dynamic interaction between the database and the interface greatly increases the chances that the data will be findable, accessible, interoperable, and reusable.

OCHRE's approach to data publication stands in contrast to other common strategies. By providing the researcher with the ability in the OCHRE app to prepare raw data in the core database (the backend) for publication, we reduce the amount of processing that typically would be performed using JavaScript or Python to develop web-based presentations and analysis (the frontend). This approach also eliminates the need to cache external files or manage exported subsets of data on a webserver since all data remains in the OCHRE backend ready to be delivered dynamically to the frontend. This is a revolutionary approach to data publication. Powerful, flexible, and accessible tools are in the hands of the researcher to configure their digital publication without significant intervention by a web developer. The black box of the database is unlocked and the entire data life cycle from capture through preservation and publication is available to the researcher.

Appreciating that each project has its own needs, the sections that follow provide selective examples of OCHRE-based digital publication strategies that illustrate the range of options available: internal or external to OCHRE, static or dynamic data. While the methods described here may challenge traditional approaches to digital scholarly publication, we hope to demonstrate that OCHRE's item-based approach leaves the doors wide open for creative and compelling publications.

Interactive, Integrative OCHRE Presentations

Internal to OCHRE is a built-in publication method, based on the Presentations category, which allows a scholar to create a lesson, presentation, or workflow to publish project data. This approach is useful if a project lacks the resources, the skill set, or the desire to publish data in HTML. It is also a useful means of viewing and navigating OCHRE data when running OCHRE in offline mode in cases where Internet access is not readily available. This style of presentation, created and

[28] https://www.w3.org/standards/.

Fig. 9.3 Marathi Online's hotspotted splash page provides links to the Lesson selections

managed entirely in OCHRE, is controlled by pre-formatted Hierarchies which provide linear breadth for a scripted presentation of a topic, as well as depth for drilling down to greater levels of detail. A selection of formatting options—splash pages, image maps, tabbed indexes, tables, side-by-side images, etc.—allows the researcher to create informative, varied, and functional presentations. The outcome is an interactive experience that runs in an OCHRE Java session (Fig. 9.3).

Our favorite example of this option is the publication of a Marathi Grammar,[29] billed as an interactive first-year course in Marathi, designed and developed by the late Senior Lecturer Philip C. Engblom, formerly of the South Asian Languages and Civilizations Department at the University of Chicago. As part of a Mellon grant (1998–2001) supporting "less commonly taught languages," Engblom converted his printed grammar (Bernsten et al. 2003) into an OCHRE Presentation which integrated lessons, an online glossary (OCHRE Dictionaries category), and thousands of audio samples (OCHRE Resources category) of native Marathi speakers. Each of the three volumes of *Marathi in Context* was represented by a separate hierarchy in OCHRE. The table of contents and well-organized lessons fell naturally and intuitively into a hierarchical framework, providing the students with a controlled presentation, while at the same time giving them freedom to explore non-linearly.

[29] *Marathi Online*: https://ochre.lib.uchicago.edu/launch?project=134c8bc4-d2b3-33c6-e23c-499f97ecb1ae.

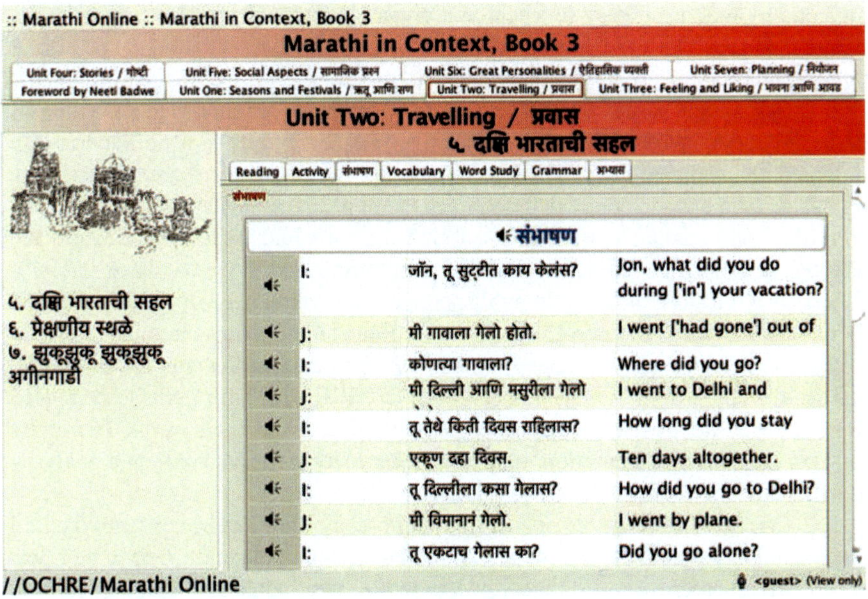

Fig. 9.4 OCHRE Presentations integrate many types of items like images, audio, and text

Using a vivid color palette and an assortment of OCHRE features to link related content, Engblom copy-pasted his grammar into OCHRE Resource and Presentation items, formatting it to his liking. As the lessons progressed, Engblom introduced more content in the Marathi language (applying a Sanskrit font that renders the characters of the Devanagari writing system) and linked in longer audio samples of full conversations. With no specialized technical skills, and needing very little technical support, Engblom created an engaging, interactive, integrative, illustrated, online resource available to students everywhere (Fig. 9.4).

Other sample publications that use this strategy include the electronic version of the Chicago Hittite Dictionary,[30] designed to mimic its print edition, and the Persepolis Fortification Archive viewer.[31]

Preparing Data for Publication

One of the goals of publishing project data, however, is to be independent of the OCHRE Java application and use traditional Web technologies that require neither OCHRE nor Java to produce public content. OCHRE supports other publication

[30] For the eCHD: https://ochre.lib.uchicago.edu/launch?project=5d506e6e-c050-f252-7e1f-e0cc86683918.

[31] For the PFA viewer: https://ochre.lib.uchicago.edu/launch?project=65801673-ad89-6757-330b-fd5926b2a685.

methods by making it easy to select and prepare content for publication from the item-based repository and present it, either statically or dynamically, on the Web or through other applications.

OCHRE's item-based approach allows for any item to be published individually, or for collections of items to be published as either Hierarchies, Sets, or Queries (all of which, themselves, are OCHRE items). For most items, the researcher need only right-click and choose "Publish item" from the pop-up menu. This granular level of control is highly valuable. If an error is found and corrected in the database, only the affected item need be republished. If new items are added to the database and published, they will join the already published material which need not be republished to include new data. Of course, it would be tedious to publish one item at a time, so we query for the items we want to publish, collect them in a Set, and have OCHRE publish the entire Set of items at once. Since OCHRE allows for items to be reused in multiple contexts, the researcher may choose to arrange items in one Hierarchy for data collection and curation, in another Hierarchy for publication and analysis, and in a custom Set to share with a colleague.

OCHRE Sets offer flexible options for publication. They can be configured based on their intended usage, either to be exported as a static collection,[32] or to be referenced dynamically for up-to-date views based on their Citation URL. In addition, the user can choose which metadata, links, and associated data to include in a published Set, creating customized presentations of the data. OCHRE utilities allow an authorized user to publish a prepared Set along with all items belonging to it. Projects often use the Events feature of OCHRE to record who published a Set, when it was (re-)published, and for what purpose. Additionally, OCHRE provides a "finalized" Event that prevents the published Set from being edited or reconfigured without the required level of project access.

Publish, from Specification

Using Sets to flatten highly granular, hierarchically organized OCHRE data into tabular structures often results in sparse data, where many of the table cells are blank. To address this issue, as well as to minimize the amount of data that needs to be fetched from the database, thereby reducing bulk or improving response time, OCHRE provides a "Publish, from spec" option.

From the site of Gobero in central Niger, where harpoon blades incongruously litter the Sahara, we queried for all artifacts having GPS coordinates and linked images, saving the resulting 427 items to a Set. We used the Table Columns option (Fig. 9.5) to specify only a few salient properties to be included—the item's Object

[32] OCHRE exports data on demand from a Set to any of many common formats including CSV (Comma-Separated Values), XML (eXtensible Markup Language), JSON (JavaScript Object Notation), Microsoft Excel, Microsoft Word, Adobe PDF, Google Earth (KML/KMZ), and Esri Shapefile (SHP) formats.

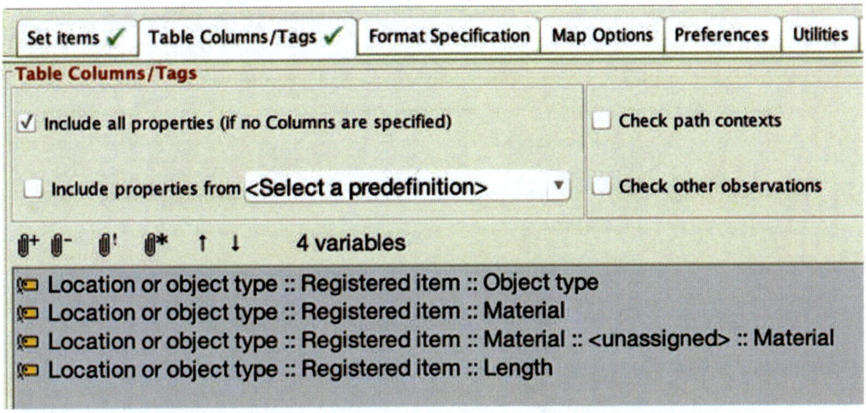

Fig. 9.5 Selected properties are used to determine the column structure of a table

Type, Material, and Length—and used the Format Specifications to request the inclusion of the Description, Coordinates, and Primary Image for each item.

By publishing using the "from spec" option, only the needed portion of the item-based data was flattened into a compact table, leaving behind all the superfluous information not required by the specification. Each column represents a requested property, each row represents an item; the table cells hold the value of the property for the corresponding item. This is a flexible and effective option when publishing selected data either to be exported to an external file or formatted as a webpage table.

Publishing Static Data Using Export Options

Publishing to Google Earth

A brief example using the Set published "from spec" just above illustrates how easy it is to publish data using widely accessible tools for a satisfying, albeit static, publication option (Fig. 9.6).

We first preview the prepared Set in OCHRE's Table View to confirm our choices. Next, we export this table to the KML (Keyhole Markup Language) format, one of the many export formats which OCHRE supports. KML is a commonly used XML-based notation used by popular applications to represent and visualize geographic information. Since we requested images to be included, OCHRE also extracts the necessary image thumbnails and packages them appropriately in the related KMZ format (a zipped archive of the KML file and its associated images). This static set of data, newly exported from the OCHRE database, is ready to be consumed by Google Earth.

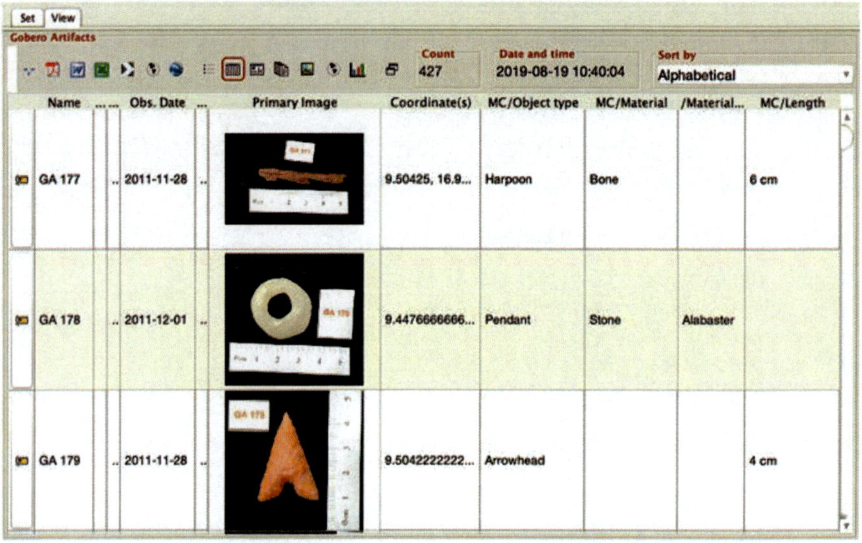

Fig. 9.6 An OCHRE Table, specified by a Set, is the basis for tabular publication formats

From this point, we simply load the resulting KMZ file into Google Earth.[33] Google does the rest. Finding coordinates that represent latitude and longitude within the KML markup, Google Earth maps the artifacts, providing access to the built-in tools which create pop-ups, display images, and allow a wide assortment of visualization options. Thanks Google, that was so easy (Fig. 9.7)!

Publishing to Esri ArcGIS Online

Viewing spatial data on Google Earth is useful; however, tagged geospatial research data can do so much more. With objects, image resources, geospatial data, and other data organized and integrated in OCHRE, the researcher can produce static publications that are appropriate for loading into the Esri ArcGIS Online workspace. In this scenario, data from OCHRE is exported as a shapefile, enhanced by an attribute table based on OCHRE properties chosen by the researcher. The resulting shapefile can be presented through a user-friendly online map, but one that is populated by data curated in and published from OCHRE. The shapefile data can be published "from spec" to include any data that exists in the OCHRE backend which is supported by ArcGIS Online, such as image thumbnails and links to other online OCHRE data.

[33] Use the "File, Open" menu option to load the file; one could also just double-click the KMZ file if the file association has been assigned.

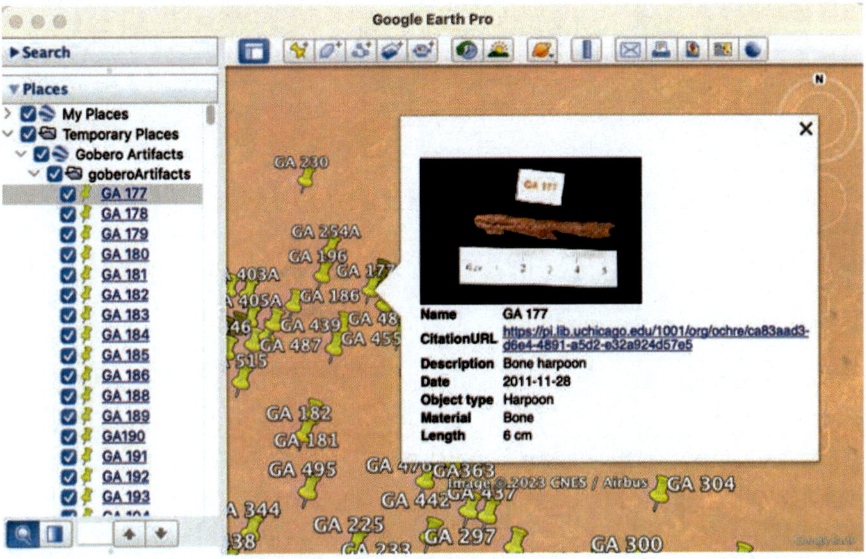

Fig. 9.7 OCHRE item properties, images, and coordinates are presented by Google Earth

Figure 9.8 shows the result of exporting several separate shapefiles of legacy data from the CRANE Megiddo project in northern Israel, configuring them in ArcGIS Online to show properties in the pop-up, and to link to "More info." Orange dots represent artifacts and their findspots managed as Spatial units in OCHRE. Data from the attribute tables is browsable, as shown at the bottom of the screenshot.[34] Thanks Esri, that was so easy!

Publishing Dynamic Data Using the OCHRE API

While easy, the above examples present static data that has been released from one format and made captive by another. This may be fine in many cases where the data has been collected and curated, the analysis has been done, and the results are being made public. But much of the project work that we support is ongoing and long term. Being able to publish data along the way is a boon to the researcher and the consumer alike. Results can be published as they become available, or in stages as they are reviewed and authorized.

Unlike with traditional database management systems, publishing data from OCHRE requires no programming or technical knowledge. OCHRE utilities

[34] https://isac.uchicago.edu/research/publications/oip/megiddo-3-final-report-stratum-vi-excavations.

Fig. 9.8 Legacy data based on the Megiddo 3 volume is published in ArcGIS Online

provide options, to any user authorized by the project, to publish data prepared as a Hierarchy or Set, or as an individual item. Once items are published, they are posted to the OCHRE *publication server* which makes the published data open and accessible to the OCHRE *application programming interface* (API). Using the API, published data can be displayed using *default publication views* built into the OCHRE platform, or processed by a web developer to *create webpages* for a custom application. Follow along as we look at this process in more detail.

The OCHRE Publication Server

The process of publishing an item in OCHRE accomplishes two steps. The first step is a concession to the highly granular, normalized (in a technical sense) XML documents at the core of the OCHRE database which are not of much use to the wider world in their raw form. They are *too* atomic for practical purposes, and replete with pointers and relationships. This internal format is intended to be managed by the OCHRE application and not intended to be comprehensible to humans or other computational processes. Remember tablet Fort. 1982–101 and its bilingual Text (Chap. 3) whose representation amounted to over 700 items? In the publication process, OCHRE gathers all the relevant details and creates a new XML document that consolidates the atomic components into a single, human-readable, self-documenting whole, where obscure pointers are substituted by their target values and links are fully exposed with labels and cross-references. This recomposed XML document is encapsulated within a single XML element, <ochre> … </ochre>, representing its *denormalized format* (DNF), in contrast to the highly normalized, atomic nature of its core representation.

Step two of the publication process posts the denormalized document(s) to the OCHRE publication server, which allows view access to the world via the OCHRE API. What we refer to as the publication server is simply a database of publicly accessible denormalized documents. This step timestamps the published document and activates the item's Citation URL—the Web-accessible, *persistent identifier* (PI) which serves as a long-lasting reference to this digital object. In the world of digital publication, persistent identifiers are only persistent if there is institutional support to maintain the architecture that associates the identifier with the correct digital object. The challenge of persistence hit home recently when following a redirected link from the Library of Congress website, where they advised "updating to the new URIS, *as we cannot guarantee a permanent redirect* …"[35] If we cannot trust the Library of Congress for persistent identifiers, whom can we trust? For OCHRE's persistent identifiers, the commitment to ensure the long-term viability of OCHRE's Citation URLs comes from the University of Chicago Digital Library Development Center (DLDC). More and more, libraries are taking on the responsibility of preserving and protecting the world's digital heritage as a natural outcome of their traditional roles, and the OCHRE platform is fortunate, and grateful, to have the University of Chicago Library fulfilling this role.

The strategy of publishing raw OCHRE data as denormalized documents to a central publication server ensures that published data served up to frontend websites are as secure and sustainable as the raw, curated backend data in the core OCHRE warehouse. There is no need for researchers, or their web developers, to create and manage a separate webserver of published documents. There is no hassle of exporting documents as a layer of "middleware" to use with web apps. There is no worry that published content will get out of date, or out of sync, having been separated from the source data. Data can be fetched dynamically, on demand, from the publication server and presented on webpages using the OCHRE Application Programming Interface (API).

The OCHRE API

An OCHRE Citation URL is enabled by the OCHRE API.[36] The OCHRE API is a mechanism to fetch data from the OCHRE publication server using the standard HTTP Web-based protocol. Simply put, using a single URL in the address bar of your browser, you can send a request for information about an item, or a collection

[35] https://id.loc.gov/techcenter/; emphasis added.

[36] The PI links of Citation URLs resolve to calls to the OCHRE API when processed by a web browser; this API call will be exposed when the PI link is pasted into a web browser.

of items, from the OCHRE database and get back a representation of that item, or items, in a meaningful format. The data returned by the OCHRE API is textual content formatted as XML (content type "text/xml") and is in the Unicode UTF-8 character encoding. Each request is independent of the next and contains in its response all the information needed to process the result of the request.[37]

The OCHRE API is called by using the base URL:
https://pi.lib.uchicago.edu/1001/org/ochre/

The OCHRE API syntax accepts other details of a request via parameters, the simplest of which is the "uuid" parameter. Such a request is securely processed by the standard HTTP GET command against the published data in the OCHRE publication server and returns an XML representation of the OCHRE item having the requested UUID. For example, the Citation URL of Ashkelon's Feature 777 triggers the following API call to the OCHRE publication server:
https://pi.lib.uchicago.edu/1001/org/ochre/33614d92-8c89-f68b-cb4a-73aaef8aa9b0

The OCHRE API call returns the published, denormalized content of the requested item, Feature 777, as XML (<ochre>...</ochre>) available to be used by a web application in the usual ways. Note that this is a live call to the live OCHRE publication server, fetching the data in real time. When new items are published from OCHRE, they are immediately available to the API and thereby to web applications (Fig. 9.9).

One typical approach to using the published XML is to style it using XSLT (the eXtensible Stylesheet Language Transformations), the W3C standard styling language for XML. Unless otherwise specified, XML returned by the Citation URL's API call will be styled using the default OCHRE stylesheet (ochre.xsl) for display in the browser, as shown here for the plaster basin from Ashkelon, Feature 777. This default OCHRE stylesheet applies a template designed to format any published OCHRE data, transforming the OCHRE data on the fly from XML to a simple HTML page for display (Fig. 9.10).

In some cases, though, a project may want to format the data to its own specifications for its own purposes. For this, the OCHRE API provides a stylesheet parameter: xsl=<name-of-stylesheet>. With a little effort, a project can add its own color scheme and presentation by creating a custom xsl file—perhaps even based on the default ochre.xsl—and calling it using the "xsl" parameter.

In addition to fetching an item using the item UUID, an XQuery can be run against the published data using the "xquery" parameter of the OCHRE API to target, specifically, data needed from the publication server. With these two options, xquery and xsl, a web designer can request data and style it appropriately to generate HTML for display in a web browser.

[37]The OCHRE API is written in PHP and is guided by the Representational State Transfer (REST) architectural style that prescribes best practice for building web services. A description of the details of a RESTful API is beyond the scope of this book, but see Bojinov (2016 ch. 1) for further details.

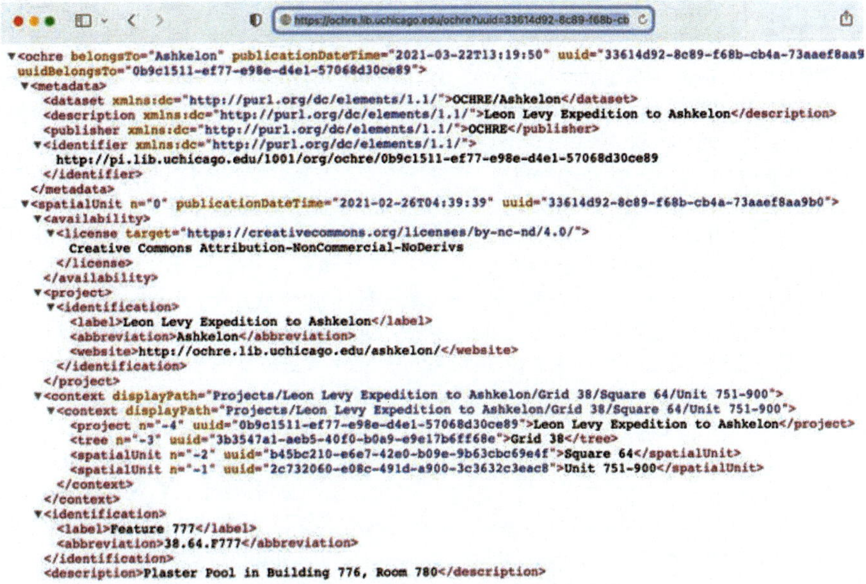

Fig. 9.9 The XML provided by the OCHRE API is well-structured, human-readable, and self-describing, as shown by this sample of Feature 777

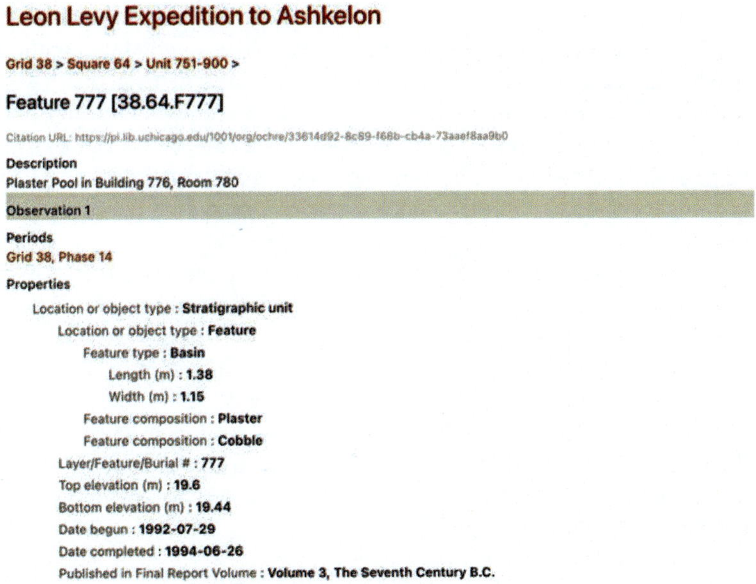

Fig. 9.10 Pasting an item's Citation URL into a browser results in its formatted display

Default Publication Views

OCHRE's built-in stylesheet, applied by default to format data fetched by the OCHRE API, is an effort to be sensitive to the needs and limitations of researchers who may choose, or be required by granting agencies, to share data in accordance with open data and FAIR principles. Often scholars who have collected the data do not have the resources to produce a website or other digital presentation to share it. For many, the time, skills, staff (funds), and infrastructure needed to produce a digital publication is a barrier to entry.

To overcome this common hurdle, the OCHRE Data Service has created a series of default publication views, applicable to any data published from OCHRE, which serve as a fallback option for publication on the web. This service includes a library of XSLT, CSS, and JavaScript templates that transform published OCHRE data into viewable HTML webpages. For example, an item with geographic coordinates will display on a page that includes a map. An item with linked images will include links to those images. A Set will display as a sortable, searchable HTML table. A Hierarchy will be presented as a formatted index. So, in the case where a project cannot dedicate resources to build a bespoke web publication, their data can still be viewable and sharable on the Web. These default views are available to all OCHRE projects and the template architecture makes it easy to replace the defaults with custom configurations or features. The OCHRE Data Service works with researchers to adopt, borrow, or customize these templates for their own project. The goal is to minimize the requisite technical skills needed by the researcher to create a digital publication to share data.

The Ashkelon project put the default publication views to good use, embedding Citation URLs as hyperlinks on references to the associated items in the PDF of the Ashkelon Volume 3 publication.[38] These links make an already engaging, award-winning publication even more interactive. As the reader clicks these links from the PDF, the published and formatted view of the item pops up, triggered by its Citation URL and freshly pulled from the widely accessible, read-only publication server (Fig. 9.11).

The CRANE project of Tell al-Judaidah in southern Turkey, directed by Lynn Swartz Dodd of the University of Southern California, built an entire website based on OCHRE's default publication views, adapting an OCHRE HTML template to create a project splash page that provides menus with links to published OCHRE Sets, image galleries, documents, and maps.[39] The rest of the site benefits from the automatic styling of data fetched by the OCHRE API on user demand to create dynamic webpages. Whenever data needs to be updated in OCHRE, the researcher can make the edit on the backend, republish the data, and the frontend views will update dynamically.

---

[38] See Stager et al. (2011) and https://hmane.harvard.edu/publications/ashkelon-3. This major feat was accomplished with the help of volunteer-on-retainer, Stuart W. Cooke.

[39] https://onlinepublications.uchicago.edu/TAJ/.

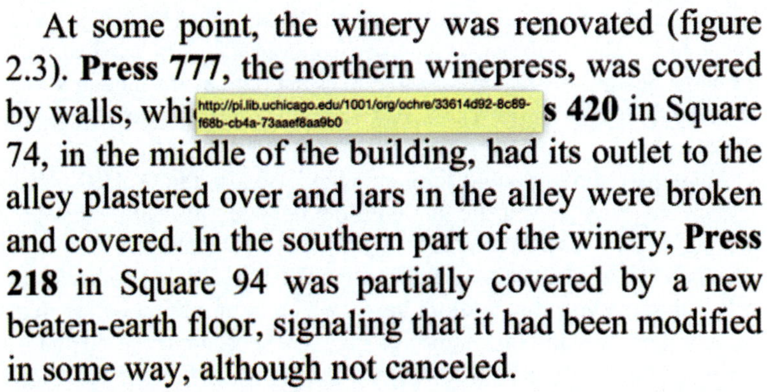
At some point, the winery was renovated (figure 2.3). **Press 777**, the northern winepress, was covered by walls, whi http://pi.lib.uchicago.edu/1001/org/ochre/33614d92-8c89-f68b-cb4a-73aaef8aa9b0 **s 420** in Square 74, in the middle of the building, had its outlet to the alley plastered over and jars in the alley were broken and covered. In the southern part of the winery, **Press 218** in Square 94 was partially covered by a new beaten-earth floor, signaling that it had been modified in some way, although not canceled.

Fig. 9.11 A partial page from the *Ashkelon 3* PDF. The text in bold indicates live links to published Ashkelon data. The OCHRE Citation URL is shown on roll-over as a tooltip

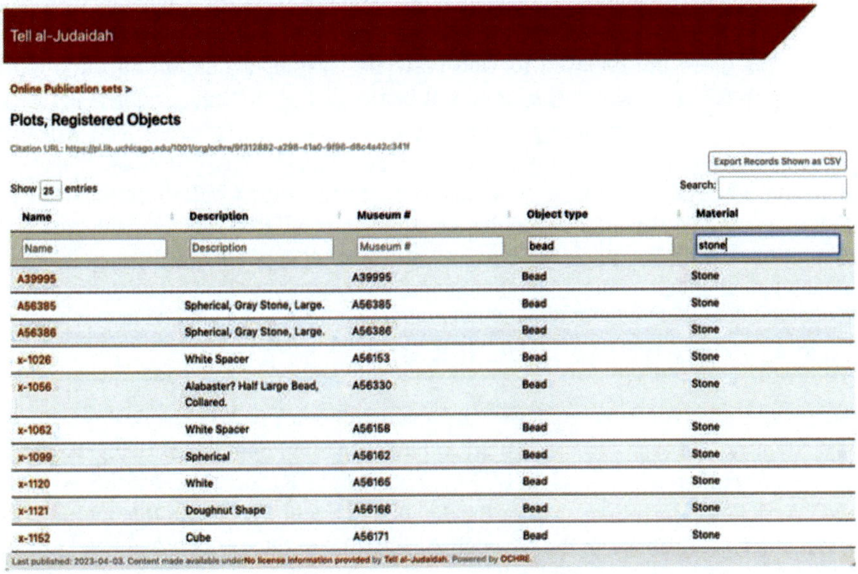

Name	Description	Museum #	Object type	Material
Name	Description	Museum #	bead	stone
A39995		A39995	Bead	Stone
A56385	Spherical, Gray Stone, Large.	A56385	Bead	Stone
A56386	Spherical, Gray Stone, Large.	A56386	Bead	Stone
x-1026	White Spacer	A56153	Bead	Stone
x-1056	Alabaster? Half Large Bead, Collared.	A56330	Bead	Stone
x-1062	White Spacer	A56158	Bead	Stone
x-1099	Spherical	A56162	Bead	Stone
x-1120	White	A56165	Bead	Stone
x-1121	Doughnut Shape	A56166	Bead	Stone
x-1152	Cube	A56171	Bead	Stone

Fig. 9.12 Stone beads from Tell al-Judaidah are fetched using the OCHRE API and displayed using OCHRE's default publication view of a Set published as a table (the Citation URL for the Set on which this table is based is: https://pi.lib.uchicago.edu/1001/org/ochre/9f312882-a298-41a0-9f96-d8c4a42c341f)

To generate the dynamic table shown in Fig. 9.12, an OCHRE Query was used to find all Season X Objects and save them as a Set. This created a static list of items, acceptable for this purpose; Season X was excavated in 1935 so there will never be new items to add to this collection. Next, the Table Column/Tags option and Format

Specification feature on the Set were used to define which properties and other fields to include. The "Publish, from Spec" option was then used to create the required table, posting the denormalized XML that defines the tabular structure to the OCHRE publication server. The Set's Citation URL is used to display the table on the Web.

The radical part about a publication strategy based on the OCHRE API is that one could create an entire website that does not contain *any* static webpages. That is, from a single URL-based API call it is possible to generate HTML dynamically that contains other API calls and/or links to the Citation URLs of other items, providing click-through potential to those items, which in turn link to other items, and so on, ad infinitum. It is no exaggeration to state that a researcher could publish their entire project using this strategy. All objects link to related bibliography, persons, texts, and images, or other OCHRE items. A single URL, representing the project, would serve as the entry point into all published project data. One need only provide a suitable XSLT document that instructs the browser how to render the data for presentation.

We are the first to admit, however, that this strategy of creating dynamic websites is *too* dynamic to suit many purposes. Web pages generated dynamically by the OCHRE API are not exposed to web crawlers, search engine optimization, and indexing in the usual way, for example. It could also be difficult, and syntactically awkward, to integrate custom graphics and design elements to create aesthetically pleasing sites, or to embed widgets that provide enhanced navigation and selection features (although, to be fair, a great deal can be done with a well-crafted, powerful stylesheet). Thus, we offer examples of using the OCHRE API to fetch data for using more familiar strategies to develop custom web applications.

Creating Webpages Using the OCHRE API

While the OCHRE API is often used in conjunction with an XSLT stylesheet to create a dynamic website, it is also used to build custom applications using standard web development tools, based on HTML, JavaScript (JS), and the Document Object Model (DOM), like the ReactJS or the AngularJS frameworks.[40] In this more traditional and typical scenario, the OCHRE API is used to fetch data dynamically from OCHRE's publication server, but the returned data is dropped into prepared structures.

---

[40] For React, "the library for web and native user interfaces," see https://react.dev/. AngularJS is a popular, open-source JavaScript (JS)-based web application framework supported by Google. In its own words, it "is what HTML would have been, had it been designed for building web-apps" (https://angularjs.org). Bootstrap is an open-source toolkit for developing with HTML, CSS, and JavaScript; "the most popular HTML, CSS and JS library in the world" (https://getbootstrap.com).

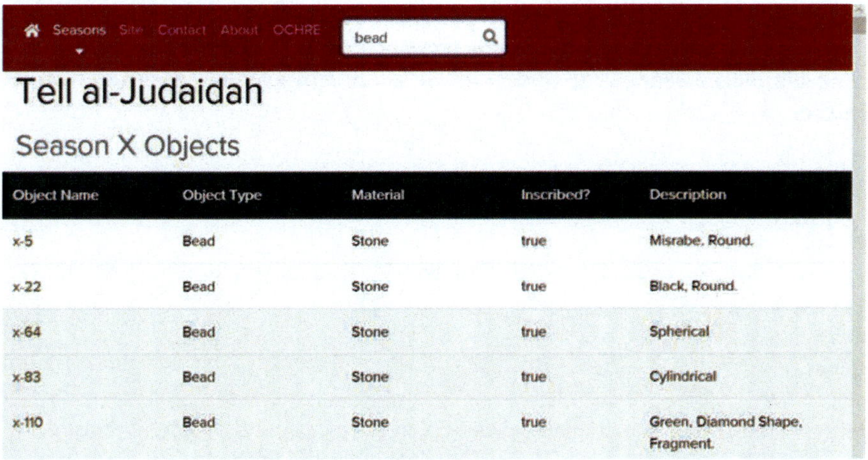

Fig. 9.13 Structured, predefined webpages fill-in-the-blanks with dynamic OCHRE data

JavaScript Code Samples

Figure 9.13 shows the same artifacts from Tell al-Judaidah, but this time through a webpage designed using HTML, Bootstrap, and AngularJS, illustrating the portability of OCHRE data for use across different web publication strategies. Although the data is fetched on demand by the OCHRE API, the returned XML is presented within static HTML elements. Widgets for sorting and filtering are built into the display using HTML tools.

In this AngularJS app, a script (JS) captures an OCHRE UUID of a Set, based on a user selection (i.e., a mouse click) of a menu option to display "Season X Objects." The script makes an XMLHttpRequest (XHR)[41] to the OCHRE API using the Set's Citation URL, retrieving the published items of this Set, formatted as XML. The script invokes the DOMParser[42] function of the browser to interpret the XML, identify the individual items (by UUID), and request details of these items from the OCHRE publication server using the OCHRE API, getting more XML in return. This provides the web page with the information needed to arrange the data into the table shown in Fig. 9.13 using standard JavaScript and AngularJS strategies. In this case, a function loops over the XML nodes in the DOM to extract data using the getElementsByTagName[43] method. The values assembled during this looping process are passed to the HTML page as a table and are inserted using AngularJS variables such as {{objectType}}. Also embedded in the table, using HTML code, are anchored href links to the UUIDs of the OCHRE items. See the code snippet below

[41] https://developer.mozilla.org/en-US/docs/Web/API/XMLHttpRequest.

[42] https://developer.mozilla.org/en-US/docs/Web/API/DOMParser.

[43] https://developer.mozilla.org/en-US/docs/Web/API/Document/getElementsByTagName.

where {{row.uuid}} is a variable that inserts the item UUID into the API URL. When the page is fully composed, the user is presented with the name of the artifact as a clickable link, creating a great deal of click-through potential from one item to another.

```
<tbody id="tableBody">
<tr class="tableRows" ng-repeat="row in rows track by $index">
<td class="Name">
<a href="https://pi.lib.uchicago.edu/1001/org/ochre/{{row.uuid}}">
{{row.Name}}
</a>
</td>...
```

In the end, the Tell al-Judaidah project opted for the more dynamic approach that uses OCHRE's default views which did not require the upkeep of an Angular app and Javascript code.

This next example illustrates for a web developer how to retrieve XML via the OCHRE API using vanilla JavaScript, in this case XMLHttpRequest. Simply provide an OCHRE Citation URL as the value of the link variable in the following script, or capture it with an HTML event, then use any of the standard JavaScript functions to parse the XML data. The rest of the script is boilerplate JavaScript for making an XHR call.

```
var link = "... OCHRE Citation URL GOES HERE ...";
function loadXML(){
XMLrequest(link);
console.log('loadXML -- OK');
};

function XMLrequest(link) {
var connect = new XMLHttpRequest();
connect.onreadystatechange = function () {
if (this.readyState == 4 && this.status == 200) {
listTexts(this.responseXML);
}
};
connect.open("GET", link, true);
connect.send();
console.log('XMLrequest -- OK');
};
```

A similar result can be achieved using the JavaScript fetch() function. Again, simply supply a Citation URL as the value of the url variable.

```
var url = "… OCHRE Citation URL GOES HERE …"
return fetch(url)
.then(response => response.text())
.then(data =>{
… DO SOMETHING WITH THE DATA …
});
};
```

With the OCHRE data stored in a JavaScript object, a web developer has complete freedom to deliver all or part of the data to the client.

A strategy of building static webpages, prepared in advance to have structures in place to receive data, and populating them with data on demand using the OCHRE API, is a useful approach. It blends the predictability of a predetermined static design with the delivery of dynamic data, which ensures that publications are never stale. It also facilitates the presentation of new data to the intended audience as efficiently as possible.

Using the OCHRE API with Other Programs

The examples shown so far have focused on fetching data using the OCHRE API for use in webpages. But the strategy of using the API to retrieve either formatted or unformatted data, dynamically from the OCHRE publication server, can be used in a variety of other contexts, beyond mere web browsers, to great effect.

Fetching Unstyled Data for Microsoft Excel

Specifying "xsl=none" as a parameter on the OCHRE API returns XML from the OCHRE database in its raw format, without any styling. Technically, this is performing XML *serialization*, which is a rather complex topic, so let us be content with the Wikipedia definition: "In computer science, in the context of data storage, serialization is the process of translating data structures or object state into a format that can be stored (for example in a file or memory buffer) or transmitted (for example, across a network connection link) and reconstructed later (possibly in a different computer environment)."[44] Data structures, transmitted across a connection, and reconstructed later—that is exactly what the OCHRE API is doing. The unstyled xml option of the OCHRE API (xsl=none) allows raw data to be fetched, dynamically, for use in other processes.

Many modern desktop productivity tools can process serialized data fetched via a URL. Take Microsoft Excel, for example, which has on its Data tab a "From Web"

[44] https://en.wikipedia.org/wiki/Serialization.

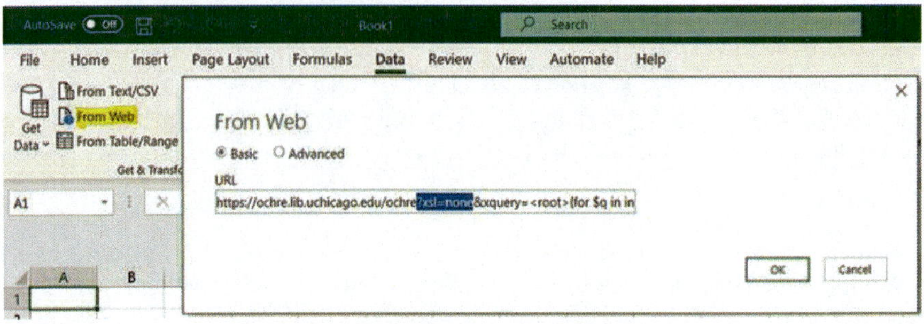

Fig. 9.14 Microsoft Excel natively handles unstyled XML fetched “From Web”

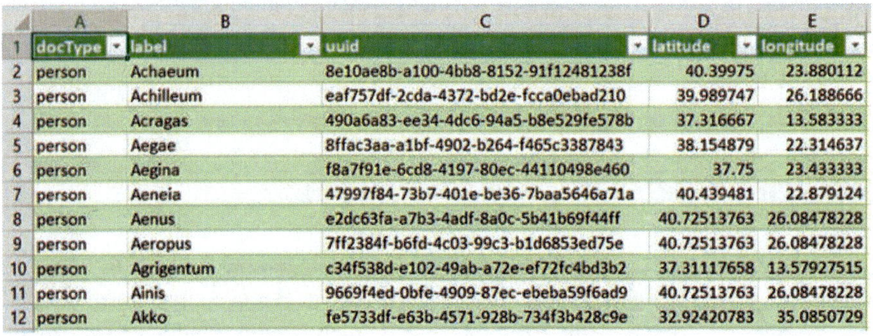

	docType	label	uuid	latitude	longitude
2	person	Achaeum	8e10ae8b-a100-4bb8-8152-91f12481238f	40.39975	23.880112
3	person	Achilleum	eaf757df-2cda-4372-bd2e-fcca0ebad210	39.989747	26.188666
4	person	Acragas	490a6a83-ee34-4dc6-94a5-b8e529fe578b	37.316667	13.583333
5	person	Aegae	8ffac3aa-a1bf-4902-b264-f465c3387843	38.154879	22.314637
6	person	Aegina	f8a7f91e-6cd8-4197-80ec-44110498e460	37.75	23.433333
7	person	Aeneia	47997f84-73b7-401e-be36-7baa5646a71a	40.439481	22.879124
8	person	Aenus	e2dc63fa-a7b3-4adf-8a0c-5b41b69f44ff	40.72513763	26.08478228
9	person	Aeropus	7ff2384f-b6fd-4c03-99c3-b1d6853ed75e	40.72513763	26.08478228
10	person	Agrigentum	c34f538d-e102-49ab-a72e-ef72fc4bd3b2	37.31117658	13.57927515
11	person	Ainis	9669f4ed-0bfe-4909-87ec-ebeba59f6ad9	40.72513763	26.08478228
12	person	Akko	fe5733df-e63b-4571-928b-734f3b428c9e	32.92420783	35.0850729

Fig. 9.15 Excel tables are created easily using unstyled data via the OCHRE API (These features may not be supported in all versions of Microsoft Word or Excel)

option. Enter the URL that represents the OCHRE API call for the requested data (Fig. 9.14).

Excel will execute the OCHRE API call thereby fetching the data dynamically from the OCHRE publication server. Excel offers a chance to Preview the result, then drops the fetched content into its table cells creating an instant table (Fig. 9.15).

Fetching Unstyled Data for the R Statistics Package[45]

For this last example, say we wanted to share or plot the ancient Greek minting authorities itemized by the Hoard Analysis Research Project (HARP). We could use one of the many convenient libraries in the R language to process and visualize the data. Those more familiar with Python will recognize that this approach would translate easily to that language.

[45] R Core Team (2018). *R: A language and environment for statistical computing*. R Foundation for Statistical Computing, Vienna, Austria. URL https://www.R-project.org/.

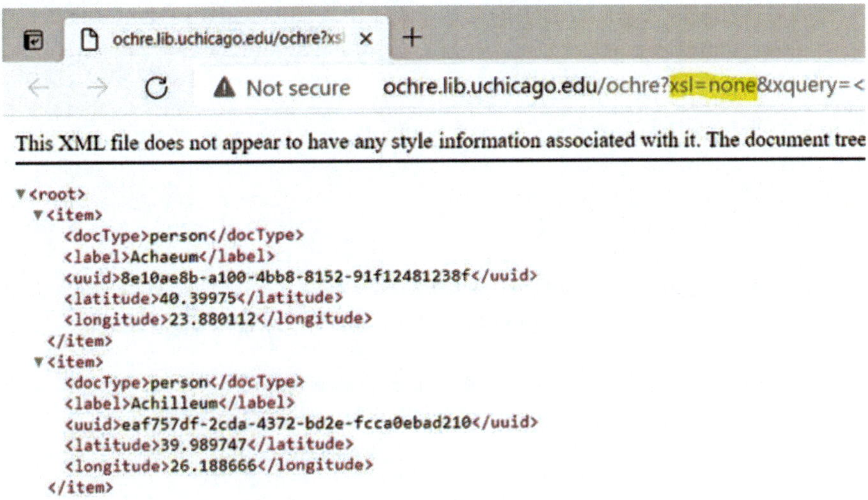

Fig. 9.16 Unstyled XML fetched from OCHRE's publication server has many uses

The following OCHRE API call provides an XQuery that asks for the document type, label, uuid (for click-through potential), and coordinates of the mints, and requests that it be left unstyled (xsl = none). The first two (of many) items returned in response are shown in a browser window in Fig. 9.16.

```
https://ochre.lib.uchicago.edu/ochre?xsl=none&xquery=
<root>
{for $q in input()/ochre[@belongsTo='CRESCAT-HARP']/person[coordinates]
return
<item>
<docType>{local-name($q)}</docType>
{$q/identification/label}
<uuid>{fn:string($q/@uuid)}</uuid>
<latitude>{xs:decimal($q/coordinates/@latitude)}</latitude>
<longitude>{xs:decimal($q/coordinates/@longitude)}</longitude>
</item>}
</root>
```

This same set of serialized OCHRE XML data can be used in the R statistics package to populate a data frame (an R data structure similar to a table). A few simple commands achieve this:[46]

1. Load the required libraries.

```
>library(XML)
>library(httr)
```

2. Assign the OCHRE API call to a variable (here with special characters converted to HTML entities as required in the next step).

```
> mintsURL <-"https://ochre.lib.uchicago.edu/ochre
?xsl=none&xquery=%3Croot%3E%7Bfor%20$q%20in%20input()/
ochre[@belongsTo=%27CRESCAT-HARP%27]/person[coordinates]
%20return%20%3Citem%3E%3CdocType%3E%7Blocal-name($q)
%7D%3C/docType%3E%7B$q/identification/label%7D%3Cuuid%3E%7Bfn:string
($q/@uuid)%7D%3C/uuid%3E%3Clatitude%3E%7Bxs:decimal($q/
coordinates/@latitude)%7D%3C/latitude%3E%3Clongitude%3E%7B
xs:decimal($q/coordinates/@longitude)%7D%3C/longitude%3E%3C/
item%3E%7D%3C/root%3E"
```

3. Use a GET function to retrieve the XML.

```
> mintsData = GET(mintsURL)
```

4. Convert the content to readable character strings.

```
> mintsContent <- rawToChar(mintsData$content)
```

5. Create a data frame `mints` with the XML.

```
> mints <- xmlToDataFrame(mintsContent)
```

6. Inspect the results in tabular format then produce a map.

```
> mints
> library(maps)
> mints$latitude <- as.numeric(as.character(mints$latitude))
> mints$longitude <- as.numeric(as.character(mints$longitude))
> map('world', fill=FALSE, xlim=c(-4, 50), ylim=c(30,50))
> title("Mints of Ancient Greece")
> points(mints$longitude, mints$latitude, col="blue", pch=20)
```

[46]The example was produced using RStudio 1.4.1106 (https://rstudio.com/). As R libraries change, this approach may need to be updated accordingly.

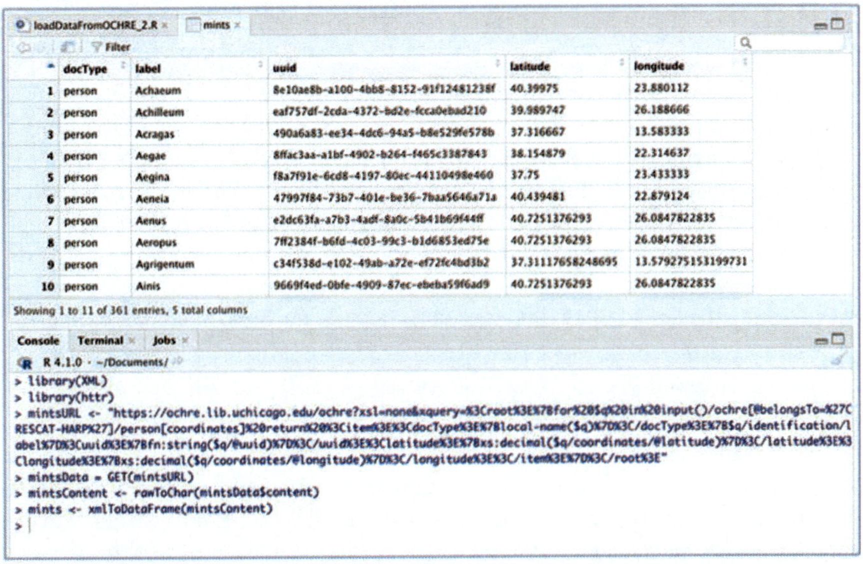

Fig. 9.17 XML data, dynamically delivered by the OCHRE API, fills an R dataframe

Fig. 9.18 An R mapping library offers a quick visualization of OCHRE's Greek mints

Once the data is in a data frame, the whole world of R libraries is available to process it (Fig. 9.17). Figure 9.18 shows a visualization created using the R "maps" library. After converting the latitude and longitude data frame fields from string to numeric values, limiting the scope of the world map to the Mediterranean region, and titling the map, the points are plotted. Thanks R, that was so easy!

OCHRE and the Semantic Web

With so much data of all kinds being published on the web—much more than can be reasonably consumed by human users trawling the Internet—there has been a shift toward making data more accessible for machine readability without compromising its accessibility to human readers. The "Semantic Web" is an architecture, established by the World Wide Web Consortium, based on a recommended stack of services, that guides how data should be formatted and delivered in a standards-compliant way.

Picking up the thread of our previous discussion of the Semantic Web in Chap. 2:

> … A 'Semantic Web,' which makes this possible, has yet to emerge, but when it does, the day-to-day mechanisms of trade, bureaucracy and our daily lives will be handled by machines talking to machines. The 'intelligent agents' people have touted for ages will finally materialize (Berners-Lee and Fischetti 2000).

Decades later, *that* dream is still a work in progress (although one could argue that other kinds of intelligent agents, like DALL·E and ChatGPT, *have* materialized). But progress has been made, and when data is published in ways that conform to the Semantic Web standards, it becomes available for discovery and use in big data analytics, artificial intelligence, or other integrative studies and publications ensuing from the research enterprise.

Underpinning the Semantic Web's stack of services are various well-known technologies: HTTP-based URIs (Uniform Resource Identifiers) for universally and uniquely identifying web resources; Unicode, for representing textual content in languages used all over the world; and RDF (Resource Description Framework), the system of structuring data and applying markup that puts the "semantic" in Semantic Web. These have been supplemented with "a set of techniques whose goal is to enrich data on the Web with more semantics in order to ultimately support more complex queries and reasoning" (Doan et al. 2012, p. 31). A discussion of these techniques follows.

Resource Description Framework (RDF)

Interestingly for us, the data model recommended for representing data published on the semantic web, as described by the Resource Description Framework—a W3C standard whose version 1.0 was published in 2004, and which was updated in 2014 to version 1.1—is a highly granular, item-based model, replete with links that create, in effect, a graph database intended to encompass the entirety of the world's knowledge. RDF is a data model based on "triples" where every bit of knowledge is broken down into a subject, predicate, and object, using vocabulary and structure defined by various metadata standards such as SKOS (Simple Knowledge Organization System).[47]

A *resource* in the RDF model is anything that can be identified, named, or described—any person, place, thing, concept, or idea.[48] A *subject* of an RDF triple is represented by a URI (a Uniform Resource Identifier) and become the nodes in the giant graph database representing the world's knowledge. Each *predicate* represents some attribute or property of the subject, or a relationship between subjects. Resources (*subjects*) are linked to other resources (*objects*) by way of *predicates* creating *linked data* (LD). Sample triples are listed here, some using prefixes to indicate their source vocabulary (e.g., dbp = DBPedia Property):

Subject—predicate—object
Zincirli—dbp:Location—Turkey
Basalt—skos:Broader—Volcanic rocks
Bracelet—isMadeOf—Gold
Coin—weighsInGrams—30

As the W3C tutorial puts it, RDF is a model where "anyone can say anything about anything."[49]

Many projects attempt to manage their *primary* data in the raw, highly atomic format of RDF, constrained by the vocabularies of specific ontologies to which they have committed. From the OCHRE perspective, although data formatted as RDF in compliance with published vocabularies is extremely important for interoperability within the context of the Semantic Web, this can be a *secondary* process, further downstream as the data matures through its life cycle. The scholar should have the flexibility and the freedom to capture and describe research data first in its most natural and ideal way, even if this means inventing new, idiosyncratic descriptors, or setting aside the adoption of any "standard"—designed by someone else, for some other purpose—at the outset. A user-defined ontology (taxonomy) might itself be a work of original scholarship. The OCHRE data model empowers scholars to represent research data primarily and meaningfully, using a graphical interface that masks the details of the underlying formats, and then map that data onto a chosen format, or indeed any number of other formats, for sharing with the wider

[47] RDF is frequently expressed as XML but can also be represented by JSON or other specialized formats like Turtle (Terse RDF Triple Language). Robert Sanderson, then Information Architect for the J Paul Getty Trust, subsequently Senior Director for Digital Cultural Heritage at Yale University, noted a dramatic upswing in the use of JSON on the web, as early as 2018 claiming then, that "10–19% of websites have JSON-LD data." https://www.slideshare.net/azaroth42/linked-art-our-linked-open-usable-data-model, p. 25 of the presentation. For Turtle, see the W3C RDF Primer at https://www.w3.org/2007/02/turtle/primer.

[48] Note that this use of the word "resource" differs from how it is used by OCHRE. Here, resource is more equivalent to OCHRE's item, and an OCHRE Resource is a much more specific type of item.

[49] Fabien Gandon and Ivan Herman, *W3C Tutorial on Semantic Web and Linked Data at WWW 2013* https://www.slideshare.net/fabien_gandon/w3c-tutorial-on-semantic-web-and-linked-data-at-www-2013.

community of researchers. In the OCHRE ecosystem, RDF would be a secondary published form of the data, valuable for interoperability, not the primary form of the data for storage.

Web Ontology Language (OWL)

The Semantic Web, through its recommended best practice and its available stack of services, encourages and enables data to be published, freely and to common standards, in such a way that consumers can process it in a meaningful give-and-take exchange. To do this, however, requires that data be published according to documented schemas. Further, it requires that two schemas can communicate in a way that make their mutual data sets interoperable. While this is no trivial task, there is a language created to generate mappings between data schemas. That official language, developed for the Semantic Web, is the Web Ontology Language, or OWL.[50]

Traditionally, the term "ontology" describes "a branch of metaphysics concerned with the nature and relations of being."[51] But the term has been repurposed by computer scientists, with credit for doing so often given to Tom Gruber who, in 1995, famously defined an ontology as "a specification of a conceptualization" (Gruber 1995). OWL is a language used to document the specifications of such an ontology within a specific domain of knowledge. As a W3C standard first published in 2004, OWL is described on the W3C website as:[52]

> ...a Semantic Web language designed to represent rich and complex knowledge about things, groups of things, and relations between things. OWL is a computational logic-based language such that knowledge expressed in OWL can be exploited by computer programs ...

Some ontologies are fairly widely used, such as the Simple Knowledge Organization System (SKOS), a W3C recommendation, and Friend of a Friend[53] (FOAF), made popular by social media apps. Others contain more technical language for a specific domain of knowledge (e.g., for biomedical, or music, or cultural heritage). Each ontology is typically associated with a unique namespace abbreviation to avoid ambiguity or resolve conflicts between terms across ontologies. That is, the SKOS namespace prefix, "skos," is used to distinguish from both the RDF schema which uses the namespace prefix, "rdfs," and the FOAF terms which use the namespace prefix "foaf." For example, the primary identifier of an item might be its SKOS

[50] https://www.w3.org/TR/owl2-syntax/.

[51] https://www.merriam-webster.com/dictionary/ontology.

[52] https://www.w3.org/OWL/. Gruber original statement: http://www-ksl.stanford.edu/kst/what-is-an-ontology.html; Gruber's updated statement: http://tomgruber.org/writing/ontology-definition-2007.htm".

[53] https://en.wikipedia.org/wiki/FOAF.

"label," referenced as "skos:prefLabel,"[54] its RDFS "label" denoted by "rdfs:label,"[55] or its FOAF term "foaf:name."[56]

Data published on the web should conform to a published ontology which defines the structure of the published data and the rules for relationships among them in a way that is understood by both human users and computational processes. OCHRE data is described by and conforms to the CHOIR ontology (introduced in Chap. 2). CHOIR is an "upper ontology" prescribing a conceptual framework for data representation. OCHRE is one implementation of the CHOIR ontology; that is, an actual (rather than conceptual) computational system that follows the rules defined by CHOIR. Any other system that also follows the ontology defined by CHOIR will be compatible with OCHRE and will be able to share data effectively. Any specific use case of OCHRE, for example an archaeology or philology project, will have an expression of the OWL CHOIR ontology that accounts fully for the description of the project's data.

As described earlier in our discussion of OCHRE taxonomies (Chap. 4), each project can customize its taxonomy, borrowing from other projects where desired and creating new variables and values where needed. Regardless of the level of customization, all project taxonomies conform more generally to the CHOIR ontology. Therefore, all projects can integrate and use data belonging to multiple projects despite differences in project-specific vocabularies.

Because every aspect of an OCHRE item (properties, links, notes, etc.) can be addressed as a separate item or XML node within an item, data published from OCHRE can be mapped to other well-known ontologies. For example, the item name in OCHRE may be associated with the dc:title element from the Dublin Core ontology. Every project chooses how to map its published data onto other ontologies. As such, we often describe OCHRE as ontology-agnostic in that it does not come preconfigured with any domain-specific ontology but can be mapped to any ontology (or various ontologies).

SPARQL Protocol and RDF Query Language (SPARQL)

With enormous amounts of data available in published formats across the Semantic Web, there needs to be a mechanism for finding and retrieving it so that it can be used for analysis or publication. Enter SPARQL, the query language developed specifically for accessing data published in accordance with the RDF specifications. Online systems that host such data, like Wikidata, DbPedia, or Getty, provide a SPARQL "endpoint" which is a point of entry through which users may request and retrieve data. SPARQL syntax allows queries to specify components of the *triples* to

[54] https://www.w3.org/2009/08/skos-reference/skos.html#prefLabel.

[55] https://www.w3.org/TR/rdf12-schema/#ch_label.

[56] http://xmlns.com/foaf/0.1/#term_name.

be searched or retrieved and to specify *joins* based on the relationships linking the online resources. Users, or developers of computational processes, design queries using the vocabulary permitted by the ontology on which the published data is based.

Here, for example, is the SPARQL syntax generated by the "Query Helper" of the Wikidata Query Service when asked to find instances of birds:

```
SELECT ?item ?itemLabel
WHERE {
 ?item wdt:P31 wd:Q5113.
 SERVICE wikibase:label { bd:serviceParam wikibase:language
 "[AUTO_LANGUAGE], en".}
}
```

Executing the query returns a far-reaching set of results, fetching everything from a *Plain-breasted brush finch* to a *Mauritanian heron*. But the generated SPARQL query syntax also indicates that "bird" is represented in the Wikidata system by the entity ID Q5113[57] and that the property "instance of" is the Wikidata term (wdt) P31.[58] This is the challenge of SPARQL. It is intended to be intuitive, issuing requests as statements in the form subject-predicate-object; for example, "find items (subject) which are instances of (P31, predicate), birds (Q5113, object)," even to the point of ending each statement with a period. But you almost need to know, already, what it is that you are looking for before you can accurately search for it. Knowing what data is available, and knowing the vocabulary with which to request it, is not always easy to determine. As with any query language, SPARQL is characterized by several non-intuitive peculiarities. For example, searching Wikipedia for the label "Duck" yields around a dozen responses including "six-wheel-drive amphibious modification of the 2-ton capacity CCKW trucks" and "fictional character from Alice in Wonderland," but no bird ducks. The query requires "duck" instead of "Duck," which is to say that SPARQL queries need to be written with care (in this example with the case-sensitive flag set to -i, insensitive). In principle, though, making data available and accessible is commendable, and as demonstrated in the next case study, the Semantic Web playground is one in which OCHRE intends to play.

Case Study: An Illustrated Taxonomy

As it turns out, OCHRE's item-based data model and its descriptive framework based on *properties* reflect an approach perfectly compatible with that of RDF. In OCHRE, a property is essentially an Item-Variable-Value triple, exactly analogous

[57] https://www.wikidata.org/wiki/Q5113.

[58] https://www.wikidata.org/wiki/Property:P31.

to an RDF triple. Such compatibility is not simply accidental, but is the natural outcome of needing a generic, flexible, sufficiently abstract, all-encompassing way to describe the world and scholars' observations of it. In OCHRE, too, anyone can say anything about anything, and OCHRE attributes the one doing the saying to what is said about the things. OCHRE's highly granular data—where every item instantly has a persistent Citation URL from the moment it is created, and where descriptive properties are documented and constrained by a project-specific taxonomy—fits naturally within the world of the Semantic Web.

OCHRE interacts most intuitively with the Semantic Web through its Thesaurus features which are available to OCHRE items in the Concept, Locations & Objects, Person, Period, and Taxonomy categories. We have already seen how OCHRE can make synonym and related-term equivalences between taxonomic values from distinct projects. Why not extend this to data beyond OCHRE, using the mechanisms of the Semantic Web? A "bird" in one OCHRE project is the same as "fowl" from another, which is the same as "ave" in Spanish, and the same as "aves" in scientific Latin. Using the OCHRE Thesaurus, we can equate the notion of a "bird" with that of a web resource (a "subject" that has a URI-handle) such as the "bird" from Wikidata identified by https://www.wikidata.org/wiki/Q5113. To address the difficulty in finding online content housed in data services and accessible through SPARQL, OCHRE provides a lookup feature on its Thesaurus links-panel to make it easier to connect OCHRE project data with data on the Semantic Web (Fig. 9.19).

OCHRE is given the means to query data available on the Semantic Web through a SPARQL endpoint by configuring a Derived Variable with the necessary information. In other contexts, Derived Variables are used to create new data based on

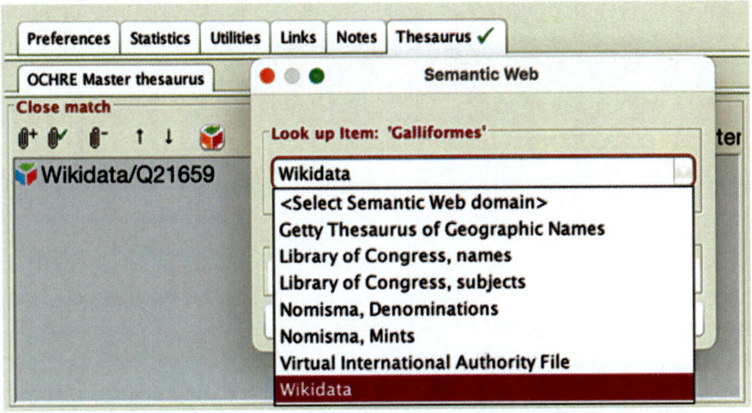

Fig. 9.19 Linking to Semantic Web data is managed in OCHRE as Thesaurus links to other published vocabularies

calculations or aggregations, for example.[59] But in this case, the Value of the Derived Variable is an item from the web, looked up by a SPARQL query, and saved as a URI. This OCHRE property—the Derived Variable along with its assigned (looked-up) Value—equates (links) an item in OCHRE with one or more datapoints from the Semantic Web.

To configure access to a specific data service, start by indicating that an Alphanumeric/String-type Variable is of the Derivation type Semantic web. Then, provide the reference to the SPARQL endpoint, for example:

```
https://query.wikidata.org/sparql?query=
```

Next, give OCHRE a template for a SPARQL query which it can execute, and which will return a list of appropriate values from the data service being configured. The template needs to contain the keyword "<Name>" which OCHRE will substitute with the Name of the OCHRE item being looked up. OCHRE documentation specifies other details of how such a template should be designed. OCHRE will look for any of several keywords in order to interpret the query results. Such queries need to be prepared by OCHRE staff or other project staff who know how to use SPARQL. If designed carefully, these queries can return information about images and coordinates to supplement core OCHRE data. In the query below, items whose "?label" matches the Name provided are fetched. The relevant snippet from the query syntax is:

```
… WHERE { ?item ?label "<Name>" @en .
```

OCHRE runs the SPARQL query against the configured endpoint and returns all matches. The user chooses the Semantic Web item which best matches the OCHRE item in question from the list of fetched results. Once saved, the OCHRE item points to the Semantic Web item using the handle, or prefix, for the URI of the items that are returned by the data service. For example, by appending the entity ID for "bird" (Q5113) to the Entity URL prefix assigned to the derived variable, in this case "https://www.wikidata.org/wiki," OCHRE generates the URI needed to reference this item.

A colorful use case of this feature is to illustrate the OCHRE Taxonomy using content from the Semantic Web. Because it is easy to cast too wide a net over the vast network of data available, we target instead the more scientific terms in the taxonomy which are often unfamiliar to non-specialists and which benefit from having supplementary information. When looking up Thesaurus links for the term "Galliformes" from the faunal analysis branch of the OCHRE Taxonomy, OCHRE formats an appropriate SPARQL query for the requested service (here, Wikidata; OCHRE substitutes "Galliformes" for "Name" in the SPARQL query template provided), sends the query through the SPARQL endpoint for that service, and in return

[59] See the Greek Coin Hoard case study (Chap. 12) for examples of Derived Variables more generally and for an example of fetching geographic coordinate data from the Semantic Web using SPARQL.

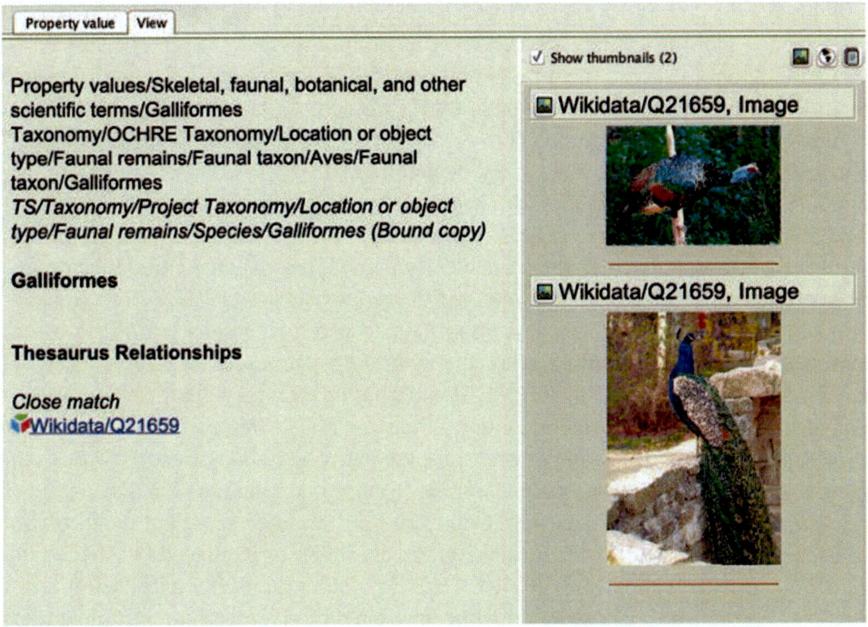

Fig. 9.20 Data from the Semantic Web is tightly integrated with core OCHRE data

gets a single hit on Q21659 with the data being sent back to OCHRE from the data service as XML. OCHRE uses the fetched information to create an appropriate Thesaurus link to this Semantic Web resource based on its derived URI. On the View of this item in OCHRE, the derived URI is displayed as a clickable link that will navigate to the item in its original context.[60] Plus, where images are available from the data service, OCHRE can often integrate them directly into the item's display. Using the checkbox to turn on the image thumbnails, the unfamiliar "Galliformes" suddenly comes to life as a magnificent peacock (Fig. 9.20).

Conclusion

The overall architecture of the OCHRE platform and its item-based approach to knowledge representation allows us to reimagine digital publication. There is very little conceptual and practical distance between the backend and frontend. Data can be published and republished quickly and easily, as often as needed. As it turns out, in the OCHRE platform, data publication for viewing, for analysis, for sharing, and for archiving are all variations of the same thing. Because OCHRE data is stored in

[60] https://www.wikidata.org/wiki/Q21659.

a highly normalized and atomized form, it can be accessed, linked, recomposed, and published in various formats for a wide variety of purposes.

Our experience has shown that digital research in the humanities is more likely to succeed if performed in conjunction with trained digital specialists within the context of a research institution. This observation is not meant to serve as a form of gatekeeping. While there are many technologically skilled researchers in the humanities and social sciences, are we to accept that digital research should be available only to those researchers who can support the technical aspects of the project themselves? Further, there are clearly many types of efficiencies when multiple projects can leverage a common set of resources. The OCHRE Data Service concomitantly makes digital publication easy to use for persons with little or no technical skills while leaving open the possibility for creative intervention by advanced users. By providing built-in, default publication formats for all data published from OCHRE and maintaining a library of HTML templates, JS code, and even R scripts for use on frontend websites, the barriers to success are reduced. Our partners at the Digital Library Development Center maintain the OCHRE publication server, host OCHRE-based websites, and are a major contributing factor in delivering security, stability, accessibility, and durability of published OCHRE data. In conclusion, the role of the OCHRE Data Service in the digital publication process is one example of a broader principle wherein digital research in the humanities launches more quickly, makes fewer false starts, achieves results more effectively, and shares outcomes more widely when performed in conjunction with a dedicated professional staff of trained computational specialists.

Chapter 10
Digital Archaeology Case Study: Tell Keisan, Israel

Introduction

It is 4:30 am, and the dome-of-the-rock alarm clock purchased in the Suq is raising an electronic call to prayer, just ahead of the call echoing across the distance from the minaret of the nearby town. Rising from the camp bed, the field supervisor instinctively reaches over to double-check that her laptop has charged fully overnight. Stopping for a quick cup of tea and a bite of bread and jam, and passing by the supply room to pick up the military-grade barcode printer assigned to her excavation area, she boards the bus for a sleepy ride to the tell.

The archaeological team's surveyor is already onsite, preparing the drone for fresh aerial photographic coverage of the excavation area just after sunrise. As tools are fetched from the storage units onsite, the tools of the digital archaeologist are set up on camp tables around the excavation square. Once the drone completes its flight, recording the latest progress, the shade cloths are raised, and work begins in earnest.

The assistant supervisor has started up OCHRE, running an offline session on the designated laptop which allows data entry only for the items related to this supervisor's 10-meter × 10-meter square. As work progresses, tags for pottery baskets are affixed with barcode labels identifying them with unique identifiers when the baskets are "opened" for collection. Small finds are collected and simultaneously entered into a small box or bag and into the database. Each object is given an automatically assigned unique identifier, a barcode label, and a brief description. With a click of the Bluetooth button in the value field of the Spot coordinates property, OCHRE plucks a coordinate from the data stream[1] broadcast by the RTK (real-time kinematic) device, an Emlid Reach Rover being held steady and level by the student

[1] The data stream, based on a protocol devised by the National Marine Electronics Association (NMEA) to communicate among networked marine instruments, includes latitude, longitude, and altitude details.

S. R. Schloen, M. C. Prosser, *Database Computing for Scholarly Research*, Quantitative Methods in the Humanities and Social Sciences,
https://doi.org/10.1007/978-3-031-46696-0_10

across the square, capturing the x, y coordinate of the object's findspot within the Israel Transverse Mercator (ITM) spatial reference, along with its elevation (z-coordinate).[2] The morning wears on and the field supervisor's musings over the day's excavation progress are logged as daily journal entries in the database.

It is a long time to second breakfast, through fruit break, to lunch. In the heat of midday, both the volunteer workers and the computer batteries are nearly spent. The bus arrives to convey the team back to the compound, the finds are gathered up, and the computers are shut down. The first stop upon arrival back at the camp is the data manager's office where the dig computers are deposited before the hungry and dirty field staff head off to lunch and showers. While the team naps, the data manager uploads the morning's work, integrating and synchronizing new data with the master database in Chicago, making the data available to the entire project.

Hours later the team gathers, refreshed, for the afternoon work session where pottery is washed, sorted, counted, and logged in the now-online database. Faunal analysis, flotation sample processing, and object registration continues apace, each item being recorded and described in its excavation context in the master database. Object photographs, captured with a high-quality digital camera, are drag-dropped onto the "Links" panels of database items; links as well as thumbnails are created before the photographs are transferred to a cloud server. GIS data is processed and integrated. A new high-resolution drone photograph becomes available as the spatially aware backdrop of a new database view. Shapes of walls and pits, traced from the high-resolution photographs, make the excavated features pop with color and symbology as top plans are prepared for the next day.

As night falls, the onsite data manager prepares the dig computers with new offline sessions for the next day. Laptops and barcode printers are settled into their charging stations as the excavation team settles down for the night, all recharging for a new day. Back in Chicago, the day's work has already been backed up and is available to project staff worldwide.

There are many configurations for using OCHRE offline in the field, depending on Internet access and speed, workflow rhythms, dig schedules, and various other factors. The daily schedule of the Tell Keisan team describes just one such scenario. And while this chapter takes a single excavation as a case study, OCHRE was not created for this specific case. Rather, the Tel Keisan project (and the other case studies that follow) adopted OCHRE as their database platform, customizing it as needed with project-specific vocabulary, spatial extents, and users; then integrated it into their broader research plan. OCHRE has been implemented for site-based excavations, region-wide survey projects, projects studying the Ancient Near East, the Classical world, pre-Columbian South America, twentieth-century America, researchers excavating at new sites, returning to previous sites, or working with previously assembled museum collections. So, when we describe a specific

[2] A team of over 80 participants from the University of Chicago, the Ben Gurion University of the Negev (Beersheva, Israel), and the Humboldt University (Berlin) pilot-tested the use of three Emlid Reach RS2 Rovers at Tell Keisan in the summer of 2022, effortlessly capturing thousands of coordinates.

implementation of OCHRE for digital archaeology, the reader should expect that the concepts and approaches of this implementation can be reimagined and customized for any type of archival or archaeological investigation.

On Digital Archaeology

If the above scenario seems too good to be true, we will be the first to acknowledge that the collection and management of archaeological data is not an easy task and presents its share of challenges on many levels. Most of the data that archaeologists would *wish* to collect has already been lost to the passage of time and the process of decay. Much more is lost to the process of selection as the dig director casts about to decide where to put down stakes. In the end, data that *is* collected is disproportionately valuable, but nonetheless is often lost again in old file formats, scattered databases, and general disorganization due to the sheer volume and complexity of the data, as well as the legitimate complexity of the archaeological enterprise. Furthermore, once an artifact has been picked up, nobody will be able to discover it anew or record where it came from after the fact. Having knocked out an ancient wall or removed a beautiful mosaic, it is well and truly gone from its original context. Archaeology, as a practical science, is inherently tangible, spatial, and data rich. But archaeology, as a destructive science, leaves no second chances to get data capture right.

There is no argument that "the way archaeological data is recorded has changed dramatically by the progress of technology and the widespread use of computers" (Karamalis 2009, p. 1420). But early use of computers in archaeology had its share of well-recognized problems due to both the wide variability in the needs of the archaeologists, and the wide variability in the types of data. Computer scientist, Athanasios Karamalis, working with excavations in Greece, presented a detailed analysis of some key technical issues, and tackled his concern that "in order to satisfy the particular data recording requirements … databases are commonly developed completely from scratch and separately for each excavation" (ibid.). He sought to design a system with more "generality" that supported multiple excavations, along with all the relevant data.

> The main purpose of such a database is to improve the capability of sharing archaeological data and knowledge of different excavations with other archaeologists, scientists and generally with other people. Also, a multiple excavation database can improve the collaboration between archaeologists, by letting them work on a specific database structure which can be indirectly modified. Another issue is the compatibility between databases and other information systems … like GIS systems, Internet applications or … different database structures. Having a database with distinct structure, information systems can be developed once and reused for any other excavation with its corresponding data (ibid., 1421).

While this team had some measure of success with the design of an application which included a more generic framework, some degree of itemization ("features" broadly defined), as well as GIS data integration and Internet accessibility, it remained stuck in the relational database paradigm which, we have argued, is not a good fit for solving the types of problems that their system attempted to address.[3]

Challenging the popularity and general acceptance of the relational database paradigm, David Schloen, co-designer of the OCHRE platform, argued for the use of a hierarchical item-based data model implemented in XML as the basis of a "flexible yet standardized data representation for archaeological research" as early as 2001.[4] Schloen, too, cataloged the disadvantages of the typical sorts of databases in use by archaeology projects:

> (1) its rigidity in the structuring of information once it has been set up; (2) its inefficiency in the use of storage space; and (3) its bias toward cumbersome and idiosyncratic alphanumeric representations of the extrinsic relationships among items in the database, which are thus treated no differently than the intrinsic attributes of the items themselves ... for example, the spatial and stratigraphic relationships among items which are so important in archaeology... (Schloen 2001a, p. 129).

But rather than trying to create just another, better, *relational* database, Schloen rejected this option in principle. "Unlike the business data for which most database applications are designed, archaeological data are spatially organized, temporally sequenced, and highly variable. It is these distinctive features of archaeological data which call for an unconventional database design for both the underlying data structure and the user interface."[5]

Preparation

Twenty years after Schloen (David) and Schloën (Sandra) first applied the item-based approach to archaeological data, the possibilities for effective data capture in the field beckon like never before. The mantra from the early days of computing—"get it once, get it early, get it right"—emphasized the need to collect data as close to the source as possible, by the people most authorized and knowledgeable to do so, with the minimum of editing, reformatting, or redundancy. What with world-wide Internet coverage, affordable technology, and computer-savvy staff, along with a comprehensive database system within which data of all kinds can be integrated in real time, digital archaeologists have all the necessary tools of the trade available, literally, at their fingertips. But the importance of adequate preparation for an archaeology project engaging in digital practices cannot be overstated. Taking along computers is not a sign that an effective data management plan is in place; neither is having an onsite "IT guy." Nothing should be left to chance.

---

[3] See Gkatzogias et al. (2005).

[4] See Schloen, J.D. (2001a).

[5] Ibid, p. 130. This paper was based on the early *Infra* implementation of the database system which later evolved into OCHRE as described in the introduction (Chap. 1).

And so it happened that the timing of the first major season of renewed excavations at Tell Keisan in northern Israel, led by David Schloen of the University of Chicago and Gunnar Lehmann of the Ben Gurion University of the Negev, coincided with significant new features in OCHRE: a revamped offline mode for data collection while out of range of good Internet access; and the Geospatially Enabled OCHRE (GEO) version, made possible by the integration of GIS tools[6] available from Esri, the leading GIS company worldwide. Armed with these advances, Tell Keisan became a testbed of digital methods. Having already performed geophysical survey and aerial photography in the summer of 2015, the project returned in 2016 with a sizeable team, comprised of mainly college students and other volunteers, for full-scale excavations. Both authors, Prosser and Schloen (Sandra), participated in the excavation that summer, over-seeing a digital dig using methods not previously available. Follow along as we share the strategies and successes of this first pilot project, and subsequent enhancements from more recent seasons, from database configuration through to analysis and publication.

Users and Access Levels

To begin, the archaeologists of the Tell Keisan team were added as **Users** to a new OCHRE project. With no prior excavation data to worry about, the database project was a clean slate. A research database consultant at the OCHRE Data Service creates and configures a new project with a Name and a Project Administrator account. Thereafter, the Project Administrator has full access to the project and can create other project Users. New users will first be added as items within the **Persons** category. A checkbox designates each one as an Authorized User. All such authorized users are collected under the Users category where the project administrator can assign access rights, by category of data. Field staff will be given Insert/Delete access to the Locations & objects category which is where the bulk of data will be entered while working in the field (Fig. 10.1).

The photographer and illustrator, for example, might be given Delete (which includes Insert) access to the Resources category so that they can add new photographs and drawings, but only Link access to Locations & Objects so that they can link their photographs and drawings to appropriate objects. Specialists might be given Edit access to Locations & Objects so that they can add an informed Observation to an existing item but be otherwise limited. The onsite epigrapher might be given full access to the Texts category in preparation for the discovery of

[6] Rooted in Java, and open to implementing special-purpose functionality based on available Java libraries (APIs), OCHRE is easily extensible. As of this writing, OCHRE uses the Esri ArcGIS Runtime Software Development Kit (SDK) for Java under a free, "Basic" license on the Windows platform. Users are not required to have any Esri products installed on their computers. See https://developers.arcgis.com/java/.

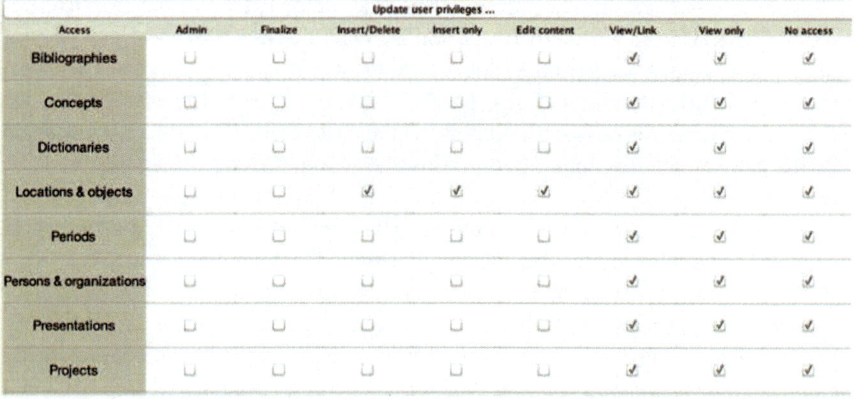

Update user privileges ...								
Access	Admin	Finalize	Insert/Delete	Insert only	Edit content	View/Link	View only	No access
Bibliographies	☐	☐	☐	☐	☐	☑	☑	☑
Concepts	☐	☐	☐	☐	☐	☑	☑	☑
Dictionaries	☐	☐	☐	☐	☐	☑	☑	☑
Locations & objects	☐	☐	☑	☑	☑	☑	☑	☑
Periods	☐	☐	☐	☐	☐	☑	☑	☑
Persons & organizations	☐	☐	☐	☐	☐	☑	☑	☑
Presentations	☐	☐	☐	☐	☐	☑	☑	☑
Projects	☐	☐	☐	☐	☐	☑	☑	☑

Fig. 10.1 An access grid lets the Project Administrator controls which Users have which kind of access to which Categories of data

that elusive archive. A colleague visiting for a few weeks to do specialized research might be given Read access to the data at large and Edit access to Queries.

Person items are used throughout the database to attribute the observer of Observations, the creator of a Resource, the editor of a Text, the author of a Note and so on. The goal is that the database will reflect the scholarly contributions of the team of collaborators and not be a repository of anonymous content.

It is worth restating that all OCHRE data is the project's data, over which OCHRE has no claim. Access to it is managed by the Project Administrator. Issues as to whether the data is kept private or made public, the licenses under which published data is made "open," or not, are not OCHRE issues. The community of scholars associated with the project make these decisions in their own way. By default, all project data is accessed by credentials and explicitly assigned permissions. No data becomes public until the project decides to make it public.

Since OCHRE manages many different projects within a common database, it is not unusual to discover that a Person already exists in another OCHRE project. The faunal, ceramic, lithics, botanical, or other specialist might contribute to many projects and already have a User account with access to other projects. Similarly, field staff may have experience with other digs from other seasons. A quick search for a Person ("Find by name") will turn up any potential matches. If a person is found to exist already, that same Person database item that represents that individual can be inserted into a new Project. We resist redundancy and reward reuse whenever possible. Access rights can be adjusted by Project, but all activity pertaining to that Person will be associated with the same uniquely identified database item. The Contexts of that Person's edit pane will list all projects where that Person is implicated.

Also, note that not all Person items need to be authorized users. Project members, or affiliated staff, not participating in the digital aspects of the dig will be listed as Persons, for the record, but will not have User accounts. A project might include data from historical projects at the same site in which case a former dig director of the site might be listed as a person, for the record, but will not need to be an authorized user. Authors or editors of related publications entered as Bibliography items will be listed in the database but will not normally also be users.

Bibliography

The site of Tell Keisan had been extensively investigated by a French team from 1971–1976, inspired by Father Roland de Vaux at the Ecole Biblique in East Jerusalem, and led by Jean Prignaud, Jacques Briend, and Jean-Baptiste Humbert. Their meticulous and comprehensive publication provides a rich backdrop for renewed investigations (Briend and Humbert 1980). This important publication was scanned as a PDF and cataloged in the Bibliography category of OCHRE, making it readily available to the Chicago team.

OCHRE provides extensive support for managing bibliography, either by using items native to OCHRE to represent bibliographic sources, or by interacting dynamically with libraries organized and styled by the popular Zotero research tool, using its application program interface (API) (Fig. 10.2).

Managing Hierarchical Data

A project like Tell Keisan which adopts the OCHRE database as their data management platform invests considerable effort well before their arrival at the site so that they can hit the ground running. In the sections that follow we review the process of setting up an OCHRE project in preparation for the digital collection of all project data and discuss decisions and plans that are best laid in advance.

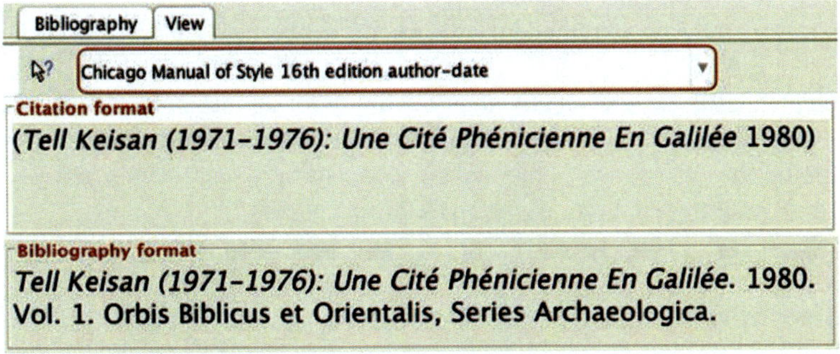

Fig. 10.2 OCHRE's tight integration with Zotero allows for a wide variety of citation formats

Taxonomy and Predefinitions

Since OCHRE is a generic platform, infinitely customizable, with no predefined structures requiring conformity, the process of tailoring OCHRE to suit a specific project involves defining the **Taxonomy** of descriptors that will constitute the project's controlled vocabulary. Recall that in OCHRE, a Taxonomy is a hierarchically organized structure of alternating Variables and their associated Values, where appropriate (see Chap. 5). Properties are Variable-Value pairs, used to describe items: Material = Ceramic; Object type = Figurine; Length = 4.73 cm. A project is free to use whatever nomenclature or organizational scheme it wishes as it constructs a hierarchy of descriptors and constraints. Tell Keisan director, David Schloen, worked with the OCHRE Data Service to construct a Taxonomy that matched his interpretive framework and would give his team the controlled vocabulary necessary to record and describe data in the field. There is no "right" way to build such a taxonomy but there are recommended practices that will make for effective data representation and efficient data entry. These suggestions are borne out of a great deal of past experiences, mistakes made, and lessons learned. Let us review some of those guidelines here.

Use Typed Variables

The use of free-form **Alphanumeric** Variables is discouraged. As much as possible, use variables of the appropriate data type instead. This will constrain data entry to values of that type, minimizing errors and triggering the use of appropriate data entry widgets to assist data entry. Nominal and ordinal variables, for example, have an associated list of allowable values, the ordinal type being an *ordered* list. Dropdown picklists will be generated using these prescribed values ensuring that only valid values are accepted. While a Tell Keisan square supervisor is documenting small finds right there at the edge of the baulk, their work is simplified and made less error-prone by these picklists. A date-picker will pop up for variables of type **Date**. A checkbox will appear for variables of type **Logical** (true/false). Numeric properties can be constrained to valid ranges of minimum and maximum **Integer** or **Decimal** values.

Apart from the data entry benefits, the use of **Values** aids querying as such items can be indexed and optimized for analysis. Finding all instances of the value Coin is much more efficient and reliable than searching for all instances of the text string "coin" (and its variations) in a character-field. If in doubt as to whether a descriptive term should be a Value, or whether a descriptive string would suffice, ask yourself: Will I ever want to search for all instances of this quality?

Reuse Properties

To resist redundancy, and duplication of both content and effort, reuse of existing properties is strongly encouraged. Taxonomy building should be done very intentionally to avoid creating a proliferation of duplicate items. New projects are welcome to A-B-C (Adopt, Borrow, and Customize) common descriptive terms—Metal, Coin, Red, Brick, Quantity, and so on—from OCHRE's centralized master Taxonomy. The OCHRE Data Service provides support to projects during the taxonomy building stage, helping draw from pre-existing arrangements of Variables and Values. A built-in benefit of borrowing taxonomic items is the resulting *automatic alignment* with other OCHRE projects. For example, if multiple projects are using the same shared property "Material = Gold" and the same shared property "Coin = Stater," then OCHRE will already, automatically, be able to find all gold staters in cross-project queries.

The Tell Keisan taxonomy is a mixture of adopted, borrowed but rearranged, and completely custom Variables and Values. Entire branches, such as the Material > Stone branch, or the Taxon > Genus > Species branches of faunal or botanical species, have been adopted wholesale. As OCHRE projects open in new geographical areas, the master taxonomy is supplemented with new values: "Llama" was added when OCHRE was adopted by a project to Peru; "Crocodile" when OCHRE was taken to Niger. Over time, extensive branches of faunal analysis, human remains description, pottery typologies, and many others have been established collaboratively and are available to all projects.

Remember, too, that an item can occur in multiple contexts. Say, for example, that a "Color" option is needed in variety of lists of values. Inserting a brand-new "Color" Variable and re-listing the relevant color Values in each list is messy and redundant. If the Value is in the project vocabulary already, just borrow the existing item and paste it into another relevant context. The Contexts of that Value's edit or display pane will reflect all instances where that Value is implicated. If the entire list of color values is needed for multiple purposes (Soil>Color; Decoration>Color; Burnishing>Color), simply link-copy the Color branch of the hierarchy into the relevant contexts.

Relate Properties

Of particular importance for archaeology projects are the relational properties that relate two items using a semantically meaningful link, especially those that maintain automatic, explicit, bidirectional links between relevant items. Take, for example, a relational property that identifies the temporal relationship between two units of excavation. If Locus B is deemed to be ***earlier than*** Locus A, it logically follows that Locus A is ***later than*** Locus B. So, if the property "Locus B is earlier than Locus A" is assigned, OCHRE will automatically and explicitly assign the inverse, related property "Locus A is later than Locus B." Alternatively, if the property "Locus A is later than Locus B" is assigned, OCHRE will automatically and explicitly assign the inverse, related property "Locus B is earlier than Locus A." OCHRE does everything it can to keep these properties synchronized (and provides an option for detecting if they have gotten out of sync) (Fig. 10.3).

Properties between and among excavation units such as these are used extensively at Tell Keisan, including properties such as "Is physically above/Is physically

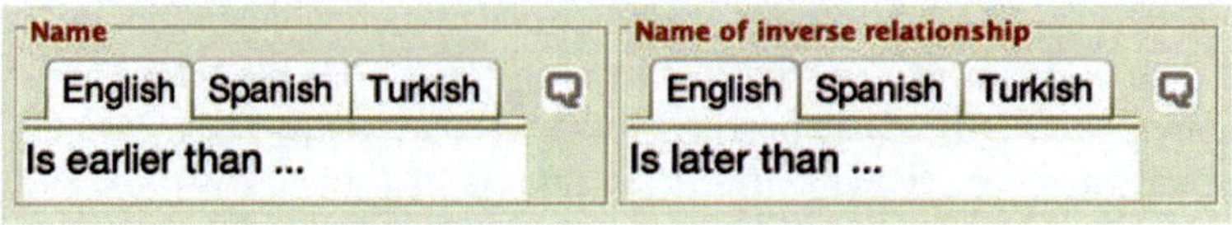

Fig. 10.3 Bidirectional, relational properties create meaningful links between two items

below," "Abuts/Is abutted by," "Cuts/Is cut by," "Is within as fill/Contains as fill," and "Is correlated with/Is correlated with." OCHRE maintains the relationship, explicitly in both directions, even though it is expressed via a single relational property and entered in only one of the directions (either one). Stratigraphic relationships such as these add to the rich network of information explicitly detailed among relevant database items. Continue reading to see how we take further advantage of such relationships (spoiler alert: exploiting them to create Harris matrices).

Recurse Properties

In Chap. 5 (Propertize), we discussed the features and benefits of a recursive structure of a taxonomic hierarchy. A hierarchy of descriptors will naturally start with more general properties that lead to more specific properties: Materials and their sub-types; forms and their sub-forms. But resist the temptation to create sub-type properties. Rather, take advantage of recursion—the ability to replicate a concept or action at a deeper level of context—and *reuse* the *same* variable at the next level of the hierarchical taxonomy. This creates a cascading list of more general to more specific Values of the same Variable, allowing the investigator to tag any item at whatever level of description is discernible. If it can be determined that the object represents the Form of an Alabastron, then tag it as such. If all that can be determined is that it is the Form of a Closed vessel, then leave it at that. Each property *inherits* all the knowledge about itself that is implicit in the hierarchical organization; that is, an Alabastron knows by inheritance that it is a Jar (and a Closed vessel) and the result of a query for Jars will include Alabastrons (Fig. 10.4).

While reusing and recursing properties, be sure to take advantage of the semantics provided by context. For example, a new "Rim diameter" property is not needed to capture the diameter of a rim. Rather, subsume the existing Diameter property within the context of the Rim designation. The same Diameter property can be reused for the diameter of the base, the diameter of the spout, the diameter of the handle, the diameter of the body, the diameter of a coin, the diameter of a loom weight, the diameter of a pestle, and so on.

Material > Stone	**Pottery form** > Closed vessel
Material > Basalt	**Pottery form** > Jar
Material > Vesicular basalt	**Pottery form** > Alabastron

Fig. 10.4 Recursive properties make "sub"-properties moot

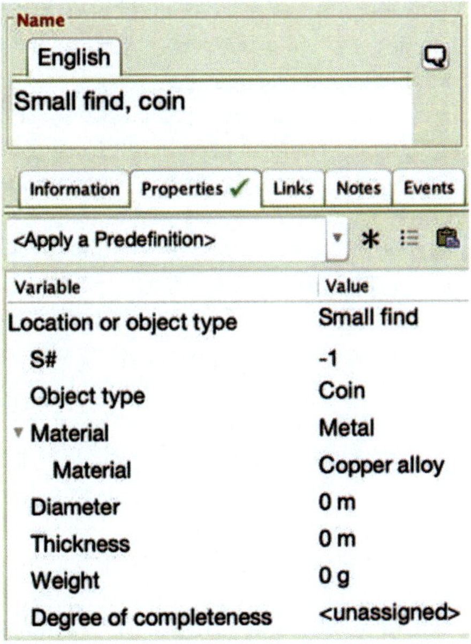

Fig. 10.5 A Predefinition reminds the registrar to measure the diameter, thickness, and weight of each coin, and to note its degree of completeness

Predefine Templates

A large excavation like Tell Keisan typically relies on the work of students and volunteers. In a predigital age, it may not have been difficult for these minimally trained personnel to record information of paper forms. To help the Keisan project record accurate data quickly and easily, the OCHRE Data Service helps the project create a series of **Predefinitions**. An OCHRE Predefinition serves as a template for data entry. It is a list of a preselected group of properties that dictates how those properties are used to describe items of a given type. By organizing the properties of interest for any type of item, the Predefinition serves to document a project's conventions while also ensuring consistent data entry. Figure 10.5 shows the properties selected for a Coin item at Tell Keisan: it is tagged as a Small find, assigned a registration number (S#), and identified as a Metal object by default. Options are also provided for descriptive characteristics such as Diameter, Thickness, and Weight.

A Predefinition sets the expectation for how items are to be described at this site and assigns the properties all at once, serving as an effective shortcut for data entry. Values of the listed Variables are generally left as <unassigned>, or preassigned to a default value, so the user can simply fill in the blanks. The use of predefinitions ensures a consistent description using a controlled vocabulary designed by the project director and the collaborating team, not prescribed by built-in database fields.

Configure Serial Numbers

While much of a project's taxonomy can be borrowed from existing projects, new variables are often needed to implement a project's specific numbering schemes. Loci, baskets, lots, and registered objects, for example, are typically assigned unique numbers according to a project's conventions. Using a Variable of type **Serial integer,** lets OCHRE automatically assign the next available number and enforce uniqueness. When a property based on a serial number is applied to an item, OCHRE will determine the next available number in the series to use as the value and will make the value read-only, preventing the user from changing it.[7] Keisan uses a serial number property, for example, to number its registered pottery items; these are diagnostic sherds that deserve further study by specialists. When a specialist pulls a stamped jar handle from the pottery table for further study, she can add this item to OCHRE to record details and attach photographs (as in Fig. 10.6). The specialist need not maintain a separate list of object numbers to see which number to assign next. The serial property will assign the next available number, in this case RP-11.

Assign Auto-labels

Predefinitions are often used in conjunction with Serial numbers and OCHRE's auto-labeling features to help assign unique names to items. Since OCHRE can generate the next available value of a serial number for a new item, OCHRE can also use this number to create a unique Name and/or Abbreviation for the item. This feature is frequently used also in conjunction with the **Concatenation**-style of derived variable which allows a formula to specify the components of the desired Name. Figure 10.7 shows the formula for a derived Variable ("Label S 2016") which was used to label the Small finds for the Tell Keisan 2016 season. It specifies that the name of the small find should be: the literal string "S16-" as a prefix, followed by the value of the Grid-Square context in which the item finds itself (inherited from its parent Locus in this case), followed by the number sign ("#"), followed by its assigned serial number (the Value of the Variable S#).

[7] Serial numbers can be unique within the project database at large, or unique among the items within the scope of any hierarchy. The unique-within-hierarchy option is needed when running OCHRE offline because the full database is not available to serve as the scope within which to generate the next-available number. Optionally, any serial-number property can be constrained to a range of numbers for a specified hierarchy, thus assisting the Project Administrator to ensure that items are uniquely identified when needed.

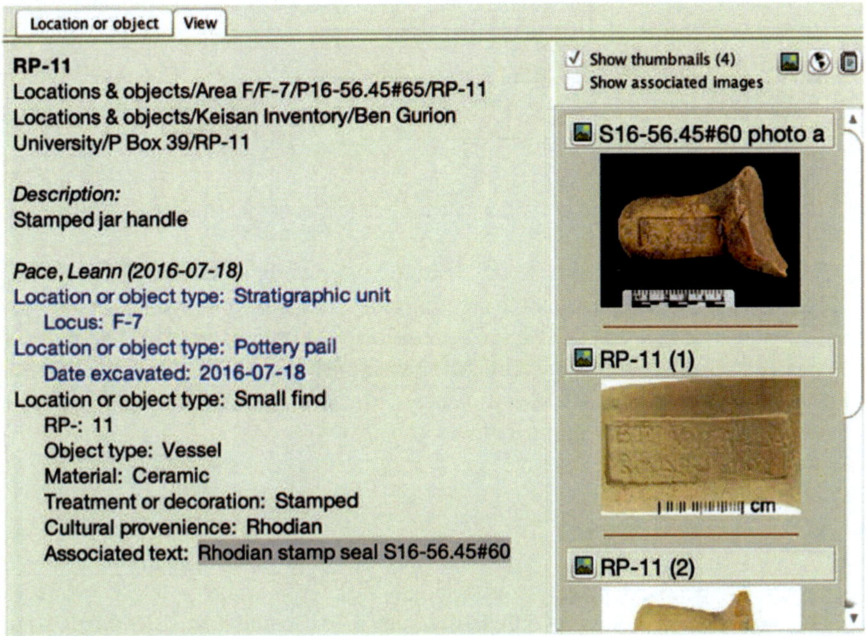

Fig. 10.6 The unique item number is assigned by a serial variable

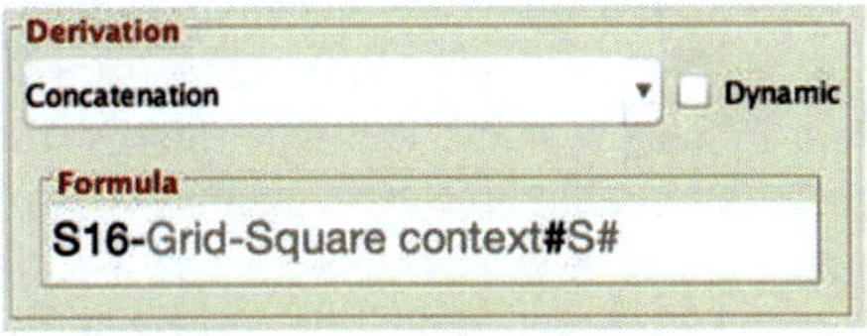

Fig. 10.7 A Formula of a derived variable generates a Name based on a given sequence of character strings

The Preferences of the Coin Predefinition specify that OCHRE should automatically label a new Coin using the Value generated by the formula of the derived Variable “Label S 2016” (Fig. 10.8). When the Coin Predefinition is applied to a new item, OCHRE will recognize the Serial number (S#) property and will automatically increment it appropriately, assigning its value to the new coin.[8] When the user saves the Properties without having given the item a Name, OCHRE will recognize that the Name is blank and that there is an auto-label specification on the Predefinition. OCHRE will use the property values to generate the unique Name based on the given formula “S16” + “46.37” + “#” + “58”: ***S16-46.37#58***.

[8] Serial numbers like “S#” default to a value of −1 in the Predefinition (as shown in Fig. 10.5). This ensures that a default value is not inadvertently assigned to an item (serial numbers are intended to be unique) and reminds the user that this value will be calculated.

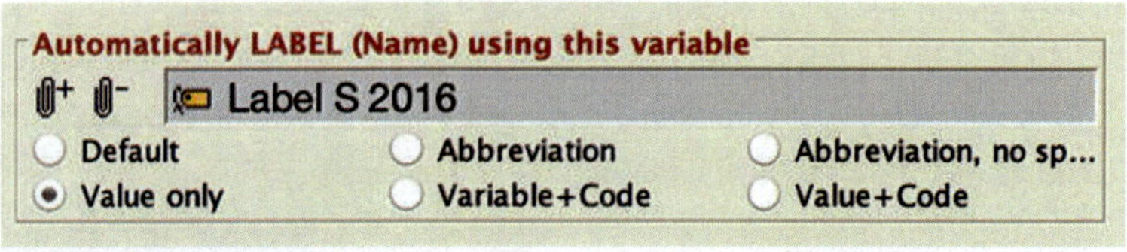

Fig. 10.8 Auto-labels are often used with serial numbers to generate unique identifiers

The preparations pertaining to the Taxonomy, Predefinitions, and naming conventions are the digital equivalent to creating and printing paper forms before a field season. The advantages to this digital approach should be coming into focus: consistency in the naming and description of locations and objects, immediate data capture, and a system that enforces project specifications while allowing for heterogeneous description and documentation.

Locations & Objects

As has already been extensively covered in the discussion of hierarchical organization (Chap. 4), archaeology is inherently spatial and contextual. But there is no "right" way to organize one's spatial items either. Projects are free to construct a spatial hierarchy in whatever way makes sense for their site. Indeed, multiple overlapping hierarchies are often useful for capturing different aspects of a project's efforts. Tell Keisan uses a primary excavation hierarchy to define the Areas of excavation, and the Loci (layers and features) excavated therein. Pottery pails, small finds, faunal remains, and other discoveries are contextualized appropriately within the relevant loci. However, the French team excavating in the 1970s used a different grid system, a different nomenclature, and different methods, requiring separate hierarchies, organized along somewhat different lines, to represent the areas which they dug. The flexibility of OCHRE allows for useful integration of legacy and modern excavations, without compromising any of their recording systems nor requiring that they conform.

For practical purposes, the excavations at Tell Keisan were laid out on a grid system, as is typical for excavations, large and small. A 1-kilometer square (Grid 46) was subdivided into 10 × 10 meter squares, creating a reference grid. A "Square supervisor" is assigned to manage the activity in each square. This is a completely artificial and arbitrary organization imposed on the area of excavation, but one that aids the recording system and the methods on the ground. A super-imposed grid that forms that basis of a recording system becomes problematic, though, when an excavated wall crosses from one square to another. In Area E at Tell Keisan, a large wall identified as E-8 crosses from Square 37 into Square 38 of Grid 46. What of the hierarchical organization then? Did we mention that there is no right way to organize one's spatial units? Consider various "solutions" listed in order from the most brute force to the most elegant, given the flexibility provided by the OCHRE data model.

Scenario A

Some projects may choose to make the grid system primary, enforcing the boundaries of each square as if they were real. The supervisor in Square 37 will assign a number to the wall as it exists in her square and the supervisor in Square 38 will assign a different number to the wall as it is represented in her square. A relational property, **Locus-corresponds-or-is-equal-to**, will link the two distinct database items to indicate that they are in fact representing the same wall. The downside to this approach is that there are two database items representing a single entity, but this is not problematic if there are other indications that they are the same.

Scenario B

Because OCHRE uses an item-based approach and allows reuse of database items in different contexts, a project may copy the database item representing the wall from its context in Square 37 and paste it into a second context in Square 38. The supervisor of Square 37 would record an *observation* on the item attributed to her where she assigns details and makes comments on the wall. The supervisor of Square 38 would record a separate observation attributed to her that details her observations of the same wall. Note that these are two separate observations on the single database item reused in multiple contexts. This database item can be edited from either of its contexts and OCHRE takes care that both supervisors are not editing at exactly the same time.[9] The advantage to this approach is that the wall is represented by a single item, eliminating the need to correlate two different items as if they were one. The disadvantage is that this can be problematic when the item is used offline. Careful workflow would be needed to ensure that only one editor had access to this item in offline sessions.

Scenario C

The option implemented at Tell Keisan removes the arbitrary grid system from the primary excavation hierarchy altogether and represents the grid system as a separate hierarchy. The argument is that this more faithfully represents the reality on the ground. Wall E-8 is within Area E, full stop. Not, E-8 is within Squares 37 and 38 within Area E. Remember, the squares are imposed simply for the sake of managing personnel and record-keeping. With the grid system as a *secondary* hierarchy, Wall E-8 links to the appropriate Grid and Squares using a cross-cutting relational property. Two instances of the property **Grid-Square system** identify

[9] OCHRE handles multiple users by putting an implicit "claim" on the item when it is edited, preventing another user from editing it simultaneously.

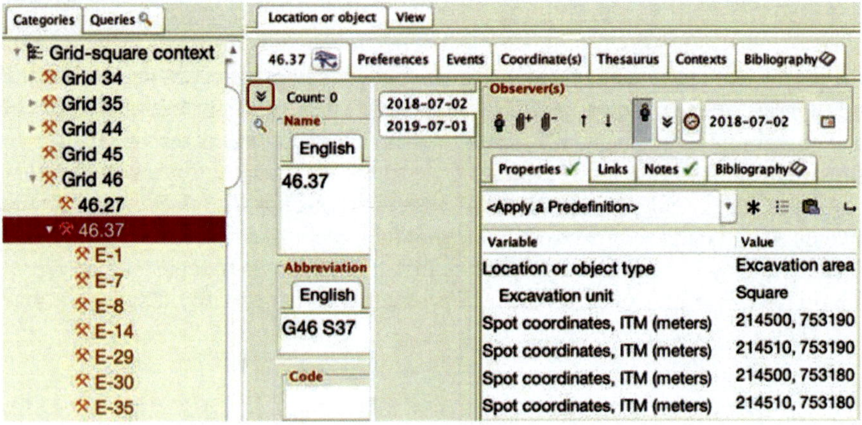

Fig. 10.9 Grid and Squares are database items with their own properties, here coordinates, and organized in a hierarchy apart from the Area, Locus, and Object hierarchy. A special query-lookup button (with a magnifying glass icon) finds and lists all items cross-referenced to the selected square, including E-8

that E-8 falls within Square 37 and also within Square 38. If the wall were to continue into Square 39, for example, it would simply require the addition of another instance of the property to note this. Under this scenario, the item exists only once and would have multiple observations for different square supervisors, with the same advantages and disadvantages as in Scenario B. In this case, though, the artificial Grid-Squares are organized in their own hierarchy, disentangled from the natural containment of the excavation hierarchy. Hierarchically contained sub-items (for any *secondary* hierarchy) are derived from a query. In this case, the contents of the square are found, retrieved, and linked based on the Grid-Square relational property (Fig. 10.9).

Any of the scenarios described here are valid and, in fact, are represented by current OCHRE projects. The choice of option would depend mostly on the preference of the excavator and practical considerations (like offline usage).

Periods and Phases

Archaeology is not only situated in space, but in time. Relevant time scales usually reference both widely applicable cultural time frames, as well as local ones, specific to a given site. The **Periods** category allows OCHRE projects to track both regional and local time frames. Organized hierarchically, like all other OCHRE items, time periods can be borrowed, if globally or regionally relevant, or customized, if locally specific. It is common to share a culturally relevant chronology among projects which work in the same cultural periods, while having a second custom hierarchy representing local periods or phases of occupation at one's own site.

Period items are used to date all kinds of items: the date of destruction of a layer of ash, a coin, a pot sherd representative of a recognizable type, and so on. Periods are assigned as simple links on an item at whatever level of specificity is possible. A coin might be known just to be "Roman" or it could be attributed more specifically, farther down the period hierarchy, to Alexander the Great. Like with other hierarchies, lower-level items inherit details of their higher-level contexts; a coin tagged as that of Alexander the Great will also know that it is Roman. Queries for Roman coins will return all those attributed to Alexander the Great and other Roman rulers or dynasties itemized as sub-periods.

At Tell Keisan, the Levels of occupation identified by the French excavations constitute a second Period hierarchy. A third Period hierarchy delineates the specific Phases of occupation noted by the Chicago excavators. These two local Period structures are itemized separately but integrate naturally within the overall structure provided by the broader cultural periods which are widely used in the Middle East (Fig. 10.10).

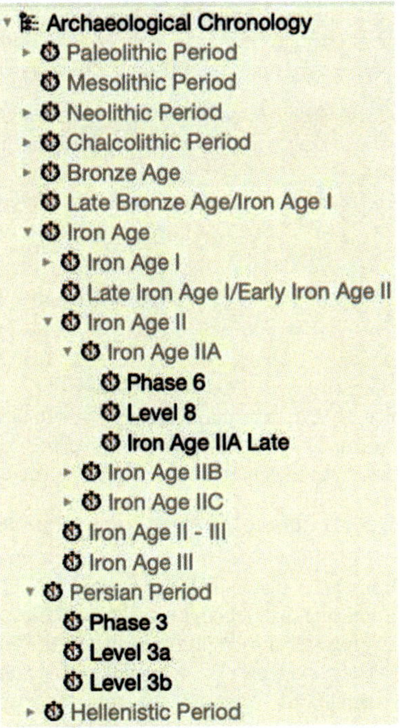

Fig. 10.10 Periods are listed sequentially at each level of the hierarchy

Cautionary Reminders

Whether space, time, or taxonomy, the hierarchical organization of items provides many benefits. But the flexibility afforded the user by the generic OCHRE framework can lead to trouble. It is worth repeating several core principles here as a reminder of best practice.

Do not mix different types of items within the same category

Consider a **Locations** hierarchy of sites being studied for a regional survey. It might seem helpful to organize them based on periods of occupation, introducing sub-headings, in effect. Resist this temptation. Is "Roman" a Location or object? No. It is better represented as a Period, and the categorize-by-period option will be achieved through appropriate Period links instead.

Locations & objects>Israel>~~Iron age~~>Tell Keisan
>Tell Megiddo
Locations & objects>Israel>~~Roman~~>Ashkelon
>Hippos-Sussita

Do not confuse items with headings

A related tendency is to organize items within familiar well-established classes of items. Resist this temptation. In the sample below, "Pottery" and "Faunal" represent classes of data, with their labels used merely as headings; they are neither a **Location** nor an **object**. Objects are described through Properties as being Pottery or Faunal items, allowing OCHRE to generate classes of items based on queries. That is, in an item-based database, organizing a collection of items by class represents a secondary option rather than a primary one.

Locations & objects>~~Pottery~~>Pottery item 1
>Pottery item 2
>Pottery item 3
Locations & objects>~~Faunal~~>Faunal item 1
>Faunal item 2

Do not conflate properties that should remain distinct

It is natural to use compound values like: Vessel type = "glass bowl," Bone type = "fish vertebra," Object type = "gold coin," Dimension = "rim diameter." Bowls may also be ceramic, stone, or metal. Vertebrae may belong to mammals, humans, or dinosaurs. Coins may be gold, silver, or bronze. By restricting ourselves to one feature per property, we maximize the reusability of the descriptive property and achieve an efficient and effective recording scheme.

Do not entangle hierarchical branches that should remain distinct

Remember that OCHRE can easily model multiple hierarchies within any given category of data. Represent distinct conceptual hierarchies separately and allow them to overlap naturally, either by sharing items in multiple contexts (as with the Tell Keisan Chicago team versus French team Periods example) or by cross-referencing using relational properties (as with the Grid System example). So, when it comes time to reorganize units of excavation into rooms, buildings, palaces, and temples, create a new hierarchy that represents the architectural analysis and assign loci, levels, layers, or features accordingly.

Atomize, organize, and propertize. Reuse and reduce. Divide and conquer.

Managing Geospatial Data

We have discussed at length the use of hierarchical organization to model the contextualization in space, time, and description of archaeological data. But by its very nature, archaeology is inherently a spatial science that generates a great deal of geospatial data; that is, data that contains Global Positioning System (GPS) coordinates, or coordinate information of some other kind, that gives it knowledge as to where it is located in space. Archaeologists have been early adopters of new technologies that facilitate the capture of geospatial data. Projects nowadays use sophisticated drone technology to capture jaw-droppingly, high-resolution geospatially aware aerial photographs of excavation progress. Ordinary digital photography can produce images with GPS data embedded. LIDAR (LIght Detection And Ranging) technology can produce stunning, spatially aware, three-dimensional models at both the microscale (e.g., a tomb) or the macro scale (e.g., a river valley). In short, much of the data collected by modern excavations is loaded with geographic information.

The high uptake in the use and capture of geospatial data poses new challenges for its management and integration. Geospatial data is often perceived to be so inherently different from other data stored in more traditional record-keeping systems that they tend to be managed separately, by project staff with a completely different skill set, overlapping only awkwardly with other project data. Information needed to describe shapes, features, layers, images, and models is often re-keyed redundantly into a "geodatabase" or omitted altogether from either the GIS system or the core database of record. But this need not be the case. The Geospatially Enabled OCHRE (GEO) version, with its item-based data model and its extensible code base, provides a unique opportunity to integrate tightly the geospatial data of a project with other core project data. OCHRE's **Map View** mode of interaction provides a geospatially aware canvas, along with a variety of interface tools and display options, with which to view and interact with geospatially aware items in conjunction with other core database items. Since spatial data is crucial to any archaeology project, it allows us to elaborate on how a geospatially aware interface combined with an item-based approach facilitates the management and integration of geospatial data.

Item-Based: Independent of Other Items

In the spirit of OCHRE's item-based approach, the ultimate goal is that each geospatially aware item in OCHRE is able to represent itself on a Map or View, independent of other items and in the relevant coordinate space. This provides maximum flexibility for creating a wide assortment of maps or diagrams based on a variety of criteria; for example, to diagram the apse and basilica of the church built atop Tell Keisan, to outline the living surfaces at Ashkelon destroyed by Nebuchadnezzar in 604 BC; to plot the distribution of coin hoards that contain Alexandrian silver tetradrachm; or to highlight all electoral districts with a specific demographic quality.

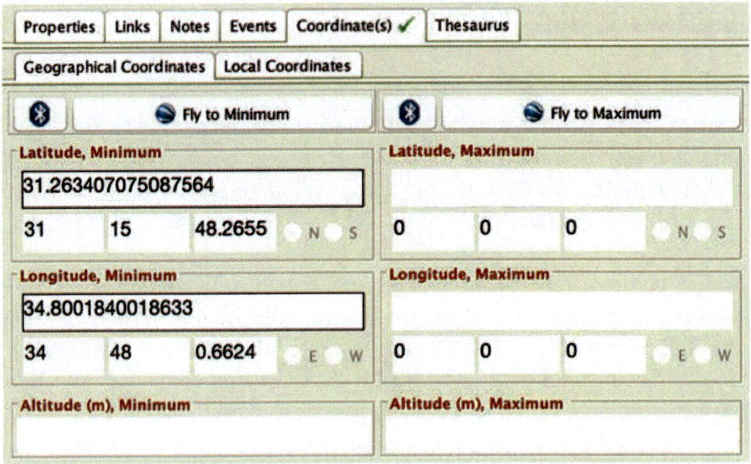

Fig. 10.11 Latitude and longitude fields let OCHRE interact with other GPS-based systems

Each wall, each floor, each coin hoard, each electoral district needs to be able to draw itself, independent of all others, on a map, on demand.

Items organized within the **Locations & objects** category are naturally expected to have geographic or spatially relevant qualities. Their spatial data is often captured as familiar latitude and longitude coordinates for which OCHRE provides built-in metadata fields and automatic integration with Google Earth (Fig. 10.11).[10] Items with coordinates can be retrieved using a query and displayed on a map.

OCHRE also facilitates the assignment of geospatial information for items managed by the **Persons & organizations** category: the laboratory at the Ben Gurion University of the Negev which stores the project's pottery, artifacts, and tools in the off-season, or the University of Chicago which is the affiliated institution of many OCHRE users and many of the Tell Keisan team members. The Coordinates metadata option is available to items in Persons & organizations to capture latitude and longitude values that can be pinned in OCHRE's Map View.

Resource items, too, are commonly spatially situated, having GPS coordinates embedded in their metadata. OCHRE can extract the embedded image metadata, thus enabling informative views such as this one showing the record of photographs taken around the site of Tell Keisan during the summer of 2015 (Fig. 10.12). Again, each item, singly, knows how to plot itself in the geographic space. Other types of files which contain geographic information, like raster images, shapefiles, or certain geodatabase formats, can be added to OCHRE as Resource items whose Type is assigned as "geospatial." OCHRE will recognize many common formats and automatically handle them appropriately.

Not all project data is based on the familiar latitude/longitude geographic coordinate system like the GPS-based metadata coordinates embedded in image files. Archaeology

[10]A fly-to button triggers the startup of Google Earth and passes along the coordinate point to be plotted there. OCHRE can also export to KML/KMZ format.

Fig. 10.12 Image Resource items plotted on a map, exploit their embedded GPS metadata

projects often capture geographic data in a more localized coordinate space to optimize the accuracy of their measurements. This is because the process of projecting the spherical earth onto a flat, two-dimensional surface results in a certain, sometimes significant, amount of distortion, by definition (picture the disproportionately oversized representations of Canada and Russia on a traditional wall map). By using a more localized projection, appropriate to the geographic area being worked in, archaeologists minimize the distortion and maximize the accuracy of the data they collect. Tel Tayinat in southern Turkey uses the Universal Transverse Mercator (UTM) 37N projection, for example. Tayinat's neighbor, Zincirli, uses a variation of the European Datum 1950 (ED50) standard. Tell Keisan, our case study project, uses a nationally adopted grid system referred to as the Israeli Transverse Mercator (ITM) projection.

Images that do not have geospatial information embedded can be made to be geospatially aware through a process call *georeferencing*. With just a handful of known reference points in a predetermined coordinate system, and the use of appropriate GIS software (such as Esri's ArcMap for Desktop or the open-source QGIS application), a scan or drawing of an excavated area can be aligned to the coordinate space of the reference points and saved with this additional spatial data.[11] Georeferenced images can then be viewed alongside other spatially aware data.[12]

---

[11] The projection information is normally preserved in side-car files associated with the original image, like the "world file" (e.g., .tfw) associated with a file in tif format.

[12] OCHRE lets a project specify its preferred (default) coordinate system and provides appropriate mechanisms for converting between different coordinate spaces. For example, an aerial view of Zincirli georeferenced in a custom ED 1950 coordinate system could be displayed along with an

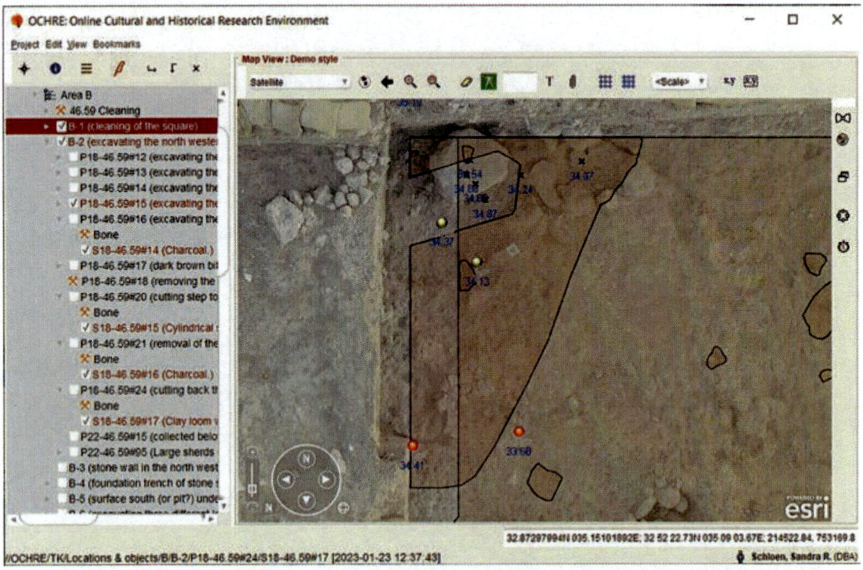

Fig. 10.13 A point scatter captures the extent and elevation of a topsoil layer at Tell Keisan. Small finds and charcoal samples are styled as colored pins, indicating findspots

It is by design that geographic content is not relegated only to built-in metadata fields. While built-in fields *are* provided for the most common and simplest case of latitude and longitude, there are many occasions when more than one such coordinate will be assigned to an item. OCHRE has the option to create **Variables** whose Type is "coordinate" and to assign to these a coordinate system of choice in order to capture coordinates in an alternate geographic, projected, or local coordinate system. For example, a "Spot elevation" variable based on the Israeli Transverse Mercator (ITM; EPSG 2039) projected coordinate system is used to capture, and convert as necessary, x-, y-, and z-values for Tell Keisan. Figure 10.13 shows a set of spot elevations for a newly excavated topsoil layer at Tell Keisan, sampled across and around its extent and comprising a veritable point cloud of information. A coordinate-type property, which can be applied to the same item over and over with different values as needed, serves as a perfect mechanism for capturing such data.

For items that are naturally represented by a single point, having an assigned coordinate—using either the latitude/longitude values in the built-in fields or a coordinate-style property value—is the easiest way to apply geospatial content. But in many cases, it is more appropriate to use lines (instead of points) to represent rivers, roads, topographic contours, and the like, or polygon-shaped areas to represent items like geographic regions or excavation features. OCHRE provides several ways to integrate shapes drawn as polylines or polygons using either the shapefile format (.shp) made popular by Esri's mapping tools or the geodatabase format

aerial view of Tayinat in the UTM 37N coordinate space on a satellite map given in WGS84 coordinates.

supported by the Esri API.[13] Points too, in fact, can be represented as shapefiles and can be fully integrated into OCHRE using the shapefile format.[14]

Integrated: Together with Other Items

It is not contradictory to suggest that each item should be able to draw itself independently of others, but in the same breath to insist that all items be integrated and able to draw themselves together or in a variety of combinations. Itemized, yet integrated; separate, yet together. For geospatial data, the integration is just as important as the itemization.

This does not mean that plans of excavation areas, maps of geographic regions with features of interest, and publication-ready views should be prepared in traditional GIS systems then integrated into OCHRE as finished products for viewing. Rather, the item-based approach requires that *each* relevant item—each individual artifact, each skeleton (or even each bone), each excavated wall or pit, each surveyed site, each cataloged monument, each political boundary, each voting district—knows how to plot itself, and only itself, independently on a map. This provides the maximum flexibility for generating a wide variety of views in response to queries and as the outcome of in-depth analysis and research. Pre-composed maps and views are just that—pre-composed by some researcher, already interpreted and discussed—not raw data available for analysis and investigation. But once the itemization has been achieved, effective integration is essential for making the whole greater than the sum of its parts.

Any OCHRE item that is hierarchically located within an OCHRE context that has been geospatially enabled can examine the relevant geospatial data made available in that context and attempt to discover additional information about itself there. An item uses this *discovery* process to query the attribute table of features in a designated geodatabase or shapefile to extract geometry data and descriptive attributes of itself. Content from these external geodatabase or shapefile features is thus integrated with their corresponding OCHRE items. A user-specified setting on the containing OCHRE hierarchy indicates which field of which feature table in the geodatabase or shapefile can be used to do a string-match on the Name, Abbreviation, or any of the Aliases of the OCHRE items within the scope of the hierarchy. OCHRE will *query* the appropriate geospatial source table (e.g., the shapefile's attribute table) to locate shapes or points of matching OCHRE items. Remember that the goal is for each item to be able to draw its own shape, along with any other items that have been requested to draw themselves, thereby providing a great deal of reusability and flexibility when creating custom Views or on-the-fly Maps in response to data analysis or exploratory research.

[13] Any software that supports the shapefile format, for example, Esri's commercial ArcMap software or the open source QGIS, can be used to create shapefiles to integrate with OCHRE.

[14] The Tel Shimron practice has been to export files of point coordinates from "Total station" capture devices into point-shapefiles and import them into OCHRE.

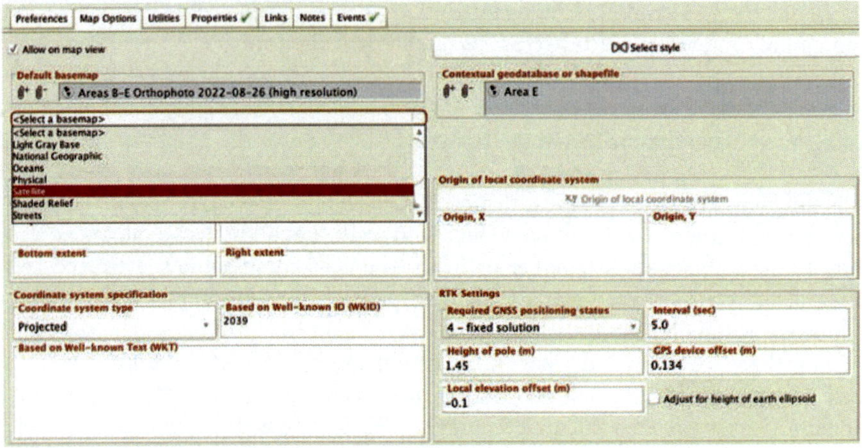

Fig. 10.14 Map Options configure a Set or Hierarchy for use in OCHRE's Map View

Configuring a Locations & objects hierarchy to be geo-enabled, say Area E at Tell Keisan, is as simple as: (1) checking on the option to allow it to be presented in Map View; (2) specifying a georeferenced raster image, a *basemap*, to use as the backdrop for Map View when a user zooms-to the hierarchy; and (3) specifying the geodatabase or shapefile in which the OCHRE items contained within the hierarchy can "discover" themselves (Fig. 10.14).

OCHRE's Map View

Each user's computer needs to be configured to enable OCHRE's GEO features from their User account by clicking the **Initialize GEO** button. Thereafter, OCHRE's Map View becomes available to a normal OCHRE session, selected as a navigation style on the View menu. Details specified on the Resources Inbox hierarchy are used to determine the initial startup configuration of the Map View environment.

From a high-resolution drone image a basemap was created that covered the region of interest—the top of the main mound at Tell Keisan. A basemap is needed as a backdrop for OCHRE's Map View and defines both the *extent* (which controls how far a user can pan in any direction) and the *resolution* (which controls how far a user can zoom in) of the geographically represented space in the project's chosen coordinate space, in this case the Israeli Transverse Mercator (ITM; EPSG 2039) projection. Each spatial hierarchy (representing a separate Area at Tell Keisan) can be configured with its own "local" basemap that provides a higher resolution option for zooming and panning (Fig. 10.15).

In Map View, rather than presenting a combination of panes, tabs, and fields, the OCHRE backdrop is a geospatially aware map. The familiar list of **Categories** from the navigation pane is available, but it presents only those items which have been

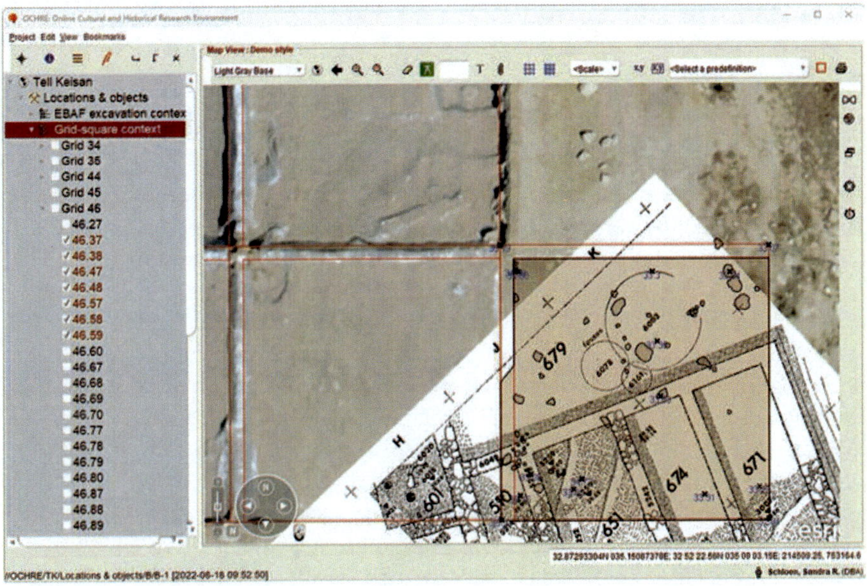

Fig. 10.15 A bird's-eye view shows excavation squares overlaid on the basemap for the mound at Tell Keisan (drone photo by A. M. Wright, courtesy of the Tell Keisan excavation) in proximity to Niveau 5 of Chantier B dug by the French team (shown by the georeferenced top plan)

selected by the project administrator to be available in this mode, thereby simplifying the interactive experience for the users.

All items that have geospatial qualities are displayed with a checkbox option so that the user can control which items to display on the map, toggling their visibility on and off as needed. Each item knows how to draw itself, and only itself, on demand, whether it is represented by a raster image, a geodatabase table, a shapefile, a coordinate variable, or a point. Note, too, that a **Query** is an item in OCHRE which can draw on (pun intended) not only the geospatial qualities of an item but also all the other property-based and string-based data as criteria for selection. The items matching the query's criteria represent a collective that can be toggled on and off as the query draws itself on demand. Similarly, a **Set** represents a collection of items—either individual items or other queries and sets—the drawing of which can be controlled as a group.

A collection of controls for panning and zooming, toggling on elevations, labels, or grid lines, controlling colors, styles, and transparency, and so on, are provided by the OCHRE interface. With geospatial data thus organized as items, and collections of items, and with a map-based environment for displaying such data, OCHRE provides essentially endless possibilities for creatively exploring and interacting with a project's itemized and integrated set of data.

Execution: Data Collected

The Onsite Data Manager

Having (almost) dismissed the notion earlier of having along an "IT guy," we are going to (almost) recant and suggest that it is an extremely good idea to have a point person designated to oversee the data collection efforts at a large-scale project like Tell Keisan. "Born digital" data collection and management is too important to be left to chance, and an onsite data manager often becomes another of the key professional personnel that make up the dig staff. Offline data needs to be uploaded to the online system or backed up and prepared for a new day; batteries need to be recharged, ribbons, and ink refreshed; photographic data needs to be integrated; mapping needs updating daily, digitally. But this is not simply a logistical or clerical position. And it is not, exactly, a technical position either. It does not involve making joins among Microsoft Access tables or coding Python scripts. But it may mean coaxing bandwidth from a cellular modem plan, disabling Windows' automatic updating of Minesweeper, Candy Crush and other apps hogging CPU, adjusting power settings on the laptops so the batteries will last all morning in the field, resetting Bluetooth connections of conflicting devices, and just being an all-around resourceful problem-solver. Over the past few years, the OCHRE Data Service has trained student assistants to embed with projects in the highly valued staff role of *onsite data manager*. An energetic, technically savvy archaeologist appreciates such a position of responsibility and recognizes the importance of this role. We highly recommend this approach and proceed in this case study on the basis of having used an onsite data manager every season at Tell Keisan.

Collecting Field Data

Preparation is done, configuration is complete, the data manager is trained, and the real work begins! Low-end, battery-powered, rugged laptops running GEO-enabled OCHRE under Windows, military-grade barcode printers with fresh ribbons, and a drone with fully charged batteries join the other tools and supplies taken out to the site. In 2022, the RTK Rovers replaced the surveyor's laser-equipped transits (e.g., "Total stations" which had needed to be calibrated every morning to known benchmarks on the site). The new RTK technology gave field supervisors and their volunteer staff the means to "shoot points," capturing accurate x, y, z coordinates without needing specialized training or know-how.

In addition, almost daily over the course of the excavation the drone would fly its programmed route, hovering at 5 meters above the ground, capturing the progress of the excavation. Using photogrammetry techniques, the resulting photographs were stitched together into 3D models. From the resulting composite, an orthorectified, high-resolution, top-down image was produced, georeferenced in the ITM

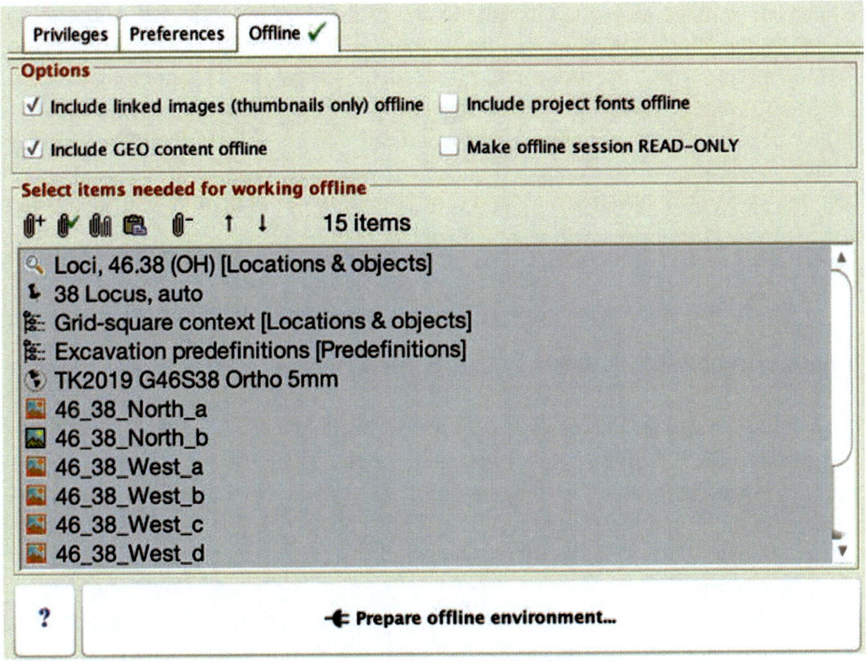

Fig. 10.16 The data manager prepares offline sessions in advance for each square supervisor

coordinate space,[15] and added to OCHRE as a record shot, providing both a bird's-eye perspective and documentation of the details on the ground. By the end of the season, this sequence of shots served as a virtual flip-book, animating the summer's progress.

Running OCHRE Offline

Many OCHRE projects work in remote areas where reliable Internet is not available onsite. In these cases, OCHRE can run in offline mode. At Tell Keisan, a laptop is assigned to each square supervisor. On the **Offline** tab of the Square supervisor's **User** profile, the data manager creates a list of all the items that need to be taken offline. This includes the Area and related units of excavation, predefinitions for data entry, and selected resources as reference (e.g., top plans or field photographs). OCHRE ensures that any dependencies are taken along (Fig. 10.16). While connected to the Internet, the data manager runs a process in OCHRE to prepare the

[15] Agisoft Photoscan software was using to process the drone images. Orthorectification adjusts the geometry of an image, removing the distortion due to differences of perspective. Georeferencing adds coordinate data to the image, so it knows where it is in space.

offline environment, allowing OCHRE to download, encrypt, and cache the needed data. Care must be taken to ensure that data is editable offline in only one offline session, but this works itself out naturally as data is segregated square by square.

Out in the field, when OCHRE is started up, it detects that there is no Internet service available and starts up in offline mode, creating a mini, self-contained OCHRE session from the prepared cache. Any needed geospatial data will have been downloaded and cached, too, and is used to present the Map View interface for the excavator. The square supervisor is now free to enter data directly into the offline version of the database while unconnected to the Internet.

Entering New Finds

Yesterday's drone photo serves as the basemap of the interactive, geo-enabled canvas in Map View. When an artifact is found, a new OCHRE item representing this new find is inserted into its logical containment context. Switching the cursor to a crosshair symbol, the mouse reports its specific location in space (within the project's coordinate system) as it is moved around the map. The supervisor clicks the canvas to capture the x, y coordinate of the findspot. A pin drops onto the map as visual feedback, confirming the location. Elevation data, the z-value, is added with a click of the Bluetooth button as OCHRE polls the Rover being held level over the findspot for a coordinate and drops it into the database field.[16] The supervisor then applies a Predefinition, using an appropriate template to describe the basic properties of this new item. The Predefinition will: attribute the supervisor as the observer of the properties[17]; time-stamp the observation; increment the unique serial number property designated to track the small finds; and automatically generate a Name for the new item based on the auto-naming formula. Here the Name includes a combination[18] of the Grid-Square designation plus the incremented serial number.

Barcode Labeling

As the new artifact is boxed or bagged for safe transport back to the lab a barcode is printed on a high-quality label, along with selected identifying human-readable information, and affixed to the box or bag. At Tell Keisan, laptops connect to rugged barcode printers via Bluetooth to produce labels on the spot. The barcode encodes the universally unique identifier (UUID) of the item which will track it throughout its life cycle, and which already forms the basis of its **Citation URL**.

[16] In prior seasons, z-values (elevations) were entered manually as readings were taken off the transit, or coded in the transit's data log, then downloaded and imported as a batch later.

[17] OCHRE has safeguards built in for offline use. For example, having the User's account designated as the item's Observer safeguards it from being edited by another user offline.

[18] That is, the concatenation-style derived Variable described earlier is used for auto-labeling, "S16-46.37#58."

Fig. 10.17 Artifacts are tagged with a unique identifier, digitally, and simultaneously with an indestructible barcode label

The process of entering new finds in the database and labeling them with barcodes repeats over and over throughout the day, again and again in each Square of excavation (Fig. 10.17).

Collecting Specialist's Data

While excavation and data collection are happening onsite, back at the dig compound members of the house staff—object registrar, ceramicists, archaeobotanists, faunal specialists, among others—are busy processing finds from the previous days' work, generating more specialized data. The dusty bone brought in from the field becomes a femur of a bovine exhibiting butchery marks. The newly washed potsherd is revealed to be a red burnished carinated bowl with everted flaring rim. It is common practice for specialists to compile their own spreadsheets or databases of their observations of the specimens, but how much better when the value added by specialists can supplement existing data about the items already collected in the master database. To maintain a record of the **Persons** contributing data, OCHRE allows multiple observations on any given item. That is, the original description by the supervisor in the field will comprise the first observation of an item. When the item is then processed by a specialist, a new observation can be added, supplementing, rather than replacing, the first. Each observation is time-stamped and appropriately attributed, creating a record of the history of discussion of the item.

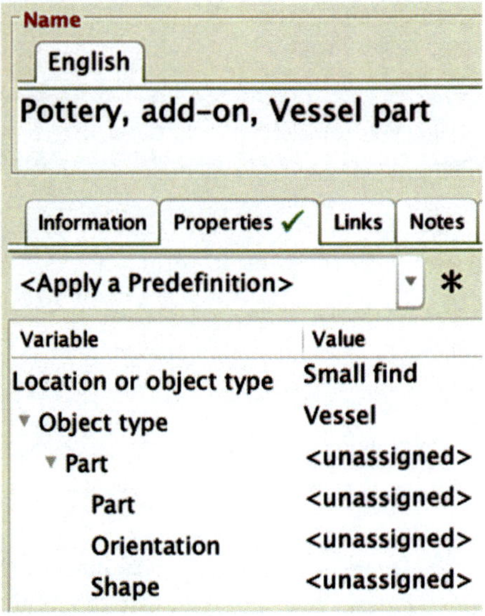

Fig. 10.18 Divide and conquer complex data entry by using a Predefinition add-on strategy

Managing *Highly Variable* Data: Predefinition Add-Ons

Given the variability of archaeological data, especially as specialists add highly detailed observations, for some items there will be many descriptors to apply; other items will have very little that can be said about them. A useful strategy is to have both a maximal predefinition which lists all the possible descriptors of an item as a form of documentation, and as a reminder to the data entry assistant, and a minimal one to use as a stub entry when there is not much to be said or the time to say it. Predefinitions can also be applied cumulatively and this, in fact, is a helpful approach (Fig. 10.18).

For a pottery item, say a Closed vessel, one can start with a Predefinition of a stub entry which marks it as a Ceramic, Vessel, with Closed Form, and which assigns a unique serial number and a name. If the rim is preserved, add-on a Vessel part predefinition and describe the shape and diameter of the rim. If the handle is present, add-on the Vessel part predefinition again, and describe the shape and style of the handle. If the base is present, add-on the Vessel part predefinition again, and describe the shape and style of the base. If the ceramic fabric is noteworthy, add-on the Fabric predefinition and specify color and inclusions. If the surface has been decorated, add-on the Treatment-Decoration predefinition and describe the treatment, color, and pattern. The intent is to describe just those features that are present for any given item, not to have a long list of place-holder values listing things that might have been said. This process results in a concise, yet comprehensive, record of highly variable data. For each item, the record indicates nothing more and nothing less than observable details.

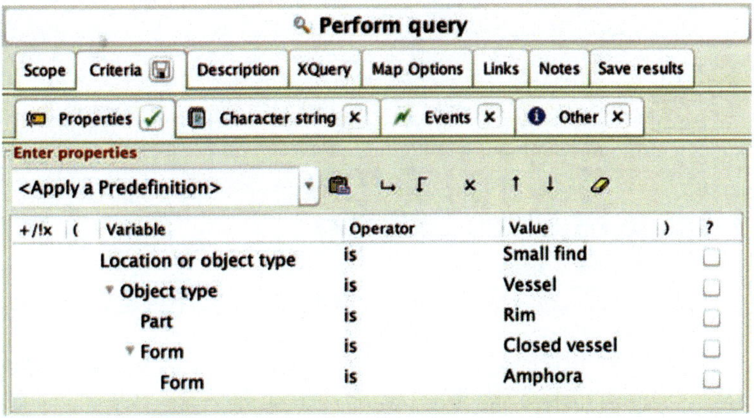

Fig. 10.19 A Query finds all Amphora Rims; matching items are saved to a Set

Managing *Highly Similar* Data: Tabular View

There may be times, though, when there are many similar items that share a common set of characteristics. A Classical Greek site might have dozens or hundreds of coins for which denomination, diameter, and weight will be cataloged. A collection of hundreds of arrowheads will share similar features. A Predefinition can be used to detail the needed descriptors then serve as the basis for a *tabular view*.

The Tell Keisan pottery collection abounds in iconic amphoras. Assume we put a student to work recording the rim diameters of these amphora. First, we identify the relevant items by running a Query and saving the results to a Set (Fig. 10.19).

Next, on the Set, we specify that the columns of the needed table should be based on the properties included in the given Predefinition, in this case the "Pottery, add-on, Rim diameter" Predefinition. On the Format Specification tab, we also check on an option to allow table editing. (Details of these steps are not pictured.)

Now, when we evoke the **Tabular View**, we have the option of editing the resulting table. It is a simple matter to navigate the table like a spreadsheet, entering the rim diameter values. Note, too, that this table is *taxonomically aware*. That is, the cells of the table represent variables still within their taxonomic context so that dropdown picklists can be generated with the appropriate contextual values. And although this view is constraining, it is not overly restrictive. If, for example, the data entry assistant notices a feature of interest, they can double-click the table row to pop-up the full entry for that item and edit it freely, adding notes or additional properties that are not represented in the current tabular view. OCHRE thereby constrains and facilitates reliable data entry, without compromising overall flexibility (Fig. 10.20).

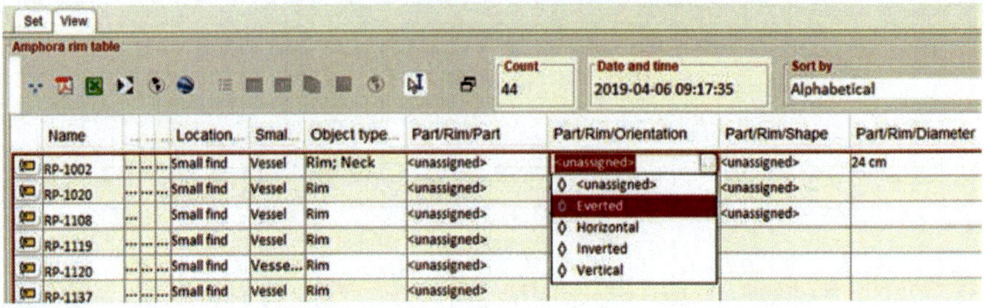

Fig. 10.20 Controlled spreadsheet-style editing of similar items is available in a tabular view

The efforts of the specialists working in house lagged the work in the field by at least a day or two, as pottery and bones were washed and dried. This allowed house staff to add data to the primary database without contention with the field staff's offline data. As specialist data was added, however, this became immediately available to the field staff in their next day's offline sessions. The excavator could see whether the pottery being found was of a significant ware or period, as identified by the expert, informing their progress in the field.

Similarly, excavators running OCHRE *offline* in the field added extensive daily journal entries describing their units of excavation. This information was synced from the field laptops to the main database in Chicago after lunch, becoming available already by the afternoon's work session to all members of the project team who were working *online*. The specialists working in-house had detailed, up-to-the minute, descriptions of the contexts from which the items had been collected, informing their analysis. This virtuous cycle of real-time data collection and integration greatly enriched the efforts of the entire enterprise.

Integration: Data Connected

Integrating the field data with the specialists' data is just the beginning. The overarching goal is to have all data generated by the project team available to all authorized members of the project within a common platform. This required integration to proceed on additional fronts.

Integrating Image Data

Throughout the season, the dig photographer was busy keeping up with photography of the collected objects, both record shots, and more detailed coverage of artifacts of special interest. These photographs were linked to their corresponding

OCHRE item using a drag-and-drop style interface almost as soon as they were shot. With a good Internet connection in the photography lab at our host kibbutz, OCHRE could seamlessly do the extra steps of creating a thumbnail and using SFTP (secure file transfer protocol) to move the image and its thumbnail to the server to be permanently stored there. This streamlined process provided an efficient and organized approach to capturing a photographic record of the small finds (Fig. 10.21).

Field photographs were also taken and hotspotted using tools provided by OCHRE. This allowed the field supervisor, or assistants, to identify regions on the image and link them to other OCHRE items. This was especially helpful for images which show the vertical cross-section of the baulks in "section drawings," thereby documenting information that could be difficult to interpret otherwise (Fig. 10.22).

Figure 10.23, a photo of the excavation team at Tell Keisan during the summer of 2016, illustrates another helpful use of hotspot links. Annotating an image, here linking to the Person items of the staff and volunteers, helps track the participants of each season's excavation.

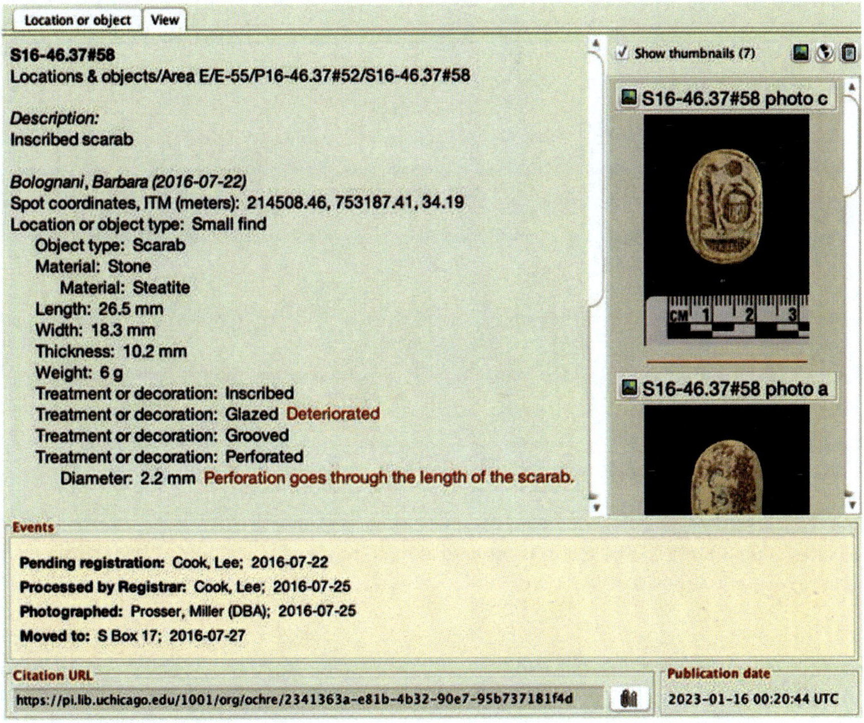

Fig. 10.21 Object photographs become available online almost as soon as they are taken

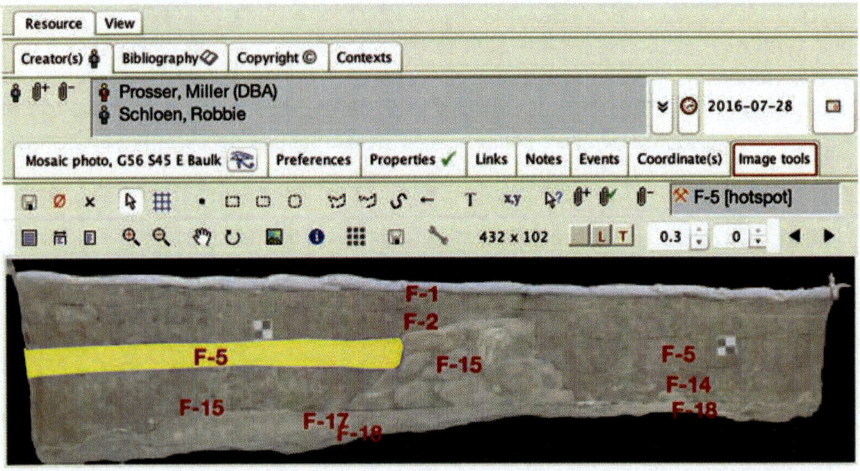

Fig. 10.22 Image tools are used to hotspot the photograph of the baulk, creating links to loci

Fig. 10.23 Hotspot links identify team members of the Tell Keisan 2016 season. S. Schloen is pictured at top-most left; M. Prosser is pictured at right-most end of the middle row. (Photograph courtesy of the Tell Keisan excavation)

Integrating Geospatial Data

As digging progressed and architecture emerged, time was allocated during the afternoon work sessions to trace from the high-resolution drone images the shapes of the visible features. The shapes were created as polygons in an ArcMap shapefile, each polygon labeled in the shapefile's attribute table by the Name of the OCHRE item it represented. That is, in the spirit of the item-based data model, *each* meaningful unit of excavation could identify the specific polygons needed to draw itself on a map.

The shapefiles of the excavated loci, one for Area E and another for Area F, were linked via the Map Options to the hierarchies representing Area E and Area F, respectively. For an item listed within Area E, for example, checking on its checkbox provided by Map View triggers a lookup of its geometry from the shapefile(s) assigned to Area E, and results in the consequent display of its shape (points, lines, polygons) on the map. With such tight integration between geospatial features and core database content, the map becomes live and interactive. Double-clicking an item on the map pops up its other related information, available to view or edit depending on access rights. Core project data need not be exported to external "geodatabase" systems, or redundantly copied into other environments, for the sake of visualizing geospatial relationships.

The itemization and integration of spatial data proved itself almost immediately at Tell Keisan to be of great value for validating the data capture process. It was obvious to tell which loci of excavation still needed to be documented, which pottery pails needed elevation readings, which small finds had not been assigned their findspot coordinates. If a checkbox was not present for an item in the navigation pane's checklist, that item did not know how to place itself on the map. Integrating the drawn shapes directly into OCHRE and overlaying them back onto the original photographs also ensured the accuracy of the drawings and made obvious any features or items of interest that had been missed.

Beyond data collection and data correction, the integration of geospatial data at the item level allows for meaningful visualization as connections are made between the core descriptive data and related polygon shapes. Map views can be generated based on queries of the primary data, targeting specific interests. In the example that follows, as architecture emerges, and the stratigraphic relationships are studied, walls, floors, and other features are assigned to "phases" represented as links to OCHRE Period items. Built-in styling tools and widgets are used to assign colors and patterns to shapes based on either Properties or Periods. The destruction phase in Area E (Phase 4) is checked "on" in the View, resulting in the styled display of only those features assigned to that phase. The slice of life from that destruction event comes into sharp relief (Fig. 10.24).

Once the excavated features had been articulated as drawn shapes traced from the photographs it was also possible to use OCHRE's Map View to print out a "top plan" as a reference for the excavator to take to the field each morning. When a wall was removed during the excavation, its corresponding OCHRE item could be toggled off the view. With a millimeter grid printed in the background, selected features displayed as outlines, scale set to 1:50, extent restricted to a 10-meter-by-10-meter square, and an optional semi-transparent photo as the backdrop, the square supervisor was doubly equipped to record the work of a new day. Although this same information was available digitally, the top plan was, for some, a welcome concession to the good old days of paper-based recording—a reassuring space for ad hoc scribbles, notes to self, and X-marks-the-spots (Fig. 10.25).

That same top plan would be returned at the end of the workday, often having been highly annotated and drawn upon. It was then scanned, georeferenced, and added back to OCHRE as a new Resource, capturing the record of that day's efforts. Tomorrow the process would repeat itself, the "paperwork" almost effortless.

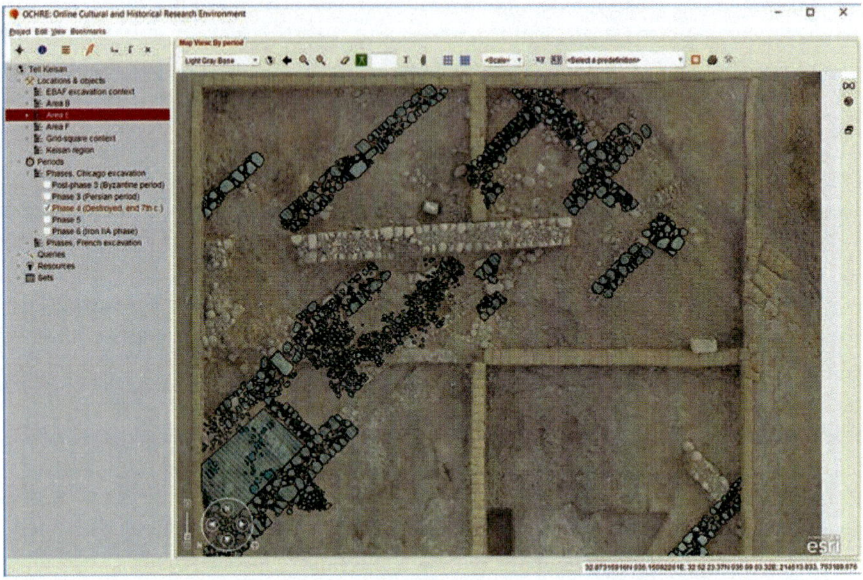

Fig. 10.24 Map styles bring to life the excavated items that are "in phase" based on Periods

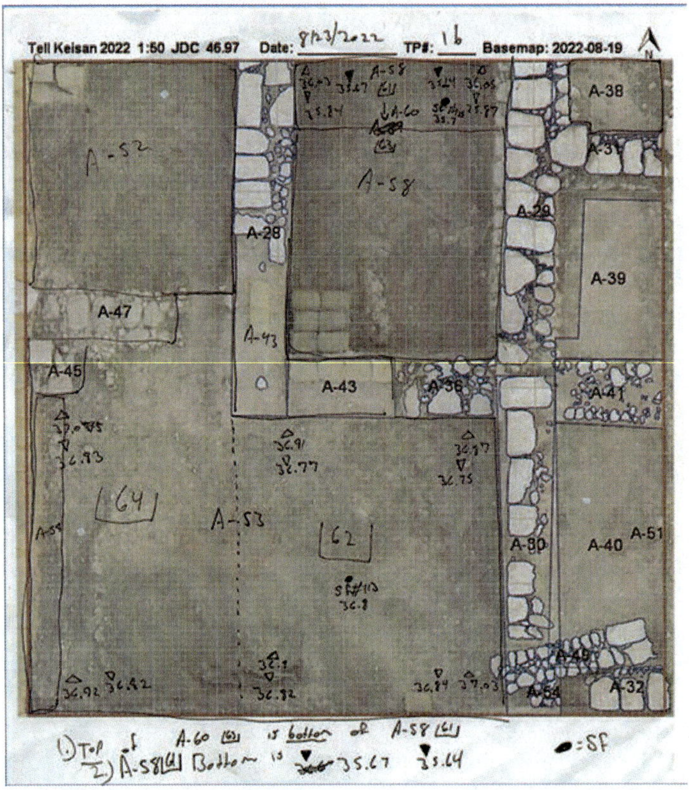

Fig. 10.25 Daily top plans for the excavation Squares were prepared in OCHRE's Map View with an overlaid grid and an underlying drone photo. (Image courtesy of the Tell Keisan excavation)

Integrating Legacy Data

Since the new areas of excavation were in proximity to the areas formerly dug by the French team, it was helpful to superimpose the new aerial photographs on the basemap along with the scanned plans of the older excavations. Were there correlations between these areas? Did the architectural features align? During the previous winter of 2015–2016, preparations had included a study of the excavation report published by the French teams which had worked the site in the 1970s. Maps published in their report were scanned, georeferenced, and added to OCHRE as "geospatial" Resource items thereby making them available to the new excavation team as reference materials. With a caveat that drawings from projects that predate modern techniques are not generally to the level of detail or accuracy available today,[19] it can still prove valuable to view legacy plans together with recent drone photographs, giving new perspectives on old data (Fig. 10.26).

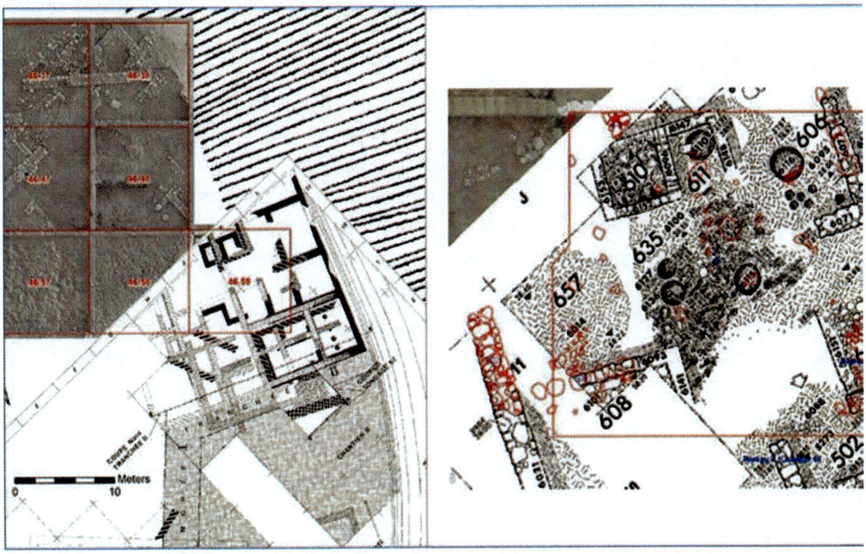

Fig. 10.26 Legacy top plans from the French excavation are georeferenced and compared to recent orthophotographs. (Prepared by A. M. Wright, courtesy of the Tell Keisan excavation)

[19] At Tell Keisan, we can still spot specific stones from the hand-drawn French plans on satellite images and aerial photographs, helping improve the accuracy of the alignment.

Evaluation: Data Corrected

Quality Control

The end of the week would find the field director online in OCHRE reading through the accumulated daily journal entries, adding notes or observations attributed to herself, studying the detailed drone photographs showing progress, and jotting down questions for the field staff for follow-up. The supervisor in one square is behind in taking elevations and needs a reminder to catch up. The stratigraphy in another square is getting interesting and more priority needs to be given to reading its pottery. The neighboring square is getting ahead of the others and perhaps workers should be re-allocated.

Meanwhile, the onsite data manager is running Queries, looking for incomplete data entry or managing workflow. Lists of items resulting from these queries can be compiled in Sets for further study or processing. Whose field photographs still need to be hotspotted? What objects are next in line for the illustrator? Can we pull all the geo-samples for the geologist coming to visit next week? Have all the photographs of the significant inscription been linked as references for the epigrapher looking at the data from Chicago? In addition, the GIS specialist updates Map View with the latest imagery so shapefiles and point clouds can be checked. There is no substitute for effectively real-time data!

The Tell Keisan project uses OCHRE's Events feature to assist with managing workflow. An event can be broadly defined, and project defined, so essentially anything can be tracked. Each Event can specify the agent (a link to a Person item), a place (a link to a Location item), or a thing (a link to any other item of any kind), along with a date (either absolute, or a link to a Period item) and comment. Furthermore, events can be paired with a fulfillment event as a counterpart; for example, the To-photograph event is fulfilled by the Photographed event. OCHRE queries can find all items whose event has not yet been fulfilled; that is, which items have been requested to be photographed but have not yet been photographed?

Inventory Control

One special event, the **Moved to** event, forms the basis of OCHRE's built-in inventory management system. Inventory is tracked by specifying, for each item, where it has been Moved to (Fig. 10.27). Storage locations are part of another, separate, secondary Locations & Objects hierarchy designated as the Inventory management hierarchy. The Tell Keisan project maintains an inventory of storage boxes at the Ben Gurion University of the Negev. Even though a given pottery vessel was found within a given Locus, it can be additionally contextualized as having been moved to a storage box. The same item is located in both locations. The Event on the item is, in effect, a link to the Inventory hierarchy. As items are moved, the inventory can be refreshed to generate a list of all items currently in storage.

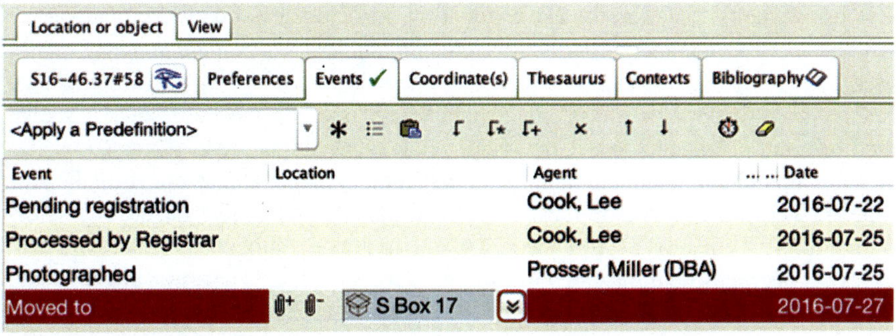

Fig. 10.27 Events track the processing of an item, identifying relevant persons and dates

During the final days of the excavation season, the registrar and her assistants set about packing up items for storage. As an artifact, or a bag of pottery, or a soil sample is packed away, the barcode scanner reads its label, pops up the associated database item, and lets the assistant add an Event, linking the item to the appropriate box, tray, drawer, closet, warehouse, or museum location that it is being **Moved to**. Despite the complexity of the logistics, as the dig disbands for the summer there is no excuse for not tracking items so that they can be found again for further study.

Although the students and volunteers have departed at the end of the excavation season, the field staff linger to finish up their final reports. All the data needed to synthesize their findings is available through their online, comprehensive, database environment—field notes, high-resolution photographs, pottery readings, faunal identifications, specialist commentary, and so on. The final reports are written, saved as PDF files, and added to OCHRE as **Resources**, available to all the project staff as they head home their separate ways (cue Ashokan Farewell).

Analysis: Auto-generation of Harris Matrices

For some projects, a key component of the final report is a Harris Matrix—a concise diagram summarizing the stratigraphical relationships among the units of excavation processed that season. Ever since Edward Harris published the definitive word on how to construct a "Matrix" for documenting the temporal succession of archaeological contexts, the Harris Matrix has been a de facto standard (Harris 1979, 1989). Harris defined the laws of archaeological stratigraphy: the law of superposition, the law of original horizontal, the law of original continuity, and the law of stratigraphic succession. With these laws as his basis, he defined a diagramming strategy to represent the stratigraphic sequence of a site. And ever since technology has shown any sign of intelligence, it has been every archaeologist's dream that the Harris Matrix could be automatically generated by an "intelligent" computational process. Allow us to illustrate how OCHRE's highly atomized, highly organized, and highly propertized items can be exploited for this purpose.

During the field season, the excavators dutifully capture properties indicating the relationship between loci of excavation. Remember how a relational property can be used to specify that "Locus B is earlier that Locus A" (which logically implicated Locus A as later than Locus B). And recall how each unit of excavation can be assigned the **Period** of occupation to which it belonged (as determined by the Chicago team).

With this detailed information at its disposal, OCHRE's ***Visualization Wizard*** (the VizWiz) provides the opportunity to auto-generate a Harris Matrix for a selection of items. Typically, a **Query** would be run to create a subset of items of interest; for example, all those units of excavation within a specified excavation area that had been assigned to a range of periods of interest. The Wizard would then prompt the user for necessary details; specifically, which are the relational **Properties** used in OCHRE that conform to the Harris notions of "superposition" (stratigraphic sequence, vertically related) and "correlation" (horizontally related) (Fig. 10.28),[20] and on which OCHRE **Period** hierarchy should the analysis be based?

In addition, the wizard gives the opportunity to create and use **Styles** to control the appearance of the resulting "graph," or matrix. Each unit of excavation (e.g., a Locus) is itemized on the graph, is clickable, and is styled according to its **Properties** (e.g., walls can be styled differently from floors or pits) and its assigned **Period**. Redundant links can be consolidated; contradictory links can be highlighted and resolved; missing links can be imputed[21]; and incorrect links can be re-assigned. The list of related items, which have not yet been assigned to a **Period**, is listed on a palette for consideration and assignment. This is not a simple static diagram. This is a navigable, interactive, customizable, and dynamic display: a dream come true (Fig. 10.29).

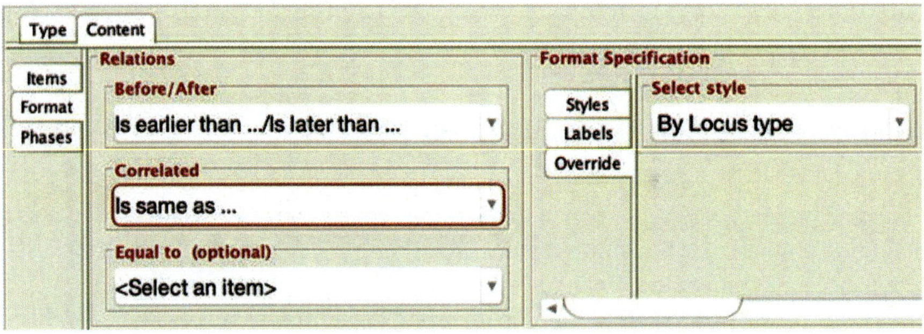

Fig. 10.28 The VizWiz prompts for details needed to auto-generate a Harris Matrix

[20] See Harris 1979, Fig. 9, p. 36. OCHRE allows for an "equals" relationship too which accommodates the case where a wall, for example, crosses an arbitrary grid/square boundary and is assigned a different number by a different field excavator. These can be equated as the same wall on the matrix diagram.

[21] If Locus A corresponds to Locus B and Locus B does not have a period assigned, we can impute that the Period for Locus B is the same as that of Locus A.

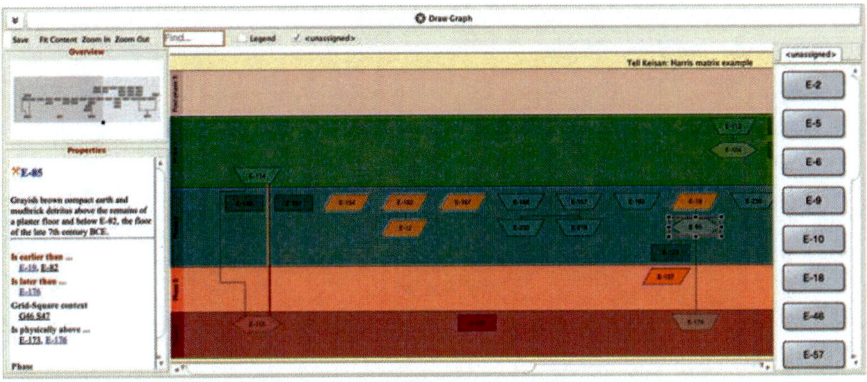

Fig. 10.29 An auto-generated Harris Matrix is derivable from field-based data capture

Analysis: Visualization of Wall E-8

To summarize the value of an item-based, integrated approach, having access to the same database item in a variety of analytic contexts—in edit mode, on a map, in a table, in a hotspotted image, and as part of a statistical analysis—consider the remains of wall foundation, Locus ***E-8***, which runs roughly East-West in Grid 46, across Square 37 and Square 38. E-8 was born digital, its database item created by Square 37 supervisor Barbara Bolognani while running OCHRE offline in the field during the 2016 excavation season, then further described by Square 38 supervisor Olivia Hayden. Both supervisors returned in subsequent years of the ongoing project to make new observations as the wall continued to be excavated. Figure 10.30 shows some of the details recorded in the field during excavation.

E-8 can be displayed in **Table View** as the result of a Query, along with all the other loci from these squares. A click on the yellow tag icon in the first column (or a double-click on the row) pops up the **Edit View** of that same database item (Fig. 10.31).

To document E-8 from alternative perspectives, its database item is later linked to field photographs using hotspots, thereby creating an interactive image (Fig. 10.32). A click on the styled orange polygon that marks E-8 in **Image View** pops up the **Standard View** of its properties, images, notes, and events.

A user-defined OCHRE Style specifies the color, pattern, or other representation of an item based on its assigned properties or periods (Fig. 10.33). Whether the item is shown in a standard view, in a map, as an image hotspot, or in a graph view, the properties or periods of the item determine how it is presented, or represented, thereby providing a consistent display of the data, regardless of the specific format or view.

Like all OCHRE links, a hotspot link is bidirectional. The **Standard View** of E-8 (Fig. 10.34) displays as much read-only information as is known about the item. This View can also list the hotspot cutouts as linked images on request. If E-8 is

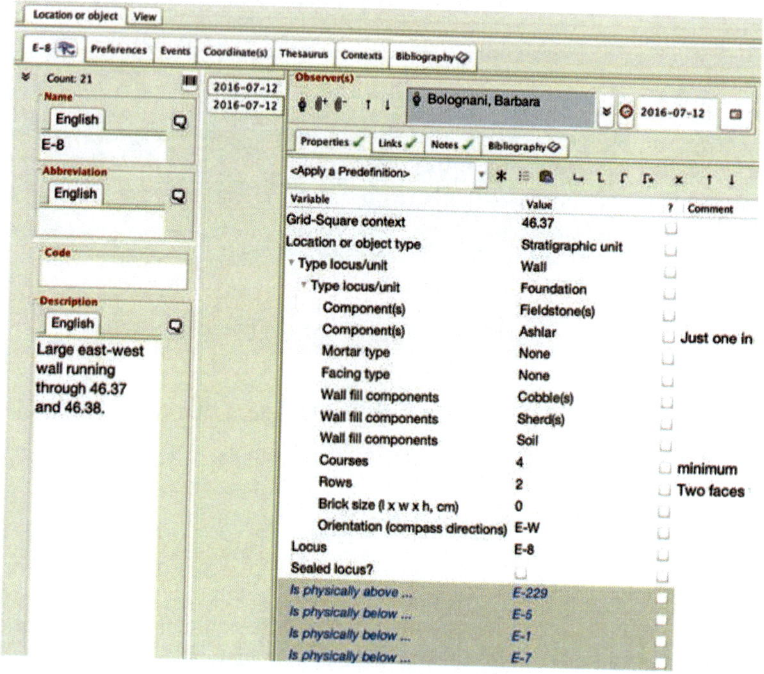

Fig. 10.30 The wall E-8 is shown in Edit View with multiple observations

Walls in Phase 3: Default table

Name	...	Description	Obs. #	Obs. Date	Observer
E-8	..	Large east-west wall running through 46.37 and 46.38.	Obs. 1	2016-07-12	Bolognani, Barbara
E-8	..	Large east-west wall running through 46.37 and 46.38.	Obs. 2	2016-07-12	Hayden, Olivia
E-30	..	Stone foundation of a wall, running parallel to E-8. Phase 3	Obs. 1	2016-07-15	Bolognani, Barbara
E-43	..	Hardened compact layer of mudbrick detritus found especi...	Obs. 1	2016-07-20	Edrey, Meir
E-50	..	A segment of a wall, one course high , built on an E-W axis ...	Obs. 1	2016-07-22	Edrey, Meir
E-58	..	ashy/burnt layers consisting of concentric, superimposed c...	Obs. 1	2016-07-25	Johnston, Philip
E-79	..	Wall foundation stub oriented NWxSE that departs from the ...	Obs. 1	2016-07-29	Johnston, Philip
E-79	..	Wall foundation stub oriented NWxSE that departs from the ...	Obs. 2	2019-07-11	Pace, Leann
E-81	..	EW stonewall foundation Phase 3	Obs. 1	2016-07-29	Bolognani, Barbara
E-81	..	EW stonewall foundation Phase 3	Obs. 2	2019-07-20	Bolognani, Barbara
E-88	..	Locus bordered by the cobble floor from the north, and by ...	Obs. 1	2018-07-03	Edrey, Meir
E-110	..	undulating pottery rich deposit under E-95 and E-96 with gr...	Obs. 1	2018-07-09	Pace, Leann
E-118	..	Soil containing several large and many small stones that wa...	Obs. 1	2018-07-11	Hayden, Olivia
E-124	..	Pottery rich, brownish gray matrix beneath E-113, with medi...	Obs. 1	2018-07-12	Wilson, Charles
E-132	..	East - west fieldstone wall in east-central area of square, pr...	Obs. 1	2018-07-13	Hayden, Olivia
E-140	..	Ash under the clay layer (E-139)	Obs. 1	2018-07-13	Pace, Leann
E-158	..	Northwest corner of the square, a splay cut by the N portion...	Obs. 1	2018-07-18	Kerr, Emma

Fig. 10.31 Multiple observations of locus E-8 are shown in Table View with other walls

Fig. 10.32 A photograph (F16–77) delimits E-8 using a polygonal hotspot, styled "By Locus type"

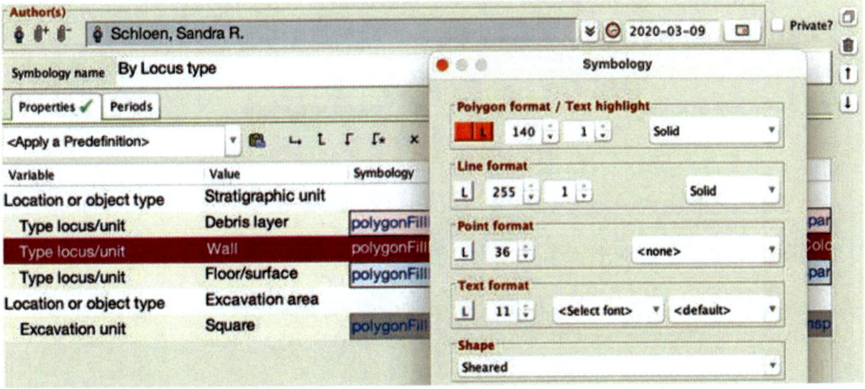

Fig. 10.33 The Style "By Locus type" colorizes items based on their Properties

accessed via OCHRE's leftmost navigation pane, all its sub-items are also available by drilling down on the Area E hierarchy, starting at the E-8 item.

Later, a GIS specialist uses a georeferenced image in mapping software to trace a vector shape representing the stones of this wall foundation. When the resulting shapefile is integrated in OCHRE and when the locus is activated in Map View, OCHRE queries the attribute table of the shapefile for the shape named E-8 to display on the map. In Fig. 10.35, the wall can be seen, properly colorized using the selected Style ("By Locus type"), running East-West across the baulk between the two squares. Clicking the shape representing the wall pops up its Edit View where details can be added. This is not a different item but a different view of the same item.

As analysis proceeds, Period links are added to the locus details which, along with relational properties indicating "earlier-than" and "later-than" relationships among the loci are used to auto-generate a **Harris Matrix View**. Although

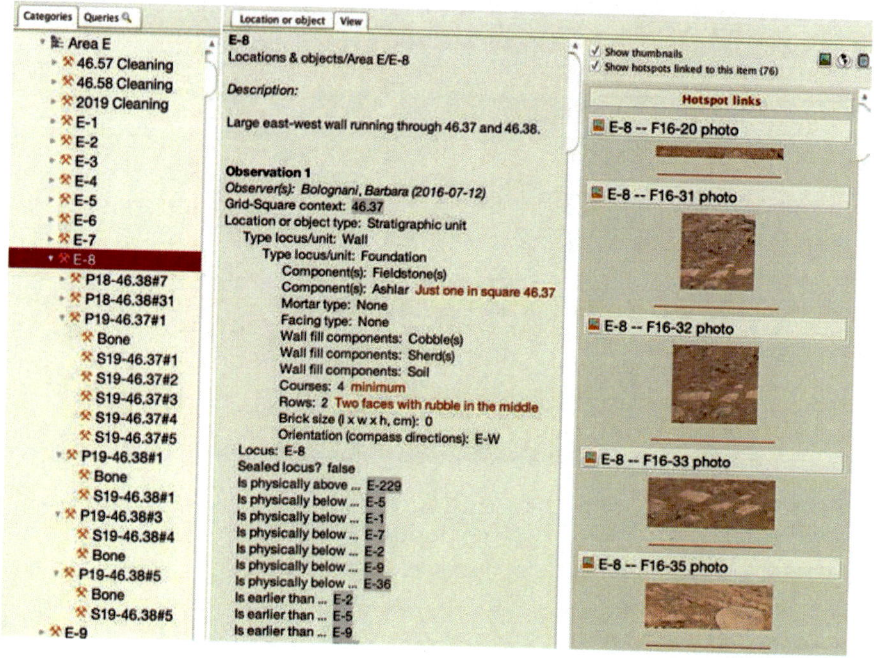

Fig. 10.34 The Standard View consolidates all details of E-8 in a comprehensive display

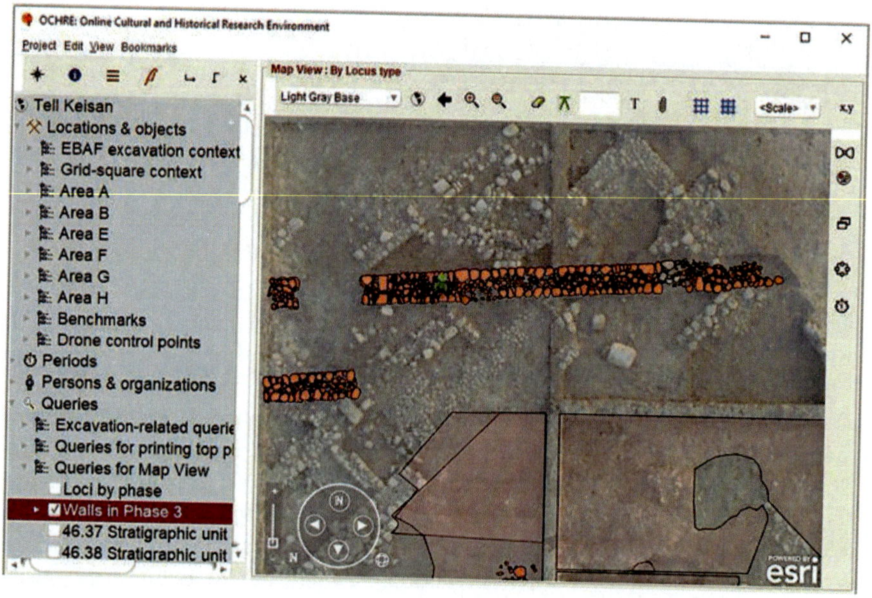

Fig. 10.35 OCHRE's Map View shows the styled extent of E-8 crossing square boundaries

relevant relational Properties are included in this view by default, a click on the still-orange polygon that marks E-8 pops up its full details, as expected (Fig. 10.36).

OCHRE's **Visualization Wizard** provides a wide variety of built-in options for visualizing statistical features of the data. A pie chart summary by locus type (Fig. 10.37) indicates that E-8, together with the other walls, makes up 3% of the loci in this excavation square.

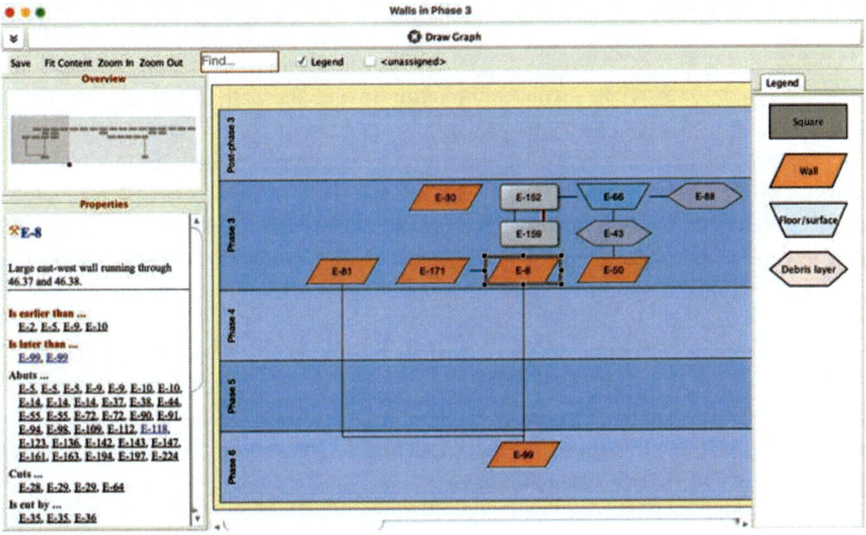

Fig. 10.36 Relationships among walls, styled "By Locus type" are shown on a Harris Matrix

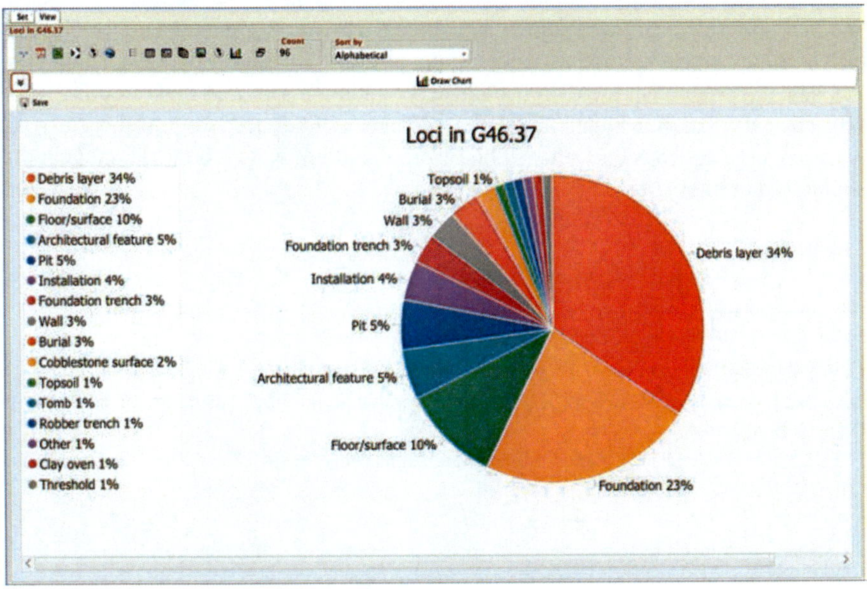

Fig. 10.37 A pie chart summarizes the types of loci in Grid 46, Square 37 (in Chart View the styling of the chart is left to JavaFx)

Instant Publication: Just Add OCHRE

Creating Web-Based Publications Using the Citation URL

There are many reasons, often valid, why it is difficult to publish the results of a summer's work. But let us not require that "slow archaeology"[22] be, in fact, slow. It is regrettable when data, having just been "born digital," reaches old age before achieving publication at the opposing end of its life cycle. In an online, item-based, environment like OCHRE, instant publication brings the data to life. **Right-click, Publish** is all that is needed to expose an item to the world or, more specifically, to the World Wide Web. Because it is born digital, each item is already primed with its universally unique, persistent identifier. Because it is online, it is available anywhere, referenced by its **Citation URL**[23] which is an HTTP version of that persistent identifier. And because it is item-based, the excavators can be selective and judicious, publishing only those items which they have chosen to make public (Fig. 10.38).

When an item's Citation URL is used in a browser, or by an HTML tag,[24] it resolves to a call to the OCHRE API which fetches the requested data for that item from the OCHRE publication server.[25] The item's published content is returned by the API as XML, by default, and is automatically styled, unless otherwise specified, by the default OCHRE stylesheet (an XSLT).

The default OCHRE stylesheet exposes related links to images or other linked content. This creates extensive click-through potential to other published items. Clicking one of the **Resource Links**, for example, triggers a call to the Citation URL of the clicked-upon Resource item, which displays its published view in another browser window. Projects can create custom stylesheets to format the OCHRE content to their own specifications or allow OCHRE's default publication mechanisms to publish the data instantly. By having a tool that makes publication both easy and fast, it is hoped that archaeologists will not need to view this stage of research as an onerous one but will be inspired and motivated to tackle publication sooner rather than later.

---

[22] See *Fast Versus Slow* in the conclusion (Chap. 13).

[23] https://pi.lib.uchicago.edu/1001/org/ochre/2341363a-e81b-4b32-90e7-95b737181f4d.

[24] For example, an item's Citation URL might be the value of the "href" attribute of an HTML link tag such as <a href = '…'></a>.

[25] See Chap. 9 for details of creating online publications using the OCHRE API.

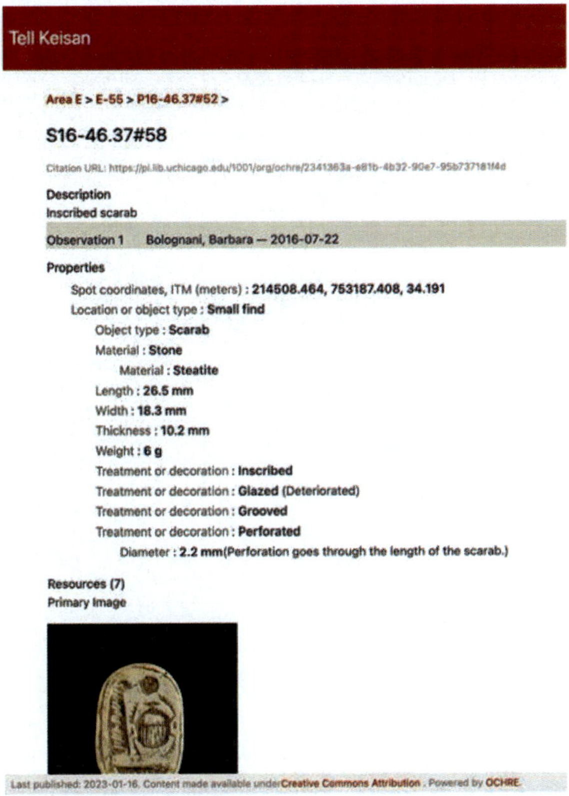

Fig. 10.38 An item's Citation URL makes it accessible to the world, in one easy step

Creating Interactive Documents Using the Citation URL

Another common use for the Citation URL is to create an *interactive* PDF document. At the end of the summer, the field director writes a final report for each Area using Microsoft Word. For every item of excavation referenced within this document, its Citation URL is copied and pasted into a hyperlink on the text representing the item. When this document is saved as a PDF, the hyperlinks become clickable. As a reader peruses the document and clicks an embedded hyperlink, the published version of the linked OCHRE item is displayed in a pop-up window, compliments of the OCHRE API (Fig. 10.39).

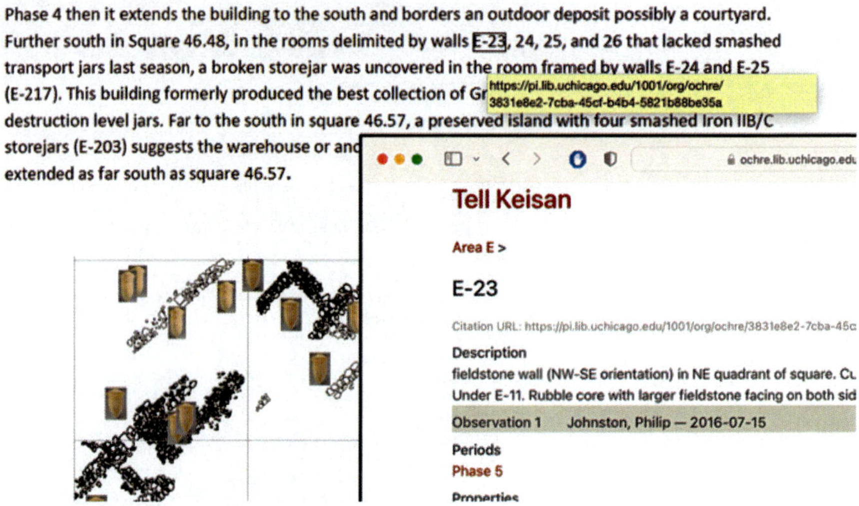

Fig. 10.39 Embedded hyperlinks based on an item's Citation URL add vitality to the 2018 Field Report (by E. Bloch-Smith)

Conclusion

Using the strategies discussed in this case study, data collected by the project was visible, editable, query-able, and accessible to all members of the project team on a day-to-day basis. This tight cycle of data collection and data integration, combined with the means of coherent graphical visualization in a common environment, greatly enabled the continuous evaluation, re-evaluation, exploration, and discussion of the excavation results in real time. The value of such integration was noted, in principle if not in practice, at the workshop on *Mobilizing the Past*:

> … the syncing of visual, spatial, and textual records as they are collected by multiple users in the field and lab prevents data loss or corruption and … enables an interdisciplinary conversation between excavators, supervisors, and material specialists that can inform not only interpretation but excavation strategy in mid-stream (Rabinowitz 2016, p. 501).

Since OCHRE is a generic, comprehensive, integrative, database platform, not specific to any one project, and not more relevant for one region of the world compared to any other, such methods could be utilized by archaeological field projects anywhere.

Chapter 11
Digital Philology Case Study: The Ras Shamra Tablet Inventory

Introduction

This case study illustrates a digital philology project, the Ras Shamra Tablet Inventory (RSTI) which is characterized by a wide range of integrated data. It consists of a catalog of inscribed objects, a corpus of digital text editions, a repository of digital images, GIS data, and much more. This case study will be of interest to scholars producing digital text editions. More broadly, RSTI will be of interest to researchers faced with a mountain of legacy data to which they wish to add new data and analysis. This is a daunting task, but this case study will demonstrate that the comprehensive, flexible, item-based approach, as implemented by the OCHRE platform, is up to the challenge.

Growing from the dissertation research of M. Prosser, and later incorporating a portion of the decades of voluminous work from co-director Dennis Pardee, the Ras Shamra Tablet Inventory integrates textual, archaeological, spatial, prosopographic,[1] and image data. The project has many research goals. At the core is an effort to create reliable text editions of the Late Bronze Age texts from Ras Shamra-Ugarit. Integrated with the textual editions is the spatial data generated over the course of nearly 90 years of archaeological excavation by the joint Syria-French Mission de Ras Shamra.[2] Pardee and Prosser, along with Robert Hawley and Carole Roche-Hawley, traveled to Syria as part of the epigraphic arm of the Mission de Ras

[1] Prosopography is the study of social and family connections among a group of people. In the absence of explicit biographical information, personal names are typically used to infer relationships.

[2] Because RSTI is currently not a collaboration with the archaeological team, any archaeological data is digitized from publications. The current members of *Mission de Ras Shamra* publish articles primarily (but not exclusively) in the journal *Syria* (Paris, Geuthner) and in the publication series *Ras Shamra-Ougarit* (Leuven, Peeters). In previous decades, the team also published in the series *Ugaritica* (Paris, Guethner) and *Mission de Ras Shamra* (Paris, Imprimerie National).

S. R. Schloen, M. C. Prosser, *Database Computing for Scholarly Research*, Quantitative Methods in the Humanities and Social Sciences,
https://doi.org/10.1007/978-3-031-46696-0_11

Shamra. In this capacity, thousands of photographs of the tablets from Ugarit were captured by this team. RSTI presently holds the world's largest repository of photos of these tablets.[3] Even though the textual data is still in the process of being added and curated, the image data has already begun to be published in standard web formats. The civil war that began in 2011 in Syria has made ongoing research and travel to this area impossible, regretfully. Many sites and objects of cultural and historic significance have been severely impacted by the war, being damaged, destroyed, or lost (Mantilla and Knezevic 2022). As a result, the photographic record preserved in the RSTI database is of unique value. This project takes seriously the responsibility both to safeguard and to publish this important digital archive.

For the RSTI project, OCHRE is more than just a data repository. It provides a variety of tools and mechanisms for integrating a wide range of data in creative and powerful ways. These tools help the investigator interrogate the data. What sort of inventive analyses can we perform when all our research data is integrated within a common platform? We can create epigraphic letter charts sorted by genre. We can visualize the various tablet archives over a backdrop of excavation reports or satellite images. We can ask an intelligent wizard to suggest words to fill in broken passages of text. On a more practical or mundane level, we can account for every word, every proper name, and every place name in every text and navigate between them. And of course, we can publish it all to the web to share with the world.

Furthermore, as implemented in OCHRE, RSTI has proven itself to be a flexible research environment to which we can add any new subset of data as we discover it. We were fortunate to inherit a large set of tablet photos from a researcher who produced them while writing a dissertation on the technical mechanism for writing cuneiform alphabetic Ugaritic (Ellison 2002). These thousands of images were added to the database along with our own image **Resources**, credited to the original photographer. Both sets of images are now available for inspection and comparison in integrated views of the text.

When a new volume of research on Ugarit is published, we can quickly and easily update the **Taxonomy** of variables and values to describe this new set of information. Whether the new publication covers objects carved from ivory, seal impressions, architecture, the divine pantheon, or even new text editions, RSTI can integrate this new subset of information with very little effort. We do not need to create a new table and configure it to relate to the already existing tables. No—we jump right in by adding these new database items into the highly flexible data model. If we are adding excavated objects, they are inserted within the **Locations & objects** spatial hierarchy of the site of Ugarit. If we need to add a new excavation area, it is easily inserted as a child of the broader containing area. Over time, the spatial hierarchy in RSTI has expanded to include all the areas excavated by the Mission de Ras

[3] RSTI also includes a large set of close-up tablet photographs generously contributed by Dr. John Ellison.

Fig. 11.1 Excavation areas at Ras Shamra are itemized in an extensive spatial hierarchy

Shamra (Fig. 11.1). There is much to say about the value of this comprehensive research environment for the RSTI project, but first some background about the impressive site of Ugarit.

An Overview of Ugarit and the Ras Shamra Tablet Inventory

Around 3200 years ago in what is now the Lattakia governorate of Syria, a small kingdom named Ugarit was about to collapse, never to be rebuilt. But let us back up another few thousand years. Beginning in the Neolithic period and continuing for roughly 7000 years, various population groups inhabited this site. Over millennia, population groups came and went. One settlement would be abandoned and a new one built on top of the ruins of the previous one. New inhabitants of the site would reuse some of what was present but might, for example, lay down a new floor over the existing floor. Eventually, this constant rebuilding and resettling process would result in a raised mound, a feature known as a tell. Throughout the countryside around modern-day Ras Shamra, one can spot others of these ancient settlement sites while driving along the highway. They are characterized by sloping sides and generally flat tops. These buttes or small plateaus are not natural geological formations, despite their hill-like appearance. They are the accumulated remains of ancient settlements.

The tell of Ras Shamra-Ugarit is formed from the deposited remains of thousands of years of mudbrick, wood, and stone structures. On the top of the tell of Ras Shamra-Ugarit, archaeologists uncovered the last phase of significant occupation dating to the Late Bronze Age (c. 1600–1200 BCE). There is evidence of limited usage of the site in later periods. In the Late Bronze Age, Ugarit was a flourishing and vibrant kingdom.[4] But with the growing instability in the region, due to multiple factors, the kingdom of Ugarit would collapse shortly after 1200 BCE.[5] Its importance would not be discovered again until 1928, when a local pastoralist accidentally stumbled upon an underground tomb at the nearby coastal site of Minet al-Beida.[6] Soon after this discovery, plans were made to investigate Minet al-Beida and later the neighboring site of Ugarit, known then by its Arabic name, Ras Shamra. In 1929, French Archaeologist Claude Schaeffer with George Chenet launched the first archaeological investigation of the site of Ras Shamra.[7] In the very first season, they discovered tablets written in a then-unknown language and writing system. Over the following 90 years, the Syrian-French mission to Ras Shamra would uncover this lost city with its rich history and culture.[8]

It is the final period of the site that most interests us because this phase of the occupation has yielded a large corpus of texts, written in various scripts and languages. About 5000 texts have been discovered to date. The local language, Ugaritic, was written most commonly in a locally invented cuneiform alphabetic script. Like all hand-written cuneiform, letters in this script are formed by impressing a stylus into moist clay to form a series of triangular wedges (Fig. 11.2).

In addition to alphabetic Ugaritic, the scribes produced thousands of texts in logosyllabic Akkadian, also written in a cuneiform script (Fig. 11.3). The texts in various genres provide a glimpse into a wide spectrum of Ugaritian culture. While nearly every excavated area of the site yielded some sort of inscribed object, the majority of texts were discovered in what appear to be the remains of ancient archives. A structure known as the House of the High Priest is located on an elevated part of the tell called the Acropolis, near two major temples. At this location, excavators discovered the famous mythological texts that recount a tale of the local storm god Baal, and epic tales of ancestral heroes Kirta, ʾAqhatu, and Daniʾilu. Excavations in the Royal Palace uncovered the personal correspondence of the

[4] For an introduction to the site in English, see Yon (2006).

[5] See the contributions (in French) in section three, "*Les derniers temps de l'histoire du royaume*," in Yon et al. (1995).

[6] For a recounting of the discovery and decipherment of Ugaritic, cf. Day (2002, pp. 37–38).

[7] See the popular report in the Illustrated London News (1929).

[8] Useful starting points are Watson and Wyatt (1999) HUS and Calvet and Yon (2008).

Fig. 11.2 RS 2.[003]+, a portion of the Kirta epic. (Photograph by M. Prosser, copyright PhoTEO)

Fig. 11.3 RS 34.141 is an Akkadian letter from Ras Shamra. (Photograph by M. Prosser, copyright PhoTEO)

kings and queens of Ugarit as well as documents produced during the day-to-day administration of the palace's business affairs. Text archives from the houses of important and affluent individuals living in the city of Ugarit but outside the Royal Palace demonstrate that the kingdom functioned as something like a large business enterprise, mostly for the benefit of the royal family. There is evidence of the transferring of raw materials to specialists and the movement of finished goods. From the mundane lists of personal names to the personal correspondence of the royal family to epic tales of heroes and gods, the texts from Ugarit paint the picture of a rich Bronze Age culture.

Preparation

Capturing an adequate picture of a rich historical culture, digitally, is easier said than done. It is tempting just to start keying data into a spreadsheet table. This quick and easy process gives a sense of accomplishment; after all, it is satisfying to see row after row of information accumulate. But it is a false sense of accomplishment. Only later do we realize that we did not atomize the data enough, that the columnar approach is difficult to reformat, or that we did not create the necessary relationships in the data. Without a careful planning stage, we run the risk of organizing data in a way that makes them difficult to query, retrieve, and reorganize. Having been through the process of creating an OCHRE project from a data set which evolved over many years—consisting of a series of unrelated Excel spreadsheets, Word documents, and a Microsoft Access database—we offer guidance, and lessons learned, in the pages that follow.

How Far Is Far Enough?

One of the most important steps in the planning process is the identification of the atomic units of study, the *minimal, meaningful parts*. This depends entirely on the research question(s) we wish to address. RSTI maximizes the atomization possible along both the epigraphic and discourse dimensions of textual data. Every alphabetic or logosyllabic grapheme visible on an inscribed object is transliterated and recorded as an epigraphic unit and organized in context, from the surface of the tablet to the column and line of text. This degree of granularity is necessary for our purposes for multiple reasons. First, we wish to track orthographic variations of words in a glossary; the spelling of a word is essentially the combination of all the graphemes used to create that word. Second, we wish to comment on the interpretations of the readings of the graphemes, some of which are broken and thus require supporting argumentation.

Not every project requires this level of atomization. The word level is often sufficient as the most atomic unit of a text. While sign-by-sign atomization may seem like overkill to some, for a project like RSTI where extensive discussion, or scholarly arguments, may take place over the interpretation of specific signs, the itemization of individual units enables careful, precise, and attributable documentation.

Slow Versus Fast

The tasks described here—representing findspots of tablet archives, transcribing detailed text editions—require a significant amount of manual effort. We are carefully reading published volumes and manually transforming data from these publications into data in RSTI. We perform this research in a "slow" manner, but we insist on using the traditional methodologies used by philologists for generations before us. When possible, we sit with a tablet in hand, under magnification. We transcribe the text sign by sign. We make copious epigraphic notes on the state of preservation of each cuneiform sign. We take pains to identify the grammatical properties of each word, the syntax of each phrase.

This all may sound distinctly un-digital. Taking the slow food movement as an imperfect metaphor, there is intrinsic value in proceeding slowly. The slow food movement was a rejection of the ever-increasing industrialization of the food production process, opposing the tendency toward a fast-food lifestyle. Some critics of digital research methodologies have taken up this movement as a model for reflecting on the nature and future of Digital Humanities.[9] What expectations should we have for the role of computers in our research? Do computers change the character of our research? Maybe it is because we are philologists, but we still wish to perform philological research. Although it is "slow," we prefer the term *intentional*.[10] We are not ready to cede to the computer the task of reading the text for the sake of expedience. Scholarship falls to the scholars in this research project. The tasks of data management, manipulation, and publication fall to the database system. At the nexus of these aspects of the research, we make use of powerful tools that can speed our research—tools that facilitate scholarship without supplanting it.

Data Integration

Spatial Data (Locations & Objects)

Digitizing Legacy Data

The first set of data imported into the RSTI project in OCHRE was a spreadsheet listing tablet numbers with findspots, publication information, and descriptions of language, writing systems, as well as tablet measurements. This spreadsheet was provided by Pardee and mirrored the data he and Pierre Bordreuil published as *La Trouvaille Épigraphique de l'Ougarit* (Fig. 11.4).[11]

The spreadsheet also provided two key pieces of spatial information about the location where each tablet was found: the general area on the site and the precise topographic point assigned by the excavators. The general area refers to a rather broad spatial area on the site, such as the Acropolis, the Royal Palace, or the Southern City. The topographic point gives a more specific location using a format

[9] See Prosser (2020) on the use of digital tools as relates to the potential for deskilling domain area specialists and to the expectation of a necessary increase in speed.

[10] On the issue of "slow archaeology," see also Caraher (2016).

[11] Even though it is out of date and in need of correction, the volume by Bordreuil and Pardee (1989) is still valuable.

Index	Inventory	Find spot	Description	Museum Number	Publication	Aliases	Images
1	RS 1.001	Acropole, Maison du Gr. Prêtre: «nid de tablettes» (= p.t. 300)	Alphabétique 110 x 140 x 35	M8214 = A2714 (AO 12.015)	CTA 34 (Syria 10 [1929], pl. LXI, no 1) RSO XII 1 Manuel 8	KTU 1. 39 UT 1	Photo CTA, pl. XXXIX ; Schweich, pl. XXIV / 1-2 (recto seulement). Exposé.
2	RS 1.002	Acropole, Maison du Gr. Prêtre: «nid de tablettes» (= p.t. 300)	Alphabétique 162 x 155 x 40	AO 11.993	CTA 32 (Syria 10 [1929], pl. LXII, no 2) RSO XII 2 Manuel 9	KTU 1. 40 UT 2	Photo CTA, pl. XXXVII; AuOrSupp 3 (1992), pl. II; Aux origines (2004), p. 269 (recto); Manuel 9 (CD-ROM).
3	RS 1.002 [A]	Acropole, Maison du Gr. Prêtre: «nid de tablettes» (= p.t. 300)	Alphabétique 18 x 19 x 2	AO 11.993	CTA 32 RSO XII 2	KTU 1. 40	Photo CTA, pl. XXXVII (petit fragment détaché). Enregistré par erreur dans pr. éd. sous le no RS 1-11.[111]

Fig. 11.4 Tabular data is ordered by tablet number and grouped by excavation season. (Excavators assigned numbers to all objects registered during the excavation seasons. A tablet from the first excavation season at Ras Shamra, for example, would begin with the number RS 1. To this prefix was added a sequential number representing the inventory number assigned by the excavators, for example, RS 1.001, the first item from the first season)

like 01:300, that is, excavation season one, point three hundred. The topographic points were usually published on excavation maps and are sometimes referenced in the daily journals and official publications of the archaeological team.

A spatial hierarchy in RSTI tracks the findspots of the inscribed objects from Ras Shamra. "Ugarit" is listed at the highest level of the containment hierarchy in the **Locations & objects** category, representing the entire kingdom of Ugarit. "Ras Shamra" is a child item beneath this spatial unit referring specifically to the site. The findspots are listed within excavation areas within the site. For RS 1.001, the excavation area is the Acropolis, an area on the northeast section of the site where the excavators uncovered temples to the Semitic gods Baal and Dagan. Working through the legacy data in our spreadsheet, we created detailed and multi-branching hierarchies of findspots. Some areas attest more highly articulated branches of subareas. For example, the full spatial hierarchy of RS 1.001 is Ras Shamra > Acropolis > House of the High Priest. In that same House of the High Priest were found 185 others tablets or tablet fragments (Fig. 11.5).

Item-Based Versus Class-Based

In the process of transforming data from the tabular style published in TEO to the hierarchical model used in OCHRE, database items were created. What had been data stored in cells in a row and column format became individual database items. This itemization process—or what may be called the process of *atomization*—is a common first step for any project converting legacy data into OCHRE-style data.

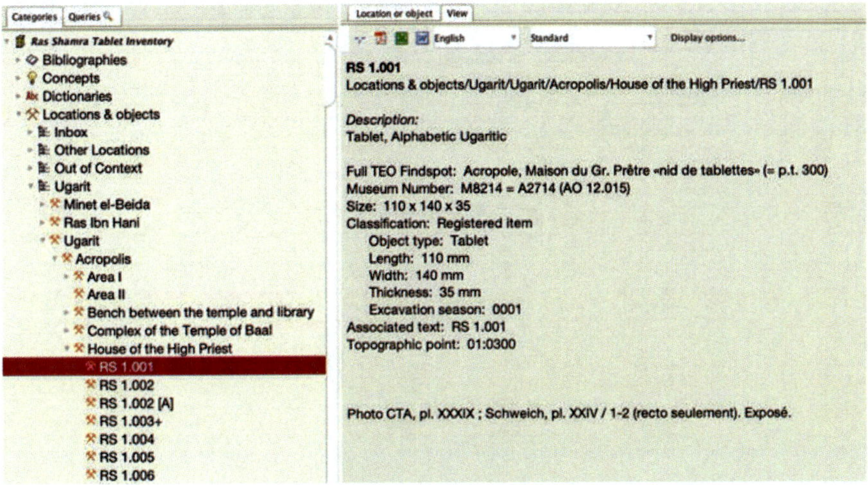

Fig. 11.5 Each row of the spreadsheet becomes its own database item, in excavation context, described only by the properties that are relevant to this item

When data is removed from tables and stored as items, it provides a great deal more flexibility to the researcher. For example, if the Acropolis requires descriptive metadata properties that do not apply to the Royal Palace, those can be recorded solely on the Acropolis item. If these two excavation areas were in the same table—or in a table of excavation areas in a relational database—a new column would need to be added for a single bit of information that applies only to the Acropolis. Those who have created relational databases will understand the difficulty this poses as the network of tables becomes more expansive, more interdependent, and as a result sometimes more fragile. The item-based approach to data eliminates this design consideration. When a researcher imagines a new metadata property, one merely adds the Variable and Value to the project Taxonomy and begins using it only on the items to which it applies.

The implication of the item-based approach is that RSTI does not store objects of the same type (class) in discrete lists. In other words, there is not an explicit list of all ceramic vessels; there is no stored list of all Akkadian tablets. However, these ceramic vessels or these tablets can be discovered in their respective item-based hierarchies using a Query, then displayed as a table of query results. As we add a new ceramic vessel to the hierarchy, we add properties to that item. The properties describe the type of object, a vessel, and can describe its other features. When the user wishes to review a list of all ceramic vessels, a query can find and display this class of items. This illustrates a philosophy of data organization practiced in RSTI and in OCHRE more generally. The list, whether a simple list or a more complex spreadsheet, is a secondary, derivative form of data—one that is meant for analysis rather than as the primary form of data organization (Fig. 11.6).

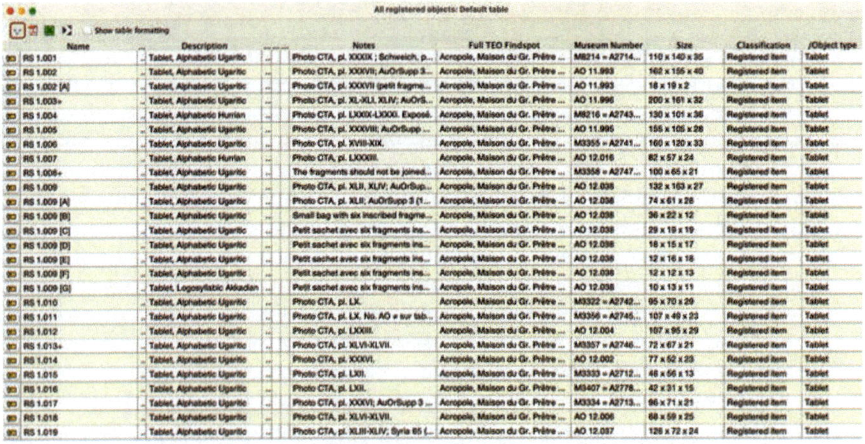

Name	Description	Notes	Full TEO Findspot	Museum Number	Size	Classification	/Object type
RS 1.001	Tablet, Alphabetic Ugaritic	Photo CTA, pl. XXXIX ; Schweich, p...	Acropole, Maison du Gr. Prêtre ...	M8214 = A2714...	110 x 140 x 35	Registered item	Tablet
RS 1.002	Tablet, Alphabetic Ugaritic	Photo CTA, pl. XXXVII; AuOrSupp 3...	Acropole, Maison du Gr. Prêtre ...	AO 11.993	162 x 155 x 40	Registered item	Tablet
RS 1.002 [A]	Tablet, Alphabetic Ugaritic	Photo CTA, pl. XXXVII (petit fragme...	Acropole, Maison du Gr. Prêtre ...	AO 11.993	18 x 19 x 2	Registered item	Tablet
RS 1.003+	Tablet, Alphabetic Ugaritic	Photo CTA, pl. XL-XLI, XLIV; AuOrS...	Acropole, Maison du Gr. Prêtre ...	AO 11.996	200 x 161 x 32	Registered item	Tablet
RS 1.004	Tablet, Alphabetic Hurrian	Photo CTA, pl. LXXIX-LXXXI. Exposé.	Acropole, Maison du Gr. Prêtre ...	M8216 = A2743...	130 x 101 x 36	Registered item	Tablet
RS 1.005	Tablet, Alphabetic Ugaritic	Photo CTA, pl. XXXVIII; AuOrSupp ...	Acropole, Maison du Gr. Prêtre ...	AO 11.995	155 x 105 x 28	Registered item	Tablet
RS 1.006	Tablet, Alphabetic Ugaritic	Photo CTA, pl. XVIII-XIX.	Acropole, Maison du Gr. Prêtre ...	M3355 = A2741...	160 x 120 x 33	Registered item	Tablet
RS 1.007	Tablet, Alphabetic Hurrian	Photo CTA, pl. LXXXIII.	Acropole, Maison du Gr. Prêtre ...	AO 12.016	82 x 57 x 24	Registered item	Tablet
RS 1.008+	Tablet, Alphabetic Ugaritic	The fragments should not be joined...	Acropole, Maison du Gr. Prêtre ...	M3358 = A2747...	100 x 65 x 21	Registered item	Tablet
RS 1.009	Tablet, Alphabetic Ugaritic	Photo CTA, pl. XLII, XLIV; AuOrSup...	Acropole, Maison du Gr. Prêtre ...	AO 12.035	132 x 163 x 27	Registered item	Tablet
RS 1.009 [A]	Tablet, Alphabetic Ugaritic	Photo CTA, pl. XLII; AuOrSupp 3 (1...	Acropole, Maison du Gr. Prêtre ...	AO 12.038	74 x 61 x 28	Registered item	Tablet
RS 1.009 [B]	Tablet, Alphabetic Ugaritic	Small bag with six inscribed fragme...	Acropole, Maison du Gr. Prêtre ...	AO 12.038	36 x 22 x 12	Registered item	Tablet
RS 1.009 [C]	Tablet, Alphabetic Ugaritic	Petit sachet avec six fragments ins...	Acropole, Maison du Gr. Prêtre ...	AO 12.038	29 x 19 x 19	Registered item	Tablet
RS 1.009 [D]	Tablet, Alphabetic Ugaritic	Petit sachet avec six fragments ins...	Acropole, Maison du Gr. Prêtre ...	AO 12.038	18 x 15 x 17	Registered item	Tablet
RS 1.009 [E]	Tablet, Alphabetic Ugaritic	Petit sachet avec six fragments ins...	Acropole, Maison du Gr. Prêtre ...	AO 12.038	12 x 16 x 18	Registered item	Tablet
RS 1.009 [F]	Tablet, Alphabetic Ugaritic	Petit sachet avec six fragments ins...	Acropole, Maison du Gr. Prêtre ...	AO 12.038	12 x 12 x 13	Registered item	Tablet
RS 1.009 [G]	Tablet, Logosyllabic Akkadian	Petit sachet avec six fragments ins...	Acropole, Maison du Gr. Prêtre ...	AO 12.038	10 x 13 x 11	Registered item	Tablet
RS 1.010	Tablet, Alphabetic Ugaritic	Photo CTA, pl. LX.	Acropole, Maison du Gr. Prêtre ...	M3322 = A2742...	95 x 70 x 29	Registered item	Tablet
RS 1.011	Tablet, Alphabetic Ugaritic	Photo CTA, pl. LX. No. AO ≠ sur tab...	Acropole, Maison du Gr. Prêtre ...	M3356 = A2745...	107 x 49 x 23	Registered item	Tablet
RS 1.012	Tablet, Alphabetic Ugaritic	Photo CTA, pl. LXXIII.	Acropole, Maison du Gr. Prêtre ...	AO 12.004	107 x 95 x 29	Registered item	Tablet
RS 1.013+	Tablet, Alphabetic Ugaritic	Photo CTA, pl. XLVI-XLVII.	Acropole, Maison du Gr. Prêtre ...	M3357 = A2746...	72 x 67 x 21	Registered item	Tablet
RS 1.014	Tablet, Alphabetic Ugaritic	Photo CTA, pl. XXXVI.	Acropole, Maison du Gr. Prêtre ...	AO 12.002	77 x 52 x 23	Registered item	Tablet
RS 1.015	Tablet, Alphabetic Ugaritic	Photo CTA, pl. LXII.	Acropole, Maison du Gr. Prêtre ...	M3333 = A2712...	46 x 56 x 13	Registered item	Tablet
RS 1.016	Tablet, Alphabetic Ugaritic	Photo CTA, pl. LXII.	Acropole, Maison du Gr. Prêtre ...	M3407 = A2778...	42 x 31 x 15	Registered item	Tablet
RS 1.017	Tablet, Alphabetic Ugaritic	Photo CTA, pl. XXXVI; AuOrSupp 3 ...	Acropole, Maison du Gr. Prêtre ...	M3334 = A2713...	96 x 71 x 21	Registered item	Tablet
RS 1.018	Tablet, Alphabetic Ugaritic	Photo CTA, pl. XLVI-XLVII.	Acropole, Maison du Gr. Prêtre ...	AO 12.006	68 x 59 x 25	Registered item	Tablet
RS 1.019	Tablet, Alphabetic Ugaritic	Photo CTA, pl. XLIII-XLIV; Syria 65 (...	Acropole, Maison du Gr. Prêtre ...	AO 12.037	126 x 72 x 24	Registered item	Tablet

Fig. 11.6 An OCHRE table lists the tablets found on the Acropolis (the result of a Query)

Lumping Versus Splitting

The item-based approach to data also solves the problem of lumping versus splitting, that of deciding which pieces of information will be recorded in the same column of a table and which will require a new column. This is a common exercise when entering data in a tabular format. For example, should object dimensions be entered in a single column as "10 mm × 25 mm × 2 mm" or should they be split into separate columns? When faced with a spreadsheet that already has two or three dozen columns, many researchers will choose to lump the measurements into a single column. But then, what do I do when I need to record the diameter or circumference of a cylindrical object? Well, I already have a column called measurements, so why not continue lumping all measurements into this column? The alternative is to split separate measurements into separate columns, one column for length, one for width, one for thickness, one for diameter, one for circumference, etc. Inevitably, one or more of these measurement columns will be mostly blank, and the spreadsheet becomes more unwieldy. Most of the objects in RSTI have length, width, and thickness measurements. Only a few objects have circumference and diameter. When recorded as columns, the circumference and diameter columns would be mostly blank. This type of sparsely populated table is cumbersome to browse.

The item-based approach to data does not create sparse data with unpopulated fields. Each item is described with only the properties that apply to the item. When there is no circumference measurement, we do not enter this property and leave it blank; we simply do not record the property at all. From the perspective of the scholar, there is a feeling of freedom in this approach to data. The researcher is freed from thinking of research data in terms of rigid table structures; free to record multiple instances of the same metadata property, like multiple types of decoration on a piece of pottery; free to record only the properties that apply to the item of observation. No circumference? No problem, leave it out. This approach is a more natural way of recording unpredictable and heterogeneous data.

Reuse Versus Duplication

The item-based approach also allows for easy reuse of data. Because the tablets in RSTI are items in a graph model and not rows in a table, they are assigned their own universally unique identifier (UUID) which makes each individual item separately addressable and reusable. For example, as one spatial hierarchy in RSTI records the findspots of the tablets, another separate hierarchy could be used to represent the current location of these same tablets in a museum storage facility. In this case, the branching hierarchy might include storage cabinets containing drawers that contain individual boxes for storing tablets. The item that represents a given tablet in the hierarchy of excavation contexts on the site of Ras Shamra, would also exist in the hierarchy that represents where it is being stored in the museum. A polyhierarchical data model, through reuse and recontextualization, allows the researcher to record data in different arrangements without having to duplicate the data.

Visualizing Geospatial Data

In addition to the thousands of objects recorded in RSTI, the Ras Shamra excavation grid is represented in the Locations & objects hierarchy. Over the course of decades of excavation on the site, the archaeological team came up with various systems for dividing up the site into a grid.[12] The still-current system, developed in 1975 by then director Claude Margueron,[13] replaced the previous system which did not cover the entire site.[14] This hierarchy is not very deep, consisting of the four main grids A-D,

[12]There is no universally adopted system for archaeological grid plans. There is a wide variety of systems, most of which use some combination of letters and numbers. Other systems rely entirely on universally agreed upon mapping systems like the Universal Trans-Mercator (UTM). A grid system is helpful for referring to excavation areas in reports and publications. See the Tell Keisan case study (Chap. 10) for further discussion of methods used for modeling excavation grids in OCHRE.

[13]Margueron divided the entire site of Ugarit into four main grids A, B, C, and D. These four main grids are arranged in a clockwise format beginning with A covering the northwest quarter of the site. B covers the northeast quarter; C the southeast; and D the southwest (Margueron 1977). In this arrangement, there is a central point, that is, the spot where the four interior corners of the grids meet. From this central point, the grid system is sub-divided into 10-meter squares. Along the x-axis, the squares are assigned sequential numbers. The squares closest to the center point begin with 1. Along the y-axis, the squares are given a letter assignment beginning with lowercase "a" and continuing beyond "z" into double letters. Even further, each 10-meter square is further sub-divided into quadrants 1–4 referring to the NW, NE, SW, and SE quadrants of the square. So, square C2m1 is in the southeastern grid of the site, the second square eastward, the thirteenth square southward (i.e., "m" along the y-axis), and the NW sub-section of this square (i.e., the final "1"). The system sounds confusing but provides an intuitive system for understanding exactly where on the site any given square might be. However, in the end there are over 24,000 combinations of small grids like C2m1.

[14]Apparently, the previous system, which used a similar strategy for naming squares along the x and y axes, decreased in accuracy as one moved away from the center point (Yon et al. 1995).

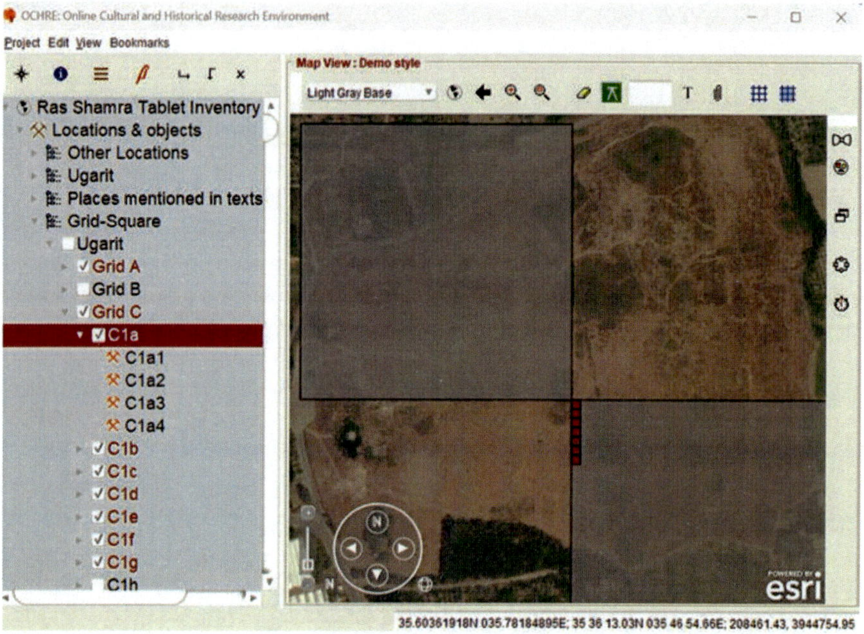

Fig. 11.7 Selected Grids and Squares can be toggled into view in OCHRE's Map View

each containing a flat list of the squares in the grid. Each square in turn contains four subdivisions of the square (Fig. 11.7).

By creating a discrete spatial unit for each excavation square, RSTI can display any square on a georeferenced map. Using OCHRE's Map View, we can view excavation plans with the excavation grids overlain as vector shape files. This serves a very practical purpose. In their publications, the excavators frequently reference progress at, or finds from, specific squares. Without this sort of interface, it is sometimes difficult to understand the narrative being presented in these publications. But with a spatially aware backdrop, and interactive tools, the reader can "zoom to" the square of interest and explore it visually. With this spatial information modeled in RSTI, we are prepared to add any new information gleaned from publications or discovered in future archaeological excavations.

OCHRE's Map View tightly integrates Esri's ArcGIS Runtime SDK for Java[15] to provide a basic level of GIS functionality directly in OCHRE while also allowing the use of shapefiles created in standalone GIS platforms such as ArcGIS or QGIS.[16]

[15] https://developers.arcgis.com/java/.

[16] Instead of trying to reinvent the many tools and features of a GIS application in OCHRE, we encourage users to continue using their preferred GIS platform for creating spatial data to be integrated within OCHRE. For more information about the free, open source QGIS application, visit https://qgis.org/.

By referencing the many valuable excavation reports published by the Mission de Ras Shamra, the RSTI team creates and edits maps, site plans, and vector graphics in QGIS, then adds these as resources to OCHRE. Polygon-shaped vector graphics have been drawn for every major excavation area on the site: one polygon represents the bounds of the entire site, one represents the Royal Palace, others represent each room in the royal palace; still others delineate streets, courtyards, houses, pits, and tombs. Findspots for pottery, seals, and other small finds are still being added (Fig. 11.8).

From QGIS, we save a single shapefile that contains shapes for all the areas on the entire site of Ugarit. We add this shapefile as a Resource in OCHRE and link it to the Locations & objects hierarchy that represents the site of Ugarit, thereby indicating that this shapefile is the source of any vector graphics used to illustrate the spatial units in this hierarchy. Since these excavation areas are itemized as spatial units using OCHRE's item-based approach, each spatial unit can be individually matched to a shape in the shapefile. In the attribute table of the linked shapefile, each polygon is given a name that matches the exact and unique name, alias, or abbreviation of a spatial unit within the hierarchy where the shapefile is linked in OCHRE. For example, "Room 28" in the Royal Palace is one shape in the unified Ugarit shapefile. It is also a spatial unit in the Locations & objects hierarchy, located within the hierarchical branch dedicated to the Royal Palace.

In OCHRE's Map View, a user can click a checkbox next to Room 28 in the Locations & objects hierarchy to display it in the View. When this checkbox is activated, OCHRE performs a query of the shapefile's attribute table to find a polygon with the name "Room 28." The query returns the shape to the View where it can be displayed along with other shapes or georeferenced maps. When OCHRE displays the polygon, it examines properties on that spatial unit to decide what type of styling

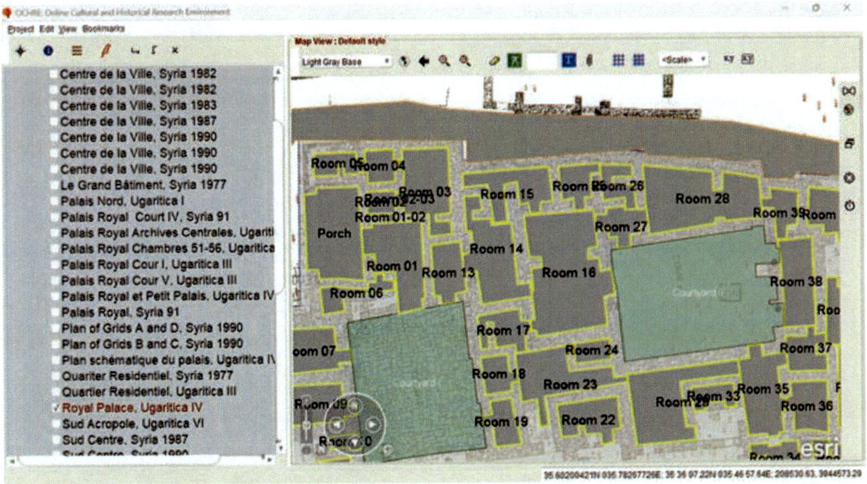

Fig. 11.8 A styled Map View brings to life the Rooms and Courtyards of the Royal Palace based on reports published by the Mission de Ras Shamra

to apply. For example, all "Room" items can be styled to display in light gray, all courtyards in green, and all streets in red. Note that these categories do not need to be reproduced in the attribute file of the shapefile. Rather, they are derived from the OCHRE properties of the items being displayed on the map. This strategy obviates the need to continually update the attribute table of the shapefile.

The findspot of most of the tablets from Ras Shamra-Ugarit were painstakingly collected and documented in TEO (Fig. 11.9). The excavation reports provided some maps which indicated findspots, the most extensive of which is a large fold-out map included with the publication *Ugaritica IV* (Schaeffer 1962). This map folds out into a 4-foot × 3-foot plan of the Royal Palace, with tiny red icons and numbers indicating findspots (Fig. 11.10). Unfortunately, there is no simple way in the print publication to cross-reference room numbers in the palace to locate a specific findspot. It is possible to use the appendices in TEO to investigate which findspots fall in which rooms of the palace. But this process requires referencing back and forth from the fold-out map, to the appendix, to a text list. It is a very tedious process.

To remedy this, we have plotted digitally in RSTI the findspots of all the tablets discovered in the Royal Palace. We began by scanning the large fold-out map and georeferencing it. The image of the fold-out map is now situated correctly in place on a satellite map of the site of Ras Shamra. Other georeferenced archaeological

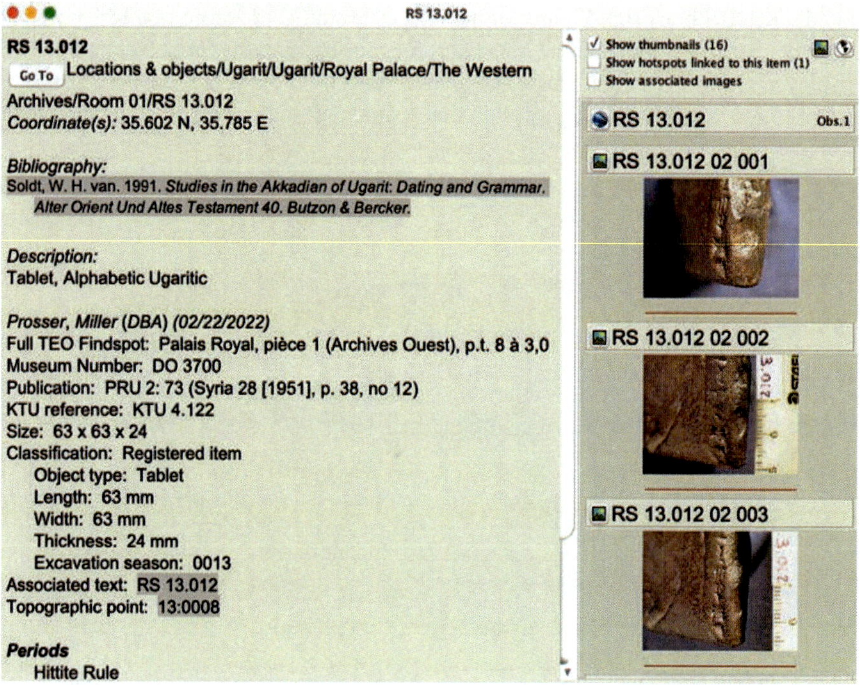

Fig. 11.9 Each tablet is assigned a Topographic point representing its findspot

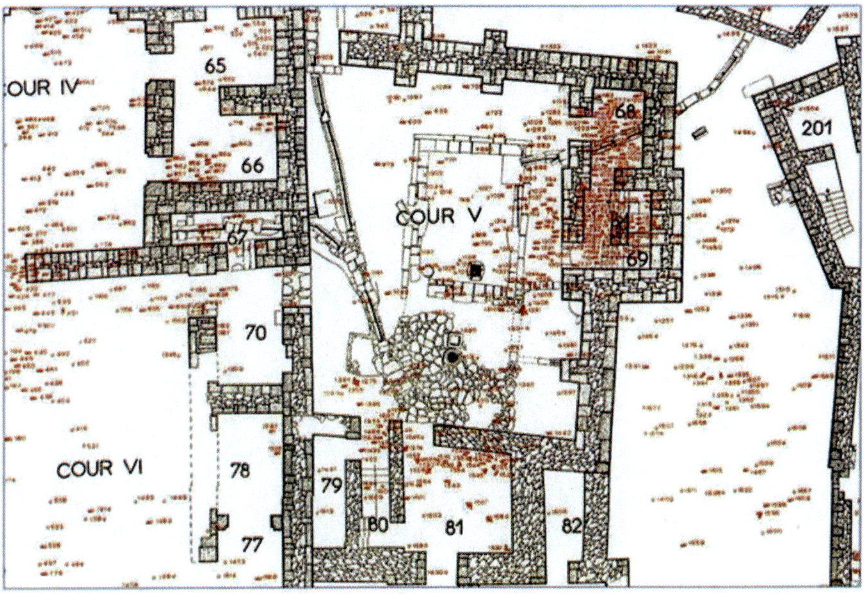

Fig. 11.10 This excerpt from *Ugaritica IV* (Schaeffer 1962) shows findspots of tablets in the Royal Palace

plans can also be layered over the fold-out map. Then, in RSTI we created a simple flat list of all known findspots as reported by TEO. Next, we associated these findspot numbers with the tablets discovered at those spots by adding a relational property on the tablet, the value of which is the findspot item.

The final step was to view the georeferenced fold-out map in OCHRE's spatially aware Map View, and to click to specify the location of the findspots. Each click assigned an x-y coordinate to the currently selected findspot based on the local UTM coordinate system. This process situated the findspot of each tablet on the digitized version of the fold-out map, capturing its coordinate.

With this network of data in place, we are then able to display tablet findspots on the site of Ras Shamra. We can choose tablets one at a time, or we can query for tablets that share common properties, such as language and genre, and plot only those. Due to OCHRE's item-based approach, where every item can draw itself (and only itself), any selection of tablets can be displayed on the map. The outcome is a dynamic and powerful visualization that helps us understand the spatial dimension of tablet findspots (Fig. 11.11).

One goal of this work on spatial data is to provide a framework into which any object can be added. As M. Prosser toured the site of Ras Shamra on foot in the summer of 2004, the ongoing and partial nature of the excavation was evident. As one would expect, some areas of the site remain unexcavated. Some of the areas that make for good tourism, such as the Royal Palace, were walkable, with open courtyards and preserved walls. Other areas were subject to active and ongoing

Fig. 11.11 Map View shows the density of findspots of tablets in the Royal Palace

excavation. The point is this: The site is not a fully known subject. It is still being investigated. To reduce the complexity of the site of Ras Shamra to a series of spreadsheets, or to a series of shape files, would be to risk losing information. Archaeology is, by definition, destruction. As excavators dig, they have one chance to record the information they find. The science of archaeology has come a long way over the course of the last century. Carefully trained professionals work hard to record and preserve as much information as possible. The method for recording this information must be up to the task of recording the necessary level of complexity.

As described up to this point, we have concentrated on the archaeological data in RSTI. While we certainly find value in understanding the findspots of the objects, our primary interest is in the texts.

Textual Data (Texts)

At the time of this writing, RSTI project personnel are actively working to add text editions to the database. Recall that OCHRE maintains a distinction between an Object and the Text recorded on that Object. An Object may be a scroll, folio, book, tablet, gravestone, or any other physical thing. The Object is related to the Text in the database by use of a relational Variable called **Associated text**, in this case. The Value of this Variable is the Text item. So, for the tablet RS 1.001, there is an Associated text named RS 1.001.[17] Not all objects have texts associated with them

[17] It is somewhat standard in Ugaritic studies to use the tablet inventory number to refer to the text, clearly the result of conflating the ideas of object and text.

of course. RSTI records various uninscribed objects like cylinder seals or ceramic vessels.[18]

In addition to a text name like RS 1.001, many other naming systems have been created over the years. For example, when a subset of texts is published together in a volume, the editors of the volume are wont to create a new numbering system. Sometimes, these numbers become the default nomenclature in certain scholarly circles. Notably, the three editions of *Die keilalphabetischen Texte aus Ugarit*, abbreviated as KTU, introduced a numbering system that has been used widely for the alphabetic Ugaritic texts.[19] These volumes present text transliterations of the Ugaritic alphabetic texts, some bibliography, but no translation and very little other commentary. The editors of KTU organize the texts into chapters according to broadly defined genres. Chapter 1, for example, is dedicated to the literary and religious texts. Each literary text is assigned a new KTU number. So, RS 1.001 is also known as KTU 1.39. Confusingly, other numbering systems have been devised over the years. In RSTI, we made the judicious decision to eschew a new numbering system. Instead, we refer to texts by their object registration number. However, we also record these other publication numbers as Aliases in OCHRE. These aliases are searchable and viewable so that a Text can be found regardless of which naming system a researcher uses.

One of the primary concerns of RSTI is to create reliable text editions. In addition to new text editions by Pardee or Prosser, RSTI also records previous text editions. Typically, if the RSTI editors have produced our own edition of the text, we will not record a previous edition. However, in cases where we have not yet been able to examine the tablet or produce a new collation, we record the *editio princeps* with necessary corrections. The original editor is credited with this work. Corrections may be based on secondary literature or on the examination of the photographs.[20]

A text edition being prepared for study or print typically has the form of a linear representation of graphemes.[21] This is usually a word processing document or PDF on the one hand, or an XML document with TEI inline markup on the other. In those representations, text is recorded in a form that replicates the linear sequence of graphemes, line by line, page by page. In large flashing lights, we wish to emphasize that the database approach to texts we describe here stands in stark contrast to

[18] This is one significant difference between the RSTI database project and the printed volume edited by Bordreuil and Pardee (1989). In their volume, they included only objects with texts written on them.

[19] For the original volume, see Dietrich, Loretz, and Sanmartín (1976). This volume is currently in its third edition (Dietrich et al. 2013).

[20] The only acceptable method for producing a text edition is a first-person inspection of the object. However, in some cases this is not possible. Sometimes we were able to photograph a tablet, but not to study it in detail. In these cases, we do not produce a final or authoritative text edition, but it seems warranted to correct any glaring mistakes by previous editors.

[21] Throughout this section, we use the technical term grapheme to refer to the smallest meaningful unit of writing in a writing system. The term "letter" becomes confusing in this context because we also discuss epistolary letters, that is, correspondence between senders and recipients of written documents.

the document (TEI) approach. Yes, we encode textual data as XML documents, but this is not to be confused with the kind of XML employed by a TEI inline markup document which is based on what we would call a document model (Schloen and Schloen 2014). The document model has its place, as we would argue, as a visual format for the researcher to publish, share, and consume the data, but a database approach allows for much greater flexibility for data representation.

Epigraphic Units

Using the database model, as implemented in OCHRE, the minimal, meaningful part of a Text is the individual grapheme, that is, the cuneiform sign or alphabetic letter. These are represented in RSTI, each by its own Epigraphic unit, and then contextualized hierarchically in a line, column, or surface where applicable: graphemes within lines, lines within columns, columns within surfaces, for example (Fig. 11.12).

Script Units

Every Epigraphic unit is verified against a pre-defined Writing system managed by OCHRE, either the Ugaritic alphabetic writing system or the Sumero-Akkadian syllabary. This ensures that only valid textual content is accepted during data entry or when importing texts. The OCHRE master project manages a variety of Writing systems which itemize and describe their allowable set of Script units. These Writing systems are shared with projects like RSTI, ranging from simpler Writing systems like the Latin alphabet, to more complex ones like the polyvalent Sumero-Akkadian syllabic Writing system—polyvalent meaning that any given sign may represent a variety of reading values. For example, the valid phonogram values across the various languages and dialects that use the Script unit IGI are: bat_5, gi_8, igi, ína, íni, ini_4, ínu, lam_5, lem, lì, lim, limi, lúm, pàn, $še_{20}$, ši, and si_{17}.[22] The valid logogram values for IGI are GANZER, GÀNZER, IGI, LIM, and ŠI. The Sumero-Akkadian Writing System in OCHRE accounts for every reading of every sign (Fig. 11.13).[23]

[22] It may be helpful to provide a few observations on the history of transliteration of the Sumero-Akkadian writing system. Throughout its long life, many signs came to be used to communicate any given syllabic value such as še, to take one example. To communicate which cuneiform sign the scribe used to communicate the syllabic value še, we transcribe the sign with either no accent, an acute accent, a grave accent, or a sub-script number. The sign we call IGI, for example, is the twentieth documented option for expressing the syllabic value še, which is why it is transliterated as $še_{20}$. So, when another scholar sees our transcription $še_{20}$, they know that we identified the sign IGI in the text and interpreted this sign as expressing the syllabic value še.

[23] In a few rare cases, we record allographic variants of letters. This does not happen regularly in Ugaritic. We have only the occasional superfluous wedge here and there. In some writing systems, such as Aramaic square script, certain letters appear in predicable allographic variation when they fall at the end of a word. OCHRE allows a project to assign an allograph to these final forms of Aramaic letters.

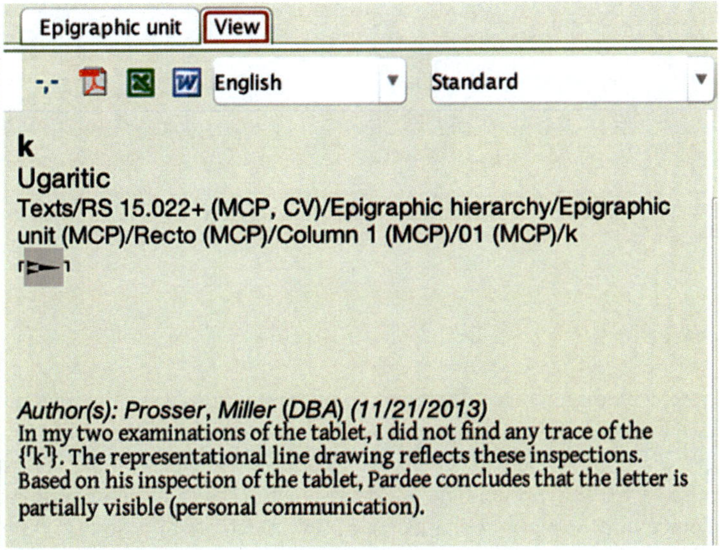

Fig. 11.12 An authored note on a single Epigraphic unit (a partially damaged "k"?) illustrates the value of highly atomized textual data

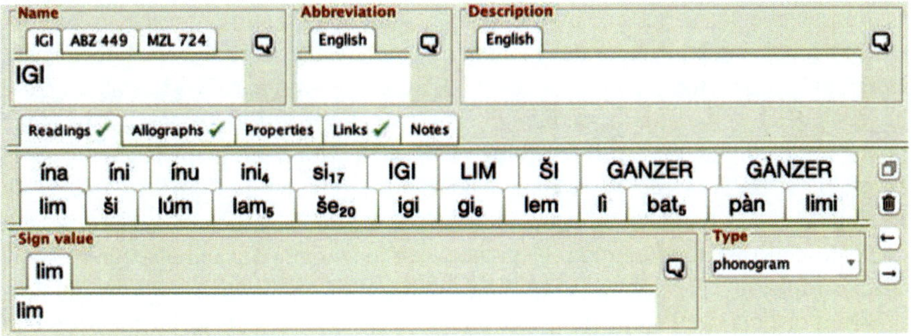

Fig. 11.13 The Script unit called IGI can be used as either a phonogram or logogram

When OCHRE encounters a value like *ši* in a word processing document being imported, or via data entry, it recognizes the italic formatting as an indication that the sign is logosyllabic Akkadian (based on the project or import specifications). Then, when OCHRE queries the appropriate Writing system for *ši*, it finds a match on the reading of the sign IGI. Back on the Epigraphic unit, OCHRE records a link to the matched Script unit from the Writing system (Fig. 11.14).

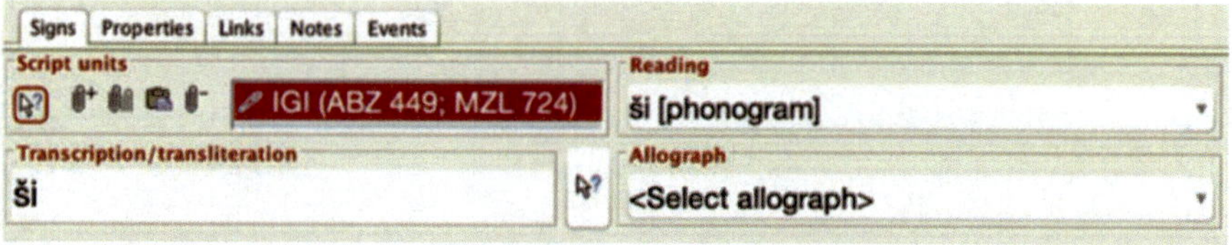

Fig. 11.14 Epigraphic units are validated by matching against Script units in the prescribed Writing system

Discourse Units

The hierarchical arrangement of textual content may raise a red flag in the mind of the reader familiar with text encoding. What happens when the graphemes that make up a word cross a line, column, or surface boundary? OCHRE's item-based data model solves this problem by making a distinction between epigraphic units and discourse units. Epigraphic units are observable units of writing, or the spatial layout of that writing, on a support. Discourse units are the further arrangement of these Epigraphic units into words, phrases, and larger units of discourse. Therefore, a Discourse unit can be composed of a sequence of Epigraphic units which reaches the end of one line and continues to the beginning of the next line. Specifically, the Epigraphic and Discourse hierarchies are two separate hierarchies cross-referenced by links between a series of Epigraphic units and the Discourse unit they compose.

A Discourse unit provides the spelling of a word—the sequence of its designated Epigraphic units. But to communicate the scholar's grammatical understanding of a Text, OCHRE allows the specification of a vocalized version of each Discourse unit.[24] For example, the word for "king" is written with three graphemes, *mlk*. The word in OCHRE is represented as a Discourse unit of the Type "word." This Discourse unit is linked to its component parts, the three Epigraphic units *m*, *l*, and *k*, creating a cross-linking relationship between the epigraphic and discourse observations of the tezt. The nominative, singular form, the word *mlk* was probably pronounced or vocalized something like *malku*. This is documented in the *discourse transcription* field where the scholar can enter a grammatical representation of the word that is otherwise not represented in the epigraphic transcription. For RSTI, a vocalized version of each noun is provided as its transcription, so *malku* instead of *mlk*. The discourse transcription is thus a sort of shorthand method for communicating our interpretation of the Text (Fig. 11.15).

[24]The discourse transcription is important for languages that use logosyllabic writing systems that poorly specify the grammatical or phonemic expression of a word. The Ugaritic language only partially records vowels (when the vowel follows an *ʾaleph* consonant). In all other cases, there is no indication of vowels in the writing system. Do not mistake our point—the spoken language obviously had vowel sounds. The ancient writing system did not, for the most part. Unfortunately for us, much of the grammatical information of the language was communicated by unwritten vowels.

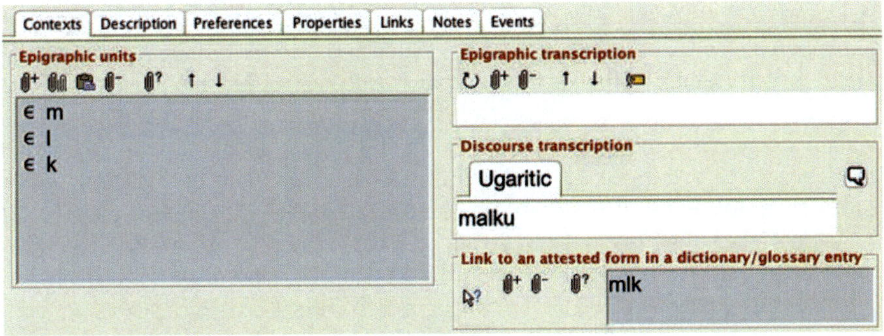

Fig. 11.15 A Discourse unit with its transcription has links to its component Epigraphic units and its related Dictionary form (as discussed below)

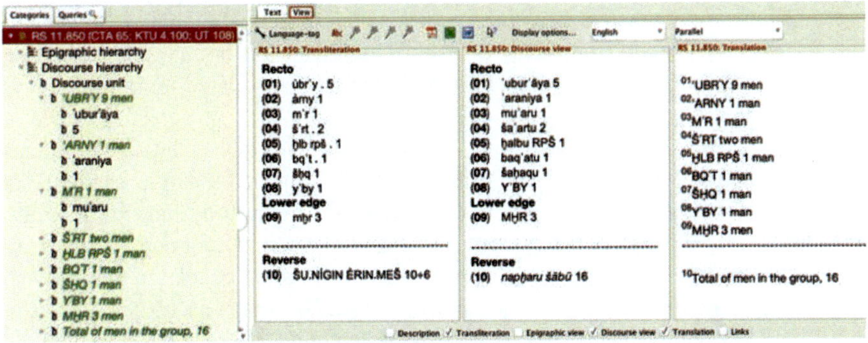

Fig. 11.16 OCHRE's Views reflect the data organization: by hierarchy, by Transliteration (epigraphic), by Transcription (discourse), and by Translation (discourse override)

From the words which are built from Epigraphic units, we create clauses, sentences, or paragraphs by grouping words into larger Discourse units. These aggregate Discourse units allow us to be intentional about providing *translations* for meaningful chunks of text. For example, instead of providing a single, overall translation of the text, we typically translate smaller phrases like an epistolary greeting or numeric subtotal. This gives us the flexibility to compare these genre-specific elements across the corpus. Conveniently for the scholar or student, these more granular units of translation make it easier to correlate the text transliteration with the translation (Fig. 11.16).

Just as we add notes to Epigraphic units, we also add notes to Discourse units to explain an interpretation, comment on an unusual word, or add just about any sort of observation imaginable. We also add a somewhat regular series of notes to the overall Text. These tend to be very long, sometimes article-length observations on the state of the tablet, the scribal hand, the tablet findspot, the structure of the text, and the interpretation of the text.

A Database Approach

Once atomized and stored in the OCHRE database, a Text no longer exists as sequential strings. The underlying format is a network of XML documents with each document recording the details of a single, atomic database item. To express that concretely, there are 513 XML documents that represent the 513 Epigraphic units that make up the Text RS 1.001. Three of these Epigraphic units identify the surfaces of the tablet: Recto, Lower edge, and Verso. Twenty-two of the Epigraphic units identify the twenty-two lines on the tablet (Line 01, Line 02, etc.). The remaining 488 XML documents record the 488 signs the scribe used to write this Text, with links to their associated Script units. For example, the first letter of the Text is 𐎄, a letter that scholars transliterate with the Latin character {d}. The XML document that records this {d} also records the relationship of this letter to the overall structure of the Text: which word it is in, which line it is in, which surface of the tablet it is on. In addition, there are 141 words that organize the 488 Epigraphic units into units of Discourse, which inherit information about their textual context from their Epigraphic units. Each Epigraphic unit and Discourse unit is thus self-aware and self-documenting, both independent from other units but related in multiple ways (Fig. 11.17).

The database approach to managing textual data solves one of the core problems with the implementation of XML used in the TEI model. A single character in OCHRE, for example the {d} in RS 1.001, can be used in multiple contexts. Because it is a single XML document representing a single letter, it is not bound to the strictures of a single hierarchy. As with the recontextualization of a tablet in findspot and museum hierarchies, this uniquely identified (UUID) letter can be referenced in multiple, conceptually overlapping textual hierarchies. Those who have worked

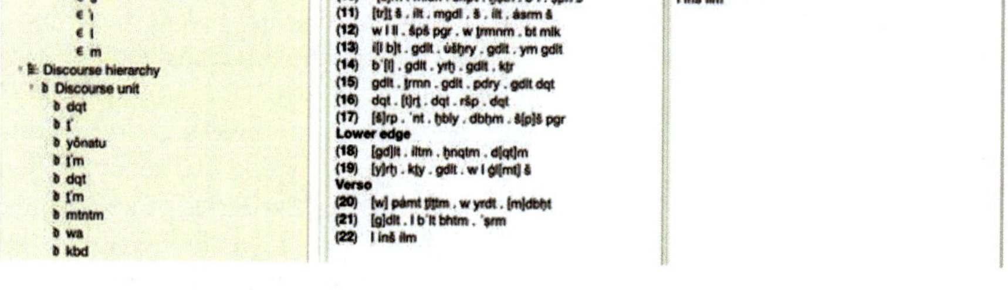

Fig. 11.17 OCHRE recomposes many atomic units into comprehensive Views of a Text

intimately with TEI will understand the freedom and flexibility this polyhierarchical strategy provides. For others, perhaps a practical example is needed. In RSTI, multiple editions of a single Text can be represented. In some cases, we wish to represent both the *editio princeps* and an updated edition. Instead of creating two entirely separate text editions, parts of the *editio princeps* can be *reused* in the newer edition, where the two agree. Only where the newer edition diverges from the original are new epigraphic units needed. By reusing data in this way, the database understands where the two editions agree and where they diverge.

Whereas the Epigraphic hierarchy allows multiple editions of the Text to be represented, attributed to a specific editor, the Discourse hierarchy allows the scholar to model multiple interpretations of these letters or signs. For example, in one interpretation, the grammatical structure of the text might be the focus of the analysis. In another, the same words might be reused and reorganized for a poetic or metrical analysis. In brief, the letters or signs from the Epigraphic hierarchy constitute words which can be used and reused in any number of Discourse hierarchies.

On a very practical level, a database approach allows for highly targeted description and analysis of atomized units, eliminates duplication of textual data needed for various or divergent views, cleanly delineates multiple, overlapping epigraphic and discourse hierarchies, and illustrates the difference between the *document model* in which an entire text is stored as a highly structured series of tagged string characters and the more flexible *database model* in which more granular textual components exist as separately defined and described items of observation and analysis.

Importation

While it would be possible to add textual content to OCHRE manually, building an Epigraphic hierarchy of surfaces, lines, and signs, then combining those elements into a hierarchy of Discourse units, it is far simpler to use the OCHRE Text import wizard to import a text document. The import wizard allows the user to start by loading a document from a local computer into an import field in the database.[25] The document typically contains only a transliteration of the text arranged into sections such as *recto* and *verso* (or, for texts not on cuneiform tablets, sections such as chapter, page, line, or paragraph).

For this example, we will start with some facts and rules that have been provided to help the import wizard interpret the conventions used in the formatted import document and see what can be learned about a new text provided in document form. We have chosen a challenging case—a text written with two writing systems and in two languages. In part, the text is written in the Ugaritic alphabetic script. In part, it is written in logosyllabic Akkadian. This is a common practice among the scribes of

[25] OCHRE can import content from Microsoft Word documents.

ancient Ugarit. In this example, most of the text is written in alphabetic Ugaritic, with a short summary statement at the end in logosyllabic Akkadian.[26]

Writing systems in OCHRE consist of Script units (signs) that define the acceptable values of the characters in that Writing system. Scholars use various schemes to transliterate Script units into formatted textual content. For this example, the following formatting conventions apply:

- Non-italicized character strings represent Akkadian language.
- Italicized character strings represent Ugaritic language: *a'rny*.
- Lower case Akkadian signs are identified as phonograms: um-ma.
- Upper case Akkadian signs are identified as logograms: ŠU.NIGÍN.
- Superscripted Akkadian signs are identified as determinatives: ^{meš}.
- Logosyllabic character strings joined by dashes or dots comprise a word.
- Words are separated by spaces.

In addition to the rules for interpreting the signs, OCHRE can be instructed how to interpret other information in the transliteration:

- Expect to find section headings.
- Do not expect to find line numbers, so provide them automatically.
- Remove the italic formatting of the Ugaritic text upon importation.
- Split alphabetic words into character-by-character units.
- Parse alphabetic words into individual characters.

The text in question is a short census of sorts.[27] It lists nine villages and counts the numbers of men from each village. The names of the villages are written in alphabetic Ugaritic. The number of men and the summary statement are written in logosyllabic Akkadian. The summary statement says: 16 men are in this group. Keep in mind that the text is written on a clay tablet, which is a three-dimensional object with a main surface (Obverse), various edges, and an opposite surface (Reverse). The text is transliterated into a document format and given to OCHRE as follows:

Obverse
u'brʿy . 1IÁ
a'rny 1DIŠ
mʿr 1DIŠ
šʿrt . 1MIN
ḫlb rpš . 1DIŠ
bqʿt . 1DIŠ
šḥq 1DIŠ

[26] Do not be distracted by the foreign-ness of these languages. Imagine a modern equivalent of two very different writing systems: a list of cities with populations in English summarized with a single statement written in Chinese.

[27] For those familiar with Ugaritic texts, the text reference is RS 11.850, also referred to as KTU/CAT 4.100 and CTA 65.

yʿby 1DIŠ

Lower edge
mḫr 1EŠ$_5$

Reverse
ŠU.NIGÍN ERÍN^{meš} 1U.1ÀŠ

OCHRE processes the text, one character at a time, using the rules specified on the import settings as a guide for processing the transliteration. Because we have instructed OCHRE to expect section headings, the entire first line is processed as a section (an Epigraphic unit) called Obverse and not as an ancient word. Subsequent section headings are preceded by an extra line break. The second line starts with a Lowercase Italic character string, *u'brʿy*, up to the first space which delimits the first word, and so it is processed as Alphabetic Ugaritic content as specified by the project settings (Fig. 11.18). Each sign becomes a separate Epigraphic unit and is verified against the Alphabetic Ugaritic Writing system. The first sign is u' and is found as a match with a Script unit in the Alphabetic Ugaritic Writing system, so a link is made between the Epigraphic unit and the Script unit. If there were a typo resulting in no match, OCHRE would warn the user that the sign was not found in the Writing system. This process repeats for all the letters in this first word. Upon reaching the first space, the wizard closes the scope of the word and creates a Discourse unit to represent the word, linking it to the sequence of Epigraphic units.

The rather odd-looking text at the end of line one is interpreted as an Akkadian Logogram, per the import specification for Uppercase, Regular text. Looking up this character string in the Sumero-Akkadian cuneiform Writing system, OCHRE learns that IÁ is the logogram that represents the number 5, basically a grouping of five small wedges on the tablet. The number 1 before the logogram is a multiplier that tells OCHRE that there is only one of these numeric logograms. This allows the database to reference the numeric value of this sign to quantify it. In this case, the simple math is 1 × 5. (The transliteration 2IÁ would result in 10, i.e., 2 × 5.)

The import wizard loops over the remaining content on the Obverse, identifying and linking each sign, organizing the signs as a branch of the Epigraphic hierarchy within the Obverse parent, creating new line items (Epigraphic units) at each line

Reading type	Case	Style	Superscript?	Language
Phonogram	Lowercase	Italic		Akkadian
Phonetic complement	Lowercase	Italic	✓ Superscript	Akkadian
Logogram	Uppercase	Regular		Akkadian
Determinative	Uppercase	Regular	✓ Superscript	Akkadian
Alphabetic	Lowercase	Regular		Ugaritic
Hieroglyphic	<unassigned>	<unassigned>		<unassigned>

Fig. 11.18 Each project can customize the formatting conventions to be used on import

break, and composing corresponding words (Discourse units) sequentially within the Discourse hierarchy. When it reaches the extra line break after the last line of the Obverse section, *yʿby* 1DIŠ, the import wizard creates a new section for the Lower edge of the tablet. After processing the text on the lower edge and creating a new section for the Reverse of the tablet, OCHRE proceeds to the first character on the Reverse. Because it is an Uppercase Regular character, OCHRE processes the string as a Logosyllabic Akkadian sign. As such, it no longer treats each character as a discrete alphabetic letter. It now looks for either a dash, a dot, or a space to mark the end of the sign. The first discrete sign found is ŠU. The format specification indicates that Uppercase Akkadian signs are Logograms so OCHRE queries the Sumero-Akkadian Writing system for a logogram called ŠU and creates the link between the Epigraphic unit (sign) in this Text and the logogram reading in the Writing system. The import wizard continues until reaching the end of the document.

The import wizard also recognizes a wide range of project-defined metadata sigla. For example, half-brackets in RSTI indicate partial damage. When the import wizard encounters input such as ⸢*m*⸣, it imports the Epigraphic unit then applies a built-in metadata property to indicate that this sign is partially broken. In other words, the half-brackets are not present in the transliteration of the sign. They are converted to metadata. This allows querying for textual data based on the presence or absence of damage. A view of the text can be generated that includes these half-brackets or that ignores them as if to present a "restored" version of the text.

In this way, the import wizard systematically transforms a line-by-line transliteration from a text document into a highly atomized, hierarchically organized OCHRE Text. The logic may seem complex, but it parallels what goes on in the mind of the scholar as they create the Romanized transliteration of a text. The scholar has been trained to record logograms as uppercase text, phonograms as lowercase signs, etc. OCHRE has been trained to do the same. But this is only the beginning. From here, a wide range of supplementary data can be added.

Lexical Data (Dictionaries)

The OCHRE Dictionary feature is easy to understand and use, as familiar as any print or digital dictionary. Words are defined with meanings, spellings, usages, and other details. Unlike a print dictionary, an OCHRE Dictionary, or simplified Glossary, is an integrated part of the entire graph data model, with links to textual content. As such, the Dictionary serves as a powerful browsing tool for finding and investigating words in Texts. For projects working with texts written in multiple languages, OCHRE allows multiple Glossaries, typically one hierarchically organized Glossary per language. RSTI maintains separate Glossaries of Ugaritic and Akkadian words attested in the texts.[28]

[28] While other languages are attested in the texts from Ugarit, they are not yet accounted for in the glossaries.

A Glossary entry begins with a Lemma, with the full list of lemmas usually grouped into headings by first letter. Lemmas can be cross-referenced to associate related words. Because each Lemma is a separate database item with a unique identifier (UUID), links can be created between them with a single click. OCHRE also provides the option to include a lengthy explanation of the cross-reference in cases where the nature of the relationship between the two items is not self-evident.

Within the level of the Lemma, the Glossary entry branches into two main hierarchies: forms and senses.[29] In the hierarchy of forms, the dictionary records grammatical forms which, in turn, might be represented by a variety of attested forms. For example, a given verb may have grammatical forms that represent the single, plural, past, present, or future conjugations of that Lemma. Attested forms of these words, which exhibit variations in spelling, for example, are organized under the appropriate grammatical form. This part of the hierarchy may be confusing to those who study languages that show little or no difference between the grammatical form and the attested form. In modern English, for example, the preterite (past tense) of the verb "to go" is "went." The grammatical form "went" will be attested in texts as "went." So, in this case there is no difference between the grammatical form and the attested form. However, some writing systems attest a high degree of variation in the orthographic expression of a grammatical form. This is particularly true for languages written using a Sumero-Akkadian cuneiform writing system where variety in phonograms, logograms, and determinatives results in potentially many attested forms for any given grammatical form (Fig. 11.19).

The other main branching hierarchy within the level of the Lemma is the hierarchy of senses or meanings. This branch of the hierarchy is recursive, allowing for the repeated use of meanings and sub-meanings. For example, if the Lemma has a primary meaning of "(1) servant," then the sub-meanings might be something like "(1a) a social subordinate" and "(1b) a servile laborer." There is no limit to the amount of subordinate nesting in this context. This hierarchy is also characterized by the use of citations and text representations to inform and illustrate the hierarchy of meanings. Any given meaning or submeaning can include snippets of text with translation or even links to textual content from texts in the project. Finally, the

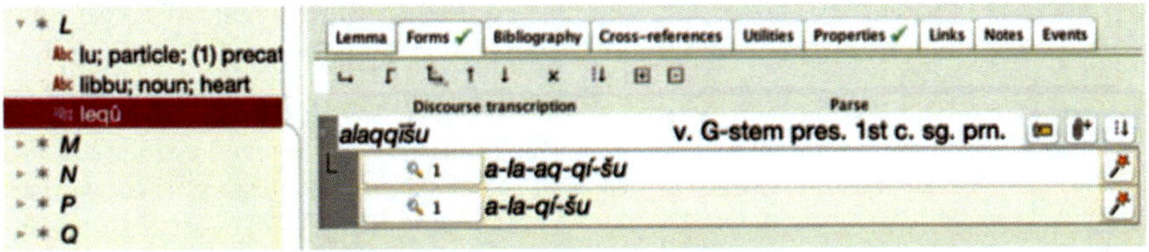

Fig. 11.19 The Lemma entry for the Akkadian verb leqû, "to take," has one grammatical form alaqqīšu, with two attested forms

[29] We introduced the Lexical Model Framework (LMF) and its use of the term *senses* in our discussion on dictionaries in Chap. 4.

researcher can include prose discussions at any level of this hierarchy to expound further on the meanings.

Presently, RSTI focuses more on morphological analysis than semantic analysis. (Once we have finished adding texts, we will be better positioned to define meanings and submeanings.) The goal of RSTI is to account for every form of every Ugaritic and Akkadian word attested in every text.[30] For each Lemma, we record a basic gloss of the word, a general part of speech, bibliography where relevant, and a few properties.[31] For each grammatical form, we record properties to identify the grammatical parsing of the word. These parse properties are entirely customizable for our project. For nouns, we maintain a Taxonomy branch of Variables and Values to identify person, number, gender, state, and nominal form. For verbs, we identify stem, conjugation, person, number, gender, tense, and a few other minor categories. As individual items, the Variables and Values can be reused in multiple contexts in the Taxonomy as needed. For example, "3rd person" exists as a subordinate Value of "Finite verb" and as a subordinate Value of "Personal pronoun" (Fig. 11.20).

In the RSTI Glossary, while it would be possible to create a grammatical form for every theoretically valid word, a grammatical form is created only if it is present in the Texts. The same holds true for attested forms which are included only if they are present in the Texts. While the Text import wizard can attempt to identify words and link them to the Glossary, we do not use this automated feature due to the high degree of homography in the alphabetic Ugaritic texts. Instead, we perform some good old-fashioned slow scholarship and identify most words manually—well, not entirely manually. OCHRE's guided lexicography wizard,[32] *TLex*, allows us to interactively identify words, insert new forms in the Glossary, add parse properties, and provide a discourse transcription. If a Lemma is already attested in the Glossary, missing grammatical and attested forms are added as needed. If the forms are already present in the Glossary, then links are made between the words in the Text and the forms in the Glossary. As the RSTI Glossary expands—that is, as we continue to add attested forms—the *TLex* wizard becomes more intelligent. *TLex* is even able to suggest matching words that are possible in broken sections, sometimes surprising us when it suggests a reconstruction that we had not previously considered.

Figure 11.21 illustrates the result of a Discourse unit having been processed by the OCHRE workflow wizards. The Text import wizard constructed the list of links to the Epigraphic units that comprise the Discourse unit. *TLex*, the lexicography

[30] At the inception of the project, we imported a table of Ugaritic lemmas with meanings from a Microsoft Access database. This served as the foundation for the Ugaritic glossary, which has since expanded greatly.

[31] RSTI makes minimal use of properties on lexemes. Other projects have a more fulsome approach to categorizing lemmas by semantic field, by category (e.g., "commodity" and "animal") or other properties. There is value in this approach, which will likely be adopted by RSTI at some point. RSTI also under-utilizes OCHRE's built-in structure for delineating sense-meanings for lexemes. Again, other projects have made extensive use of this feature, separating out meanings of lexemes into 1, 2, 3, etc. and sub-meanings a, b, c, etc.

[32] See Chap. 8 for a detailed description of the guided workflow wizards that help OCHRE users analyze Texts.

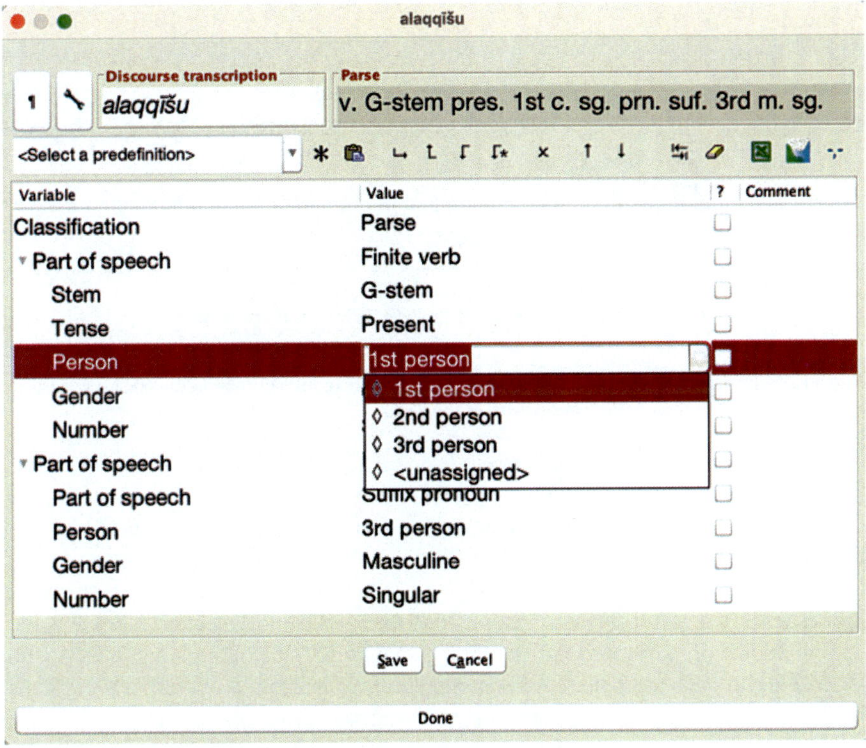

Fig. 11.20 Metadata properties are assigned to grammatical forms in the Glossary

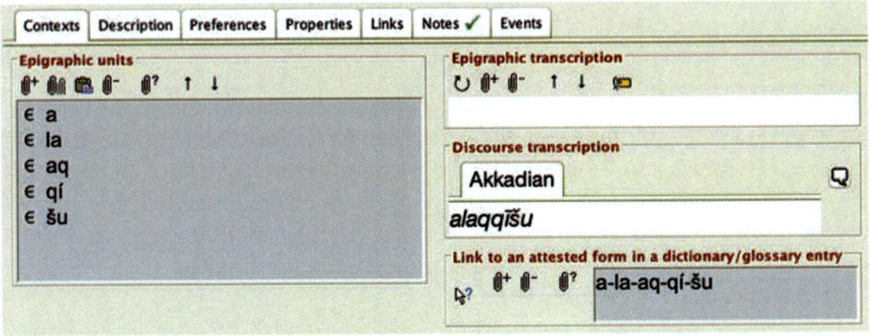

Fig. 11.21 This word (logographic, Akkadian) is one node in a graph of data, atomized into its component Epigraphic units (in turn linked to their associated Script units) and linked to its Dictionary form

workflow wizard, linked the word to its corresponding attested form in the Glossary, and let the scholar assign a discourse transcription, that is, the vocalized word.

Since parse properties are added to every grammatical form in the Glossary, once the words in the Texts have been linked to the Glossary, they inherit, in effect, the properties assigned to their linked form. In short, we parse the word once in the

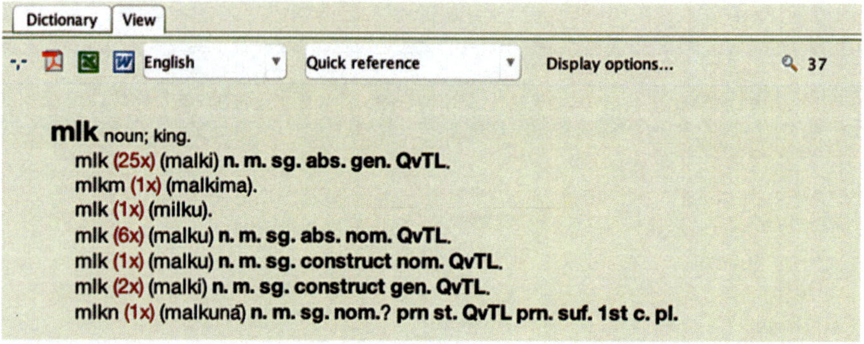

Fig. 11.22 Counts of the forms of the words (alphabetic, Ugaritic) in the Glossary are generated on the fly, based on their actual attestations in the Texts

Glossary, then leverage this information when identifying words in Texts. To review, the word in the Text links to the attested form in the Glossary, which is organized as a subordinate item to the grammatical form, which is described with grammatical properties. As a result, we can search for words in texts that attest very specific combinations of parse properties, things that would be interesting only to an Ugaritologist, such as G-stem prefix conjugation verbs from a I-y verbal root. As an additional outcome, as words are related to specific instances of analytical forms, the Glossary serves as a dynamic accounting of words from the Texts (Fig. 11.22).

Prosopographic Data (Persons)

Persons can refer to any individual, ancient or modern, real or fictional, and even to project personnel. Over the years, RSTI has been fortunate to benefit from the work of various students and volunteers. These contributors are added as Persons in the Persons & Organizations hierarchy. The project administrator can grant or restrict access to specific parts of the project to each user. This simplifies the user experience for occasional workers and gives the project administrator discretion over what materials are available to casual assistants.

While the Persons & organizations category is used by different projects for a wide range of purposes, for RSTI it is used primarily to track proper names mentioned in the texts in hopes of creating a prosopography of these persons, further expanding the network of data created by integrating textual and lexical content. The texts from Ras Shamra mention thousands of ancient individuals. Our goal is to identify persons mentioned in multiple texts and gather as much data as possible about their biography and social network. This includes occupations, family relationships, social standing, and anything else discernible from the texts. We devised a branch of the RSTI Taxonomy to include prosopography-related Variables and

Values in order to systematically capture the features of interest of these ancient people.

By way of review, a Person is an OCHRE database item which is uniquely identified (UUID), has a Name, Aliases, and a Description, and can be described by Properties, Links, Notes, and Events. RSTI uses Properties to distinguish between historical actors and literary characters. Historical actors are the Persons attested in the letters, contracts, and other non-fictional texts. Literary characters are the heroes, gods, and other characters from the mythological and epic stories. When the name of a Person occurs in a Text, the Person database item which has that name is linked to the Discourse unit (word) that represents the name in the Text. This link is recorded as a relational Variable on the properties of the Discourse unit (Fig. 11.23).

As multiple attestations of a given Person are discovered in the Texts, and after the relational Variable links are added, we can View the Person and see a summary of all known attestations (Fig. 11.24).

Note that we keep separate the Person linked to the word (Discourse unit) and the glossary Lemma that represents the name. The Lemma is meant to collect all attested and grammatical forms of the word, for all Persons sharing this name. No attempt is made in the Glossary to disambiguate individuals. The Glossary entry also records any etymological observations we wish to make about the name (Fig. 11.25).

In the Ras Shamra corpus, any name may be written in various scripts or languages, primarily alphabetic Ugaritic or logosyllabic Akkadian. Further, in these languages a given name may be attested in various spellings. All attested spellings are recorded as aliases of the Person. Take for example one of the kings of Ugarit, ʿAmmiṯtamru. His name shows the typical type of variation we would expect in Akkadian: *a*-MIŠ-*tam-ru*, *a-mi*-IZ-*tam-ru*, *am*-ME-EŠ-*tam-ru*, *am-mi*-IZ-*tam-ru*, *am-mi*-IŠ-*tam-ru*, and possibly more. The alphabetic spelling of his name even shows some variation: ʿmṯtmr and ʿmyḏtmr. We track these various spellings not just for academic interest. OCHRE uses these Aliases to find matches in Texts. The Prosopography wizard, *ProTo*, will search all attested names to suggest possible matches to the scholar. The more spellings we add, the smarter the wizard becomes. Despite the variety of orthographic forms attested in the Glossary, we take these names all to refer to the king of Ugarit. Therefore, for each Discourse unit,

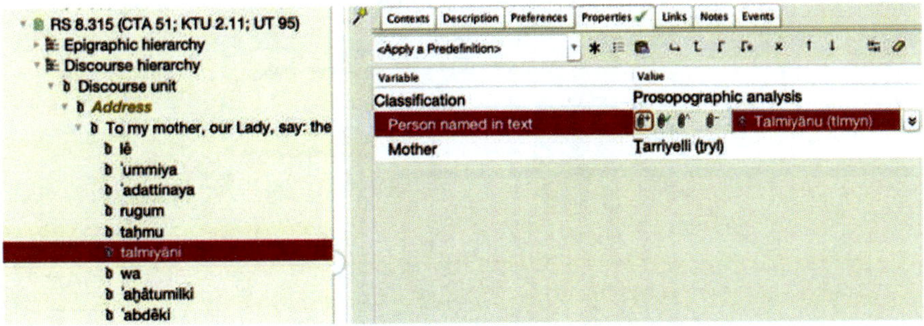

Fig. 11.23 Properties on a Discourse unit link the proper name Talmiyāni to a Person

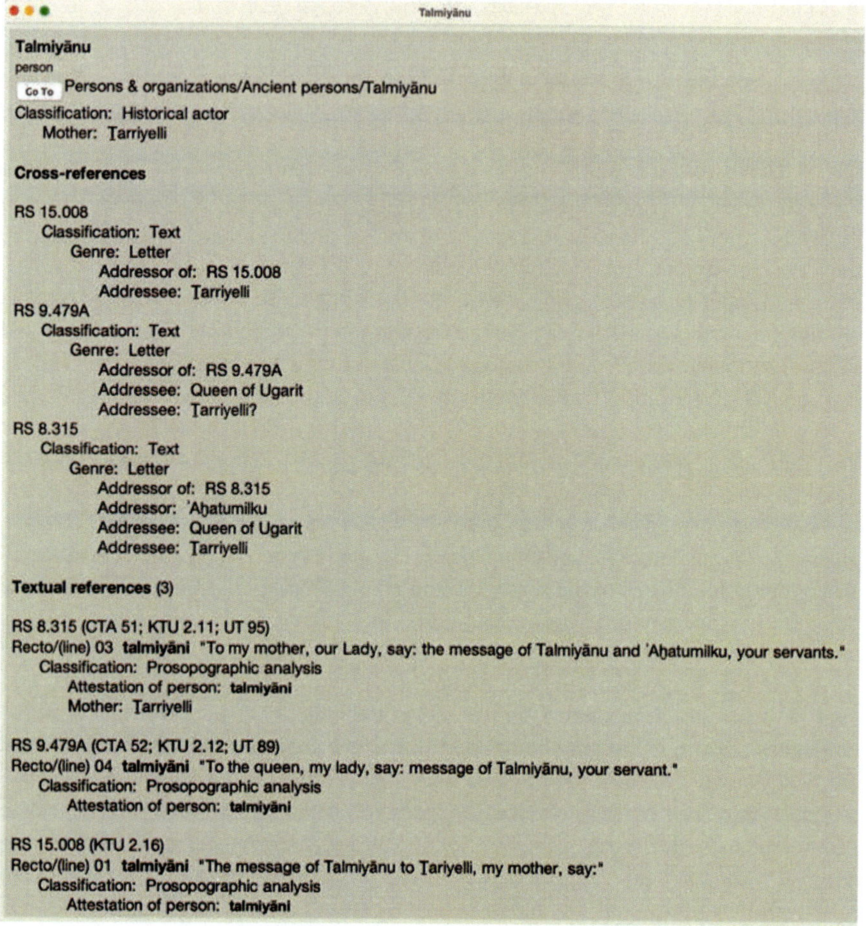

Fig. 11.24 The Comprehensive View lists all references to the Person named Talmiyānu

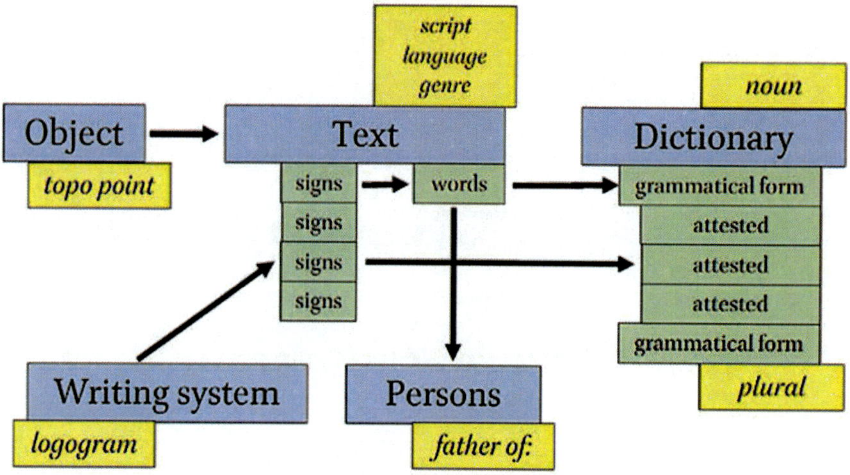

Fig. 11.25 Radical atomization of textual and lexical data supports prosopographic studies

regardless of spelling, we use a relational property to link to the Person item that represents the king ʿAmmiṯtamru. As with Talmiyānu, this network of links allows us to view the Person item and see at a glance all known attestations in the Texts.

We also see in the Comprehensive View the role the king plays in the Texts. These roles are recorded as properties on the relevant Discourse unit in the Text. For example, we may record that the king is the recipient of a letter. This is a localized property that is placed on the specific Discourse unit that references the king by name as the recipient in a specific context. These are not facts about the king that are stable; rather, they are contextualized within a specific transaction or incident. As for the properties that are more durable, we record these on the Person item. For example, where we know familial relationships, we record them with relational Variables on the Person item: Person A is-son-of Person B. These relationships are also reciprocal such that they need be assigned only once for the pair of Persons. The inverse relationship (has-son) applies to Person B and displays in the property pane for that database item. As descriptive details accumulate on the Person items, and as they are linked to activities and transactions in the Texts, new perspectives on an ancient society gradually emerge.

Bibliography

Bibliography is a critical part of any research. RSTI maintains an online Zotero bibliography library.[33] Zotero is a popular bibliographic tool for which OCHRE provides full integration. From within OCHRE, a user can query for and link to bibliography references in the online RSTI Zotero library. The researcher is then able to link these bibliographic references to Texts within RSTI, clicking through to see the full citation presented in the Chicago Manual of Style format. RSTI opts for this style, but OCHRE interacts with the Zotero API to provide a nearly limitless list of other citation formats. For texts in RSTI, we cite the *editio princeps*, all later significant studies of the texts, and usually additional citations about specific words or focused topics in the text (Fig. 11.26).

Personal Aside on Notetaking

RSTI has evolved to serve as my primary notetaking platform on all things Ugaritic. While I am reading a new publication, RSTI is open in the background. For each notecard I wish to make, I create a new "internal document" (an OCHRE Resource item) linked to the text, lemma, architectural unit, or ancient person mentioned in the publication. With a quick query to the Zotero API, I can add citations to the notecard. Over time, I have accumulated a large collection of digital notecards

[33] Zotero is a free online, open-source bibliography management tool. See https://www.zotero.org/.

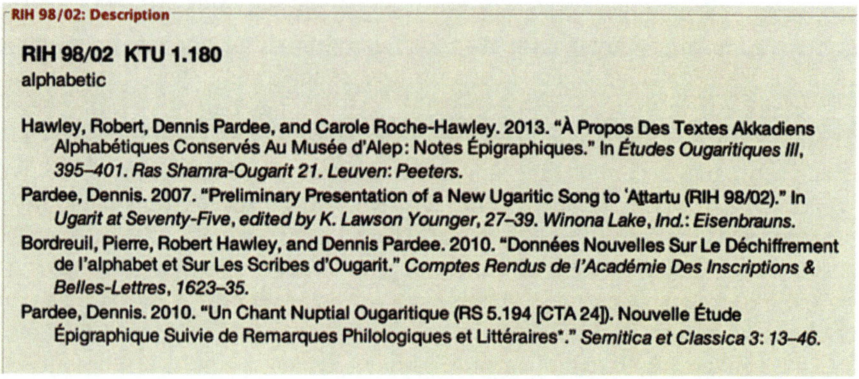

Fig. 11.26 Bibliography entries on a Text are entered and styled using the Zotero API

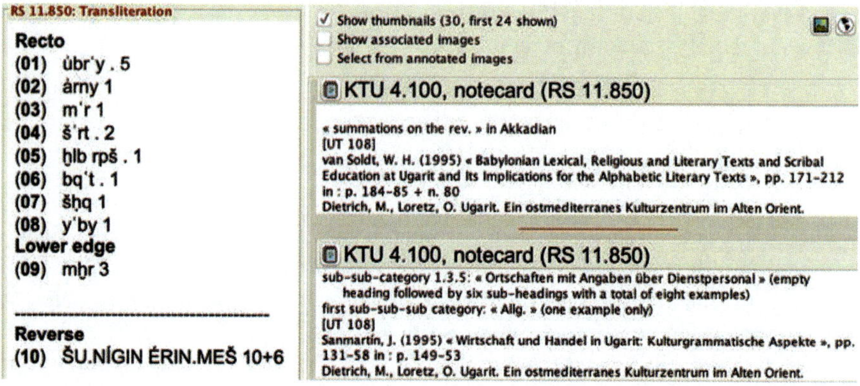

Fig. 11.27 Prosser has amassed thousands of notecards, linked in profusion, to supplement the content of other database items. (As of March 2023, there are 23,173 notecards catalogued and linked in the RSTI project. The vast majority of these were imported from spreadsheets contributed by Pardee)

which are organized so that they are readily accessible from the item of interest. The notecards are also searchable using a character-string based Query. So, even if I am not sure where the notecard may be linked, I can search for text strings in all the notecards and browse through the results (Fig. 11.27).

Temporal Data (Periods)

We are interested in various vectors of time as they relate to ancient Ugarit, and so we represent multiple, overlapping hierarchies of time Periods including (1) archaeological levels I-V at Ras Shamra; (2) an historical outline of Ugarit with kings' reigns; (3) reigns of the Hittite rulers; (4) reigns of the rulers of Carchemish; (5) reigns of the Assyrian kings; and (6) an Egyptian chronology. It should be obvious that we could track other chronological schemas and no doubt we will in the future.

Most of these OCHRE Period items are defined by start and end dates. Admittedly, we cannot be precise in many cases, but it is still valuable to be as accurate as possible. By linking a Period to a Spatial Unit or a Text, we assign a chronological context to that item. This allows us to create chronological sequences of excavation units, of historical actors, or even of texts that refer to historical events. For Texts, this is possible usually because we can identify well-known Persons in the Text. Otherwise, we are left to extrapolate by comparing content between Texts. For Spatial units, we rely on the conclusions of the excavators to assign temporal sequence to excavation units. Most of the Ugaritic Texts date to the very end of the historical sequence at Ugarit, which means that we do not gain much analytic information from the Period hierarchies as we might otherwise (Fig. 11.28).

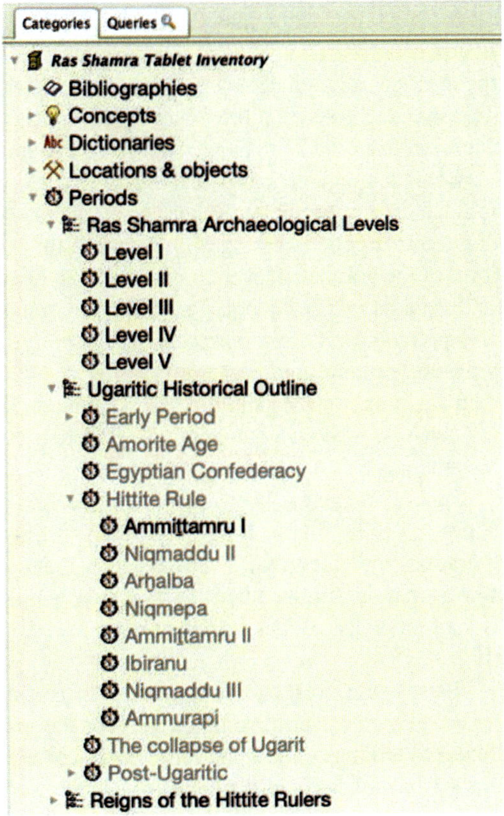

Fig. 11.28 Texts, Persons, and Spatial units can be analyzed based on any number of defined chronologies

Other projects make more extensive use of Periods. For example, an archaeology project will assign excavation phases to ceramic vessels discovered throughout the site. This allows the researchers to query for the location of all pottery by Period, resulting in an effective temporal analysis of the data.

Image Data (Resources)

We are fortunate to have accumulated the largest set of photographs of the tablets from Ras Shamra. The Ras Shamra team produced many of these images during research trips to Damascus, Aleppo, and Paris. Others were donated to RSTI by scholars no longer working on this subject matter. Because every Resource is a separate database item, it can be linked to any other database item. For RSTI, we decided that resources would be linked to Texts. We may well have decided instead to link images to tablets (the objects). This decision was purely pragmatic in that when viewing a Text, we usually want to see the available images; and we typically view Texts more frequently than tablets. In some way, this is a bit misleading. After all, the image represents the physical object, not purely the message written on that object. This distinction may be more semantic than purely about data modeling, but in any case, our choice demonstrates the flexibility of the OCHRE data model and the utility of a graph database approach to the problem. In practice, any given RSTI Text may be linked to a few images or to a few hundred images. Each image can be accessed from the Text View, making consultation convenient.

With its image hotspotting tool, OCHRE provides a unique mechanism for linking data to a region in an image. Any database item can be associated with a user-defined region of a photograph. Because the RSTI textual data is atomized to the level of the grapheme, each grapheme is an item that can be addressed individually. In this case, we draw a polygon shape on an image and associate this polygon with an Epigraphic unit that represents the sign outlined by the polygon. OCHRE provides an intuitive and easy-to-use interface for selecting the Epigraphic unit and then for drawing the polygon on the image. The polygons are separate from the image and can be styled, hidden, displayed in various colors, shown with the grapheme name, etc.

Once an image has been hotspotted, the Text can be presented in a **Synchronized View**, which highlights a polygon when an Epigraphic unit is selected in the transliteration, and vice versa. The translation that corresponds to the selected letter also shows up as highlighted because the letter is linked to a Discourse unit (a word) that is part of a larger Discourse unit (a phrase) where we record this translation (Fig. 11.29).

Because the hotspots are linked to distinct database items, they can be queried based on their descriptive properties (or the properties inherited from their parent Texts) to produce epigraphic letter charts. We hope also eventually to identify various scribal styles if not the hands of specific scribes (Fig. 11.30).

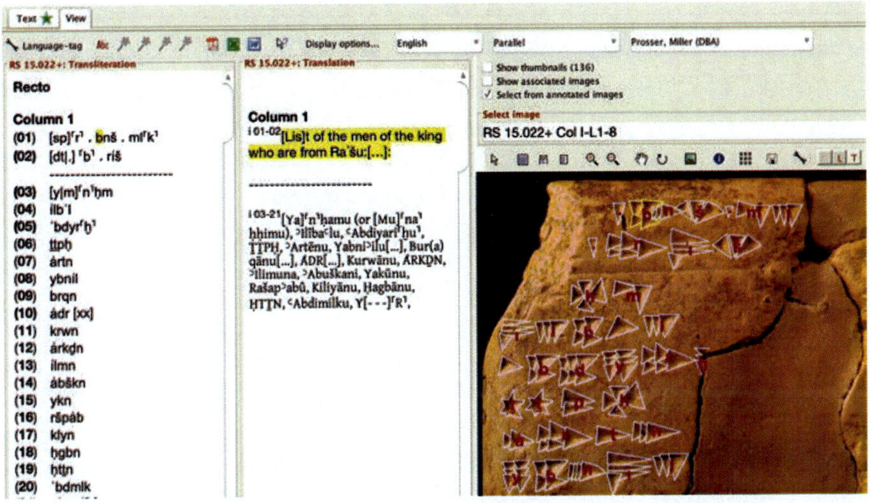

Fig. 11.29 OCHRE traverses a network of data to discover and display relationships

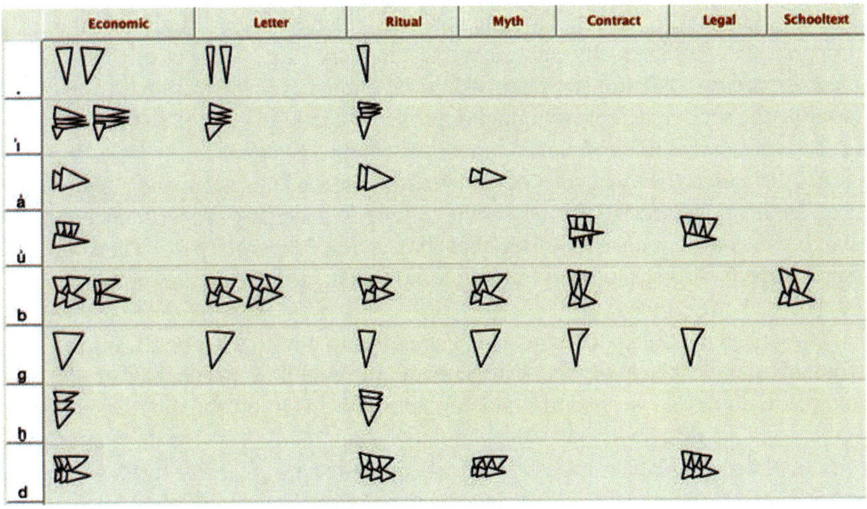

Fig. 11.30 An Epigraphic Letter Chart compares the forms of the alphabetic cuneiform letters from various genres

Analysis: Social Networks

A carefully curated corpus of content consisting of a catalog of objects and editions of texts can serve a variety of other research goals. For example, we are investigating the social and economic organization of the kingdom. What are the rules that serve to organize power? What are the primary structures of the society and what

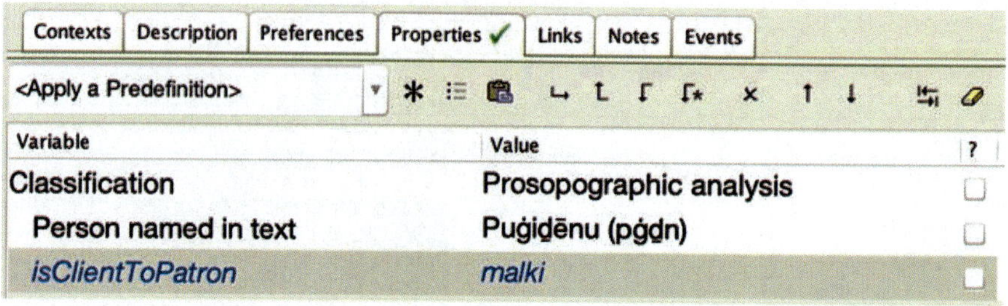

Fig. 11.31 Properties on a Discourse unit identify Puġiḏēnu as a client of the king (*malki*)

role does each actor play? Prosser's current hypothesis is that a unique version of a patron-client system played a role in structuring trust at Ugarit (Prosser 2022). To address these broad questions, we begin with the highly granular data in the texts. Where possible, properties are added to Discourse units—primarily to proper names, occupations, or words for other social groups—properties that identify that entity's role in the social transaction that led to the writing of the Text. In some cases, this is very clear. Some Persons are clearly described as supervisors, and so they are tagged as such. Others, as shown in Fig. 11.31, are described as clients of the king (isClientToPatron). The shaded styling of the property indicates that this property also automatically applies to the king, the target of the link, where the inverse property, isPatronToClient, would be shown. These relational properties, along with the assigned prosopography properties, can be queried to yield a study of the professional roles of named individuals in the archive.

In other cases, the exact roles of persons and relationships between persons in the texts are not as clear. OCHRE allows the scholar to make any property uncertain by clicking the relevant question-mark checkbox on the Properties pane. Then, when it comes time to aggregate this information through a query, uncertain properties can be included or excluded.

This endeavor is an attempt to establish nodes of power at Ugarit. Can we identify individuals who clearly work in the realm of royal power on behalf of the king and his family? Can we identify brokers, who serve as middlemen between power centers and persons lower down the hierarchy? And finally, who are the people who we call clients in the patron-client system? Are there specific terms for these clients in the native language? OCHRE's built-in network analysis feature lets us visualize this data. By adding meaningful properties, nodes are defined in a network of dyadic relationships. We then query for all Discourse units in Texts that are tagged with the appropriate properties and pass the results to OCHRE's **Visualization Wizard** which prompts for some decisions on how to understand the data then generates a visual representation of the network (Fig. 11.32).

It is important to remember that these processes represent acts of scholarship. No matter how well-organized, the data will not otherwise provide answers to these questions. Intentional, or even slow, scholarship plays a critical role in the research process. Computers may have changed our methods, introducing new and improved tools into our toolbox, but they have not eliminated the role of scholars and of

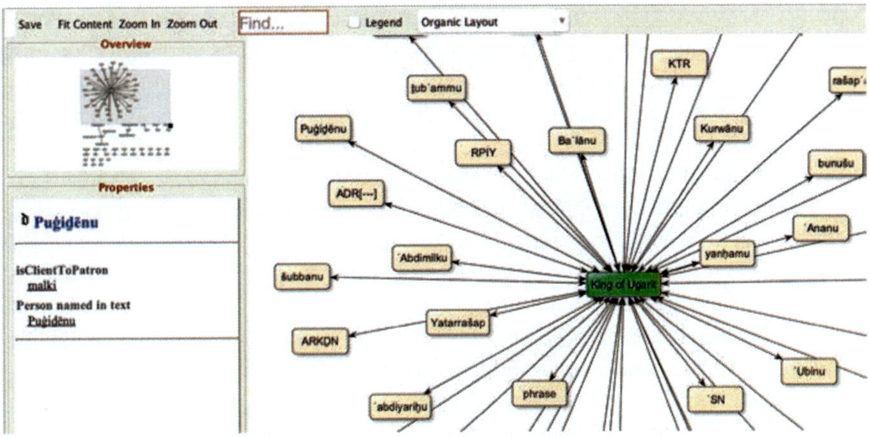

Fig. 11.32 OCHRE's network graph tool helps visualize Patron-Client relationships

traditional analysis. It can be a challenge to determine which tasks should be, or can be, automated and which are better achieved through a high degree of human intervention. In RSTI, as elsewhere in OCHRE, we employ various automated tools and are guided by workflow wizards that handle a portion of the automation but require scholarly interaction. On the other end of the spectrum, we perform tasks that can only be categorized as manual. As computer processes advance, no doubt some of these manual tasks will become more and more automated. However, when it comes to identifying a named individual in a 3000-year-old cuneiform text as either a patron, broker, or client, one struggles to envision a future where an algorithm has been sufficiently trained to address such a question.

Publication

RSTI makes extensive and effective use of the OCHRE API to make data available for viewing online through a traditional web browser or through mobile apps.[34] The complete catalog of inscribed objects has been published, essentially creating an

[34] Instead of listing a traditional-looking URL for the RSTI website, here is the persistent identifier for the entire project. This address is supported by the Digital Library Development Center of the University of Chicago. Whereas a web server is likely to change, this address will be more stable or "persistent." In OCHRE, this persistent ID has been configured to resolve to the current RSTI web server. At the time of this writing, the persistent URL https://pi.lib.uchicago.edu/1001/org/ochre/46ccab46-9c3f-4448-8476-2bf18236791e resolves to https://onlinepublications.uchicago.edu/RSTI/. If the location of the website ever changes, we need only update the field in RSTI that records the new location of the web server. The persistent ID for the project's website will then resolve appropriately to the new location. This strategy provides flexibility and stability, minimizing the possibility of broken links.

updated—now digital—version of TEO. To mimic the published version of TEO, RSTI collects the inscribed objects into Sets by excavation season which are the basis for an interactive HTML-based appendix of objects by season. Each Set is published as an addressable item and all the items in each Set are also published. The OCHRE API fetches the Set, based on its unique identifier (UUID), delivering to the web app an XML file of the Set and its contents. An XSLT style sheet transforms the XML delivered by the API into an easy-to-use table, embedding navigable links behind the name of each item. The embedded links provide click-through access to the individual items, also fetched by the OCHRE API to be presented as simple HTML pages.

The general strategy is that any item or aggregated Set of items in OCHRE is "self-publishing," whereby it is called dynamically via the OCHRE API and styled for immediate presentation in a web app. In this approach, we are not required to manage a web server of static HTML pages. In fact, we are not required to manage *any* content files on a web server. The web server directory for the RSTI digital TEO page contains only a short list of HTML pages, some CSS and JavaScript, and a few icons and images. This dynamic approach to publication simplifies the process immensely. Once an item is published from OCHRE, it becomes available to the API immediately. If later edits are needed, an item can be updated in OCHRE and republished individually (Fig. 11.33).

To publish the tabular appendix of the inscribed objects at Ras Shamra in the RSTI web app, we first run a Query for all inscribed objects from a given season. OCHRE fetches the matching items from their assorted hierarchical contexts and we save the results as a Set. In this case, the Query for objects excavated during Season 15 found 238 items. OCHRE lets the user define which Variables from the project Taxonomy should be included as columns in the resulting table. On the

TEO Season 15

Citation URL: [illegible]

Description
Season 15

Show 25 entries

Name	Description	Object type	Museum Number	Full TEO Findspot
Name	Description	Object type	Museum Number	Full TEO Findspot
RS [Varia 7]	Tablet, Logosyllabic Akkadian	Tablet	AO 27.987	unknown
RS [Varia 8]	Tablet, Logosyllabic Akkadian	Tablet	AO 27.986	unknown
RS 15.001	Tablet, Alphabetic Ugaritic	Tablet	DO 3894	Palais Royal, pièce 53 (Archives Est), p.t. 72, 73, à 0,70
RS 15.002	Tablet, Alphabetic Ugaritic	Tablet	DO 3895	Palais Royal, pièce 53 (Archives Est), p.t. 72, 73, à 0,70
RS 15.003	Tablet, Alphabetic Ugaritic	Tablet	DO 3896	Palais Royal, pièce 53 (Archives Est), p.t. 72, 73, à 0,70
RS 15.004	Tablet, Alphabetic Ugaritic	Tablet	DO 3897	Palais Royal, pièce 53 (Archives Est), p.t. 72, 73, à 0,70
RS 15.005	Tablet, Alphabetic Ugaritic	Tablet	DO 3898	Palais Royal, pièce 53 (Archives Est), p.t. 72, 73, à 0,70

Fig. 11.33 Inscribed objects from Season 15 are fetched dynamically and presented in a sortable, filterable, searchable HTML table in the RSTI web app

configuration pane of the Set we select: Object type, Museum number, Findspot, Associated text, Script, Language, and Size. With a click of a button all the items in the Set are published, making each one accessible through the OCHRE API. The click of a second button publishes the Set as a single collective item.

The OCHRE API accesses the published Set using a persistent identifier (PI):

https://pi.lib.uchicago.edu/1001/org/ochre/7e5dbd07-bbfb-47ca-8fc1-13a0717bf464.

The first portion of the URL is the same for every OCHRE item. The URL is unique based on the item's UUID at the end of the base URL. Specifically, the published Set includes the UUID of each item along with the Values of the Variables selected as table columns.[35] The API delivers this content to the client browser as a highly structured XML document that can be manipulated in the HTML.

The strategy we use to publish a digital version of TEO is only one of the many ways a frontend application might process data published from OCHRE. Because each item can be fetched as an individual document, a user might decide to embed persistent identifiers as links in a PDF or other digital document. In this way, a digital publication can be enhanced with clickable links that allow the reader to explore the data in ways that could not be expressed in a traditional publication. For example, if we were to publish a text edition in a scholarly journal, we may wish to include more figures than the journal is willing or able to print. Or we may wish to provide full color images, which some journals are unwilling to publish. These additional resources could be made available to the reader of the journal through links based on the OCHRE API.

Digital publication opens doors to many new and interesting modes for delivering data to our audience. In the humanities and social sciences, maps can serve as vital and powerful tools for visualizing data. Online tools such as ArcGIS Online[36] can consume data packaged and published from OCHRE to create compelling and engaging applications. In RSTI, we are creating GIS vector shapes to represent the various areas, buildings, and rooms on the site of Ras Shamra, and we are including GIS points to represent the findspots of inscribed objects. From OCHRE, we export this GIS information as shapefiles that can be used to create interactive maps in ArcGIS online. Note that rather than creating these maps in QGIS and uploading them directly to ArcGIS online, by using OCHRE, we can include metadata about the inscribed objects in the exported shapefile. This strategy reimagines a common approach whereby GIS users treat the attribute table of a shapefile as an ersatz database for storing metadata about the objects. This approach suffers from the limitations a spreadsheet imposes on data which we need not reiterate here. By using OCHRE to generate the attribute table of the shapefile according to various export specifications, we retain the flexibility and utility of the OCHRE data model for

[35] For the digital version of TEO, we configured the Set to include only a list of the UUIDs of the items in that Set. We then use an Angular JavaScript app to create the tabular appendix.

[36] ArcGIS Online is a tool from ESRI that can be used to create GIS maps for display in Web apps.

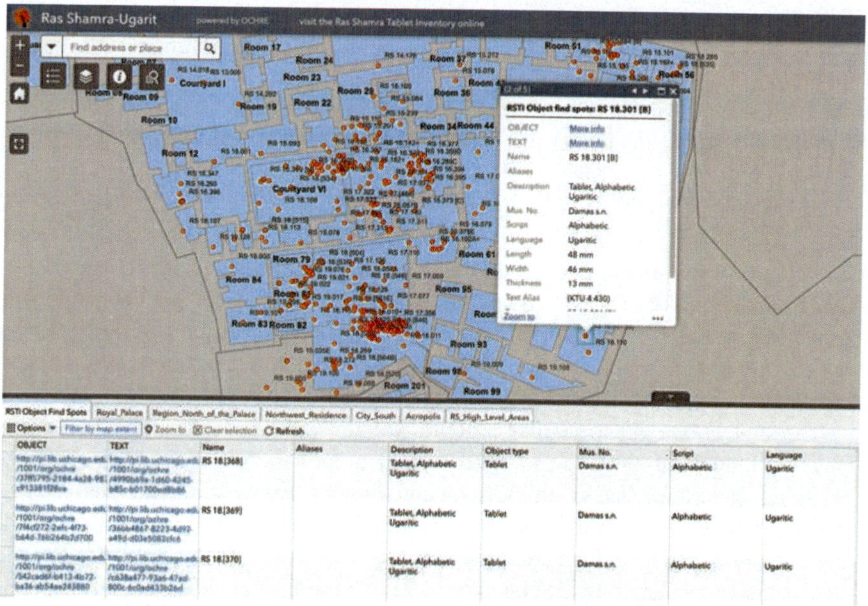

Fig. 11.34 An ArcGIS Online app is greatly enhanced by data published from OCHRE

managing our complex data. The information exported from OCHRE to the attribute table is accessible to the ArcGIS web application and can be used for querying and filtering. The persistent ID of each item is also included as an attribute, allowing the web map to provide click-through links from the map to detailed views of the items (Fig. 11.34).[37]

Finally, we consider the use of the OCHRE API for publishing text editions. OCHRE produces TEI-compliant XML that can be accessed by the API and customized by various export parameters. The Text Encoding Initiative (TEI) maintains a standard for representing texts digitally which includes rules for how elements and attributes may be formatted to represent texts as XML documents. To be clear, the storage of textual data as highly atomized XML documents in the OCHRE database is not based on the TEI standard. However, XML documents published using the OCHRE API can be made to be TEI-compliant.

Some projects may wish to retrieve a published XML document that contains highly granular textual content where each character is accessible as a separate XML element. Others may need a more flattened document with words and lines recomposed for easy display. The text publication parameters allow for these and other variations of published XML to be accessed through the API. Like other items

[37]The RSTI ArcGIS web mapping application is available at https://onlinepublications.uchicago.edu/RSTI/maps.html.

published from OCHRE, a Text is accessible via its persistent identifier. Its component parts can be published, and accessed, separately or in the aggregate. Having a common strategy for publishing all OCHRE data greatly eases the process by which OCHRE data comes to life in web applications.

Conclusion

RSTI is a work in progress. We began by importing a large set of legacy data into OCHRE, integrating previously dispersed sets of descriptive and image data, then added born-digital text editions amplified with classificatory properties. Through queries, analysis, and publication, we continue to expand this data set, both in traditional ways and by innovating new avenues of inquiry not previously imagined.

RSTI fully leverages OCHRE's data model and the possibility of a radical degree of atomization. Every inscribed object is itemized as a discrete database item, described using a custom hierarchical taxonomy of itemized Variables and Values, and contextualized by findspot in the Locations & objects category. In this way, a complex branching tree of nodes representing the entire excavated site of Ras Shamra has been created. Texts, too, have been fully atomized for both epigraphic and discourse analysis, and for the creation of a corpus-based Glossary. In a very real way, the database of research is built up from individual graphemes to texts and objects, to persons, time periods, glossaries, and ultimately to a vast network of data. RSTI currently records nearly two million epigraphic units that comprise nearly six hundred thousand discourse units in nearly five thousand texts recorded on objects found in hundreds of locations on one ancient site.

Where does RSTI go from here? The answer to this question is the best argument for adopting an item-based approach. Whatever new directions we pursue, the database does not stand as a structural hinderance. After the initial import of data, we focused on integrating the GIS-based spatial component of RSTI. We were also motivated to explore the identification of personal names in the texts. Neither of these tasks was explicitly in our initial plan. Once our various data sets were integrated in a common platform, it became apparent that these research efforts would be valuable. In the early days, we did not plan on publishing subsets of our data to the web, and yet now the OCHRE data model and the OCHRE API makes this very easy.

As of this writing, RSTI is pursuing a research partnership to study the poetics of the epic texts from Ras Shamra. Because our texts are not limited by a restrictive data model, we can accept this new challenge; the underlying data need not change. New analysis can stand alongside our previous work. Our research data is already in a format that is flexible enough to be used and reused for many purposes. The level of abstraction and granularity makes this possible and creates unlimited potential for future studies and collaborations.

Chapter 12
Digital History Case Study: Greek Coin Hoards

Introduction

While excavating as a volunteer during the summer of 1989 at the site of Ashkelon on Israel's southern coast, S. Schloen lucked into an amazing discovery. The gentle workings of the handpick in the corner of a room loosened the soil around some long-corroded flecks of metal. Although this lowly peon was hastily reassigned to make room for the professional archaeologists, what emerged was a hoard of silver tetradrachmas, which bore the profile of Alexander the Great. Buried with it was a laurel-wreathed diadem and a silver bracelet, adding to the allure and mystique of this remarkable find (Fig. 12.1).[1]

Coin hoards are found all over the Mediterranean world and the importance of such goes far beyond the romantic imaginations of a novice summer archaeologist. The study of how and why collections of coins come to co-locate and the reasons as to where and why they co-circulate and come to be intentionally deposited together are of great interest to experts looking to enhance their understanding of commerce and trade in the ancient world.

CRESCAT-HARP Overview

The Hoard Analysis Research Project (HARP) is a subproject of the CRESCAT initiative[2] under the direction of Alain Bresson, a professor of Greek economic history in the Department of Classics at the University of Chicago. In order to

[1] See Stager (1991). The hoard was found in Grid 57, Square 68, Room 341 in "a small pit cut into the floor" (MC 31620). Ashkelon 1, p. 322.

[2] CRESCAT: A Computational Research Ecosystem for Scientific Collaboration on Ancient Topics began in September 2015 with generous support from a National Science Foundation (NSF) grant,

S. R. Schloen, M. C. Prosser, *Database Computing for Scholarly Research*, Quantitative Methods in the Humanities and Social Sciences,
https://doi.org/10.1007/978-3-031-46696-0_12

Fig. 12.1 Coin hoards, like this collection of silver tetradrachmas found at Ashkelon, raise challenges for data representation. (Photograph by C. Andrews, courtesy of the Leon Levy Expedition to Ashkelon)

represent the project accurately, we restate here the research goals summarized in the original project proposal.

> Coin hoards are a rich source of evidence for economic and political history because they reveal patterns of exchange that reflect economic trends and political relationships. However, numismatic researchers lack a computational tool to easily perform global analyses of the circulation patterns reflected in many thousands of spatially and temporally distributed hoards. This project will develop such a tool using network analysis methods in conjunction with other statistical methods (e.g., principal components analysis) to detect clustering patterns among hoards at various geographical and chronological scales. The effects of geographical proximity (or transportational proximity based on least-cost routes by land and sea) will be compared to clustering of hoards that may override the effects of geography and reflect important economic and political relationships. This will allow us to identify the cities (mints) that played more or less important roles as connectors within the network in a given period.

We will not attempt to answer these research questions in what follows. Far from it! We will leave that to the experts on the Greek economy and society. Rather, we will show how a suitable computational platform that provides rigorous data modeling

---

Award 145,045. UChicago archaeologist, David Schloen, was the PI; Walter Shandruk (PhD '16, Classics UChicago) was the postdoctoral researcher; Bresson, now retired, is the Robert O. Anderson Distinguished Service Professor Emeritus in Classics, History, the Oriental Institute, and the College (https://www.nsf.gov/awardsearch/showAward?AWD_ID=1450455).

and integration in conjunction with appropriate tools can support such research effectively. Follow along as we analyze the project's data needs, implement a database solution using an item-based approach, and experiment with tools that will help the scholars achieve their goals.

Background

The initial set of data on which this research is based came from a series of good, old-fashioned books. The *Inventory of Greek Coin Hoards (IGCH)* (Thompson et al. 1973) is the definitive work on the subject. However, having been published by the American Numismatic Society (ANS) in 1973, it is significantly out of date. The *IGCH* catalogs Greek coin hoards by assigning to each a unique number and listing their provenance and date. It also lists, where possible, the contents of each hoard, itemizing the quantity, denominations, and mints of groups of coins of different types (Fig. 12.2). A follow-up series of ten books in the "Coin Hoards" (CH) series by the Royal Numismatic Society has updated the IGCH, taking into account new discoveries and further analysis of the known coin hoards.[3]

The coin hoard data is a case in point of how humanities data is qualitatively different from data produced by the hard sciences. We often deal with incomplete data, working with only part of the picture. We should not let this discourage us from asking hard questions about the data. But there is often a gap between the state of the data and our ability to use the data for analysis. Bridging this gap is a very real challenge. Allow us to highlight just some of the variation, ambiguity, and complexity of which we are well aware, which make this data problematic.

First, there is a wide range of coinage of different denominations representing different values up for comparison. Many of the hoards list rather imprecise counts

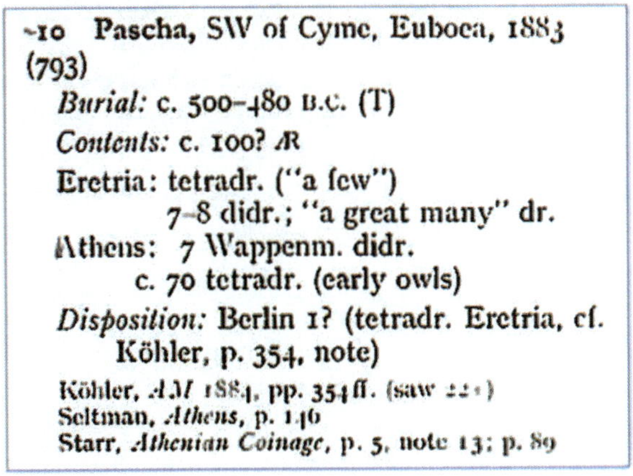
~10 **Pascha,** SW of Cyme, Euboea, 1883
(793)
Burial: c. 500–480 B.C. (T)
Contents: c. 100? AR
Eretria: tetradr. ("a few")
7–8 didr.; "a great many" dr.
Athens: 7 Wappenm. didr.
c. 70 tetradr. (early owls)
Disposition: Berlin 1? (tetradr. Eretria, cf. Köhler, p. 354, note)
Köhler, *AM* 1884, pp. 354ff. (saw 22?)
Seltman, *Athens*, p. 146
Starr, *Athenian Coinage*, p. 5, note 13; p. 89

Fig. 12.2 IGCH 0010 provides a semi-structured description of this hoard found in Pascha

[3] See Royal Numismatic Society of Great Britain (1981).

of the coins in the hoard ("a great many"). Find spots are sometimes also imprecise, specified only as a broad region. In addition to the locations of the hoards, we have a second set of location information: the mints. The project wishes to understand the relationship between the minting location of a coin and the hoard find spot. They are interested in which kinds of coins from which mints end up co-circulating. Did low-value coinage circulate differently from high-value coinage, and in what kinds of networks? The researchers would benefit from effective visualization strategies to help illustrate these processes. Were it not for this variation, ambiguity, and complexity, we could use Excel or FileMaker. The item-based, hierarchical approach of OCHRE helps to bridge the gap between the difficult nature of the data and the research goals for learning from it.

When the CRESCAT-HARP project started in 2015, the printed *IGCH* data set, representative of the "document model" of pre-digital days, was complemented by an online version of the entries in the *IGCH* made available through a website managed by the American Numismatic Society (ANS). At that time, the ANS site was essentially a transcription of the hoard descriptions from the printed coin hoard volumes. As such, it was limited in its support of research by virtue of the inherent limitations of a page model of data. Data was served to the web browser a page at a time in response to human-user interaction providing a user experience typical of web applications that involves navigating through linked data.

More recently, a new and improved Coin Hoards website has been released, which "provides primary data and other information on 2,387 hoards of coins produced by Greeks and other non-Roman peoples in the Mediterranean and adjacent regions between ca. 650 and 30 BCE. In addition to a basic description, users will find on the page devoted to each hoard mapping tools for the findspot and mint(s) where the coins found in the hoard were produced, bibliographical references, and a list of the hoard contents."[4] CoinHoards.org now uses Linked Open Data (LOD) protocols to present much more granular data highly itemized and richly linked in the spirit of an item-based approach (Fig. 12.3).

The CRESCAT-HARP project aimed to confront additional questions like: how to quantify the hoard data, in either weight or value; how to handle incomplete, uncertain, or approximate descriptions and valuations in the legacy data; how to build a meaningful network of relationships between mints and the minted coins; how to find patterns of distribution, or co-circulation, of coinage geographically or by time period?.

[4] http://coinhoards.org. The CRESCAT-HARP team would like to thank and acknowledge the collaborative efforts of Dr. Peter van Alfen and Ethan Gruber from the American Numismatic Society.

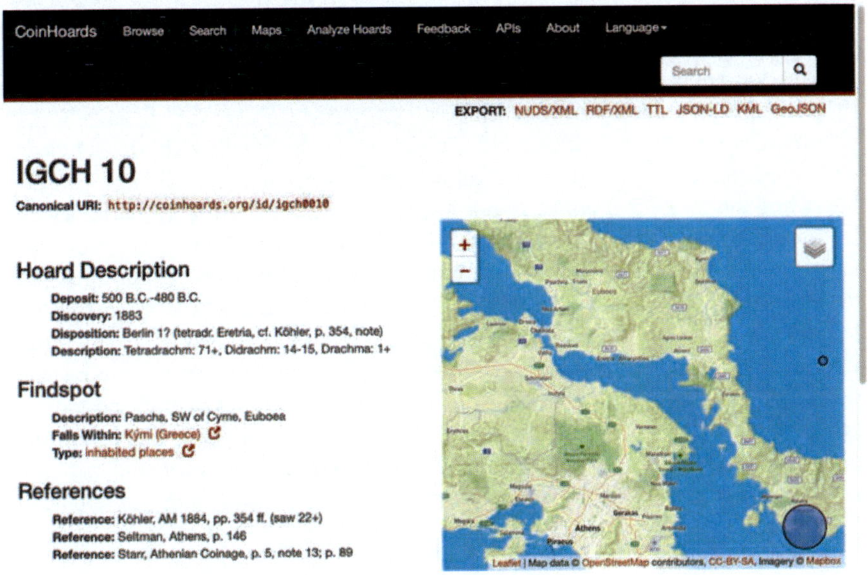

Fig. 12.3 Coin hoard IGCH 0010 is described, itemized, and geolocated on the Amencan Numismatic Society's website (http://coinhoards.org/id/igch0010)

Preparation

It was important at the outset of this project to pause and reflect on the research questions and how the data can address those questions. It is tempting to get started as quickly as possible. It feels good to make progress. However, sometimes, quick starts turn into false starts. In the CRESCAT project, we took time to reflect on the nature of the data and how best to represent it in OCHRE. In the sections that follow, we will review how we reanalyzed and restructured this data set along the outline of the principles discussed in this book. This will illustrate how the item-based, hierarchical data model as implemented in OCHRE allows us to extract a much richer set of analytic data from this same legacy data set, and we will demonstrate assorted analysis and publication options that this approach makes possible.

Atomize and Organize

Locations & Objects

First things first. What *is* the "minimal, meaningful" unit being described by this data? This turned out to be less obvious than it seemed. While a "hoard" was the basic unit of investigation, itemizing at that level would have left out too much information about the coins themselves that might be claimed. But in answering the question *How far is far enough?,* we had to be realistic about the nature of the available data which is highly summarized and already aggregated, not giving much information about individual coins. Instead, we find details like "7–8 didr. from Eretria" or "c. 70 tetradr. from Athens."

Taking at face value the published listings of *groups of coins* within each hoard, we settled on the notion of a "Coin group" as an intermediary item between the coin hoard and the individual coins. In our analysis, a **Coin group** represents a subcollection of coins of a single denomination from a specified mint of a given metal type (any of which might be uncertain or unknown). If any of these factors differed—the denomination, the mint, or the metal—we would create a new coin group. This resulted in database items that mimicked the descriptions like "7-8 didr. from Eretria" and "70 tetradr. from Athens"—an accurate but more granular representation of the data as reported by the *IGCH.* Students set about identifying the coin groups represented in each of the hoards, untangling the inconsistently published descriptions, making explicit any implied information (e.g., inferring the Mint for a list of items from the same mint), and nesting the coin group items hierarchically within their hoards.

This process raised the question: How should we label these coin group items? It was overkill to give each of them a unique identifier as a Name (e.g., Coin group 1, and Coin group 2); OCHRE already automatically assigns a universally unique identifier (UUID). And it was unnecessarily laborious to type out a description like "7-8 didr. from Eretria," redundantly, to use as a name. And so, we coined the Name "Coin(s)" to serve as an all-purpose label for all of the coin groups (Fig. 12.4).

In the sections that follow, we will discuss assorted variations and complications inherent in the data being captured, but the notion of coin groups sent us down a productive path. Note that this model does not preclude the possibility that some other scholar might wish to do a future investigation of individual coins. This was not the focus of the current research, but should a scholar wish to study individual coins from the hoards, this model would extend naturally. Any individual coin could be pulled from its coin group and nested within it hierarchically as its own item. Modeled in this way, an individual coin would inherit everything known about its contextual ancestors—its coin group, its parent hoard, and its geographic context.

The hoard items are spatial in nature, as we have seen, but not all have findspot coordinates. Yet, we do not want to ignore that which we can know about each hoard spatially. Sometimes the hoard location is defined in relation to the closest city, and sometimes, even, just the region is noted. A hierarchically organized geographic

IGCH 0010; Greece/Pascha : Hoard : IGCH 0010 : c. 500-480 B.C. : -500 : -480 : Quantification : Silver : 100 : c. QtySum: 129 SumTetrdr: 77.000 tetradr.
Coin(s); Pascha/IGCH 0010 : Hoard item : Coin(s) : Athens : Quantification : Silver : 7 didr. ValTetrdr: 3.5 tetradr.
Coin(s); Pascha/IGCH 0010 : Hoard item : Coin(s) : Erétria : Quantification : Silver : Tetradrachm : Few
Coin(s); Pascha/IGCH 0010 : Hoard item : Coin(s) : Erétria : Quantification : Silver : Drachma : Great many
Coin(s); Pascha/IGCH 0010 : Hoard item : Coin(s) : Erétria : Quantification : Silver : 7 didr. : 8 didr.
Coin(s); Pascha/IGCH 0010 : Hoard item : Coin(s) : Athens : Quantification : Silver : 70 tetradr. : c.

Fig. 12.4 The hoard IGCH 0010 is itemized into Coin groups in OCHRE context can provide the means to capture whatever level of information is provided, without suggesting too much or saying too little. Hoard items are assigned their coordinates where available, but where not available, they are listed within their nearest stated geographic location, whether a city or a region. It is important to keep in mind that sibling items in a containment hierarchy are not necessarily of the same category—hoards are intermingled with subregions or cities. The location Cyprus (Fig. 12.5) contains sub-locations (Amathus, Athienou, etc.) and it contains objects (IGCH 1273, etc.). (Be careful not to confuse a spatial containment hierarchy with a kind of hierarchy where each child is a more specific type of the parent item like Coin>Stater>Gold stater.)

Periods

Configuring **Periods** for this project was a simple matter of creating Period items for each of the Archaic and Classical periods. Since we were limiting the scope of the current study to items from just these two periods, this was all that was needed.

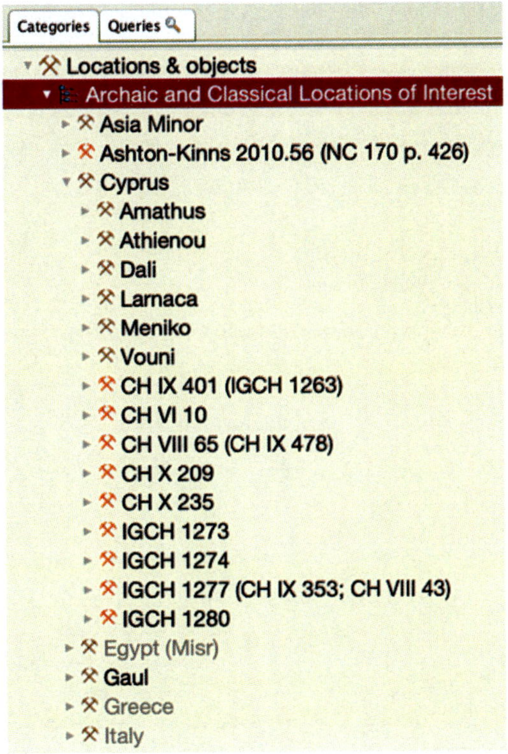

Fig. 12.5 The branching of the Coin Hoard spatial hierarchy allows for a mix of different kinds of items at different spatial levels

Persons & Organizations

Next, we set about entering and organizing the mints. These must be "Locations" too, right? But while Athens and Eretria are indeed locations, there are other jurisdictions listed in the IGCH and CH volumes under which coins were minted such as Alexander I or Philip II. These are not simply determined by a dot on a map. So, rather than listing the mints as locations, we conceived of them as Minting authorities, whether a specific city or a ruler, and identified them in OCHRE as **Persons & organizations.** Since OCHRE supports spatial characteristics for Persons & organization items, the project assigned coordinates to most of the minting authorities, and so, no further hierarchical organization was needed (Fig. 12.6).

Concepts

Having identified persons, places, and things, what remained was to devise a strategy to model the system of currencies represented by the coin groups in these hoards. We wanted to remain faithful to the data as recorded, and also to be able to analyze the coin groups quantitatively with respect to the quantities listed, their weights (based on scholarship from the field of Classical studies), and their monetary value. We also wanted to be able to compare the values (or weights) of the hoards even when the hoards contained coins of differing denominations. To manage that, we needed to establish the relationship between the various coin denominations and convert to a standard unit so as not to be guilty of comparing apples to oranges, or (as the French say) *comparer des choux et des carrottes*.

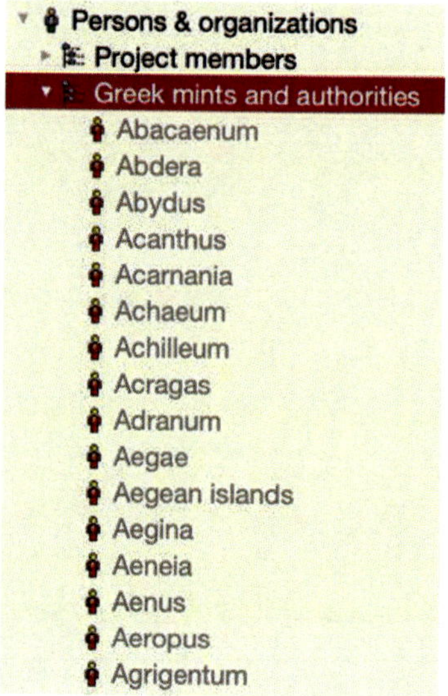

Fig. 12.6 The list of Minting authorities remains flat

For this, we turned to OCHRE's **Concepts** category. Each coin denomination was represented by a Concept item with its denomination specified as its unit of measure. This is analogous to how we use Concepts to model other measurements. When specifying Length, for example, we can record measures in millimeters, centimeters, meters, or kilometers and relate them all to the standard unit, *meter*, for comparison. When recording Weight, as another example, we can measure in milligrams, grams, or kilograms, and relate them all to the *kilogram* standard unit.

Choosing somewhat arbitrarily the tetradrachm as a standard unit, we organized the remaining currencies as subitems subordinate to it. We then related the concepts to the tetradrachm standard using an appropriate conversion factor. Note that we could just as easily have used the stater or the shekel as the standard measure. In fact, competing standards could be set up using OCHRE's ability to model multiple, overlapping hierarchies, allowing the user to run analyses under different conditions.

Propertize

To build in basic logic regarding currency conversion, we exploited OCHRE's property mechanism which allows us to describe items of any kind with any number of properties of any kind. Working through this case study, we will show how we *propertize* not only the Concepts (coin denominations) but also, primarily, the Locations & objects (hoards and coin groups) to capture as much detail as possible for each of these categories of items.

Concepts

To facilitate currency conversion and other numeric analysis, we added special intelligence to a predefined OCHRE decimal property called **Conversion Factor**. Any project can use this property, borrowed from the master OCHRE project, to set up its own system of related measures. Current uses of this property include: converting currencies among US dollars, Euros, and British pounds as the sale of artifacts at auction houses is tracked; converting the volume of dry liters of commodities like barley and dates among Old Assyrian traders passing through the ancient city of Kanesh in central Anatolia (modern-day Turkey); converting feet to meters and acres to hectares as data is captured from old archaeological paperwork; converting weights measured in grams of ballista balls found at a Classical Greek/Roman site to minaes and libras for comparison on a common scale. For each Concept (denomination) in our list of currencies, we assigned an appropriate Conversion factor with respect to the tetradrachm. Different currencies can then be converted easily to the tetradrachm unit, and to each other, by way of the tetradrachm unit (Fig. 12.7).

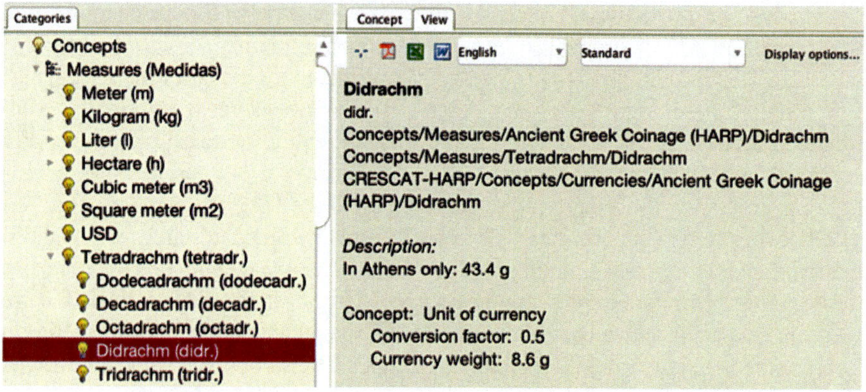

Fig. 12.7 Currency values are organized hierarchically as Concepts and related to a chosen (parent) standard using a Conversion factor; here, two didrachm make up a tetradrachm

Locations & Objects

Even though we restricted our current study to the hoards from just the Archaic and Classical periods, the data entry effort produced 1056 hoards. Each combination of *denomination-plus-mint-plus-metal* constituted a coin group itemized within its hoard. In all, we realized a total of 4249 coin groups. While not exactly “big data,” it is certainly enough with which to do interesting quantitative analysis.

Identifying Hoards

Hoards were identified with the property Location or object type = Hoard. The ICGH or CH identification number was used both as the item’s Name and as a property. While this will seem somewhat redundant, having the Hoard ID available as a *property* (rather than just as a *label*) allows the subcoin groups to *inherit* this detail, making it useful for querying or other analysis.

The date the hoard was buried, insofar as it was reported, was listed in the publication under the “Burial” label as either a specific date, a date range, or an approximate date. We created an alphanumeric property to capture this legacy string as a reference. But string-matching would be an inadequate method for finding hoards based on their burial date and so we used parallel properties that represented the given date as a numeral or a numeric range. Year BC, earliest, and latest were defined as integer properties that would allow querying, for example, for all hoards where the earliest (or latest) burial date was prior to 500 BC or within a specified range (Fig. 12.8).

Having qualified the hoards to be selected for this study based on their date, each hoard item was tagged as either an Archaic or Classical hoard by being linked to the appropriate Period on its Links tab. As it happens, IGCH 0010 is represented in both the Archaic and Classical periods, and so both Periods are linked.

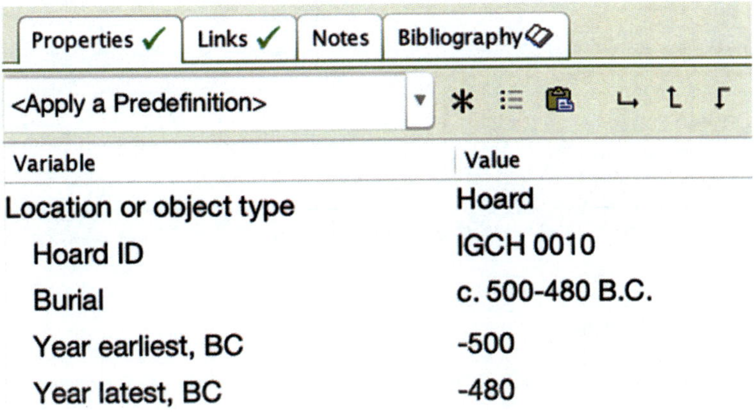

Fig. 12.8 The Year was specified as a negative value to indicate that it is BC

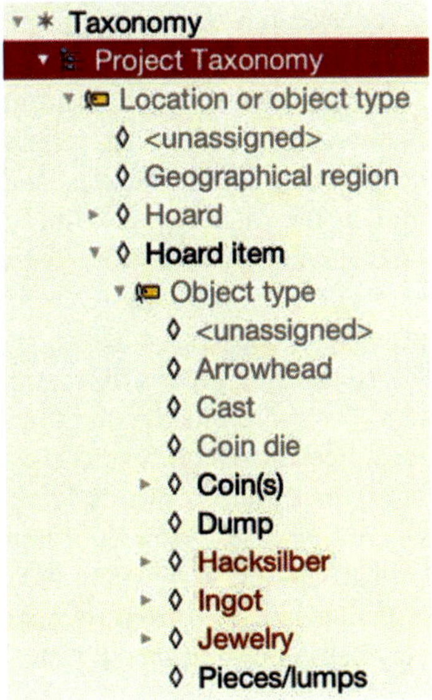

Fig. 12.9 Some taxonomic Values (shown in red or grey) were borrowed from the OCHRE master project; others were added as unique to this project ("Pieces/lumps")

Identifying Hoard Items

Every coin group, labeled Coin(s), was created within its containing hoard and described with the property Location or object type = Hoard item. While doing data entry, we noticed that the published coin hoard volumes noted other kinds of objects that were found within these hoards, so we tagged these too. The initial branch of the descriptive taxonomy thus allowed for various type of ingots, hacksilver, jewelry, etc., to be listed as other Hoard items, where applicable, along with the coin group items (Fig. 12.9).

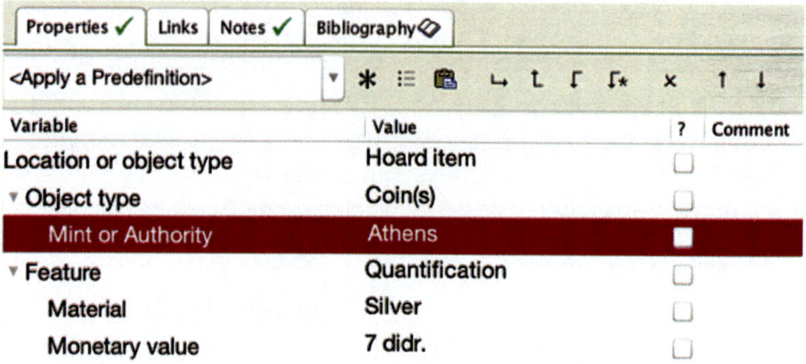

Fig. 12.10 The relational property, Mint or Authority, defines a Person & organization item, the mint, as a valid target link

By definition, each coin group was associated with a mint. The Other Links tab could be used to make this connection, much like the Periods are linked, but there is a better option. A *relational property* provides a mechanism to link two items, not loosely on the Links tab, but as a targeted link, where the relational property ascribes semantic value to the link. In this case, we called the relational property Mint or Authority, to identify the relationship between the Locations & objects item (the coin group), and the Persons & organizations item, the mint. Selecting the required mint as the value for the Mint or Authority relational variable, we thereby create a link between the two. Note that this is a bidirectional link; the coin group is associated with the mint, and consequently, the mint item is associated with the coin group (Fig. 12.10).

All the coin groups that were minted in Athens are linked to the same database item that represents the mint in Athens. Finding all coin groups minted in Athens, regardless of which hoards they appear in, is a simple matter of following those links. In addition, hoards were assigned their findspot coordinates in OCHRE, where available. Two sets of latitude/longitude coordinates are thus relevant to any coin group: one assigned to its related mint, representing where it was minted, and the other inherited from its hoard, representing where it was found, in effect, the very beginning and the very end of the coins' circulation.

The Challenge of Quantification

Confident that we could identify the items under consideration and locate them in time and space, we were left with the more complicated problem of quantifying both the hoards and the coin groups. On one level, it seemed straightforward as we set out to capture "5 staters" or "7 didrachm." A decimal property, **Monetary value**, was created, its Units associated with the tetradrachm standard of measure defined as a Concept. When a Coin group's Monetary value was entered, a recognizable Unit of measure was needed. The Unit would be the Abbreviation of the relevant

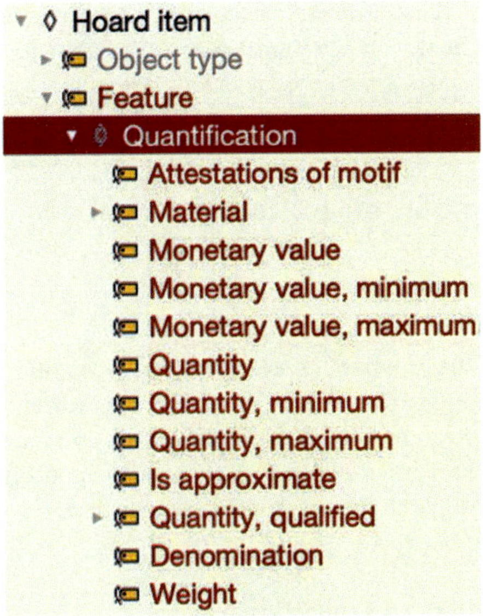

Fig. 12.11 The Quantification branch of the Taxonomy was established for the Hoard items but is re-used, as is, for the Coin groups

currency denomination documented as a Concept item; for example, five staters would be entered as "5 st.," seven didrachms as "7 didr." Each specific value was recorded in its *original* units, remaining faithful to the published record, but the currency Concepts related each Monetary value to the *standard* unit (Fig. 12.11).

This approach handled the ordinary cases where both an amount and a denomination are given, but within the published record, there are many cases that are not so precise. In the sample hoard IGCH 0010 alone, there are notations like "a few" tetradrachm, "7–8" didrachm, and "a great many" drachm all minted in Eretria, along with "c. 70" tetradrachm minted at Athens. It would be overstepping, and a misrepresentation, to force these less-specific forms of quantification to adhere to the more exact nature of the Monetary value data capture. But to ignore these less precise descriptions also seems misleading.

It is worth mentioning, too, that this is not just an issue with the recording method or the publication standard. The hoards, themselves, are archaeological objects, corroded, dirty, worn, broken, stuck together in clumps. It is simply not possible in many cases to say more than "approximately 70" or "a great many." And so, we created additional properties to capture more faithfully the ambiguity and vagueness of the published data, which correctly represents the ambiguity and uncertainty of the coin hoards.

A property representing Quantity was used instead of Monetary value to capture the cases where the amount was recorded, but not the coin denomination. Properties representing minimum and maximum amounts covered values like "7–8," "at least 100," and "300 + ." A Boolean property, "Is approximate," recorded vagueness. Properties for Material and Denomination were used either singly or together when all that was listed was "Silver" or "obols" or "Silver tetradr" (with no quantities specified). And finally, an ordinal property was designed to enumerate the qualitative characterizations ranging from "few" to "great many." Armed with the means to represent faithfully the wide range of published notations, the research assistants set to work.

Data Integration and Analysis

Analysis

We promised at the outset that we would not pretend to be Classicists with answers to the research questions. But we do want to illustrate how the data that results from a carefully organized item-based approach, extensively documented by meaningful properties, along with tools that support integration and interaction, can support the research requirements of this project.

Derived Properties

Having carefully captured the various ways to quantify either a hoard or a group of coins, how then can we usefully apply quantitative methods to such a diverse set of tagged data? This is where OCHRE's derived properties come into play.

To avoid comparing cabbages and carrots, it was necessary to resolve the separate coin groups into a common currency of choice, in this case, the tetradrachm. For this, we used a Derived Variable, of the **Conversion** derivation type provided by OCHRE, which we called "Monetary value, Tetradrachm." Inherent in a Conversion-style Variable is the logic of a **Selection**-style Variable. This provides an option to create a list of Variables in order of priority. OCHRE will select the first Variable it detects as having been applied to the given item and will use its Value. Because there were several different ways in which the Monetary value might have been expressed (an absolute, a minimum, or a maximum), the user can pick the order in which OCHRE should find and evaluate them. Given the list of Variables shown in Fig. 12.12, if an item has the *Monetary value* property, OCHRE will use that. If not, it will check for a *Monetary value, minimum*. Lacking that, it will look for a *Monetary value, maximum* before giving up. If the user wants to run an analysis more conservatively, the "minimum" value can be given precedence. Alternatively, for a more aggressive approach, the user can promote the "maximum" value.

Given all the ways we ended up with to calculate the Quantity of a Coin group (or hoard), we needed to use a Selection-style property to prioritize the outcomes. The **Based on variables** list reflects all the different ways that were available to yield a count on a coin group, and it lists them in priority order. The Selection-style derivation was applied to this property to check each coin group for any of the Variables listed and extract the corresponding Property Value of the first one encountered (if any) (Fig. 12.13).

To include the quantities of coins which had been described qualitatively, rather than quantitatively, we devised a strategy to allow the user to specify a numeric equivalent for a descriptive string, allowing OCHRE to thereby *impute* quantitative

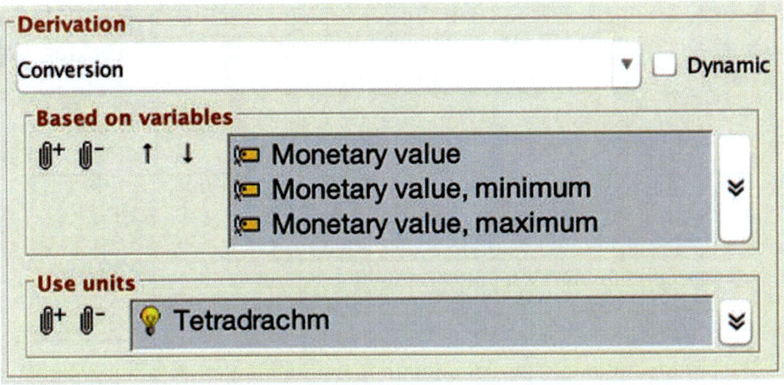

Fig. 12.12 The Conversion derivation directs OCHRE to convert the stated (tagged) values to the specified unit, here the Tetradrachm, based on assigned conversion factors

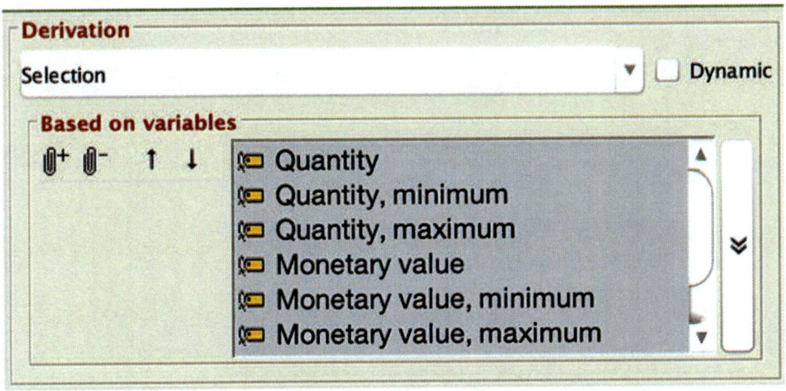

Fig. 12.13 The Selection-style derivation evaluates the Property Values in order of priority given to the Variables as specified by the user

value to a qualitative property. The user can experiment with assigning imputed values, providing conservative estimates, or not, depending on the analysis at hand; for example, "a great many" might mean 50 or 100. As long as such substitution is applied transparently so as not to be misleading in the analysis, it is a powerful option for incorporating data that would otherwise be lost altogether.[5] Note that an imputed list of qualified quantities would normally be listed lowest in priority by the

[5] This **Substitution** feature was implemented with the blessing of Francois Velde, economic advisor to the CRESCAT project. It was he who provided the term "Imputed value" in affirmation of the strategy during discussion at the CRESCAT Workshop, March 2017, in Chicago. The ANS Coin Hoards website acknowledges the incompleteness and uncertainty of the record (http://coinhoards.org/pages/about), but does not attempt to account for qualitative descriptions like "a few" or "a great many." Hence, in their analysis (with "uncertain" counting as 1), the total count of IGCH 0010 comes to "86–87 coins" (http://coinhoards.org/id/igch0010), whereas with specific quantities imputed to "a few" and "a great many," our total comes to 129 coins. In both cases, caution and transparency are needed in any analysis.

Selection-style property of the controlling Variable—a fallback strategy to quantify the coin group in the event that there is no other numeric information provided (Fig. 12.14).

In the end, an **Aggregation**-style Derived Variable was used to total the number of coins in each hoard, insofar as it was possible, given the information provided, by adding up the counts of each of the hoard's coin groups. Similarly, a second Aggregation Variable summed the converted valuations of each of the coin groups to derive a total value (in tetradrachm) of each hoard. Here, then, is the full description for the sample hoard IGCH 0010 (Fig. 12.15).

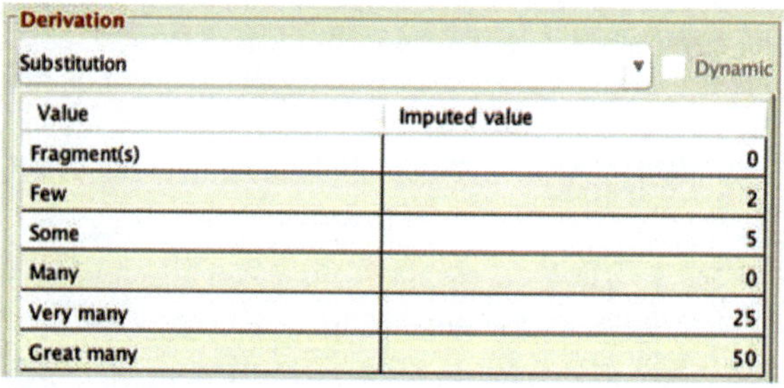

Fig. 12.14 The Substitution-style derivation is a mechanism for salvaging descriptive content for numerical analysis by imputing values to descriptive terms

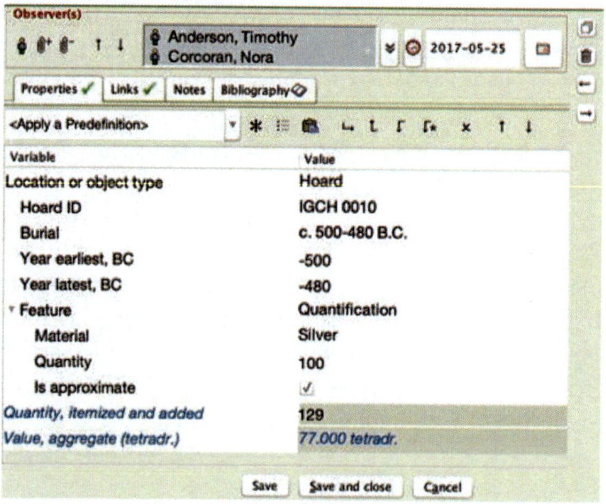

Fig. 12.15 The IGCH 0010 Properties pane shows intrinsic qualities of the hoard itself along with calculated values of the quantity and value of its coin groups

Queries and Sets

Having transformed descriptive data into numeric data, these values can be queried against and used to perform numeric analysis. In order to resolve the given assortment of currencies to the tetradrachm standard for comparison, OCHRE is asked to fetch the **Monetary value** recorded in the original units of each coin group, then apply the **Conversion factor** identified by the Concept denominations which represent those units. It is fifth-grade math, but virtually impossible without an item-based model that carefully defines each part of the equation and itemizes each component in a rigorous way.

Items that match the query Criteria, and which therefore constitute the result set of the query, can be saved as a Set in OCHRE for further analysis (Fig. 12.16). A Set is simply a collection of items saved as a convenience so that a group of items of interest does not need to be generated on the fly each time. A Set can be configured by a variety of Format Specifications which are commonly used to produce tables with columns that represent the values of any of the properties, or any of the *derived* properties, of the items in the Set. The ability to use formulas (derived properties) alongside core project data is a powerful feature supporting further data analysis (Fig. 12.17).

Dynamically Generated Maps

Sets of data, or Query result sets, can also organize items along the geospatial theme, as is especially helpful with the coin hoard data, situated as it is geographically around the Mediterranean region. OCHRE's tight integration of mapping features[6] allows for map-based visualization of any of the spatially contextualized content. Shown in Fig. 12.18 are the high-value Coin(s), from the Set created above,

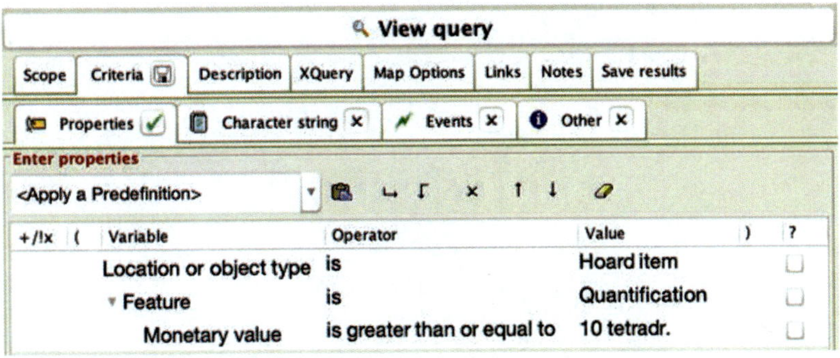

Fig. 12.16 Apparently, only 523 of our original 4500+ coin groups represent coin groups having a monetary value of 10 or more tetradrachms

[6] See the Tell Keisan case study (Chap. 10) for more information about Map View.

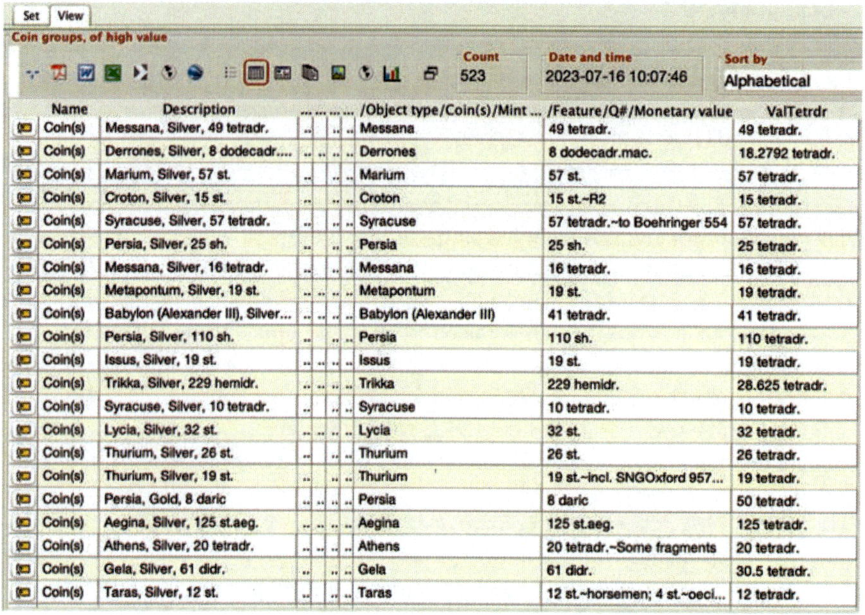

Name	Description	... ...	/Object type/Coin(s)/Mint ...	/Feature/Q#/Monetary value	ValTetrdr
Coin(s)	Messana, Silver, 49 tetradr.		Messana	49 tetradr.	49 tetradr.
Coin(s)	Derrones, Silver, 8 dodecadr....		Derrones	8 dodecadr.mac.	18.2792 tetradr.
Coin(s)	Marium, Silver, 57 st.		Marium	57 st.	57 tetradr.
Coin(s)	Croton, Silver, 15 st.		Croton	15 st.~R2	15 tetradr.
Coin(s)	Syracuse, Silver, 57 tetradr.		Syracuse	57 tetradr.~to Boehringer 554	57 tetradr.
Coin(s)	Persia, Silver, 25 sh.		Persia	25 sh.	25 tetradr.
Coin(s)	Messana, Silver, 16 tetradr.		Messana	16 tetradr.	16 tetradr.
Coin(s)	Metapontum, Silver, 19 st.		Metapontum	19 st.	19 tetradr.
Coin(s)	Babylon (Alexander III), Silver...		Babylon (Alexander III)	41 tetradr.	41 tetradr.
Coin(s)	Persia, Silver, 110 sh.		Persia	110 sh.	110 tetradr.
Coin(s)	Issus, Silver, 19 st.		Issus	19 st.	19 tetradr.
Coin(s)	Trikka, Silver, 229 hemidr.		Trikka	229 hemidr.	28.625 tetradr.
Coin(s)	Syracuse, Silver, 10 tetradr.		Syracuse	10 tetradr.	10 tetradr.
Coin(s)	Lycia, Silver, 32 st.		Lycia	32 st.	32 tetradr.
Coin(s)	Thurium, Silver, 26 st.		Thurium	26 st.	26 tetradr.
Coin(s)	Thurium, Silver, 19 st.		Thurium	19 st.~incl. SNGOxford 957...	19 tetradr.
Coin(s)	Persia, Gold, 8 daric		Persia	8 daric	50 tetradr.
Coin(s)	Aegina, Silver, 125 st.aeg.		Aegina	125 st.aeg.	125 tetradr.
Coin(s)	Athens, Silver, 20 tetradr.		Athens	20 tetradr.~Some fragments	20 tetradr.
Coin(s)	Gela, Silver, 61 didr.		Gela	61 didr.	30.5 tetradr.
Coin(s)	Taras, Silver, 12 st.		Taras	12 st.~horsemen; 4 st.~oeci...	12 tetradr.

Fig. 12.17 Despite the variety of denominations represented by the original values, OCHRE makes it possible to compare them using a chosen standard denomination, in this case, the tetradr

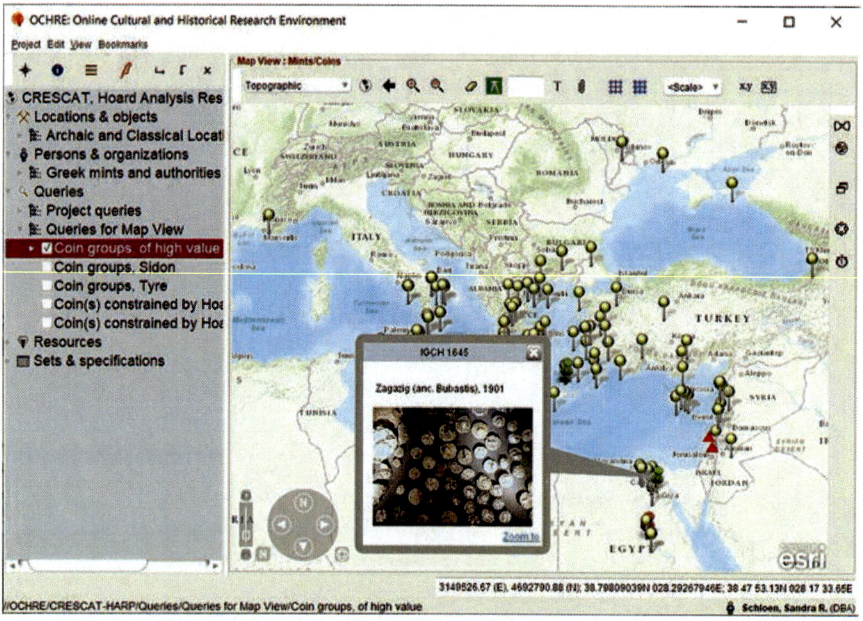

Fig. 12.18 Although coin groups have not been assigned geographic coordinates, they inherit this information from their spatially aware parent hoard item (The image of the Zagazig hoard is from the exhibit in the Bode-Museum, Berlin, Germany. This work is in the public domain because the artist died more than 100 years ago. Photography was permitted in the museum without restriction (https://commons.wikimedia.org/w/index.php?curid=45758304))

plotted on a map using OCHRE's built-in Map View. This map was requested simply by clicking the globe-icon (for Map View) instead of the table icon (for Table View) from the Set's toolbar. Since the underlying database entities are all items, and are not already predefined maps, or tables, or documents, they can be presented easily and dynamically in an assortment of Views.

Map content can be manipulated based on interactions with OCHRE's core data. Content might be filtered based on item type (e.g., plot coin groups compared to the Mints represented by the coins in the group), or based on property values (e.g., show tetradrachm minted in Athens), or based on derived, calculated properties (e.g., show a map of high-value hoards compared to low-value hoards), or based on context (e.g., plot hoards where coins minted in Tyre co-occur with coins minted in Sidon). OCHRE's powerful query facility, which produces highly granular, itemized results regardless of the item type, along with the ability to style such items based on any number of intrinsic or applied characteristics, allows for a wide array of complex visualization scenarios.

Visualization

Although many powerful visualization features are built into OCHRE, it cannot compete with the rich feature sets of more highly specialized, single-purpose software, and so, every effort is made to make it easy to interact with other applications, supplying good data to facilitate further analysis and visualization. A few examples follow.

Creating an Instant Visualization Using Google Earth

For a first, simple example, the toolbar button with the Google Earth icon is used to export the table of coin hoards shown in Fig. 12.19 as KML (Keyhole Markup Language)—Google Earth's XML-based format for describing geographic information. Google Earth allows for non-spatial supplementary XML-based content to be included in the KML format, so OCHRE packages the property data listed in the Table specification, along with the geographic data, into an appropriately formatted KML file. If images are included in the Format Specification of the Set, OCHRE will also create the companion KMZ file which contains a zipped folder of images referenced by the XML.

Saving the exported file locally, then double-clicking it, starts up Google Earth. The selected OCHRE property data, the corresponding image, and the persistent Citation URL of each item are instantly available to visualize in this popular application (Fig. 12.20).

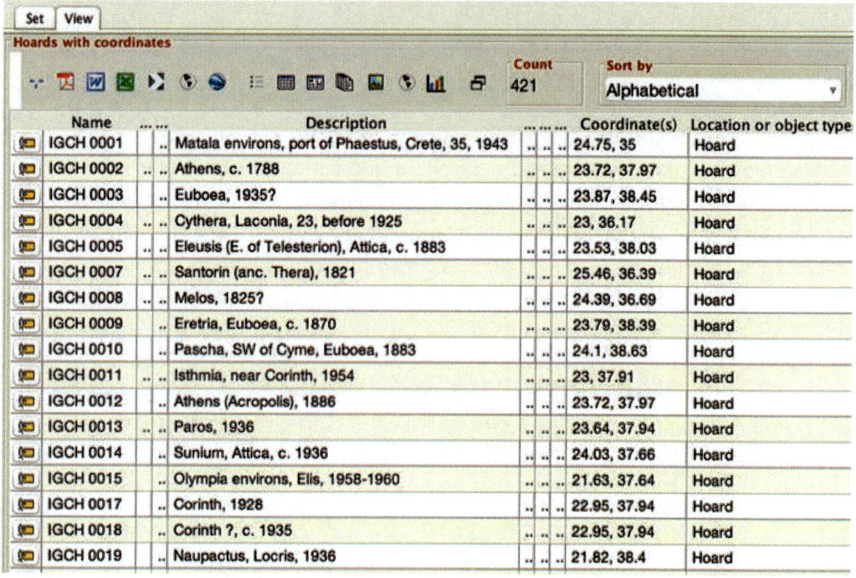
Set View
Hoards with coordinates
Count 421
Sort by Alphabetical

Name	Description	Coordinate(s)	Location or object type
IGCH 0001	Matala environs, port of Phaestus, Crete, 35, 1943	24.75, 35	Hoard
IGCH 0002	Athens, c. 1788	23.72, 37.97	Hoard
IGCH 0003	Euboea, 1935?	23.87, 38.45	Hoard
IGCH 0004	Cythera, Laconia, 23, before 1925	23, 36.17	Hoard
IGCH 0005	Eleusis (E. of Telesterion), Attica, c. 1883	23.53, 38.03	Hoard
IGCH 0007	Santorin (anc. Thera), 1821	25.46, 36.39	Hoard
IGCH 0008	Melos, 1825?	24.39, 36.69	Hoard
IGCH 0009	Eretria, Euboea, c. 1870	23.79, 38.39	Hoard
IGCH 0010	Pascha, SW of Cyme, Euboea, 1883	24.1, 38.63	Hoard
IGCH 0011	Isthmia, near Corinth, 1954	23, 37.91	Hoard
IGCH 0012	Athens (Acropolis), 1886	23.72, 37.97	Hoard
IGCH 0013	Paros, 1936	23.64, 37.94	Hoard
IGCH 0014	Sunium, Attica, c. 1936	24.03, 37.66	Hoard
IGCH 0015	Olympia environs, Elis, 1958-1960	21.63, 37.64	Hoard
IGCH 0017	Corinth, 1928	22.95, 37.94	Hoard
IGCH 0018	Corinth ?, c. 1935	22.95, 37.94	Hoard
IGCH 0019	Naupactus, Locris, 1936	21.82, 38.4	Hoard

Fig. 12.19 A Set representing the collection of hoards for which there are coordinates is viewed as a table then saved for display in Google Earth

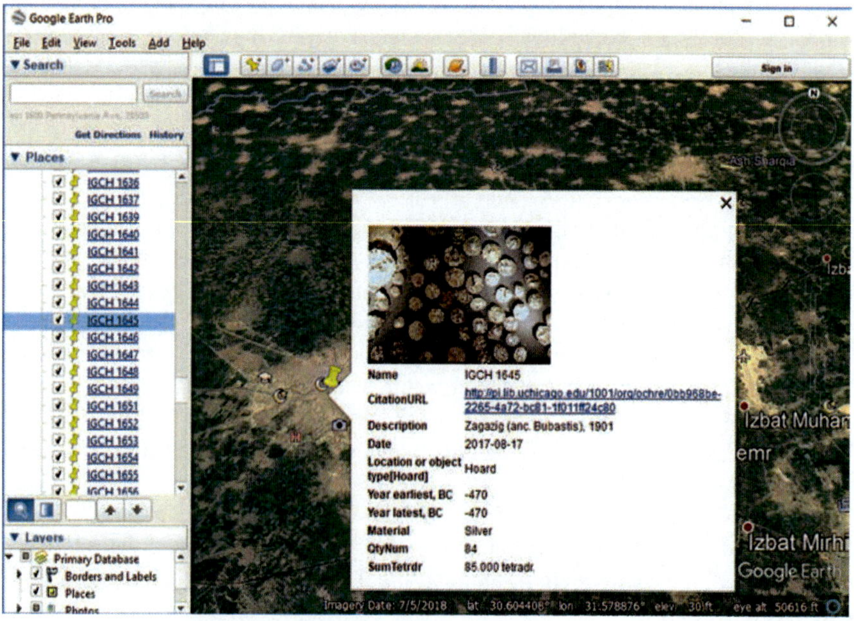

Fig. 12.20 Exported data for the Zagazig hoard is viewed in Google Earth

Spatial Analysis Using Web AppBuilder for ArcGIS, by Esri

In this next example, we go to a little more trouble to create a sophisticated visualization. We start in OCHRE by running a Query and creating a Set … three times, in fact: once for all mints, once for all hoards, and again for all coin groups. Each time, we added to the Set specification as many intrinsic descriptive details as possible to provide the maximal set of data available from OCHRE. We then produced the Table View for each Set based on its Format Specifications.

On the Set View menu bar is an option to **Save as Shapefile**. This process will succeed only if the members of the Set have geospatial information appropriate to the shapefile format; that is, if the items can be represented by polygons, polylines, or points. OCHRE produced three point-style shapefiles representing coordinates, one each for mints, hoards, and coin groups, and packaged them for hosting as feature layers on ArcGIS Online. The corresponding attribute tables of the shapefiles were populated with other property data from OCHRE. This supplementary data included the derived properties which calculated converted and aggregated values, with and without units. The values in the attribute tables are thus available for filtering, sorting, and display in a map application.

We then turned to the powerful ArcGIS Web AppBuilder by Esri[7] to develop an interactive web application[8] for exploring this rich data set. Each of the feature layers (mints, hoards, and coin groups) is available for zooming and selection, filtering and graphing, and other analytical tools, alone or in combination (Fig. 12.21).

We have only scratched the surface in demonstrating the use of this tool. You can imagine the range of possibilities and the powerful analysis that can be supported by such an interactive and data-rich environment.

Network Analysis Using Gephi Graph Visualization Software

There are many kinds of relationships other than spatial ones that one might wish to explore using research data such as the coin hoard data. Our own limited expertise does not permit an in-depth treatment of network analysis here, but it seems worth a simple example, at least, to illustrate the value of an item-based approach.[9] We have explained already how the coin hoard data, having been itemized and related in OCHRE as hoards, coin groups, coins, mints, currencies, and time periods, can be collected in Sets of items of interest based on Queries. Here, we explore the roles and relationships of two mints, Sidon and Tyre, strategically located at the eastern end of the Mediterranean during the Archaic and Classical periods. We will find all the hoards which contain coins minted at either Sidon or Tyre and identify the coin

---

[7] https://developers.arcgis.com/web-appbuilder/.

[8] https://datacomestolife.maps.arcgis.com/apps/webappviewer/index.html?id=48a70a51abae4dbdabbc874c06e0c9eb.

[9] See Freeman (2004), Knappett (2011), and Scott and Carrington (2011).

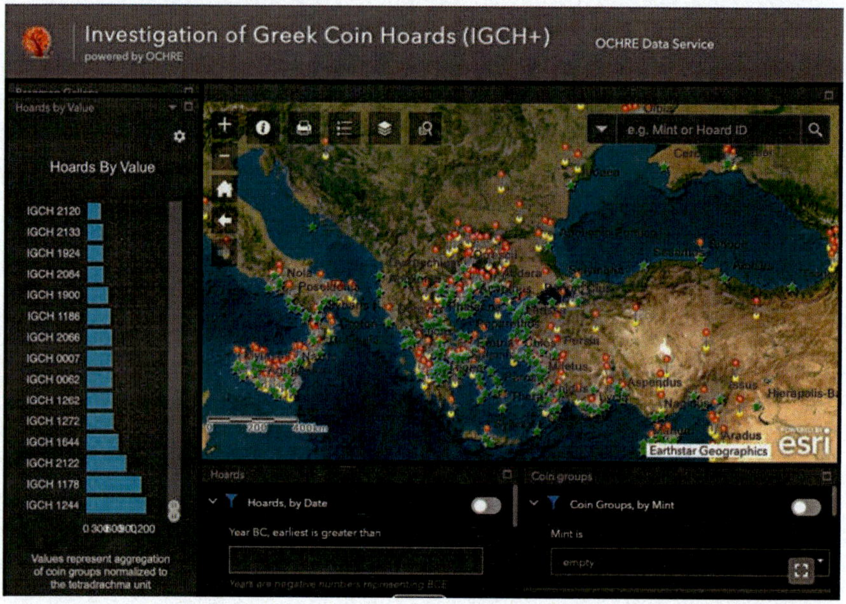

Fig. 12.21 Intelligent quantification that valuated coin groups and resolved differences of denominations makes possible meaningful infographics like the plot of Hoards by Value

groups they contain—both the coins minted at these two mints of interest and also the coins that co-circulate with them—and then extract their related information to tables which can be used as source data for a tool such as Gephi.[10]

We start by using OCHRE's **Query Designer,** which provides a mechanism for contextual queries that leverage the hierarchical, containment relationships central to the OCHRE data model. Hoard items "that contain" coin groups minted in Tyre are saved to a Set that is used to constrain the next query. To find the other coin groups that co-circulate with coin groups from Tyre, we query for the Coin(s) that are "within scope" (the "Nature of constraint") of this constraining Set of already-identified hoards; that is, those that contain coins minted at Tyre (use the "Constrain by Set" option, not pictured) (Fig. 12.22).

This process generates a Set that contains all the Coin(s) from all the hoards that have any coin group minted in Tyre. The derived Monetary value property that calculates the value of the coin group based on the tetradrachm standard is included in the Set specification. This ensures that the numeric values are comparable. Using the Set to generate a Table View, we export the table to Excel. Repeat for Sidon (Fig. 12.23).

OCHRE exports more than what we need in this case, so we do basic manipulation first in Excel. We create a list of all the mints to use as *nodes* in our network

[10] "Gephi is the leading visualization and exploration software for all kinds of graphs and networks. Gephi is open-source and free" https://gephi.org/.

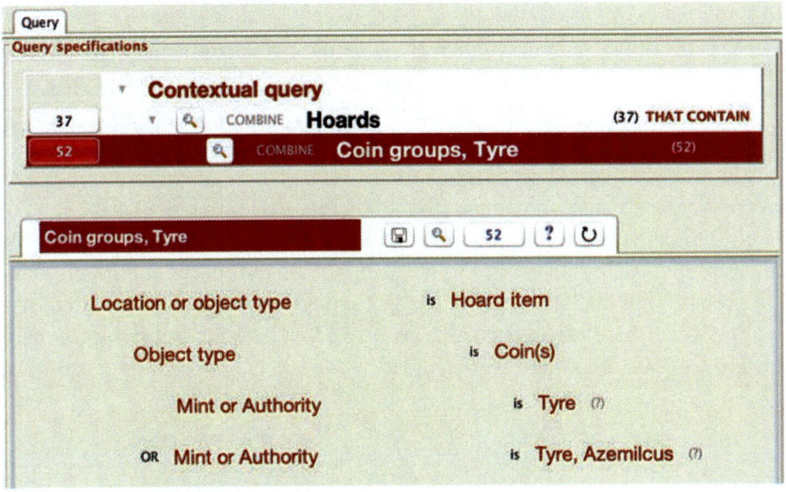

Fig. 12.22 Using the "THAT CONTAIN" operator, OCHRE can find all Hoard items that contain coin groups whose Mint or Authority is Tyre

A	C	H	I	L	
Name	Description	Mint	Val	Val (Base Value only)	Path -1
Coin(s)	Athens, Silver, 8 tetradr.	Athens	8 tetradr.	8.0	Ismailiya 1983
Coin(s)	Aegina, Silver, 1 st.aeg.	Aegina	1 st.aeg.	0.7	Ismailiya 1983
Coin(s)	Tyre, Silver, 1 sh.ph.	Tyre	1 sh.ph.	0.8	Ismailiya 1983
Coin(s)	Ascalon, Silver, 1 tetradr.	Ascalon	1 tetradr.	1.0	Ismailiya 1983
Coin(s)	Philistian, Silver, 1 tetradr.	Philistian	1 tetradr.	1.0	Ismailiya 1983
Coin(s)	Philistian, Silver, 1 dr.	Philistian	1 dr.	0.3	Ismailiya 1983
Coin(s)	Cyrene, Silver, 1 hemidr.	Cyrene	1 hemidr.	0.1	Ismailiya 1983
Coin(s)	Imit. Athens, Silver, 2	Imit. Athens			IGCH 1492
Coin(s)	Cyzicus, Silver, 1	Cyzicus			CH VIII 158
Coin(s)	Tyre, Silver, 4	Tyre			CH VIII 158
Coin(s)	Imit. Athens, Silver, 1 dr.	Imit. Athens	1 dr.	0.3	IGCH 1649
Coin(s)	Tyre, Silver, 1 st.	Tyre	1 st.	1.0	IGCH 1649
Coin(s)	Philisto-Arabian, Silver, 2 tetradr.	Arabian	2 tetradr.	2.0	IGCH 1649
Coin(s)	Athens, Silver, 54 tetradr.	Athens	54 tetradr.	54.0	IGCH 1651
Coin(s)	Sidon, Silver, 8 2.sh.ph.	Sidon	8 2.sh.ph.	12.0	IGCH 1651
Coin(s)	Tyre, Silver, 1 sh.ph.	Tyre	1 sh.ph.	0.8	IGCH 1651

Fig. 12.23 Data exported from OCHRE is used for network visualizations

graph, removing duplicates, and save this as a spreadsheet to import into the node list in Gephi. To create the *edges*, we add a column in the Tyre-results that specifies Tyre as the target mint (Node), and similarly, a column in the Sidon-results that specifies Sidon as the target mint (Node). We use the base value (which represents the coin group's value converted to tetradrachm) as the *weight* of the edges.[11]

[11] We also cleaned out items where mints were missing or where values were blank or zero, since blank or zero weights are not allowed in Gephi.

In Gephi, we imported the nodes and edges in a **Workspace** of the **Data Laboratory**. Helpfully, the weights were consolidated as the edges were imported; that is, multiple instances of coin groups between the same **Source** and **Target** mints had their weights summed. Even with just a default graph, we can see right away that each mint has a distinct community of related mints, but also that there are a considerable number of additional mints represented among the coin groups which co-circulated with coins minted at both Tyre and Sidon (Fig. 12.24).

As with the Esri tools, there is much that can be done with a powerful network visualization and manipulation tool like Gephi. An item-based approach makes it easy to prepare input tables of nodes (items) and edges (links) along with meaningful weights (e.g., here monetary value resolved to a common currency) generated from highly atomic, quantifiable, clean data.

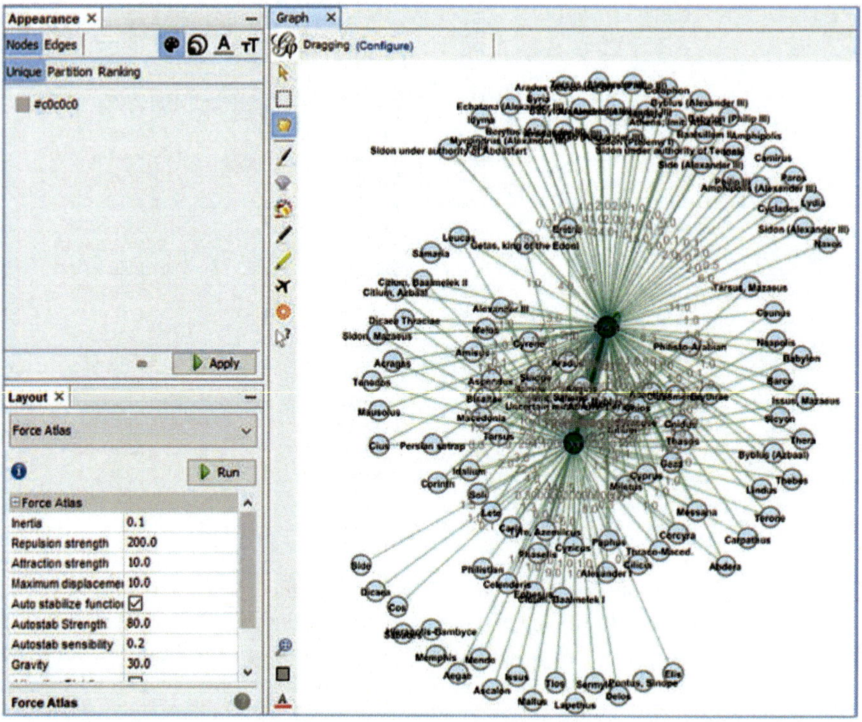

Fig. 12.24 Gephi's Force Atlas layout gives an immediate sense of the two centers, Tyre and Sidon, and their respective communities

Integration

While the coin hoard data is essentially a stand-alone data set, coins have been found all over the Mediterranean world by many project teams, some of which also use OCHRE to manage their data. In addition, the coin hoard data is highly contextualized geographically and has been extensively studied. These factors provide the opportunity to illustrate some integrative strategies facilitated by an item-based approach: first, that of integrating coin data across multiple projects having potentially different recording schemes; secondly, that of interacting with the wider world of linked open data; and finally, that of interfacing with powerful bibliographic tools to track related research.

Cross-Project Analysis

The item-based approach where property descriptors—Variables and Values—are *themselves* items which can be shared allows different projects to align naturally as they use descriptive properties in common. Far from having to align sets of idiosyncratic tables manually or explicitly, each designed based on the style and conventions of a specific project, OCHRE can find common ground as the branches of item-based, user-defined taxonomies overlap naturally within a shared, collaborative framework. Hoards and coins from sites all over the greater Mediterranean world can be analyzed together. Any OCHRE data made public by excavation projects could integrate directly with the coins and hoards of the HARP project as contextual hierarchies connect across projects or as items from one project are grafted into branches of another. Figure 12.25 shows the Ashkelon hoard found by our

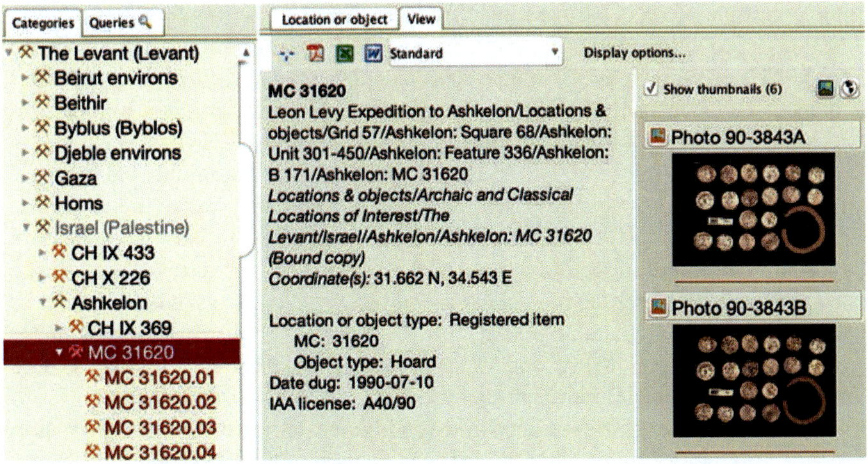

Fig. 12.25 Access to borrowed-in content is restricted based on access granted by the owning project, here view-only (hence colored red)

lowly volunteer, bound-copied into the geographic context of the HARP project to be listed alongside all the other hoards native to the HARP project.

Thesaurus Mapping

When property descriptors are not shared at all due to either a preference or a difference, OCHRE provides a **Thesaurus** mechanism, based on links, to match a Value from one project to a Value from another, either as a close match (synonym) or a related match (broader or narrower). Since each Value is a database item, the thesaurus is, in effect, a simple network of links among Values that expands the graph of knowledge available to OCHRE for querying and analysis.

When the Tel Shimron project team, working in northern Israel, invited a specialist to study their modest collection of coins, they were pleased to find a comprehensive list of relevant mint authorities already documented in OCHRE which they could borrow. The Hippos Excavations Project team, on the other hand, also working in northern Israel but in one of the great cities of the Decapolis, had spent years already cataloging a collection of over 1200 coins using a specially coded list of mint authorities described in their own way. This gave OCHRE two distinct items representing the mint at Tyre, two distinct items representing the mint at Sidon, and so on. In addition, the Hippos Excavations Project used their own "Mint" Variable while the other projects used the HARP "Mint or authority" Variable. A search for coins minted at Tyre based on the shared taxonomy would find the Ashkelon, Tel Shimron, and HARP coins, but not those cataloged at Hippos. To complicate matters, the Ashkelon and Tel Shimron projects tag coins as Registered items; the Hippos project shares the "Coin" Value but contextualized within Baskets; and the HARP project records coin groups as Hoard items within hoards. With so much variability in recording schemes and terminology, queries designed to find coins among multiple projects seem doomed from the start.

Allow us to illustrate how a query among collaborating projects can succeed using OCHRE's integration strategies by designing a query to find, say, all coins minted at Tyre. To start, OCHRE's Thesaurus mechanism lets the Hippos project's mint at Tyre ("Mint #7") be aligned with the shared OCHRE master mint at Tyre as a synonym (close match) in the **OCHRE Master thesaurus** via a simple link (Fig. 12.26). Similarly, the "Coin" and "Coin(s)" property Values are aligned as synonyms, and the "Mint" and the "Mint or authority" property Variables are aligned as synonyms, all within the same Thesaurus. This Thesaurus is then linked into the Query as the source of synonyms and other related terms, ensuring that the Query will find coins matching on "Coin" or "Coin(s)," mints matching on either "Mint or Authority" or "Mint," and "Tyre" matching on either the Tyre from HARP or "Mint #7" from the Hippos project.

To accommodate the differences in taxonomic context, we use the Query **skip** operator. Any of the valid nested contexts can be used to target the needed property criteria as long as the top-most level(s) are skipped. Since the Hippos project has identified these contexts primarily as **Baskets**, the Ashkelon and Tel Shimron

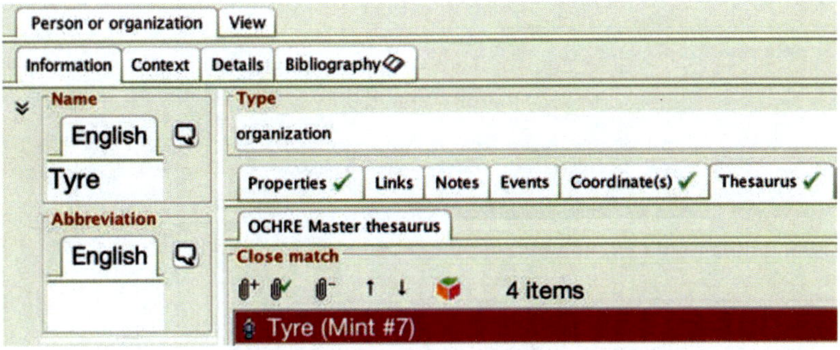

Fig. 12.26 Taxonomic or descriptive Values (here a Person or organization item used as the Value of a Link property) can be linked via a Thesaurus as synonyms or related terms

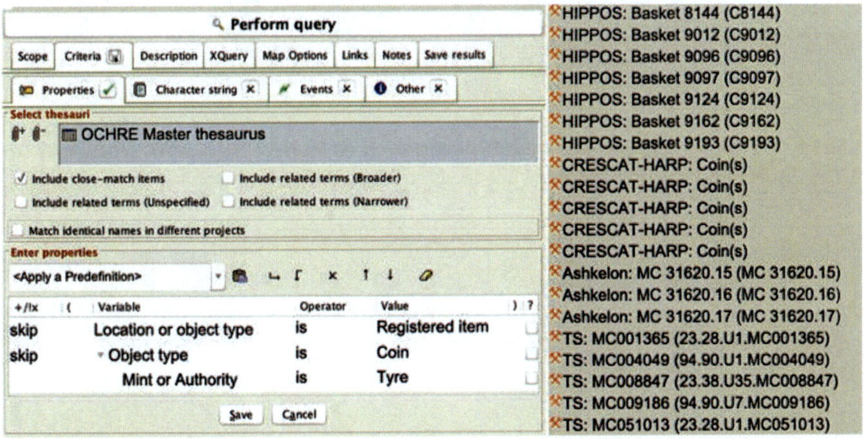

Fig. 12.27 Integration strategies make it possible to find common ground among projects using different recording schemes

projects have identified them as **Registered items**, and the HARP project has identified them as **Hoard items**, we can use *any* of these criteria to specify the level where the **Mint** is recorded, as long as we use the skip operator to disregard the levels where the specific variable used might be different. In this case, the Registered item context is used but skipped; it is effectively ignored by the Query logic (Fig. 12.27).

Setting the **Scope** to the projects of interest and performing the Query yields Coin items from Baskets minted at Mint #7 from Hippos, hoard items minted at Tyre from the HARP project hoards, and Registered items from Ashkelon and Tel Shimron. Given the diversity of the original source projects, and the variability of the descriptions of the coins, this is a triumph of data integration! (Fig. 12.28).

Rather than forcing projects to conform to a common taxonomy or descriptive scheme, the item-based approach lets us overlook differences and focus on commonalities. Cross-project analyses such as the one demonstrated here have proven

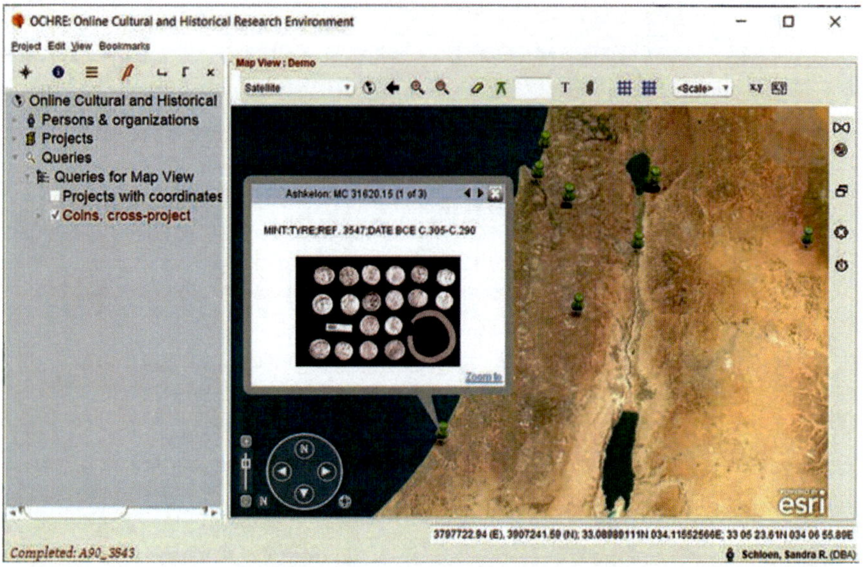

Fig. 12.28 Running the Query in Map View plots the results, converting the ITM coordinates of the Tel Shimron coins on the fly to latitude/longitude to plot them on a basemap

to be fruitful in other fields of specialized research, such as ceramic studies, faunal studies, and radio-carbon dating studies, where specimens or samples from different sites, described under different recording schemes by different researchers, can be compared and studied together despite differences in the data.

Linked Open Data and the Semantic Web

Far beyond the project data within the OCHRE repository lies a world of Linked Open Data (LOD). The American Numismatic Society was an early player in the world of the Semantic Web. In collaboration with other like-minded parties, they "provide stable digital representations of numismatic concepts according to the principles of Linked Open Data (LOD)."[12] The Nomisma site is a window to a wealth of data, both numismatics concepts and relevant linked resources, documented by a published ontology (expressed as RDF/XML), exposed as stable URIs via the Nomisma namespace (nmo), and accessible through a SPARQL endpoint. Data published in accordance with a prescribed vocabulary and presented via the stack of services that together constitute the Semantic Web are accessible to computational processes—like OCHRE—in predictable ways. OCHRE, too, can map onto

[12]As stated on the ANS Nomisma website: https://nomisma.org/.

the item-based Semantic Web in the field of numismatics, helpfully enriching the set of data available for scholarly research.

First, why would a project wish to connect to Linked Open Data on the Semantic Web? In short, the Semantic Web is a growing source of networked data that can be used to supplement your own project data. When working with well-known locations or concepts, metadata about these things can often be found on the Semantic Web. You may find spatial coordinates for locations, alternate names for cities and countries, or even thumbnail images of objects and concepts. For HARP and other projects, it made sense to develop a mechanism in OCHRE for leveraging data from the Semantic Web as a supplement to other project data.

As it turned out, the most natural way to interact with linked data on the Semantic Web from OCHRE is through a Derived Variable. We have already explored several varieties of Derived Variables that create new data via conversion, concatenation, substitution, or aggregation. This time, we teach a Variable how to send a SPARQL query to an endpoint, returning the query results as its new Derived Value.[13] New concepts, resources, and properties, fetched by a query from the Web, can be linked, just like other links within OCHRE, to core Concepts, Resources, Persons, Periods, and Taxonomy items, via the OCHRE Thesaurus.

OCHRE uses a designated hierarchy in the Property Variables category of the OCHRE master project to organize Derived Variables of the Type **Semantic web**, representing LOD vocabularies or ontologies that become available to all OCHRE projects. The Variable's Abbreviation specifies its namespace prefix, and its **Entity URI** provides the prefix for its base URL. For example, we created a Variable called "Nomisma" with an Abbreviation of "nmo" and an Entity URI of http://nomisma.org/id/. When this Property Variable is assigned to an item, its corresponding Property Value is looked up (via a SPARQL query) and then used to complete the Entity URI prefix. The Derived Variable also provides the information needed to run a SPARQL query against a data set of interest. This includes a reference to the SPARQL endpoint of the targeted data set, and a SELECT command that serves as a query template. OCHRE requires that the query template include the special field "**<Name>**" as part of the lookup options. When an OCHRE item attempts to use the configured query to find related information from the targeted data set, it will substitute its own Name in place of the <Name> field.

This next example demonstrates how to target Nomisma's extensive lists of coin denominations and relate these as synonyms to the denominations that were set up as Concepts in OCHRE. The handle to the Nomisma SPARQL endpoint is formatted as a URI, which submits a SELECT statement to the query engine:

```
http://nomisma.org/query?query=SELECT ...
```

Notice in Fig. 12.29 that the WHERE clause uses the special <Name> field as a match on the "skos:prefLabel." In ordinary language, this means that the query will target the Nomisma data set looking for items whose preferred label (as identified

[13] See Chap. 9 for another example of using a SPARQL query with OCHRE.

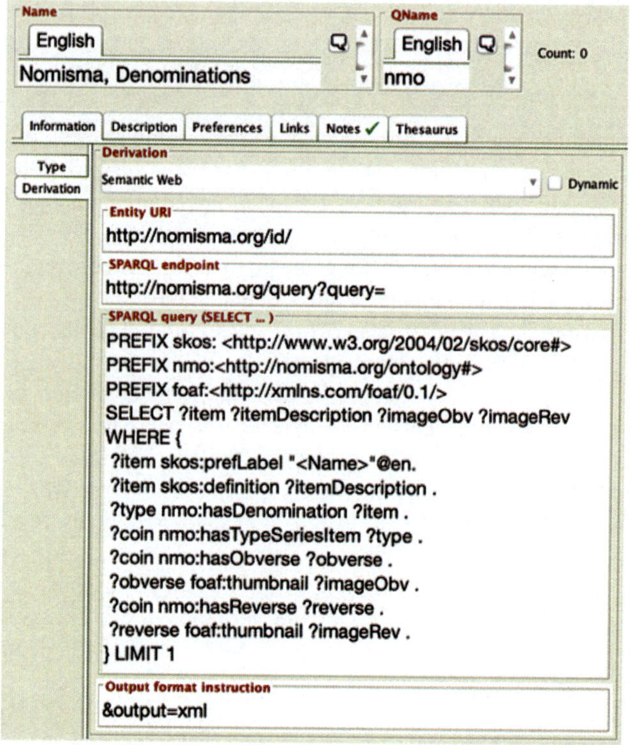

Fig. 12.29 This SPARQL Query references several W3C-recommended vocabularies: "skos," the Simple Knowledge Organization System; "nmo," Nomisma; and "foaf," Friend of a Friend

by the skos property "prefLabel") is a match on the Name of the OCHRE item being looked up.

The OCHRE Data Service helps projects design queries to return meaningful data. Additionally, OCHRE has been taught to look for certain keywords upon return, including **id**, **item**, **subject**, **image**, **lat**, and **long**. The id, item, or subject keywords must provide the unique identifier of the matching item from the data set. OCHRE will add this identifier to the Entity URI prefix to compose the official URI for the fetched item based on the targeted namespace. The stable URIs published by Nomisma look like this, for example: http://nomisma.org/id/obol.

The SPARQL query fetches the item which matches the given denomination, along with thumbnail images of both its obverse and reverse sides. From the Thesaurus tab of an OCHRE denomination (a Concept item, here the Obol), we use the Semantic Web button to trigger a lookup. A list of Web domains for which OCHRE has been given the needed Semantic Web details is presented as a picklist for the user. The Obol item substitutes its own Name ("Obol") for the <Name> field, and then, OCHRE fires off the query to the SPARQL endpoint. A list of return values—here just one from a targeted query—is presented. Accepting the result creates an OCHRE link to the Semantic Web data (Fig. 12.30).

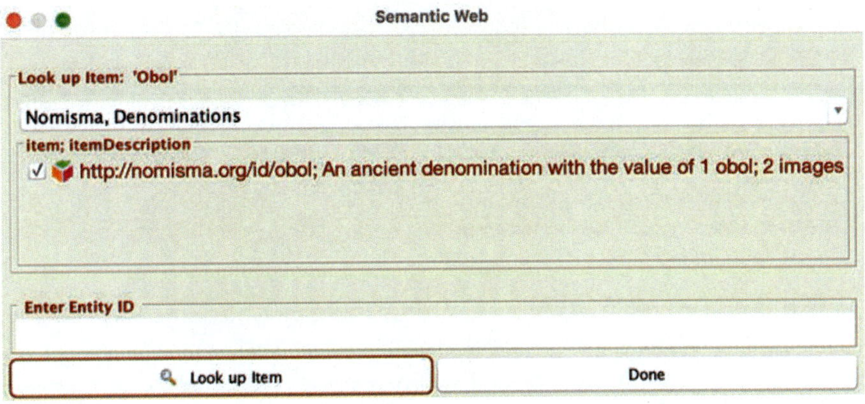

Fig. 12.30 A SPARQL query returns the "?item" that matches the value "obol" from the Nomisma endpoint

OCHRE appends the returned value ("obol") to the Entity URI prefix, thereby creating the official URI for this Nomisma item: http://nomisma.org/id/obol. OCHRE also creates a Thesaurus link to this Nomisma item as a synonym; it is now linked data. View the OCHRE Obol item to see the link to the Nomisma obol presented as a hyperlink which, when clicked, directs the viewer directly to the Nomisma source page on the Web (Fig. 12.31).

Another brief example illustrates a variation on the Nomisma configuration, targeting instead their extensive data on mints in the ancient world. The minting authorities, having been itemized and listed as individual entities in OCHRE, can be related to entities defined by Nomisma for use on the World Wide Web. A simple query that matches on the preferred label (skos:prefLabel) of the Nomisma mint (nmo:Mint) and returns the item, its description, and its coordinates (optionally; that is, if available) is shown here.

```
PREFIX nmo:<http://nomisma.org/ontology#>
PREFIX skos:<http://www.w3.org/2004/02/skos/core#>
PREFIX geo:<http://www.w3.org/2003/01/geo/wgs84_pos#>
SELECT ?item ?itemDescription ?lat ?long
WHERE {
 ?item skos:prefLabel "<Name>"@en ;
  skos:definition ?itemDescription ;
  a nmo:Mint .
 OPTIONAL { ?item geo:location [geo:lat ?lat ; geo:long ?long ] }
}
```

In making a Semantic Web link, the OCHRE mint of "Tyre" substitutes its own Name (for <Name>) for lookup then triggers the SPARQL Query and its response. OCHRE creates a Thesaurus synonym (technically, a "close match") between the OCHRE Person or organization of Tyre and the Nomisma Mint of Tyre. OCHRE

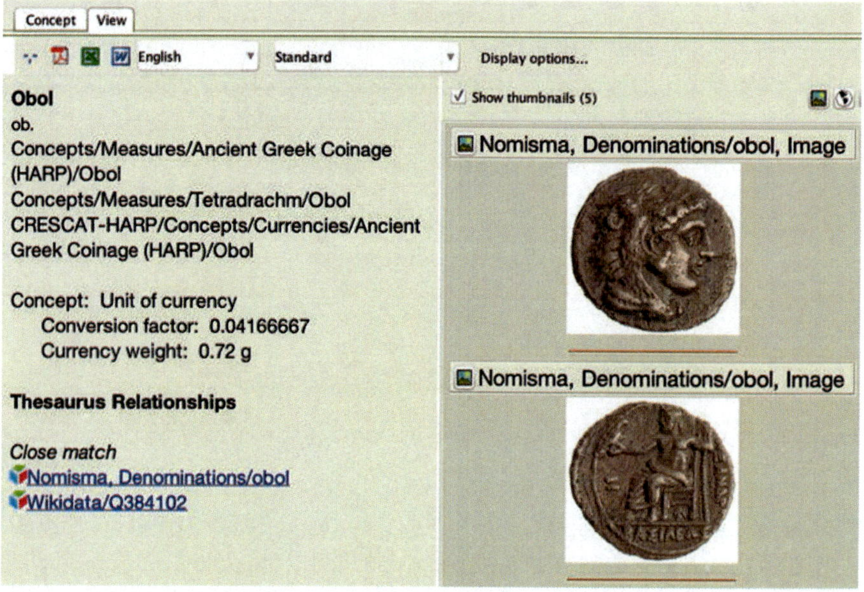

Fig. 12.31 If images are included in the SPARQL query results they are fetched *on the fly* to supplement the OCHRE View

also drops the fetched **?lat** and **?long** as coordinates into OCHRE's Coordinates tab as metadata and composes the URI for the mint at Tyre as defined by the Nomisma Entity URI prefix (http://nomisma.org/id/tyre) to use as a hyperlink (Fig. 12.32).

It goes without saying that data on the web is not all created equal. One would want to reference domains and ontologies that are reputable and relevant sources of linked data with which to complement one's own project data. But there is no limit to the possibilities this opens up. The wider world of linked open data awaits your discernment and imagination!

Bibliography

The IGCH and later Coin Hoard volumes include many bibliographic references. OCHRE has a built-in bibliography management tool, but it can also manage bibliography created in the free, online bibliography management tool Zotero,[14] a web-based management tool with built-in formatting specifications based on the Citation Style Language (CSL). Instead of reinventing thousands of bibliographic formats, OCHRE interacts directly with Zotero libraries via the Zotero API (Application

[14] "Zotero is a free, easy-to-use tool to help you collect, organize, annotate, cite, and share research" https://www.zotero.org/.

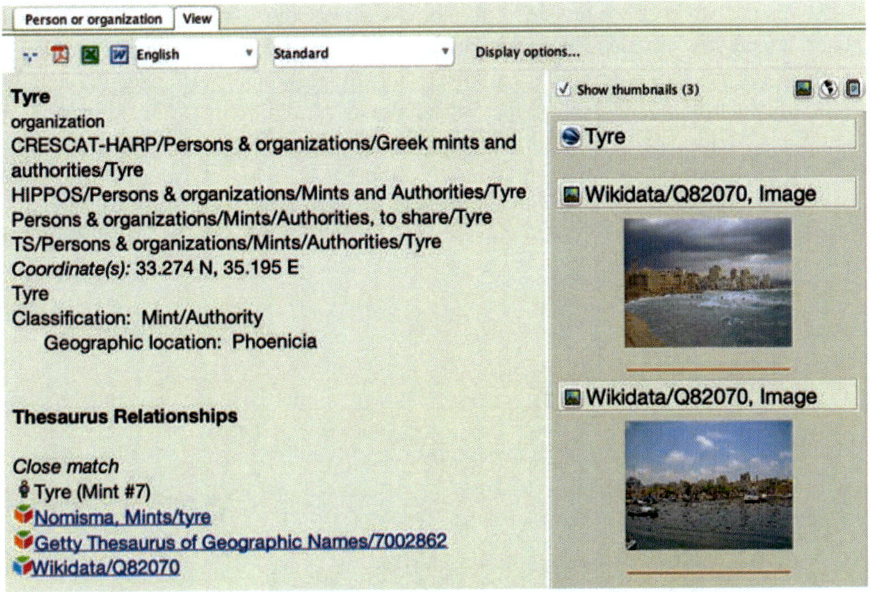

Fig. 12.32 Images for the Mint at Tyre were supplied by a Wikidata SPARQL query

Programming Interface) and calls on Zotero to format OCHRE's bibliographic citations.

One of our dedicated volunteers[15] carefully tracked down the many and complex references in the *IGCH* volumes and added them to a Zotero library. The HARP project was then able to integrate the bibliographic references by linking them directly, based on their Zotero key, to the hoards in OCHRE. Zotero styles the bibliographic data according to the user's preferred style and delivers the formatted output to OCHRE where it can be displayed as a citation.

Publishing HARP Coin Data

When data is represented using an item-based approach, there is a great deal of flexibility available for publishing it. Some might think too much flexibility, in fact, as it is often desirable that many of the granular bits come together into a more comprehensive and generally intelligible format for wider consumption. The user community needs to see walls and rooms and houses and neighborhoods, not just bricks. With items as building blocks, we can build tables and maps as we have already seen, along with documents and webpages as familiar constructs. In this section, we

[15] With thanks to Sharon A. Taylor of Pittsburgh, PA, a retired librarian.

will consider several options for publishing OCHRE data, or item-based data in general, using the famous Zagazig hoard found in Egypt as an example.

OCHRE provides a default View which consolidates on a single page the details of the Spatial unit that represents the Zagazig hoard including its Name, hierarchical Context, Coordinates, Description, and other descriptive Properties. Bibliography items are linked in for reference, styled by Zotero. Its Period is listed for temporal context, and it is illustrated by a photograph represented as a Resource item (Fig. 12.33).

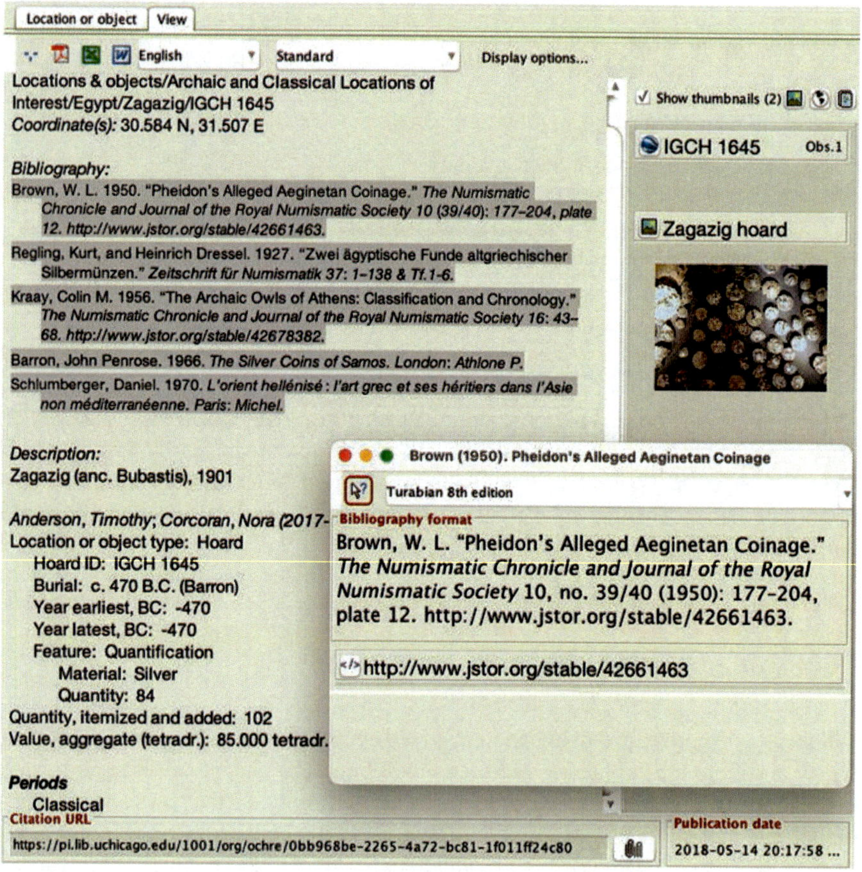

Fig. 12.33 More than twenty-five items in all are fetched from the database for OCHRE's View of the Zagazig Hoard

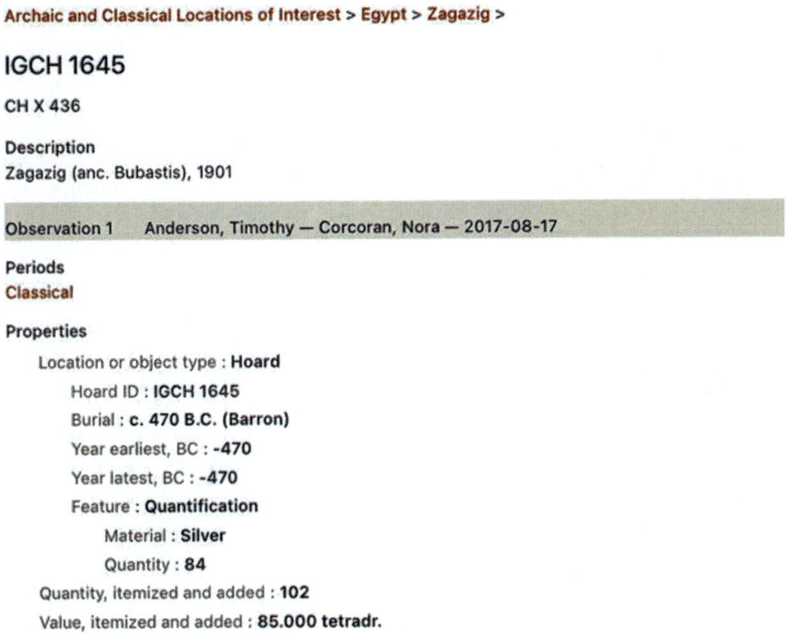

Archaic and Classical Locations of Interest > Egypt > Zagazig >

IGCH 1645

CH X 436

Description

Zagazig (anc. Bubastis), 1901

Observation 1 Anderson, Timothy — Corcoran, Nora — 2017-08-17

Periods

Classical

Properties

Location or object type : **Hoard**

Hoard ID : **IGCH 1645**

Burial : **c. 470 B.C. (Barron)**

Year earliest, BC : **-470**

Year latest, BC : **-470**

Feature : **Quantification**

Material : **Silver**

Quantity : **84**

Quantity, itemized and added : **102**

Value, itemized and added : **85.000 tetradr.**

Fig. 12.34 OCHRE's default publication option uses a stylesheet (XSLT) to transform OCHRE's XML into HTML for display

Instant Publication and the Citation URL

When data is ready for publication apart from OCHRE, making it accessible to users on the World Wide Web, a Project Administrator can decide which parts of the data to publish. Publication can be done surgically and highly selectively, one item at a time; or, it can be done *en masse* by publishing an entire hierarchy or Set of data (see Chap. 9). OCHRE's publication process time stamps each item and activates its Citation URL—the Web-accessible, persistent identifier which serves as a long-lasting reference to this digital object. Here, for example, is the Citation URL for the Zagazig hoard, based on the item's UUID (universally unique identifier), which guarantees the URL to be unique. Open this Citation URL with any standard web browser to view a published form of the item based on readily available web development tools (Fig. 12.34).

https://pi.lib.uchicago.edu/1001/org/ochre/0bb968be-2265-4a72-bc81-1f011ff24c80

Scrolling down to the rest of the page, we see the Subitems displayed (Fig. 12.35). These are the coin groups found within the Zagazig hoard, which have been consolidated within the published XML document for handy reference and exposed via the styled XML. Bibliographic references related to this hoard complete the published view.

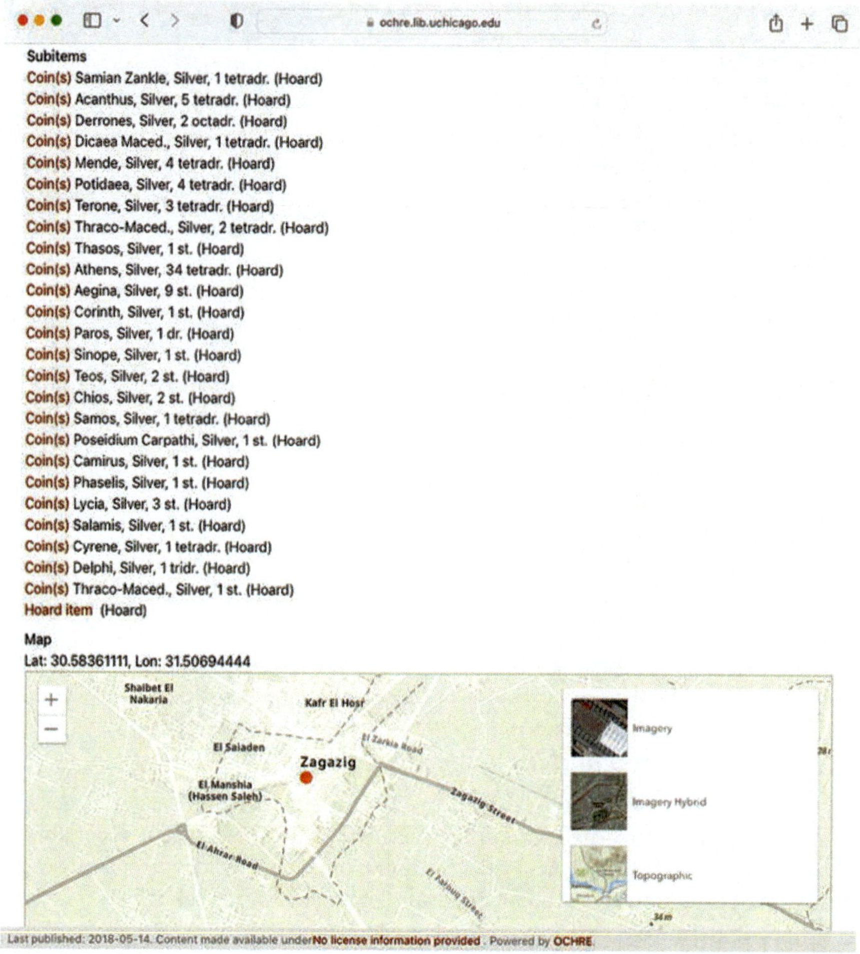

Fig. 12.35 An item-based approach to publication facilitates click-through potential for exploring a network of related data

Rethinking Published Data

Remember that at the start of this analysis, we opted to use the generic name Coin(s) for each of our coin groups. As we looked at the published results, we regretted this decision; you will notice that we rectified our blunder. While OCHRE could find and recognize each group of coins based on their unique identifiers, the list of coin groups displayed on the published page—Coin(s), Coin(s), Coin(s)—was meaningless to the viewer. As a remedy, we derived a Concatenation-style Variable called **Coin group label** that generates a descriptive label using the

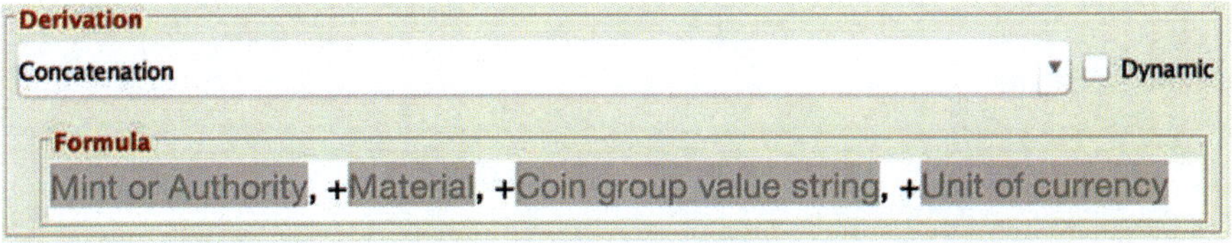

Fig. 12.36 A Derived Variable transforms a great many silver drachma from Eretria into a meaningful label: Eretria, Silver, great many, Drachma (dr.)

mint-plus-material-plus-coin-group-plus-currency of the coin group. Another, the **Coin group value string**, resolves the assorted options for describing the quantification of the coin group into a concise string (Fig. 12.36).

By querying for the coin groups and including the Coin group label as a column in the requested Table View, we triggered the creation of this newly concatenated descriptive string for each coin group. We then turned around and exported-then-imported this label back in as the official Description of each item. Much better!

Publishing Dynamic Websites Using the OCHRE API

The OCHRE Citation URL is not only a *persistent* identifier but an *actionable* one, made possible by the OCHRE API. The API provides access to any published OCHRE data using a simple syntax. Behind the persistent identifier is an API call that requests the data for the Zagazig hoard using the **uuid** parameter, which looks like this:

https://ochre.lib.uchicago.edu/ochre?**uuid=**0bb968be-2265-4a72-bc81-1f011ff24c80

This call to the API returns the well-formed published XML of this item. It is human-readable, and usable in all the ordinary ways in the world of web development, as verified by inspecting the source of the webpage (Fig. 12.37).

Unless otherwise specified, the default OCHRE stylesheet will be applied to format the fetched XML appropriately. In this next example, we will fetch all the published hoards and their hoard items and format them as a table in a webpage. To do this, we use the stylesheet parameter of the API, **xsl** = <name-of-stylesheet>, in tandem with the **xquery** parameter. Applying these two options results in a custom set of data returned from the publication server based on the given query and formatted in a custom way based on the given stylesheet.

```
https://ochre.lib.uchicago.edu/ochre?xsl=xsl/All_pubs_dt.xsl
&xquery=for $q in input()/ochre[@belongsTo='CRESCAT-HARP']/
spatialUnit return <project> {$q/project/identification/abbreviation}
<item> {$q/@uuid} {$q/identification/label} </item></project>
```

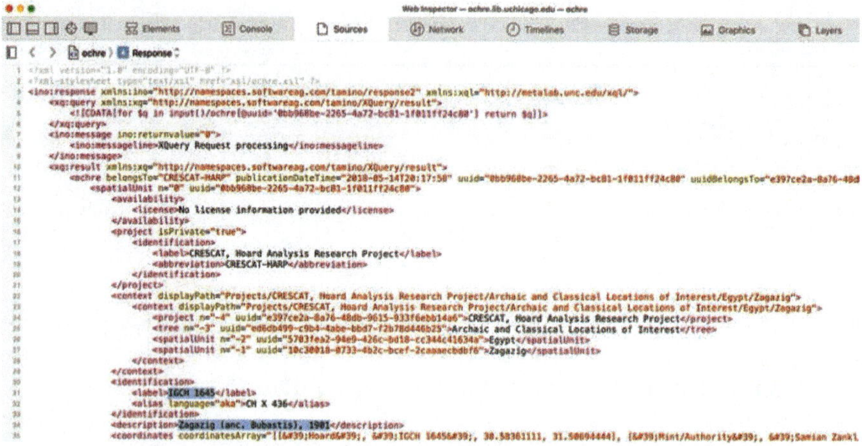

Fig. 12.37 A careful eye can pick out details such as the <label> and <description> of the hoard item from the published XML

Since many (most!) OCHRE projects do not have the luxury of having dedicated web developers on staff to present project data, OCHRE tries to make it easy to produce published results in useful formats for display on the Web. The Format Specification of a Set lets a user define columns for a Table View using any of the properties available to any items in the Set or any other items *from which they inherit* or *to which they are related*. OCHRE does a "join" in effect, sparing the user from needing to learn SQL or XQuery syntax. The inclusion of a Derived Variable (Monetary value) in the specification will trigger the calculation of the Variable's value. The resulting table can be "Published, from spec" based on the user-defined specifications. OCHRE's default stylesheet will format the published XML into a pageable, searchable, filterable, sortable, and downloadable (if permitted) HTML table for display in a browser (Fig. 12.38).

https://pi.lib.uchicago.edu/1001/org/ochre/7e11e552-ebdc-4251-b2f6-9901b472d0cc

Like the coins which we have tracked from their beginnings at the mint to their ends in a deposited hoard, so too we have come a full circle, back to the issues of web publication from which we started this investigation. It seems important to emphasize that webpages created using this method of selective, dynamic web development do not exist apart from the output generated *on the fly* by the actionable OCHRE Citation URL. The web browser sends requests to the OCHRE API which generate XQueries against the live, published data. The data returned in response is then formatted within HTML syntax generated by the given XSLT for display in the browser. This strategy is especially useful for data sets that are being used for active research and which are growing or are subject to ongoing edits and enhancements.

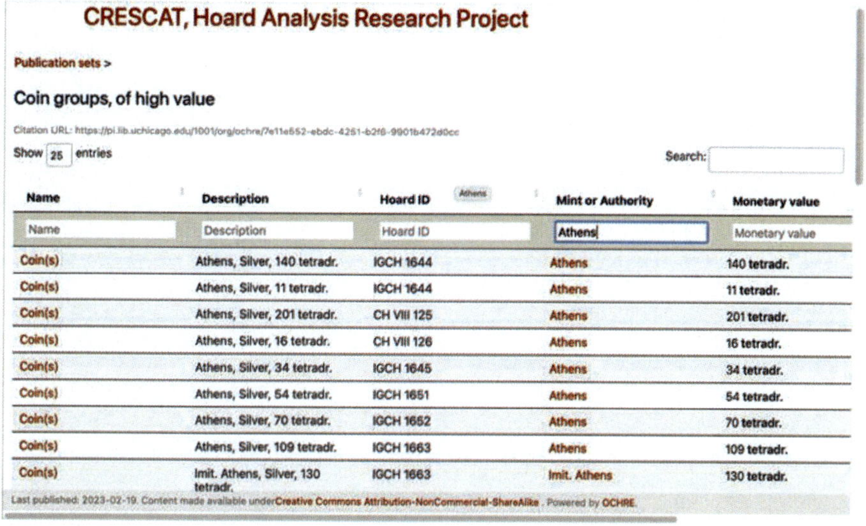
CRESCAT, Hoard Analysis Research Project

Publication sets >

Coin groups, of high value

Citation URL: https://pi.lib.uchicago.edu/1001/org/ochre/7e11e552-ebdc-4251-b2f6-9901b472d0cc

Show 25 entries

Search:

Name	Description	Hoard ID	Mint or Authority	Monetary value
Name	Description	Hoard ID	Athens	Monetary value
Coin(s)	Athens, Silver, 140 tetradr.	IGCH 1644	Athens	140 tetradr.
Coin(s)	Athens, Silver, 11 tetradr.	IGCH 1644	Athens	11 tetradr.
Coin(s)	Athens, Silver, 201 tetradr.	CH VIII 125	Athens	201 tetradr.
Coin(s)	Athens, Silver, 16 tetradr.	CH VIII 126	Athens	16 tetradr.
Coin(s)	Athens, Silver, 34 tetradr.	IGCH 1645	Athens	34 tetradr.
Coin(s)	Athens, Silver, 54 tetradr.	IGCH 1651	Athens	54 tetradr.
Coin(s)	Athens, Silver, 70 tetradr.	IGCH 1652	Athens	70 tetradr.
Coin(s)	Athens, Silver, 109 tetradr.	IGCH 1663	Athens	109 tetradr.
Coin(s)	Imit. Athens, Silver, 130 tetradr.	IGCH 1663	Imit. Athens	130 tetradr.

Last published: 2023-02-19. Content made available underCreative Commons Attribution-NonCommercial-ShareAlike . Powered by OCHRE.

Fig. 12.38 Interactive tables with click-through potential are presented by OCHRE's default stylesheet for effective publication on the Web

Conclusion

When the CRESCAT-HARP project began, it was faced with legacy data in print and digital formats that required considerable attention to be used in a study of coin circulation. HARP leveraged the OCHRE data model to atomize and organize the data into individually identifiable items—hoards, hoard items, coin groups, and coins—contextualized in space and time. The project borrowed from existing taxonomic metadata properties and created customized variables and values where necessary—the data landing soundly in an ultimately rigorous and intuitive representation within the OCHRE platform, becoming available for meaningful, quantitative analysis and publication.[16]

While HARP was a narrowly focused project, it involved experts from a wide variety of backgrounds, from Classics to modern monetary theory to data analytics and computing. The OCHRE Data Service played a major role in advising on data management and in performing much of the data curation, integration, and publication, helping to bring this data set to life.

[16] See Chap. 9 for a discussion of how HARP data is exported from OCHRE for analysis using R.

Chapter 13
Final Thoughts

Introduction

In the time it has taken us to write this book, we have witnessed profound changes that remind us of the tenuousness of technology in our lives and also our dependence on it. When we started, quite a few years ago, Adobe Flash was prevalent across the Web,[1] premium services from Google and others were free, IBM's Watson was all the rage in AI, and we were part of a select club that routinely worked remotely with collaborators all over the world. Since then, drones and GPS devices have become commonplace toys, making sophisticated technology available to the masses; DALL-E, ChatGPT, and a new generation of generative AI have taken the world by storm, causing us to question our educational practices and our ethics; Facebook has become Meta, reflecting a trend toward virtual reality and other novel technologies; the seemingly monolithic Twitter has imploded and the tech industry has lost its luster among a glut of layoffs; and a global pandemic has made working remotely a norm (Fig. 13.1).

On a more personal, and positive, note, from our beginnings in a specialized area of research at the University of Chicago's Oriental Institute (now the Institute for the Study of Ancient Cultures), the OCHRE Data Service has become part of a growing and thriving team of digital humanists within the Forum for Digital Culture of the University of Chicago. From this base, we have taken on many more projects that extend to fields of study far beyond our early emphasis on archaeology, including the history of science (*Capturing the Stars*, in collaboration with astronomers and historians), manuscript studies (*Peripheral Manuscripts*, a digitization project by midwestern English professors), social science (*Primed to React*, a study of

[1] The "Adobe Flash EOL General Information Page" confirms that the once very popular Flash Player was retired, once and for all, as of December 31, 2020. (https://www.adobe.com/products/flashplayer/end-of-life.html).

S. R. Schloen, M. C. Prosser, *Database Computing for Scholarly Research*, Quantitative Methods in the Humanities and Social Sciences,
https://doi.org/10.1007/978-3-031-46696-0_13

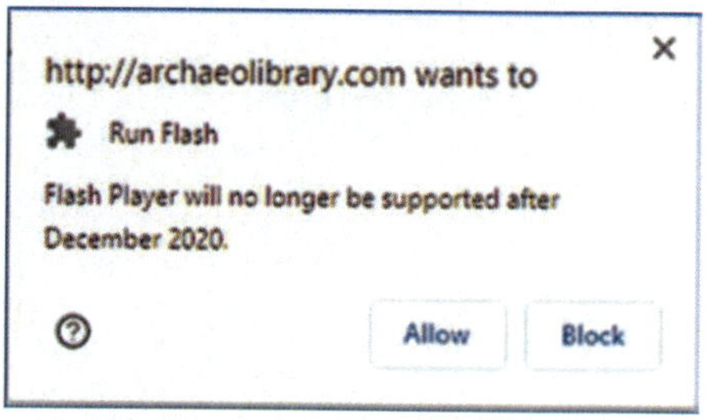

Fig. 13.1 A death sentence is delivered to the once immensely popular Flash Player

police response in Chicago), digital media (*Cinemetrics*, a crowd-sourced collection of movie takes), human genetics (*Genomes, Migration, and Culture*, a collaboration of archaeologists and geneticists), and musicology (*Village Harmony*, an annotated collection of works of culture-bearing musicians around the world), among many others, illustrating that an appropriately generic item-based approach can support research of all kinds.

But despite the inexorable passing of time that continued to delay this writing project, we persisted for a couple of reasons. First, the *problem* of managing data for humanities and social science research has not gone away, ChatGPT- (3, 4, … N) notwithstanding. While projects in fields of academic research can adopt, and greatly benefit from, advancing technologies—creating 3D models of excavation contexts, using advanced OCR to transcribe historical documents, training deep learning methods to read cuneiform tablets, etc.—such tools are not a panacea for the ongoing challenge of responsible data management. Second, the validity of the *principles* discussed here has not changed. The strategy of an item-based approach remains a legitimate and effective solution regardless of the specific technology used to implement it. And finally, having used OCHRE (and its predecessors) as a database platform in *practice*, for what amounts to a lifetime in the technology industry, we have gained helpful perspectives.

And so we conclude this book with a reflection on some of these perspectives and how they have influenced our outlook in the hope of giving others a head start with wrestling with the inherent problems of research data in the humanities and social sciences. While we do not claim the final word on these topics, many years of experience have provided insights, informed the implementation of OCHRE specifically, and guided our approach to research data more generally. We have learned that researchers working with digital tools and computational processes must remain open to *change* and ongoing learning, open to *complexity* and the reality that such work often lacks clear-cut solutions, open to fruitful *collaborations* that inspire and motivate, and ultimately, open to new *challenges*.

Open to Change

As soon as we close the pages on the writing of this book, it will surely be already out of date. There is no stopping the momentum of continuing advances, no way to avoid upgrading, no escaping the reassessment of project needs, and no excuse for

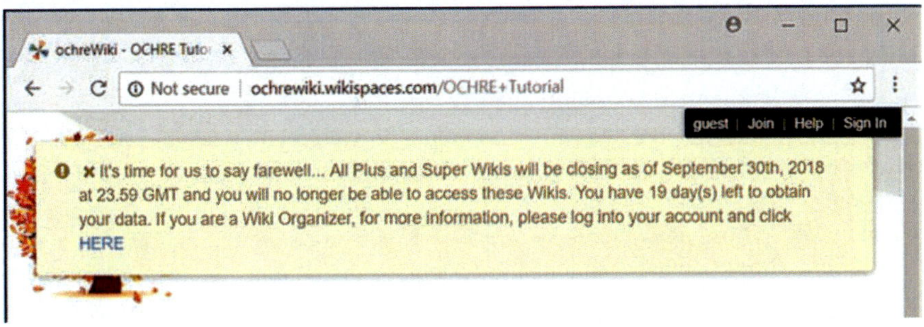

Fig. 13.2 Wikispaces closes with a poignant message: "It's time for us to say farewell"

being stuck in the past. Details of implementation, availability, and functionality of tools will change. Not so long ago, the popular platform we used for our wiki was closed because it lacked the resources for updating to match the features of new players in this space (Fig. 13.2).

Digitized data is susceptible to the march of time. A recent consultation with an emeritus professor unearthed four external hard drives of documents and images containing a vast amount of research that dated back to the early days of personal computers. Much of this was nearly unreadable by current software programs. Only the long-outdated Macintosh system on life support in his office could process this data. File formats were old and not recognized by modern operating systems. Fonts based on non-Unicode character sets were no longer supported. Time was running out for this digital treasure trove. This was no fault of the careful scholar who was used to being organized and to paying attention to details. We have come through a time of rapidly changing technology, and for those for whom the technology was a tool of the trade, rather than the trade itself, it has been incredibly difficult to keep pace. Individual scholars and research projects alike need to take stock of their data stores to ensure that they are not falling into disarray and need to be intentional and vigilant about watching over their data.

The item-based approach exemplified by the OCHRE platform supports change. While OCHRE represents a specific implementation, the principles and practices are not dependent on specific products; any enterprise-level, XML-based database technology would do. XML, as a readable, nonproprietary data format, is easily transformable into whatever new format comes next. The highly atomic data model which is the basis of the "backend," like stem cells or bricks, is adaptable and flexible for the creation of new structures. A strategy of dynamic publication which is the basis of the "frontend" allows data to be more easily migrated, shared, and republished. The strength of our institutional support structures reassures us of long-term sustainability. Despite the challenge of constant change, we are confident that our strategies are as future proof as can be reasonably expected.

Open to Complexity

Applying technology to help with one's research is challenging and there are many barriers to success. There are complex options to weigh and decisions to be made. How does a scholar chart a clear course through a technological landscape that is constantly changing and without clearly defined rules? Which digital tools should be selected? Whose advice is to be trusted? This is not a simple matter, and we do not have a simple answer. But in the following discussion, we highlight several attitudes, misconceptions, and issues that raise contrasting points of view that, at least, should be well considered.

Innovation Versus Conformity

We have decried Procrustean efforts to force-fit data to unnaturally conform to a given standard or to an artificial or theoretical format devised by someone else. This will inevitably compromise one's data in some way, making the data less useful for the research for which it was intended. In addition, would-be standards are often inadequate or have not been widely accepted by the targeted research community. Yet, in the highly connected environment in which we all work, it seems prudent to try to ensure that one's data will interact nicely with other data, both within the same project or from other researchers. And it seems logical to expect that structurally similar projects, or multiple colleagues trying to solve essentially the same problem, should be able to get good mileage out of a one-size-fits-all approach. But no one should be forced to use research methods, recording schemes, and prescribed terminology simply because "the computer" requires it.

Scholars who react against conformity, choosing instead to rightfully exercise their prerogative to be their own semantic authority, often try to roll their own solution. But what is passed off as innovation becomes another instance of reinventing the wheel. Yet another bespoke FileMaker database is developed: the data entry fields have different names, the fill-in forms have different layout designs, and the linked tables have different formats. Yet another website is launched with a custom MySQL database dishing up pages of indexed data featuring new tables of data, new sliders, buttons and other widgets for interaction, and newly designed publication formats. These efforts are often impressive and may fill an immediate need for a specific project, but they often limit collaboration and undermine the ability to share our data sets.

The OCHRE approach has been to tread a middle ground, offering a highly generic platform where the ontology of persons, places, and things allows a high degree of customization, but where core structures (e.g., hierarchy) can be shared, and where reusability (e.g., of taxonomic branches) is encouraged. Instead of adopting standards that fit only partially, it is better to model data in its most granular form such that it can be reconfigured to align with a variety of standards. Features that offer flexibility and customization are key to any good database solution and can enable efforts to conform to a common approach.

Novice Versus Expert

Scholars looking for advice on putting a computer to work on behalf of their research goals will encounter a wide range of experts. Some technology experts will be out to lend a hand to the poor scholar who is supposedly in over their head. Such experts often have a short attention span and other more remunerative fish to fry. When the novelty of the academic project wears off, or when the exciting excavation season is over, the scholar may be left high and dry. Others might truly be expert regarding the technology, but will not take the time to truly understand the research, resulting in a misapplication of the technology to the subject matter.

Some scholars, not expert with respect to the technology, will be satisfied with rudimentary forms of digitization, thinking that they have done due diligence in applying modern technology to the research process, but they could stand to be more ambitious with respect to data capture and more informed as to appropriate data representation. Others will expend a disproportionate amount of energy, time, and/or money to get results. Manually combing through inadequate data, they key and re-key, file and re-file, sort and re-sort, copy and re-copy, and count and re-count. Often, the result is no better than an old-fashioned paper record. The medium might be digital, but if data is not transformed into an analytically useful, manipulable format, then it might as well have been recorded on tablets of clay. Their efforts are laudable, but call into mind the catchy advertising slogan of a familiar home improvement chain: "you can do it; we can help." Put technology to work for you. We can help!

The do-it-yourself crowd often seems motivated by the sense of satisfaction that comes from doing it themselves and, perhaps too, a misplaced confidence that they know what they are doing. But technology is more complicated than drywall. The field of digital humanities, and the wider world of the Web, seems rife with examples of the Dunning–Kruger effect, a psychological phenomenon that explains "why people fail to recognize their own incompetence." As social psychologists, David Dunning and Justin Kruger, describe it:

> …poor performers in many social and intellectual domains seem largely unaware of just how deficient their expertise is. Their deficits leave them with a double burden – not only does their incomplete and misguided knowledge lead them to make mistakes, but those exact same deficits also prevent them from recognizing when they are making mistakes and other people are choosing more wisely (Dunning 2011).

Their studies are fascinating as they explore this deeply rooted human tendency. Dunning and Kruger declare us all to be "confident idiots" and observe:

> what's curious is that, in many cases, incompetence does not leave people disoriented, perplexed, or cautious. Instead, the incompetent are often blessed with an inappropriate confidence, buoyed by *something* that feels to them like knowledge (Dunning 2017).

Recognition of what we do not know is difficult to attain in the sphere of technology. A new user who has experienced success with a relational database, or a geographic information system (GIS), or a JavaScript plug-in, should be rightfully enthusiastic and buoyed by a sense of accomplishment and also cautiously aware of the limitations of their abilities.[2] An online webinar, a YouTube demo, or a Stack Overflow account is no substitute for proper training or for the assistance of an expert who has been years in the making.[3] After extensive research, Dunning et al. conclude that Confucius' observation rings just as true as it did twenty-six centuries ago: "real knowledge is to know the extent of one's ignorance."[4]

Our point here is not to criticize limited technological expertise, nor the good intentions of technology experts, but to suggest that it is not just a matter of understanding the technology but also a matter of understanding the nature of good data. We have seen technology experts make a hash of research data and have watched projects run by highly decorated computer scientists die on the vine because there was not the time or trouble taken to understand the data properly or to fully appreciate its intended use. We have also seen amateur, self-taught users create simple but elegant database systems with carefully formatted, blissfully consistent, and well-organized content.

We also understand deeply that the relationship between a nontechnical scholar and their technological partners requires a considerable amount of trust. For those without technological expertise of their own, it is difficult to evaluate the merits of their advisors. A good track record of previous applications or implementations, positive recommendations from other users, and official credentials, can help allay concerns, but in the end, a scholar is at the mercy of the skills and commitment of their collaborators. The technology advisor should make substantial efforts to include meaningful training, to make regular progress updates, to create data that is not locked into an otherwise inaccessible format, and to pass along whatever access or control can be given to the principal investigators, in order to bridge the gap between the novice user and the expert consultant.

[2] Dunning and Kruger (1999) go on to explain that "improving the skills of the participants, and thus increasing their metacognitive competence, helped them recognize the limitations of their abilities."

[3] See Ericsson et al. (2007), "Making of an Expert" and the bibliography therein.

[4] See Dunning et al. (2003).

Realistic Versus Visionary

Some scholars have wildly unrealistic ambitions for their data which exceed the current practical reality. They tend to be impatient (if cheerfully), easily sidetracked, and often frustrated by both the process and the results. Yes, we need to be dreaming of better tools and imagining a world where technology will take our breath away, and we always welcome scholars who have high ambitions for their research. But there is no getting around the fact that for now, at least, there remain a lot of hard work, tedious effort, and the application of our own human intelligence to create useful research data. We sometimes forget that comparatively arcane topics like archaeology and philology cannot be studied with the same methodology as fields that have at their disposal ready-made data sets. A researcher studying modern American novels can feed millions of words into a statistical algorithm, not caring too much about the level of noise in the data because the sample size is so large. But these types of advanced analytical methods are less appropriate in fields where every piece of data is precious and none can be considered insignificant. So, while we can learn from these visionary tools, we try to remain realistic about the nature of our research. While impressive AI is redefining what we consider to be realistic, we cling to the value of the incumbent, traditional, and slow process called thinking.

Fast Versus Slow

William Caraher, an academic familiar with digital field practices for archaeology, and a proponent of "slow archaeology," challenges "any claim that gains in efficiency through the use of digital tools is sufficient reason alone to incorporate them into the archaeological workflow" (Caraher 2016, p. 437). Along the same lines, Adam Rabinowitz, a Classical archaeologist with a long-standing interest in digital methods, reflects on a technological revolution that has left us "addicted to digital speed" (Rabinowitz 2016).

Make no mistake—we are all in favor of "the time-saving possibilities and increases in efficiency [that] are notable and real" (ibid., p. 432). As such, we applaud reports of major efficiency gains, like these reported as a result of using the *PaleoWay* digital workflows:

> Using off-the-shelf hardware and applications we achieved notable productivity gains, both in the field and in the time it took to go from field to deliverables. Utilizing all team members, each with their own role in the process and each inputting data to their own device, the recording of a lithic scatter went from over an hour in the paper era to under 15 minutes … The time spent recording an isolated artifact went from 10 minutes to less than a minute. … The move from field records to deliverables went from two weeks to two days" (Spigelman et al. 2016, p. 410).

Caraher reminds us not to use digital tools uncritically for the sake of speed, but "to recognize the particular emphasis on efficiency, economy, and standardization in digital practices within the larger history of scientific and industrial knowledge production in archaeology" (Caraher 2016, p. 423). He wonders on his blog "whether archaeologists have confused the importance of data collecting with the importance of question answering."[5] Regardless of our discipline, we need to consider not just *how* we are using technology, but *why* we are using it, and always with the aims of advancing our research (Prosser 2020).

Fragmentation Versus Integration

Caraher's slow archaeology perspective also recognizes the complexity of data collection, both with regard to the number and variety of collaborating staff and specialists, and with regard to the variety and complexity of the accompanying hardware and software tools:

> The fragmented, if more comprehensive, records created by digital practices in archaeology almost always require reassembly after the archaeologist leaves the field … As the information collected in the field has become more granular and more digital in character, the tools and techniques required to reassemble it have become more complex … Compared to the relative simplicity of an excavation notebook, which requires almost no particular technology to read and understand, the modern excavation or survey dataset is a virtually meaningless mass of encoded data (Caraher 2016, pp. 432–433).

Caraher identifies the intersection of three critical themes: granularity, comprehensiveness, and reassembly. As we have argued, data should be recorded in the most granular form required for a project's research needs. We wholeheartedly agree that a project should strive for as comprehensive a digital record as possible, and we have illustrated the importance and power of reassembly—what we would call integration—analysis, and publication. But a "meaningless mass" of data is not inevitable, not true by definition, and not the fault of technology. We also challenge the assertion that an excavation notebook naturally provides meaningful data, being reminded of Stephen Ellis at Pompeii who observed that "almost all of the recorded fieldwork for the American excavations at the Panhellenic sanctuary at Isthia…was scribbled down by well-intentioned novices. For my own legacy data project at that site, barely 10% of the recorded, stratified contexts from the 1970s excavations can be reassembled…" (Ellis 2016, p. 63). He goes on to suggest this is "hardly unique" and that "it is rare to happen upon a legacy data project that reports skillfully crafted, paper-based datasets" (ibid.). If, instead, we use a system designed from the outset to be granular, comprehensive, and integrative, we can most certainly affect positive outcomes, even to the point of making it look easy.

---

[5] https://mediterraneanworld.wordpress.com/ 2015/03/03/mobilizing-the-past-workshop-review-part-2/.

Born-Digital Versus Legacy

To be sure, dealing with legacy project data, the work of previous researchers, does raise additional challenges. In the best of all worlds, a project will build upon previous scholarship and the database environment should accommodate the integration of these legacy data even if intensive, manual, digitization effort is required to convert paper to digital media. Old maps should fall into place right alongside newly produced, spatially aware, born-digital images. A new project, returning to an old excavation area, will find a history of the site already in place. The discovery of a new manuscript may transform what is already known of a historical author.

A collaborative data management system needs to be sufficiently flexible structurally to allow for the representation of multiple, attributed observations from different points of view. This handles, exactly, the situation where a project team from the past has recorded observations of the same space but in a different time. Keep in mind that the nature of the data will reflect the standards of the day. We cannot help but notice that the data collected from projects, say, in the 1930s differs greatly from that of modern-day excavations. In those early days, it was the whole pots, the complete figurines, the intact scarabs, that were kept and recorded (and brought home to American and European museums, but that is another story). By today's standards, most projects pick up every scrap and broken fragment of … whatever … and log it in their databases, just because they can, or more fairly, in the spirit of being more scientifically rigorous. Statistical analyses of data from these projects, contiguous in space but separated over time, would not be meaningful (Fig. 13.3).

Also, remember that there were no high-precision instruments on site at Persepolis, no high-flying drones capturing spatially aware photographs to centimeter-level accuracy. We cannot expect legacy data to meet the standards of modern-day collection and recording. Tagging the source of an observation as to its date and authorship gives the users of the data the necessary context by which to judge it.

Even though historical data does not meet the standard of current data collection, we would not rule out legacy data as useful and meaningful for research. We generally recommend exposing as much data as possible, say, for example, by making scans of the field notebooks, and linking those as images or PDF documents to the relevant database items. In this way, data is preserved as part of the official record and is available as a reference, at least. Sometimes, it is tempting to transform the original record. Perhaps transcribe the content of a letter which is hard to read in an inked longhand script typical of days gone by. Perhaps geo-reference an old map or hand-drawn plan, accepting some vague level of inaccuracy. Perhaps expend an appropriate level of effort to do basic tagging from free-form descriptions; a first pass to distinguish "Wall" from "Tomb" can go a long way to maximizing hits of a query. If a project has available resources and personnel, we consider it to be absolutely worthwhile to digitize and integrate legacy data in a manner such that it can be leveraged for future research. In so doing, we salvage and perpetuate the efforts

Fig. 13.3 A large team of workmen at the site of Persepolis keeps only the good stuff. (Photograph courtesy of the Institute for the Study of Ancient Cultures of the University of Chicago)

of the past. An appropriately flexible and comprehensive database platform will embrace and enable this.[6]

Fun Versus Boring

A common misconception that lies in wait for the computer user is to imagine that the use of a computer in digital research eliminates all tedious and time-consuming work. The opening paragraph of the online edition of a popular book called "*Automate the Boring Stuff with Python*" (Sweigart 2015) suggests that the computer can do tedious tasks for you.[7] However, the tendency to think that one should never need to perform manual tasks repeatedly in a digital environment can lead to two traps. First is to believe that if one were to search online long enough, a script to solve the problem would be found. Some problems are so unique that the answers have not yet been posted to GitHub or Stack Overflow. Second is the trap of spending an excessive amount of time writing a script to perform an isolated task that

[6] The current authors deal with this specific issue in further detail in (Prosser and Schloen 2020).

[7] https://automatetheboringstuff.com/.

could have been completed manually in less time than it took to write the script. After all, is that not more fun?

The old adage "haste makes waste" also comes to mind. The Critical Editions for Digital Analysis and Research (CEDAR) project[8] at the University of Chicago has scholars from its Divinity School poring over Greek, Hebrew, and other biblical manuscripts using OCHRE to render accurate digital editions of each manuscript as faithfully as possible. This is tedious work, "slow philology," transcribing word by word, character by character, and yes, even accent by accent from hard-to-read scans of often poorly preserved manuscripts. We are often asked: why not just OCR the manuscripts? Why not create a special utility to import them all into the database? Would that not achieve 90–95% accuracy? But, for this carefully curated scholarly resource, even 95% accuracy is too low a bar. Finding what was missed or done incorrectly by a computational shortcut, and then correcting it, would be much more laborious than getting it right, intentionally, the first time.

More importantly, this thinking could lead to a digital humanities perspective that removes the role of the philologist, the archaeologist, the scientist, and the historian from the process. Digital tools should amplify scholarship, not replace it, and while we encourage the use of computers to automate the boring stuff, we are quick to point out that a specialist may well be needed to train the database to become intelligent in the first place.[9] We are counting on the biblical scholars to apply their training, expertise, and thoughtful intentionality to the process. Even if we look forward to achieving the lofty, and automated, goal of "artificial intelligence," scholars will still be needed as a check on computer-generated results and as the providers of meaningful analysis and interpretation.

Effort Versus Payoff

A consequence of slow scholarship is the constant tension between effort versus payoff. Sometimes, it seems that the work of the data janitor is never-ending, literally, never ending. The light at the end of the tunnel is nowhere in sight and we long for magic. Is it worth representing an ancient text cuneiform-sign-by-cuneiform-sign so we can argue over the legibility of the ones along the broken edges? Is it worth itemizing and detailing all the attested variations of all the words in the dictionary, linking these to every occurrence within our corpus of texts? Is it helpful to trace the excavation's contexts and features stone by stone or will a rough outline do?

The United States Library of Congress initially committed to archiving all Twitter tweets as part of the national record—approximately 21 billion tweets

[8] https://cedar.uchicago.edu/.

[9] See the discussion on the DeepScribe project (Chap. 8) for our efforts to apply AI to the tedious and difficult task of reading cuneiform tablets.

dating from 2006 to 2010. Subsequently, overwhelmed by the magnitude of the task and the staggering amount of data, it seems that reasonable minds have since prevailed. The effort of archiving every public tweet was not worth the payoff. After twelve years, the Library backtracked, committing to "only collect Tweets it deems of historic importance" (Daley 2017). In 2020, Google issued a warning that "Google Drive's trash has changed. Items will be automatically deleted forever after they've been in your trash for 30 days."[10] Apparently, the effort (cost) is not worth the payoff of retaining deleted items "forever" for nonpaying customers.

Rabinowitz gives an example of an observable change in archaeological practice by the project at Chersonesos, weighing effort over payoff, influenced by the adoption of digital tools that skewed, in this case, the perception of scale and relevance:

> [I]nstead of ignoring tiny pebbles that cannot be represented in a 1:20 pencil-drawn plan, team members digitizing context plans from orthorectified photographs in ArcGIS tended to zoom in to vectorize all of them, without making a conscious decision about whether it was actually useful to preserve the position of those pebbles (Rabinowitz 2016, p. 506).

When is it "actually useful" information and when is it data for the sake of data? Each project must make this decision. No two projects may agree, and no two projects need agree (Fig. 13.4).

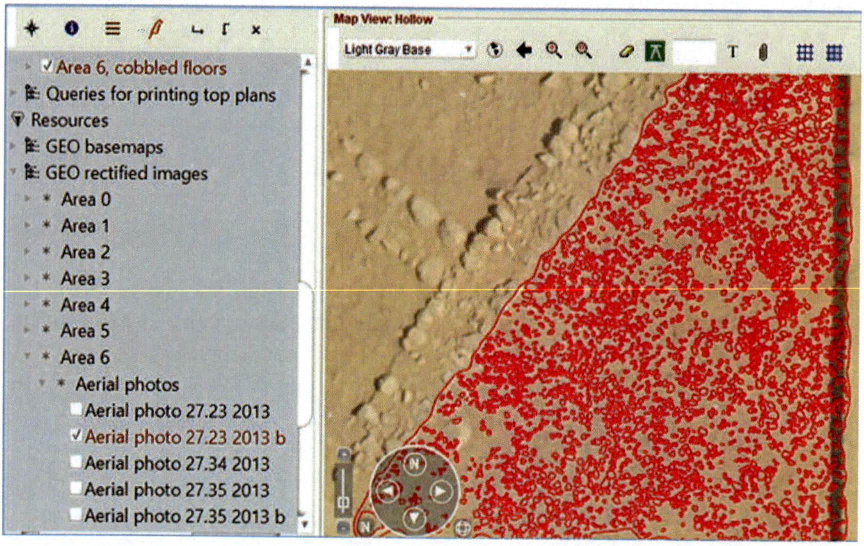

Fig. 13.4 Is it worth manually tracing a cobblestone floor stone by stone? You be the judge. (Zincirli, L13–6040 in OCHRE's Map View, drawn by volunteer D. Ridge)

[10]As of December 2020, https://support.google.com/googleone/answer/10214036.

Custom Versus Commercial

Which digital tools to use is perhaps the most complicated question. There are both open-source and proprietary, both custom and commercial, tools that we find essential to our work. Participants in the *Mobilizing the Past* workshop proposed, demonstrated, and critiqued the uses of a variety of tools. When asking "What is the right tool for the job?," we should be thoughtful and intentional regarding the implications, limitations, and outcomes related to the choices that are made.

If we deplore how "the uncritical use of technology can potentially privilege processes and uniform types of data collection, which can fragment and narrow archaeologists' perspectives" (Gordon et al. 2016, p. 19), then let us not use digital tools that encourage uniformity and fragmentation.

If we lament how "as digital tools accelerate the pace of archaeological work, more aspects of archaeological practice become obscured by technology" (Caraher 2016, p. 434), then let us not use digital tools that obscure for the sake of efficiency.

If we "remain skeptical that archaeology [insert 'research'] will benefit from tools that offer greater efficiency, consistency, and accuracy alone" (ibid., 423), then let us use tools with added value.

If we worry that our digital tools are "black boxes" that "hide certain processes or maneuvers either owing to their complexity, their routine character, or their location outside of the expertise of disciplinary work,"[11] then by all means, let us use digital tools that are transparent, customizable, and that do not require the smoothing over of variations.

If we disapprove of "the growing pressures…to produce results at the pace of development and capital" (Caraher 2016, p. 434), sacrificing quality (among other things) for the speed and quantity of industrial or scientific processes, then let us not choose digital solutions created *by* industry and business, *for* industry and business.

If we resent the system of capitalism "that is responsible for the design and production of the digital tools we use" (Rabinowitz 2016, p. 495), and our "dependence on tools that are not necessarily made for our benefit" (ibid., 498), let us commit to not using such tools uncritically and instead to bend them to our will.

Tools/Toys Versus Solutions

We like to think that we are building *tools* for scholars rather than automated *solutions*. A good example of this is the set of text-processing wizards that we have built into OCHRE to enable scholars to step through the words of a given text, examine them, parse them by attributing grammatical properties, identify them as

[11] Caraher (2016, p. 421), citing Latour (1987, pp. 1–21).

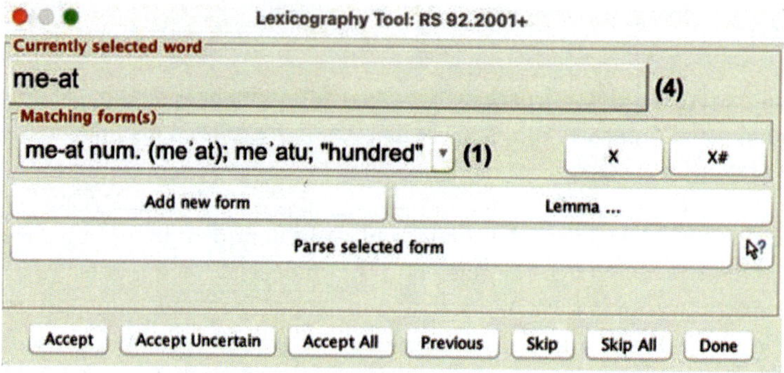

Fig. 13.5 An OCHRE wizard helps the scholar to create a network of database knowledge

proper nouns (e.g., personal, divine, or geographic names), and link them to lemmas in the project dictionary. Watching a student work through a text, it almost looks like magic. With OCHRE doing database lookups behind the scenes, matching on known information, following links, making suggestions, it seems that the automated process could be set in motion and then left to finish on its own (Fig. 13.5).

But what of homonyms? What of unusual forms of a word? What of broken sequences? What of other assorted ambiguities? While the tool can guide the scholar and make it easy to access the known information, the scholar's own intuition and judgment must still be the ultimate arbiter of knowledge. We do not seek to replace scholarship with technology. We would do well to beware the black box and avoid technology "that just works" (Caraher 2016, p. 434).

Some scholars cannot resist the temptation just to play with the technology, often to the point of distraction. Dabbling with the latest download is stimulating; trying out the new tech toy is a nice diversion; the proof-of-concept is fun to show off. But it is easy to underestimate the work involved in creating a robust research "solution" and to fail to appreciate the ultimate complexity of a well-designed, comprehensive system. Good technology looks easy. Creating it is not.

We also must buck the perception that using a "solution" like OCHRE will take the fun out of implementing one's own system. Not at all! There is much creative work and technical challenge involved for those who want to take it on: data to wrangle, taxonomies to build, files to corral, websites to publish, and research to support. OCHRE provides the environment and the tools to manage and manipulate beautifully organized data, howsoever it might have been collected. OCHRE provides a backdrop upon which many different views or analyses can be projected. The scholar provides the imagination and the intelligence to make it meaningful. Even for the most experienced Python data analytics expert or web developer, there is a role in an OCHRE-based project. Why reinvent the system for modeling and managing the data when time and resources can be spent on more productive tasks? We do not wish to steal all the fun, but why start from scratch?

Open to Collaboration

Starting from scratch can be an expensive proposition and many research projects in the humanities and social sciences tend to be underfunded. Limited budgets are quickly drained by the costs of hiring qualified personnel with technological skills to develop software or implement computational solutions. And once funds have been sunk into a bespoke "solution," the need to upgrade as technology advances, or even to maintain the status quo, typically requires ongoing costs. More often than we like to think, such projects run aground when grant funding is exhausted. Granting agencies, however, are enthusiastic about supporting systems that are widely applicable, both in principle and in practice, to a wide range of use cases, offering more bang for their buck. When multiple participants can collaborate in supporting a common research environment, without losing control of the research process or compromising the structure of the data, it feeds a virtuous process of shared development and sustainability. Each new project brings a new challenge or a new wrinkle; enhancements, in turn, are available to all. Each project contributes as budgets permit, then piggybacks on the common endeavor when circumstances change. This is the ideal on which the OCHRE Data Service operates, where no project is left behind when the money runs out.

Collaboration, while typically encouraged in academic contexts, also needs to be handled sensitively, especially when data is managed in a common platform. A scholar's data might reflect new ideas or groundbreaking research; it might have been collected under creative or difficult conditions; credit for it might be needed to attain tenure or promotion at one's institution. But one of the goals of a scholar, or a team of scholars, is to share data with interested colleagues and disseminate research results to a wider audience. Data thus needs to be collected in such a way that ensures proper scholarly attribution and safeguards a scholar's expectation to be recognized for their research contributions; needs to be secured until it is time for dissemination; and needs to be made accessible in a controlled manner to relevant parties. Recognizing that not all data should necessarily always be "open," OCHRE was designed to restrict access to any user at the level of the category at large, or a hierarchy more specifically. In addition, any item, hierarchy (group of items), note, or event can be kept private (i.e., excluded from publication options). Collaboration is enabled, but in conjunction with discretion (Fig. 13.6).

Fig. 13.6 A project administrator has fine control over who can access which data

Open to New Challenges

Might we suggest that many of the tensions described here, many barriers to success, and any disgruntlement that ensues from the use of digital tools, stem from inappropriate uses of inappropriate technology to achieve research goals? What if there were a digital platform that simply, granularly, comprehensively, and transparently modeled research data? What if it were extensible, scalable, customizable, sustainable, secure, and affordable? What if when the archaeologists happened upon the archive of texts, the very same system could comprehensively manage the textual material, in context, and integrated? What if when the philologists studied, analyzed, interpreted, and built glossaries, their scholarship could be managed by the very same integrative platform? What if the historians could access source data to compare and synthesize as they paint a picture of the past? What if research tools for analysis and publication were only a right-click away? As we hope to have illustrated, perhaps it really does come down to using the right tool for the job.

A Grand Challenge

We have argued elsewhere (Prosser 2020) that OCHRE is positioned as an ongoing answer to the "grand challenge" presented by Jeremy Huggett in his keynote address to the 2012 Computer Applications in Archaeology (CAA) conference in Southampton, UK (Huggett 2015b). To restate the topic briefly, a grand challenge is a proposed goal in a field that many might acknowledge as a significant achievement—"something that is self-evidently difficult and challenging to achieve … 'hard enough' both to warrant the name and the investment of time, energy and resources into achieving it and yet not 'too hard' such that it is situated in the realms of science fiction or fantasy" (ibid., pp. 81–81). A grand challenge represents an innovative, measurable, fundamental paradigm shift involving "the creation of new technological capabilities and ways of knowing."

This book sought to demonstrate how OCHRE is a significant step forward in the field of digital data management for academic research projects, motivating scholars to engage productively with their data, and inspiring collaborative efforts across multiple disciplines. This is due in part to the underlying data model designed on an item-based approach, and to the user application which has been long in the making. But it is also due to a support team of professionals with an appropriate education and background (computer science and the humanities); a history and track record of over two decades of continuous experience; the many people who have contributed ideas and expertise to the system (with deep thanks to them all!); and the wide range of projects currently benefiting from their use of the platform. With this backing, we feel confident in claiming that OCHRE is one answer to the grand challenge of digital research that can be applied to the entire life cycle of a project's research data.

The Ultimate Challenge

A recent headline from the Wall Street Journal caught our eye: "99% of big Projects Fail. His Fix Starts With Legos" (Cohen 2023). The story is about Bent Flyvbjerg, an economist who has spent decades studying "megaprojects" and who has advice for getting them right: "Think slow, act fast, and build brick by tiny plastic brick." His book, *How Big Things Get Done* (Flyvbjerg and Gardner 2023) introduces the "Iron Law of Megaprojects," which explains how megaprojects cost too much, take too long, and time and again fall short of expectations. Although he is not referring to research projects specifically, his reflections resonate with academics:

> Humans are optimistic by nature and underestimate how long it takes to complete future tasks. It doesn't seem to matter how many times we fall prey to this cognitive bias known as the planning fallacy. We can always ignore our previous mishaps and delude ourselves into believing this time will be different. We're also subject to the power dynamics and competitive forces that complicate reality, since megaprojects don't take place in controlled environments, and they are plagued by politics as much as psychology Take funding, for example. "How do you get funding?" he said. "By making it look good on paper. You underestimate the cost so it looks cheaper, and you underestimate the schedule so it looks like you can do it faster" (Cohen 2023).

Flyvbjerg's book, however, focuses on success rather than failure and he offers two valuable pieces of advice. The first, "think slow, act fast" emphasizes the need for "meticulous planning." Each of the case studies presented earlier began with a section on *Preparation*—categorizing data elements, identifying atomic units of observation by asking *How far is far enough?*, building a Taxonomy, configuring Users and access, cleaning data. A slow start is a good start which enables progress.

With his second piece of advice, we sent up a cheer! Flyvbjerg says that the key to succeeding in massive undertakings is to find a "Lego," a small task that simplifies a big project and makes it modular—"profoundly modular, built with a basic building block"—in short, an item-based approach. Such projects, claims Flyvbjerg, can then "scale up like crazy, getting better, faster, bigger, and cheaper as they do."

Think of *your* research as the next big idea, the next grand challenge, the next megaproject. Then, following Flyvbjerg's urging, ask the questions every project leader should ask. What is the small thing we can assemble in large numbers into a big thing? What is our Lego? To succeed in building the "bridges, tunnels, office towers, airports, telescopes and even the Olympics," consider taking an item-based approach tackling the big idea one item at a time, then scale up, like crazy, getting better, faster, bigger, and cheaper. Who can resist the challenge?

Citations

Aguinaga, S., Nambiar, A., Liu, Z., & Weninger, T. (2015). Concept hierarchies and human navigation. *2015 IEEE International Conference on Big Data (Big Data)*, 38–45. https://doi.org/10.1109/BigData.2015.7363739

Ambuel, D. (2015). *Turtles all the way down: On Plato's Theaetetus, a commentary and translation* (1. Auflage.). Academia Verlag.

Bachman, C. W. (1973). The programmer as navigator. *Communications of the ACM*, *16*(11), 653–658. https://doi.org/10.1145/355611.362534

Barrett, A. (2001). Databases Embrace XML. *Server/Workstation EXPERT*, *12*(8), 43–47.

Berners-Lee, T. (2009). *Linked Data—Design Issues*. https://www.w3.org/DesignIssues/LinkedData.html

Berners-Lee, T., & Fischetti, M. (1999). *Weaving the Web: The original design and ultimate destiny of the World Wide Web by its inventor* (1st ed). HarperSanFrancisco.

Berners-Lee, T., & Fischetti, M. (2000). *Weaving the web: The past, present and future of th world-wide web by its inventor*. Orion Business Books.

Berners-Lee, T., Hendler, J., & Lassila, O. (2001). The Semantic Web. *Scientific American*, *284*(5), 34–43. https://www.jstor.org/stable/26059207

Bernsten, M., Paranjpe, S., Badve, N., & Engblom, P. C. (Eds.). (2003). *Marathi in Context* (2nd, revised ed.). Associated Colleges of the Midwest.

Berson, Alex., & Dubov, Lawrence. (2011). *Master data management and data governance* (2nd ed.). McGraw-Hill.

Blanchard, G., & Olsen, M. (2002). Le système de renvois dans l'Encyclopédie: Une cartographie des structures de connaissances au XVIIIe siècle. *Recherches sur Diderot et sur l'Encyclopédie*, *31–32*, 45. https://doi.org/10.4000/rde.122

Bode, K. (2018). *A world of fiction: Digital collections and the future of literary history*. University of Michigan Press.

Bojinov, V. (2016). *RESTful web API design with Node.js: Design and implement efficient RESTful solutions with this practical hands-on guide* (2nd ed.). Packt Publishing.

Bordreuil, P., & Pardee, D. (1989). *La Trouvaille Épigraphique de l'Ougarit 1: Concordance* (Vol. 5/1). Éditions Recherche sur les Civilisations.

Borger, R. (2004). *Mesopotamisches Zeichenlexikon*. Ugarit-Verlag.

Brachman, R. J., & Levesque, H. J. (2004). *Knowledge representation and reasoning*. Morgan Kaufmann.

Briend, J., & Humbert, J.-B. (1980). *Tell Keisan (1971-1976): Une cité phénicienne en Galilée*. Éditions Universitaires.

S. R. Schloen, M. C. Prosser, *Database Computing for Scholarly Research*, Quantitative Methods in the Humanities and Social Sciences,
https://doi.org/10.1007/978-3-031-46696-0

Bryant, J. (2002). *The Fluid Text.* University of Michigan Press. https://www.press.umich.edu/12020/fluid_text

Burns, W. (2016). Apple's "Practically Magic" Advertising Campaign Feels More Like A Sleight Of Hand. *Forbes.Com.* https://www.forbes.com/sites/willburns/2016/10/18/apples-practically-magic-advertising-campaign-feels-more-like-a-sleight-of-hand/#23f6f0a7217c

Calvet, Y., & Yon, M (eds). (2008). Ougarit au Bronze moyen et au Bronze récent: Actes du colloque international tenu à Lyon en novembre 2001, Ougarit au IIe millénaire av. J.-C. État des recherches. Travaux de la Maison de l'Orient et de la Méditerranée 47, Lyon.

Calzolari, N., Monachini, M., & Soria, C. (2012). LMF - Historical Context and Perspectives. In G. Francopoulo (Ed.), *LMF Lexical Markup Framework* (pp. 1–18). John Wiley & Sons, Incorporated.

Caraher, W. (2016). Slow Archaeology: Technology, Efficiency, and Archaeological Work. In E. Walcek Averett, J. M. Gordon, & D. B. Counts (Eds.), *Mobilizing the Past for a Digital Future* (pp. 421–441). The Digital Press, The University of North Dakota.

Codd, E. F. (1970). A Relational Model of Data for Large Shared Data Banks. *Communications of the ACM, 13*(6), 377–387.

Cohen, B. (2023, February 2). 99% of Big Projects Fail. His Fix Starts With Legos. *Wall Street Journal.* https://www.wsj.com/articles/lego-megaprojects-bent-flyvbjerg-big-things-11675280517

Corballis, M. C. (2014). *The Recursive Mind: The Origins of Human Language, Thought, and Civilization - Updated Edition.* Princeton University Press.

Cox, A., & Verbaan, Eddy. (2018). *Exploring research data management.* Facet Publishing.

Daley, J. (2017). *The Library of Congress Will Stop Archiving Twitter.* Smithsonian Magazine. https://www.smithsonianmag.com/smart-news/library-congress-will-stop-archiving-twitter-180967651/

Date, C. J. (2004). *An introduction to database systems* (8th ed.). Pearson/Addison Wesley.

Dave, T., Athaluri, S. A., & Singh, S. (2023). ChatGPT in medicine: An overview of its applications, advantages, limitations, future prospects, and ethical considerations. *Frontiers in Artificial Intelligence, 6.* https://doi.org/10.3389/frai.2023.1169595

Day, P. (2002). Dies diem docet: The Decipherment of Ugaritic. *Studi Epigrafici e Linguistici, 19*, 37–57.

De Morgan, A., De Morgan, S. E., & Smith, D. E. (1915). *A budget of paradoxes* (2d ed). The Open Court Publishing Co.

Dietrich, M., Loretz, O., & Sanmartín, J. (1976). *Die keilalphabetischen Texte aus Ugarit* (Vol. 24/1). Butzon & Bercker, Neukirchener.

Dietrich, M., Loretz, O., & Sanmartín, J. (2013). *The Cuneiform Alphabetic Texts from Ugarit, Ras Ibn Hani and Other Places (KTU3) Third, Enlarged Edition Edited by Manfried Dietrich, Oswald Loretz, and Joaquin Sanmartin.*

Doan, A., Halevy, Alon., & Ives, Z. G. (2012). *Principles of data integration.* Morgan Kaufmann.

Dobrova, V., Trubitsin, K., Labzina, P., Ageenko, N., & Gorbunova, Y. (2017). Virtual Reality in Teaching of Foreign Languages. *7th International Scientific and Practical Conference "Current Issues of Linguistics and Didactics: The Interdisciplinary Approach in Humanities" (CILDIAH 2017)*, 63–68. https://doi.org/10.2991/cildiah-17.2017.12

Dreyfus, H. L. (1992). *What Computers Still Can't Do: A Critique of Artificial Reason.* MIT Press.

Dreyfus, H. L. (1997). *What Computers Still Can't Do: A Critique of Artificial Reason* (5th ed.). MIT Press.

Dufton, J. A. (2016). CSS For Success? Some Thoughts on Adapting the Browser-Based Archaeological Recording Kit (ARK) for Mobile Recording. In E. Walcek Averett, J. M. Gordon, & D. B. Counts (Eds.), *Mobilizing the Past for a Digital Future* (pp. 373–398). The Digital Press, The University of North Dakota.

Dunning, D. (2011). Chapter five—The Dunning-Kruger effect: On being ignorant of one's own ignorance. In *Advances in experimental social psychology, Vol 44* (pp. 247–296). Academic Press. https://doi.org/10.1016/B978-0-12-385522-0.00005-6

Dunning, D. (2017). *We Are All Confident Idiots*. Pacific Standard. https://psmag.com/social-justice/confident-idiots-92793

Dunning, D., Johnson, K., Ehrlinger, J., & Kruger, J. (2003). Why People Fail to Recognize Their Own Incompetence. *Current Directions in Psychological Science*, *12*(3), 83–87. https://doi.org/10.1111/1467-8721.01235

Eifrem, E. (2021, June 17). Neo4j Raises the Largest Funding Round in Database History. Neo4j Graph Database Platform (blog). https://neo4j.com/emil/neo4j-raises-largest-funding-round-database-history/

Ellis, S. J. R. (2016). Are We Ready for New (Digital) Ways to Record Archaeological Fieldwork? A Case Study from Pompeii. In E. Walcek Averett, J. M. Gordon, & D. B. Counts (Eds.), *Mobilizing the Past for a Digital Future* (pp. 51–75). The Digital Press, The University of North Dakota.

Ellison, J. L. (2002). *A Paleographic Study of the Alphabetic Cuneiform Texts from Ras Shamra/Ugarit* [Ph. D. Thesis]. Harvard University.

Ericsson, K. A., Prietula, M. J., & Cokely, E. T. (2007, July 1). The Making of an Expert. *Harvard Business Review, July–August 2007*. https://hbr.org/2007/07/the-making-of-an-expert

Flyvbjerg, B., & Gardner, D. (2023). *How Big Things Get Done: The Surprising Factors that Determine the Fate of Every Project from Home Renovations to Space Exploration, and Everything in Between*. Penguin Random House.

Francopoulo, G. (2012). *LMF Lexical Markup Framework*. John Wiley & Sons, Incorporated.

Francopoulo, G., & George, M. (2012). Model Description. In G. Francopoulo (Ed.), *LMF Lexical Markup Framework* (pp. 19–40). John Wiley & Sons, Incorporated.

Freeman, L. C. (2004). *The Development of Social Network Analysis: A Study in the Sociology of Science*. Empirical Press. http://moreno.ss.uci.edu/91.pdf

Garcia-Molina, H., Ullman, J. D., & Widom, J. (2008). *Database Systems: The Complete Book* (2nd ed.). Pearson.

Gkatzogias, M., Karamalis, A., Pyrinis, K., & Politis, D. (2005). GIS Driven Internet Multimedia Databases for Multiple Archaeological Excavations in Greece and the Region of South-Eastern Europe. *Proceedings of the 9th WSEAS International Conference on Systems*.

Gordon, J. M., Walcek Averett, E., & Counts, D. B. (2016). Mobile Computing in Archaeology: Exploring and Interpreting Current Practices. In E. Walcek Averett, J. M. Gordon, & D. B. Counts (Eds.), *Mobilizing the Past for a Digital Future* (pp. 1–30). The Digital Press, The University of North Dakota.

Green, J. (2019). *Turtles All the Way Down* (Reprint edition). Penguin Books.

Griffith, E., & Metz, C. (2023, January 7). A New Area of A.I. Booms, Even Amid the Tech Gloom. *The New York Times*. https://www.nytimes.com/2023/01/07/technology/generative-ai-chatgpt-investments.html

Gruber, T. R. (1995). Toward principles for the design of ontologies used for knowledge sharing? *International Journal of Human-Computer Studies*, *43*(5), 907–928. https://doi.org/10.1006/ijhc.1995.1081

Güterbock, H. G., & Hoffner, H. A. (Eds.). (1997). *The Hittite dictionary of the Oriental Institute of the University of Chicago: Volume P*. The Oriental Institute of the University of Chicago.

Haigh, T. (2016). How Charles Bachman invented the DBMS, a foundation of our digital world. *Communications of the ACM*, *59*(7), 25–30. https://doi.org/10.1145/2935880

Hallock, Richard T. (1969). Persepolis Fortification Tablets. Vol. 92. Oriental Institute Publications. Chicago: University of Chicago Press.

Harris, E. C. (1979). *Principles of archaeological stratigraphy*. Academic Press.

Harris, E. C. (1989). *Principles of archaeological Stratigraphy* (2nd ed.). Academic.

Harrison, G. (2015). Tables are Not Your Friends: Graph Databases. In: Next Generation Databases. Apress, Berkeley, CA. https://doi.org/10.1007/978-1-4842-1329-2_5

Hauser, M. D., Chomsky, N., & Fitch, W. T. (2002). The Faculty of Language: What Is It, Who Has It, and How Did It Evolve? *Science*, *298*(5598), 1569–1579. http://www.jstor.org/stable/3832837

Hawking, Stephen. (1988). *A brief history of time: From the big bang to black holes*. Bantam Books.
Hernandez, D., & Fitch, A. (2021, February 20). IBM's Retreat From Watson Highlights Broader AI Struggles in Health. *Wall Street Journal*. https://www.wsj.com/articles/ibms-retreat-from-watson-highlights-broader-ai-struggles-in-health-11613839579
Herrmann Rimmer, V., & Schloen, J. D. (Eds.). (2014). *In remembrance of me: Feasting with the dead in the ancient Middle East* (Vol. 37). Oriental Institute.
Hockey, S. M. (2000). *Electronic texts in the humanities: Principles and practice*. Oxford University Press.
Huggett, J. (2015a). A manifesto for an introspective digital archaeology. *Open Archaeology*, *1*(1), 86–95. https://doi.org/10.1515/opar-2015-0002
Huggett, J. (2015b). Challenging Digital Archaeology. *Open Archaeology*, *1*, 79–85.
Hunger, M., Boyd, R., & Lyon, W. (2021). *The Definitive Guide to Graph Databases*. 35.
Jackson, J. (2004, February 2). *Taxonomy's not just design, it's an art*. GCN. https://gcn.com/articles/2004/02/03/taxonomys-not-just-design-its-an-art.aspx
James, B. (2021, May 11). Top 5 Graph Analytics Takeaways from Gartner's Data & Analytics Summit. *Neo4j Graph Database Platform*. https://neo4j.com/blog/top-5-graph-analytics-takeaways-gartners-data-analytics-summit/
Kansa, E. C., Kansa, S. W., Burton, M. M., & Stankowski, C. (2010). Googling the Grey: Open Data, Web Services, and Semantics. *Archaeologies*, *6*(2), 301–326. https://doi.org/10.1007/s11759-010-9146-4
Karamalis, A. (2009). Databases for Multiple Archaeological Excavations and Internet Applications. In J. Erickson (Ed.), *Database Technologies: Concepts, Methodologies, Tools, and Applications* (pp. 1420–1445). IGI Global. https://doi.org/10.4018/978-1-60566-058-5.ch085
Kay, A. (1993). The Early History of Smalltalk. 28:69–95. https://doi.org/10.1145/155360.155364
Kintigh, K. W., Spielmann, K. A., Brin, A., Candan, K. S., Clark, T. C., & Peeples, M. (2018). Data Integration in the Service of Synthetic Research. *Advances in Archaeological Practice*, *6*(1), 30–41. https://doi.org/10.1017/aap.2017.33
Knappett, C. (2013). *Using network thinking to understand transmission and innovation in ancient societies*. https://api.semanticscholar.org/CorpusID:55244144
Knappett, Carl. (2011). *An archaeology of interaction: Network perspectives on material culture and society*. Oxford University Press.
Kruger, J., & Dunning, D. (1999). Unskilled and unaware of it: How difficulties in recognizing one's own incompetence lead to inflated self-assessments. *Journal of Personality and Social Psychology*, *77*(6), 1121–1134. https://doi.org/10.1037/0022-3514.77.6.1121
Lang, M., Carver, G., & Printz, S. (2013). Standardised Vocabulary in Archaeological Databases. In G. Earl, T. Sly, A. Chrysanthi, P. Murrietta Flores, C. Papadopoulos, I. Romanowska, & D. Wheatly (Eds.), *Archaeology in the Digital Era, Volume II*. Amsterdam University Press.
Latour, B. (1987). *Science in Action: How to Follow Scientists and Engineers Through Society*. Harvard University Press.
Lau, K. W., & Lee, P. Y. (2015). The use of virtual reality for creating unusual environmental stimulation to motivate students to explore creative ideas. *Interactive Learning Environments*, *23*(1), 3–18. https://doi.org/10.1080/10494820.2012.745426
Lidgard, S., & Nyhart, L. K. (Eds.). (2017). *Biological individuality: Integrating scientific, philosophical, and historical perspectives*. The University of Chicago Press. https://catalog.lib.uchicago.edu/vufind/Record/11274078
Lipka, L. (1992). An Outline of English Lexicology: Lexical Structure, Word Semantics, and Word-Formation. In *An Outline of English Lexicology* (2nd ed.). Max Niemeyer Verlag.
Lohr, S. (2014, August 18). For Big-Data Scientists, 'Janitor Work' Is Key Hurdle to Insights. *The New York Times*. https://www.nytimes.com/2014/08/18/technology/for-big-data-scientists-hurdle-to-insights-is-janitor-work.html
Loshin, D. (2006). Defining Master Data. *BeyeNetwork*. https://web.archive.org/web/20070510063838/http://www.b-eye-network.com/view/2918

Mantilla, L. F., & Knezevic, Z. (2022). Explaining intentional cultural destruction in the Syrian Civil War. *Journal of Peace Research*, *59*(4), 562–576. https://doi.org/10.1177/00223433211039093

Margueron, J. (1977). Ras Shamra 1975 et 1976 Rapport préliminaire sur les campagnes d'automne. *Syria*, *54*(3/4), 151–188. http://www.jstor.org/stable/4198125

McGann, Jerome. (2004). "Marking Texts of Many Dimensions." In A Companion to Digital Humanities, edited by Susan Schreibman, Ray Siemens, John Unsworth, and Jerome McGann, 198–217. Blackwell Companions to Literature and Culture. New York: John Wiley & Sons.

McGann, J., & Buzzetti, D. (2006). Critical Editing in a Digital Horizon. In L. Burnard, K. O'Brien O'Keeffe, & J. Unsworth (Eds.), *Electronic Textual Editing* (pp. 51–71). The Modern Language Association of America.

McGrath, L. B. (2019). More Specific, More Complex. *Post45*. https://post45.org/2019/05/more-specific-more-complex/

Metz, C. (2022, August 5). A.I. Is Not Sentient. Why Do People Say It Is? *The New York Times*. https://www.nytimes.com/2022/08/05/technology/ai-sentient-google.html

Mikołajczak, T. K. (2018). *The Accounting Texts and Seals in the Persepolis Fortification Archive* [Ph.D. Dissertation]. The University of Chicago.

Morales, A. (2020). The 25 greatest Java apps ever written. *Java Magazine*. https://blogs.oracle.com/javamagazine/the-top-25-greatest-java-apps-ever-written

Nelson, T. H. (2015). What Box? In D. Dechow & D. C. Struppa (Eds.), *Intertwingled: The work and influence of Ted Nelson* (pp. 133–150). Springer.

Newman, M. E. J. (2003). The Structure and Function of Complex Networks. *SIAM Review*, *45*(2), 167–256. https://doi.org/10.1137/S003614450342480

Nietzsche, F. W. (1968). *The will to power* (W. Kaufmann & R. J. Hollingdale, Trans.). New York: Vintage Books.

Pardee, D. (2009). A New Aramaic Inscription from Zincirli. *Bulletin of the ASOR*, *356*, 51–71. https://doi.org/10.1086/BASOR25609347

Perry, S. (2015, April 2). Why are heritage interpreters voiceless at the trowel's edge? A plea for reframing the archaeological workflow. *SARA PERRY*. https://saraperry.wordpress.com/2015/04/02/why-are-heritage-interpreters-voiceless-at-the-trowels-edge-a-plea-for-reframing-the-archaeological-workflow/

Pinker, S., & Jackendoff, R. (2005). The faculty of language: What's special about it? *Cognition*, *95*(2), 201–236. https://doi.org/10.1016/j.cognition.2004.08.004

Prosser, M. C. (2018). Digital Philology in the Ras Shamra Tablet Inventory Project: Text Curation through Computational Intelligence. In *CyberResearch on the Ancient Near East and Neighboring Regions: Case Studies on Archaeological Data, Objects, Texts, and Digital Archiving*, volume 1, edited by Vanessa Bigot Juloux, Amy R. Gansell, and Alessandro Di Ludovico pp. 314–335. Digital Biblical Studies 2. Leiden: Brill.

Prosser, M. C. (2020). Digging for Data: A Practical Critique of Digital Archaeology. In R. E. Averbeck & K. L. Younger (Eds.), *"An Excellent Fortress for His Armies, a Refuge for the People," Egyptological, Archaeological, and Biblical Studies in Honor of James K. Hoffmeier* (pp. 309–323). Eisenbrauns.

Prosser, M. C. (2022). Patrons, Brokers, and Clients at Late Bronze Age Ugarit. In H. H. Hardy II, J. Lam, & E. Reymond (Eds.), *"Like 'Ilu Are You Wise": Studies in Northwest Semitic Languages and Literatures in Honor of Dennis G. Pardee* (pp. 55–71). Oriental Institute.

Prosser, M. C., & Schloen, S. R. (2020). Unlocking Legacy Data: Integrating New and Old in OCHRE. In E. Aspöck, S. Štuhec, K. Kopetzky, & M. Kucera (Eds.), *Old Excavation Data: What Can We Do? Proceedings of the Workshop held at the 10th ICAANE in Vienna, April 2016* (pp. 39–52). Austrian Academy of Sciences.

Prosser, M. C., & Schloen, S. R. (2021). The Power of OCHRE's Highly Atomic Graph Database Model for the Creation and Curation of Digital Text Editions. In E. Spadini, F. Tomasi, & G. Vogeler (Eds.), *Graph Data-Models and Semantic Web Technologies in Scholarly Digital Editing* (Vol. 15, pp. 55–71). Books on Demand. https://kups.ub.uni-koeln.de/55226/

Rabinowitz, A. (2016). Mobilizing (Ourselves) for a Critical Digital Archaeology. In E. Walcek Averett, J. M. Gordon, & D. B. Counts (Eds.), *Mobilizing the Past for a Digital Future* (pp. 493–520). The Digital Press, The University of North Dakota.

Randall, N. (1997). XML: A Second Chance for Web Markup. *PC Magazine Online*, *16*(19), 319–322.

Robinson, I., Webber, J., & Eifrem, E. (2015). *Graph Databases: New Opportunities for Connected Data* (2nd edition). O'Reilly Media.

Ross, C. (2018). Infinite Regress Arguments. In E. N. Zalta (Ed.), *The Stanford Encyclopedia of Philosophy*. Metaphysics Research Lab, Stanford University.

Royal Numismatic Society (Great Britain). (1981). *Coin hoards*. Royal Numismatic Society.

Schaeffer, C. F. A. (1962). *Ugaritica IV: découvertes des XVIIIe et XIXe campagnes; fondements préhistoriques d'Ugarit et nouveaux sondages; études anthropologiques; poteries grecques et monnaies islamiques de Ras Shamra et environs. Mission de Ras Shamra XV*. Imprimerie Nationale.

Schaeffer, C. F. A. (1929, November 2). A New Page Opened in Ancient History: Sensational Discoveries in Northern Syria: An Unknown Language; Royal Archives, Tombs, and Treasures of the 13th and 14th Centuries B.C. *Illustrated London News*, 764–767.

Schloen, J. D. (2001a). Archaeological Data Models and Web Publication Using XML. *Computers and the Humanities*, *35*(2), 123–152. https://doi.org/10.1023/A:1002471112790

Schloen, J. D. (2001b). *The House of the Father as Fact and Symbol: Patrimonialism in Ugarit and the Ancient Near East*. Eisenbrauns.

Schloen, J. D. (2014). The City of Katumuwa: The Iron Age Kingdom of Sam'al and the Excavation of Zincirli. In V. R. Herrmann & J. D. Schloen (Eds.), *In Remembrance of Me: Feasting with the Dead in the Ancient Middle East* (Vol. 37, pp. 27–38). Oriental Institute.

Schloen, J. D., & Schloen, S. (2014). Beyond Gutenberg: Transcending the Document Paradigm in Digital Humanities. *Digital Humanities Quarterly*, *8*(4). http://digitalhumanities.org:8081/dhq/vol/8/4/000196/000196.html

Schloen, J. D., & Schloen, S. R. (2012). *OCHRE: An Online Cultural and Historical Research Environment*. Eisenbrauns.

Schöning, H., & Wäsch, J. (2000). Tamino—An Internet Database System. In C. Zaniolo, P. C. Lockemann, M. H. Scholl, & T. Grust (Eds.), *Advances in Database Technology—EDBT 2000* (pp. 383–387). Springer. https://doi.org/10.1007/3-540-46439-5_26

Schreibman, S., Siemens, R., Unsworth, J., & McGann, J. (Eds.). (2004). Marking Texts of Many Dimensions. In *A Companion to Digital Humanities* (pp. 198–217). John Wiley & Sons.

Scott, John., & Carrington, P. J. (2011). *The SAGE Handbook of Social Network Analysis*. SAGE Publications.

Shakespeare, W. (n.d.). *Hamlet, from the Folger Shakespeare* (B. Mowat, P. Werstine, M. Poston, & R. Niles, Eds.). Folger Shakespeare Library. Retrieved July 1, 2021, from https://shakespeare.folger.edu/shakespeares-works/hamlet/

Sharma, J., & Herring, J. (2018). Geography Markup Language. In M. T. Özsu & L. Liu (Eds.), *Encyclopedia of database systems: Vol. G* (Second edition, pp. 1605–1608). Springer. https://doi.org/10.1007/978-1-4614-8265-9

Shirky, C. (2008). Ontology is Overrated: Categories, Links, and Tags. *Clay Shirky's Writings about the Internet*. https://oc.ac.ge/file.php/16/_1_Shirky_2005_Ontology_is_Overrated.pdf

Simon, H. A. (1969). *The sciences of the artificial*. M.I.T. Press.

Software AG. (2015). *Tamino: Advanced Concepts*. https://documentation.softwareag.com/webmethods/tamino/ins97/print/advconc.pdf

Spigelman, M., Roberts, T., & Fehrenbach, S. (2016). The Development of the PaleoWay: Digital Workflows in the Contet of Archaeological Consulting. In E. Walcek Averett, J. M. Gordon, & D. B. Counts (Eds.), *Mobilizing the Past for a Digital Future* (pp. 399–418). The Digital Press, The University of North Dakota.

Stager, L. E. (1991). When Canaanites and Philistines Ruled Ashkelon. *Biblical Archaeology Review*, *17*(2), 2–19.

Stager, L., Master, D., & Schloen, J. D. (Eds.). (2011). *Ashkelon 3: The Seventh Century B.C.* Eisenbrauns.

Stanek, W. R. (1998, May 26). Structuring Data with XML. *PC Magazine* (pp. 229–238).

Stevenson, K. H., & Jandl, H. W. (1986). *Houses by mail: A guide to houses from Sears, Roebuck and Company*. Preservation Press.

Stolper, M. W. (2007). Persepolis Fortification Archive Project. In G. Stein (Ed.), *Oriental Institute 2006-2007 Annual Report* (pp. 92–103). University of Chicago.

Stratford, E. (2017). *A Year of Vengeance. Volume 1: Time, Narrative, and the Old Assyrian Trade* (Vol. 17). de Gruyter.

Struble, E. J., & Herrmann, V. R. (2009). An Eternal Feast at Sam'al: The New Iron Age Mortuary Stele from Zincirli in Context. *Bulletin of the American Schools of Oriental Research, 356*, 15–49. https://doi.org/10.1086/BASOR25609346

Sun Microsystems. (2001). *Web Services Made Easier The Java TM APIs and Architectures for XML, A Technical White Paper.*

Sweigart, A. (2015). *Automate the Boring Stuff with Python: Practical Programming for Total Beginners*. No Starch Press.

Thompson, M., Mørkholm, O., Kraay, C. M., & Noe, S. P. (1973). *An inventory of Greek coin hoards*. Published for the International Numismatic Commission by the American Numismatic Society.

Thornton, R. Fuller. (2004). *The houses that Sears built: Everything you ever wanted to know about Sears catalog homes* (2nd ed.). Gentle Beam Publications.

University of Chicago. Oriental Institute, Güterbock, H. G., & Hoffner, H. A. (Eds.). (1980). *The Hittite dictionary of the Oriental Institute of the University of Chicago*. The Oriental Institute.

Walcek Averett, E., Gordon, J. M., & Counts, D. B. (Eds.). (2016). *Mobilizing the Past for a Digital Future*. The Digital Press, The University of North Dakota.

Wallis, J. C., Rolando, E., & Borgman, C. L. (2013). If We Share Data, Will Anyone Use Them? Data Sharing and Reuse in the Long Tail of Science and Technology. *PLOS ONE*, *8*(7), e67332. https://doi.org/10.1371/journal.pone.0067332

Watson, W. G. E., & Wyatt, N. (1999). Handbook of Ugaritic Studies. Handbuch Der Orientalistik 39. Leiden: Brill.

Wilkinson, M. D., Dumontier, M., Aalbersberg, Ij. J., Appleton, G., Axton, M., Baak, A., Blomberg, N., Boiten, J.-W., da Silva Santos, L. B., Bourne, P. E., Bouwman, J., Brookes, A. J., Clark, T., Crosas, M., Dillo, I., Dumon, O., Edmunds, S., Evelo, C. T., Finkers, R., ... Mons, B. (2016). The FAIR Guiding Principles for scientific data management and stewardship. *Scientific Data*, *3*, 160018. https://doi.org/10.1038/sdata.2016.18

Williams, E. C., Su, G., Schloen, S. R., Prosser, M. C., Paulus, S., & Krishnan, S. (forthcoming). *DeepScribe: Localization and Classification of Elamite Cuneiform Signs Via Deep Learning*. Journal on Computer and Cultural Heritage.

Yardney, S., Prosser, M., & Schloen, S. R. (2020). Digital Tools for Paleography in the OCHRE Database Platform. *TC: A Journal of Biblical Textual Criticism, 25*, 129–143.

Yon, M. (2006). *The Royal City of Ugarit on the Tell of Ras Shamra*. Winona Lake: Eisenbrauns.

Yon, M., Sznycer, M., & Bordreuil, P. (1995). *Le Pays d'Ougarit autour de 1200 av. J.-C.: Histoire et Archéologie: Actes du Colloque International, Paris, 28 juin-1er juillet 1993*. Éditions Recherche sur les Civilisations.

Zeng, M. L., & Qin, J. (2016). *Metadata* (2nd edition). Neal-Schuman.